*Title page of the Raccoon and
Penns Neck Church Register*

*Pages from the Raccoon and Penns
Neck Church Register (Swedish Text)*

The Records of the Swedish Lutheran Churches at Raccoon and Penns Neck

1713 - 1786

American Guide Series

Translated and Compiled by the
FEDERAL WRITERS' PROJECT OF THE
WORKS PROGRESS ADMINISTRATION,
STATE OF NEW JERSEY

With an Introduction and Notes by
DR. AMANDUS JOHNSON
Director of the American Swedish Historical Museum,
Philadelphia, Pa.

Book Publishers

Southern Historical Press, Inc.
Greenville, South Carolina

This volume was repropuced from
a personal copy located in the
Publisher's private library
Greenville, South Carolina

Please direct ALL correspondence and book orders to:
www.southernhistoricalpress.com
or
**Southern Historical Press, Inc.
PO Box 1267
Greenville, SC 29602-1267
southernhistoricalpress@gmail.com**

Originally published: Elizabeth, N.J. 1938
ISBN #978-1-63914-021-3
All Rights Reserved
Printed in the United States of America

Works Progress Administration

HARRY L. HOPKINS, *Administrator*
ELLEN S. WOODWARD, *Assistant Administrator*
HENRY G. ALSBERG, *Director of Federal Writers' Project*

The New Jersey Commission to Commemorate the 300th Anniversary of the Settlement by the Swedes and Finns on the Delaware

SENATORS: D. Stewart Craven, Salem, Chairman; Albert E. Burling, Camden; Robert C. Hendrickson, Woodbury; George H. Stanger, Vineland.

ASSEMBLYMEN: Millard E. Allen, Laurel Springs; Lawrence H. Ellis, Haddonfield; Norman P. Featherer, Penns Grove; Howard B. Hancock, Greenwich; Rocco Palese, Camden; John G. Sholl, Pitman.

COMMISSIONERS: Frank I. Liveright, Newark, Vice-Chairman, North Jersey; Loyal D. Odhner, Camden, Vice-Chairman, South Jersey; Harry C. Hallberg, Orange; George de B. Keim, Edgewater Park; Karl J. Olson, East Orange; Samuel H. Richards, Collingswood.

SECRETARY: Ann G. Craven, Salem.

PREFACE

The Federal Writers' Project of New Jersey has been pleased to join with the New Jersey Commission established to commemorate the three hundredth anniversary of the Swedish and Finnish settlement of the Delaware by preparing this volume of translations of the records of Swedish Lutheran Churches at Raccoon and Penns Neck.

This book marks the entry of the project into two new fields. It is the project's first publication of authentic source material for the benefit of historians as well as the general reading public. It is also the project's first venture in the translation of important documents and records.

In order to spare the old record books of the Raccoon Church at Swedesboro, N. J., from frequent handling during the preparation of the manuscript of this volume, the text was reproduced on microfilm. For the use of scholars the Federal Writers' Project has presented microfilm copies of the records to the following institutions: the Royal Archives of Sweden, Stockholm, Sweden; the Archives of the Republic of Finland, Helsingfors, Finland; the Library of Congress, Washington, D. C.; the New Jersey Historical Society, Newark, N. J.; the Historical Society of Pennsylvania, Philadelphia, Pa.; the Free Library of Philadelphia, Philadelphia, Pa. and the Gloucester County Historical Society, Woodbury, N. J.

We are grateful to the Episcopal Churches at Swedesboro and Churchtown for permission to make the translation and to Dr. Amandus Johnson, director of the American Swedish Historical Museum, for reading and annotating the manuscript.

IRENE FUHLBRUEGGE,

State Director.

INTRODUCTION

When the Swedish Lutheran Mission on the Delaware was re-established in 1697, a considerable number of Swedes and Finns had settled on the Jersey side of the River, principally at two centers, Raccoon and Penns Neck (upper and lower), Matts Mattson, the father-in-law of the Rev. Andreas Rudman, being "the first to build a home at Raccoon". These colonists were accustomed to attend services in the old church at Tranhook (near present-day Wilmington) and at Tinicum Island, depending upon the location of their farms, the settlements around Penns Neck going to the southern church and those living about Racoon Creek attending on Tinicum Island.

It is likely that the worshippers would congregate near Penns Neck and about the mouth of Raccoon Creek and from there go in companies by canoes to service on Sunday mornings or on Saturday, in which case they would stay overnight with relatives or friends near the churches. The journeys across the Delaware in those days were hazardous, yes impossible at certain seasons of the year, and tragedies occurred more than once. Besides, the journeys consumed much time and kept the able-bodied men away from work during harvest and at other periods, when the farms needed most attention. As a result the attendance of these far-off settlers at the churches on the east side of the river was poor and many never attended services at all.

When Rudman and Björk built their churches at Christina (Wilmington) and Wicaco (Philadelphia), the Jersey Swedes desired to have a church erected on their side of the river also. The pastors found these plans impractical, as the settlers were few and not in affluent circumstances. The settlers on the Jersey side then agreed to help in the erection of places of worship on the Pennsylvania side of the river if the people living there, in turn, would help them, when the time came and when they found themselves numerous and strong enough to build their own chapel. The old divisions were of course retained, the lower colony at Penns Neck being assigned to Christina (Wilmington) Church, the upper section at Raccoon Creek to Wicaco.

In order to keep the people together and prevent them from falling

[iii]

away from the church, Rev. Björk stationed a school teacher at Raccoon, Hans Stålt. Rev. Björk, and possibly Rudman, visited the Jersey settlers occasionally, preaching in the homes of the Swedes and Finns and performing other pastoral duties. Parish meetings of a sort were also held with the people on that side of the river, which were quite similar to the meetings of the members of Christina Church, living on the Pennsylvania side. One of these meetings was held at the home of Jacob Van de Ver on November 28, 1701. The minutes of the gathering are recorded in the Church Records of Holy Trinity, like the regular meeting of the members of the church. Such meetings helped to give the people a feeling of independence and importance and contributed. to their desire for a separate church organization and a building of their own.

The employment of a school teacher also helped to foster their idea. When Björk could not preach on the Jersey side (and he seldom could), the people were advised to go to Raccoon Creek every Sunday and Holiday, and Stålt, the teacher, was instructed to read the selections for the day from a collection of sermons on the Epistles, by Lukerman. These "lay services" tended to center the people's minds on Raccoon as the meeting-place for the Jersey Swedes. It is possible that a log cabin was erected for a school, which was used for services by the people on Sundays and Holidays.

About the time of the meeting at Van de Ver's, mentioned above (November 26, 1701), another Swedish pastor, Lars Tollstadius, arrived in Philadelphia and presented hmself to Rev. Rudman as his duly appointed successor. He carried no papers of identification, pretending that he had left these in New York with his other effects, which were to follow him. Rev. Rudman was somewhat suspicious at first, especially as he had heard from postmaster Thelin in Gothenburg, that his old friend, Andreas Sandel, would soon arrive to take his place. Rudman, however, was in poor health and consequently engaged Rev. Tollstadius for a period of six months on trial, at a salary of £25, apparently paid in advance. (It seems that he was allowed to occupy the parsonage at Manayunk, while he served the church). But on March 18, 1702, long before the six months were up, Rev. Sandel arrived, carrying an official appointment as pastor of the parish and a written report about Tollstadius, detailing all circumstances in the case, why he could not obtain a commission and why the Consistory had forbidden him to depart for America.

Tollstadius now had to relinquish his place to Sandel and was left without employment. He had entirely misrepresented his case to Rev. Rudman. While living in Stockholm he heard about an opening in America and applied to the Consistory for the post, even offering to pay his travelling expenses. The Consistory thought well of his plan and encouraged him; but it seems that he had been involved in some matter, which "caused a bad report to be spread about him" which reached the Consistory, and "he was declared unsuitable for the position" and told not to leave Sweden. However, he departed on his own responsibility and managed to reach New York, presumably on an English ship.

With the coming of Tollstadius we must begin the history of the Swedish Lutheran Church in New Jersey. During the service in the Wicaco Church he apparently made many friends on both sides of the River, especially in New Jersey, where some "began to hang to him, and he to them". When he was obliged to give up his charge in the Wicaco Church, he was warned by "the regular pastors" not to preach in these parts or do anything else "that would cause a scandal"; but if he should remain for a time, waiting for a ship to Europe, or for other reasons, he could "take himself a school," presumably at Raccoon, and thus help the other pastors in their work. But Tollstadius had other plans. He obtained a passport to Europe as he pretended that he desired to go there and a testimonial of good behavior from Rev. Rudman, but instead of returning to Sweden he went to Raccoon in a canoe which was waiting for him at Manayunk, not far from the old parsonage, where he seems to have lived while he served the church. He promised the people to preach for them and to perform all other services "that a pastor can do," and a great many of the Swedes and Finns on the eastern shore of the Delaware received him as their pastor and promised to support him. He succeeded in forming a congregation in the late Summer or early Fall of 1702. A letter was drawn up by him to the Consistory signed by the members of the newly-founded organization and requested that he be appointed their pastor. Tollstadius went to New York with the letter, but "on account of various misfortunes which befell him" he was unable to depart and returned to Raccoon in five or six weeks. It is likely that Tollstadius sent the letter to Sweden by boat and Rev. Björk wrote to the Archbishop giving him the details of the controversy. Tollstadius continued to preach and most of the members that belonged to the two churches on the other side of the River, went to the services. Rev. Björk held meetings with the members, advising them not to accept Tollstadius, but to await orders from Sweden and do everything in the regular way. In the fall, Tollstadius was taken seriously ill and his work lapsed for many weeks, but he recovered and began collecting subscriptions for a new church before an answer had arrived from Sweden. A parcel of land was purchased for £12 (deed dated September 1, 1703), containing ten acres and bordering on Raccoon Creek.

Later two and a half acres of meadow land purchased for five shillings were added to the tract. On this land the Swedes near and around Raccoon Creek built a log church which was dedicated by Tollstadius on the Third Sunday after Trinity, 1705. The other pastors, Björk and Rudman, were invited, but did not accept, Rev. Björk giving a long explanation about his refusal. It was undoubtedly a great day for the New Jersey Swedes and Tollstadius, who performed the dedication exercises according to Swedish Lutheran custom. From now on it is likely that services were conducted regularly in Raccoon and the main holidays like Christmas, Easter and New Year, were observed in the Swedish manner.

But the joy was not for long. Tollstadius seems to have been somewhat irregular in his habits and his indiscretions caused disturbances in the congregation and led to conflicts between him and his parishioners. He was accused of having illicit relations with Ole Persson's daughter, Katharine, and "was bound over to the Court" at Burlington in the spring of 1706. But the case never went to trial. On the 29th of May, Tollstadius came to an untimely end. It seems he had been on a visit to Philadelphia to buy a plowshare. His canoe drove ashore with his travelling cloak and plowshare in it, while his body was found at Uppland the seventh of June, nine days after the accident.

Rev. Björk now assumed that the Raccoon congregation would scatter and that the people would return to their old church, but in this he was mistaken, and he complains that the Jersey Swedes were more "obstinate and spunky than ever," although a few, on account of the "ruinous state of things" came back to his own church. The Raccoon Congregation called Rev. Jonas Aurén, who had accompanied Björk and Rudman to the colony. He had come here to gather information about the people and obtain a map of the country, and then was to return home to report to the King. But the King died, the wars of Charles XII were setting northern Europe aflame, and other circumstances intervened to make a change in Aurén's plans. He remained here, went to

Conestoga and other places and even tried his hand at missionary work among the Indians. On his sojourns, especially at Lancaster and Ephrata, he came in contact with the Seven-Day Dunkars (an off-shoot of the German Baptist Brethren) and soon adopted their faith. To help spread the new gospel he wrote a pamphlet (which Acrelius called an *almanack* (almanac), entitled *Nae Dufwa* in which he presented his newly adopted faith, especially about Saturday as the real day of rest. The tract caused much confusion and probably turned some away from the Swedish Lutheran churches. At any rate Björk felt obliged to answer it by publishing *A Little Olive Leaf, put in the mouth of that so called Noach's Dove, and sent home again to let her Master know, that the waters are abated from off the face of the ground, and that for the sake of Jesus Christ, whose servant to the end of my life I shall endeavor to be.* (Those were days of long titles.) "This work," says Acrelius, "which is composed with a mature understanding and with powerful reasons accomplished much good among the people, but hardly more with Mr. Jon. Aurén than that he indeed preached on Sundays for others, but kept Saturday holy for himself."

About 1704, Rev. Aurén settled at Elk River, Maryland. Here he preached to an English congregation on Sunday and apparently conducted missionary work on Saturday and other days for his Baptist Brethren, possibly among the Swedes who lived there, as well as others. He considered the call to Raccoon seriously and went there in the autumn of 1706 to consult with them about the charge. He also discussed the situation with Björk. As he found that Rev. Björk was not enthusiastic about the call, and as he felt that he could not leave his post at Elk River abruptly, nor without "more maturely considering the matter," he went back to his home in Maryland. In order not to leave the Raccoon Swedes without religious instruction (Rudman at Wicaco was in poor health and could not serve them) he arranged for his relative, Brun Johan, to be their school teacher and lay reader, Brun Johan or Brunjan (a corruption of some sort) was apparently a Seven-Day Dunkar. He had been with Aurén two years or more, perhaps helping him to spread his religious views in the community. In the spring of 1707 the Raccoon Swedes became more insistent in their call, and finally Aurén accepted, especially as Björk gave his consent to the arrangement. The congregation applied to the Governor of New York to permit them to engage him. It seems that he was "cited before the Governor on certain grave charges,"[1] but after the hearing, at which he presented a special communication from Björk and other evidence "he was acquitted and granted permission to act as minister" at Raccoon.

"Now directly after this those below Jacob van de Ver's down to Pumking Hook began a movement to obtain Herr Aureen to preach every Sunday for them. He did not consent, nor come to any agreement with them, but came over himself finally to confer with me [Björk] about it, but I bade him be still for I would never agree to his going over there to give me further trouble, for he had already got a bit of my bread, which I had given up in compassion for his circumstances, and therefore he should let the remainder alone."

As a result of the consultations, Rev. Björk was to serve the Swedes in the lower section about Penns Neck and on August 12, 1707, he arranged to go there "once a month" for an increased salary, "on the condition that they in all things should remain united to Christina as heretofore and help pay for the support of the Church and the parsonage, etc." About two weeks later (August 29), Björk began his work among the Jersey Swedes (at Penns Neck) and apparently kept it up quite regularly. As it was difficult for Björk to get across the River and back again, the congregation hired Sven Kolberg to ferry him over whenever he should set a time to preach. Later Hendrick Jansson was engaged for the purpose and on May 23, 1711, John Mink undertook to take the pastor across the River and back again when he wished to go there to perform his duties. Björk continued to serve Penns Neck quite regularly until December 5, 1712, and occasionally until he returned to Sweden in 1713.

On May 1, 1712, Rev. Abraham Lidenius, arrived from Sweden as the assistant to Rev. Andreas Hesselius, who was appointed pastor in the Christina Church (Wilmington). In the beginning of December, 1712, Lidenius went to Penns Neck and took charge of the congregation there, preaching regularly on Sundays and holidays, and performing all other pastoral duties.

Aurén remained quietly in Raccoon with his family and performed his work faithfully and well. He kept on good terms with Rev. Björk, visited his congregation occasionally, helped him to organize the church vestry, buried one of his children, and did other favors. He died on

---

[1] It is not quite clear what these "certain grave charges" might have been. Perhaps they were of a theological nature and hence considered "grave" by Björk, from whom I have quoted the above statement.

February 17, 1713, and was buried by Rev. Lidenius on the 24th, leaving a wife and two sons behind.

The Raccoon people were again without a pastor. Rev. Sandel from Wicaco went there occasionally, but he was too busy in his own parish to help them much. Arrangements were therefore made with Rev. Lidenius in Penns Neck to preach every other Sunday in Raccoon. From now on the two congregations really formed one parish (although they were still considered annexes to the Christina and Wicaco Churches) and at this point the church records begin.

* * *

The translation and publication of the church records of Raccoon and Penns Neck Swedish Parishes is an event of importance to every student of American colonial history. These documents are the earliest Church Records from this section of the Delaware Valley, and as such possess special value and importance. They not only form an invaluable source to the genealogist and local historian by their accounts of births, baptisms, marriages and deaths; they also give many interesting glimpses of the cultural, religious and material life of people at the time, by the reports of parish meetings, by the account of disputes and disagreements, and by their statements about buildings, fences, the collecting of materials, etc. In some cases the pastor inserted part of their diaries in the church book, giving interesting glimpses of their experiences. Official letters from the Consistory, from the King, from the Archbishop and from the Bishop of Skara, that were received by the congregation or the pastor, were written into the churchbook, thus preserving original records and papers of the period.

The financial conditions of the New Jersey colonists was usually poor and few had more than their daily needs. Although they showed considerable interest in church work, the pastors were poorly compensated for their labors, and even the small salaries allotted to them were not regularly paid, sometimes not at all. Those in poorest circumstances would pay up at least part of their subscriptions, while the members who could best afford to do so, never paid at all. When subscriptions for the pastor's salary or for expenses connected with the church were made, the members usually would be asked to give a bond for the amount, and the sums could be legally collected. In fact once or twice the law was invoked to collect the pastor's salary, but this caused so much bad feeling that it was seldom attempted.

The amount of subscriptions considered proper and fair may be measured by the statement that a woman who worked for her living should donate one week of her income toward the pastor's salary. In other words, one fifty-second, or about two percent of a man's total income was considered a fair donation towards the pastor's maintenance,—not a small amount, if measured by standards of today

Many circumstances combined to make matters difficult for the pastors. Sometimes epidemics played havoc in the settlements, and we are told that many families removed to distant places, reducing the members of the congregation.

Just as today a congregation will often buy an automobile for the clergyman, especially in the country, so in those days the congregation bought a horse for the pastor, which reverted to the parish, if the preacher should accept another call and move away.

In spite of the fact that the settlers in this district were not very religious and many did not go to church at all, it seems that they were anxious to bury their dead in the churchyard and not in their own fields, as was done in Maryland and elsewhere at the time. They had no compunction apparently about secretly burying their dead in the graveyard, so as to avoid paying the fee to the congregation, as we find references to this fact in the churchbook.

Much of the work in building the churches, schoolhouses, and the parsonage, and the necessary repairs were done by volunteer labor of the members. The fences around the church and the churchyard were likewise erected and repaired by the members, a certain section of the fence being assigned to a certain member, while gates, hinges, etc., were also supplied by the members. In many cases, however, subscriptions were raised and materials and labor paid for.

A few members of the congregation did most of the work, while others were simply on committees,—human nature does not change! Disagreements among the members of the congregation often arose and there were violent quarrels about pews and the seating arrangement.

In the records we find the prices of food at the time, the amount of wages paid for various kinds of labor, and the value of materials, such as bricks, lumber, shingles, mortar, etc. (In 1770 we are told that nails could not be obtained as the Non-Importation Convention prevented nails from reaching the country from England.) In many cases workmen would be paid by the job or by piece-work. In some cases board or board and lodging were supplied as part of the agreement.

Rum was one of the necessary requirements of the period and regularly supplied to workmen.

The church services were not always treated with due respect. Some of the pastors complained that the people would run in and out during the sermon. It seems that children were not taken to the services by their elders as was the custom in Sweden, and here also in a later period. They were allowed to play and make a noise outside the church, disturbing the services and causing the pastors to complain.

The Consistory in Sweden instructed the congregations here to organize children's schools. This was done, and a schoolhouse was erected near Swedesboro, probably the oldest parochial schoolhouse in the State. A singing school was also organized as church singing was almost forgotten, even by the older people, when the mission was first established. At times violent quarrels and dissention arose between people of various opinions and the Herrnhuters caused much trouble. In 1744, some of the trustees and church wardens of Raccoon became Herrnhuters, or Moravians, and others had to be elected in their places. In fact in 1745 it seems that the majority in Penns Neck adhered to the Moravian faith.

As time went on, English words or expressions crept into the Swedish language written and spoken here and we find many such in the churchbook, as for instance *resa lönen til, resa något mer lön. Resa* here is the English "raise," in the one case, and "collect in the other. The Swedish would be *höja lönen til, samla något mer lön,* etc. In 1742 it was decided that Swedish should no longer be preached in Penns Neck church and later Acrelius proposed that the Latin script should be used in recording minutes in the Church Book, as the Swedes had forgotten how to read the old script.

AMANDUS JOHNSON.

A NOTE ON CONTENTS AND ARRANGEMENT

The contents of this volume were derived from five record books dealing with the history of the Raccoon and Penns Neck churches from 1713 to 1786. The major portion of the text consists of entries from the book begun in Raccoon in 1713, which contains both Raccoon and Penns Neck entries. Material was also drawn from two additional Raccoon books, containing minutes, leases and other documents, and from two volumes with brief entries pertaining to the Penns Neck congregation. The Raccoon books are in the vault of Trinity Episcopal Church, Swedesboro, N. J., and the Penns Neck books are in the possession of Mrs. Sarah Jacquett, of Churchtown, a descendant of Jean Jaquet, donor of the land for the church built in Penns Neck in 1717.

The material has been rearranged to give a chronological account of the churches' history in terms of (1) minutes of parish meetings and entries in pastors' journals which contained church business; (2) documents; (3) records of baptisms, marriages and deaths. Documents which related closely to events in the church minutes have been left in their original place in the record.

Such arrangement was necessary because the haphazard manner in which the books were kept resulted in considerable confusion of subject matter and an almost complete lack of continuity. In the early years, pages were occasionally left blank to keep the records of the two parishes in consecutive order on opposite pages. This ultimately led to the present disordered state of the books. Paper was very expensive in the eighteenth century and every available space had to be used as the book began to be filled up. Thus an account of a parish meeting in the time of the Revolutionary War would be inserted on a page left blank half a century earlier. Or some of the writers would begin a document on a blank half page and then be obliged to continue it several pages ahead in the book because the intervening pages had already been used. In the same way, birth, marriage and death records were frequently inserted not along with the accounts of the parish meetings of the year in which they occurred, but wherever space permitted.

Every effort has been made to preserve the flavor and character of the original books. The actual form of the entries has been altered only when a need for clarity dictated a change; this was especially necessary with the financial accounts and the records of the labor contributed on the cooperative building enterprises. All explanatory matter inserted by the editors has been enclosed in brackets

The first part of the book was written in "the old Swedish script," probably by the pastors, beginning with Lidenius. In 1732, during the rectorship of Rev. Tranberg, Latin letters were used and the entries are in English until 1741. In 1741 a new form is started, on the right hand page, thus: "Racoon and Pens Neck, 1741". The Swedish language with the old script is now used again, and both pages are filled consecutively. Some pages are in English, however, probably written by a clerk. The Swedish is perhaps by Malander. In 1750 the Latin script and Swedish text are again introduced, on the advice of Rev. Israel Acrelius. The Rev. Johan Wicksell, who became pastor of the churches in 1762, used Swedish for the parish minutes until 1763; thereafter the majority of his entries were in English. His successor the Rev. Nicholas Collin used English almost exclusively.

The Raccoon and Penns Neck Churchbook which contains the largest part of the text of this book is bound in parchment. The covers are badly worn. The back is broken and the parchment is removed from it. The book has been badly repaired by pasting muslin strips across the back to keep the covers from falling off. There is no fly-leaf. The title page is loose and worn, and has been repaired, the title *Racoon Creek och Pens Neck Kyrkjobook* being legible, but some of the table of contents below being worn off and in places unreadable. This title and contents have been written in at a later date, probably about 1750. Some of the first few pages are worn on the edges, but little of the script has been lost. In some cases the inner edges of the pages have been damaged by sewing when the book was repaired and some of the text has been drawn in or sewn in too far, so that it cannot be easily read. This is the case in the first twenty pages. After the first forty or fifty pages the book is in fine shape. The last forty or fifty pages are likewise worn and damaged on the outer edges.

The Rev. Nicholas Collin made some annotations and a few translations throughout the book. Some are signed, the others are easily recognized by his handwriting. The end of the book is in the handwriting of Nicholas Collin, marriages being reported in his hand from October 1, 1773. At the very end of the book are some loose pages badly worn, giving the names and amounts of the donors to the new church in 1786.

CONTENTS

MINUTES OF PARISH MEETINGS AND SUPPLEMENTARY HISTORICAL ENTRIES

PENS NECK 1714 [1]

ON the 6th of April there was held a Parish Meeting concerning the [location of a] Church building, about which they had great difficulty in coming to an agreement, some insisting on one place, and some on another. However, since the Germans,[2] who adhere to the Swedish congregation, already had a burial place [laid out] where many of their dead lie buried, it was finally decided, after much difficulty, to build a Church there, that is, on Johannes Casper's land, down by the River. A German, Regner von Aist, undertook the construction of the Church, to build it 24 feet square, for 24 pounds, old money.[2a]

Also, were chosen for Vestrymen: Jacob Hindersson, Jacob von Devair, Johan von Neeman, George Litzen, Lucas Petersson and Johan Minck. But since nothing was accomplished of what had then been decided, a Parish Meeting was again called and held on the 3rd of December, when they all agreed to build a Church which should lie as near the middle of the Congregation as was possible, namely, on the

---

[1] Headings from the original books appear in upper case throughout the book, with the exception of a few uses of italic. Headings inserted by the editors are in upper case, enclosed in brackets. Question marks have been inserted where the date or location of the entry is doubtful. The manuscript titles are in the old spelling, "Racoon" and "Pens Neck" or, rarely, "Pensneck". The inserted headings use the modernized versions, "Raccoon" and "Penns Neck".

[2] Several German immigrants settled near the Swedish colony in New Jersey at an early date. They were apparently Lutherans and many joined the Swedish churches.

[2a] Considerable inquiry into the exact meaning of the terms "old money" "new money" has failed to produce a definite explanation. Authoritative works on the subject of colonial money such as *The Money Supply of the American Colonies Before* 1720, by Curtis Putnam Nettels, and *The History of Currency in the British Colonies*, by Robert Chalmers, and general histories of New Jersey make no mention of these terms. Their information on the monetary situation suggests three possible explanations:

1. "Old money" and "new money" may refer to the acts of Parliament of 1704 and 1709 fixing the value of foreign silver coins in the British colonies. If so, the differentiation would be between the value of the foreign coins before and after this legislation.

2. Paper money was first issued in New Jersey in 1709. Possibly these terms are used to distinguish between coins and paper issue.

3. Following the union of the provinces of East and West Jersey in 1702 under the Governor of New York, the official rate of currency in the province was that of New York. Nevertheless, in western New Jersey foreign coin continued to circulate at the higher Pennsylvania rate. The terms may thus refer to the New York and Pennsylvania rates.

land of Jean Jaquet,[3] near the King's Highway, whereunto Jean Jaquet promised to give, as he also did, 4 acres of land. It was then also decided to cut logs that winter and cart them over, so that building [operations] might begin in the Spring. The logs were to be hewn 32 and 22 feet long, and were hewn and carted over by the following:

	Logs		Logs		
Marten Jansson	2	Jean von Neeman	2	Guarret von Neeman	
Olof Nillsson	2	John Bertillsson	2	John Minck	
Lucas Petersson	2	Zacharias Bertilsson	2	Cornelius Corneliusson	
Jacobus von Devair	2	Henric Petersson	2	Peter Billerback	
Philip Franssen	2	Jacob Savoj	2	John Savoj	
David Savoj		Hinric Billerback	2	Abrah: Savoj	
John Billerback	2	David Billerback	2		

[RACCOON 1714]

After the death of Mr. Jonas Aureen [Aurén][3a] on February 16, 1713, the people of Racoon Creek were without a pastor, excepting for what service Magister Pn. Sandell[4] rector of Wicaco could render them, until they came to an agreement with the people of Christina to secure the help of one of their ministers, who was to preach in Pens Neck. After the Rev. Hesselius[5] had consented to this and Mr. Abra-

---

[3] Jean [John] Jaquet, undoubtedly a descendant of John Paul Jaquet, a French Protestant refugee who came to America and became Governor of the Delaware colony in 1656. He had several distinguished descendants such as Major Jaquet in the Revolution, Reverend Joseph Jaquet and others. Jean Jaquet's daughter married Baron Isaak Baner

[3a] Reverend Jonas [Aureen] Aurén, was sent to America in 1696 and given four hundred *dalers* as "travelling money" by the King. He was to accompany the two pastors, Rev. Rudman and Rev. Björk to the Delaware to collect information about the country and the people, obtain a map of the district and then return home to report to the King. He remained here, however, to the end of his days. For a time he did missionary work among the Indians. After the death of Rev. Tollstadius he was called to serve the Raccoon parish in the summer of 1706, but he did not assume his duties there until the spring of 1707. He was a man of some parts and a popular pastor. He died on February 16th or 17th, 1713, and was buried on February 24th. (The Records of Holy Trinity Church at Wilmington state that his death took place on February 17th.)

[4] "Magister (Master of Arts) P[roste]n (Dean) Sandel. Andreas Sandel was born in Hållnäs parish, Roslagen, November 30, 1671.

He was suggested by his old friend, Andreas Rudman, Rector of Gloria Dei or Wicaco Church, Philadelphia, as his successor, and the Archbishop acted on this proposal and appointed Sandel "missionary on the Delaware." He was ordained in July, 1701, and shortly thereafter left for America. He served as pastor at Philadelphia until June, 1719, when he returned to Sweden. While in America he married Maria Dahlbo, of an old Swedish-American family, and had several children with her. He died on May 11, 1744.

[5] Andreas Hesselius was born in Klingsbo on May 8, 1677. He entered the University of Uppsala in 1690 and became master of arts seventeen years later. On June 23, 1711, he was appointed pastor "in the American Mission" and was ordained on September 3rd, the same year. As Rev. Björk remained in the congregation for some time, he did not assume his duties in the Old Swedish Church

ham Lidenius[6] had come over to Pens Neck to be there steadily, Stephen Jönsson and Anders Hoffman went there and, with the consent of the People of Pens Neck, Mr. Abr: Lidenius was given permission to preach for them every 3rd Sunday. This continued from October 20th, 1713, until April 4th, 1714. Then Dean Björck,[7] at the request of the people of Racoon Creeck, and with the consent of Mr. Lidenius, arranged for them to have services every other Sunday, like those who lived in Pens Neck.

RACCOON CREEK [1714]

On May 14 a Parish Meeting was held regarding the Church, which decided among other things, how it was to be kept up. It was decided that it should be covered on the outside with boards and whitewashed on the inside. Peter Lock undertook to secure boards from Chester.

Some time after that they received an answer from Peter Lock that there were no boards in Chester. Wherefore some of them got together, without the knowledge of the Pastor, and made an agreement with Sam: Robbinsson of Philadelphia, who undertook to whitewash the Church both inside and out for 54 pd. new money [which]

---

in Wilmington (variously called "Old Swedes", Christina—the original Swedish name for Wilmington—and Holy Trinity) until the Spring of 1713. On September 15, 1723, he preached his farewell sermon in Wilmington and departed for Sweden in October.

[6] Abraham Lidenius was appointed assistant to Andreas Hesselius in 1711 and arrived in Wilmington on May 1, 1712. Later he was stationed at Pens Neck and Raccoon and thus became the first regularly appointed pastor of this parish. His work was successful and he was able to erect a second church at Penns Neck, in spite of the fact that the members of the Christina congregation did not fulfill their obligation and promise of contributing to the building of a chapel on the Jersey side, when this should be necessary.

Lidenius was a faithful pastor of great merit who did his duty and more, although his salary was never paid regularly, sometimes not at all, and he often suffered privations and want. He returned to Sweden in 1725 and became pastor in Umeå. While here he married Maria Von Neaman, of an old Swedish-Dutch family, and had two (or three) children with her, among them Johan Abraham, who later became pastor in his father's congregation, as is stated below, p. 84, note 78.

[7] Eric Biörk (Björk) was requested to go to America in 1696 and given 500 Swedish *dollars* for travelling expenses. In company with Rev. Rudman and Rev. Aurén and Anders Printz as companion, he left Stockholm on August 4, 1696, and arrived at Elk River, Maryland, on June 24, 1697. He built the Old Swedes' Church in Wilmington, Delaware, which was dedicated on July 4, 1699, today probably the oldest church in America still continuously used for services.

He married Christina Stalcop in Wilmington, Del., on October 6, 1702 (a descendant of one of the old Swedish families). On July 29, 1714, he left America for Sweden and became pastor at Falun on his arrival in his native land. He died on August 21, 1741.

was promised. The list of their contributions was left at the home of Jacob Lukas, and therefore was lost.

[RACCOON 1714]

On October 30, Mr. Abraham Lidenius was appointed by Dean Andreas Sandel to the Church of Racoon Creek, to be rector of Racoon, [and] Pens Neck, according to Bishop Swedberg's[8] direction and warrant, which here follows:

> *To the Christian Congregation at Pens Neck and Racoon Creek, we wish much grace and blessing of God Almighty in the Name of Jesus Christ!*

The Christian congregation's Welcome letter, dated Racoon Creek [*Ratkungskyhl*], March, 1714. I have recently received from Dean Björck [Biörck], and from it, as well as from Dean Björck's both written and oral detailed relations, I perceive that it is your desire for the sake of your own and your children's spiritual welfare, to have your own Congregation [and] Minister, namely Mr. Abraham Lidenius, whom you promise honorably to support and reward.

I have given careful consideration to your request, and Mr. Björk's information, and found it to be very reasonable. Inasmuch as Racoon Creek and Pens Neck are so far distant from Christina Church; and whereas in the fall, winter and spring, they are scarcely able to get across the River to you without danger to life; and whereas they, by the grace of God, have acquired still another teacher besides the two Ordinary teachers: so it is Christian that they form themselves into a separate congregation and be ministered to entirely by Mr. Abraham Lidenius, call him, and promise properly to support him. But Racoon Creek and Pens Neck must come to an amicable agreement with their teacher, Mr. Abraham, first, as to where their Church is to be, and afterwards about the Services. It would be most advisable that they build a nice Church halfway between these [two] places, and likewise a parsonage in the same place, so that, as far as possible, they arrange to have the church stand in the middle of

---

[8] Bishop Jesper Svedberg (1653-1735) was one of the great names in Swedish ecclesiastical history, and father of Emanuel Swedenborg. He helped to revise the old translations of the Bible and he was one of the principal workers in preparing the new psalmbook of 1695. This edition was withdrawn from circulation on account of "heretical expressions" in it, but many copies were sent to America in 1696 to be used among the Swedes on the Delaware. He became Bishop at Skara in 1703 and was one of the most active and enthusiastic supporters in Sweden of the Swedish Lutheran Churches in the Delaware Valley. He wrote many books, among them *America Illuminate*, 1732; *En Gudelig Barna Cateches*, etc., 1723; *Nova Svecia* (*New Sweden,* translated but not yet published).

the Congregation. Then they may, as was said, in a friendly manner, agree amongst themselves, either for each parish to take one Sunday, or for the one to have somewhat more than the other; according as they find it most convenient. Let everything be done in mutual sincerity, Christian charity, and brotherly confidence. If afterwards they could build a serviceable school[9] there, beside the Church, it would be well.

For the rest, I wish to assure you all that as long as I live I shall not neglect to pray God for you and your welfare, to work with my Gracious Sovereign all that I am able, to promote your best interests. I shall furthermore do whatever I can to procure for you the needed religious books, and take great care to send them over to you.

Hoping that you will always so conduct yourselves that you and your children may have ample grace and good favor to derive from God and the King, and that they may thereby be strengthened and encouraged, to still further keep watch over your welfare. Wishing you and myself all God's grace and blessing in the Name of Jesus, Amen.

I remain, steadfastly, with sincere pleasure,

The Christian Congregation's
Most devoted servant,

Jesper Swedberg.

[Brunsbo]   2 [?]
1714.
1715.

Bishop of Skara: and also of the Swedish Lutheran Churches of London in England and of Lisbon in Portugal as well as in America.[10]

[RACCOON 1714]

On November 3 was held a Parish Meeting, at which it was discussed how the Minister should be supported, and he was promised, by each one, as much as seemed to them equal to 6 [sh ?] and for 2 Men to be chosen, namely, Åke Helm and Elias Fish, who were to receive the money, and since the congregation had no parish clerk, it was decided that the Vestrymen should pass around the collection bag

---

[9] A schoolhouse was erected later near the parsonage. This was burned by the English in the Revolutionary War.

Several schoolteachers taught Swedish and gave religious instructions among the Swedes in New Jersey during the 18th century, such as Stält, Jesper Svedberg, Jr., and others.

[10] Bishop Jesper Svedberg was appointed by the King in 1702 to have special supervision of the Swedish congregations on the Delaware, and he occasionally calls himself "Bishop of Skara and of the congregations . . . in Pennsylvania in America."

six days each.[11] With this Anders Hoffman was to make a beginning next Sunday. Furthermore, Johan Cock was made Church warden in the place of his father, Cock, who was doing the congregation no good.

The Minister's salary was promised, as follows:

ALL OLD MONEY

	pd.[11a]	sh.		pd.	sh.
Anders Hoffman	1	10	Michael Laikian	10	
Jons Coln	1	⁓	Herman Halm		
Hans Petersson	1	--	Stephen Jonsson	1	4
Åke Hellm		15	Hans Halton		10
Johannes Seneck		12	Olof Petersson		15
Fredrick Hoffman		15	Johan Cock		15
Joh: Nilsson		15	Joh: Georgen		10
George Kyhn		15	Eric Mulicka		12
Nils Qwist		12	Anders Mulicka		12
Anders Dahlbo		12	Elias Fish 2 pairs of shoes[12]		
Lars Dahlbo	1	5	Clemens Corinna		6
Matts Mattson		12	Lars Cock		12
Thoms Dinneh[s]		10	Peter Cock		15
Måns Halton		10	Jons Halton		10
Laurentz Hollsten		12	Johan Mulicka		12
Manne Dircksson		12	Berthil Supply		6

pd.

Michael Hommen
Gunnar Arched
Olof Mulicka
James Guarring
Anders Mattson
John Hoffman, Jr.
John Y. Hoffman
Lars Petersson
Fredrich Dinneh
Gabriel Petersson   1

    Total   26

Also received of Thom. D.[ennes] on behalf of the Church . . . . for 1 linen cloth . . . .

[RACCOON 1715]

On February — a Parish Meeting was held with Racoon Creek [congregation], regarding where the Pastor could live in case he wished

[11] That is, each one of the vestrymen should pass around "the collection bag" at the services, six Sundays in succession. The collection bag was attached to a handle about five feet long, making it possible for the vestryman to reach far in between the pews.

[11a] pd, "pound sterling", is the abbreviation used in the original for pound, contrary to the more usual abbreviation of "£".

[12] Fish was probably a shoemaker.

to get married. To which the Congregation gave answer that since they had, and the people of Pens Neck had not, any house and [land], that the Pastor ought to live there [in Racoon], to which the Pastor [objected that there he] could not expect any grain crop and he was quite unwilling [to do it] since he [received] far too small a salary to live on without it. Could he not induce the people to build for him other houses in some other place in the country, where the ground was somewhat better? For this reason it was decided that Gabriel Petersson, who had a vacant farm in Pens Neck, should dedicate[13] it to the Pastor until the Congregation had time to look around, they promising to build a cabin for him to live in, if the people of Pens Neck would cart the logs for it, and provide floors and Cellars as well as [a] Fireplace. This was lived up to by the people of Racoon Creek, but not so by those of Pens Neck.

[PENNS NECK 1715 ?]

On March 4, a Parish Meeting was held as to when and who should begin to build the Church, and it was decided that Jan Minck, Lucas Peterson, John von Neeman and Jacob Hindersson should undertake to build it. This was done during the first days of May, the others coming one day each to help them heave up the logs; But Jacob von Devair was there to help them every day. Jean Jaquet carted over the corner-stones. It was then also decided to finish the inside work on the Rectory, when the people of Racoon Creek had put it up and roofed it; but very little [of this promise] was kept. The Pastor did most of it himself, paying for bricks, the making of the fireplaces, and the boards [and] glass.

PENS NECK 1716

Since the first of May, 1715, after the erection of the Church, nothing more was done to it. For that reason a Parish Meeting was held on the 24th of February, at which [contributions] were promised for its completion by the following:

NEW MONEY

	sh.		sh.	
Jean Berthilsson	6	Jacob Hindersson	6	Jean v. Neiman
Lars Petersson	6	Olof von Neeman	6	Hans Shiere
Guarret von Nieman	6	Lucas Petersson	6	Jean Minck
Jean Savoj	6	Philip Fransson	6	Jacob v. Devaire
Zacharias Berthilsson	6	Jean Jaquet, paid,	6	Peter Billerback,
Hindric Petersson	6	Cornelius Corneliusson	6	not paid
Jacob Savoj	6	Eric Jansson	6	George Litzen
				Abraham Savoj

---

13 *inviga thet åt Predikanten. Inviga*, "consecrate", "initiate", "open", "dedicate". Here "to assign", "to allow the pastor to use".

At the same time it was decided that Jacob von Devair should arrange for the Shingles, which [duty] he voluntarily assumed, and the same winter, with the help of Jacob Savoj, Paul Jansson, Henric Billerback, Zacharias Berthilsson, Henric Petersson and Philip Fransson he made 2,000 shingles of Chestnut wood. But since these were not sufficient, more were made by Erik and Olof v. Neeman, Erik Jansson, Jacob Hindersson and Guarret von N.[eeman].

The same day it was also agreed that Lucas Petersson and Jean Minck should roof the Church for 12 pd., old money, but the congregation were to help them raise the rafters and provide them with nails, all of which was thus arranged.

For the nails, a bond was drawn up on Olof Stahlkopp, which he owed Dean Björck, and which the latter, before his departure, had given, towards the building of a Church, which amounted to 4 pounds 10 shillings, old money.

It was also decided that Jean Minck, or some other of the Vestrymen, was to secure a carpenter who could make the Pulpit and Altar the Congregation to do all the rest itself.

[PENNS NECK 1716]

On October 8th, the members of the Congregation came together to plane and lay the Church floor. Jean Minck having brought along a carpenter, Jacob Artwood, who contracted with the Congregation to make the Altar and Pulpit for 7 pd. 16 sh. new money. This was promised by those that follow [below]. For this money Jacob v. Devair and Jacob Hindersson gave to Jacob Artwood their bond, and he his, in return, for the satisfactory completion of the work.

NEW MONEY

	sh.		sh.	
Jacob Hindersson	10	Jacob von Devair	10	Jean von N.
Eric Jansson	10	George Litzen	10	Hans Mu[licka]
Jean Mink, paid in		Marta Guilliamsson	6	Marta Jansson
work	10	Seneck Senecksson	6	Jean Berthilsson
Olof von Neeman	6	Cornelius Corneliusson	6	Lars Petersson
Jacob Savoj		Philip Fransson	6	Johan Hindersson
Abraham Savoj	6	Guarret von Neeman	6	Hindric Peters[son]
Hindric Guns	6	Zacharius Berthilsson	5	Hindric —
Elizabeth Guilliamsson	7	Lucas Petersson	10	

[RACCOON 1716 ?]

On September 27, a Parish Meeting was held in the presence of Dean Sandell. At which time the Minister complained that his salary came in so irregularly that he had hardly anything to depend upon. Whereupon the Dean, with many arguments, exhorted them to arrange

[8]

with all diligence so that their teacher be not obliged either to do his work with sighing, or to leave them entirely. Whereupon the congregation unanimously promised improvement which, nevertheless, by many, has not been complied with.

The complaint was also made that very few wanted to answer their teacher, when he questioned them about their religious faith;[14] and it was asked whether the Young People, divided into different districts, could not come forward into[15] the choir? To which consent was given, and it was done. It was then also promised that benches should be made in the Choir, for the children to sit on during the Service, but that is said not to have been done

At the same time also this Church-book was bought by the Rev. Dean Sandell, in Philadelphia for £1, 11 sh. 6 d. new money, and paid for by the people of Racoon Creek:

It was also decided that the Church meadow should be rented out for 5 Shillings a year.

Also, that Lars and Gabriel Dahlbo should sit with Anders in their father's pew.

[PENNS NECK 1717 ?]

On January 6, a Parish Meeting was held, wherein it was considered how the benches in the Church were to be made. The Pulpit and the Altar were now ready. The men of the Parish had before always thought of making them themselves, but now they thought it would be [better] if a carpenter made them. They therefore made a new agreement with Jacob Artwood to construct benches like those in Racoon, or Christina, for which he asked 20 pounds, which also was promised him. And since they were afraid that the boards would not suffice, he promised to saw several logs, which were lying at the Church, if the Congregation would have his saw mended, and get him a man to help him. Which was promised and kept. For his payment for the benches, moreover, they subscribed as follows:

	pd.	sh.		pd.	sh.
Jacob Hindersson		15	Marta Jansson		12
Lucas Petersson		15	Philip Fransson		10
Jean von Neeman		15	Seneck Senecksson		10
Hans Shiere		15	Johan Hinricsson		10
Eric Jansson	1	00	Marta Guilliamsson		10
Cornelius Corneliusson		10	Jean Philpot		8
Olof v. Neeman		10	Thom. Wiggorie		6
Guarret von Neeman		10	Abraham Savoj		7
Henric von Neeman		10	Henric Geens		10
Joh. Shogen		10	Margareta Billerback		5
Jacob Savoj		7	George Litzen		9
Johan Berthilson		8	Christina Göransson		

[14] *Christendoms stycken*, "Christian knowledge", "articles of faith".
[15] Sit in the choir.

Olof Stahlkopp's Mother-in-law gave to the Church_____ 3 15
Gave also Olof Stahlkop a steer, which Jean Minck got for the windows
and doors of the Church, and [for] Jacob Artwood's board.
Thom. Wiggorie gave a heifer which the Vestrymen gave to the Minister as partial payment towards the inside work on his house.

PENS NECK 1717

On the 31st of March the Church was dedicated by Dean Andreas Sandell and called "St. George."

[PENNS NECK 1717]

On the 24th of May a Parish Meeting was held, at which time the Churchyard was measured off, and it was decided to enclose it, which was done the ensuing week by the following:

Eastern	Southern	Northern	Western side
Jean Minck	Jean v: Numan	Abraham Savoj	Jacob Hindersson
Joh: Shogen	Marta Jeansson	Jacob Savoj	Philip Fransson
Simon Eaton	Hans Shiere	John Savoj	Jonas Shagen
Hinric Geens	Jacob v. [De]vaire	Henric Billerb :16	Christiern Petersson
	Hinric Petersson	Peter Biller	Johan Berthilsson
	Zacharias Berthilsson		

Lucas Pettersson and Eric Jansson made the Gates,
Lucas [making] 2, Eric, 1, at the northern side.

RACOON CREEK 1717 AND 1718 [17]

On April 10th a Parish Meeting was again held with reference to the churchyard which was very badly dilapidated, and it was then decided that each one should repair his portions, or panels, [of the fence], which was not performed properly, there being some who did no more thereunto than to set up the old and weather-rotten rails. Jacob von Cöln and Elias Fish moreover left their gates unmended, so that the Churchyard still lies open for Swine and everything, in spite of its being often and earnestly preached about. At the same time Åke Helm promised to spade the Churchyard, which he also did.

[RACCOON 1718]

On February 1 a Parish Meeting was held, at which again the Churchyard was discussed, but little was accomplished. Later, also there was discussion about a porch for the Church, and since everyone was not able to come and work on it, it was decided, with the consent of

16 Henric Billerback.
17 Two dates were used because the birth, marriage and death records which in the church records are listed along with the minutes of the parish meetings frequently covered two years.

all, that a man should be hired for it, who could put it up and roof it. The arrangements for this were left in the hands of Måns Kyhn and Matts Mattsson. Towards autumn, these contracted for it with John Rambo, Junior, who was to receive £2, 10 shillings, new money, for it from the Church funds.

The Congregation then also considered, and the major part of them agreed to pay for the horse which Jacob von Cöln, Stephen Jones, and Anders Hoffman had bought, on January 2nd, for the Minister, who otherwise had none which he could ride upon, in doing them service, and it was paid by the people of Raccoon and Pens Neck together (costing £9, 5 shillings, new money) as follows:

RACOON CREEK

	Shs.	pce.		Shs.	Pce.		Shs.	Pce.
John Reehn	6		Lars Coch	7	6	Pehr Cock	4	
Gabriel Petersson	3		Måns Kyhn	4	8	Eric Mulicka	2	
Laurens Hollsten	2	4	Jacob v. Cöln	4	6	Jacob Mattsson	4	6
Stephen Jönsson	4	6	Matts Mattsson	4		Peter Long	3	
Peter Justice	4	6	Abr. Lid[enius]	4	6	Lars Lock	2	
John Mattsson	3		Michael Hoffman	3		William Cobb	2	4
Åke Helm	3		Carl Dahlbo	3	2	Fredrick Hoffman	2	
Hans Petersson	4	6	Manne Dirchsson	3				

PENS NECK

Jean v. Numan	6	Henric Petersson	4	Olof von Numan	5
Jacob v. Devaire	4	Simon Eaton	5	Marten Johnsson	5
Jean Minck	4	Jonas Shagen	4	Jean Savoj	4
Philip Fransson	4	Cornelius Corn		Zacharias Berthil-	
Hinric v. Numan	4	[eliusson]	3	sson	3
Henric Geens	3	Abraham Savoj	4	George Litien	3
Lucas Petersson	6				

[PENNS NECK 1718 ?]

On March 12, a Parish Meeting was held, and it was decided to build a porch for the Church, 10 feet long and 8 feet wide. For which Olof v: Numan, Joh: Shagen, Zach: Berthilsson, Jean Savoj, Simon Eaton, Jean Berthilsson and Jonas Shagen were to make Shingles and Clapboards, and to cart them over. Henric Petersson, John von Numan, Henric v. Numan, Abrah. Savoj, Marta Jansson, and Henric Geens, were to make stulps, sills, and laths, which Cornelius was to cart over. Lucas Petersson, Jean Minck, Jacob Hindricsson, Jacob von devair, Philip Fransson, set it up and roofed it.

All of which was thus arranged and done.

It was then also decided to buy boards with which to line the Church, and that a well should be dug.

RACOON CREEK 1718 AND 1719

As the plaster on the northern wall began to fall off, a Parish Meeting was held on March 1 [to consider] how it should be mended. The pastor's suggestion was to let it all fall off, and then line it with boards. But as the majority thought that, when the three other walls were whitewashed, there was no use in having the fourth one different. It was therefore agreed to have a plasterer come from Philadelphia who could plaster [and whitewash] the wall over again. This was left for Peter Mattson to arrange, which he also did. And the cost amounted to £4, new money, which was paid out of the Church money, which Åke [Helm] had charge of.

Matts Mattsson and Michael Laikian were then also appointed Churchwardens in the place of Thom. Dinneh and John Kock.

RACOON CREEK 1719

On April 18, a Parish Meeting was held, at which the following was discussed:

1. It was proposed by the Pastor: Whether the congregation did not think it necessary that the age of the children who were baptised, and the names of their god-parents should be presented [to the pastor] on the morning of the christening, so that the pastor could then put down the children's ages, and disapprove of those god-parents who were not suitable for assuming responsibility for the children's baptism. To this it was replied, that they were willing to give in the ages of their children after the Sermon, but as far as godparents were concerned, it was impossible for them to get such as were found competent in all respects, because the congregation was small, and only the smallest part thereof was rightly concerned about what appertained to their salvation. Wherefore everyone either had to get such godparents as he could, or else be without them. From which it may be seen that godparents heretofore have served more to uphold custom than to be of use to the children.

2. There was talk of a Glebe, since the land which the Parson was living on was neither his own nor the Congregation's. To which it was replied that they wanted to build on the land which lies at Racoon Church, if the Parson would live there. But since the soil was only sand, and, besides that, the way to the other Church in Pens Neck was too long, the Parson asked whether, if he would live at Racoon Creek, they would give him grain, besides the small salary which he had by the year, and which they knew to be entirely too little, and whether, with the help of the people of Pens Neck, they would make a bridge over Old Mans Creek, in order to make the road between the two Churches shorter. But as "no" was answered to that by the majority, the parson therefore [declared that he] would not,

[12]

and could not, live at Racoon Creek. Wherefore also that talk was ended for this time.

Whereas Jacob Lundbeck, who had recently arrived from Sweden, had nothing much to count on, therefore the Congregation was asked whether they would not take him on as Parish clerk, and give him each a bushel of grain a year, and this was approved by the Congregation. Whereupon Jacob Lundbeck was called in and asked whether he was willing to assume the office of Parish clerk under those conditions. To which he answered "yes" and took the keys.

Finally it was asked how floors, doors and shutters, together with the benches, were to be made ready for the Porch of the Church, and Elias King replied, that he would make all of them, if someone who lived near the church would provide him with board. This Åke Helm promised to do, and it was thus arranged.

PENS NECK 1719

On June 5th was held a Parish Meeting at which it was first asked by the Minister, who was to have the Church Keys, since they had no Parish clerk and it was not convenient for the pastor to have them, as he was so many times called away from the Church and furthermore lived inconveniently.[18] To which it was replied that it seemed most appropriate for one of the Vestrymen who lived near to the Church to take them and be at hand to unlock the Church, not only on Sundays, but also on other days when any such necessary occasion arose.

It was also decided that he who had the keys was to pass around the Collection bag and have the money in his keeping. This Lucas took upon himself to do for one year

After that Timothy Damsey was asked whether he would join our church; to which he answered "yes" and promised to give £3 new money to the Church for a seat in the 7th pew.

After that the pastor complained that the children, on Sundays, made a dreadful noise outside the Church. To prevent this the Vestrymen agreed to take turns about going out of Church to look after it. Jacob v. Devair was to make a beginning with it next Sunday.

There were also chosen for Vestrymen in place of those who had died: Hindric Petersson, Marta Jansson, Olof von Numan.

Finally the question was put: Whether the Congregation preferred to plane the boards, or to tar them? To which they answered "tar

---

18 *och bodde eljest helt oläliget,* "and besides lived quite inconveniently." The idea is that the pastor lived too far away from the church and it was therefore inconvenient for the members to get the keys, if they should want them, when the pastor was not at the church.

[them]." Whereupon the 13th of June was appointed[19] for coming together again to nail up the boards and sheathe the Church.

Whereupon Timothy Damsey promised to procure 14 pounds of nails, which he also did, out of what [the money] he had promised to the Church.

On June 13th the parishioners came together again, wainscoated the Church and dug a well, but did nothing more to the well.

The boards were paid for by the following:

NEW MONEY

	Ss		Ss		Ss
Olof von Numan	6	Philip Fransson	6	Marta Jansson	6
Guarret v: Numan	6	Anna Shiere	6	John Bertillson	6
Cornelius Corneliusson	4	Jacob Hindersson	6	Hindric Peterson	6
Johannes Shagen	3	Zacharias Berthilsson	6	John Savoj	6
Jonas Shagen	4	Abraham Savoj	6	Jacob Savoj	6
		Henric Geens	6		

Henric Billerback also paid on an old debt to the church	1
Bal[ance]	1

[RACCOON 1720 ?]

On January 16, at the request of Anders Hoffman, a Parish Meeting was called, and held by the Pastor, regarding the Parsonage. No great number were in favor of the land around the Church, and yet no one was for [building] the bridge over the Creek. When the upright [among them] insisted that it was impossible for the Minister to live on that land, with the small and uncertain salary he had, the answer was made by Jacob Cöln, on his own and others' behalf, that the Minister had to have time to experience the same conditions, and be content like other farmers who lived on the same kind of land, without considering [the fact] that the Parson could not even afford to hire a workman, and hardly even a maidservant all the year through. However, it was at last agreed by the more intelligent of them, that 4 men should be chosen for all [the rest] to go and see what land would be the most serviceable for a Glebe, whether that at Racoon Church, or Anders Dahlbo's which he wishes to sell, and which lay in the middle between the Churches. The men who were chosen for this business were: Måns Kyhn, Peter Lock, Fredrick Hoffman and Michael Laikian. Three of these were quite willing that the Minister should live at Racoon Creek. But when they had carefully inspected both properties, they came back to the Congregation with the following answer: that Racoon Creek's parsonage land would not do at all,

---

[19] *Hwaruppå blef appointed d.* 13. English words are found occasionally in the original, as *appointed* in this sentence

but that the other land was as good and suitable as any they knew of. Whereupon, at their request, a Parish Meeting was called by the Minister for the 13th of February.

RACOON CREEK 1720

When the 13th of February came, not all came who had promised to meet together. Some respectable men remained at home on account of illness, and other hindrances. The Pastor then took the greatest pains to exhort the people to be generous for [the sake of] their own and their children's welfare. But all this to no avail. So this Parish Meeting was held and ended to the great vexation and annoyance of the pious. And few indeed were they who would promise anything equal to purchasing the Glebe. Hermanus Helm, who has 100 pounds put out at interest, had not the heart to promise more towards it than 36 shillings, whereas Manne Didricsson, who had a hard enough time making his living both promised and gave more. Pehr Cock, who one can imagine purposely makes fun of everything, promised 5 shillings. In fine, this Parish Meeting was so disappointing that the Pastor assured them he never wanted to hold another with them about any Glebe, before they showed a great and noteworthy improvement.

The Pastor thought herewith that the whole plan was over until Mr. Jesper Swedberg[19a] came down to [see] him, and said that he himself and Måns Kyhn had been [around] to each and all in the congregation of Racoon, and had gotten from them a list of 120 pounds and that they were obliged on fine of 10 shillings, to come in on February 27, each one to give a Bond to 4 Men for what they had promised towards the purchase of the Glebe. He furthermore assured the Pastor: That all had asked for his presence.

On the day appointed, the parishioners came, and everything was fulfilled which they had promised Mr. Swedberg when he and Måns Kyhn united with them. Four men, namely Stephan Jansson, Anders Hoffman, Jacobus von Cöln and Matts Mattsson, were chosen by the Congregation to buy and make arrangements for the Glebe. To these men the others gave a Bond for the payment, which Mr. Swedberg wrote out.

The pastor also was present, at their request, but he did nothing else than to remonstrate against their hardness and their blindness, reading aloud to them the Queen's letter from Sweden, which had been delivered to him the previous day by the Dean, the Rev. Hesselius, begging them not to abuse the tenderness which the Government of Sweden so undeservedly entertains towards them. The letter follows on the next page.

19a Jesper Svedberg, Jr., the brother of Emanuel Swedenborg, and son of Bishop Svedberg, spent several years here as a schoolteacher. He was also given a commission for handling books that were sent from Sweden to the churches here.

Ulrica Eleonora, by the grace of God, Queen of Sweden, of the Goths, and the Wends, Grand Duchess of Finland, Countess of Skania, Esthland, Liffland, Carelia, Bremen, Werden, Stettin, Pomerania, Cassuben and Wenden, Duchess of Rugen, Lady over Ingermanland and Wismar, Countess of the Palatinate at the Rhine, in Bavaria, of Gulich, Cleves and Bergen, Countess, etc., also Landgravine and Hereditary Princess of Hessen, Princess of Hirtsfelt, Countess of Posen, Elmbogen, the Diet of Zingen, Hayn, Widde and Schämnburg, etc.

Our approval and gracious disposition with God Almighty: We have noted with gracious pleasure, oh well beloved Swedish men and Inhabitants of Pensilvania, the steadfastness, with which you have always maintained your Faith and Christianity towards God, as well as your love and loyalty towards Us and Your Fatherland.

We are therefore disposed, immediately, at the commencement of our reign, graciously to make known to you, through this our letter, that we have had you in gracious remembrance, and are resolved in every way to promote your welfare and to maintain it, and in the meantime we have ordered Bishop Swedberg to come to your assistance with some religious books which he will send over by two clergymen, who, by our gracious command, he is sending out to you, to serve you in your religious exercises and which will be delivered unto you. Wherewith we commend you graciously to God Almighty. Ulrica Eleonora. Issued [in] Stockholm, April 15, 1719. D. Von Höpken. To the Swedish Congregation
    in Pennsylvania.

RACOON CREEK 1720

On March 2, the 4 Men whom the Congregation had chosen went down to Anders Dahlbo to buy his farm for a Glebe, which he was obliged to sell on account of a great amount of debts which he was daily paying interest on. This same farm had a little while before, been offered for £112; but when Anders Dahlbo heard that the Congregation wanted to buy it, he demanded £150, which all four did not agree on, that day. However, since it was not a great sum which divided them, the Pastor, Anders Hoffman and George Kyhn, went again to Anders Dahlbo the following morning, and offered him the whole sum, the Pastor also permitting Anders to live on the farm and work it for nothing for one whole year, until the Pastor himself should come up there to live, and in the meanwhile Anders Dahlbo could look around for another place

This Anders Dahlbo consented to, and he made an agreement with Anders Hoffman to bind himself thereto in writing on the 14th of the same month. Before that time [however] Anders Dahlbo changed his mind, thinking, undoubtedly, that the Congregation was so anxious for his farm that he could get more for it than ever it was worth, wherefore the Congregation left off its land-purchasing with him and came to an agreement with George Kyhn to buy his plantation, which took place on the 21st, and cost 145 pounds.

NB. Anders Dahlbo is said afterwards undoubtedly to have regretted what he had done [namely] that he had not stood by his deal, for not only was he forced to sell his land for 100 pounds, but he also had to pay interest on the money he owed for two more years.

PENS NECK 1720

On the 13th of April, it was decided that Jacob Hindersson and Jacob v: Devair were to go around and collect Subscriptions for the Glebe, and afterwards to go up to Racoon Creek and give their Bond to those who bought it,[20] for as much money as had been promised them. They went around to [collect] it, but since little resulted from what Jacob Hindersson was doing, therefore another Parish Meeting was held on May 20th. Then both Jacob v: Devair's and Jacob Hindricsson's districts signed up to pay to Jacob v: Devair.

On the 9th of May, Henric Petersson, Lars Nilsson, and Matts Shagen went up to cut timber for a house on the Glebe.

Jacob v: Devair and Jac[ob] Hindersson now again promised to go up to Racoon Creek on June 7th, to give their Bond to Stephen Jones, And[ers] Hoffman, Matts Mattsson, and Jacobus Cöln, who had bought the land, but they did not keep this [promise], wherefore the Racoon Creek church-book shows it caused great confusion.

Those who promised [money] for the Glebe subscribed as follows:

NEW MONEY

	Pd.	Shs.		Pd.	Shs.		Pd.	Shs.
John Savoj	1	10	Philip Fransson	1	0	Lars Nilsson		10
Jacob Savoj	2		John Liffsen			David Billerbäck	2	10
Andrew Hindrics-			Standly		15	John Minck	2	10
son		15	Henric Petersson	1	10	Abrah. Savoj	2	
Zacharias Berthills-			John Berthillsson	2		Guarret von Num.	2	5
son	1	10	Olof von Numan	2		Henric Billerb.	2	10
Hinric Guns	2		Lucas Petersson	2		Ezechiel Jansson	1	10
Cornelius Corneli-			John Shagen	1		Marten Jansson	1	10
usson	1	10	John Senecksson		10	Peter Berthilsson		15
Jonas Skagen	2		Timoth. Damsey		15			

This maketh in ye whole the full Sum of[21]_____ £38 10

---

20 The original is very confused. It probably means that Olof von Nurman and Jonas Shagen gave a bond of £50 to Jacobus Cöln and Matts Mattson.

21 Thus in the original.

When the time came for this to be paid [erasure], [Cornelius Corneliusson] caused great confusion among the people, which brought the Congregation into dissention, and gave their teachers much worry and many a sleepless night. The reason for it was that Cornelius advised them not to pay, which the majority of them obeyed, until, by the Pastor's letter of advice, [Cornelius Corneliusson] was arrested by Jacob v: Devair and sentenced to pay himself. This put fear into the others. For this, however, the Pastor has borne more insults and sweat from [the subscribers] than anyone could possibly believe, excepting those who have heard and seen it. God forgive him for it, and may no others fall into his sin.[22]

RACOON CREEK 1720

On April 19, the books mentioned below, sent from Sweden, were distributed, and it was decided that 2 Shillings should be given for each Bible, and 6 pence for each Psalm-book, and 4 pence for each Catechism and Compendium. Of which moneys Mr. Swedberg should have 1 Shilling for each Bible, for his trouble in taking care of them. The remainder was to be for the use of the Congregation and to pay the Freight.

	Bibl.	Pcb.	Cat.	C.H.[22a]		Bibl.	Pcb.	Cat.	C.H.
John Rambo	1	3	–	–	Stephen Jones	2	3	1	–
Peter Mattsson	1	2	–	–	Samuel v: Neeman	1	1	–	–
Manne Dirksson	1	2	–	–	Åke Helm	1	2	1	–
Matts Mattsson	1	2	–	–	Olof Petersson	1	5	–	–
Nils Qwist	1	1	–	–	Fredrich Hoffman	1	1	–	–
Thomas Dinneh	1	2	–	–	Anders Hoffman	1	3	–	–
Johan Seneck	1	1	–	–	Hans Halton	1	2	–	–
Lars Halton	1	–	–	–	Johannes Georgen	1	1	–	–
John Mulicka	1	2	–	–	Olof Mulicka	1	2	–	–
Eric Mulicka	–	1	–	1	Henric Henricsson	1	1	–	–
Peter Steehlman	1	1	–	–	Charles Dahlbo	1	3	–	–
Gunnar Arched	1	1	–	–	John Arched	1	1	–	–
Manus Helm	1	1	–	–	John Halton	1	1	–	–
Anders Dahlbou	1	3	–	–	Jacob Mattsson	1	1	–	–
Hans Steehlman	1	–	–	–	George Kyhn	1	1	–	–
Lars Lock	1	–	–	–	Peter Justice	1	1	–	–
Pehr Cock	1	–	–	–	Matts Homan	1	1	–	–
John Reehn	–	1	–	–	Jonas Björström	1	1	–	–
James Guarring	–	2	1	–	Jacob Lundbeck	–	1	–	–
Jacob Forssman	–	1	–	–	William Cobb	–	2	–	–
David von Neeman	1	1	–	–	Guarret v: Neeman	–	–	–	1
Gabriel Dahlbo	–	2	–	–	Peter Dahlbo	–	2	–	–
John Dahlbo	–	1	–	–	Olof Steehlman	–	3	–	–
John Mattsson	–	1	–	1	Anna Runnels	–	1	–	–
Påwel Kempe	–	1	–	1	Pelle Kock	–	3	–	–

[22] Fall into the error of having members of the congregation arrested for non-payment of debts.

[22a] *Pcb*, "psalmbook", "hymnbook"; *cat.*, "catechism"; *C.H.*, "compendium of Hesselius".

	Bibl.	Pcb.	Cat.	C.H.
Lars Sträng	-	1	-	-
Peter Long	1	1	-	-
Gabriel Petersson	1	3	1	-
Lourence Hollsten	1	2	-	-
John Hoffman	1	1	-	-
Elias King	1	-	-	-
Peter Lock	1	2	-	-
Johannes Hoffman	1	1	-	-
Michael Hoffman	-	1	-	-
And: Petersson	1	-	-	-
Jacobus v: Keuhlin	1	4	cat	-
Måns Keehn	2	3	1	-
Johannes Nilsson	1	2	-	-
Mans Halton	-	1	-	-

	Bibl.	Pcb.	Cat.	C.H.
Eric Kock	-	2	-	-
Hans Petersson	-	2	-	-
Tim[othy] Stedham	-	3	-	-
Michael Homan	1	3	-	-
Måns Laikian	1	1	-	-
Michael Laikian	1	1	-	-
John Lock	1	1	-	-
Gustaf Lock	1	2	-	-
John And: Hoffman	1	-	-	-
Matts Mattsson	Book of sermons			
Lourence Cock	1	2	-	-
Lars Petersson	1	-	-	-
John Cock	-	3	-	-

RACOON CREEK 1720

On June 29, the freight for the books was paid out of the book money, as the following receipt shows:

The undersigned has received from His Honor, the Rev. Mr. Lidenius, three pounds, 2 shillings and 7½ pence, on behalf of the Rev. Dean Samuel Hesselius, for freight, and for advance payment on the Bibles and Hymn-books, which have arrived for the Congregations in [New] Jersey.

Andreas Hesselius.

Christina, June 29,
1720

[PENNS NECK 1720]

On May 26, the books enumerated below [being some] of those which arrived from Sweden with the Rev. Mr. Lydman[23] and Mr. Samuel Hesselius,[24] donated by his Majesty King, Charles the XII., were distributed [as follows]:

[23] Jonas (Lydman) Lidman took charge of the Gloria Dei Church in the fall of 1719. He was a man "of small gifts" but he worked hard and a "more faithful servant of the Lord", as was said about him, never officiated in the Swedish churches on the Delaware. It appears that Lidman returned to Sweden on November 14, 1730.

[24] Sameul Hesselius (1692-1753) was appointed pastor of Gloria Dei by Charles XII on December 23, 1717. Later, however, a change was made. Lidman was appointed pastor and Hesselius his assistant. Samuel Hesselius worked at Manathanim, Upper Merion, Pennypack Creek, Neshaminy and other places in Pennsylvania. He served as pastor of the Old Swedes' Church in Wilmington from 1723 until 1731, when he left America.

Cornelius Corniliusson, 1 Bible, 1 Hymn book, I Large Catechism
John Minck, 1 Bible, 1 Hymn book
Lucas Petersson, 1 Bible, 1 Hymn-book.
Abraham Savoj, I Bible, 1 Hymn-book
John Savoj, 1 Bible, 2 Hymn-books
John Seneck, 1 Bible, 1 Hymn-book
Marten Jansson, 1 Bible, 1 Hymn-book, 1 *Compendium Hasselii*
Olof v. Numan, 1 Bible, I Hymn-book, 1 *Compendium Hasselii*
Guarret v. Numan, 1 Bible, I Large Catechism
Henric Geens, I Bible, I Hymn-book
Jacob Savoj, I Bible, 1 Hymn-book
Jonas Shagen, 1 Bible, I Large Catechism
Zacharias Berthilsson, 1 Bible
Henric Petersson, 1 Bible, 1 Large Catechism
John Berthilsson, 2 Hymn-books, I Large Catechism
John Shagen, 2 Hymn-books
Lars Nilsson, 1 Hymn-book
William Pukman, I Hymn-book
Anders Hindersson, 1 Hymn-book
Philip Fransson, 1 Hymn-book
Peter Billerback, 1 Hymn-book
Elizabeth Jansson, 1 Hymn-book
Thom[as] Wiggorie, 1 Hymn-book
Tim[othy] Damsey, 1 Hymn-book

It was then decided that everyone who received books should give for each Bible, 2 shillings, for each Hymn-book, 6 pence, and for each Large Catechism, or *Compendium Hasselii*, 4 pence. Of this, Mr. Swedberg who had charge of them, was to have for his work 1 Shilling from each Bible. The rest of it was to go towards the Freight and for the benefit of the Congregation, which also was so done.

At this Parish Meeting it was further decided that those who for [a] year and a day[25] either had not helped the Church, when it was needed, or else did not pay the pastor's salary, within [such and] such a time, should lose their seat in the pews and should have no service to expect of the pastor, unless they could show good reasons for their neglect, such as sickness, etc.

[PENNS NECK 1720]

On August 18, the Congregation hired Henric v. Numan, and Abraham Savoj to form or fit the logs which had been cut the preceding May for a parsonage. Each one worked his 2 weeks at this, so that their pay amounted to 18 shillings per man, out of which Henric v[on] D[evaire] gave 15 Shillings to the Glebe. The remaining 3 Shillings and the half part of Abraham Savoj's work, which was 9 shillings, was paid from the balance remaining from Pen's Neck's accounts for the year 1719; the other 24 Shillings having been spent for glass.

---

25 *på åhr och dag*, "for [a] year and [a] day", for some time", "for a long time", it may also mean "within a stipulated time"

	p.	sh.
To Henric v. N[uman]		3
To Abraham Savoj		9
To glass	1	4
Total	1	16
To 20 pd. nails		17.6

[RACCOON 1720]

On December 26th, a Parish Meeting was held, in which it was decided that, since the Glebe needed a great deal of work [on it], which was very dilapidated when it was bought, and since it was impossible for a few [men] to set it to rights again, and put it into order, therefore each one who could work should, whenever his Churchwarden summoned him, go with him, without [offering] any excuse, and do whatever he was told. This has been fairly well kept, with the exception of Peter, Lars and Eric Kock, in the district of Mantals Creek.

It was also afterwards decided that all the men of the Parish should pay the Pastor's salary at the time due to none other than the Churchwardens, and that the Pastor should not receive anything of it before he got the whole salary for half a year at once, in order that the people might see whether his pay was not entirely too small. This showed the Congregation what they had taken in, and it did not amount to 8 pounds. Whereupon the whole Congregation promised improvement. It was also proposed by And. Hoffman and Åke Helm that a Bond be written, and everyone who wanted to pay should sign his name to it.

[PENNS NECK 1721]

On January 1, after the Service was finished, a Parish Meeting was held. Here Jacob Hindersson and Jacobus von Devaire by reason of their ill health and age were excused from their duties on the Glebe, and in their place two others were chosen by the congregation, namely, Olof von Numan and Jonas Shagen, who came up to Anders Hofman on the 9th of January, and gave him Jacobus Cöln and Matts Mattsson their Bond for 50 pd. new money.

by both [parties], and Anders Hoffman undertook to make an agreement with a mason about it, which was so done.

[RACCOON 1721]

On September 16, a Parish Meeting was held, at which it was decided that the people of Racoon Creek should engage a mason to make 3 fireplaces and a cellar, which they would pay for, if the people of Pens Neck would engage and pay a carpenter. This was agreed to

[PENNS NECK 1721]

On September 30, a Parish Meeting was held at which it was agreed, that since the people of Racoon Creek had undertaken to pay the mason who had done the masonry work on the fireplaces and cellars of the parsonage, those of Pens Neck should hire and pay a carpenter to do the interior work on the houses.

This Jonas Björström[26] was willing to do, if the people of Pens Neck would pay his debt to Regner Rowden in Salem, which was £6, new money.

This was granted by those present. For which reason Jonas did the interior work and Olof v. Numan guaranteed his debt to Regner. But as all were not present, therefore the others were consulted about it the following day, and all gave their approval thereto. Nor did it come to more than 6 shillings, new money, per man, which was subscribed by those who were present, as follows:

	Sh.		Sh.		Sh.
Olof von Numan	6	Jean Minck	6	Lucas Petersson	6
Simon Eaton	6	Seneck Senecksson	6	Philip Fransson	6
Guarret von Numan	6	William Markander	6	Henric Guns	6
Jonas S'hagen	6	Marta Jansson	6	Henric v. Numan	6

PENS NECK 1722

On April 21, was held a Parish Meeting, at which the Minister, with good arguments, showed the Congregation not only his own condition, as it then was, but also how miserable would be the [condition of] the Congregation, unless a different order was established between the members of the Congregation and the Pastor, for not only would he be obliged to leave them, on account of poverty, but also that many people would force themselves into the Congregation who never intended to do it any service. For this reason the Pastor asked whether the Congregation thought it advisable that an agreement, which the Pastor read, should be signed by [all] those who, after this, wished to belong to the Congregation, so that the Pastor might thereby know his Sheep, and know which ones he had to care for, or not. This was approved by all those who were present, who then, immediately, signed it and delivered it into the hands of the Church wardens, who were to visit the others in their homes, and see who wished to do the same, or not.

Here follows the Agreement, and those who signed.

---

[26] Jonas Björström (Bjurström), joined Rudman, Björk and Aurén in 1696, taking the place of Andreas Printz who mysteriously disappeared. Bjurström thus became the "attendant in common" of the three pastors on the journey to America, and arrived here with them in June, 1697. See Acrelius, *Beskrifning*, p. 231, 232 ff.

Knowing that every one, that doeth preach y Gospel is according to the order of God to live by y Gospel, we all the signers of this present doe hereby towards Y maintenance of our Ministers, binde us in a double Sum to what we here do Set our names to, to pay yearly to the Churchwardens of our Congregation in Pens Neck at or before y 20th day of Octobr. every year during our life or abode here, making by this the Churchwardens and every one of them, whoesoever they may be, duly authorized to call arrest or Sue for at every time of y appointed terms as much as will be here Subscribed and promised of lawfull proclamation money for y use and Support of every minister, that now or hereafter, Shall by a lawfull sending administer unto us y means of our Salvation. And for y better performance hereof, we doe Sett hereunto our owne hands or Marcks, this 21 day of April in y year of our Lord 1722.[27]

	Sh.		Sh.		Sh.
Lucas Petersson	18	Jean Minck	12	Henric Petersson	8
Seneck Senecksson	12	John Seneck	8	David Billerback	8
John Jaqvet	10	Lars Nilsson	10	Tim: Damsey	15
William v: Neeman	15	Marten Johnsson	12	Garret v: Neeman	15
Ezechiel Johnsson	10	Albert Billerback	10	Oney Standley	6
Tobias Caspersson	10	John Philpot	10	Johannes Gaspersson	8
Josias Pennington	6	Matthias Starte	4	Thom: Lamstone S.	6
Jacob Hindricsson	12	John Guransson	6	Marta Guilliamsson	9
William Philpot	5	Jacob v: Devaire,		Jacob Savoj	6
Cobus Danielson	12	Jr.	6	Matthias Shagen	6
Henric Billerback	8	Henric Jeany	9		
		David Savoi	6		

Zacharias Berthilson	10	[pce.]
Abraham Savoj	10	
Henric V. Neeman	10	
Jonas Shogen	8	
And[ers] Hindricsson	6	
Henric Winny	4 _ 6	
Joseph Hawkes	8	
Thomas Wiccorie	11 _ 3	
William Stahlcop	11 _ 3	
John Shogen	7 _ 6	
John Standley	4 _ 6	
And[ers] Hindricsson	4 _ 6	
Philip Fransson	11 _ 5	

RACOON CREEK 1722

On May 14, a Parish Meeting was held together with the people of Racoon Creek, in which the Pastor described his miserable condition, because very few paid up his Salary, which made it impossible to live with them any longer. It was therefore asked whether the

[27] Original in English as above.

Congregation did not want to take [pity] upon his need, and pay properly the little they had promised him, since otherwise he would have to go his way. It was also proved by the Pastor that he would have to suffer from both hunger and nakedness in case, his condition were not improved. But although this was presented with many arguments, there was no change except that some person or other now and then came in with a few Shillings, which did not happen often. Since, however, God touched some of them who sent food and drink for his household, the Pastor remained, but the others also remained in their unwillingness.

[RACCOON ? 1722 ?]

On September 29, a Parish Meeting was again held, at which it was again asked, whether the Congregation either would let the Minister leave them, or make a better arrangement for his support. But as there were very few present, and those few said they were unable to do anything more than what they were doing, it was therefore requested by the Minister that those few would sign a letter, which the Minister would send home to Sweden, asking for help, since the greater part of the Congregation were unwilling [to help], and the remainder were too weak. But since this proposition was opposed, therefore another one was presented by the Minister, namely, that he set up an agreement which every one who wanted to belong to the Congregation should sign his name to and, after their names, [put down] as much as they intended to give their teacher, annually. To this some of them agreed. And since their arguments, together with the Minister's, seemed the best, therefore an Agreement was written by him and delivered into the hands of the Churchwardens, to get each one's signature, but since the Churchwardens got an unceremonious reception from almost every one, therefore the matter was dropped, and the Minister remained in his former condition. He appealed to God in his need, and the Congregation's distress, which was working its own Destruction, because by this they make it plainly evident that they would rather be without a Minister than give him the assurance of their support.

RACOON CREEK 1723

Because the Minister saw the Congregations's reluctance towards his first proposition for their consolidation, and that furthermore those who formerly united with him with very few exceptions, thereby were set at variance, he thought to let the matter drop entirely, and to say no more about it. Wherefore, also, he left everything in the hands of God, who best knows the conditions of all, desiring with all his heart that God would vouchsafe to show him some way out which might make it feasible for him to remain and tend those few Souls who were ready to do him and the Congregation some service. In the meantime the Minister, namely Abraham Lidenius, received a summons from Bishop Swedberg to return home to Sweden, who also promised to send another [minister] in his place. At this the Minister was dismayed, knowing how little his Successor, whoever it might be, could get along unless another and a better arrangement were made before he went away, especially since he knew what trouble he had had in working the Congregation into the condition it now was in, pitiable as that was, at the best, and that it would nevertheless become worse unless some further and firmer union were established between the members of the Congregation. He therefore called a Parish Meeting on January 19, taking care to explain to them, with many reasons, the use and necessity for an Agreement such as he read to them, being very hopeful that they would then be accommodating, since they would see that the Minister, who was about to depart, did not do it for his own sake but for theirs. But however well this was intended and presented, nevertheless it was not signed by them all; some giving one excuse, some another, which put together mean nothing but this: *they did not want to*. For if this is a lawful excuse, namely: "He who will not take my word, he need not," or this: "There have been Ministers here before who have not demanded any such thing", then everything is an excuse.

Here follows the Agreement itself and those who signed it:

Knowing that every man that preacheth the Gospel is by the orders of God to live by ye Gospel, we all the Signers of this, belonging to the Swedish Church at Racoon Creek, Situated in Gloucester County, in the Gouvernment of west New Jarsey, doe hereby binde ourselfes, each of us to pay the Sum of Currant lawfull money, or such value thereof, as can be agreed upon, yearly and every year, as will be sett downe at our names, in two intire payments, viz. half of it at ye beginning of May, and ye remaining halfe at the beginning of Novembr, every year during our abode or Stay here at this aforenamed congregation; Giving also by the Same, unto all Churchwardens of the Same Church, that either now be in place or hereafter will be chosen, full power to call arrest and sue for, of every person that Sum, which that person hath sett or caused to be Sett downe at his owne name so that no bodie is to be molested for ye others neglect, but the neglecting person himself, and this for no other use, than for Such a minister as is both lawfully called, ordained and sent. To the which performance, we doe binde our selfes freely, by setting our hands to this present. Racoon Creek the nineteenth of Januarii, in the nincth year of the Reigne of our Souvaraigne King and Lord, King George, anno Domini, 1723.[28]

---

[28] The original in English as above.

Marcks	Pd.	ss.	d.		Pd.	ss.	d.
Stephan Jones	1	4		Lars Cock	00	10	
Gabriel Peterson	1	3		Hermanus Helm	00	12	
Peter Lock		12		John Jones	00	8	
Manna Dirckson		9		Thomas Dinneh	00	11	
John Hoffman		6		John Arched	00	8	
Alexander King		8		David von Neeman	00	12	
Gustaf Lock	00	10		Samuel von Neeman	00	8	
Eric Steehlman	00	6		Jacob Mattsson	00	7	
Elias Fish	00	12		Nicolas Hoffman	00	6	
Jonas Biurstrom	00	12		Bartholomew Supply	00	5	
Jonas Biurström	00	12		Michael Homman	00	8	
Lourents Holls[t]en	00	12		Hans Stechlman	00	8	
Michael Laikan	00	10		James Guarring,			
Lourents Lock	00	8		Sen:	00	6	
Isaac Senec	00	5		Jonas Kyhn	00	10	
Mons Laikan	00	12		Mons Halton, Sr.	00	10	
Mons Kyhn	00	15		William Peterson	00	8	
Jacob Lundbeck	00	6		Johannes Hoffman	00	6	
Hans Peterson	00	15		Nicolas Justice	00	8	
Nicholas Layman	00	10		Desiderius V:			
John Hoffman	00	8		Neeman	00	6	
Anders Mattsson	00	6		Jacob Fosman	00	6	
Hindric Hindricsson	00	10		Peter Peterson	00	6	
Eric Mulicka	00	9		Andrew Hoffman	1		
Hans Halton	00	7	6	Timotheus Stedhman	00	9	
Lourents Halton	00	9		Michael Hoffman	00	6	
Stephan Mulicka	00	8		Elias King	00	6	
				George Keehn	00	10	

[RACCOON 1724]

PARISH MEETING

None was held after this year, because the pastor expected to journey to Sweden, and therefore the one which was held on the 15th of February, 1724, may here be inserted. At this, 54 persons were present, who, because of the plastering on the outside of the Church having fallen off, promised to bring thither 50 clapboards per man, of six inches width and 4 foot length, wherewith they would line the Church; which clapboards they promised to deliver by the 29th of February.

Here also a smith came in, by the name of Herman Richman, who asked to be allowed to buy himself a burial place, which was permitted him by the Congregation, under the condition that he would take care of a portion of the fence around the Churchyard, to which he agreed.

The Churchyard having for a long time been lying open for all kinds of cattle as well as swine, which carried on pitiably with the graves of the dead, it was now first agreed that it should be better fenced in and more properly taken care of, for which reason also it was more carefully than ever divided up among each and every one.

And as each one received only one Post and one length of fence [rails], it was therefore found good that each one should mark his post, which he sets up, with his name or mark.

Buerring places[29]

Afterwards, because a large portion had not chosen any burial places, which often caused not a little confusion, the pastor this time finally induced them to do it, and the places were divided up among them, beginning at the Western end of the Churchyard and running from North to South in the following manner:

First row:
Herman Richman, Anders Hoffman, Joh: Jansson Hoffman, Mons Kyhn, Gabriel Petersson, Lars Halton.
Second row:
Alexander King, John Jones, Mons Lock, Olof Petersson, Hans Petersson.
Third row:
Anders Fredrickson Hoffman, Fredrick Hoffman, Jacobus Kulen, Peter Lock, George Kyhn, Peter Justice, Lourentz Hollsten.
Fourth row:
Hans Halton, John Arched, Johan Fredr: Hoffman, Gustaf Lock, Johannes Geörgen, Lars Lock.
Fifth row:
Carl Sträng, Lars Påwelsson, Thomas Dinneh, Jacob Lundbeck.
Sixth row:
Lars Sträng, Lars Hoffman, Fredrich Dinneh, Michael Homman.
Seventh row:
Anders Sträng, Swen Homman, Gunnar Arched, William Cobb, Manne Didrickson.
Eighth row:
John Andersson Hoffman, Peter Homman, Hindric Hindricksson, James Guerring.
Ninth row:
Nicolas Hoffman.
On the Southeast side of the third row, Hermanus Helm, beside the panels [fence].

Item, Anders Dahlbo, laid at the Southwestern side, by the rail fence, just near the gate, his burial place.
Down by the road, on the North side of the Church, took the following: Nils Gustafson, Jacob Forsman.
At the Eastern end of the Church: John Mulicka, Erik Mulicka, Olof Mulicka, and, at the southern Church-door, Johan Seneck.

PENS NECK 1724

PARISH MEETING

Here is inserted a Parish Meeting which was held on February 22 1724, wherein the following was decided:
1. That the Church should be pinned under with stone, which

---

[29] Thus in the original.

should be carted up from the shore. Jonas Shagen promised to cart them over, if others would come and help him to load them off and on. And because everyone promised his help towards this, [the foundation] was masoned with clay on March 3rd; the promises were kept, and everything was accomplished.

2. There was talk of [putting in] a window in the fore part of the church, since those who have their pews there are advanced in years and can not very well see to read or to sing, wherefore also one Shilling per man was promised for making it.

3. The repairing of the Churchyard was discussed, and those who had dilapidated palisades promised that they would mend them.

4. Lucas Petersson and Jonas Shagen each promised a lock for the Churchyard gates, so that anyone and everyone might not secretly put their corpses therein, as had hitherto been done.[29a]

5. Whereas Johannes Shagen proved reluctant in paying what he owed to the Church, the others, by the Pastor's advice, gave a promise that they would never persuade or importune a laggard, but would let him be until he was ashamed of himself, or saw his fault and, in the meantime, they themselves were to do what was needful.

6. Guarret von Numan was made Church warden in the place of Philip Fransson.

PENS NECK

Anno 1727, on May 25, a general Parish Meeting was held in Pens Neck, when the following matters were transacted:

1. Vestrymen were appointed, namely: Luke Petersson, Olof von Jman [von Neeman], Martin Johnson, Senekson and Henry Guans Churchwardens—Cornel. Cornelson, John Senekson.

2. It was decided that a general Parish Meeting should be held yearly on Ascension Day, and that anyone who then is absent without legitimate cause should pay a fine of 4 Shillings to the church.

3. That every woman who goes out working should give the Minister one week's work a year.

4. Each one chose his burial place in the Churchyard.

5. They were advised that at Child Baptisms and christenings, the Godparents announce themselves in time, in order that the Minister may be informed whether they are suitable for it or not, so that the Parents of the children do not take any and every chance [acquaintance] for a Godparent.

6. William Mecum bought David Billerbak's pew, and paid 40 Shillings [for it].

[29a] *at icke som här til skedt war, hwar och en måtte stjäla therinn sina lyk*, "might steal therein their corpses". *Stjäla* means "to steal", but here the meaning must be that no one might stealthily or secretly bury their dead in the churchyard so as to avoid paying the fee.

7. If anyone who did not belong to our Congregation, should wish to be buried in the Churchyard, he had to pay 15 Shillings, 9 pence to the Minister, and 6 [shillings] to the Church.

Here ended what happened in this Congregation during the time that the Rev. Mr. Windrufwa had it in his care. NB.[30]

[RACCOON]

ANNO 1727

On March 19, the Congregation met together to hold a Parish meeting, at which it was decided that they should give both their Teachers such support as would be somewhat sufficient to help them out.

This was done, in the following manner:

1. That Racoon should pay the Pastor's salary according to the subscription which they had raised among themselves shortly before the departure of the Rev. Mr. Lidenius.

2. Since the Glebe was not provided with a good fence, but lay open it was therefore asked that the Congregation put the place into good order; afterwards the one who lived there should keep it up. It was thereupon decided that those who did not desire to work on the Glebe that year, should give five Bushels of grain in the place of five days' work.

3. That they should pay the Rev. Mr. Windrufwa's board as heretofore. Very few from Pens Neck came to this Parish Meeting, not more than four. A portion of those who stayed away were not satisfied with what was decided, although it had been previously generally agreed that whatever the Vestry and the Churchwardens decided was to be fully effective. This also resulted in very few from there paying their grain, and none of them any work. But Racoon erected the fence and cleared the land. In this the following fulfilled their promise as to the grain and work:

[30] The Rev. Andreas Windrufwa in company with Peter Tranberg (see Raccoon meeting July 6), set sail from Gothenburg on September 1, 1725. They were wrecked on the coast of Norway, but after many adventures made their way to Amsterdam and from there to London. They arrived in Philadelphia in the Summer of 1726.

Rev. Windrufwa was stationed at Penns Neck, while Tranberg was assigned to Racoon, where he was installed on June 30, 1726.

Windrufwa began his work with much promise. He was to receive twenty pounds annually, "a house and provisions, together with a horse for his services". He became popular with many in the congregation and married a daughter of Jaquet, but he died a little more than two years after his arrival (November 5, 1728).

RACOON		PENSNECK
Gabriel Petersson	John Fredrick	Olle Von Eman
Hans Petersson	Anti Hofman	Guarrit von Eman
Lorens Holsteen	Ake Helm	Marta Janson
Mans Keen	Manna Dedriks	Henrik Guans
John Hoffman	Gunnar Archiet	Jonas Skaggen
Alex King	William Cobb	Senek Seneckson
Mattis Mattisson	John Archiet	John Eaton
Cobus Culen	Pet. Lock	
Pet. Justice	Gustaf Lock	
Jons Halton	Henrik Henrickson	
Nils Justice	Mich. Homman	
Thom. Denny	John Jones	
Paul Kamp	Sam. Von Eman	
Hans Halton	Stephan Jons	
Olle Petersson	David von Eman	
	Herm[an] Helm	

Note: The hard winter which was that year, threw both the ministers and the members of the Congregation into straightened circumstances.

RACOON CREEK 1727

On July 6 was held a Parish Meeting, the Congregation being then asked if they would support Mr. Windrufwa, for the time being, until some better arrangements could be made for him, so that, in the meantime, Divine Worship could be conducted every Sunday, both in Racoon and in Pens Neck. To this the Congregation was entirely agreeable and answered, just as they had on the previous Sunday, when Dean Lidman made them the same proposition, that Racoon should [collect] or make up forty pounds for Mr. Tranberg,[30a] and Pens Neck twenty pounds for Mr. Windrufwa, and pay his board, and buy him a horse. When the Parish Meeting for this was called, only half of them came. Those who came there were of entirely different minds. Some followed their conscience and gave more than they had formerly been in the habit of giving, since they saw that they were to have Divine Worship every Sunday. But some, not so. Indeed, they made nothing of

[30a] Rev. Tranberg became pastor in both congregations in 1728. However, he did not confine his labors to his own parish, but extended them as far as Egg Harbor and other distant places, preaching to the Germans, English and Swedes, as he was, for a while, the only Swedish pastor in America. On his request a commission for his transfer to Wilmington was issued by the King, on October 5, 1739, and in 1741 he entered upon his duties there. Even there he extended his work to remote places, going as far as Lancaster,—a great distance in those days. He acquired a perfect mastery of English and also seems to have been able to preach in German without effort.

He died on November 8, 1748, on a visit to his old congregation at Penns Neck, having served in this country for twenty-two years. He was buried in Wilmington (Holy Trinity) Church on November 10.

He married Anna Catherine Rudman (daughter of Rev. Rudman) and had four children with her, Andreas, Rebecca, Elizabeth and Peter.

what they had formerly subscribed themselves as willing to give to the Pastor who will succeed the Rev. Mr. Lidenius; when they noticed that they had to get together a few shillings for Mr. Windrufwa's horse and board, some reduced [their subscriptions] by four, some by five shillings. All this was done by the people of Racoon, but Pens Neck stood by the former subscription.

After this had been decided, the following were appointed for Vestrymen and Churchwardens:

Vestrymen	Petter Lock Måns Keen Thomas Denny Mattis Mattisson Petter Lock Lorents Holsten	Churchwardens	George Keen Jons Halton Johan Kock And. Mattisson

As to Mr. Windrufwa's horse, it was decided that it should be left behind, after his departure.

At last it was granted by all that, after this, when a Parish Meeting was to be held, only the Vestrymen and the Churchwardens should be obliged to meet with the Pastor, and that no one has the right to complain about whatever is then decided.

ANNO 1728 RACOON CREEK

On February 2, which was Candlemas Day, a Parish Meeting was held at the end of the Service, the preacher finding it necessary to announce the following to the Congregation:

1st. The Rev. Mr. Windrufwa asked them whether those in Racoon would support their Teacher, in which case he would content himself with those of Pens Neck. Which the people of Racoon were willing to do and made arrangements for George Keen and Lorens Holsteen to go around and see what salary they could raise. But this did not help matters very much, because a great many of them insisted on having it as they had it at the time of the Rev. Mr. Lidenius.

2nd. The Congregation were admonished to lay aside the bad habit of running in and out of Church during the Sermon.

3rd. To make frequent use of the Holy Supper, and not to neglect it, as very many had done.

[RACCOON 1728]

On May 18, still another Parish Meeting was held, solely concerning the people of Racoon and their Teacher. Since very many appeared so reluctant in paying their Minister's salary that 24 of them were owing for both years, it was therefore asked whether those who were dependable would raise their contributions somewhat, so that the Minister could have his salary assured, instead of its being uncertain, as formerly, in which case he would still continue. But at this, some of them, to begin with, had the idea that the Vestrymen and the Church-wardens should issue warrants against such slow payers, without the Minister having the least hand in it, or be blamed for it. This, indeed, at first, seemed advisable enough, but in order to avoid the tongue of the scandalmonger, this was postponed, and the demand was made that they be given time, and a chance to re-consider payment.

Afterwards, all the people of Racoon made up a new subscription, which was not to be effective any longer than while Mr. Windrufwa was at Pens Neck, and both Churches had a Sermon every Sunday. The Subscription is as follows, wherewith let the reader observe that wherever this mark occurs (†) the preacher has not received any salary all the years, up to now, that he has been with the Congregation.

	Shill.		Shill.		Shill.
Gabriel Petersson	35	Fredrick Hofman	15	Pet. Dahlbo †	10
Hans Petersson	30	Lars Pavelson	10	Pet. Lock	20
Lorens Holsten	15	Hans Halton	15	His Sons Lars and	
Lars Lock †	9	David Kock †		Carl	10
Måns Hoffman	20	Anders Strang	10	Gustaf Lock	16
And. Stalcop	12	Carl Streng	6	Henrik Henrikson	20
John Senekson †	12	Pet. Lajement	10	Mich. Homman	12
And. Dahlbo	15	Lars Strang	10	Hans Stillman	16
Lars Halton	9	Pet. Homman	6	Stephan Mullicka	10
Ephry Kock †		Gustaf Homman	5	Erick Mullicka	12
Georg Keen	15	Mattis Skaggen	10	Olof Mullicka	12
Måns [Mons] Keen	25	Paul Kamp	9	John Mullicka	15
John Hoffman	12	Enok Enokson	20	Elias Fish	25
Alex King	10	Åke Helm	30	Tim. Stedom	9
Mattis Mattisson	25	John Ronolds	6	Jacob Forsman	10
Cobus Culen	25	Erick Ronolds	5	Dishe von Eman	9
Olle Culen	10	William Ronolls	10	John Jones	12
Peter Justice	10	Gilbert Ronolls	5	Sam von Eman	16
Anti Hoffman	8	James Guarron	10	Erik Stillman	12
Jani Hoffman, Jr.	8	Edward Niclas	5	Lars Hoffman †	6
Jons Halton	15	John Niclas	10	Mich. Hoffman	6
Nils Justice	15	Gabriel Enockson	5	Stephan Jones	26
Thom. Denny	16	Olle Homman	8	David von Eman	30
Olle Petersson	15	William Cabb	12	Herm. Helm	20
John Fredrick	7	Manna Dedrikson	20	Jonas Kock †	
Carl Halton †	8	John Rambo	12	Erik Kock †	10
Nils Laikan	10	Pet. Rambo	10	Gabriel Rambo	6
Mans Laikan	10	And. Rambo	10	Per Kock	15
Mich. Laikan †	12	Peter Halton	5	John Culen	15
Guarriet von Eman	5	Måns [Mons] Lock	5	Thom. Bull	8
Hans Stellman,		Gunnar Archiet	14	And. Jones †	10
Junior	10	Israel Lock	8	Zach. Laikan	5
Lars Lock		John Archiet	12	Lars Hoffman	6
John Hoffman	12	Jonas Keen †	6		
And. Hoffman	8	And. Mattson	10		

The Rev. Mr. Tranberg was well pleased with this subscription, and promised that, if the Congregation would pay correctly, according to the same, things could remain as they had been. But if they did not fulfill their promises, neither could he hold his.

This held for only a half year, when a change occurred through the removal by death of the Rev. Mr. Windrufwa, which happened on the 5th of November, 1728, and after that time the Congregation paid the salary of its Minister according to the subscription which was customary before.

PENS NECK 1729

On January 6th, Mr. Tranberg held a Parish Meeting at which he brought the following points to the notice of the Congregation:

1. Whether they would hereafter stand by what was decided at the Parish Meetings which were held by the deceased Rev. Mr. Windrufwa: to which each one spontaneously answered "Yes."

2. How the trouble could be settled which had arisen between Racoon and Pens Neck concerning Mr. Windrufwa's horse, which had been purchased with the end in view of leaving it with the Congregation after his departure, but it was subsequently allowed, by a great many, that the horse was to be his own. This dispute they tried to settle in the following manner: that even as they had given Mr. Windrufwa his horse, so they would also give Mr. Tranberg his, if he, like Mr. Windrufwa, should die in the Congregation. But should he be called to any other Congregation, then the Horse was to belong to this Congregation. Although this seemed to be a most impartial [settlement], nevertheless Racoon would not consent thereto.

3. At the same time an investigation was held to find out how the case was with the prevailing state of confusion which had arisen between Simon Eaton and Mattis Nilson, his Stepson, with regard to the pew, and it was found to consist in this: 1. That the Church-book showed that whatever money Simon Eaton had paid out was done on Olle Nilson's Orders, which he gave before his death, and it was found, by the Church-book, that said Simon Eaton had not given much at all towards the entire Church building or any other expenses. 2. There were reliable witnesses present, such as Guarrit von Jman [Neeman], Henry Guanse, and Luke Peterson's Written Statement, which he had made during his life-time, unanimously testifying that the right to the pew belonged to Mattis Nilson, and they proved that not only had the former Pastor, Rev. Mr. Lidenius himself said that the pew should belong to Mattis Nilson when he came of Age, and that Simon Eaton was only allowed to make use of the pew during the years of the owner's minority, and that he had been put on the list of pews with that end in view, but also that said witnesses could show that Mattis Nilson's Mother, before her death, had asked that her Son might not in any way lose this right. As a conse-

quence of this it was rightfully found that said Mattis Nilson may, for himself and his Heirs, keep said pew as his lawful property.

4. On the same occasion the pew-list was read aloud from the Church-book, as it had been drawn up by Rev. Mr. Lidenius. But it can be believed that it caused not a little consternation on the part of some who had of old been sitting in pew-seats other than their own. Cornel Cornelson's wife and Peter Peterson's wife were so impudent as to believe of their teacher that he had changed the list at his own good pleasure, and so they went not to church for a year and a day, cut off the Pastor's salary, and bore towards him continually a secret illwill, in spite of the fact that he permitted them, if so the Congregation would have it, to keep the pew-seats by old custom used by them, and to change the list in accordance with the way they were sitting. But since the Congregation felt hesitant about changing [anything] in the church-book, that had once been put down, these insistent women were dismissed with the word that they may, for their life-time, sit wherever they had formerly been sitting, but that their children, after them, must sit as they had been put down in the Church-book.

5. *Item*, it was decided that Pens Neck should buy a horse and Racoon another for the use of the Pastor, which also was done. Anders Peterson sold them, down in Pens Neck, a black young horse for £7.

[RACCOON 1731 ?]

At a general Parish Meeting it was unanimously agreed that a gallery for the use of the Young People should be built, and Christophor Taylor and Cobus Culen undertook the duty of constructing it, they afterwards contracting with Allover Vessland and Gabriel Enokson for 22 pounds of these moneys. And, in order to collect said money, the pew-seats were given out at the following prices: The 1st pew, 20 shillings, The 2nd pew, 15 shillings, The 3rd pew, 12 shillings, The 4th pew, 10 shillings. Those who redeemed the pew-seats were the following:

PEW 1
Christopher Taylor, Zacharias Peterson, John Rambo, William Culen, John Månson Keen, Peter Justice, Erik Ronolls, Alexander King.

PEW 2
? Hoffman, Jr., Gilbert Runolls, Jacob Mattson, James Hanson Steelman, John Orcherd, Andrew Mullicka, Lars Lock came in the place of Lars Hofman, and the money is to go to the church.

PEW 3
Hans Hanson Steelman, Guarit von Jman, John Hoffman, Israel Hindrikson, Nicholas Keen, Peter Fredrikson Halton, Charles Lock, Gunnar Kock.

PEW 4
Nils Justice, Lars Cock Larson, Olof Larson Cock, Peter Halton, Andrew Hoffman.

Note: Since many have moved away, others have taken their places, and that is the reason that the Bench-list has been altered.

Since no Bench-list can be found in the Parish Register, therefore the same was set up by those present at this Parish Meeting, as follows:

PEW 1
Zach[arias] Peterson, Måns [Mons] Keen, Henrik, Jon. Henrikson, David von Jman, Lorens Halton.

PEW 2
Carl Dahlbo, Peter Dahlbo, Christopher Taylor, Lars Lock, John Jones, Hans Hillman.

PEW 3
Johan Hoffman, John Lock, Abraham Jones, William Cabb, Thom. Denny, Israel Lock, And.[ers], James Halton, Måns Hoffman, Manni Connor, Niclas Dahlberg, William Gerhard.

PEW 4
Peter Lock, Jonas, Gustaf Lock, Sven, And.[ers] Strang, Lorens String, Lars Halton, Gabr[iel] Dahlbo, Måns [Mons] Lock, Gabriel Dahlbo, Eric Ronnols.

PEW 5
Håkan, [Hokan], And[ers] Helm, John Kock, Lars Kock, Desiderius von Jman, And[ers], Lars Påvelson [Paulson], Gabriel Peterson, Israel Helm, Enok Enokson, Lars Kock (is permitted, for a time, to sit in Johannes Nilson's seat).

PEW 6
[Paul], James Steelman, Manna Dedrickson, John, Anders Mattson, Nils Justice, Cobus Culen, Erik, Manne Fredrikson, Richard Lorence, Edward Lorence.

PEW 7
John Rambo, Peter, Lorens Holsten, Mounce Keen, Olle Mullicka, Nils Keen, Erik Mullicka, Hermanus Helm, Åke Helm, Gabriel Peterson, Hans Steelman, Jr., Jacob Forsman.

PEW 8
Elias Fish, Jonas Jones, John Georgen, Hans, James Guarron, Povel Peter Hindrickson, Niclas Hoffman, Måns Homman, Olle Homman, Michal Homman, Peter Homman, Swen Homman, Anders, John Reeyn, Fredrick Georgen.

PEW 9
Denny, John, Hans Halton, John, James Guarron, jun., Jesper Lock, Hans Georgen, Stephan, John Senekson, Michel Logkon [Laikian?], Morten Stille, Georgen Keen, Peter Pet. Lock, Samuel von Jman,[31] Andrew Gustafson Lock, John Helm.

PEW 10
Gunnar Orchert, Lars Hoffman, John Mullicka, Hoffman, Andrew Israelson Lock, Lars Peterson, Israel Orcherd, Jonas Kock.

PEW 11

[It was] decided, that there be 8 persons to every pew. The three fatherst pews, on the men's side, are for the use of the Young People.

---

[31] The spelling, even of proper names, was very irregular in Europe and in America until the beginning of the 19th century, when the newspapers and schools began to standardize the spelling. *von Iman*, is a phonetic spelling of von Neeman (Voniman)

Henrik Henrikson's wife is to sit in the same pew as Peter Lock's wife.

On the same occasion it was asked that some of the Elders in the Congregation, who sat farthest down in the church, would take the front pew seats, and give a little something to the church for it, which was to be paid when the church needed money. Those who redeemed said pew seats, and what they owe the church for it, are these:

David Von Jman [Neeman]	50 sh.	Niclas Dahlberg	40 sh.
Mounce Keen	50 sh.	Jacob Forsman	30 sh.
Henrik Henrikson	50 sh.	Samuel von Jman	30 sh.
		John Jones	50 sh.

A Final Speech to the Reader[32]

I lay now down my penn & shut up the book, having no more to write or say, but according to orders must go to another Parish. The Lord of Heaven be with us all, & grant that when the Records of our Stewardship shall be laid open before men and Angels, we may be found faithfull Stewards & hear that blessed invitation written by St. Math. ch. 25. v.21. Are the hearty prayers of your most humble servant.

Pet. Tranberg,

Late Pastor of these Churches

GOD SAVE KING GEORGE II

RACOON AND PENSNECK, 1741

In order that After-Ages may know with certainty, and not be left in the darkness of ignorance respecting the revolution and change which has occurred in these Congregations, it is found good here to insert the following:[33]

On the 9th of July, 1740, being last year, there arrived in Philadelphia, to the Honorable Mr. Jöns Dylander,[34] dean of Wicaco, the following Letter from the Bishops and Consistory of Sweden:

---

[32] English in original.

[33] This material covering the pastorless period of the churches was probably inserted by several different members of the congregation and visiting pastors.

[34] Mr. Jöns Dylander, usually Johan (or Johannes) Dylander. *Jöns* is an abbreviation of Johannes with progressive umlaut.

Dylander acted as pastor of Gloria Dei Church 1737-1741. He was the most popular and able pastor the Swedish Government ever sent to America in the early days, unless Wrangel should be excepted. A remarkable linguist, he usually preached two sermons in the morning, the first one in German to the Germans, and the second in Swedish to the Swedes. In the afternoon he delivered a third sermon in English to an English congregation. His popularity with the English caused the English pastors to complain to the governor.

Honorable and Very Learned Dean:

Whereas His Royal Majesty, by his gracious letter and answer of October 25th last, left it to the Disposition of the Consistory, for the good of the Congregations in America, to arrange about Dean Tranberg's Succession to Christina after Pastor Eneberg,[35] who will now betake himself home to Sweden, and also about Dominus Malander's ordination into the Ministry: Therefore, in consideration of the circumstances cited by said Dean Tranberg, and by Your Honor, the Consistory finds it reasonable and just that Mr. Tranberg be transferred to Christina, and also deems it needful and good that Dominus Malander be ordained by your Honor and the several Swedish Ministers at present in America, with the usual Ceremonies, into the Holy Office of Pastor, in order that the congregations of Racoon and Pens Neck may not come to suffer for lack of a teacher: The Consistory therefore kindly wishes hereby to bring your attention to this matter. Furthermore, the Consistory has applied to Mr. Gustaf Celsing, Secretary of State for the Royal Foreign Office, to procure His Royal Majesty's Transportation warrant for said Dean Tranberg, and to forward it, together with this letter, and also a communication from the Consistory, to Dean Eneberg. We remain

Your Honor's

Most obliging [servants]

Joannes Steuchius.

Upsala Nov 7 1739.

Olof Celsius, Er[ic] M. Melander, A. Winbom.

Matts Asp. Magn[us] Beronius.

Eric Waldius.

RACOON AND PENS NECK 1741

In consequence of this letter (: the preceding, given on the last page:) and by virtue of the Royal Warrant, which followed along with it, Mr. Tranberg removed from here to Christina, in the month

---

[35] Johan Eneberg entered the University of Uppsala in 1708, where he studied theology. Before he was ordained he fled from Sweden to escape punishment for "an accidental murder", and made his way to England, where he offered his services to the Swedish churches on the Delaware. He was ordained in London by a Swedish Lutheran clergyman and, while waiting for his commission to the Swedish churches in the Delaware Valley, he was appointed pastor of a German church. Later he made his way to America and preached for the Germans in Philadelphia and probably at other places in Pennsylvania.

In 1730, Rev. Eneberg gave up his work among the Germans to take care of Gloria Dei church, which had been left vacant by Rev. Lidman. He also visited Christina once a month, during the vacancy of this church. On July 4, 1732, he was appointed pastor at Christina by King Frederik. He officiated here until 1741 when he returned to Sweden

of July, in the Summer of 1741, after Mr. Eneberg had departed for Sweden: the result of which was that this congregation [which at that time had already rather declined and diminished],[36] began to be highly offended and entirely scattered. For the people here who were libertines and accustomed to living without any law, fancied that Mr. Tranberg was now their bond-Servant, since he had served them for such a long time, and that neither King nor Bishop in Sweden had anything to do with him, but solely they themselves. And now, when this opinion proved wrong, some of them said, with great bitterness and malice, that they would never more have anything to do with any Swedish Pastor.

But some weeks later Charles Lock from Rapapon came up to Philadelphia, and related that they had quieted down and were willing to accept Mr. Malander,[37] requesting that he come over and preach for them; which Malander did, and was received by the majority of Racoon's congregation (about 20 families, and almost as many bachellors), who promised to pay him and requested that he be ordained a Minister, in accordance with the Consistory letter. But when the time came, which had been set for the ordination (which was the first of November), Mr. Dylander was dead, and Mr. Tranberg was left sole Swedish Minister in America. No ordination therefore took place. Nevertheless Malander served the congregations after that, both in the Swedish and English Tongues, in such things as the Rev. Mr. Tranberg, saw fit to permit in so great an emergency, and which the following letter shows:

To the Christian and Honorable Congregations in Racoon and Pens Neck we desire the Grace and peace of God the Almighty.

Since through the departure by death of the Dean of Wicaco, the late Honorable and Most learned Reverend, Jo[h]annis Dylander, the ordination of Mr. Malander has not been possible of accomplishment, at the appointed time, therefore I have found it advisable to announce hereby to the Christian Congregations in what matters said Mr. Malander, as their appointed Teacher, may serve it. The following, therefore, is herewith to be observed:

[36] Translation here adapted from Johnson *Journal and Biography of Nicholas Collin*.

[37] Olof Malander arrived here in November, 1737, in company with Rev. Johannes Dylander. As he was a student of divinity "well exercised in preaching", he was recommended for ordination, which was to take place on November 1, 1741; but Rev. Dylander's death prevented the execution of this plan. Malander served the New Jersey churches for some time after the death of the pastor, but because of his leaning toward the Moravian faith, he failed to gain the confidence of his people. Finally, poverty and other circumstances, compelled him to leave. After spending some time in Philadelphia in Benjamin Franklin's printing shop and doing other labors, he removed to Rhode Island in September, 1742. Here he organized a congregation and built a church. He died in the summer of 1744.

1. That he may conduct Worship with Prayer, Praise, and Preaching.
2. Marry Betrothed couples.
3. Bury the dead.
4. Receive church-going Wives.
5. Baptise Children in emergency.

Whatever else remains, I myself will assist with, when the occasion demands, until he has been Ordained a Minister; hoping that the Christian Congregation will let itself be contented herewith, until an opportunity for Ordination can be found, I remain,

The Christian and Honorable Congregation's
Most obedient Servant,
Pet. Tranberg.

Wilmington,
Nov. 9 1741.

But those who undertook and promised to pay Malander were far too few, and the greater part of them were poverty-stricken; so that his salary amounted to so very little that he was unable to live on it: Therefore the Elders agreed to buy him a beast[38] to slaughter for the winter. And so, with their approval, a cow was bought and slaughtered for him that autumn. Måns Keen bought the cow for 3 Pounds 5 shillings, paying for it with 3 Pounds out of the Collection Money from Racoon, the pastor himself paying the rest. But the Congregation of Pens Neck gave nothing, although they received the same service as Racoon; with the exception of William Garret and Henry von Nieman who were very helpful.

RACOON AND PENS NECK 1742

On May 27, which was Ascension Sunday, a Parish Meeting was held in Pens Neck, at which time the pastor stated that he could not serve them any longer with so little salary as he had; and therefore must leave them, and go to make his living wherever he could, unless they could give him something to live on. (For all that the preacher had received, up to this time, from the congregation of Pens Neck, for eight months' Service, was no more than 13 shillings, when nevertheless in a Subscription of last fall, on October 4th, they had promised over 6 Pounds a year, etc., so little do these people keep their promises:) Then answered those Swedes who were present at the Parish Meeting: That since the congregation was now mostly English, they wished, after that day, to have their services always in the English language, and to give up their Swedish church entirely to the Service of the English people, in order that the Congregation might be better enabled to support their teacher. (But as to when they would pay

---

38 *ett kreatur*, "a beast", "an animal", here meaning a cow or steer.

that which formerly had been promised, nothing was said). It was then decided that, after that day, no Swedish Services should be held any more in the church of Pens Neck, but always English, with Prayers and Ceremonies according to the Church of England; which also is done.

Thereafter much indeed was promised, but little was kept; 'twas a sign that the Word of God, alas, was despised; 'twas hard to get out a few Shillings, from time to time; and the pastor, with a wife and tender babe, lived in the misery of hunger and thirst; for they could not drink water alone, as is here quite customary, without becoming sick thereby.

The pastor now saw that he could not get on for long with the salary he received, which was, indeed, too small. (In fact, for half a year, or more correctly for 8 months, from his arrival towards the end of August, 1741, until May, 1742, he received about 9 Pounds in Racoon, and only 13 Shillings in Pens Neck.) However, in the hope of an increase for the following half year and in the future time, which always was promised, he remained quiet, doing his best according to his talent and endowment, to rightly, purely and plainly dispense the Word of Truth for the good of the people.

But after he found in the long run, that his salary was still more diminished, and that the people, quite contrary to his hopes, in part, were becoming cold-hearted, he was obliged to leave and relinquish the congregation, about the end of the month of September, 1742, sorrowing over the small success of his service, wishing his Successor better fortune, and praying for the welfare of these congregations.

[RACCOON 1744]

On the 6th of February, a General Parish Meeting was held. It was then proposed by Master[39] Åke Helm that, since a great many of the congregation here in Racoon had allowed themselves to be seduced into departing from the pure Lutheran doctrine, hitherto preached here in Racoon, to the Zinzendorff, or Moravian [doctrines]; Therefore other Trustees and Church-wardens would have to be chosen in the place of the former, who are pure Lutherans, and well disposed towards the welfare of the holy doctrines of the Lord, and for their own souls as well as those of others.

Of those who have remained and who, with upright hearts' confession, still wish to continue Lutheran, the following are now chosen for Trustees:

---

[39] *Mäster Åke Helm, Mäster (mästare),* "master", "craftsman", "expert". Here it means "craftsman"

1. Åke Helm, as previously, (N.B. Mast[er])
2. Hans Stillman
3. Gabriel Frenne
4. Hindrick Hindricsson, previously a Churchwarden.

For Churchwardens were chosen:
1. Joannes Hoffman
2. Gustav Gustavsson
3. Lars Lock
4. Eric Runnels

It was unanimously decided and decreed that Mr. Anders Hoffman was to remain parish-clerk, on account of his general praiseworthy character.

It was here decided that every Sunday, between each of my visits, the Congregation should come together here in the House of God, at the proper time, to praise and glorify God with harmonious mutual love, with reflections upon God's Word from a Postilla, and with Psalms. The lay-reader to be

John Hoffman.

* * * * *

Inasmuch as I, Gabriel Näsman,[40] have actually, by My Most Gracious King in Sweden, been put in charge of the Philadelphia congregation on the other side of the River, but whereas this Congregation unfortunately is without any commissioned Pastor, sent hither from Sweden, therefore the Members of the Congregation, desiring me to minister unto them with preaching, until they are able to agree about calling hither a Pastor from Sweden, which I, in Jesus' name, truly also will do, for a suitable reward about which some other time we can agree.

dated as above   John Hoffman

Gabriel Näsman   Åke Helm   Andrew Hofman

---

[40] Gabriel Näsman (1714-1777) was appointed pastor of Gloria Dei, Philadelphia, on August 9, 1742.

The so-called Herrnhuters (Moravians) made inroads into the Swedish congregations, especially on the Jersey side of the Delaware River. Besides, personal controversies developed between the pastor and Mr. Peter Kock, an influential Swede in Philadelphia, about the advisability of a union between the German and Swedish Lutheran churches. Peter Kock proposed the plan and worked energetically for its adoption, believing that it would counteract the influence of the Moravians. Rev. Näsman opposed the idea and won out. But because Kock was involved in the financial management of the church, ultimately Rev. Näsman's influence was almost entirely undermined in the congregation. Many joined other churches and the Swedish congregation was on the point of disappearing. After his recall to Sweden, he remained here for some time, earning a living by preaching in New Jersey and other places, and conducting a language school in Philadelphia. He left America in 1751.

1. On August 6th, the Members of the Congregation were assembled; it was then decided to make a humble appeal to His Royal Majesty and the Arch Bishop of Sweden to secure a Minister thence for the Congregation here in Racoon. Since Pens Neck always adhered first to Mr. Tranberg, and afterwards to the Moravians, they have never requested that a Minister be written for. It was decided now that a letter, previously handed in, requesting support for a Minister, should be properly drawn up and sent over to Sweden.

2. Andrew Hoffman has hitherto kept the Church book at his house, not being willing to deliver it, at the request of the Elders of the Congregation, on necessary occasions, either to them or to the Pastor, but wanting to keep it to himself, on the claim of the people of Pens Neck. Mr. Åke Helm called to mind that they had not paid anything along with Racoon, for this book, and that they could always get information here at the Church, or from the person here in Racoon who lived nearest to the Church, into whose care the members of the Congregation would entrust it. It seemed to them most reasonable for Mr. Åke Helm to keep it, and not to give it out excepting with the approval of the Elders of Racoon Church.

3. Mr. Gabriel Frenne asked to be relieved of the Office of Trustee, and that the Congregation would elect another in his stead; Mr. Jacob Forssman was then appointed by the Congregation in his place.

Gabriel Näsman
Pastor of Wicaco

Åke Helm
John Hoffman

[ENTRIES BY THE REV. JOHAN SANDIN] [40a]

In Nomine Jesu Crucifixi

After the application, mentioned on the preceding page, had reached the Very Reverend Arch Bishop, Doctor Jacob Benzelius,[41] at Upsala, in the month of March, 1746, and he, through various letters from this place, had become acquainted with the confusion which the Congregations of Racoon and Pens Neck, as well as practically the entire Swedish Lutheran Church in general, had fallen into, through certain Swedish so-called Moravian Brethren,[42] who had been instructed and

---

[40a] For Sandin see note 47, p. 45.

[41] Jacob Benzelius (1683-1747), a man of great learning, became archbishop in 1744, succeeding his brother.

[42] Moravian Brethren, or Moravian Church, originated in Moravia (now a part of Czechoslovakia) as a result of the Huss Reformation. The movement passed through many vicissitudes and was revived by Germans who joined the sect and became its real leaders.

In 1722 persecutions caused many Moravians to flee into Germany (the members being largely Germans) and settled on the Hut Mountain on a site presented to them by Count Zinzendorf. Here they founded the village of Herrnhut in Saxony and began to be called the Herrnhuters. In 1730 the movement

brought up in Count von Zinzendorff's School, and who were fore-mostly Pastor Daniel Bryzelius,[42a] who had come over here in the year 1741, with Count Peter Abraham Reinke,[43] born in Stockholm, but residing in Germany since his fourteenth year, and Swen Rosen,[44] of Gothenburg, who had formerly, namely in 1740, been driven out and exiled from Sweden, on account of his adherence to the views of the Dipple and the Pietist Confessions,[45] said Bishop, therefore, being tender and zealous for the honor of God and the purity of the Lutheran religion, could do no otherwise than take such measures, together with

---

was given new life and organized form by Count Zinzendorf and from that time on they were more often called Herrnhuters than Moravian Brethren.

The sect was established in Sweden by K. H. Grundelstjerna (1701-1754), who on a journey through Saxony became acquainted with Count Zinzendorf and accepted his religious views. Arvid Gravin, lecturer at the University of Uppsala, Rev. Tore Odhelius, Jonas Hellman, Peter Werwing, Karl Rutström and others worked for the spread of the Herrnhut religion in Sweden. In 1741 the movement was recognized in Stockholm and Uppsala as Lutheran. A hymn-book, *Sions Sånger*, "The Songs of Sion", was published and the movement had considerable success. In 1745, however, the teachings were forbidden in Sweden and some of its leaders exiled. The movement spread to most countries in Europe, mainly through the great efforts of Count Zinzendorf.

In America the sect is known as the Moravian Church (or Moravian Breth-ren). The sect was established in Pennsylvania, where Bethlehem was built in 1741 (see Israel Acrelius. *Beskrivning*, who made a visit to Bethlehem in 1741 The sect obtained a foothold in North Carolina in 1754, through a friend Zinzendorf, Frederick Wilhelm von Marschall, who founded Salem in 1760, which became the center of the Moravian Church in the South.

[42a] Paul Daniel (Brizelius) Bryzelius, born in Häradshammer, Sweden, ordained by David Nitschman, a Moravian bishop, in January, 1743, was sent by Count Zinzendorf to preach among the Swedes in New Jersey. He had a winning personality and drew many away from the Swedish churches the first years of his missionary work here. The serious quarrels and strifes are indi-cated in the letters from Sweden printed here.

Bryzelius finally left the country and the Moravians (Herrnhuters) were forbidden by law from preaching in English and Swedish churches in New Jersey.

[43] Peter Abraham Reinke (1712-1760), a native of Sweden, adopted the Moravian faith while studying in Jena, Germany. In the fall of 1744 he left Amsterdam for New York and preached among the Swedes in New Jersey for some time. He lived in Philadelphia until 1747 and spent some time in Lancaster and Bethlehem, visiting Philadelphia for a second time in 1751.

[44] Swen (Sven) Roseen (Rosén) (1708-1750), a man of great gifts and strong religious convictions, was a force in the liberal religious life of Sweden in his day. He became acquainted with the pietistic movement in Germany (see footnote 45), especially with the Moravian Church, which he joined in 1743. When his leadership of the Moravians in Sweden increased the strength of the sect, he was banished in January 1741. Sent to America in 1746 to labor among the Swedes of New Jersey, as well as among other people, he died at Immaus, Pennsylvania, in 1751, and was buried there.

[45] *Dipple and Pietist Confessions.* John Konrad Dippel (1673-1774), theo-logian, chemist, and alchemist, discovered Prussian Blue and prepared "Dippel's animal oil", which had a great vogue for a long time and was used for the cure of even nervous ailments (hysteria, etc.). Dippel became best known for his theologian writings, expressing a pietist faith, stressing "the inner life, the

[43]

the Consistory, as he thought might serve to quell this disturbance and preserve pure Doctrine among our Swedish Brethren in Faith, here in this country. For this reason, therefore, he did, on the 16th of April last, remit to His Majesty, the most gracious monarch of the Realm of Sweden, King Freidrick I.,[46] his proposal for what was believed to be the best way of settling this matter, in order to attain a happy solution. But inasmuch as this proposal involved some incumbrance on the part of the Government, His Majesty was unwilling to commit himself or make any comments about it before he had communicated the matter to the laudable Estates of the Realm of Sweden, which were expected in Stockholm, in the Month of September. As they were now convened, the proposition was remitted to them, and they subsequently sent it to the Secret Committee, which took it up for their enlightened consideration, and on behalf of all the Estates of the Realm, gave it their approval, in the Month of January, 1747, with the humble request to His Majesty, that he deign to give it His gracious approval. This was done, whereupon the Arch Bishop was immediately advised to present his suggestion for a person to fill the new office, graciously granted. Now he had indeed, from the very beginning, namely on April 21, 1746, called him, who also afterwards was appointed, to the service of Racoon Church, but various circumstances, beyond anyone's control, kept him from undertaking so hazardous an office and journey, and besides, so much time passed before there was a decision from official sources, that he declared himself willing rather to accept the most modest employment in the service of God's Church in the home country, if it be God's pleasure, than to receive this one, which seemed more honorable, in a strange land. But when the matter became urgent, and it weighed upon his conscience whether he ought to refuse so useful a nomination he also found that a righteous servant of Christ ought not to allow any worldly advantages and physical considerations

---

word", making man independent of "the word of the Bible" and even of Christ. His writings greatly influenced the pietist movement all over Europe, and he had many followers in many countries.

In 1726 he visited Sweden where he gained many followers. As usual, a strong opposition arose against Dippelanism (as his teachings were called) and he was expelled from Sweden in 1728. He died, "misunderstood even by the pietists", in 1734.

Pietism (a term of ridicule applied to adherents of the movement), a reform movement in the Lutheran Church, arose in Germany toward the end of the 17th and the beginning of the 18th centuries. It stressed individualism and religious subjectivity in opposition to orthodox objectivity and collectivism. "Inner light" and "inner personal experience" were substituted for orthodox tenets. Moravianism really received its greatest inspiration from the pietist leaders and from the teachings of Dippel and others of that period.

[46] King Freidrick (Fredrik) I, of Sweden, was born at Kassel, April 28, 1676. In March, 1715, he married the Swedish princess Ulrica Eleonaro and in 1720 he was elected King of Sweden. He died at Stockholm on March 25, 1751. He was a brave general, taking part in many battles, and was quite popular among the Swedes.

to restrain him from the calling to which God had appointed him, through those men he has raised up, to be the Stewards of his Church. His consent was therefore given, whereupon this open Warrant of His Majesty was immediately issued, which here follows, namely:

We Friedrich, by the Grace of God, King of Sweden, the Goths and the Wends, etc., Landgrave of Hesse, Prince of Hirshfield, Count of Catzen-Ellenbogen, Dietz, Zingenhayn, Nidda, and Schannburg, etc, etc.

do hereby make known: that inasmuch as we have graciously found good to appoint a Dean to have charge over the Swedish Lutheran Congregations in America, and whereas the Master of Philosophy, our well esteemed Johan Sandin, on account of his learning, skill and good standing, has been humbly recommended for this, as well as for filling the vacant Pastorate of Racoon and Pensneck in the same place:

We do therefore, herewith, and by the Power of this Our open Warrant, graciously desire to appoint him, the Rev. Johan Sandin[47] to be Dean over the Swedish Lutheran Congregations in America, and Pastor of the aforesaid Evangelical Congregation of Racoon and Pensneck, wherewith we desire graciously to grant him, besides the advantages which he may derive from the Pastorate, and which his predecessor has rightfully enjoyed, also an additional Fifty pounds sterling, annually, as Provost over the Lutheran Congregations in America. Let all concerned obediently observe this.

For further certainty we have signed this with our own hand, and confirmed it with Our Royal Seal.

Stockholm in the Council Chamber, May 25, 1747.

Friedrich

L.S.   Fred W. Steenhagen.

As soon as this Warrant was issued, the person concerned realised that the time was over for flattering himself with the hope of remaining at home, and for that reason he committed himself to the Lord, and prepared himself for the journey. During these preparations in Stockholm, he came across a translation, into German, of the letter which the Arch-Bishop and Consistory had given to the merchant,

---

[47] Johan Sandin was appointed pastor on the Delaware May 25, 1747, and he was made the first Dean or Provost (prost) of the Swedish churches in America. His voyage to America was stormy and dangerous, lasting eighteen weeks. He finally landed in New York with his wife, and made his way across the country to Philadelphia, where he arrived in March, 1748. He delivered his first sermon here on Palm Sunday, in the Raccoon Church. His success was immediate and by keeping clear of all controversies he soon won the respect and love of his parishioners; but his activities were cut short by death on September 22, 1748, after but six months' service in the country.

Mr. Peter Kock,[48] of Philadelphia, in answer to his question concerning the Moravian Brethren. This translation had been in the hands of Count Von Zinzendorff,[49] and he had made certain comments on the explanations of the Arch Bishop and Consistory. For this reason he [i.e. Sandin] thought it advisable to give this translated letter, together with the Count's notes, into the hands of the Consistory, in order that they might explain it, so that the falsity might be brought out, and the truth be defended, and thus they might free themselves of the Count's harsh judgment; wherefore, also, since what is treated of in the letter happened to the Swedish Congregations at home, therefore, before the aforesaid letter is inserted here, it is first necessary, for the sake of connection, to insert the letter to Mr. Kock, which is as follows:

COPY OF THE LETTER FROM THE ECCLESIASTICAL CONSISTORY AT UPSALA TO MR. PETER KOCK, MERCHANT OF PHILADELPHIA

The Consistory has recently received a letter from You, Mr. Merchant, dated Philadelphia, in America, August 22, 1744, and from this, as well as still more from other accounts which have arrived here in Sweden from the same place, we have noted, with much repugnance and disturbance of mind, the distressing condition which has arisen in our Swedish Lutheran Congregation there, on account of the serious attacks and actions of the so-called Moravian Brethren, or Herrnhutters,[50] in that the latter are taking pains to propagate their doctrines in the Congregations, wherever possible, in order to destroy the Lutheran Church and set up their own in its stead.

Two persons specifically, belonging to that sect, who have come from Sweden here, [namely] Paul Daniel Briselius and Pet. Nyberg,[51]

---

48 Peter Kock (Cock) (1704-1749), a sergeant in the Swedish army during the period of Charles XII, became a trader and finally settled in Philadelphia. Here he grew wealthy, measured by standards of those days, and became an influential citizen, not only among the Swedes but among the other settlers as well. He was a native Swede but possibly of German extraction. At any rate, he had large commercial relations with Germans and favored them, as some thought, more than the Swedes. He was pious and religious and greatly influenced by the so-called Hallensian or Pietist movement, violently opposed to the Moravians, and a strong advocate of close relations between the German and Swedish Lutheran churches. (See notes 40 and 42.)

49 Count Nicholas Zinzendorf (1700-1760) became interested in the Moravian Brethren, adopted their faith, and became the real founder of the sect, as a world religion. His idea was not to establish a new church, but to work within the Lutheran Church, effecting, as he thought, necessary reforms. He travelled widely through many countries, visiting Sweden in 1735 and America in 1741-42. (See note 40.)

50 See note 42.

51 Pet. Nyberg. His name was Lars Nyberg and not Pet. Nyberg was educated in the Lutheran faith and ordained as a Swedish Lutheran pastor. He came to America with Rev. Näsman in October, 1743, to work among the German Lutherans in Lancaster and Conestoga. Soon he joined the Herrnhuters

the former born in Norrköping,[52] having previously joined these Moravian Brothers and accompanied Count von Zinzendorff to America, and the other, a native of Westrogothia, having been ordained some years ago, at the request of the Skara Consistory, to be chaplain for a prominent house in Stockholm, and immediately thereafter being sent to serve the American Congregation in Lancaster. Not only do these men make proselytes and attract pupils to themselves by going around in the homes, but, still further to promote their supposedly Apostolic mission, and to lead the simple astray, they do also exhibit a number of fictitious letters as written by various prominent men here in Sweden, and especially by the Zinzendorffian Missionary, Arvid Gradin,[53] wherein it is stated that their doctrine was approved and accepted by some of the most prominent teachers here in the country, so that the Moravian Brethren already had the privilege of preaching it and spreading it all over Sweden. Furthermore, aforementioned persons are said to have had the audacity to introduce and establish their new religion through public preaching and the administration of the Sacraments in the Congregations of Racoon and Pensneck, whereby a disturbance has arisen between those who have been led astray and those who have not yet joined the Moravian party, so that this whole case, to the [great detriment of] religion and particularly to the detrimental opinion of the English as to our Lutheran Churches, has burst out into open disturbance, quarreling, vituperations, the hewing to pieces of the Church doors, and occasionally to fighting, both outside of the Church and even inside the very Church itself, and such things, unheard of among Christians, which can do no otherwise than arouse a heartfelt distress over the disturbance which these peculiar people, by their injurious actions, have occasioned among this weak and far-distant flock of Christ. Under such circumstances and because the heretical spirit has so taken the upper-hand among the member of our Lutheran Congregations in that place, that soon the simple will not know what they are to believe, or what doctrines they are to adhere to, whether to those that their former Ministers, sent out from here, have presented to them, or to those that these new Teachers now seem to want to force upon them, and which have now been finding special favor ever since the American Pastor, the Rev. Nyberg, — in whom the Congregation supposed that it was able to have confidence, he being a reg-

or Moravians and through the aid of the civil authorities was expelled from his post as Lutheran pastor in Lancaster. Later he went to Bethlehem, Pa., and from time to time visited the Moravian congregation in Maurice River, N. J.

[52] Norrköping, one of the leading manufacturing cities in Sweden with a flourishing trade. It is often called the "Manchester of Sweden".

[53] Arwid (Arvid) Gradin, for a time lecturer at the University of Uppsala, adopted the Moravian (Herrnhuter) faith and became a strong advocate of the sect in Sweden. He was expelled from the country about 1750 and it was feared that he would try to go to America to proselyte among the Swedes on the Delaware. See letter from Acrelius to the Consistory at Uppsala, September 29, 1750.

ularly called and sent teacher — has adopted this new doctrine, and both secretly and openly has spread it, under the excuse that it was accepted here in this country. For this reason You, Mr. Merchant, on behalf of yourself and your brethren, have asked the Consistory to give a plain statement as to whether, and how far, our Brothers in Faith out there may join with these Moravians in Religion and worship, and entrust their Churches and Congregations to them?

Furthermore, inasmuch as there are some differences in Church Discipline and Ceremonies both in the German Lutheran congregations in America, among themselves, and also between the German and the Swedish [Churches], it is perceived that harmony, in this matter, would greatly contribute to good order, both in Divine worship and in the Discipline, as well as in promoting God's Church and the pure doctrine here, in this country, for which reason you, Mr. Merchant, on the occasion of a proposition being made by certain worthy German Preachers in America, with reference to the setting up of a Church order and Agenda which could be generally adopted by all Lutherans, both the German and the Swedish Congregation there, have also wanted to obtain the Consistory's opinion and statement about this, as to whether it is permissible for our Swedish Ministers to join with the Germans in the event of such matters, namely, as forming such Church orders, and adopting such Ceremonies, as are most serviceable for your welfare?

The Consistory acknowledges with much gratification the praise-worthy zeal and care which You, Mr. Merchant, in this way, evince for God's dearly bought Church, and the preservation of the purity of Worship, under these deplorable temptations and infestations, and we wish, Mr. Merchant, at your request, to give the following brief and kindly answer and information:

Therefore be it known that: as regards these Moravian Brethren, in general, although, time and again, they and also those more recently known under the name of Herrnhuter Brethren, wish to be regarded as Lutherans, nevertheless they have always refused to accept the Augsburg Confession, and have expressed themselves as opposed to it, and they still utter contemptuous opinions and judgments concerning Our Symbolical Books, hardly acknowledging any other Confession of Faith than their so called *Gesangbuch*[53a] which, although it has been changed once or twice, nevertheless contains, not only a quantity of dark and ambiguous expressions, but also all kinds of Popish, Calvinistic, Fanatic and other similar gross heresies. A few brief remarks may serve as proof of this fact, which has furthermore been amply demonstrated and explained by our Evangelical teachers—while nevertheless it is gladly admitted that not all of this sect profess them, nor do they equally participate in them. It is found that, besides the Holy Bible, they make much fuss about a so-called internal word, an internal light, internal revelation, *et cetera*, setting this up above the Holy Scriptures,

[53a] *Gesangbuch*, "hymnal", "songbook", of the Moravians.

so that they presume to judge and override God's pure and living word, according to an internal word of this kind, when yet they should rather instead test and inform themselves according to the latter, as to whether their supposed inspirations are not altogether both unnecessary and unfounded. Then again, neither are they satisfied with our Lutheran Bible-version, but have recently undertaken to collect and publish first one and then another, which, as they imagine, is more complete, when nevertheless it is of no better quality, with its vague and stupid interpretations, than that it has occasioned much confusion and distress in God's Church. They hold that God created all creatures out of his own being, and that man, as part and parcel, belongs to God's nature, becoming, as a consequence, when converted, as they say, changed and turned into a divine nature. They will not admit that the Father, the Son, and the Holy Spirit are three separate Persons in a Divine being, but only three such names, which designate certain qualities in God, and thus they do not use the expressions which, in consequence of Holy Scripture, have, from time immemorial, been commonly used in the pure Church, to express this most correct heavenly doctrine, as for example, God's being, God's essence, God's nature, the Persons, etc. Especially do they pass by in silence, the personality of the Holy Spirit, so that it is not known with certainty how far they differ from and how far they approach to the views of the Old and New Heretics in this respect. As concerns Christ's Intercessor-Function they differ from our Evangelical truth in speaking more about Christ in us than about Christ for us, not recognizing any difference between these, but they take great pains about Christ's suffering as an example which we ought to follow in our Christian conduct, rather than regarding it as an actual redemption from our sins and a merit for our salvation. They believe that Christ is come to release the damned from hell. They teach that man, after the fall can, by his own innate powers, and without any further idea or knowledge of any other order of salvation, aquire eternal life, so that any one, indeed, without God's word, can learn to know Christ. In another place they say that God will unite and communicate Faith only to the chosen, and to those whom He, of eternal judgment, has pre-ordained to life and salvation. They mix together the personal union of the two natures in Christ with the doctrine of the spiritual conjunction of the faithful with Christ, and they say, among other things, that man, in justification, essentially assumes the human nature of Jesus Christ. They make no correct distinction between the new birth, justification and regeneration, and base justification upon the crucifixion and mortification of the flesh and on the contempt of the world, the denial of self, and other such things. Also, in the doctrine of saving Faith, they leave out Christ as the object, and trust in his worthy merit and reward, accepting, on the contrary, such things as belong to the fruits of faith, but not to its right nature and proper quality.

So, also, they have not any correct idea about true conversion and reformation, teaching furthermore that man is saved by means of Faith and good works together. The Holy Sacraments they regard more as a mere Ceremony than as any means of salvation, and for that reason they deny their necessity, so that they also call the Holy Supper a bread-breaking in remembrance of Christ. They say that a man who has once fallen into a deadly sin can not again be converted. Wherefore, also, they maintain that regenerated and true Christians have a perfect salvation, and that the Congregation of Christ consists of such entirely holy, and no longer with-sin-infected persons. They make an example of Purgatory in a methodical manner. As far as they are able, they willingly allow every single member of the Church, without distinction of class, freedom and right, to conduct priestly functions, openly, and as if properly called thereunto, wherefore also they censure the regular Priestly Office and pour forth against it bitter invectives. And neither do they [consider the authority of the] Politic Estate but, since they would gladly be free of all worldly subordination, they also burst forth against the proper Authorities in every kind of disparaging expressions. Their separatist spirit, and, in fact, their having no spiritual use for our Evangelical Church, is easily seen in this, that while they do, indeed, want to be regarded and tolerated as our religious Brothers, they nonetheless are exclusively attached to the communion of their Herrnhutter Brethren, indeed, even so far as to insult our Evangelical Church, while, on the other hand holding their own to be the only, true, right and unfalsified Church here on earth. Also, as regards their Ceremonials and Church discipline, in spite of the fact that their improvisations, newly-invented ordinances, forms of worship, and other religious offices manifestly differ, in many ways, not only from their old Bohemian and Moravian Brethren's manners and customs, but also from the order of God's Church both in the Old and the New Testament, they none the less maintain that their Church discipline is the most perfect, and forthwith despise all other Christian Churches who refuse to follow their institutions in such measures.

Now, as to what you, Mr. Merchant, and others have related further concerning their recently started disturbance in America, it is particularly confirmed by the similar procedure which they have practiced in other places, especially in Poland, against the Evangelicals, and thereby have given evident proof of their custom of not dealing uprightly with our Brethren in Faith, but as often as there is an opportunity, they become their most violent persecutors, and under the false appearance of Church discipline, they do the Evangelical Church more harm even than the Papists themselves were ever in the habit of doing.

There is now no longer any doubt about what idea one ought to entertain about this sect, since in recent times, they have begun to take root in several places, and thus, by abundant experience, the opportunity has been given to perceive how the toleration of them by the Evangelical, as well as the Reformed [Church] has resulted in their noisy demonstrations and doings usually having to be checked and governed by the Authorities. On this account, the attempt which they made in the year 1741, to gain acceptance here in Sweden, could have no other outcome than that Arwid Gradin and Martin Dober,[54] who were sent here as Missionaries, had to turn back with unaccomplished errand, this circumstance, on this occasion, being so much the more remarkable as it brings to light the unwarranted and groundless tales which Brizelius and Nyberg have related to the Congregations out there about the acceptance of the Zinzendorffian doctrine here in this Country, and at the same time it reveals the unscrupulous principles that these persons have tried to make use of, in order to injure our Evangelical Swedish Church in America, and by usurpation, establish themselves there instead. On such a notable occasion, a more convincing proof of the artful attempt of these teachers, and of their extravagant actions could scarcely be advanced than the very fact that, in such a serious work as they consider this, their supposedly Apostolic mission to be, they were not ashamed to base it upon such gross untruths and calumnies. And, although this disturbance, which they have aroused, can have no other effect than that of thoroughly distressing and grieving the Evangelical congregation in general, nevertheless our domestic Swedish Church feels this very deeply since—with the benevolent intention of providing the innocent Children of the Faith in such far-distant congregations with a true and upright teacher,—they have had the misfortune of choosing this Nyberg, who, against conscience and his given priestly oath,—by which he has bound himself to God and his Holy Evangel, that in his work of preaching he shall neither secretly for himself, nor openly before his listeners, spread and preach any other doctrine than that which is based on our Holy Bible and which is briefly written down and explained in our Symbolic Books,—nevertheless, instead of building up the congregation entrusted to him, seeks in every possible way to divide it, and consequently to destroy it. In a situation of this kind, the Consistory cannot fail, by humble application to His Royal Majesty and whatever else has been done in this case, to take such measures as may tend to the prevention of any further trouble of this kind, and they therewith wish to supply the congregations, in the place of Nyberg, with a teacher in whom they may have every trust, assurance and confidence, in a work so tender as that which touches the pure knowledge of the truth.

From this, which has now been so briefly related here you, Mr. Merchant, together with your amiable Brethren in the Faith, may easily see what answer the Consistory ought to make in reply to the question: Whether our Swedish Lutherans may, in religious matters, unite with these Moravians, and entrust to them their Churches and Congrega-

---

[54] Martin Dober, a Moravian, was expelled from Sweden. It was suspected that he had in mind to go to the Delaware to do missionary work among the Swedes there.

tions? Namely, that such a thing by no means can, nor ought to be done, without losing the pure and unfalsified Evangelical Truth, and on the contrary, would plunge many souls into a direful darkness and soul-deadening delusion, which may God mercifully avert!

It is far more the duty of the Consistory, in consequence of its calling, and the care of these Congregations, with which it is thereby entrusted, not only truly to desire them, but also, on God's behalf, to warn and admonish them all in general, and each one in particular, to be thoroughly on their guard against such false Brethren, and their harmful attempts and machinations, to be steadfast in the faith and the Evangel which, through the merciful regard of [God] the all highest and the tender care of our Majesty, during such a long time, even from the first beginning, has hitherto been preached and upheld by our faithful teachers sent from Sweden; and not to follow any doctrine other than that which God, the Holy Spirit itself, has dictated and taught in His word, and which is accepted by the whole Evangelical Church, as contained and written in the Symbolic Books. The Consistory wishes you, in this work, the gracious help and support of God, and makes use of the injunction, which the faithful Apostle Paul gave to the members of the Thessalonian Church, when these also were being attacked, in the same manner, by false breathren: "Now, we beseech you, brethren, by the coming of our Lord Jesus Christ, and by our gathering together unto him, That ye be not soon shaken in mind, or be troubled, neither by spirit, nor by word, nor by letter. . . "Yea, we thank God," with the same Apostle, "as often as we think of You, that ye are partakers of the Gospel from the first day even unto now. And grant us the same, that it has begun in you a good work, he shall finish it unto the day of Jesus Christ."

For the rest, as the question of a new Church discipline, and the institution of a new Agenda, while there is much in this matter which, according to various impelling causes and conditions, could either be kept or changed, nevertheless, as this is a work which possibly involves greater difficulties than one may at first imagine, since experience amply teaches, how the changing of even trifling things often paves the way for such dissentions as may disturb the peace and serenity of a Congregation, therefore the Consistory thinks it more wholesome for our Swedish Congregations in America, with regard to the aforesaid matter, that in the future, as in the past, they do follow, as nearly as possible, the Liturgy and Church order which is customary here, in the Kingdom. Herewith the Consistory remains, ever, with all faithful affection and love, etc.

Jacob Benzelius

Olof Celsuis,[55]   Matth. Asp.   Magnus Beronius
Upsala, September 4,   Eric Waldius.
     1745

---

[55] Olof Celsius (1670-1756), was a Swedish theologian, scholar, botanist, traveler, author, and specialist in the Greek and Oriental languages.

EPISTLE TO THE SWEDISH LUTHERAN CONGREGA-
TIONS IN AMERICA /: ON MATTERS WHICH HAVE BEEN
MENTIONED BEFORE, AND DEALING WITH THE CRIT-
ICISMS OF THE COUNT:/ FOR WHOM WE ASK THE
GRACE AND PEACE OF GOD OUR FATHER AND SAVIOUR,
JESUS CHRIST.

Whereas His Royal Majesty, the gracious reigning King of
Sweden, the Goths and the Wends, out of laudable concern and
zeal for the Congregation of God, even in the regions of America,
and for their increase and growth, has most graciously been
pleased to appoint Rev. Mr. Jöran[56] Sandin to be Pastor in the
parish of Racoon and Pensneck, and to endow him with power
and authority, the better to obtain good form and order and, as
Dean, to have supervision over the other Swedish Lutheran Congregations in America, and whereas said Dean and pastor is now
starting out on his journey, to take over the important work entrusted to him, therefore the Consistory considers it to be their
duty to publish His Royal Majesty's most gracious letter in the
firm assurance that it will be regarded as a convincing evidence
of His Royal Majesty's extraordinary care in the guardianship and
government of the American congregations, and [he desires] that
the Rev. Sandin, whom the Consistory has found to be a benevolent, zealous, and pious man, be received as a pastor and Teacher
sent by God; the Consistory also wishes to nominate and highly
recommend him to all in general and to each one in particular.

On this occasion, and because there has come into the hands
of the Consistory a German translation of the letter which was
sent out from here to Pennsylvania, on September 4, 1745, to
which Count von Zinzendorff has added a few remarks by means
of which he supposes himself to have refuted the well-grounded
opinions and thoughts of the Consistory, concerning the Moravian
brethren, both now and formerly, who retain the name "true doctrine" and as to whether they differ from our Lutheran Church
and the true Faith, and since it seems likely that Count Zinzendorff either himself, or through others, will probably circulate said
translation, with the aforementioned notes, throughout the Swedish Congregations in America, and in this way, slander the Consistory in order to bring himself less under suspicion and to gain
a freer hand for the accomplishment of his newly-laid attempts
and plans; therefore the Consistory can not neglect sincerely warning and advising all the Christian Swedish Lutheran Congregations
in America, from in any way letting themselves be drawn away
from the Word of our Lord Jesus Christ, and from the Doctrine

---

[56] Rev. Mr. Jöran Sandin. *Jöran (Göran)* is the Swedish for George and
hence a mistake here. Sandin's Christian name was Johan. See note 47.

concerning Piety, which is sure, and which is able to instruct them, and we advise them to remain steadfast in the Evangel which was taught them in the beginning, and which they, by the grace of God, have accepted, and by means of which alone they may be saved.

For the rest, as to what concerns the aforementioned notes, although every righteous and unpartisan man without difficulty can see that they are more swollen up with bitterness and calumniations, the strongest weapons of these presumptuous people, than with well-grounded arguments; and for this reason the Consistory, in consideration of this fact, may pass them by in silence, and leave everything, with a prayer for the Count, to the examination of the Learned and the judgment of God; however, since the salvation of no less devout souls from a threatened destruction also belongs to the Consistory's rightful honor, therefore the Consistory wishes to mention, for the better information of their Brethren in Faith in America, one or two things, by means of which the matter itself may be placed in a clearer light, and the treachery, which Count Zinzendorff harbors, may be the more clearly seen. And the Consistory believes that this can be accomplished with the least difficulty when one pays attention only to the fact that the greater portion of the written notes rest upon a very smooth and slippery foundation, and have no other basis than a continual submission to everything that Learned and erudite men of the Moravian Brotherhood have stated [which are] delusions. And although the Consistory sincerely wishes that the Count, on his own and others' behalf, would and could make a heartfelt denial of this, nevertheless the Consistory can with so much the less assurance, rely on that denial, since the truth of the matter has been found out and been exposed by those who—by reason of proximity and other circumstances—have had the opportunity of becoming more closely acquainted both with their doctrinal teaching and with their artful plots, to the disturbance and persecution of the Church of Christ. Count Zinzendorff can scarcely demand that the Consistory shall attach greater faith to him and his tales than to those of others, especially since Doctor Baumgartner of Halle,[57] in the twenty-fourth of his *Theologische Bedäncken*,[58] has

[57] *Baumgartner*. There have been several prominent Germans by the name of *Baumgartner*, but the man meant here is *Baumgarten*. Sigmund Jacob Baumgarten (1706-1757), eminent German theologian, educated in the school of Spener and Franke, and hence a student of the Pietistic movement of the day. He was far more scientific in his theological writings than the exponents of the pietistic school, some of whom regarded him as their teacher. He is looked upon as the forerunner of Rationalism in Germany which found its first prominent exponent in Baumgarten's greatest disciple, J. S. Semler

[58] *Theologische Bedänken*, in seven volumes, by Sigmund Jacob Baumgarten, were published at various intervals from 1732 until 1750.

both plainly and painstakingly shown that the Count acted by pure deceit and falsehood, means which his adherents also treacherously use for the propagation and spread of their doctrine, and which sad experience also has made manifest in all the places where they have stayed for any length of time, for such purpose. The Consistory gladly refrains from advancing any examples of this, since the Christian Congregations in America themselves, and all the disturbances and distress which these deceptive people have caused, are witnesses to it. However, the Count beseemingly denies this, of course, as well as everything else in his written remarks of the oft-cited letter of the Consistory, which throws not a little suspicion upon him and his adherents. They probably find themselves convicted of having insinuated themselves into the flock of Christ under a false mask, but they have shown their wolf-nature more than a little, and since this can have no other effect than that of hampering them in their objective, and opening the eyes of others to see the soul-destruction which they cause, therefore no other way remains, than to deny everything that they are reasonably accused of, and to express themselves in disparaging terms against those who, out of pure and unfalsified zeal, in order that Souls may not so easily be deceived by them and induced to believe falsities, disclose the cunning which they wish to hide under the appearance of piety.

The Count denies those errors which have been ascribed to him and his supporters; he denies the tumult and disturbance that his adherents have aroused in our Swedish Congregations in America, which has finally resulted in Unchristian fighting outside and within the churches. He denies the fictitious letters which his Missionaries have looked to for the support of their false claim about the acceptance of the Zinzendorffian Doctrine in this Country, and other things; and they therefore think they have sufficient reason to accuse the Consistory of sin against the eighth commandment and freedom to do the same as he condemns others for doing. But although the Consistory, both now and in its former statement, admits that all who acknowledge the tenets of this Sect are not equally participant in the aforementioned errors and are not only willing, out of Christian Charity, to judge more lightly concerning the Zinzendorffians in respect to some of their doctrinal teachings, but also eagerly longs, to hear that all these, and such as are against God and the doctrines contrary to his pure Word, both all in general and each one in particular, the farther off [they have been] the more they have renounced and become simplified—nevertheless we have much reason at least to suspect them [their intentions] inasmuch as they have entirely denied the truth of such things as are quite well known, and about which the Consistory possesses proof in hand, making for themselves a screen of deceit and taking refuge in lies.

One thus perceives that the Count, in his attempts and doings for the confusion of the American Congregation, is not satisfied with Doctor Alfwin, the present Bishop of Wäxiö, having given the Missionary, Arvid Gradin, freedom to preach in Stockholm, in the Great City Church,[59] but either the Count does not know, or else he keeps silent about the fact, that this took place by means of a deception, and that Doctor Alfwin, when he gave his permission for it, did not as yet know Gradin to be an adherent of the Zinzendorff Sect. That he was entertained by Dr. Alfwin as a friend, in no wise proves that he was endeared to him as a Zinzendorffian, or that the Doctor approved of his purposes and delusions, for which the aforementioned Doctor, no less than other learned men in the Kingdom here, both had and have a horror, no less proper than it is just, and on all occasions strives to demonstrate its contagious nature. For this reason also it happened that, when Gradin tried to preach in Gothenburg, this was denied and forbidden him, which, together with some other circumstances, fully proves that he was not thought so well of here, in this Country.

For the rest, as regards Arch Bishop Jacob Benzelius—whom God, to the great regret of the Kingdom and God's Church recently called hence by the temporal death—and the bitter and slanderous remarks about him with which the Count, here and there, has interlarded his barren statements, and even filled up one entire letter, which the Count sent off to some of his Friends,—that deceased Gentleman's deep insight, learning, experience in and zeal for the glory of God and the welfare of the Church, which made him universally beloved, honored and praised, speak so much in his defence that the Consistory does not need to add anything to it. At least the sainted Arch Bishop need not be blamed for having mistrusted Count Zinzendorff, for it is not yet known [even now] that he was appointed and called by God to take care of the Congregation, but indeed that he, uncalled (and against the interdiction of God's Spirit,) has taken upon himself that honor, and forced himself in, to scatter and to destroy it. Wherefore also, in the Chronicles of the Consistory, and in the hearts of all righteous men, it will stand written, to the everlasting credit of the Sainted Arch Bishop, that he sought, with all his might and main, to serve God's Church and to suppress all the disturbance which his enemies had tried to cause, in order to oppress it and he has even given our Brethren in Faith, in America, noteworthy and convincing proofs of his praiseworthy zeal and care for their welfare, let the Spirit of scorn, through its instrumentalities, speak against him as much

---

[59] *Stora Stats Kyrkia* Usually called *Storkyrkan*, "the large church", still standing and in good repair at Stockholm.

as it likes or is able. Who will some day meet him by necessity, and find who is to be punished for having entertained evil and secret intentions and conspiracies for the disturbance and destruction of the Church of God?[60]

Finally, the Consistory prays that God, from whom all grace cometh, will through his Word and Spirit, manifest his power in the American Christian Congregations, by strengthening the right-thinking, by converting the erring, by comforting and consoling the afflicted, and may He keep all the hearts and souls of His people in Christ Jesus, our Lord!

The grace of our Lord Jesus Christ be with you all! Amen, Upsala, August 12, 1747.

Olof Celsius   Engelb. L. Halenius
Gabriel Mathesius   Petrus Alm.

Now when we had finished preparing as well as we could for the journey, it was commenced on August 4th, after we had taken leave of our Relations, Friends, and Patrons at Hammarby Works in Ofwansiö Parish in Gestrikland. We arrived at Stockholm on the 7th, having the previous day taken leave of the members of the Consistory and the other Professors in Upsala. We remained in Stockholm until the 26th to arrange about books for the use of the Congregations out here, so generously presented by His Majesty, and to await the clearing of the Ship. The Consistory letter had arrived previously, on the 19th, together with the Ministerial Instruction and the above [document], in two copies, for the Congregations out here, as well as one each for the Pastors here, in Wilmington and Wicaco. From the 26th of August until the 14th of October we were on our journey to London, in England, during which time we encountered much storm and contrary winds, and hardly a day were we in health, since no one, in our little family, was used to the sea. The Ship was a small Brigantine [from] Suffolk, which was commanded by one Anders Falls. When the most necessary things had been attended to in London, we put out from there on November 8th, for Gravesand, and came safely to harbor at Plymouth on the afternoon of the 15th, with [a boat] called *Simon, Sir Lester*,[61] destined for New York and commanded by Captain John Colshaer [?], a good and kindly man. After the ship had taken on more cargo there in Plymouth, of powder and muskets, we were still unable, because of contrary winds, to put out to sea

---

[60] This sentence is very confused in the original.

[61] "med Simon Herr *Lesters kalled*". It is difficult to know what the name of this ship may be. Perhaps *Herr* is a proper name and not the Swedish *Herr*, "Sir", "Mister", in which case the name would be *Simon Herr Lester*.

before the 6th of December. From the 10th on (when, because of a violent storm, we were separated from our company of 4 to 5 other ships), until the 9th of March, the following year, 1748, we were in dread of enemies, and in almost continual N.W. and S.W. storms.[62] But on that day it pleased Our gracious God to put us all on land, with life and health, at the time of noon in New York. What misery and difficulty, during such a long journey, in time of winter, man and wife suffered, no one can believe except one who has tried a maritime [journey].

On shipboard [provisions] ran so short that, had we been a very few days more on the sea, God's meed of bread and other food had run out, especially as, at the last weighing-out on March 7th, only a few small cakes remained. Except for the Captain's precaution of timely forethought, we had all starved to death long before that time; for he commenced giving out rations on the sixth week. On the 12th, we afterwards went by boat to Brunswick, from there, on the 21st, to Trintown (Trenton) by coach, and finally, on the 27th, from there by boat to Philadelphia, where we arrived on the 28th, at eight o'clock in the evening. In the meantime, in passing, we had waited upon the Governor of [New] Jersey, Jonathen Belcher, Esqr.,[63] and shown him His Majesty's of Sweden Warrant and Traveler's Pass, and since that Gentleman had served under His Majesty at the time that he was General for the Allied army in the Netherlands, he had great consideration for his Majesty's recommendation. Wherefore he gave his Secretary orders to send the following letter to the Congregations and Vestries of Racoon and Pens Neck, namely:

Gentlemen[64]

His Excellency the Governeur has ordered me to notify Your Congregation, that the Bearer, Mr. John Sandin, Missionary to the Swedish Church at Racoon et PensNeck in this Province has waited on him, and produced to His Excellency the Credentials, Passport & Recommendation from His Swedish Majesty now in alliance with the King our Master, and being therewith fully satisfied has licensed him to officiate as Minister in the said Churches, et all others in this Province, by the consent of their particular Pastors, & has kindly promised to give him protection.

You are therefore to conduct him to Mr. Ladd at Glocester

---

[62] The seas were unsafe at this time. On March 15, 1744, France declared war on England, bringing her into the so-called War of the Austrian Succession (in America called *King George's* War). The war raged in America as well as Austria, Bavaria, and Netherlands.

[63] Jonathan Belcher (1681-1757), merchant, politician, adventurer, was governor of Massachusetts and New Hampshire from 1730 to 1741 and was appointed governor of New Jersey in 1747.

[64] This and the letter succeeding are of course in English in the churchbook.

or to Mr. Gibbons at Salem befor he officiates, & lett him be attended by some Gentlemen capable of interpreting to him, the Oaths w[h]ich Mr. Ladd or Mr. Gibbon is authorized to administer.

Gentlemen
    I hope you will in an exemplary manner recommend yourselves to the further Care of His Swedish Majesty by a gratefull Return to His present Favour in assisting Mr. Sandin in everything as far as your Circumstances will permit & beg leave to recommend union & decency in your Church as the proper means of preserving a good Reputation here & hereafter eternal felicity:

Burlington 28th   I am
    March 1748   Gentlemen
To the Vestry & Congre-   t
    gation at Racoon &   your very humble serv-
    PensNeck in New Yersey.   Charls Reed

    Now, inasmuch as Mr. Näsman [Naesman], at Wicacoa, had informed those of Racoon of my near approach, therefore on April first, Hindrick Hindricksson, Hans Steehlman and Lars Lock came up to Philadelphia to see about my arrival, and in that case to bring me down. Since I now had arrived, I went with them in the evening, and took my oath with Mr. G. Ladd, [?] and the following day, which was Palm Sunday, I gave a short sermon. Afterwards I went back, and on the 8th [?] I came down with my whole household, and found a house for us at Mårten Hill's, on Old Man's Creek. On Easter, the 10th, I gave up my inaugural sermon, and the Fourth day of Easter, the 13th, I preached at Pens Neck. Thereupon on the 17th, being the following Sunday, in the same Church, I was publicly declared Pastor through His Majesty's Warrant, by the Rev. Peter Tranberg, Pastor in Wilmington, and the Rev. Gabriel Näesman of Wicacoa. But because a great many of those in Pens Neck declared that they did not any longer desire to have a Swedish Minister, but Services in the English Language; and neither does His Majesty of Sweden force any Swedish Minister upon them, even he who comes supplied with a Warrant; therefore it was asked and decided that the people of Pens Neck might meet with those of Racoon in the Rectory at Piles Grove on April 25, so that a decision might be arrived at, as to whether the members of both Congregations should join together in supporting a Minister and the upkeep of the rectory as formerly.

[PILESGROVE 1748]

    On the day appointed, April 25, the greater part of both Congregations met at Piles Grove when unanimously,
    1. It was decided, in humble gratitude, to accept the Min-

ister sent to be their Teacher by His Majesty of Sweden, and that both Congregations should receive the same service as to preaching, since they also wished equally to participate in the Rectory building and other things, just as before.

2. It was decided that the Congregations purchase a horse and saddle for the Minister, for their common service. The horse was bargained for by Sebulon Lock for 13 Pounds, to be paid by the month of August, and the Saddle was ordered through Måns Keen. The Saddle cost 3 Pounds and the bridle 4 Shillings. Hans Steehlman had also procured, on behalf of the Congregations, two cows, which the Minister was to leave after him *in natura,* at the Parsonage, if, in the future, he should move from there to some other place.

3. That the Twenty Pounds, and 8 Bushels of wheat, which still remained unpaid as Rent for the years that the Parsonage was rented to John Keen, should, when they were paid, belong to the Minister that, with them, he might put his household in order.

4. The woodshed and fences were inspected. The latter were to be set up by John Keen, but as to the houses with broken roofs and windows, there was no decision about them, as to how or when they were to be repaired.

On the same occasion the Members from Pens Neck who were not present, and who for the most part were English, presented, through Jacob von Neeman and Cornelius Corneliusson, the following written statement, which they had signed with their own hands, as follows:[65]

We the subscribers being of the Congregation of Pensneck are informed that you are desired by the Congregation at Racoon to continue your service wholely in their Church, or Chiefly, for the greatest part, that is two Sundays in three. But we pray that, as the Swedish Society has been pleas'd to appoint you S^r to have the care of our Church in PensNeck as well as that at Racoon, we acknowledge Our selves thankfull for the pastoral and Fatherly care they have had of us in sending so worthy a Gentleman as we conceive You to be S^r to have the Care and Government of our Church. Our desire is that you would be pleased to proceed in Your services among as Mr Tranberg the other Swedish Minister have done for time past, and your Compliance S^r with our request will oblige Your Humble Servants

---

[65] The following document in English in the original.

Synnick Synnich
John Sawoy
Cornelius Corneliusson
Mathias Lambson
Jonas Stalkup
Mathias Johnson
Jacob Van Neeman
Archibald Cranford
Oliv^r Webbe
Peter Peterson
Peter Bilderback
Nicholas Harman
Enok Gill Johnson
Andrew Synnickson
Gabriel Donaldson
Daniel Bilderback
Thomas Lambson
Erich Johnson
Mattis Sulven
James Congelton
Laurence Jöranson
Thomas Wickory
Thomas Elwell
Ann Corneliusson
John Marshall
Jerimiah Baker
Eben Ezer Erichson
Cha. Erichson

Thomas Corney
James MacGenis?
Måns Anderson
John Monsen
Jacob Van de War
Mattis Nelsen
Peter Peterson
Samuel Conner
William Meums
Eben Ezer Dione
of Don
John Cornelus
Henry Peterson
Carpenter
Nicholas Nelson
Charls Corneliusson
Nicholas Philpot Senr
Samuel Whitehorne
Janes Barkley
Timothy Connar
John Corneliusson
Matthias Starck
Josiah Pennington
Andrew Standle
Aaron Butterworth
Allen Congelton
Thomas Penington
John Bilderback

John Parke
Erich Sheer
Francis Miles
Hanry Gill Johnson
Joseph Hawke
Michael Miller
Påvel Jaqwatt
Sarah Shadock
Mary Graffay
Gunly Felgute
Lourence Holton
Andrew Bartelson
William Bett
Henry Peterson
John Gill Johnson
David Strohen
Henry Peterson
Gabriel Peterson
Martin Minck
Henry Wan de Ware
Lucas Peterson
Mathis Hollsten
Michael Lambson
Joseph Pennington
Thomas Gilchrist
Margaret Meauris
Margaret Wan Nemen
Jona Scott

On the same day, namely on April 25, it was also decided that we should move over to the Rectory as soon as possible, which also was done on the 28th following. Gustaf Justice and Johan Hoffman, assisted with dray-horses. However, we had to live in a very crowded way, because we had to allow Niclas Keen, who was living at the Rectory after his sickness, to remain there with his household, until he was able to look around for a more secure place.

[ENTRIES BY THE REV. ERIC UNANDER] [65a]

In accordance with the good pleasure of an all-wise God, once more the Congregations of Racoon and Pens Neck had to lose their good and beloved Teacher, Dean Johan Sandin, after a resi-

[65a] Erik Mathias Unander was born in 1720 in the parish of Wätö, Roslagen. He entered the University in 1732 and was ordained on October 18, 1747. On May 29, 1747, he was appointed assistant pastor in the Swedish American Mission. In company with Acrelius he left Stockholm on July 20, 1749, and arrived in Philadelphia on November 6th of the same year.

He was received with great joy by the people of Raccoon and Penns Neck and was later made their rector (1751). Unander had a difficult time at Raccoon, as his salary was not regularly paid, sometimes not at all. As a consequence, he accumulated debts and at times did not have enough for his ordinary wants. "Often he had to go to bed hungry" and wore clothes that nearly fell off. In

dence among them of only 5 months, for on the 23rd of September, 1748, he was removed from this world by reason of a severe illness[66] which attacks nearly all who come over here from Europe. This great and noteworthy loss our merciful Lord has in some measure relieved, for the comforting of these Congregations, by the Professor of Economy from Åbo Academy in Finland, Mr. Peter Kalm[67] (now known throughout almost the entire world, for his learning), who had come, at the command of His Majesty, our Most Gracious King of Sweden, to see this country, who not only wrote immediately to Sweden, and to the Venerable Consistory of Uppsala, at the request of the Congregation of Racoon, asking for another Minister; but furthermore, very kindly assumed the care of the Congregation by preaching for them the whole winter through, in spite of the many interruptions [it caused] to his own work. Now, as soon as the letter from here, about the late lamented

---

1756 he was transferred to Christina to succeed Acrelius, who left for Sweden, and he preached his farewell sermon at Raccoon on September 26th.

He was recalled to Sweden in 1758 but he remained at his post for two years, due to various circumstances. His debts increased and he had troubles with the new Dean of the churches, and others. On July 6, 1760, he delivered his farewell sermon in English, and on the 21st in Swedish. On Sunday, July 28th, the ship on which he was to return to Europe with his family was ready to weigh anchor. A large crowd had assembled to say farewell to their pastor. Before he went on board he delivered perhaps the most eloquent and most touching sermon of his career. The Twenty-first and One Hundred and Twenty-second Psalms were sung in unison, and the assembled multitude was touched to tears; the old animosities and quarrels were forgotten. For eleven years Unander had worked unselfishly among his people and made many friends. His consuming jealousy was his great fault and caused most of his many troubles.

On his way between Gothenburg and Stockholm he was shipwrecked and lost all his property and all his papers. On his arrival at Stockholm he was treated as liberally as Acrelius, but he was apparently unable to handle money and he was always in financial straits. Finally, after long waiting, he became pastor in Nora parish, Ångermanland, in 1764, where he died April 30, 1766.

In America he married Maria Hesselius (September 19, 1750), a daughter of the famous painter, Gustav Hesselius, the father of American painting. He has descendants still living in Sweden.

66 *brännesjukan* (dialectic), "burning sickness", "continuous fevers", "severe fever".

67 Professor Per (Peter) Kalm, naturalist, scientist, economist, educator (of an old Swedish-Finnish family), was born in Ångermanland, Sweden, in 1716. He entered the University of Åbo in 1735, where he became interested in the natural sciences, especially botany which he later studied at the University of Uppsala. In 1747 he left Sweden for America to study the flora of the country, in those parts where the climatic conditions resembled those of Sweden. He remained in America until February, 1751. During this time he travelled extensively here and in Canada. During the winter of 1750 he lived in the parsonage at Racoon and preached in the parish (Racoon and Penns Neck) almost every Sunday, "also performing other services"

After his return to Europe he published the results of his journey in three volumes, *En resa til Norra America, etc.* (1753-1761), ("A Journey to North America," etc.). In November, 1752, he became professor at his old university, and died at Åbo on November 16, 1779

Dean Sandin's death, came before the Venerable Consistory of Uppsala, they did, with great kindness assume [the care of] these Swedish congregations, proposing to His Majesty a most worthy and deserving man to be Dean of the Swedish Lutheran congregations, and Pastor of the Congregations of Racoon and Pens Neck, [namely] that most Honorable and Learned gentleman, the Rev. Mr. Israel Acrelius.[67a]

In this, the Venerable Consistory has manisfested a new proof of its tender care for their Brethren in the Faith in the Swedish Congregations, humbly submitting to his Royal Majesty how necessary it is that an assistant, having Royal Warrant and salary, may hereafter continually be supported here in the Congregations, who, in case of sickness overtaking the regular pastor or in the event of a vacancy, in the former case would assume the care of the Congregation, and in the latter case would, with a Royal Warrant, immediately succeed to the Pastorate. His Royal Majesty, in his most praiseworthy zeal for the glory of God, has [therefore] both appointed the Rev. Mr. [Acrelius] to be Pastor and Dean here with the necessary Warrant and fifty pounds Sterling annual salary, and also (not without noticeable expense to the kingdom), has appointed me, Eric Unander, by most gracious Warrant, to the position of Preacher extra-ordinary and supplied me with the necessary money for travel and with an annual salary of Twenty-five pounds Sterling.

Now, when we were almost ready to depart, there came to the Venerable Consistory the recent letter from the Congregation in Christina, with the request that they be given a pastor for themselves, in the place of the Rev. Mr. Tranberg, who also had died. By virtue of the letter of appointment, whereby the Venerable Consistory has made it incumbent upon me to exercise my precious Office in God's Church in this place (which, together with the Warrant I will insert here in the Church Record book), I and no other ought to have been proposed by His Majesty as the pastor for the aforesaid Church. But inasmuch as His Reverence the Dean considered this position more advantageous

---

[67a] Israel Acrelius (1714-1800), studied at the University of Uppsala and was ordained in 1743. In 1747 he was appointed Admiralty Pastor and in 1749 he was selected by Archbishop Henrik Benzelius to go to America to take charge of the Swedish churches on the Delaware, as Provost (Prost), or Dean. He served here with great success as pastor of Holy Trinity, in Wilmington, until November, 1756, when he returned to Sweden through ill health. He went home by way of England, where he remained during the winter to study the University conditions at Oxford

Acrelius published a number of speeches, sermons and dissertations, but his most famous publication was his Beskrifning, a history of the Swedish churches in America, issued at Stockholm in 1759. The book is of permanent value, based on extensive researches and written in a careful and scholarly manner. It was poorly translated into English with an introduction by Reynolds and published jointly by the Historical Societies of Pennsylvania and Delaware in 1874.

to himself, and especially more suitable for the better execution of the office of Dean, he was, at his request, and at the suggestion of the Consistory, provided by his Royal Majesty with the necessary Warrant of Transfer. In this matter I kept entirely passive, my respect for my superior office also keeping me entirely bound.

Copy of the Consistory's Letter of Appointment for me to be Preacher extra-ordinary in the Swedish Lutheran Congregations in America!

Sir
Worthy and Most learned Gentleman!

Whereas His Majesty, at the humble request of the most honorable Arch Bishop, has seen fit to graciously order that an assistant preacher shall be sent here from Sweden for the service of Swedish Lutheran Congregations in Pennsylvania, who, in case of the eventual illness of the regular preacher there, or of an actual vacancy there, shall, in the former case, assume the care of the Congregation, or in the latter case shall, by Royal Warrant immediately succeed to the Pastorate, which has become vacant (to which end not only will the necessary money for travel graciously be granted,) but also a certain annual salary will be bestowed until he can be appointed to a regular pastorate elsewhere. The Consistory does therefore hereby call your honor to the office of assistant Preacher in Pennsylvania, with the assurance that, as soon as seven years have been passed in this place, your honor shall, whether you have by then come into a regular office or not, if you so desire, be recalled home, and be promoted to a charge, etc.
Upsala on April 15, 1749. Your honor's most obedient servants,
Olof Celsius,   Eng. Halenius,   Gab. Mathesius,
L. Benzelstierna,   Lour. Norin.

Copy of His Royal Majesty's gracious Warrant

We, Friedrich, by the grace of God, King of Sweden, the Goths, and the Wends, etc., etc. LandGrave of Hesse, Prince of Hirschfeld, Count of Catsen-Ellenbogen, Dietz, Zingenhayn, Widda and Schäumburg, etc., etc.
Do hereby announce that: Whereas We have been pleased to appoint an extraordinary Preacher for the Swedish Lutheran Congregations in America, and whereas the Rev. Eric Unander, in consideration of his great learning and edifying conduct, has been humbly proposed:
Therefore, by force of this Our open Warrant, we do graciously appoint him, Eric Unander, to be assistant Preacher for

the Swedish Lutheran Congregations in America, and we wish to assign thereunto Four Hundred dahlers in Silver, yearly salary. Which let everyone whom it concerns obediently observe.

For further certainty we have let this be confirmed by the signature of Our Own Hands, and by Our Royal Seal. Stockholm, in the Council Chamber, May 29, 1749.

Friedrich

L. S.

C. Rudenschöld.

Copy of the Consistory Letter to the Congregations of Racoon and Pensneck.

To the Christian and honorable Swedish Evangelical Lutheran Congregations in Racoon and Pensneck we desire Grace and Peace of God, our Father, and our Lord Jesus Christ!

From your [recently] arrived letter, the Consistory has learned that the Dean of the Swedish Congregations in America, Pastor in Racoon and Pensneck, during his life the Worthy and Learned Rev. Joh. Sandin, was called hence by death, on the 23rd of September last. The Consistory regards his departure as so much the greater privation and loss, and the more deeply deplores it, as they not only do perceive by Your Own letter that he was a welcome, faithful and beloved Teacher, who through the mediation of God's precious mercy, brought forth among you, a blessed fruit; but also because, from His own accounts, sent over from time to time during his short sojourn in America, we have been informed of his Divine aim and solicitous provisions. And they do delightedly perceive, from these accounts how, in all that he did, he had regard to the spiritual growth and improvement of the Congregation which, had God granted him the favor of a longer lifetime, would undoubtedly have produced much good amongst you.

Now in order that such a good work, through the dear grace of the same God, may still further be advanced for the edification of Souls, His Royal Majesty of Sweden, our Most Gracious King, upon the humble petition of the Consistory, for the general good of the Congregations, has appointed the Dean of Christina, the Rev. Israel Acrelius, to be Dean over these Swedish Congregations in America, and has supplied him who now is departing from Sweden with a gracious warrant and an annual salary. The Consistory has also thoughtfully provided for being able now again to supply you in the congregations of Racoon and Pensneck, with a right-minded, faithful and zealous teacher and Pastor, in the place of the Rev. Mr. Sandin, but since it is impossible to arrange this matter so hastily as for him also to be ready for the journey, at once, therefore, in the meantime, they have spared no pains in the watchful guardianship of souls, wherefore now an assistant preacher, Ericus Unander, is now leaving, provided with a Royal Warrant and travel money, who will assume the care and management of these Congregations until a regular Pastor and Dean has had time to arrive. This tender and Fatherly guardianship which His Royal Majesty, Our most gracious King, in this manner assumes, now as ever before, for these far-distant Swedish Lutheran Congregations, can not fail to arouse in you the praise and admiration of the great God, and a venerable gratitude towards our Most gracious King, and also (inasmuch as all this solely and entirely looks to the spiritual welfare of Your Souls, and their edification in Faith for eternal salvation,) do ye also, each one, watch that ye, with obedient hearts, do embrace the word which will be preached, worthily partake of the Holy Sacraments, which the Saviour, Jesus, hath ordained, and so dispose and conduct yourselves in all things as properly pertain to rightful Christians, that God's name may thereby be hallowed, and faith and devotion become evermore rooted in your hearts.

With God's grace, it would contribute much to this end if you would lay it upon your own hearts, (as also your Christian duty demands,) that you keep your children, from their earlier years in Schools, that they may imbibe the knowledge of Christianity, and afterwards take them with you to the general and public Services in your Churches, in order that they may in time become accustomed to the practice of devotion, and learn to reflect what a blessing it is, rightly to know God and correctly to serve Him and pray to Him.

To this end our gracious King, as a token of the fondness with which His Royal Majesty embraces these Congregations, has now sent along some books, even as has formerly [been the custom] whenever any Ministers have been sent over from Sweden. The Rev. Acrelius may therefore distribute said [books] for the service of the Congregations, as circumstances arise and as there is need of them; and the Consistory assures you that more will be sent over at another opportunity; if only, in the meantime, it is seen that these, and those which have formerly been sent to you, have been properly utilized and that more of the same kind, or of another kind, are desired.

As for the rest, the Consistory desires God's merciful grace and blessing upon the Christian and Worthy Congregations and will always, in its prayers to God, include the Congregations as

[66]

to all spiritual and bodily welfare. We remain always and continually,

Christian and Worthy Members

· of

The Congregations of Racoon and Pensneck,

Your most obedient servants,

Upsala June 19, 1749   Henric Benzelius.[68]

Olof Celsius,   Matthias Asp,   Eng. Halenius,
Gabriel Mathesius,   L. Benzelstierna,
Laur. Norin.

When, after a successful journey of four months, we arrived on November 6, in good health, at Philadelphia, Master Hans Steelman and Master Eric Ronnols, having received word of our arrival, were sent out to meet me on the 10th, of the same month. I was obliged to accompany them immediately, the same night, to administer the sacred rite of baptism to two little children who were very weak. The following Sunday, the 25th after Trinity, I was introduced in the Church of Racoon, and the next Sunday after that in Pensneck

[RACCOON 1749]

On the 28th of the following November, a Parish Meeting was held in Racoon, which the Rev. Dean Acrelius opened with a very suitable and quite moving speech for the occasion, and then the following matters were brought up and decided.

1. It was stated that, whereas some of the Trustees and Churchwardens had departed this life, it was first necessary for the Congregation to choose others in their stead, which also was done, the following Worthy men being, by the consent of all, appointed:

Mounce Keen,
Trustees: Messrs: Zacharias Pettersson,
Thomas Denny
Churchwarden: Master Petter Rambo

II. It was proposed and decided that necessary repairs on the Church should be made at the first opportunity, by arrangement with the Trustees.

III. The Congregation requested the Provost to compose a letter, in their name, to the Venerable Consistory, to permit them to retain the assistant preacher, Eric Unander, for their

---

[68] Henrik Benzelius (1689-1758), succeeded his brother, Jacob, as Archbishop in 1747

Pastor, (Note: there were also delegates from Pensneck present, who made the same request on behalf of that Congregation.) In consideration of which the following letter was written by the Dean, which was signed, on behalf of all, by the Foremost [members] of the Congregations:

Copy   S. T.
                          Kind Sir!
We acknowledge with deep reverence the tender care which the worthy Father, at the very outset of his accession to the Archbishopric entrusted to him, has been pleased to bestow upon our poor Souls, in sending such faithful and zealous teachers over to our Congregations, and by so favorably negotiating with His Royal Majesty, the most gracious King of the Realm of Swe[den], for the increase of the Swedish Mission in our country, and also by coming to their relief with the necessary Swedish Books, and many other things serviceable to the future spiritual welfare of us and of our children.

Especially do we wish to express our sincere joy for the extraordinary or assistant Teacher, the honorable and very learned Rev. Mr. Eric Unander, who has now been sent to us to preside over our Congregations, until some regular Pastor is appointed! And although we do in nowise doubt that we will even hereafter continue to be included in the same loving care, of which we have already seen so many proofs, so that we will, in the future, be provided with such a Pastor as seeks the salvation of our souls, nevertheless we take the liberty, in the meantime, of presenting this humble petition to be permitted to retain as our Teacher and regular Pastor the assistant preacher, Mr. Unander, whom we, in our simplicity, have learned to regard as very learned and as being a good example for our lives, and in every way most necessary and useful.

We humbly beg that this benefit may not again be taken away from us, which we have already received, and we assure you that he will be loved by us, honored and supported by his hearers in the manner that so righteous a Teacher deserves. Awaiting your favorable approval of this petition, we remain, with all due reverence, etc.

IV. A Subscription to the Pastor's salary was set up:

Mounce Keen	0	10	0
Hance Steelman	1	00	0
Zacharias Peterson	0	15	0
Thomas Denny	0	10	0
Peter Rambo	0	16	0
Gustav Gustavson	0	12	0

Laurence Lock	0	15	0
Erik Ronols	0	15	0
Gunnar Kocks	1	00	0
Morton Stille	0	15	0
Jonas Cox	0	10	0
Morris Conner	0	15	0
John Fish	0	10	0
And: Hendrickson	0	10	0
John Halm	0	10	0
Nils	0	15	0
Jonas Hendrickson	0	10	0
John Mulica, Sr.			
Johan Mulica, Jr.	0	10	0
John Keen	0	10	0

V. It was thereupon decided that the Minister should live with some member of the Congregation the first year, and that the Place [i.e. the Rectory] be rented, and that the Members of the Congregation should pay his board by contribution.

After that the Members of the Congregation took a friendly leave of one another and went to their homes.

[LETTER TO RACCOON CONGREGATION FROM DEAN ISRAEL ACRELIUS]

Willmington, ye 2 Aug. 1750.

Salvo sit:

My beloved Brethren in the Lord:

Together with various Orders pertaining exclusively to the Clerical Office, I received on the 12th of July last, from the Right Reverend Doctor and Arch Bishop and the Venerable Ecclesiastical Consistory at Upsala, the following announcement:

We have been informed, not only through written accounts, but also from printed documents, that the Zinzendorfian disturbance and the Herrenhuter Sect has commenced to spread more and more in America. The Consistory, therefore, can not neglect, on this occasion also, to encourage you, Mr. Dean, and also the other Swedish Ministers, to keep diligent watch, calling on the Most High God for mercy and assistance, and also to warn their listeners and faithfully admonish them to remain steadfast in the Doctrine and the wholesome example of God's Word that they have heard from their former zealous and praiseworthy Teachers, and which they have thus themselves learned and comprehended from their Youth. The Consistory, in this connection, does not wish to pass by without notice, now that the well known Missionary, the Rev. Arwid Gradin, from Herrenhut, who has now been staying here in Sweden for some time—now that his doings have been publicly and properly examined—, although being [indeed] a native of Sweden, nevertheless, by solemn Royal order has been banished from the Kingdom, never again to return, and has been transported, under guard, beyond the confines of the kingdom. The Consistory is so much the less disposed to pass this by as it has reason to surmise that, under these circumstances, said Gradin probably will turn his steps towards America, in order to disturb the Evangelical Lutheran Congregations there, it may even be under an assumed name, inasmuch as similar deceptions are not uncommon amongst this people. For this reason it is necessary for you, Mr. Dean, with the help of the other Ministers, to keep a watchful eye upon the herd, that the enemy take not advantage of this to sow tares there, as he diligently endeavored to do here, by means of Gradin's sojourn.

Praying that the Teachers, as well as their hearers, may be kept faithfully under the protection of God, the most high, that the purity of Doctrine may be sustained, and that Christian morals may be uncontaminated,
Upsala, February 28, 1750.

we remain,

Honorable Mr. Dean,

Your most obliging servants,

Henric Benzelius,

Olof Celsius, Matthias Asp, Engelbert Halenius,

Gab. Matthesius, L. Benzelstierna,

Laur. Norin.

We now see, my beloved Brethren, how the Lord God at last tramples Satan under our feet, in spite of his occasionally permitting him to raise his head. Let us therefore diligently watch and pray that, through Christ, we may fight and win. To keep our Church records, after this, in Swedish, as heretofore, proves absolutely necessary, without the intermixture of English, unless such documents are to be inserted as do not bear translation, wherewith, hereafter, the Latin style is always most serviceable:

1. In order that those of our people who understand Swedish and write English may thus be enabled easily to read the Church Records, since no Swedish-American understands the Swedish style of writing any longer. 2. In Sweden, this

style is very much in use for Swedish, and is continually growing, so that in time it is likely that no other will be seen, and by this means the style which was formerly used, both for writing and printing the Swedish language, will come into the pristine form, which it undoubtedly had before the Munks deteriorated it by their changes. 3. A group of Swedish Hymnbooks in the said style has been sent over with me, by order of the Doctor and Arch Bishop, as an example. Since they seem desirable as to style, we have written for several more. A humble request has likewise been made that, in the future, all books for the use of the congregations may be of the same kind, for the easier instruction of the young people. For this reason I have felt called upon to adopt this Latin Style myself, in the Church Records of Christina Congregation, presuming that my beloved co-brethren, in consideration of the above Reason, will do likewise in their Churches. Our successors, who will still more see the Fruit of this will, I hope, never depart from this Order, adopted by us, and for the rest, in every conceivable way, will endeavor to keep up their mother tongue, which is almost at the point of becoming extinct. I remain with all conceivable affection,

Salvo sit:

> My beloved co-brethren
> Your faithful servant,
> Israel Acrelius.

[RACCOON AND PENNS NECK 1751]

The Tenth Sunday after Trinity, which was the 11th of August, Erick Unander was introduced as Dean of the congregations of Racoon and Pensneck, having received the Royal Warrant dated Stockholm, July 9, 1750, which the Assistant Preacher, Mr. Johan Abraham Lidenius, had recently brought over on his arrival, and which reads as follows:

> *We, Friedrich, by the Grace of God, King of Sweden, the Goths and the Wends, etc. etc. Landgrave of Hesse, Prince of Hirschfeld, County of Catzen-Ellenbogen, Dietz, Zingenhayn, Nidda and Schaumburg, etc. etc. Hereby maake known,* That inasmuch as the position of Dean over the Swedish Lutheran Congregations in Racoon and Pensneck, in America, has become vacant, and whereas the Extraordinary Preacher, Eric Unander, in recognition of his great Learning and Exemplary Life, has been humbly proposed for filling the vacancy; Therefore We do hereby, and by Power of this Our open Warrant, graciously appoint him, Eric Unander, to be

Dean over the Swedish Lutheran Congregations in Racoon
and Pensneck, in America, wherewith We do also Graciously
grant him all the Advantages and Rights, which his Predecessors in the Pastorate have and rightfully ought to enjoy.
Which let all concerned obediently observe. For further certainty We do confirm this with our own Signature and with
our Royal Seal. Stockholm, in the Council-chamber, July 9,
1750.

Friederich

(L.S.)   O. Rudenschöld.

*The following Letter from the Right Reverend Arch Bishop and
the Venerable Consistory, dated July 25 of the same year, was also
read to the Congregations:*

*To the Christian and Honorable Swedish Evangelical Lutheran
Congregations in Racoon and Pensneck we desire the Grace and Peace
of God our Father and of the Lord Jesus Christ!*
From the Consistory's Letter to You, issued on June 19th last, you
have probably noticed that, although circumstances then would not
permit us immediately to provide these Congregations of Racoon and
Pensneck with Regular Teacher and Pastor, in the place of the departed
Rev. Sandin, nevertheless the Consistory has taken to heart the care
and guardianship of Your Souls, and has, therefore taken steps to
have the Assistant Preacher, Eric Unander, assume that [responsibil-
ity]. The Consistory now perceives with pleasure from your letter,
dated November 22, of the same year, which arrived here last week,
on the 12th of June, that said Unander, immediately at the commencement of his official duties, has won the Love and Confidence of you
all. In consideration whereof You do request and desire that he be
appointed your regular Teacher and Pastor. For this reason the Consistory has also humbly informed his Royal Majesty of this matter,
whereupon His Majesty has caused his gracious Warrant to be issued
for this Pastorate for said Unander, your request being, in such
measure, now granted. And as it may clearly be seen from all this
that His Royal Majesty, our most gracious King, is graciously pleased
to do all that His Royal Majesty feels, in one way or another, con-
tributory to the well-being and edification of these Congregations.
Therefore the Consistory may not omit, on this occasion also, encour-
aging You to Laud and Praise God and moreover it expects you, in
consideration of the Grace thus shown you, time and time again, that
you make good use of this, for the good of your own Souls, and the
spiritual Welfare of your Children, obediently following the Advice
of your Teachers and their wholesome admonitions. Being also pleased
to adopt the manners and customs in practice here in Sweden, in such
matters as concern the management of the Congregation. But by all

means diligently and piously attend the public Services, partake worthily of the Holy Sacraments, present yourselves willingly for examination in the Cathecism, and for instruction, and institute Schools for Children among you. For all this is of use, by the mercy of God, in order that your Souls may be strengthened in Faith, steadfast in hope, and grounded in charity. In this way, also, you confirm Your Calling and choice, and in that measure there will be given you a full entrance into the Heavenly Kingdom of our Lord and Savior, Jesus Christ.

Hereby is the joy of your Teachers fulfilled, whose work therefore is not uselessly spent among you; hereby also is the Divine End of the Consistory accomplished, and His Royal Majesty, our most gracious King, will undoubtedly, in the future, as heretofore, spare no pains for your [welfare].

Faithfully commending you to the Care and providence of the Most High God, we remain,

Christian and Worthy Members of the Congregations of Racoon and Pennsneck,

Your most obliging servants,

Upsala, July 25, 1750.   Henric Benzelius.

Olof Celsius,   Matthias Asp,   Eng. L. Hallenius,
Gabriel Mattesius,   Laur. Norijn

[PENNS NECK 1752]

In the year 1752, on May 18th, there was held a Parish Meeting when the following matters were brought up and decided.

I. The Dean brought up the impropriety of the freedom that the Congregation in general were taking upon themselves in the assumption of Godparentage at the Baptism of Children; and by a suitable Address he tried to bring them to a consideration of the necessity of Godparentage and its Need, especially in this country. God grant that it had some good effect!

II. Two new Churchwardens were chosen in the place of Jacob van Neeman and Cornelius Corneliusson, who earnestly insisted on being relieved of the trouble, namely: Jacob Corneliusson and Olof Van Neeman.

III. It was requested by the Congregation that the Churchwardens, without negligence, or regard for Persons, should collect the usual fee (four shillings and sixpence) for strangers who were buried in the Churchyard.

IV. It was decided that the Collection money should be counted in the presence of the Minister, be taken care of by the Churchwarden Olof van Neeman, and that an account thereof should be exhibited annually at the parish meetings, and be included in the record-book of the Church.

V. It was related by the Minister how that the People of Racoon, at a Meeting the previous year, had given the Minister the horse and the two Cows as his own, requesting that this Congregation also would agree to the same, to which all freely consented.

VI. It was shown how necessary it was to get new Poles for the Churchyard fence, with which end in view a subscription was started and the money given into the hands of Churchwarden Olof van Neeman.

VII. Complaint was made that the Minister did not get his Salary, and for that reason Mathias Lampson and John van Neeman undertook to collect what remained outstanding.

To God's Congregations in Wicacoa, Christina, Racoon and Pensneck, in Pensilvania, [sic] who have received the same precious faith as ourselves (the sanctuary called saintly through Christ Jesus,) and to all those who call upon the Name of our Lord Jesus Christ, in each and every place, their and our Grace be with You, and the Peace of our Father and of our Lord Jesus Christ!

The very agreeable and welcome letter from the Congregations dated Pensilvania [sic], September 6, 1752, I had the pleasure of receiving on the 20th of the following November; and I wish to thank kindly everyone in general and each one in particular of the honorable Members of the Congregations, for the kindness and favor which they were pleased to express towards me.

It should indeed be recognized as a clear and never sufficiently lauded sign of grace from the merciful God, that the pure Evangelical Doctrine has come to shine in its clearness among You, in a Place far distant from the rest of the upright adherents of the Augsburg Confession, where ye are daily exposed to dangerous snares from Your spiritual enemy, who through his instrumentalities neglects not to use the greater diligence in scattering the flock of Christ, the more open an opportunity he finds for so doing.

In Your letter ye also seem, not without astonishment, to recount the adventurous attempt which certain erring spirits, have instituted among you, with devilish cunning, to entice you from your simple faith in Christ, especially at the time when the Divine Providence was pleased to call hence by death two of Your Pious and zealous Teachers. But that this wicked attempt nevertheless did not succeed in gaining its desired end, namely that of drawing you away from Evangelical grace into spiritual darkness, that is not Your work, but the Lord's, for which Ye owe Him humble and reverent sacrifices of thanksgiving upon the Altars of your hearts.

Ye know, beloved Brethren (and Your hearts ought to be filled with sincere acknowledgment thereat,) that the Kings of Sweden, inclined and prompted by the King of Heaven, like true providers and care-takers, have taken to heart the guardianship of Your Souls, and have taken the necessary precautions that Ye may not be lacking in spiritual food for your souls, from the Holy Word of God, in unfalsified purity. Ye know this, and I do rejoice over the gratitude Ye express thereat, both towards the late King, His Majesty, Friedrich I., glorious in memory, in supplying You, by Royal Grace, not only with other right-thinking Teachers in place of the deceased, but also, over and beyond this, being pleased most graciously to increase the usual number of Your Ministers. The Lord grant You Grace to use so precious an advantage for the honor of God and for the salvation of Your Souls!

Our present reigning Monarch, the most gracious King, *ADOLPH FRIEDRICH,* who from his first accession to the Swedish Throne, has let the Evangelical Church experience a more than fatherly tenderness, has also, at our humble request, graciously assured us, that he will always regard You, one and all, with Royal Mercy, even as did his high Predecessor in the Government, and that Ye, under the Government of His Royal Majesty, will enjoy the privileges, in respect to spiritual guardianship, which Ye have had graciously granted and conferred upon you by former Swedish Kings. In confirmation whereof we send over the enclosed, His Royal Majesty's Gracious Resolution, concerning your humble Petition, which ought to be of strong encouragement to You to be ardent in your Prayers and Solicitations for the continually flourishing happiness and prosperity of His Royal Majesty and the whole Swedish Royal House.

The love which Ye declare that Ye bear for your present well-disposed Teachers is good occasion to me for satisfaction and joy, because I conclude thereby that they have regard for the Office which they have received from the Lord, and that they are performing it aright. I also have confidence in You, my Beloved Brethren in Christ, that between You and Them there will remain a fond and deeply rooted affection, the undoubted result of which will be that you embrace, with obedient hearts, what they, on God's behalf, present to you, making constant your faith, and exercising a life such as is pleasing to God, such as is proper to the Heavenly Doctrine, and such as is an ornament to the name of Christian among your neighbors.

Your affectionate statement, concerning Your former Pastor the Rev. Mr. Naesman, now called home, confirms me in my purpose, long before this resolved upon, (and which is also my duty), to contribute in every possible way, towards his promotion, and I am fully convinced that His Royal Majesty will keep in gracious remembrance His faithful work among You, and kindly recollect the difficulties he sustained for many years.

I really do not know the reason why he has not yet arrived, or why he has not taken advantage of such a good opportunity [i.e for travel] as has already been afforded, and by which your kind Letter came safely over to London. This much I do know, and my conscience is a good witness to it, that I have so cleared the way for him that, at his homecoming, he may not have any occasion for disappointment, and I shall also continue still further in the same kindness, upon his arrival home, God being willing to extend my life to that time.

For the rest, I commend you to God and His Merciful Word, that Ye may grow into a holy temple in the Lord! Test all things, and keep what good is; But the God of Peace Himself bless you above all, so that your Spirit, Soul and Body may be preserved from punishment at the coming of our Lord Jesus Christ! This is the wish, faithfully and constantly of Your

benevolent friend and servant,

Henric Benzelius.

Upsala, January 26,
     February 6
       1753.

Royal Majesty's Gracious Resolution regarding the humble petition of his faithful subject and Arch Bishop, the Honorable and Very learned Doctor, Henric Benzelius, as well as the Evangelical-Lutheran Congregations at Wicacoa, Christina, Racoon and Pensneck in America, and Pensylvania, and also the appointed Ministers of the aforesaid Congregations, together with the Swedish Congregation, Ulrica Eleonora in London, concerning the confirmation of privileges formerly granted to the congregations and the Clergy. Issued in the Council Chamber, December 7, 1752.

His Royal Majesty has caused to be read both the Arch Bishops humble Petition in the aforementioned matter and the humble petition presented by the congregations and the Clergy. And since His Royal Majesty holds for the Evangelical Lutheran Doctrine's support and propagation a no less tender affection than His Glorious Predecessor on the Royal throne of Sweden, therefore His Royal Majesty also will always regard said Congregations and Ministers with Royal Favor, and wishes to assure them that, under the Government of His Royal Majesty, they will enjoy the same privileges, in respect to the guardianship of their Souls, as was graciously granted and given them by former Swedish Kings. Thus the Ministers, after the lapse of a few years, will be allowed to return home to their Fatherland and be rewarded with suitable Offices, other experienced Clergymen being sent over for the care of the congregations. Which all concerned must obediently observe. For further certainty we have signed this with Our Own Hand, and confirmed it with Our Royal Seal. *Ut Supra.*

Adolph Friedrich

(L.S.)   O. Rudenschöld.

Adolph Friedrick, by the Grace of God, King of Sweden, the Goths and the Wends, etc. etc. etc. Heir to Norway, Duke of Schlesswig, Holstein, etc. etc.

Our favor and gracious benignity with God Almighty, Trusted servant, Arch Bishop and Pro-Chancellor. Your humble petition of June 20, concerning the affairs of the Swedish Congregation in America has been duly brought to our attention and, in compliance with Your humble recommendation we have, under this date, given the Clergyman Johan Wiksell[69] Our Gracious Warrant to be assistant Pastor in the aforementioned Congregations. We have likewise ordered Lidenius, the present Dean of the Congregations of Racoon and Pensneck, to be recalled home, and that, for his return journey, he use the money for travelling expenses granted to the Assistant Pastor Nordenlind,[70] and not yet used, and that Wiksell, now retiring, may, for the present, take charge of said Congregations, thereby made vacant, with the salary of Thirty-three Pounds Sterling, which have been graciously granted to him as Assistant Preacher. All of which you are free to arrange, in a proper manner. And we commend you graciously to God Almighty. Stockholm, in the Council Chamber, July 6, 1761.

Adolph Friedrich

(L.S.)   M. V. Hermanson   S.K.

[Secretary to the King]

By virtue of the preceding Royal Warrant and Consistorial Decree I did enter upon my valued office in these graciously entrusted Congregations of Racoon and Pennsneck, on July 11, 1762, and the same day, after the sermon, I was introduced by the Dean, Doctor Wrangel, into the Church and Congregation of Racoon, in the presence of the Dean, Mr. Borell. And I held my inaugural sermon in Racoon on the following Sunday, and in Pensneck on the Sunday after that.

---

[69] Johan Wicksell was born on March 31, 1727, in Vaddö parish. He entered the University of Uppsala in 1747. In 1749 he went to Russia, and later to Viborg, in Finland. After his return to Sweden he served four years in the Customs office. Later he resumed his theological studies and was ordained on December 26, 1760. On July 6th, the following year, he was appointed pastor on the Delaware, and arrived here on May 3, 1762. He was installed in Raccoon church on July 11th, and preached his first sermon in Penns Neck the following Sunday. Wicksell became the Dean of the Swedish churches after the death of the Rev. Andrew Borell, in April, 1768. Having been recalled to Sweden, he took a warm farewell of his colleagues on October 6, 1773, and on October 30th, the same year, he left America.

[70] Eric Nordenlind was appointed pastor of the Swedish churches in America by Royal Commission, dated October 20, 1755. Due to the Seven Years' War, he was obliged to spend the winter in Stockholm and "consumed some of his travelling money". He was finally able to leave, and reached London safely. Again the war kept him from continuing his journey, increasing his debts. Finally he found opportunity to leave London with his wife, and he landed in Philadelphia on September 2, 1756. His wife died on the very day of their arrival, before the ship cast anchor. In June, 1758, he was appointed pastor of Raccoon and

Lord God, for the sake of Jesus, grant me the grace of thy spirit, to perform this, my precious office in these Congregations zealously, vigilantly and faithfully, and with the blessing of God!

Johan Wicksell[71]

[PENNS NECK 1762]

1762, July 25. Held my Inaugural sermon in Pensneck, in Swedish, and the next time in English.

[PENNS NECK 1762]

Whereas the Church at Pensneck was found to be in a condition of great dilapidation, with roof, gables and windows missing, I first turned my attention to its repair. For this purpose a Parish Meeting was held on August 22, after the Service, when it was decided by the elders of the Congregation, to set up a Subscription list, in order to collect money, and to appoint Peter Boon, to see to its being carried out. But for lack of carpenters, and because of all kinds of other delays, nothing was done about it before late in the fall of the following year.

[PENNS NECK 1762]

October 17, 1762. After the sermon there were chosen: Andrew Senex,[72] Matthias Lambsson, Peter Bonde, and Andrew van Neuman as Trustees, and Hance Lambsson, Francis Miles, Hindrich Petersson and John Beetle as Churchwardens. It was then decided that the Keys to the Church should be entrusted to Hance Jaquette, who was to dig the graves, for 4 shillings in payment for an adult, and for two [shillings] for a young corpse, and to keep watch that no strangers were buried in the churchyard, (the poor excepted)

Penns Neck, but the congregations did not wish a change and Rev. Nordenlind was not anxious to go there. He therefore remained as assistant pastor in Wicaco Church where his unsuitability resulted in his recall. Shortly afterward he fell ill on a visit to Raccoon and died on September 30, 1760. He was buried in the Old Swedes' Church at Wilmington on October 2nd, by Rev. Wrangel.

[71] From 1762 to 1767 Wicksell set down the records of both the Raccoon and Penns Neck parish meetings in the record book at Raccoon. In 1767 he came into possession of the separate Penns Neck book which had been started by Eric Unander (see Penns Neck 1767 entry, p. 93). He apparently made an effort to bring this book up to date for the period of his pastorship for he made several entries of Penns Neck meetings already recorded in the book at Raccoon. These later accounts have been inserted in the text in their chronological order and are designated by footnotes.

[72] Senexsson.

without the knowledge of the President, and before payment for the ground has been made.

Whereas the Palisades round about the churchyard of Racoon were, on my arrival, for the most part decayed and dilapidated and everything lay open for the cattle: It was therefore decided in consultation with the Elders of the Congregation, that a day should be appointed when all who had burial places there should come together, on pain of losing them, to put up and repair their fences. And for this purpose the 25th of October, 1762, was announced and appointed. At that time a great number of people assembled and with great pains, we were able to repair it so that it was possible to keep it shut in and enclosed for a short time again, until we were able to think out some better method of keeping the Churchyard in regular order, which could not be accomplished in the old way, because many families had died out and many had removed to far distant places.

[PENNS NECK 1762] [73]

On October 17, the same year, I held the first Parish Meeting in this Congregation, on which occasion the following Members were chosen for Trustees and Churchwardens, namely:

Trustees:	Church wardens:
Anders Senickson	Francis Miles
Mats Lambson	Hanu Lambson
Peter Bonde &	John Beetle
Anders v. Neuman	Henry Petersson

On this occasion I first explained to the whole Congregation, and afterwards to this chosen Vestry, the necessity for having their church repaired, because both gable ends were found entirely open and broken down, there were no windows, and the roof on the sunny side, was absolutely rotten. It was then decided that a Subscription list should be drawn up for that purpose, and that the Churchwardens should take pains to get up a Subscription, and get it collected as soon as they were able to do so, so that the work could go forward, if possible, this fall.

But this, in the beginning, met with many difficulties, which, for the most part, had their origin in, or were derived from, the false idea mentioned,[73a] so that these repairs was not completely finished before 1764, in the spring. Then this congregation began noticeably to increase, and collect itself again, after the scattered and dispersed condition into which it had fallen, a long time before my coming. With what danger and difficulty divine worship was

---

[73] Another account of the above meeting, written in the Penns Neck book by Wicksell

[73a] The statement above that "many families had died and many had removed to far distant places"

held in this open Hen House the first two winters, attended with what sorrow and distress for the Pastor, it seems best here merely to mention.

On this occasion, since there was no parish clerk to rely on, the Keys to the Church were given into the keeping of Hance Jaquet, and also the charge of the burials, with the injunction not to permit any strangers to be buried here without the consent and permission of the Trustees, and that hereafter he would get 4 shillings

RACOON 1762

On December 14, 1762, the first regular Parish Meeting was held in Racoon, which at the Pastor's request, the Members of the Congregation were asked to attend to a man. The reason was that the Petition for the securing of a Charter [or Privileges of Incorporation] (which the Dean had long before promised to have drawn up by a Lawyer in the City,) was now to be signed by the Congregation. But when the Dean came, he did not have it with him, for the reason that it was not yet ready, the Lawyer having been sick. So nothing was done about the matter at that time.

Whereas several of the English and German Lutheran members of the Congregation, together with some of the young Swedish families had, time and again, requested to be given burial places in our churchyard at Racoon, and whereas I had inquired of the Elders their opinion on this matter the preceding fall, when the fences were being repaired, at which time they had agreed to it. Therefore, for the attainment of this end, it was decided to add three rows of new ground on the left side, and two on the north, which also was done. The 10th of January, 1763, was then appointed as the day on which these lots should be apportioned, which also was done by Esquire Denny and myself. But the [price] and the conditions, which were then given orally, were to be put down on another occasion.

[RACCOON 1763]

On May 11, 1763, at the request of the Dean, a general Parish Meeting was announced in Racoon, for the purpose of signing the long-promised Application for securing a *Privilegium* [or Charter]. But just as little was done about this matter this time as on previous occasions. And the Dean gave as his excuse that the Lawyer had not yet had time to draw it up. On the same occasion I asked the assembled Vestry or Elders, whether they did not find it good to slightly lower the price of the ground-rent for the lots which were to be rented, in order to encourage the first Settlers, and in this way to promote the quicker carrying out of the Plan, since everyone complained that the price was too high. But since the Dean and the majority of the Vestry were against it, alleging that it was low enough, Therefore I, being still a stranger, could not in any way set myself up against it, but, for the present, it remained as they had previously settled it.

[PENNS NECK 1763]

On the following day, Divine Service was held and a Parish Meeting in Pens Neck. On this [occasion] the members of the Congregation were asked by the Dean whether they wished to share equally with the Congregation of Racoon in the building of a Rectory. If not, then they could no longer enjoy an equal share with them in the service, if the people of Racoon were obliged to build alone.

They answered that they were satisfied to lose their former rights in the services. But as for assuming half the costs with the people of Racoon, they thought they were too few. They were willing to share in proportion to their number. But the Dean did not think he could be satisfied with that, but gave them further time for reflection, to talk the matter over with the rest who were absent.

[PENNS NECK 1763] [74]

1763. On May 12th, a Parish Meeting was held at Pens Neck after the sermon. Dean Wrangel, being present, explained to the Society the Advisability, if they wanted to have the same Service in Racoon, of their also taking an equal share in the building of the Rectory at Racoon. To this the Pens Neck people replied that they were much fewer, and could not go halves with them on the Expenses. Nevertheless they did wish to do what they could, and in the meantime they asked for time to think it over, which they already had until the 28th of May next year, when a Parish Meeting was again announced there, on the same subject. However, no one but Anders v. Neuman came to it. For which reason Dean Wrangel ordered me from that day on, until further reply could arrive from Sweden, to preach two Sundays in a row at Racoon, and the third in Pens Neck, which was, in fact, put into practice by me, after it had been unanimously approved at the next Parish Meeting. This step, certainly in the beginning, caused some misunderstanding, but it will gradually improve.

And this Congregation began to increase, yearly, more and more, so that the people could not nearly find room in the Church, a circumstance which led the people to consider a balcony and the building of a new porch, which also soon afterwards was done.

---

[74] See note 73.

[SWEDESBORO 1763] [74a]

On July 11, a special Parish Meeting was held to come to an agreement with the carpenter and the mason about the building of the house and the cellar. And, after much bargaining, it was thus agreed: That the Carpenter was to have 5 shillings a day and free board, for himself and his apprentices, and that this agreement should apply, only with reference to the outside work. The mason was to have 4 shillings a *pearch*,[75] and keep himself in food, and all other assistance.

On September 28, 1763, I took the Subscription list for the Church repairs in Pens Neck away from Peter Boon and gave it to Andreas van Niuman, living at Salem Creek, requesting him to collect the remainder of it, for the making of the repairs, with which he promised to do his best.

[SWEDESBORO and PENNS NECK 1764]

On February 13, 1764, a general Parish Meeting was held, to consider the completion of the Rectory in respect to the inner work, which still was not done. The Carpenter was asked what he demanded for said work. After having made an estimate, he demanded, and declared that since he was to provide his own board, as they desired: one hundred and fifteen pounds. But he afterwards came down to an even 100. But now came the second question: from whence these moneys, or the Total amount, was to be secured?

The Swedish Congregation in Racoon had already collected as much as they could, many, indeed giving above their means. Nothing more could be expected or demanded of them. The English and German congregations helped very little towards it, and they were unwilling to give any more than they had already subscribed to, which amounted to only between £30 and £40. Under these conditions and pressing circumstances the elders hit upon the only way out and asked me, if I would not show the Congregation the charity and kindness to allow the Carpenter [who wanted to rent the Rectory]: [to] have it rent-free for five years, during which time, the rent being £20 a year, which answered to the Sum demanded, they would make up the same Sum to me annually, which would make it much easier for them. As for me, it was a matter of conscience, seeing the house, built as to walls and roof, standing half-finished, thus being held up to scorn and ridicule by other sects. I therefore at once agreed to their request, safe in the trust that the Lord would provide for my support and worldly living, even if that Sum never should be made good to me, which I had grave reason to doubt. And it was thus decided that the Carpenter, Johan Keen, should have a lease on the Rectory for 10 years. The first 5 years without pay, for the afore-said work; but

---

[74a] The name of Raccoon was officially changed to Swedesboro in 1763.

[75] *Pearch*, obsolete form of *perch*, a measure of length containing 5½ yards.

[82]

the latter five years he was to pay £25 a year. However, inasmuch as he now was paying the rent for all the 5 first years at one time, through his work, therefore he claimed that he ought also to profit by the interest on it. Namely, in such wise that something be drawn off from the Sum for the last 5 years, which was granted him, so that for the last 5 years also, he pays no more than £20 a year, just as for the first. The remaining conditions, and the improvement of the place, will be found inserted in the lease, or Rental-Contract. The same was drawn up by my Predecessor, Pastor Lidenius, (although not to my present satisfaction in all parts). A copy of which ought here to be inserted.[76]

THIS INDENTURE Made the 23d Day of February in the year of Our Ld. 1764, setteth forth, That we, Minister Trustees & Wardens of the Sweed Lutheran Church at Racoon & Pensneck, have leased and put out, as we hereby, do lease & put out the Parsonage place belonging to said Church & situated in Pilesgrove Town, Salem County & W.N. Jersey, to Jonas Keen of s[ai]d place Carpenter, for him to have, hold, repair, & improve, for the Term, Lease and possession of Ten years, agreably to the following articles between us agreed viz.

1st. The Lessee, Jonas Keen, is to have, keep, improve, & repair the above mentioned place for the term of ten years, namely; from the first day of March this present year, to the same date of same month of the year 1774: four, inclusive & successively.

2d. Whereas the congregation has agreed with Jonas Keen, about finishing the Building of the Parsonage House allready by him begun at Racoon, & the Congregation is indebted to him for some worck he has done & has yet to finish, Therefore Jonas Keen shall enjoy the leased place for the Term of five years & get a receipt in full for the payment of Rents for sd. first five years, when he according to bargain has finished the out & inside works; The bargain being changed & at the fullfilling thereof challenged by & between the parties concerned, But the —

3d. Article sheweth, that all the work included in the bargain ought to be done & finished at or before the last of June next insuing, Sickness excepted; and when that is fullfilled, then Jonas to have no Claim against the Congregation on account of sd. [said] House, except the receipt just mentioned.

4th. When the first five years are, in this above specified manner lawfully answered on both sides, then Jonas to pay for the remaining five years the full & lawful sum of Twenty pounds each year, at such Seasons, as parties concerned can fix & settle, at least in two payments, one in June & the other at Christmass.

5th. At the end of these Ten Years, the Lessee to have the place in good Tenantable Order and Repair, & to have the Refusal, if he chuses to stay longer, or quit the place, as also to hawl away his last grain in & with the straw.

6th. The Lessee shall clear at least two acres of Swamp on the Crick each year; But if he chuseth to clear the whole or half at once, it is for his own interest. Should any New Improvement be necessary on the upland, then both parties further to agree about the Spot or Spots.

7th. No timber to be cut, or barked, but for the repair of the place & for fire. But if any curled maple or other curious tree, be found, then when cut down, to be equally shared between the Minister & the Lessee.

[76] This indenture in English in the original

[83]

8th. The Lessee to pay the land & poor Taxes during his time of possession. To these Eight Articles above mentioned & lawfully to be held & fullfilled on Both sides between the Lessors & the Lessee, we have interchangeably put our Names & Seals the day & year as above— John Wicksell. R. P.
    Sealed and delivered in the presence of us.

John Abr. Lidenius	John Lock	Lawrence Streeng
James Halten	Thomas Denny	X [his mark]
Andrew v. Neuman	John Helms	Jonan Keen

Feb. the 18th Went Esqr. Denny and myself down to the Parsonage place in Pilesgrove and he run it out this day and settled the lines both sides & made an entry of it for Record.

[SWEDESBORO 1764]

October the 6th this year did the present Church Wardens and Vestry men of this Congregation viz. John Lock, John Helms, John Rambou,[77] John Derixson, Lawrence Lock, Charles Lock, Moses Hoffman, and Thomas Denny, Esqr., as their Attorney, meet at Thomas James's House in Sweedesborough, in order to overlook the Subscription Lists, to take proper methode for [to] get in the arrieares, to settle the accounts with the workmen on the parsonage House and for to make provision for the several articles yet wanting towards the finishing of the said Houses. Then it appeared by comparing the several lists, that fourty pounds were yet unpayed by some subscribers, which were ordered to be got in as quick as possible, without suing of the people, if gentle means could prevail. Farther did Esqr. Denny now pay to Jonas Keen £7 S. 1 & 6 p. from monney in his hands. And as good many small articles of material now were wanted towards the finishing of the House: as painting, glass, Locks etc. to answer This immediate want did John Derixon and Charles Lock advance Ten pounds to Jonas Keen, who was ordered to buy these articles himself and bring in his account thereof duly verified at the next meeting, and meanwhile finish off the Building compleatly, which he did also accordingly. And the said Derixon and Lock were to make themselves payed from the yet unpayed subscriptions which were left to their own care to drive in with all possible speed.

[SWEDESBORO 1765]

This winter did the Revd. John Ab: Lidenius[78] keep Sweede and English School in Repapo and the children were greatly profited by his teaching especially in the Sweede Tongue.

---

[77] The spelling is unusual. The common form is *Rambo*.

[78] Johan Abraham Lidenius was born in Raccoon, his father being the Swedish pastor there, Abraham Lidenius, and his mother Maria von Neaman. In 1723 he was taken to Sweden by his parents. Here he was given a theological education and in due time ordained. In July, 1750, he was appointed pastor at Raccoon

March the 14th did I move from William Matsson, my good and exceeding kind Benefactor for 19th month, into the Parsonage House near Racoon Church, which now was finished according to bargain by the Carpenter Jonas Keen. And was conducted and introduced by great many of my loving Hearers.

Since Thomas Denny, Esqr., in Nov: last year, obtained our Deeds back from Mr. Galloway, the Lawer at Philadelphia, and proper application was made upon the desire of this Congregation, by me & said Denny to the Honorable Charles Read, Secretary of this Province & one of his Majestys Council, to draw up a Petition for this Congregation, to our Governour and Council for getting the Members of this Congregation incorporated and a Royal Charter obtained for this place; Accordingly had the said Gentleman drawn up and sent down to our Speedy signing a Such Petition, By reason of the Counsils quick and imediate meeting, which the Stamp Act. Concern in particular hastened; And for this reason was it imediatly signed without the least delay; by the Several members of this Congregation viz on the 17th day of March 1765. When the Congregation met the first time after Divine Service in the New Parsonage House. Our desire and application was at first, that both Racoon & Pensneck Congregation should be included in one and the same Charter; but this could not be granted by reason of their laying situated in two different Counties. I then proposed the next time to Pensneck Congregation, to make application for themselves in the same concern. But they could see no necessity or moving cause for the purpose, and therefore I dropped urging it any further.

---

and Penns Neck. As he had been born in America and learned the language as a child, great hopes were placed in him by the Archbishop and Consistory in Sweden.

He arrived in America on July 21, 1751, and preached his first sermon in Raccoon on the Tenth Sunday after Trinity. He visited Raccoon and Penns Neck on alternate Sundays and also preached in other congregations, at Maurice River, Manatawning, Reading, Little Conestoga, and other places, and for awhile he preached at Marcus Hook, Marlborough, and Fagg's Manor. He was recalled to Sweden and actually began preparations for his journey, preaching his farewell sermon in the Autumn of 1752. Rev. Wrangel gave him thirty pounds for his passage, but he squandered the money and later determined that he would never return to the land of his forefathers. His many troubles cast a shadow over his life and he was finally expelled from the church and prevented from preaching in any of the Swedish congregations along the Delaware. As stated above, he taught school for a while at Rappapo (Repaupo). It was said that he was a skillful teacher. He accumulated debts and was finally unable to take care either of himself or his family. He died in the winter of 1765.

For *Rappapo*, see Johnson, *Journal and Biography of Nicholas Collin*, pp. 265, 300, 306.

[SWEDESBORO, 1765]

On the 17th of March, 1765, the members of the Racoon Congregation met for the first time in the new Rectory, into which I had moved on the previous Thursday. On this occassion the Congregation had the pleasure of signing the Application which Carl Read, the Government Secretary, had drawn up for them, to the Governor and the Council, concerning the granting of Privileges [a Charter] for the Congregation of Racoon and Pen Neck to be incorporated into a political Community, for the administration of their Churches and lands, according to English law, etc. etc.

1765. March the 20 & 21. Had each of these days 15 hands for clearing of the Lot and gardeen Spot, most all Sweeds, and particularly must [note] here the readiness of Dennys, the Several Locks, Mattsons, Jurissons, Archards, Derixon, Cocks, Urians, Homans and Hindrichsons famillies be remembered, which also at the clearing and improving of the pasture ground and at all other occasions, were both willing & ready to lend their helping hand. These famillies it were also, who hawled the logs for the house from the Ceder swamps and the other materials and this all gratis.

[SWEDESBORO 1765]

May the 12th after Divine Service were following members chosen by the Congregation for Trustees and Churchwardens this ensuing year viz. Thomas Denny Esqr. and John Lock Trustees. And James Stillman, John Derixon, John Rambou, John Helms, Lawrence Lock & Charles Lock Churchwardens. May the 26th this year I urged and tendered the repair of Pensneck Church to this Congregation in the strongest manner in my power.

[SWEDESBORO 1765]

On the 2nd of June of this year a ministers' conference was held here at Racoon, at which the Rector Dr. Wrangel,[79] Pastor

---

[79] Carl Magnus Wrangel, a nobleman of an old family, was appointed Dean of the Swedish churches in America in 1758.

On Easter Sunday, April 15, 1759, he delivered his first sermon in Gloria Dei. He was recalled to Sweden after many years' service and engaged passage to Europe in 1766; but his church would not let him go and he remained here until the fall of 1768. Wrangel was probably the most eloquent preacher Sweden ever sent to this country, equally proficient in English, Swedish, German and Latin.

Borell[80] of Christina, and the Rev. Mr. Hegblad[81] were present. At this conference we, the last mentioned ministers, found it unavoidable to warn Dr. Wrangel, in writing, that we could no longer associate with him, nor show him that confidence and respect which we owed him as a colleague, and in particular, as the rector, appointed for this Mission. The reasons on our side, for a step of such importance, are so complicated and delicate that they neither can nor aught to be cited, but rather be left to be buried in oblivion.[82]

[SWEDESBORO 1765]

August the 27th [I] Went up to Burlingtown in Order to consult personally with the Secretary Charles Read concerning the Charter, but did not find Him at home; then went to his office and perused Brundwick Charter, made my Remarks on this, and in a letter to His Honour Read desired, that those circumstances & clauses might be brought in which were comunicated to Him in my last Letter, and such as I now mentioned excluded, which did not suit the Constitution of our Church. Some of these clauses or to the most part were afterwards granted and incerted in the Charters, but some could not, as being contrary to His Excellencys Our Governors Instruction.

The 26th of Octobre this year we received our Charter[83] by the hands of Thomas Denny Esqr. who had payed the usual fees to the Governour, Attorney general and the office, due for a such Priviledge, out of his own pocket. The next meeting did the Members of the Vestry, myself, Denny, James Stillman William Homan & a few of the Sweedes more, make up the said expense & charges to Esqr. Denny, and the whole did not amount to more than six pounds ten shillings. But the Reason was this; Because Secretary Read, who drew up both the Petition and the Charter, He generously did it gratis, knowing the Circumstances of this Congregation, and as He was pleased to say, in return for some small serv-

---

80 Anders (Andreas) Borell was appointed assistant in the Swedish mission in America two years later. In the Spring of 1759 he arrived in Philadelphia in company with Rev. Carl Magnus Wrangel. In 1760 he became pastor in the Old Swedes' Church in Wilmington, where he remained until his death on April 4, 1768. He was made Dean in 1765 of the Old Swedish churches on the Delaware. For a time he preached once a month at Penns Neck Church and also visited the other Swedish churches in the Delaware Valley.

81 Johan (Johannes) Häggblad became Rev. Wrangel's assistant in Philadelphia, in September, 1763. Although Wrangel befriended him, Häggblad caused him much difficulty by siding with other pastors who were Wrangel's enemies.

82 This paragraph in Swedish in the church records

83 For text of the charter see p. 125.

ices, the present Rector of this place, occasionally had the pleasure to show Him.

[PENNS NECK 1765]

In the fall. It was decided in the Church Council, at the request of many, that a Gallery and a new porch should be built, and a Subscription List be drawn up for that purpose, which also was done. Money was therefore collected for this during the winter, and in the spring, 1766, the work was completed and paid for.

Nov: the 4th Went up to Burlington in order to wait on the Governors Council, for to return the sincere & humble thanks of this Congregation and my own, for the many & signal favours and Priviledges granted to our Society By this Charter; and also for to get a couple of hard expressions therein altered: viz. 1. the unlimited and undue Power granted this Vestry to turn out their Minister at their own good pleasure; into this moderate controul, that the said power should at leest be lodged in the breasts of the Major part of the whole Congregation, if ever the necessity should urge a such harsh step to be taken without the previous & usual Remonstrance to the King of Sweeden by the Arch Bishop and Consistory at Upsala, as the genuine and lawful Judges over this Royal Sweedish Mission. 2. That the approbation & confirmation of a Sweedish Missionary at this place, 'by his Exellency the Governor of this Province, called in question, the Reserve in the cession of this Colony, as also the appointment and Dignity of his Sweedish Majesty, and therefore appeared to be improper Terms in a Priviledge of such a Nature.

The 5th I had the Honour & good luck to wait on his Excellency in Council met, and returned my humble Thanks to them All, and represented the above concern to their most affectionate consideration; But the misfortune was, that Governor & Council were this day exceeding bussy about the Stamp Act, so that they had not time sufficient to weigh this subject. Still They altered the first, most to my purpose, But the Second point His Excellency said, was not in his power for the present to alter.

[SWEDESBORO 1765]

Nov: the 8th At a meeting of the Rector, Church Wardens and Vestrymen of the Sweedish Lutheran Congregation in and about Sweedesborough, assembled and met at the Parsonage House of said Congregation present, John Wicksell Rector, p. t. Thomas Denny, Esqr. & John Denny, Church wardens; and John Lock, John Derixon,

Laurence Lock, John Helms, & John Rambou, Vestrymen, p. t., were following concerns relative to this Congregation, transacted. viz.:

1. It was proposed and Resolved, that the 30th day instant, be the day appointed for setling the accounts concerning the building of this parsonage house, with all the several persons concerned therein. Which also was done, as the general account of this day, in the account Book of this Incorporation sheweth.

2. Proposed & Resolved, that public notice be given to the Respective Members of this Congregation that they amend and repair the decayed Church Yard-pales, if they chuse after the old methode. / : each one his pannel : / or some new measures shall be taken by this Incorporation, that answers better the end, and can promote more speedily and regularly the work, viz. by a small subscription from every owner of the Lots, as often as any repair thereon is necessary. This last measure I recommended as more expedient, than the old irregular way.

3. Was Resolved, that all English and Deutch, who kept to our Church should have liberty to take lots in our Buring ground upon following terms viz—1^0. That they must help from time to time to keep the Church Yards-pales in good repair. 2^0. They must help to build the Church and maintain the lawful Minister of this place. They must profess the principles and be subject and observe the Orders and Rules of this Society.

And 4. If such person, persons or famillies should happen to move away from these parts, then and in all such cases, fall their Lots to the Church again, without that, such moving or dying persons, shall have the leest power to sell conveigh or transfere their Right, or any other, but their lawfull Heirs that remain in this place, and observe these mentioned rules.

At this meeting was also Resolved, that the three Roes next to the pales on the east end of the yard should allways serve for Strangers and the poor; But no such person be burried there without the previous knowledge and consent of the present Rector, and whenever the stranger was able, then and in every such case were his friends or Administrators to pay, to the Rector of this Church, for the breaking of the ground, from Ten to five Schillings, according to their Several abilities, *Besides the Clercks* fees.

4^0. Proposed and Resolved, That every other lot from Thomas Denys House to the Ministers garden, or on the west side of the Roude be let, at the rate of Twenty Schil: pr. acre. And those of the east side for Twenty five dito pr. acre, and to extend down to the Run.

On the 8th of November 1765, the same year, the Charter was read to the members of the congregation in the Rectory.[84]

---

[84] This entry in Swedish in the original. Wicksell's main entries from 1762 to 1763 were in Swedish; thereafter he used English.

[SWEDESBORO 1765]

Nov: the 30th Met the Vestry at Parsonage House in Sweeds-borough according to appointment, and setled the accounts concerning the House building with them who came in; but the general account would not be drawn up this time, because several persons concerned did not attend.

[SWEDESBORO 1766]

January the 2d. met following members of the vestry at the parsonage house in Sweedsborough viz. John Lock, John Helms, Lawrence Lock, Charles Lock and Mounce Keen and in the presence of and with the consent of their Rector were following business transacted viz.

1. James Stillman present, made application to the vestry desiring to take upon ground rent, a little piece of the churchland in Sweedsborough that fronts the creek below the bridge, in order to build a wharf hereon, offering to pay therefore 30 shil: yearly ground rent and a free landing of all church goods. The vestry went down and willed the desired spot, and pointed out the line and course according to Mr. Stillmans desire, and after due, consideration accepted of Mr. Stillmans offer proposed; ordered him to have it run out by Thomas Denny, esqr. and lease drawn up, which the vestry promised to sign to him sometime this spring or as soon as this and the other leases could be ready —

2. Was the desire of Doctor Bodo Otto, Senr. and Mr. James James, merchant, proposed by the Rector, and debated in the vestry, viz. who of them should have the lot next joining to Thomas James and it was resolved with the consent of the Doctor, who was present, that James James should have one acre and a half joining his brothers lot and the Doctor two acres next joining James James; and this on terms that they both should build and improve their respective lots at least within the space of two years from the present time.

3. Was proposed by the Rector and consented to by the present members, that a book in folio should be bought from the purse money, wherein the charter, leases, rules and other acts of this incorporation should be properly entered and recorded, which concern the rector was desired to execute, which also he did. J. W.[85]

[SWEDESBORO 1766]

Feb: the first was a general meeting of the whole Congregation both Sweeds, English and Deutch. Now was sufficient ground for three New Roes on the west end taken into the church-Yard, By reason of many wanting lots therein. The Poles were

---

[85] The initials stand for J[ohan] W[icksell].

accordingly moved out, mended put up and closed up again. And Thomas Denny, Esqr. Run out the whole yard into twenty Nine Roes, Twelf lots in each Roe, and every lot of 14th by 7th feet biggness; and He made a map upon a great sheet of parchment over the Yard, marked out the Roes accordingly, and so we took down the Names of those owners who were present, which did not amount to the quarterpart, altho' I took peines to publish this concern a whole month before hand, with a strict warning, and afterwards, I have layed hold on every opportunity, to get the neglectful owners properly recorded on this mapp; But as yet, have not been able to bring it farther. The Parchment and the trouble & peine, did the said Denny, according to his usual generosity and afection for his Church & Brethren, give and do gratis.

The 3d of this month did my kind and ever affectionate Sweedes in Rapapo cut down and draw out to the Edge, 66 cedar poles, in James Stillmans Swamp, which he gave gratis for a stable.

The transactions of this vestry for the following years are recorded (P. 116) in the New book of this incorporation, as the papers of this is to much blouting.[86]

Since sufficient room here before is left for the entering or recording of the several leases, which hereafter from time to time may be granted by this incorporation. Then has the present rector of this place thought proper, to give the transactions of this incorporation, for the present and remaining time of his rectorship a fair and true record on these following pages: under the sincere and hearty prayer and with, that every measure may lend for Gods glory, and the eternal wellfare of every soul belonging to this church and society and be a satisfactory information to our succeeding generations to the latest future ages.

[SWEDESBORO 1766]

April the first, being the yearly election day of church Wardens and vestry:men for the Sweedish Lutheran Congregation in and about Sweedsborough upon Racoon Creek, let the old vestry of this incorpation and good many members more at their parsonage house in the said Borrough, and in the presence, and with the consent of their present Rector John Wicksel, voted in following members, as church wardens and vestrymen for this next insuing year, viz:

John Lock & John Derixson } Church Wardens

Lawrence Lock
James Stillman
John Rambou
Charles Lock
Mounce Keen
John Helms
} Vestrymen

---

[86] This refers to a second book of the Raccoon parish, which contains the charter received in 1765 and many church leases.

At this meeting were following concerns proposed by the Rector and agreed upon by the whole vestry. viz.

1. Resolved, that the several subscribers towards the parsonage house who has not yet payed their subscription, should be warned by the present wardens and in case of none compliance be sued after a certain appointed time by the vestry.

2. Were Lawrence Lock and John Helms appointed, to inspect the parsonage place or glebe in Pilesgrove, inforce the lease, and at the next meeting, give in a true report to the vestry concerning the state of this place and the tenants conduct and behaviour.

3. Application was made to the rector by two men, for getting a lease for the lot opposite the church, but the proposal was this time denied; because the vestry were of opinion that the congregation would not as yet part with the use of that lot, by reason of their horses, before proper provision was made for the building of a stable where their could have shelter in fowl weather, and necessary have in summer season, and thereby it remained for this time.

4. Was proposed by the rector: whether any means could be found out to get the church marsh canked in this spring? But none could be found as yet by order of the vestry.

John Wilksel, P.R.

5. It was proposed by the Rector, whether it would not be expedient to have the design and plan of our charter and incorporation as verfied in the newspapers for some considerable time, which by the vestry was though proper, agreed upon, and provided for.

6. Was proposed and agreed upon, that the leases of this place, must build a house, in order to answer the ground rent, on their respective lots, or make some other considerable improvements answering the same purpose, within the term of one year, from the leasing time, or at least within two. The said House to be build in a decent suitable manner for a town, either of stone, brick, frame, or log, and the dimentions of it, to be, at left, 20 by 16 or 16th feet.

7. Agreed, that any absent member of the vestry or one coming more than one hour later than the appointment, since due notice been given, should pay one shilling fine, to be imployed for proper purposes, signed in the minute by the above mentioned vestry and by want of a clerk brought into this book by the p. R. as above. J.W.[87]

[SWEDESBORO 1766]

December the 3rd. was the whole vestry appointed to meet at the parsonage house in Sweedsborough, in order to sign and execute the several leases granted from time to time in the years passed; but unluckely it happened that the most part of the members were at pres-

[87] "the p[resent] R[ector] as above J[ohan] W[icksell].

ent taken sick, and for this reason must this urging concern also for this time be defered til another time.

It must be mentioned here, that the Rector could not attend at this present years election day; because he was the night before expressly called over the River to Willimingtown, to visit his friend Andrew Borell the Sweedish Commissary of this Royal Mission, who then laid on the point of death, and very desirous to see him, before his departure, but still did the vestry in their respective offices for the next insuing year also and the minutes of the day were taken down by Thomas Denny, Esqr., according to my request to him, left in writting at the parsonage house.

[PENNS NECK 1767]

As this Church record-book[88] did not come into my hands before the end of the year 1767, from my Predecessor [colleague] in the office, Johan Abram Lidenius; Therefore my official transactions for the previous period of office were not able to be put down in it; Especially since I did never know of it, but I put them down in the Church record-book of Racoon, in the old way. Nor do I think it apropos, for the sake of convenience, to break off that Order, but I have continued with the same transactions in the book mentioned where my Warrant, etc., is found inserted. However, I have found it needful to here introduce the Parish Meetings, resolutions, and economical improvements, which have been held and undertaken during my time, in this Congregation, which, in the beginning, was very much opposed to me on account of a false rumour which had been spread there by malicious people, namely: That I was not to be regarded as their Minister; But that I had been sent for the service of the Racoon Congregation only. This false prejudice, however, disappeared, as soon as I had, for some time, been preaching there every other Sunday, equally with Racoon. But the reason why this order was subsequently changed will be told, or put down, in its place.   [Johan Wicksell].

[SWEDESBORO 1767]

January the 5th met the present vestry at the parsonage house in Sweedsborough, in order to setle the accounts concerning the building of the parsonage house according to previous notice given to all persons concerned, which all to the most part now attended and accordingly the general account was drawn up by Thomas Denny esqr, the chosen manager of this building, and laid before the vestry to be inspected before the next meeting, the balance, and the state of this large account properly setled, so, that it could be brought in to the Book of accounts of this incorporation, and in order to promote this purpose, were the wardens ordered by the vestry, to get friendly

---

[88] This is Wicksell's first entry in the Penns Neck book. See footnote 71.

sumons issued out against all subscribers that had not payed, to meet the 24th instent here at Sweedsborough, in order to pay or to acknowledge judgement before the magistrate or their respective sums which also was done on the said days.

At this meeting was Erick Cock appointed clerk of the Sweedish Congregation, with the usual fees attending this office, during good behaviour in his trust, and impowered to dig the graves, and charged to observe well the roes after the new map, and to be carefull in any absence of the Rector, that nobody be burried in another mans lot.

[SWEDESBORO 1767]

March the 28th met the old vestry and several other members of the Sweede Lutheran Congregation upon Racoon Creek, at their parsonage House in Sweedsborough, and then were following members elected church wardens and vestrymen for the next year, by the approbation and consent of their Rector, viz.

John Lock and } Church wardens Joh Helms } and		John Dericson Lars Lock Charles Lock Mounce Keen } VESTRY MEN	

Then they proceeded to following business viz.

1. They signed and executed following leases viz. Number 1. To Thomas Denny, Esqr. No. 2 to Peter Lock, Junr. No. 3 for James James. No. 4 to Thomas James, Inkeeper. No. 5. To James Hellman, Farmer.

2. Were John Helms and Mounce Keen appointed by the vestry to be present and attend a meeting at Woodstown on the 7th of April next, in order to prevent a road being laid out over the parsonage glebe in Pilesgrove; and if not able to prevent it, then to see it executed in the most advantagous manner for the place, and also, at the same time to inspect the said glebe and report the situation and conduct of the tenant to the vestry at their next meeting.

3. Resolved, that a book of accounts be bought from the purse money, wherein the accounts of this incorporation for time to come should be entered and regularly kept. Which concern the Rector undertook to provide for.

4. Did John Rambou the late vestryman point out and bespeak two lots of ground, one each side of the road, and asked the favour of that time he intended to build on the [lots], if he recovered his former health. Which was granted. But else, his engagement to be void.

[SWEDESBORO 1767]

April the 21st being the day appointed by charter for the yearly election of church wardens and vestrymen of the Sweede:

Lutheran congregation on and about Racoon Creek, then met the old vestry and several members more of the same society, at the parsonage house in Sweedesborough and in the presence of, and with the approbation and consent of their present rector, they chose following members for church officers for the ensuing year; since it was previously agreed upon by them, that the number this year, should not exceed six, besides the Rector; because several leases were to be granted and executed, and therefore the multiplicity of names to be avoided as much as possible. Accordingly were—

John Lock &
John Helms

appointed church wardens

and John Rambou
Lawrence Lock
Charles Lock &
Mounce Keen, Junr.
were appointed vestrymen
for the next year.

present also Thomas Denny, Esqr.,
our trusty friend and wellwisher.

1. Resolved and ordered that the subscribers to the parsonage house pay their subscriptions before the 8th day of June next, or be sued for the same, by the proper persons mentioned in the list.

2. Ordered that the several persons who have obtained grant and taken lots in Sweedesborough, now to have them enactly run out and lawfull leases executed for the[m], by Thomas Denny surveyer deputed, yet on the cost and expense of the leases and a day be appointed as soon as these leases be drawn for the proper executing and signing of them.

3. Ordered and agreed upon, that the respective ground rents or the leased lots be payed on the election yearly and forever.

4. Did the vestry at this meeting settle with Thomas James, inkeeper near Sweedsborough, about the arrear rents on his two lots, and accepted of his offers of seven pounds for the whole, for which sum he gave a note to the wardens, payable within 12 month, with the interest from this day. And a lease, according to his desire, was ordered to be drawn up for him.

5. Were John Helms and Charles Lock ordered as a committee to carefully inspect the parsonage place in Pilesgrove and report the situation of the same to the whold vestry at their next meeting—

6. Was a bargain made with Erick Cock to make new sales for the land or front side of the churchyard, and from the old to mend up the other sides, and to look for his pay from the respective owners. He was to have five shill: for every new parcel and payed by day to the Rect.

[SWEDESBORO 1767]

October the 31st. Met following members of the vestry at the parsonage house in Sweedsborough, viz. John Lock, John Helms, Lawrence Lock, Mounce Keen, Junr. and Thomas Denny, Esqr. and John Derickson were also present, as concerned in the business of the day and following concerns were proposed by the Rector, viz.

1. What steps must be taken for to get in the unpayed subscriptions of the parsonage house? And it was resolved that John Derickson should sue those in Gloucester, and John Helms do the same with those in Salem County.

2. The respective leases would not be executed because they were not as yet drawn up by Thomas Denny, Esqr., by reason of his preecedent sickness; but he promised now to do it as quick as possible and to deliver them to the Rector, in order to have them by good time entered into this book of the incorporation, that they might be executed, at least, at our next election day.

3. The repairing of the church windows was proposed and found to be absolute necessary before the winter set in and John Lock the warden was ordered to see the work done at the cheapest rate, and the Rector promised to make a small collection towards defraying the expenses, which he had already begun with success.

4. Had the rector payed to Erick Cock at sundry times £4.s.15 6p. towards the pay for the sales, which he took pain to gather in himself, this sum was acknowledged by Erick, and a list of the names of those who had payed, was now given by the Rector to Erick, and he ordered to get in the remainder himself according to bargain.

5. Proposed, whether the fees for digging the graves should not be increased and a fixed distinction made betwixt old, young, and a babe? But this concern was defered to another time and a fuller vestry. By order of the present members.

John Wicksel, P. & R.[88a]

[PENNS NECK 1769]

In the spring of 1769 I laid before the Congregation and the Church Council the necessity of the third improvement: namely the boarding-in of the outside, and the sealing, or plastering of the interior, the laying of new floors, the improvement of the Benches, the making of new Seats for the porch and passage, (which were still often needed, when the weather was fine,) and the mending of the roof on the other side. This also was considered necessary by the Congregation and the Church Council, and

---

[88a] P[astor] and R[ector].

Andrew Senekson, Esquire, undertook to draw up an Article of Subscription, or List, which was to be presented to the people this fall and the following winter, by the Churchwardens, in order to collect a Sum sufficient for the accomplishment of this object. But inasmuch as the putting into effect of this matter went too slowly for them, I myself took charge of the List and, riding around for three days in the lower and upper Neck, collected a Subscription Sum which we thought sufficiently large to cover the Cost of aforementioned improvement.

[SWEDESBORO 1770]

April the 17th. Met the old vestry and few members of the congregation besides, at the parsonage house in Sweedsborough at which occasion following members were elected church wardens and vestrymen for the next ensuing year viz.

John Lock and John Helms	} Church Wardens and	Lars. Lock John Derixson Mounce Keen Jacob Jones Charles Dalbou Charles Cock	LAWFULLY elected vestry- men, for the ensuing year

At this meeting were following business transacted. viz.

1. Was a lease granted and signed unto Erick Cock, the clerk, for a piece of Swamp above the ministers pasture on the same run; and also two acres of ground in Sweedesborough, joining my garden, This last was granted, no farther, than til such a time, as some body took up the lot joining the ministers garden, which must intend to Lads line, and in such a case all ways be at the free disposal of the vestry, and for the farther conditions must be looked to the lease itself.

2. Did the wardens setle their accounts with Thomas James, both concerning the arriariers, as also concerning the latter ground rent for his lots now due, for which he gave a note to the wardens payable after two month from the present date.

3. Did Doctor Bodo Otto, Senr., make application to this vestry for getting half an acre of ground this side of his former lots yet added, and included in his lease, which also was granted him by the present vestry, and resolved that the lease should be ordered accordingly.

By the order of the vestry, John Wicksel, P. & r.

[PENNS NECK 1770]

And in the month of August, 1770, the Congregation chose John Beetle and Charles Green for managers for the carrying out of this work; it was then also decided to plaster the Church on the inside instead of Sealing it. And in September a Parish Meeting was held as to what absolutely had to be repaired on the Church, when the aforementioned was found needful. On this occasion Charles Green was asked, in consultation with Esquire Senicksson, to buy the necessary materials for the work, and to bargain with the craftsmen. And John Beetle undertook to collect the money. But when they were ready to proceed with this work there were no nails in the country, and therefore the work had to be postponed until the next spring, when enough nails were expected from England again, since the Non Importation Convention had now already been abolished.

The Subscription Lists for the three repairs mentioned will be correctly given below, if they can ever be got out of the hands of those in question. If not, may posterity hold me innocent in this case, if they are left in ignorance of it.

As for the collection money in this Congregation, during my time, it was disposed of as formerly, namely, Anders v. Neuman, on Salem Creek, had charge of them the first 6 or 7 years, and from time to time dispenced them for the small needs and repairs for of the Church, without giving any formal Account of them. There is no doubt, however, about his good Trust or use of them. John Beetle has taken care of them during recent years in the same way. He has paid various small repairs out of them, to old Brown for the needs of the Churchyard, and the repair of the fences, bought wine for the Holy Supper, and kept a glass of wine constantly in the Church for the minister after the sermon, which, in later years, I have found to be absolutely necessary for the preservation of health, at certain times of the year, especially when heat and cold is extreme, and for a minister who is not accustomed to a heavy breakfast; for the lack of which, during the first 6 or 7 years I, for my part, often injured my health.

In this Congregation I have never been able to get any steady parish clerk, for the reason that, in the beginning, there was said to be no one who understood English Singing: Therefore I have been obliged to get along here, as well as I might, sometimes with, and sometimes without singing, especially during the first years, until I got to know the people better, and there was an opportunity to arrange Singing Classes, among them, the first of these beginning in Manathan; after that time I have almost never failed to find some one who could sing. However, Hance Lambson, in the lower Neck, sang during the first years, when he was at home, as well as he was able, and he responded to the Service.

N.B. I have not been able to secure from them the Subscription List for the Gallery; when I asked, I was told that during the collection it went through so many hands that it was worn out, or had been mislaid by someone and lost.

And since the third of the aforementioned Repairs has finally been completed this spring, and the greater part of the payment for the work has already been paid, what remains [outstanding] soon ought to be collected now for the satisfaction of the one Carpenter, Dennie, and for making good other unpaid accounts, the other Carpenter, Erich Philpott being already paid. The Congregation has to settle this account with John Beetle, the widow Green, and Hance Lambsson who have had said Subscription List amounting to some 40 Pounds or more, in their hands, the whole time.

Below follows the first Subscription List of Pensneck Church repairs as to gables, windows, window-shutters and roof on the Sunny side, drawn up by the Trustee Andrew Senickson, on August 30, 1762. Those who have paid their Subscriptions are the following, to wit:

	£	S.	d.		£	S.	d.
Andrew Senickson, Esqr.	3	0	0	Hance Jaquet	0	7	6
Peter Boon	2	0	0	Andrew Standly	0	10	0
Mathias Lambsson	2	0	0	Solomon Olman	0	6	0
Peter Bilderback	2	0	0	Andrew Helms	1	0	0
John Hickman	0	10	0	William Rynolds	0	3	9
William Van Neuman, Jr.	0	7	6	Andrew Hoffman	0	7	6
Andrew Van Neuman,				Moses Keen, Jr.	0	7	6
Salem Creek	2	0	0	John Procter	0	5	0
Hugh Davis	0	10	0	Andrew v. Neuman, Jr.	0	10	0
Hance Lambsson	0	10	0	Nicholas Nilsson	0	5	0
John Holstine	0	7	6	Albert Bilderback	0	7	6
Cornelius Boon	1	0	0	Henry Petersson, Sr.	0	15	0
Thomas Lambsson	0	5	0	Laurence Holten	0	5	0
Annanias Elvill	0	5	0	John Beetle	0	15	0
Tobias Caspersson	0	7	6	William Mecum	0	10	0
Alexander Congelton	0	7	6	Thomas Miles	2	0	0

[SWEDESBORO 1771]

April the 2d. Met following members of the Vestry of the incorporation of Swedesborough at the parsonage house in the said Bourough, on their yearly election day viz. John Lock, John Helms, the old church wardens, and Lawrence Lock, Mounce Keen, and Charles Cock the old vestrymen, and whereas they made a majority according to charter, they proceeded upon following business, the other three members absent were all sick.

1. Were the old church wardens John Lock, and John Helms confirmed in their office as wardens for the next year, and Lawrence Lock, John Derixeon, Mounce Keen, James Stillman, Charles Cock and Charles Dalbou were elected and confirmed to be vestrymen for the said year.

2. The desolate state of educating children in these parts having long laid at the heart of the present Rector and very desirous to remove ignorance and excile darkness and carcarity, he now tendered to his vestry: Weither a lease, could not be granted, on a half acred of ground, in this bourough, for the use of a public schoolhouse, free from all manner of ground rent forever. The form of a lease for that purpose, was drawn up by the rector, and read to the present vestry; and after a due consideration a debating of the subject it was approved of, and resolved to be executed.

3. Did Doctor Bodo Otto, Snr., resign his right and claim on the lots, which he heretofore had obtained a grant of and in part taken in possession, to this incorporation by reason of his having a design to move up to Philadelphia, and the incorporation accepted of his resignation willingly, as several made application for to take and improve the said lots.

4. Did Mr. Robbert Brown make application, for to take on the fixed ground rent, two acres of ground on the east side of the Kings roade, joining to Thomas James' lots, which request was granted to him and a lease ordered to be given and executed, yet on the express reserve of his building on, or improving the said lots within a years time, so as to secure their respective ground rent.

5. Did John Rambou, farmer and late vestryman, make application to this vestry, for to take on the fixed ground rent, four acres of ground one on the west side, and three on the opposite side of the roade, which three last lots, he desired might lay undertermined for his account, til after next court; so, that he then might have liberty, to lessen the number according to his own pleasure, in case he should miss of obtaining a licence, and accordingly it was resolved as to answer these his purposes.

6. Did Abram Keen Taylor, likewise make due application to this present vestry, for to take on the fixed ground rent, one acre of ground; on the west side of the roade joining to John Rambou and Asa Becks lots, which request was also granted to him on the above mentioned terms, and a lease ordered to be given and executed.

7. At the same time, did Asa Beck likewise make application to this vestry, desiring to take on the fixed ground rent, one acre of ground joining to Thomas Dennys, Esqr., and the said Abram Keens lots, which also was granted him on the above terms and a lease ordered to be given and executed.

8. Was proposed by the rector, that the glebe and house in Pilesgrove should be carefully inspected in regard to the marsh, fields, roads and the house itself and see how the lease is executed, the necessity and enspediency of this concern appeared plain to this body and appointed John Helms and Mounce Keen for this purpose, and to give in a true account thereof, at the next meeting of this vestry.

9. Was Joseph Devenport's lease for his lot now ready drawn up by Thomas Denny, Esqr., and presented to the Vestrys percesal and approcation,[88b] but it could not be executed at this occasion, as it was not given, time enough, into the hands of the Rector, for to get it duly entered into the incorporation book, and therefore refered to the next meeting

Day, year, and place as above mentioned.

JOHN WICKSEL, P. R.

[SWEDESBORO 1772]

The 21. day of April met following members of the old vestry of the Swede-Lutheran Congregation, at the Parsonage house at Swedesborough viz. Joh Lock, and John Helms, church wardens; and John Derixon, Lawrence Lock, Mounce Keen, Charles Cock, Vestrymen of the last year. And then were following business transacted: viz.

1. Were the old members unanimously chosen to serve for the ensuing year in the said office, and James Steelman and Charles Dalbou were added and returned to the number of vestry men for the said year which office they also accepted of.

2. Was the lease for John Rambous lots duly executed.

3. Was a subscription list drawn up by the Rector, for to raise sixty pounds towards paying of the remaining ballance of building the parsonage house, or repairing the house at the glebe in Pilesgrove, and defraying the costs attending the deed for the church marsh upon Racoon Creek, which the rector allready had payed out of his own pocket to Thomas Denny, Esqr., and this subscription was begun by the Rector, and the present members of the vestry.

4. Was Mathew Gill's desire, to get the lot opposite the church on ground rent, proposed to the vestry; but they did as yet not see cause to let it for a while, as the congregation could not spare the use of it.

5. Was John Helms and Mounce Keen appointed as a committee to inspect the parsonage glebe at Pilesgrove, and to give in their report thereof at the next meeting.

6. Did Asa Beck make application for another lot of one acre of ground on the east side of the roade; his desire was granted, and a lease ordered to be executed for him the next session place year & day as above, L: Secret; John Wicksel, P. & Rect.

[88b] Vestry's perusal and approbation.

[SWEDESBORO 1773]

The 13th day of April met following members of the old Vestry of the Swede-Lutheran Congregation at the Parsonage house in Swedesborough viz. John Lock, John Helms, Church Wardens; and John Derixon, Lawrence Lock, James Steelman, Charles Cock, Mounce Keen, and Charles Dalbou, vestry men, and then were the said members re-elected and refirmed to serve as church wardens and vestry men for the next year and no business were incumbent or laid before the vestry at this meeting: Only, that Hance Cock by the hand of Lawrence Friend made application to get a lease for the spot of ground between the church yard and Mr. Browns warf which proposal the vestry would answer and grant at another meeting, if they found him able to build a snug house thereon, such as that front lot of the borough did require. Place, year, and day, as above. L: Secret:

John Wicksel P. & Rect:

[SWEDESBORO 1773]

August the 19th according to appointment and proper notice given by the Rector, did following members or vestrymen of the Swede-Lutheran Incorporation meet at their parsonage house in Swedesborough viz. John Helms, Church Warden, and John Derixon, Lawrence Lock, James Steelman, Mounce Keen, Charles Cock and Charles Dalbou, vestrymen. At this meeting were following business laid before this vestry, by their present rector. viz. such as followeth—

1. Was the letter from the whole Swede Lutheran Minstry Co. which last Sabbath had their usual yearly meeting in this vestry upon Delaware in North America, concerning His present Majestys, King Gustaf the 3d. at Sweden, gracious answer and confirmation on their former privileges enjoyed under the reign of His glorious ancestors read to this vestry the Sunday before was red after the Swede service to the whole congregation containing an account of the present change within this mission, now made by his majesty the King of Sweden, along with the moving exhortation from the Arch-Bishop and consistory at Upsal, duly to acknowledge these renewed royal grants and signal favours.

2. It was proposed by the said rector, by what means and manner this vestry thought proper, that the remaining ballance attending the building of the parsonage house at Swedesborough should be made up? And it was resolved, that the members of Raccoon congregation should do it among themselves and the rector was desired to try his best to execute this design and to requaint the vestry of his success at the next meeting.

3. Did John Rambo, Inkeeper at Swedesborough, apply to the vestry for a spot of ground above the bridge, joining the creek and bounding upon the Kings roade from the creek up to a black oak sappling, and from thence, straight line, to a large black oak, standing on the edge of the marsh, and from thence in a pararel line with the mentioned Kings roade to the creek again, which spot was granted him by the majority of the present vestry and a due lease thereon, ordered to be executed for him before the next meeting.

4. Did the said Rambo offer himself to take up the deceased Erick Cocks lease before granted to him, on the branch above the ministers pasture ground, which also was granted to him John Rambo, on the same terms; yet, with this farther addition, that he should emprove the said branch within two years, and put it into the best grass the said can afford, and so have the possession and benefit of its 7 years from next spring.

5. The Sweede. Congregation being without a clerk by the death of Erick Cock, the rector proposed Hance Urian to supply his place, at the usual allowance of 18 pence or a half bushel of grain, yearly salary from every Swede familly, for the usual service, and even to attend the church at English service, which was granted to him, and he accepted of, for digging of graves, his fees, after this day, were allowed to be three shil. and 6 p. from those families that pay him yearly salary and from strangers and others, who are able to pay, but pay him no yearly salary, he is to be allowed 5 shil. currency.

6. Did several members of the vestry resolve to go and inspect the glebe in Pilesgrove, next saturday come two weeks, attended by me and Mr. Collin if time permitted. Year and day as above.   John Wicksel, P. & Rector.

RECORD FOR THE TIME OF NICHOLAS COLLIN [89]

The year 1779 several vestrys were held on account of the plantation in Pilesgrove,[90] but nothing effectually was done partly throu the fraud of the tenant, and partly throu the difficulty of assembling

[89] Nicholas Collin was born in 1746, and ordained in 1767(?). He was appointed pastor in America in 1769, and arrived in Philadelphia from Sweden on May 12, 1770. He first served in New Jersey, later in Philadelphia. He was a many-sided personality, writing on Philosophy, Philology, History and other subjects. He made inventions of various kinds and received the Gold Medal of the American Philosophical Society, some of his papers being published in the transactions of the Society. He was a trustee of the University of Pennsylvania, and he received the honorary degree of D.D. from that institution. He was one of the most faithful members of the American Philosophical Society and present at nearly all of its meetings. He died in 1831, having served in America as pastor of the Swedish churches here for more than 61 years.

[90] This refers to property owned by the church.

a majority of vestrymen, and of making them pursue vigorous measures. The lease was expired the 1st. of March this year. The tenant ought therefore to have had warning three months before that time, but so it happened that no satisfactory agreement could be made with him til it was too late. He did, however, promise the minister that he would pay at least twenty five pound for keeping the place one year after the term of the lease, but after having eluded the appointment of meeting him and the vestry in order to have the agreement formally drawn and sealed, when he at last came to Swedsborough Christmas day 1773 he in the presence of him and Lawrence Lock and John Dericson Vestrymen absolutely deny'd his bargain, and refused to sign any agreement whatever. Tho this man might have been forced away, yet as this would have been attended by a great deal of trouble and expence, and as the glebe in the condition it was, would not have been let to advantage, the minister thought it most adviseable to drop the matter. The next summer the Rector with the vestry set a foot a list of subscription for draining the swamp on the said glebe, which agreeable to the lease given to Jonas Keen ought to have been improved before the expiration of the term, yet had only been cleared, and was now again so wild as ever. Nor could any suit be brought for damages, because the lease was not drawn up in form of law. The little money could be got in, yet the Rector had the land drain made before fall. It was now time to think of letting the place, and it making now a better figure several tenants offered themselves. For want of a majority nothing, however, could be done til the last of November, when the Rector and of the Vestry Lawrence Lock, John Lock, William Homan and Mounce Keen met at the said plantation. Three and thirty pound a year was offered by two men who would rent it jointly, and cash for two years if desired. Tho this was a very good offer, yet as the vestry had before promised the old tenant to have the refusal of the place, provided he would come up to what should be offered; and he now cheerfully engaged to pay the said yearly sum and fullfill all the articles presented to him, lamenting besides the hardship he should undergo if obliged to remove, he was accepted. The articles were before drawn up by the Rector and rehearsed to him, and agreed to in the presence of witnesses, and a compleat lease was to be formed from them in order to be signed and sealed within a short time.

[SWEDESBORO 1775]

The year 1775 second day of Jan: the vestry met at the Rectors house. The tenant came but refused to stand to his agreement, and would even not declare whether or no he would give up the place. Such a piece of deceit astonished us. We told him that we should either prosecute him or else get a writ of ejectment against him. It had been the best to have had done with this man before now, but one great reason why he obtained the tenement was the avoiding of peoples blame, who would not have failed of giving the minister the epithets of covetous, unmerciful, revengeful, and what not, if the old man had been forced off the place when he had made reasonable offers. But it was now high time to get rid of him; accordingly after a few day's the Rector accompanyd by two evidences went to the plantation and warned him off within the 25th of March next following; He promised to go; and thus offer paying his rent in the spring, we were delivered from this troublesome man.

[SWEDESBORO 1775]

The 22d of February a majority of the vestry met in Swedsborough to treat with Richard Sparks who wanted to rent the plantation, and after a good deal of caution on both sides the bargain was made and a pair of indentures of lease signed and sealed mutually delivered. Better conditions could not be obtained, the inferior to what had before been offered; but considering that the place was at present much out of order and would require a great deal of expence in order to be improved, no great reason can be to complain.

Year 1776

The 9th day of April being third day of Easter the vestry and part of the congregation met, and after divine service the minister and vestry entered upon business, present Lawrence Lock, John Hellms, John Dericson, James Stillman, William Homan.

A mo. was taken into consideration the petition of Hans Cox to have the lease for his lot signed, which was expected by reason of its not being survey'd, but unanimously agreed to sign the same as soon as this should be done.

2. The following additional members of vestry were chosen by common consent. John Rambo, William Matson, Isac Jeffrs, and Peter Lock, son of Charles Lock, deceased.

3. Mr. William Homan petitioned for an acre of ground on the west side of the road, being part of the minister's garden, to begin with the side next the pinegrove, and to go straight to the line; for which he offered quitrents of twenty shillings a year. This was agreed to, and a lease promised after the lot should be survey'd.

4. Was confirmed the agreement made last fall between the minister and the vestry, by which he was to improve the swamp below the old meadow down the line, and between the fences extended so far in a strait line, and thus taking in all the low land; and to have the possession and benefit of this piece of ground at least for seven years.

The year 1777

The 1st. day of Apr. the vestry met as usual, present Lawrence Lock, John Hellms, John Dericson, Mouns Keen, James Stillman, William Homan, John Rambo, William Matson. The vestry appointed two of their members to collect the ballances of ground rents in Swedsborough.

The year 1778

The usual vestry meeting on the 3d day of Easter could not be observed, because of the general distraction produced by the war. Militia and continental troops on one side, and refugees with British on the other were frequently skirmishing, and both allmost equally distressing the country. Plundering, Marauding, Imprisonment, and burning houses, with Aher horn'd except were frequent from the beginning of Spring til July when the British arms evacuated Philadelphia. In the morning of Easter Sunday, a man who had traded with the British, was tied to a pine near the burying ground, and cruelly whipped. He died after a short time. On the 4 day of April, some hundred of English Marines and refugees came to Sweedsborough early in the morning to purpose the militia. Being disappointed they burnt the schoolhouse, alledging for a reason that some loyal subjects had been imprisoned therein some weeks before.

The year 1779

The 6th day of April the Rector was gone to Philadelphia on business concerning the mission. Only five of the vestry met.

The year 1780

The 28th day of March being third day of Easter the vestry met according to the chartre: present Lawrence Lock, John Hellms, John Lock, John Dericson, John Rambo, James Stillman, William Homan, Charles Cox, Peter Lock.

The rector represented the unhappy situation of these congregations, which after his leaving of them must for many years be destitute of a Minister, because there is no possibility of supporting one when the rents of the church lands are become mere nothing by the alarming depreciation of the paper currency, which is now in exchange sixty for one. He desired them, if they had a sincere concern for their own spiritual wellfare and for that of their children and fellow christians to device some expedient for preventing so great a calamity, perhaps the utter ruine of the congregations, and proposed to petition the assembly, that it would be pleased to obligate the tenants of the church lands to pay the rents according to the old rate of money, either in specie, or at the current exchange. This appeared reasonable. It was therefore unanimously resolved, that the Rector should draw up an address, in terms fully expressive of the justice and weight of the subject, set with due discretion and complacence; which on being approved of and subscribed by the vestry should be delivered to the assembly at the next session.

This adress was accordingly formed and signed. Andrew Sinnicson, Esq., promised to recommend it to government, but we dropt this matter, as other similar adresses had met with no success.

The year of our Lord 1781

The 17th day of April being the third day of Easter, the vestry met according to the Chartre. Present Nicholas Collin, Lawrence Lock, John Hellms, John Lock, Mounce Keen, John Dericson, James Stillman, William Homan, Charles Cox, William Matson, Peter Lock.

1. As the lot behind the church, which had been leased to Robert Brown the year 1776, had not yet been signed, it was now properly done by the members which had granted the same.

2. As there was one vacant seat in the vestry the Rector proposed three worthy members of the church as candidates for the same, to wit Benjamin Rambo, Andrew Henricson and Peter Lock, son of Mr. John Lock. The vestry unanimously found them all worthy of this trust, and chose the first mentioned, Benjamin Rambo, who is therefore hereby duly elected.

The year of our Lord 1783

The third day of Easter the vestry met as usual, and resolved upon the following matters.

1 mo. Hans Urian and Lawry Friend having cleared the burying ground of bryars and other rubbish, and also moved the pates of one side, and made new additions at the corner of the same, so as to take in the fourteen feet reserved for this purpose, made a charge of three pounds, which the vestry thought reasonable, and ordered a list of subscription to be drawn up for the collecting of this sum, and for paying six shillings and two pence for the nails used in the said work.

2 mo. Whereas people have begun to build vessels in the grove on the church ground, which is not only a benefit to those concerned, but some disadvantage to most of the congregation that put up their horses and waggons there, it was determined that for the present, they shall pay for every vessel twenty shillings, and that this sum may be raised hereafter, if the vestry shall see fit.

3. It was agreed, that the new lots now taken in shall be dispossed for twelve shillings and six pence apiece.

The year of our Lord 1784

The third day of Easter, being the 13th of April, the vestry met according to the charter. Present the Revd. Nicholas Collin, John Hellms, Lawrence Lock, John Lock, James Stillman, Mounce Keen, John Dericson, William Homan, Benjamin Rambo, when the following business was transacted.

1 mo. Mr. Andrew Henricson was unanimously chose vestryman in leu of Charles Cox, deceased.

2. Mr. Nicholas Collin and Mr. John Hellms undertook to visit the glebe in Pilesgrove, in order to settle the lines, and in case the old marks are not nearly discernible, it was resolved to employ a surveyor.

3. Whereas the gove is found incumbered with planks and other materials to the prejudice of people that want room for their horses on coming to church; it was resolved that no person shall hereafter spread those materials too much, nor put them too near the trees, so as to make the shade useless, but place them in such vacant places as will be assigned by the Rector or any of the Vestry, and that all except such as pay for the building of vessels as before is determined, shall give some reasonable satisfaction for such priviledge.

Year of our Lord 1785

The third day of Easter being 29 of March, was as usual a meeting of the vestry, present John Hellms, John Lock, Mounce Keen, William Homan, William Matson, Andrew Henricson.

In the place of John Dericson deceased, was proposed for a vestryman Peter Lock, son of John, and unanimously chosen.

YEAR of our Lord 1786

The third day of Easter the Vestry met as usual. As by the charter members of the vestry may amount to 14, inclusive of the 2 Wardens, and as such a full complement is an ornament and support to the church: it was agreed to choose a sufficient number of new members for this purpose.

In consequence whereof, Thomas Denny, Esq., Charles Lock, Isac Van Neaman and Peter Lock were chosen Vestrymen, with the unanimous consent of all present.

DOCUMENTS

[PENNS NECK 1714]

To All Christian people to whom these presents shall come, I John Jaquet, of Pens Neck in the county of Salem and province of New West Yearsy, yeoman, send greeting. Know ye that I, the above said John Jaquet, for y consideration of the love and good will I bear towards my loving Friends and neighbours here in Pens Neck, and County aforesayd, have given granted and by these presents doe freely clearly and absolutely give and grant to y Swedish congregation of y said province, four acres of land joyning to y land of Jonas Shogen, beginning from y hill below y King's road and lo uppward, to build a church upon, and likewise to have y remaining part thereof for a church yeard, and other convenient use for y church, bestowing thereupon all y timber of y said four acres of land, to ye benefit of the said church or no other. And I, the said John Jaquet, my heirs, executors administrators or assignes, doe shall and will warrant, all the afore bargained promises, without any manner or condition, and that forever.

In Wittness whereof I have hereunto lett my hand and seale this eight day of Januarii in y year of our lord $17\frac{14}{15}$ [91]

Signed Sealed and Deilvered
   in the presence of us,
      Abraham Lidenius
      Henrii James
      Nicolas Moore   John Jaquet, LS

RACOON CREEK 1715

Bishop Swedberg's Order for Mr. Abraham Lidenius

Worthy and Most Learned Mr. Lidenius:

Your letter, written from Christina, in Pennsylvania, 1714, on April 8th, I received from Dean Björck 14 days ago. It is with great pleasure that I hear from those of Racoon Creek, on the other side of the river, that they have called you to be their special Teacher, and that they, and the rest on that side, such as Pens Neck, etc., wish to join together into a Congregation. I have carefully informed myself, from Dean Björck, about all this, and find it reasonable and Christian to assent to their just demands, as is shown by my letter to them. And be you now, appointed in the name of the Lord Jesus, in compliance with the congregation's call, and by virtue of the office which God and the King have commissioned me, to be rector and pastor for that portion which is on the other side of the river, where Racoon Creek, Pens Neck and other farms are situated. It being your duty to work in the Lord's dearly bought Vinyard, to the utmost of those powers which God may be pleased to grant you, to win many souls to

---

[91] Thus in the churchbook.

God and Christ Jesus, for the Honor of God, for the Congregation's temporal and eternal blessing, and for Your own peace of conscience and rich reward of grace, here and there forevermore. Amen, Amen! Let me now see that I always hear what is gratifying and Christian of you. I shall always follow your welfare as long as I live.

I have written to Dean Sandel to visit you and properly initiate you into the congregation. Books I shall secure for you. I have no time to write any more now. With many sincere greetings to the Congregation, and faithfully commending you to God's merciful care, I remain, continually,

Honorable Mr. Rector,
Your most obliging Servant,
Jesper Swedberg.

[Bruns]bo, the 24th [—],
    1714.

PENS NECK 1717

On March 30 the bench-seats were apportioned in the following manner, and those were first who most had worked for, or given to, the Church.

The first pew: Jacob Hindersson, Jacob v. Devair, Lucas Pettersson, Hans Shiere, Jean Jaqvet, Jean Minck, Jean von Numan, Eric Jansson, Hinric Petersson.

The second pew: Cornelius Corneliusson, Olof v. Numan, Simon Eaton, Olof Stallkopp, Lars Petersson.

The third pew: Johan Berthillsson, Marta Jansson, George Litien, Zacharias Berthillsson, Jonas Shogen.

The fourth pew: Guarret v. Numan, Philip Fransson, Marta Guilliamsson, William Minck, Jacob Savoj.

The fifth pew: Henric Geens, Seneck Senecksson, Johan Hinricsson, Joh: Shagen, Johan Savoj.

The sixth pew: Henric v. Numan, Thom. Wiggorie, David Savoj, John Seneckson.

The seventh pew: Tim Damley, Andrew Petersson, Jacob Danielsson, Andrew Boone, Peter Boone.

THE WOMEN'S PEWS

The first: The pew of the Pastor's Wife.

The second: Jacobus V. Devair's Wife, Jacob Hindersson's Wife, Lucas Petersson's Wife, Simon Eaton's Wife, Regina Savoi.

The third: Jan Von Numan's Wife, Hans Shiere's Wife, Hinric Petersson's Wife, Jean Minck's Wife, Johanna Jaquet.

The fourth: Eric Jansson's Wife, George Litien's Wife, Elizabeth Guilliamsson's Wife, Christina Guar[ron's] Wife, Olof Von Numan's Wife.

The fifth: Jan Berthillsson's Wife, Cornelius Cornel's Wife, Lars Petersson's Wife, Zacharias Berthilsson's Wife, John Savoi's Wife.

The sixth: Marten Guilliamsson's Wife, Marten Jansson's Wife, Jonas Shagen's Wife, Sarah Seneck, Thom. Wiggori's Wife.

The seventh: John Philpot's Wife, Albert Billerback's Wife, John Shagen's Wife, Guarret Von Numan's Wife, Jean Hindersson's Wife.

The eighth: Annica Fransson, Annicka Seneck, Helena Boone, Fransensy Boone, Beata Petersson.

The ninth:

[PENNS NECK 1717]

Expenses for the Church

For boards - - - 200:
For 200 feet *dito*
To Jacob Artwood
For glass windows
[To] Jacob Hindersson [for] sills
For Nails, besides
Stahlkop's bond

For lime and
For Church locks
[For an] Altar cloth
For hinges for the benches
To Lucas Petersson,
    a trunk
To Lucas and J —
    Simon Eaton paid
married Olof Nilsson's widow
which Olof Nilss. promised
the Church before his death.

[RACCOON 1720]

Here follow the Days' Work done on the Glebe[92]

This is an account of days work done on the Glebe.

Nich: Collin.[93]

Those who carted logs for a house, also rafters and beams and laths: Anders Hoffman, 1 (day); Jacobus v. Keuhlen, 2; Gabriel Petersson, 1; Hans Petersson, 1; Johan Mattson, 1.

Preparing the Beams and rafters: Johan Mattson, 1 (day); Stephan Jones, 4; Jacob Forsman, 1; Matts Mattsson, 2; Eric Mulicka, 1; John Thom, 1.

Those who nailed on the laths and braces, and fitted the rafters: Laurents Hollstein, 2 (days); Måns Laikian, 2; Johan Cock, 2; Anders Laikian, 2.

On erecting the house: Johan Arched, 6 (days); Laurens Hollstein, 2; Lars Lock, 2; Anders Petersson, 6; Hans Petersson, 2.

On setting up the rafters and nailing on the laths: Åke Helm, 4 (days); John Rambo, 4.

---

[92] *Här följa dagwärcken, som äro gjorda på Prästlandet.*

[93] This is a translation of the above in Collin's hand (Rev. Nicholas (Nils) Collin), who was pastor of the Raccoon and Penns Neck Churches from 1770 to 1786.

[113]

On trimming the walls: Michael Hoffman, 1 (day); Thomas Dinneh, 1; Johan Hoffman, Sr., 1; Lars Hoffman, 1; Gabriel Petersson, 1; Påwel [Paul] Kempe, 1.

On the sawing off of the corners and the under-pinning[94] of the house: Peter Justice, 1 (day); Johan Hoffman, 1; Johan Hoffman Andersson, 1; Lars Lock, 1; Johannes Fred: Hoffman, 1.

On preparing the shingles: Måns Kyhn, 1 (day); Nicholas Hoffman, 1; Hindric Hindricsson, 1; Johan Hoffman, Sr., 1; Peter Petersson, 1; Påwel [Paul] Hoffman, 1.

On the carting of bricks: Anders Hoffman, 1 (day).

RACOON CREECK, 1720

As Anders Hoffman saw that it was impossible to cart the bricks such a long and difficult way, since a great many would be needed for so large a fireplace, it was decided to make a fireplace out of clay until the next year, when bricks could be made at home, on the grounds, for this and other needs, and the claystove was therefore constructed by the following:

The following persons made a chimney of clay for a temporary use, hauled shingles, and hewed the walls.   N. Collin

Matts Mattsson, 1 (day); Nils Qwist, 3; George Kyhn, 1; Peter Cock, 1; Johan Matsson, 1; Peter Mattsson, 3; Pelle Cock, 1; Anders Hoffman, 1.

[Work] on carting over the shingles: Hans Petersson, 2 (days); Jacobus von Reulen, 2.

[Work] on trimming off the outside of the house: Gunnar Arched, 2 (days); Anders Mattson, 1; Jacob Mattsson, 1.

The following exhibits the expenditure of the money subscribed on the land, buildings, etc.   N. Collin.

Money expended

	Pd.	Sh.	pce.
On payment for the land	102		
For the Deed	1	8	6

Money expended from the book-funds of the people of Racoon and Pens Neck together:
For the inside work in the lower part of the House, namely for floors and cellars,

	Pd.	Sh.	
Doors and windows	2	10	
For Window-sills	0	6	
For bricks of	0	6	
For door-hinges	0	8	
For an oven and baking-oven for the hearth	0	9	
For 4 pounds of Nails		3	6

[94] *Till knutarnes nedsågande och husets underpinnande.*

[114]

Here follows the list of those whom Mr. Jesper Swedberg and Måns Keen visited, and [who] promised [contributions] to the Glebe, and gave their Bills or Bonds for payment on February 27:

The following is a list of those who subscribed for the purchase of the parsonage in Pilesgrove, and gave them bonds,[95] duly translated, witnesses Nich. Collin, May 20, 1790

Name	pds.	shs.	pce.	Name	pds.	shs.	pce.
				Transport	£61	00	06
Hans Petersson	5	00	00	Gabriel Petersson	4	00	00
Stephan Jones	4	00	00	Fredrich Hoffman	3	00	00
Anders Hoffman	3	00	00	Måns Kyhn	3	00	00
Lourents Hollstein	3	00	00	Peter Long	3	00	00
David von Neeman	2	10	00	Jacobus von Keulin	3	00	00
John von Neeman	1	00	00	Sam v. Numan	1	00	00
Guarret von Neeman	1	00	00	John Rambo	3	00	00
Peter Matsson	3	00	00	Mans Helm	2	00	00
Åke Helm	2	00	00	Charles Dalbow	2	00	00
Manna Dircksson	2	10	00	Nils Qwist	2	10	00
John Koch	1	15	00	Peter Cock	0	12	00
Matts Mattsson	2	05	00	Elias King	2	00	00
Olof Petersson	1	10	00	Måns Halton, Sr.	1	10	00
Hans Halton	1	10	00	Thomas Dinneh	2	00	00
Jonas Bjurström	2	00	00	Jöns Halton	2	00	00
Johannes Hoffman	1	10	00	Olof Mulicka	1	10	00
John Mulicka	1	10	00	Eric Mulicka	1	10	00
Måns Laikian	1	5	10	Michael Laikian	1	5	00
John Mattsson	1	10	00	Peter Steehlman	1	00	00
Clemens Corinna	00	10	00	Lars Cock	1	00	00
Gustaf Lock	1	00	00	Måns Cock and his			
John Hoffman	0	10	00	son Gabriel	2	00	00
John Jones	1	4	00	John Reehn	1	5	00
Jacob Mattsson	1	00	00	Jonas Jones	1	00	00
Lars Hoffman	1	00	00	Nicolas Hoffman	1	00	00
Måns Halton, Jr.	1	00	00	Alexander King	1	00	00
Eric Cock	00	10	00	John Anderss. Hoffman	00	12	00
Peter Petersson	1	00	00	Gabriel Dahlbow	1	10	00
James Guarring, Jun.	00	10	00	John Arched	0	10	00
Hans Steehlman, Jun.	00	06	00	Charles Halton	0	10	00
George Kyhn	2	00	00	Henric Henricsson	2	00	00
Peter Lock	1	10	00	Matthias Homan	1	10	00
Tim: Stedham	1	10	00	Gunnar Arched	1	10	00
Lars Halton	1	00	00	Lars Lock	1	2	00
Eric Steehlman	1	00	00	Andrew Mattsson	1	00	00
James Guarring, Sen.	1	00	00	Hans Steehlman	1	00	00
Peter Justice	1	00	0	Johannes Georgen	1	00	00
				Fredrich Georgen	0	10	00

On December 26 Jöns Stuhleman came up to Racoon Church and voluntarily gave to the Glebe — 1 15 6

Carry forward	61	00	6
The Whole	120	16	6

[95] "and gave them bonds", apparently should be "and gave their bonds".

PENS NECK, 1720 and 1721

Besides this the [following] day's work have been done by Pens Neck [parishioners] :[96]

	days
On September 22, Cornelius Corneliusson helped the parson to move	1
Item, Guarret v. [von] Numan, to lift logs	1
Guarret von Neeman	2
[Work on] Sloping boards, Clapboards, Laths, on October 10,	
Jacob von Devaire	1
Anders Bonde	2
Johan Seneck[sson]	1
[Work on] shingling and roofing [on] the 24th:	
Jean Minck	3
[Work] on the clay fireplace:	
Olof von Neeman	2
On October 3, [they] began to build, and built [as follows]:	
Henric Petersson	6
Ezechiel Jonsson	6
[Work] on lifting Logs and Props, and driving them home:[97]	
Olof v. Numan	2
Jacob Savoj	1
Philip Fransson	1
Peter Billerback	2
David Billerback	1
October:	
Lucas Petersson	3
Guarret von Numan	1

PENS NECK 1721

DAYS' WORK DONE ON THE GLEBE:

Working on clearing the swamp: Olof von N[uman], 1 (day); John Minck, 1; Philip Fransson, 1; Jacob Savoj, 1; Marten Jansson, 1; Stephen Wainam, 1; Guarret von Numan, 1; Zacharias Berthilsson, 1; Johan Savoj, 1; Lucas Peterson, 3; Henric Guns, 1; Anders Hindersson, 1; Jonas Shagen, 1; John Berthilsson, 1; Henric Petersson, 1; Johan Senecksson, 1; Lars Nilsson, 1; Seneck Senecsson, 1.

To carting fencing material: Olof Hoffman, 1 (day); Jacob v. Devaire, Jr., 1; Simon Eaton, 2; Olof v. Numan, 1.

To logs: Zacharias Berthilsson, 1 (day); Stephan Starck, 1; Abraham Savoj, 2; Anders Bonde, 1; Simon Eaton, 1; Hinric Petersson, 1; Hinric Billerback, 2; Marten Jansson, 1; Jacob Danielsson, 1; John Standly, 1; Guarret von Numan, 1; Anders Hindersson, 1; John Danielsson, 1; David Billerback, 1; Seneckson Seneck, 1; Henric v. Numan, 2; Zech Jansson, 1; Joh Senecksson, 1; Lars Nilsson, 1; Jacob c. devaire, Sr., 1.

To the placement of the logs: Olof v. Numan, 1(day); Eric Shiere, 1; John Jaquet, 1; Olof v. Numan, 1.

To beams: Peter Berthilsson, 1 (day).

To rafters: Jonas Shagen, 1 (day).

To carting of logs:

---

[96] *Thes utan äro dagswärcken gjorde utur Pens Neck. Utur Pens Neck,* "out of Pens Neck", "by those from (out of) Pens Neck".

[97] *lyfte Stockar och Stöts at kjöra them hem, Lufte (lyfta),* "to lift", here means "to load".

To carting planks: Olof and Guarret, each 2 (days).

To laths and clapboards: Lars Nilsson, 1 (day); Jacob von devaire, 1.

To putting together the rafters, to nailing on the laths, and to making ready for the roofing: Ezeckiel Jansson, 4 (days).

To wood for burning of bricks and top beams for the porch: John Senecks, 1 (day); Marten Jansson, 1; Zacharias Berthilsson, 1; Philip Fransson, 1; David Billerback, 1; Matts Shagen, 1; Seneck Senecksson, 1; Henric Guns, Jacob v. Devaire, Sr., Abraham Savoj, Peter Billerback, 1; Johannes Shagen, Marten Guilliamsson, 1; Lucas Petersson, 1; Jacob v. devaire, Jr., 1; Jacob Savoj, 1; Henric Petersson, 1.

To carting of wood: Olof v. Numan, 1 (day).

To digging the cellar: Jacob Danielson, 1 (day); Benjamin Stedham, 2; Anders Bonde, 1; Cornelius Cor., 1; And. Hindricsson, 1.

To water for bricks: Guarret Von Numan, 1 (day); Ezech. Jansson, 1; John Seneckson, 1; Anders Bonde, 6; Lucas Peterson, 2.

To frames for the cellar door and vents:

To posts for the porch, for nailing up the clapboard:

To setting up the bricks:

For burning: Peter Von Numan, 1 (day).

To setting up the posts and nailing the supports, and to covering one of the floors, and half of the porch: Jean Minck, 2 (days); Jean Savoj, 2.

To measuring out clay bricks: Ben Stedham, 2 (days).

In Ye Whole Days Work: 106 (days).

RACOON CREEK 1721

Days-work done upon the Glebe 6 s—following persons.

N. Collin.

The days-work of those who worked upon the Glebe, on which was built a house and vestibule, the swamp was cleared, fences made, bricks made, and fireplace built and cellars dug and masoned.

[Work on] fences: Peter Lock, 1 (day); Michal Homan, 1; Åke [Oke] Helm, 1; Johan Dahlbo, 1; Lars Halton, 1; Påwel [Paul] Hoffman, 1; David von Neeman, 2; Stephen Mulicka, 1; Hindric Hindricsson, 1; Gustaf Lock, 1; Manna Didricsson, 1; Hans Steehlm[an and] Peterss[on], 2; Gustaf Qwist, 1; Hans Halton, 1; Anders Laikian, 1; Olof Mulicka, 1; Hans Steehlman, 1; —— Jönsson, 1; James Guarring, 1; William Cobb, 1; Johan Reehn, 1; John Hoffman, 1; Lars Lock, 1; Zacharias Laikian, 1; William Runnels, 1.

[Work] on the carting of fencing-material: Anders Hoffman, 1 (day); Carl Halton, 1; Johan Seneck, 1; Hans Petersson, 1; Anders Dahlbo, 1; Gabriel Petersson, 1; Lourentz Hollsten, 1.

[Work] on putting up the fences: Timoth: Reehn, 1 (day); Peter Guarring, 1; Peter La Shamet, 1.

[Work] on the carting of fencing-material, and putting it up on the other side: Måns [Mons] Kyhn, 1 (day); Nicholas Hoffman, 1; Elias King, 1; Michael Laikian, 1; Michael Hoffman, 1.

Working on clearing the meadow: Gunnar Arched, 1 (day); Lourentz Hollsten, 2; Anders Dahlbo, 1; Elias King, 1; John Hoffman, 1; Peter Mattsson, 1; Påwel [Paul] Homan, 1; Johannes Seneck, 1; Jöns Halton, 1; Charles Dahlbo, 1; Olof Petersson, 1; Charles Halton, 1; John Hoffm. Sr., 1; Peter Justice, 1; Matts Mattsson, 1; Måns [Mons] Laikian, 1; Johannes Georgen, 1; Swen Homan, 1; Johan Jones, 1; Thom: Dinneh, 2; Michael Hoffman, 2; Lars Hoffman, 2; Sam:von Neeman, 2; Lars Påwelsson [Paulsson], 2; John v: Keuhlin, 1; Fredrick Dinneh, 1; Fredrick Petersson, 2.

[Work] on the carting of logs, beams and spars, and also on boards and corner stones: Anders Hoffman, 2 (days); Johan Mattsson, 2; Gabriel Petersson, 2; Jacobus von Keuhlen, 2; Hans Petersson, 2; Anders Dahlbo, 1.

[Work] on the planing of beams, and the digging up of cornerstones: Lars Halton, 2 (days)

[Work] on the erection of the house: Thom: Dinneh, 2 (days); Peter Justice, 2; Henric Hinricsson, 3; Lars Hoffman, 2; Åke [Oke] Helm, 3; Johannes Georgen, 3; John Hoffman Anderss, 2; Jacob Mattsson, 3; Johan Hoffman, Sr.

[Work] on making a shed for the bricks and preparing a place for making them: James Guarring, 3 (days); Påwel Hoffman, 3; Hans Halton, 3; Matts Mattsson, 3

John Hoffman, 1 (day); Charles Halton Månsson, 2; Lars Påwelsson, 1; Charles Sträng, 2. Hans Petersson looked after how it was to be done; for instance, he covered the shed over again, it being too flat the first time.

RACOON CREECK 1721

The foregoing acct continued.   N. Collin.

Repair of Church

[Working] days in the making of laths and clapboards for the gable ends and the entrance-hall: Elias Fisk, 4 (days); Peter Dahlboo, 2.

[Work] in carting over the boards from Salem: Lars Lock, 2 (days); Timoth Stedham, 2.

[Work] in constructing the buttresses: Peter Mattsson, 2 (days); Måns Laikian, 1; Zacharias Laikian, 1.

[Work] in nailing up the laths and dormer windows and the setting up and covering of the spars: Johan Rambo, 2 (days); Manus Helm, 2; Jonas Biurström, 6.

[Work] in sawing off the corners: Manna Didricsson, 2 (days); Peter Guarring, 2.

[Work] in the making of floor sills:

[Work] in carting over the porch-beams and setting them up: Zacharias Petersson, 2 (days); Matts Mattsson, 1; Lars Påwelsson, 1; John Mattsson, 1; Jacob von Keuhlen, 1; Nicolas Laikian, 2.

[Work] in the making of mantelpieces, and the pulling down of the clay fireplaces: Anders Mattsson, 2 (days); Jonas Kyhn, 1.

[Work] in trimming off the walls with an adz: Lars Hoffman, 1 (day); Michael Laikian, 1; Eric Mulicka, 1.

[Work] in the laying of the porch floor: Påwel [Paul] Kempe, 1 (day).

[Work] in the digging of the cellar: John Hoffman, 1 (day); Jonas Kyhn, 2; Peter Justice, 1; Gustav Qwist, 1.

[Work] in kneading the clay and carrying off the Bricks which Göstaf Lock made, which were 19,000 in all: John Reehn, 4 (days); William Runnels, 4; Jonas Biörström, 4; Eric Steehlman, 2; Isaac Seneck, 2; Swen Homan, 3; Lourens Hollsten, 6.

[Work] in carting over the wood for the brick-burning: Matts Mattsson, 1 (day); Lars Halton, 1; Hans Petersson, 1.

[Work] in carting over the sand and the lime for the Brick-maker and the Mason, besides what Hans Petersson, Lourenz Hollsten and Gabr[iel] Petersson brought by horse: Måns [Mons] Kyhn, 2 (loads); Carl Halton, 4; Elias King, 2; Jonas Kyhn, 2; Hans Petersson, 1; Lourentz Hollsten, 1.

[Work] in [making] steps for the cellar: Elias King, 1 (day).

[Work] in the laying of floor-beams over the cellar: Gunnar Arched, 1 (day), John Arched, 1.

[Work] in the making of eaves, and for setting them up: Nils Nilsson, 1 (day); Swen Homan, 1; Timoth: Reehn, 1; Peter Petersson, 1; Peter La Shamat, 1; Johannes Fred: Hoffman, 1.

[Work] in setting up the bricks for burning: Gabriel Petersson, 2 days); Måns Kyhn, 1; Lourentz Hollsten, 2; Elias King, 1; Johan Seneck, 3; John Hoffman, Sr., 1.

NB. Anders Hoffman is not so often mentioned here, perhaps, as some others, but he has been here and taken charge of all the work, so that there is no one here who has had as much trouble as he has.

RACOON CREEK 1721 AND 1722

Account of expenditure by Andrew Hoffman Churchwarden.

N. Collin.

Money expended by Anders Hoffman.[98]

	(£)	(Sh.)	(Pc.)
To Gustaf Lock, who made the bricks	4	10	–
To Gustaf Qwist, who worked with the brickmaker	–	11	3
To Jonas Biurström, for work	2	–	–
To 20 pounds nails	–	17	6
To 2 pounds *dito*	–	1	10½
To the Mason	8	10	–
To one cow for the mason's board	2	–	–
To 4 bushels of lime	–	6	–
To rum for the brickmaker	–	4	2½
To rum and sugar for the mason	–	10	–
To 2 hogsheads of lime	2	–	–

RACOON CREEK 1722

Money expended out of the Collection Money by Åke Helm, from November 3, 1714, until now.

	£	Sh.	d.
For Jacobus Kuln	2	4	–
For the Church windows	2	12	–
For improving and plastering of the Church	4	–	–
For window-hinges	–	4	–
For boards	2	–	–
For a vestibule for the Church	2	10	–
To wine in the Church several times	–	15	–
To window-hinges in the Rectory	–	4	4
To a Church spade	–	7	–
For nails	–	5	3
For nails for the Rectory	1	7	11
To Mr. Swedenborg	–	18	–
To Måns [Mons] Kyhn, for nails	–	7	1
To Peter Rambo, for glass	–	9	7
To Gabriel Rambo, for hinges	–	4	6
To wine for the Church, several times	–	18	–
To hinges and nails several times	1	9	1
To paper and wine for the Church	–	12	3
Total	21	7	9

---

[98] Translated by Nicholas Collin.

Money expended by Måns Kyhn namely,
To Boards for the Rectory houses_____ 1   14   11

Money expended by Åke Helm for the Church and the Glebe

	Pd.	Sh.	pce.
To Abraham Lidenius for the Mason_____	-	12	10
For a lock _____	-	4	-
For hinges _____	-	5	-
For boards _____	1	3	-
For wine _____	2	4	-
For nails _____	-	4	-
For books _____	-	2	6
For nails _____	-	1	8
Total	4	17	-

[RACCOON 1722]

There were also this year taken into the Church two whores,
namely Maria Sträng on July 15, and Brigitta Halton on September 30.

[PENNS NECK 1722]

Money laid out for the use of the Church and Parsonage.
N[icholas] Collin.

Money laid out for the use of the Church and the Parsonage by
William v. Numan and Guarret v. Numan:

	Pd.	Sh.	d.
For Purchasing the Glebe _____	50	-	-
For the deed[99] _____	-	6	6
For Rum for the Brickmaker_____	-	6	9
For Logs _____	-	1	6
For Molasses _____	-	1	4
For Rum[100] _____	-	3	9
For the Carpenter _____	6	-	-
For Nails _____	-	10	-
To Henric von Numan for kneading clay_____	-	7	6
For Boards _____	1	14	11
Total	59	12	3

Paid out by Guarret for the Church:

	Pd.	Sh.	d.
For wine at several times[101]_____	-	9	6
For nails for the Parsonage _____	-	9	-
Total	19	-	-

---

99 *Til Grundbrefwet eller deeden. Grundbreg (grundbrev),* "deed".

100 Rum was one of the necessities of life in those days and nearly always
furnished to workmen.

101 *Til wyn, at several times,* thus in the original.

[PENNS NECK 1726]

Anno 1726, on June 30, [Rev.] Mr. Pet[er] Tranberg was initiated by the Dean, Rev. Jona[s] Lidman,[102] as pastor and Dean of Racoon and Pens Neck, according to His Royal Majesty's Warrant, thus worded:

We, Friedrich, by the Grace of God, King of Sweden, of the Goths and of the Wends, etc. do announce [that]: Inasmuch as we have been humbly informed that the Swedish Evangelical Congregation in Pennsylvania is greatly in need of being supplied at the first opportunity with a faithful and skillful pastor, unless it is shortly to suffer for want of Divine Worship, And whereas the proper authorities have humbly proposed the Rev. Peter Tranberg for this position, on account of his learning and exemplary life; Therefore, by force of this our open Warrant, be he, Peter Tranberg, hereby graciously appointed to be Pastor and Dean of aforesaid Evangelical Congregation. Which all concerned will obediently observe.

For further certainty we have signed this with our own hand, and confirmed it with our Royal Seal.

Stockholm in the Council Chamber, January 11, 1725.

Friedrich.

[L.S.]   J. Von Höpken.

[RACCOON 1726-28]

The following has been spent out of the Collection money during 1726, 1727, and 1728 by Peter Lock, then Trustee.

Anno 1726

	Lb.	Sh.	d.		Lb.	Sh.	d.
For wine	0	7	6	For a cow	2	10	0
item for wine	0	5	0	For wine	0	1	0
For "butcher-money" for the Pastor[103]	0	5	0	For wine	0	2	0

1727

	Lb.	Sh.	d.		Lb.	Sh.	d.
For wine	0	1	0	For wine	0	1	0
For an altarcloth	1	2	9	For ink	0	1	0
For wine	0	2	0				

---

[102] See note 23.

[103] *Slagtepen*, is either compounded from an English and Swedish word, *slagt*, "slaughter", plus *pen*, "slaughter-pen", or *pen* might be an abbreviation for the Swedish *penningar*, in which case it would mean "butcher money" or money for butchering.

1728

	Lb.	Sh.	d.		Lb.	Sh.	d.
For wine	0	0	6	For wine	0	2	0
For wine	0	1	6	For wine	0	1	0
For 1 Almanac	0	0	6	For wine	0	1	0
For a log for fences	0	3	0				

[RACCOON 1729]

Church Expenses

	Lb.	Sh.	d.		Lb.	Sh.	d.
Bought wine for	0	18	6	For repairing the			
For nails	0	15	0	Church windows	0	11	0
For paper	0	01	8	Total	2 Lb.	6 sh.	2 d.

[RACCOON 1730]

Church Expenses

	Lb.	Sh.	d.
For a silver goblet, with paten, which was purchased out of the Collection money, and those Shillings which were taken in when the Hymn-books were distributed, there was spent	7 Lb.	7 Sh.	4 d.
For wine, for the entire year	0	18	0
Total	8 Lb.	5 Sh.	4 d.

[RACCOON 1731]

Church Expenses

	Lb.	Sh.	d.
For Wine	1	0	0
For the horse	0	6	0
For paper	0	1	0
	1 Lb.	7	0

[RACCOON 1732 ?] [104]

	Lb.	sh.	d.		Lb.	sh.	d.
A sack for a pall	0	04	6	item, wine	0	01	0
For nails	0	02	0	item, wine	0	02	0
For wine	0	00	9	item, wine	0	01	0
item, wine	0	02	0	For a glass	0	00	8
item, wine	0	00	6	Almanac	0	00	6
item, wine	0	01	0				
item, wine	0	01	0	Total		16 sh.	2 d.

[104] It is assumed that this entry is for 1732, because it is the only undated entry in a series dated from 1726 to 1735.

RACOON 1733

	lb.	sh.	d.
Bought a spade for	0	7	6
A Mattock	0	7	6
8 Pints of wine at Sundry times		8	
For a Broom & Allmanack	0	0	11

Lb. 1 3 Sh. 11 D.

After the Church was rubbed of [robbed] wicked hands from a biurring [burying] Pall, Surplice chalue [chalice] and the minister of his Gown which never could be dis-covered. Then Henrick Henrickson from Rapapy made a present of a biurring [burying] Pall to the Church. [A] surplice [was] bought of the Church money but not thought on a gown. [there was no thought of buying a gown].

[RACCOON 1734]

Charges

	Sh.	d.
for an Allmanack	0	6
for a Comb	0	6
To gabriel Enoks for helping Willm. Cabb to make the communion table	10	6

[RACCOON 1735]

Charges

	lb.	sh.	d.
for wine	0	4	0
for an Allmanack	0	0	6

These are to Certifye whom it May Concern that Hannah Nevil the Daughter of Wm Nevile of the Citty of York in England but now lives at Raccoon Creek in Gloster County West New Jersey and David Jones of the sayd county were lawfully Marryed to geather according to the Canon of the Eccliasticall Constitution of the Church of Eng-land at Racoon Creek the tenth day of 9ber [Novem-ber] 1740 given under my hand the 4th Day of 9ber 1740.
Witness   Pet. Tranberg.

[INVENTORY OF RACCOON AND PENNS NECK BOOKS][105]

In over-abundance do witness to His Majesty of Sweden's tender-ness and care for the instruction of these Congregations, now and for all time (wherever such grace is not despised) the many and costly books, such as Bibles, Hymnals, and Catechisms, which not only are

[105] Made in 1748 by the Rev. Johan Sandin.

to be distributed to those Members who have need of them, in all the Congregations, but also those which have been especially given to these Churches of Racoon and Pens Neck, and are to be continually in the possession and care of the Minister, to be both for his own use, and for lending out to those in the Congregation who desire more thorough instruction, and still further improvement in their religion. They were the following, which, together with the Church Book, are to be put down as a perpetual inventory, namely:

1. Doct[or] Gezelius' *Explanation of the Old and New Testament,* consisting of 2 Volumes in folio. The one, on the Old, in an entirely new French binding, and the other, on the New, in parchment, rather well used.

2. Dean Laurence Hallenius' *Swedish and Hebrew Concordances, of the Whole Swedish Bible,* in all new parchment Bindings, 3 volumes in folio.

3. *The Symbolical Books of the Lutheran Church,* in Swedish, in new French binding, in quarto.

5. The Late Doctor Arnd's *True Christianity,* in Swedish, printed in Norköping in octavo, French Binding.[106]

On June 25, Cornelius Corneliusson, on behalf of the People of Pensneck, paid the cost of the Saddle and Bridle, namely Three Pounds and Four Shillings.[107]

ERICK UNANDERS ACCNT. TO BOTH THE CONGREGATIONS RACOON & PENSNECK FOR BUILDINGS AT THE PARSONAGE PLACE.

Debt:	£	Sh.	d.
To boarding the Men for cutting the Logs for the Barn ____	1		
To two Galn. of Rum @ 3/6/ p. Gn. _____		7	
To And: Mattson for sawing the Joices _____		7	6
To bording the Brick Layer, manding the cellar & a Men tending him Two Days _____		3	
To Wagas for the Men @ 2 sh: p. day _____		4	
To Joseph Applin for a Hogs Head of Lime _____		15	
To 900 Shingals for the Barn @ 50 sh: p. 1000d. _____	2	5	
To Abrahm. Barber for building of the Barn _____	3		
To Ditto for framing & Covering the House _____	6	2	6
To bording Abm. Barber his apprentice 10 Weeks @ 10 Sh: P. Week _____	5		
To Robt: Mattocks for the inside work _____	10		

---

[106] Dr. Johann Arnd (or Arndt), one of the foremost theologians of the protestant world, was born in Ballenstedt, Germany, in 1555 and died in 1621. He has been called "the Reformer of the Reformation" and two of his works have been translated into practically all of the languages of Europe.

[107] This purchase was for Sandin. See p. 60.

Debt:	£	Sh.	d.
To bording him & his apprentice 13 weeks @ 10: sh: p. Week	6	10	
To Wm. Craig for building a Chimbly and Plastring the house in part of pay	3		
To a Team for haling the timber, Sand & Lime	1	10	
To Wages for a Men tending the Brick Layer		9	
To bording him, his apprentice & the Men. tending him		13	
To Richard Wister for Glass, Spricks & Lath Nails etc.	2	17	
To More Lath Nails eight penny & double Ten Nails		18	4
To Singel Ten Nails from Jeremiah Wood	1	10	
To Locks, thumlages etc. from Thoms: Maul		15	
To Hooks & Hinges from Joy: Redman		6	9
To Erand Silver for haling the bords	1	16	
To Sundry pair Hooks, Hinges, Bolts, Rivetts and Spikes	1	15	
To Rum for all the Work Mens about the house 10 Galn. @ 3 £ 6 p. Gn	1	15	
To Nails from Joseph Sharp		11	3
To One Thousand Foot of Bords	3		
	£56	10	4

Errors ye Piles grove Eric

ERICK UNANDERS ACCNT. TO BOTH THE CONGREGATIONS RACOON & PENSNECK FOR BUILDINGS' AT THE PARSONAGE PLACE.

Credit	£	Sh.	d.
Per Contra.			
From Racoon			
By Gounnar Coxe	1	10	
By Hance Stehlman Senior	2		
By Peter Rambo	1		
By Andrew Hindrickson		15	
By Hinrick Hindrickson		5	
By John Helm in Clemel	1	5	
By Thom: Denny of the Purse Money	1	16	
By Zacharia's Petersen on Peter Stilleys account		19	6
By Thom: Denny of the Church Money	3	10	
By Jeremiah Wood for the Logs	12	10	
By a note from Thoms: Wilkens	10		
By John Lock		7	6
By Thom: Denny	1	6	
By Lawrence Lock		7	6
	£37	11	6

From Pensneck

	£	Sh.	d.
By Matthias Lambson	1		
By Peter Boon		10	
By Andw. Sinnickson	1		
By Wm. Vanneeman Money for the Church Yard	1	2	6
By Mounce Keen Jn.		7	6

Credit	£	Sh.	d.
By John Mounsson _____		10	
By Thmas Wickery _____		5	
By Timothy Morray _____		2	6
By Cornelius Corneliusson _____		10	
By Gvarret Vanneeman Church Money _____		9	9
By John Vanneeman _____		17	6
By Andw. Vanneeman _____		10	
£:07 :04 :09	44	16	09
Ballance due to me Erik Unander _____	11	14	01
	£56	10	04

Excepted
29th day of Sepembr. Ao. Dni. 1756
    Unander

COPY OF THE CHARTER OF THE SWEDES CHURCH AT RACCOON

George the third by the grace of God of great Britain, France and Ireland King defender of the Faith Sc: To all to whom these presents shall come Greeting: Whereas we have been informed by the humble petition of our living subjects the Reverend John Wicksell, Thomas Denny, John Denny, Lawrence Lock, John Lock, John Rambo, James Steelman, John Helm, Benjamin Rambo, Jonas Keen, Erick Cox, Jacob Archer, Isaac Tushison, Gilbert Renelds, Gabriel Strang, William Homan, Peter Matson, Peter Keen, Andrew Jones, Hans Urian, John Hoffman, Lawrence Strang, John Derricksson, Charles Lock, Erick Renals, Jacob Jones, William Matson, James Halton, Andrew Lock, Moses Hoffman, Charles Fuller & Andren Vanneman, in behalf of themselves and others Inhabiting near Raccoon Creek in the County of Gloucester in our Province of New Jersey, presented to our trusty and well beloved William Franklin Esquire Captain General and Governor in Chief in and over our Province of New Jersey and Territory thereon depending in America Chancellor and Vice Admiral in the same &c. That some pious and well disposed of person have heretofore appropriated lands and given them in trust for the use and benefit of a Swedish Reformed Church to be erected near Raccoon Creek aforesaid in order thereby to raise a Fund for keeping the said Church in repair and to support a minister of the Reformed Church that Divine Service might be performed therein, with becoming Reverence and decency: But as the said land could not be Leased out managed and improved, nor the Rents collected or other services done with convenience fornant of their being Incorporated and made a Body Politick.

WHEREFORE to the end the said petitioners and their successors shall be secured in the quiet & peaceable proffession and enjoyment of said church and also be erected and made a body politick & corporate the better to and for the glory of God and the pious uses intended thereby they prayed our Royal Charter to grant such power and priviledge as have been usually granted to the churches within this colonay, and to make them capable of holding and enjoying such lands and receiving such personable state, as may be given to them for the use of the said Church and to constitute the Minis. Ser. church wardens and Vestry-men one body politick & corporate in Deed, fact and name by the name and stile of the Rector, church warden and Vestry-men of the Swedish Evangelical Lutheran Church in the Town of Sweedsborough near Raccoon Creek, and we being willing to give all due encouragement and promotion to the pious intention of our said subjects and to grant their reasonable request in their behalf KNOW YE that we of our especial grace certain knowledge and meer motion have made, ordained, constituted granted and declared AND by these presents for us our Heirs and successors DO make, ordain, constitute, grant and declare that the said John Wicksell, Thomas Denney, John Denney, Lawrence Lock, John Lock, John Rambo, James Steelman, John Helm, Benjamin Rambo, and the rest of the Communicants of the said church, be, and they and their successors. Shall be from time to time and all times hereafter a body corporate and Politick in Deed. Fact and name by the name and stile of the Rector, church Wardens and Vestry-men of the Sweedish Evangelical Lutheran Church in the Town of Sweedsborough near Raccoon Creek: a Body corporate and Politick in Deed. Fact and name really and fully, but if it shall that there be no Rector incumbert or Presbyter of the said church duly qualified, instituted and inducted into the cure of the said church then and in such case the said church wardens and Vestry-men of the said church inhabitants of Sweedsborough aforesaid and places adjacent and their successors shall be from time to time and at all times hereafter as often as such vacancy shall happen and during the continuance thereof a Body Corporate and Politick in Deed, fact and name by then and stile of the church wardens and Vestry-men of the Sweedish Evangelical Lutheran Church in the town of Sweedsborough near Raccoon Creek, Really and fully and we do for us, our Heirs and successors erect make, constitute, declare and create by these presents, and that by one or either of the same name or names as the said body corporate shall happen to be circumstanced, they and their successors shall and may be persons able and capable in the law to sue and to be sued, to implead and to be impleaded, to answer and be answered unto, to defend and to be defended in all courts and elsewhere, in all and singular suits, causes, quarrlls, matters, actions, demands and things, of what nature or kind soever. And also that they and their successors, by one or either of the same name or names as the said body Corporate shall then happen to be circumstanced be and shall be forever hereafter capable and able in the law to take accept, have, hold, and enjoy in fee for ever, or for life or lifes or for year or years, or in any other manner any missuages, buildings, lands, tenements given, granted, leased, released devised bequeathed, bargaind or sold by any former gift grant, bargain, sale or patent or by any other ways or means what soever to any person or persons whom soever for the use of the said church or parsonage of the Town of Sweedsborough aforesaid and so bring suit or suits, in all courts or elsewhere for the recovery and obtaining the same by all lawfull ways and means whatsoever. And also that they and their successors by one or either of the same name or names as the said body corporate shall then happen to be circumstanced be and shall be forever hereafter capable and able in the law to take accept of accquire and purchase receive, have, hold, and enjoy in fee forever, or for life or lifes, or year or years, or in any other manner any messuages, buildings, houses, lands, tenements Hereditaments and real estates and all or any part of the messuages buildings, houses, lands, tenements, hereditaments and premises aforesaid, to lease for one or more years or to grant, alien, release bargain, sell and dispose of for life or lifes or in fee simple, under certain yearly rents and also to accept of, take possess and purchase any goods chattels, or personal estate, and the same to hire, lett, sell or dispose of at their will & pleasure and all this as fully and amply as any other corporation or body Politckwithin that part of our Kingdom of Great Britain called England or this our Province of New Jersey, lawfully may do PROVIDED that such missuages and real estates, as they or their successors shall have are or may be entitled unto, shall not at any time exceed the yearly rent of Five hundred pounds lawfull money of Great Britain over and above the said church and ground on which the same stands.

PROVIDED ALWAYS notwithstanding the power and authority herein before given and granted or construed to be herein or hereby given and granted to the Rector, church wardens and Vestry-men of said Swedish Evangelical Lutheran Church, that nothing in these presents is meant or intended to authorize or impower all or any of them at any time hereafter, to bargain sell, dispose, change or alter any lands tenements good or chattels given or granted to the said body corporate or Politick, or that was given or granted unto them from the use or purpose for which the donation was made, given or granted, contrary to the true intent and meaning of the donor or donors, but that all such bargains, alienations, sales, or misapplications of such donations they and every of them and their and every of they executors and administrators shall be accountable for and lyable to make satisfaction for the same to each and every succeeding Rector church wardens & Vestry-men of the said Sweedish Evangelical Lutheran Church. AND FURTHER we do will and grant that the said body corporate and Politick & theirs successors shall and may forever hereafter have a common seal to serve and use for all matters, causes, and things & affairs whatsoever of them, and their successors, and full power and authority to break alter change and new make the same or any other common seal from time to time at their will and pleasures as they shall think fit and further we will and ordain and by these presents for us our Heirs & successors do declare & appoint that for the better ordering and managing the affairs and business of the said corporation there shall be one Rector or Parochial Minister duly ordained for the cure of Souls two church wardens and six or more Vestry-men not exceeding the number of twelve from time to time constituted and chosen in manner and form as is hereafter in this presents expressed, which Vestry-men or the major part of them and the two church wardens or one of them to gether with the Rector for the time to time and at all times hereafter apply themselfes to take care for the best obtaining, receiving and disposing, governing and ordering the general business and affairs of an concerning the said church, and all such lands tenements, hereditaments, real & persons estate which shall or may be hereafter accquired as aforesaid. And we do will and ordain for us our Heirs & successors that the aforesaid John Wicksell shall be and we do hereby constitute and appoint the said John Wicksell to be the present Rector of the said Parochial church of Sweedsborough and we do further will and ordain that upon his death or removal and untill another rector ordained by any consistory of the Lutheran Church in Sweeden, and well recommended from thence, shall be appointed in his stead by the honorable society for propagating the Gospel in foreign parts and approved and inducted by the governor of our province of New Jersey for the time being that the two church wardens and the major part of the vestrymen of the said church for the time being upon the refusal or neglect of the said society after application made to them by the said church wardens & Vestry men in appointing a minister ordained as aforesaid to be the rector of the said church shall from time to time and at all times hereafter whan and as often as such vacancy shall happen have the right and power of calling, receiving, and accepting such minister ordained as aforesaid to be the Rector of the said church as they with the approbation and consent of our said governor shall think fit who shall continue to be the minister of the said church as long as the said church wardens and vestry-men with the major part of the members of the congregation from time to time shall think fit and no longer and that the said church and the said Lawrence Lock, John

Lock, John Rambo, James Steelman, John Helm, and Benjamin Rambo be the present Vestry-men of the said church which said church wardens and vestry-men are to continue in the said several offices untill the Tuesday in Easter week next ensuing or untill others be chosen in their room, in such manner as is herein after expressed.

And further we will and by these present for us our Heirs and successors do ordain appoint and dire it that the Rector of the said church for the time being shall and may from time to time upon all occassions assemble and call together in a publick manner the said church wardens & vestry-men for the time being and with them or the Major part of them at least and not otherwise consult, adivise, do and perform the business and affairs of the said church and of and concerning the premisses aforesaid, and to hold vestry's for that purpose, and in case of the death absence or refusal of the said minister for the time being, then in either or such cases during such vacancy absence or refusual the church wardens for the time being or one of them may call and hold such vestry's in manner aforesaid and do and perform in the absence, vacancy or neglect of the said Rector and not otherwise every matter and thing relating to the premisses, as if done by and with the order consent and approbationg of the Rector of the said church. And further our will and pleasure is and we do for us our Heirs and successors establish appoint and direct that the choice as well of the vestry-men as of the church wardens of the said Church shall be annual, and that yearly once in the year forever that is to say on Tuesday in Easter Week in every year at the said church in the manner following (to wit) that the rector for the time being shall appoint one of the congregation of the said church to be one of the church wardens and the congregation of the said church or the major part of them then present shall elect choose and appoint one other of the congregation of the said church to be the other church warden and the said congregation or the major part of them so met as aforesaid shall elect and choose six or more persons, not exceeding twelve of the said congregation to be vestry men for the ensuing year, which church wardens and vestry men so chosen shall immediately enter upon their respective offices from the respective times they shall be so chosen untill fit persons be respectively elected in their steads and places and shall by these present have full power & lawful authority to do execute and perform their several and respective offices in a full and ample manner as any church wardens or vestry men in that part of Great Britain called England or this our Province of New Jersey have or lawfully may do. And if it shall happen that any or either of them the said church wardens or vestry men so to be annually elected shall die, or be removed or deny refuse or neglect to officiate in the said repective offices of church wardens and vestry men before any of their times for serving therein be expired then and in every such case it shall and may be lawfull to and for the congregation of the said church for the time being or the major part of them to proceed in manner aforesaid and make a new election of one or more of the said congregation in the stead and place of such officer or officers so dying removing denying refusing or neglecting to officiate in his or their respective offices as aforesaid and so often as the case shall happen or require. And our further willed pleasure is that it shall and may be lawfull to and for the present or any other succeeding rector of the said church by and with the advise and consent of the church wardens for the time being or one of them and by and with the consent of the vestry men for the time being or the major part of them in vestry met and assembled to nominate and appoint a clerk, sexton or bellringer to and for the said church also a clerk & messenger to serve the said vestry at their meetings and such other under officers as they shall stand in need of to remain in their respective offices so long as the said Rector, church wardens and vestry for the time being or the major part of them shall think fit.

AND WE DO further of our especial grace certain knowledge & mere motion give and grant unto said Rector, church wardens & vestry men and their successors forever that the rector church wardens or one of them and vestry men of the said church for the time being of the major part of them in vestry met & assembled shall have, and we do hereby give & grant unto them full power and authority from time to time and at all times hereafter, to make ordain, and constitute such rules, orders & ordinances for the good discipline and order of the members of the said church and corporation as they or the major part of them shall think fit, so that these rules, orders & ordinances be not repugnant to the laws of that part of our Kingdom of Great Britain called England or of this our Province of New Jersey, but as near as may be there to which rules, orders and ordinances shall be from time to time fairly entered in a book or books to be kept for that purpose.

AND LASTLY we do for us our Heirs & successors ordain and grant unto the said rector, church wardens & vestry men of the said Sweedish Evangelical Lutheran Church in the town of Sweedsborough near Raccoon Creek aforesaid and their successors by these presents that this our grant shall be firm, good and effectual and available in all things in the law to all intents constructions and purposes whatsoever, according to our true & intent meaning herein before declared and shall be received, deemed, taken, construed and adjudged in all causes most favorable on the behalf and for the best benefit and behoof of the said rector church Wardens & vestry men of said Sweedish Evangelical Lutheran Church in the town of Sweedsborough near Raccoon Creek in the province of New Jersey aforesaid and their successors although express mention of the yearly value or certainty of the premisses or any of them in these presents, are not named or any statute ordnance provision, proclamation or restriction hereafore had made enacted ordained or provided, or any other matter cause or thing, whatsoever so that contrary thereof notwithstanding IN TESTIMONY where of we have caused these our letters to be made and patent and the Great Seal of our said Province of New Jersey to be hereunto affixed WITNESS our Trusty and well beloved WILLIAM FRANKLIN Esqr. Captain General & Governor in Cheif in and over our Privince of Nova Casaria or New Jersey & territories thereon depending in America Chancellor and Vice Admiral in the same Sc: at our city of Burlington the twenty fifth day of October in the fifth year of our Reign anno: Domini one thousand seven hundred and sixty five.

READ

> I have inspected the within charter and find nothing
> therein inconsistant with His Majesty's Honour or
> interest.   CORT. SKINNER.
>   Att. Gen. II.

Burlington
Oct. 23rd, 1765

> Recorded in the secretary's office in Burlington Lib:
> Comm: A A A fol. C. Read, Secretary.

CONSTANT COMMUNICANTS OF THE SWEDISH CONGREGATION IN RACOON

During my time,[108] were the following, namely: Erich Cock, Gilbert Runnals, Erich Runnals, Maria Runnals, the wife; Widow Elisabeth Gyrgon, Gustaf Justisson, Anna Justisson, his wife; Magnus Dragström, Widow Maria Matsson, Widow Cathrina Linberg, Laurence Lock, Widow Maria Orchard, Elisabeth Matson, Widow Elisabeth Hindrickson, Anna Homan, Jonas Lock, Widow Beata Cock, Widow Sarah Lock, Andrew Lock, Debora, his wife; Carl Lock, Helena Lock, his wife; Britta Homan, Olof's wife; Hance Urian Rapapo, Hellena Urian, his wife; Widow Cathrina Lock, Lars Sträng [Strengh], Rebecca Sträng, his wife; Carl Sträng, Maria Sträng, Gab's [Gabriel's] wife; Daniel Sträng, Widow Anna Angelow, Maid Britta Petersson, Beata Homan, John's wife; Widow Cathrina Halten, James Halten, Cathrina Halten, Peter's wife; Widow Maria Hoffman, Widow Judith Mattson, Rebecca Cock, Carl's wife; John Lock, Sara Lock, his wife; Enrich Mullicca, John Mullicca, Widow Cathrina Hindrichson, Zebulon Lock, Drusilla Lock, his wife; Widow Britta M'Carty, Widow Christina Lundbeck, John Richards, Cathrina Richards, his wife; Benjamin Richards, Johanna Richards, his wife; Widow Elsa Stillman, Widow Christina V. Neuman, Måns [Mons] Keen, Sr., Elisabeth Keen, Niclas' wife; Lars Paulhson, Anna Paulhson, his wife; Widow Magdlena Cock, Olof V. Neuman.

The English Congregation's are the following: William Sharpe, George Clarck, Margreta Clark, his wife; Märta [Martha] Beette, John Pinter, John Jemesson, Mary Jamesson

Note: Those who have taken the Holy Supper only once, or on their death-bed are not mentioned here

---

[108] This list made by Wicksell.

REGULAR COMMUNICANTS OF THE SWEDISH CONGREGATION IN PENS NECK

During my time were the following, namely: The Widow Hellena Månsson [Monsson] or Bonde, Deborah Bonde, Peter's wife; Maria Petersson, old Henry's wife; Niclas Nilsson, Isabella Hantsson, William's wife; The Widow Cathrina Beetle, Elizabeth Weithorn, Michel Mathews, a Finn; Jacob v. Neuman, Old man William Beette.

The reason why there are so few communicants in Pens Neck, seems to have been the bad epidemic which 40 years ago killed off the greater part of all the old Swedes there, and they thereby losing the proper understanding, remembrance and use of this precious means of grace.

[RACCOON 1765-1768]

An account of the purse monney collected under my time followeth here, the collections of the three first years were kept by Lawrence Lock one of the Church Wardens til in the beginning of the year 1765 when I was necessitated to take it into my own hands, being too troublesome to him, as not knowing to write, and very Serviceable to me, as being my only cash some times for two and three month together and the account of, and for, it, stands thus.

Debet	£	S.	d.	year day 1765	Credit	£	S.	D.
1765. May the 20th Received of Lawrence Lock the old Collection for this year	4	6	2	May 18	Laid out for a hochsaid of lime for the house	0	19	10
				the 22	For a burring line	0	3	6
					For 200 hosties	0	2	0
				June 2	Towards one quart of wine for Com:	0	2	0
This and the Collection amounts to	7	2	9½	Oct. 14	Towards a half Rime of paper	0	10	6
				Nov: 17	Tow: one quart of wine for Comun.	0	2	0
				Dec: 25	Tow: dito for dito use	0	2	0
					The whole sum	2	1	10
The whole sum	7	2	9		Ballance due	5	0	11½
				1766				
The collection in the year 1766 amounts to	1	17	4½	Januar. 1	Towards a quart of wine for the Comun:	0	2	0
				March 30	Towards dito for dito	0	2	0
				April 10	Towards a spade for the church	0	5	0
				the 20	Towards building of an oven	1	5	0
				Sept. 28	Towards one quart of wine for the comun	0	2	0
				Nov. 7	Towards a half Rime of paper	0	11	0
					Ballance due me	0	9	7½
the whole sume	1	17	4½		The whole sum	2	7	0

Debet	£	S.	d.	year day 1767	Credit	£	S.	D.
The collection in the year 1767 amounts in all to ____	2	16	5½	Januar: 1	Towards a quart of wine for the comun.	0	2	0
				April 19	Towards dito for dito use _____	0	2	0
				Sept. 8	Towards dito for dito _	0	2	0
				Decemb: 25	Towards dito for dito use _____	0	2	0
					The whole sum ____	0	8	0
					The ballance due to the congregation _	2	8	5½
The whole sum	2	16	5½					

				1768				
The collection in the year 1768 amounts in all to ____	3	0	10	Januar: 30	Towards six quarts of wine the whole year for both cong: ____		12	0
					Towards a Counting book for the Incorporat[ion] _____	0	10	0
				dito dito	Towards a half Rime of paper _____	0	11	0
				Feb. 4	Towards nails for repairing the church pales _____	0	1	0
					The whole sum ____	1	14	0
					The ballance due to the Congreg[ation]	1	6	10
The whole sum	3	0	10					

[ACCOUNTS OF THE PARSONAGE HOUSE AT SWEDESBORO]

Here you find truly recorded the names and different sums of monney of those members and friends, who Subscribed and helped towards the Building of a Parsonage House in Swedesborough near Racoon Church in the year 1763 for the Sole use of a Sweede-Lutheran Minister, lawfully commissioned and sent by his Majesty the King of Sweden, and ordained by the Lord Arch Bishop and consistory of Upsala which building of Cedar logs 33 foot long and 23 feet broad, two Storys high, thre room on each flour with other conveniencies and a comodius garret, was finished late in the faul 1764 and the present Rector, who heretofore lived with the exceeding kind William Matsson, moved into it the 14th of March 1765. And here I will observe the due distinction betwixt the Sweede, English and Deutch Subscribers, and also afterwards mention what famillies helpt to dig the stones, and to hawl the logs from the cedar Swamp, the boards, the bricks lime, and other materials and this, all gratis. viz.

	£	S.	P.		£	S.	P.
John Wicksell the present Rector gave up five years rent to it__	100			Thomas Denny Esq. (Besides his trouble of management) _____	5		
John Lock _____	10			Charles Stillman _____	5		

	£	s.	d.		£	s.	d.
Peter Homan	10			Zebulon Lock	1	10	
William Homan	10			Jacob Mullica	0	10	
James Stillman	10			John Denny	1	10	
Erick Mullica some				Moses Cox	1	10	
paid by fraight	8			Samuel Linck	3		
William Matsson	8			James Halten	1		
Charles Lock	5			William Forssman	1		
Jonas Lock	5			John V. Neuman			
Lawrence Lock	6			Clemell	0	15	
				Charles Cock	1		

	£	s.	d.		£	s.	d.
Gustaf Justisson	4			Jonas Denny	1	10	
Charles Hoffman	3	5		Jacob Matsson	1		
John Derixon	3			John Hoffman	3		
John Reynolds—payed				Jonas Hindrickson	2		
in part by work	3			Cathrine Hindrickson	1	10	
Lawrence Strang Senr.	3			Oke Helms	2		
Andrew Lock	2			Charles Magn:			
Pacob Archard	3	10		Wrangel D.D.	3		
Hance Urian Rapapo	3			Benjamin Rambou	2	10	
John Strang	2			Christiane V. Newman			
				Clemell	1		
Brought Over	195	15	0	Brought over	38	5	0

	£	s.	d.		£	s.	d.
Carried over	195	15	0	Carried over	38	5	0
Mounce Keen Junior	2	0	0	Gilbert Rynalds	5	0	0
John Helms	1	0	0	Andrew Justisson—			
Gabriel Strang	1	10	0	Pensneck	1	0	0
Lawrence Strang Junr.	0	10		Daniel Strang	1	10	0
William V. Neuman—				Jonas Dalbou	1	0	0
Pensneck	3	0	0	Gabriel Dalbou	1	0	0
Charles Dalbou	3	0	0	John Rambou	1	10	0
Peter Lock Senior—				Thomas Rambou	0	10	0
Repapo	2	0	0	Israel Matsson	0	15	0
Benjamin Angelou	2	0	0	Andrew Matsson	0	15	0
James Georgen	1	0	0	John Holton	0	7	6
Moses Hoffman	1	10	0	David Angelou	0	7	6
Friedrick Hoffman	0	12	0				
	213	17			51	0	0
				The whole makes	264	17	0

Here Followeth the Subscribers of the English Congregation

	£	s.	d.		£	s.	d.
Robbert Clarck	1	0	0	Joshua Lord	0	10	0
George Clarck	1	0	0	Alexander Ware	0	12	0
James Clarck	1	0	0	Bartholomu Supply	1	0	0
Benjamin Harden	0	5	0	John Delavow	0	10	0
William Wallis	1	0	0	Joseph James	1	10	0
Elias Böys	1	0	0	Nathan Boys Junr.	1	0	0
John Jemesson	0	10	0	Lenherd Stanten	2	0	0
Alexander Randle				Nathanael Thomsson	0	7	6
Esqr.	2	5	0	Henry Michel	0	5	0
Francis Batten	3	0	0	Joseph Schute	1	0	0
Nathan Böys Senr.	0	10	0	Meradith Jones	1	0	0

	£	Sh.	d.		£	Sh.	d.
Thomas Allen (never payed)	1	0	0	William Sweeten	1	0	0
Abram Lord	0	12	0	John Thomas	0	5	0
John Richards	1	0	0	Robert Thomas	0	10	0
John Sweeten	0	10	0	Dennie Burgan	0	5	0
Francis Robbinsson	0	10	0	William Sharpe	0	15	0
Haatsson Springer	0	10	0	Robbert Briant	0	3	0
James Bright	0	10	0	William England	1	0	0
Abram Laidden	0	10	0	John Erven	0	7	6
Joseph Richards	1	2	6	James Mathewth	0	10	
Thomas Clerck Clemell	0	10	0	William Hug	1	0	0
William Shoote	0	15	0	John Kemble	0	10	0
William Harrisson	5	0	0		16	1	0
Simon Sparcks	0	12					
	24	11	6	The whole makes	40	12	6

	£	Sh.	d.
Carried over the Sweeds Cap. S.	264	17	0
and the English Cap: Sum	40	12	6
Now followeth the Deutch Subscribers viz.			
John Goldsmith	0	10	0
John Higner	0	10	0
Joseph Applin	1	0	0
John Light	0	10	0
Jeffry Clarck	0	10	0
The whole Capit: sum Amounts	308	9	0

Besides this 308 pounds, 9 Shill. and Six pence, errors excepted, there is some small matter fallen into Thomas Dennys hands, in part from those who have been suied, and also from a few who have not set down their names on the Subscription papers, and whereof he will give the account himself and discount it, whenever the congregation can pay off the ballance due to him. And it will appear from his general account, which is here recorded on the following pages.

THE GENERAL ACCOUNT OF THOMAS DENNY ESQR.

Chosen Manager by the Sweede Lutheran Congregation at Racoon, for building their parsonage House in Sweedsborough, near Racoon Church, laid before the Vestry of the Said Congregation to their examination, at their first meeting in the year 1767 on the 5th day of January.

DEBT.	£	Sh.	d.
Cash payed for 2000 foot of boards	7	0	0
Cash payed for 2000 foot of dito	9	0	0
Dito for Lime	2	19	6
Cash Payed to Hezek: Goodens for House logs	20	0	0
Dito for 218¼ ℔ of nails at 8 d. ½ per ℔	7	13	10
Dito for 1000 heart boards	6	0	0
Dito to Erich Cox for the Carpenters diet	1	10	0
Dito for hawling of logs	1	7	0
Dito to Peter Dalbou	0	10	7
Dito to Erich Cox for diet	1	18	6

	£	Sh.	d.
Dito to dito	0	4	8
Cash layed out for an half gallon of Rum	0	2	0
Dito to Erich Cox for diet	1	19	8
Cash payed for 1000 foot of boards	4	0	0
Cash payed for the Scantling	20	0	0
Cash payed to Gabriel Dalbou for hawling and other work	6	0	0
Cash payed for 500 Shingels	2	0	0
Cash payed for 110 foot of heart planck	1	5	0
Dito to Erich Cox for diet	1	4	8
Dito to Isaac Von Neuman	1	0	0
Dito for hawling planks and shingels	0	3	0
Dito to Erich Cox for diet	4	18	0
Dito to Dito	3	19	11
Dito to Gabriel Dalbou for hawling 1000 foot of heart-boards	0	16	0
Dito to Jonas Keen the Carpenter	5	0	0
Dito to dito	20	8	0
Dito for 200 shingels	0	16	0
Dito to Samuel Pressin for diet	7	0	0
Dito to Erich Cox for diet	1	0	0
Dito to dito	1	2	0
Cash for 10 ℔ of small nails	0	10	0
Cash for 1000 of sprigs	0	4	9
Dito for 1000 of Cedar boards	4	10	0
Dito for 25 ℔ of nails at 10 p. pr. ℔	1	0	10
Brought over	147	3	11
	£	Sh.	d.

	£	Sh.	d.
Carried over	147	3	11
Cash payed for 24 ℔ of Shingel nails	1	0	0
Dito for Smiths work, as hinches spikes etc	5	15	11
Dito for a hogshead of lime	1	4	4
Dito to Jonas Keen the Carpenter at three different times	15	2	6
Dito to Isaac and Andrew Z. Newman the masons	4	7	1
Dito for more spikes to the house	0	9	0
Dito for hawling of logs	1	0	0
Dito to Jonas Keen	2	10	0
Dito to Peter Lauderback for 7700 of bricks	11	11	0
The whole Capital sum Errors except: is	190	3	9
The same brought here	190	3	9

CREDIT

	£	Sh.	d.
Per Contra. Received of following Subscribers & Collectors			
Cash viz of John Derixon collector of the one list	15	15	0
Received of Hezek: Gooden on account of William Homan	2	0	0
Dito of Lawrence Lock	3	0	1
Dito of Francis Batten collector of another List	10	0	0
Dito of John Derixon	17	14	0
Dito of Thomas and Joseph James their Subscriptions	2	10	0
Dito of Benjamin Richards another collector	4	17	6
Dito of Charles Hoppman his Subscription	3	5	0
Dito of John Hoffman his Subscription	3	0	0
Dito of Isaac Justisson his Subscription	3	0	0
Dito of Gabril Dalbou in Worck	1	0	0
Dito of Charles Cock his Subscription	1	0	0

	£	Sh.	d.
Dito of Jonas Denny his Subs: _____	1	10	0
Dito of William Homan part of his Subscription _____	7	0	0
Dito of Hance Urian in Rapapo part of his Subscription___	1	10	0
Dito of Lawrence Lock part for himself & part on Subscription _____	4	0	0
Dito of John Derixon on Subs: _____	4	0	0
Dito of Lawrence Streeng Senr. part of his Subs: _____	1	10	0
Dito of Benjamin Richards on Subs: _____	1	10	0
Dito of John Cox for one years ground rent on his lot __	1	10	0
Dito of Lennert Stanten part of his Subscript: _____	1	10	0
Dito of Benjamin Rambou his Subs: _____	2	10	0
Dito of Christiane Van Newman her Subs: _____	1	0	0
Dito of Benjamin Richards on Subs: _____	3	12	6
Dito of William Matsson his Subs: _____	8	0	0
Dito of Peter Keen his Subs: _____	1	0	0
Dito of Samuel Laiden his Subs: _____	0	10	0
Dito of Joseph Applin his Subs: _____	1	0	0
Dito of Joseph Rumford as Subs: _____	0	15	0
Dito of John Derixon on Subs: _____	13	0	0
Dito of Dito _____	2	0	0
Dito of Moses Hoffman _____	1	5	0
Dito of Charles Lock of his Subs: _____	1	15	0
Dito of Andrew Lock in Rapapo his Subs: _____	2	0	0
BROUGHT OVER _____	129	19	1

	£	Sh.	d.
Carried Over _____	129	19	1
Received of Gabriel Streeng his Subscription _____	1	10	0
Dito of John Jemesson his Subs: _____	0	10	0
Dito of Hugh Forbes _____	0	3	0
Dito of John Derixon on Subs: _____	1	10	0
Dito of Moses Hoffman _____	1	12	0
Dito of Benjamin Richards on Subs: _____	0	12	6
Dito of Nathan Boys Junr. _____	1	4	4
Dito of Alexander Randel Esqr. _____	1	0	0
Dito of Nathan Boys Senr. _____	0	10	0
Dito of Abram Boys _____	0	10	0
Dito of John Cox one years ground Rent for his Lot __	1	10	0
Dito of John Lock part of his Subs: for the rest he provided shingels _____	1	10	0
Dito of Samuel Linck his Subs: _____	3	0	0
Dito of William Harrisson his Subs: _____	5	0	0
Dito of Benjamin Richards _____	1	0	0
Dito of Dito on Subs: _____	1	5	0
Dito of William Hugg his Subs: _____	1	0	0
Dito of John Helms his Subs: _____	1	0	0
Dito of Mounce Keen junr. his Subs: _____	1	10	0
Dito of James Urian his Subs: _____	1	0	0
Dito of William Forssman his Subs: _____	1	0	0
Yet my own Subscription _____	5	0	0
The whole Capital Sum, Errors excepted sum _____	162	15	11
The Ballance due to the Said manager is thus _____	27	7	10

In April 1772 did the Rector, with the approbation and consent of the Vestry draw up a new Subscription list, for to make up the ballance yet remaining in Charge to the Congregation, to the Rector & to Several members, who had advanced monney towards the building of the parsonage house & as yet were unpayed, and also towards some repair done on the house in Pilesgrove, if it be Sufficient and the Subscribers towards these purposes, are these as followeth.

	£	S.	P.		£	S.	P.
John Wicksell the present Rector	2	0	0	Robert Clarck dito	1	0	0
Samuel Hulling	2	0	0	James Clarck dito	0	15	0
John Helms	2	0	0	George Vanleer Esqr.	1	10	0
Mounce Keen	1	10	0	Gilbert Rynolds by Denny Esqr.	5	0	0
John Lock Senior	0	10	0	John Helms again	1	0	0
Lawrence Lock	1	0	0	James Steelman	1	0	0
John Derixon	1	0	0	Samuel Tonkin	1	0	0
Charles Cock	0	5	0	George Sommerwill	1	0	0
John Rambo	1	0	0	Samuel Linck	1	0	0
William Homan	1	0	0	John Helms Jnr.	0	15	0
Daniel Sutherland	1	0	0	Peter Homan Rapapo	1	0	0
Dr. Bodo Otto Jnr.	3	0	0	Andrew Kewtin	0	15	0
John Conrod	0	10	0	Peter & John Lock Juniors	1	0	0
John Collins	0	10	0	Linnert Stanten	1	0	0
David Hindrickson Rapapo	4	0	0	Alexander V. Newman	1	0	0
Jonas Hindrickson dito	1	0	0	James Talman	1	0	0
Sarah Hindrickson the widdow	1	0	0	Conrade Shoemaker	0	15	0
Jacob Jones	2	7	6	Charles Dalbou	1	0	0
Andrew Jones	2	15	0	Isaac Justisson	0	15	0
Andrew Hindrickson	1	0	0	Moses Cox	0	15	0
Joseph Richards	0	15	0	William Matsson	0	10	0
John Richards	0	15	0	Isaac Van Newman	2	0	0
Robert Brown	1	2	6	Jacob Archard Senr.	0	15	0
William Sweeten	0	10	0	Jacob Calm	0	10	0
Thomas Clarck of Pilesgrove	1	0	0	Thomas Dodd	0	7	6

Now followeth the name of those famillies, who at all occasions in general, are free and willing to assist and work both for the church and the Minister, when he has occasion to call upon them; and who shewed themselves forward in particular at the building of this House, by digging, hawling, and working; at the clearing, grubbing & fancing of this Lot, the garden Spot, the pasture ground, the building of the Stable and by getting the poles cut and hawled; and at the clearing of the Church marsh. They are as followeth viz. Thomas Dennys famillie Esqr, William Matson, William Homan, John Lock, Lawrence Lock, Charles Lock, Andy Lock, John Derexon, Jacob Orchard, Peter Homan, Isaac Justisson, Peter Lock, Junr., Charles Cock, Eric Mullica, Andrew Hindrickson, David Hindrickson, Enkan [widow] Sara Lock i[n] Rapapo, Hance Urian i[n] Rapapo, Zebulon Lock, Isaac Justisson, Erick Cock, Anders Matson, Isaac V. Newman, Hance Geörgen near Sweedesborough, John Hoffman, John Rynalds, Peter Matson Senr., and Jacob Mattsson. These famillies distinguished themselves in a particular manner, at these above mentioned occasions. Jacob and Andrew Jones' and good many of the English and Deutch did also a little towards it, but in no comparison to the other above mentioned who bore willingly the burden: And the same must be said of them in regard to their generosity and singular Kindness, in providing provision for their ministers. They behaved allways very kind benevolent and in the most effectionate manner towards him, and his least want was allways a grief and sorrow to them. Their names shall therefore be in high esteme and a worthy Remembrance, both of him and all his good and affectionate successors. N.B.

N.B.—The two Doctors Bodo Ott Senr. & Junr. were exceeding kind & generous towards me, at all occasion, likewise Robert Brown & John Halton Esqr. at Sundry occasions.

The above mentioned famillies, along with James Stillman, Mounce Keen Junr, John Rambou, and Moses Hoffman it were, who payed and bore the charges of the Charter granted to this Society, by his Excellency the Governor of This Province, the Honorable William Franklin in the year of our Lord 1765, which may be here justly observed. The cost of it amounted only to Six pound ten shillings, since the Secretary Colonel Read gave in his usual fees both for the Drawing up of the Petition, as also for the Charter itself, which if payed, would have come to a great deal more. And the motives to this his particular favour and generosity is mentioned in the book of Incorporation

N.B.—fully in the same number hand John Helms, James Stillman, Jacob Fisler, Linnard Stanten, Moses Hoffman, Charles Dalbou, William Dalbou, Cornelius & Peter Boon, Anders Helms, Henry Peterson Senr., John and William Beetle, George Augustine, & Erick Peterssons and the several Senicksons, Lambsons, Bilderbacks, Newmans, Greens & Standlys in the Lower Neck.

Here is recorded the last Settlement concerning the remaining Balance attending the building of the Parsonage house here in Swedesborough in the year of our Lord 1764. And which balance did arise partly from thence, that the cost exceeded a good deal the Subscription; Because the materials, and the wages of the workmen, and the bourding of the same were extreemly high & did run away with a great Some of monney, and 2dly. Because, the Congregation did loose on the Subscription raised for that purpose, upon the Several Lists, in all, about 45 pounds currency, by Subscribers, that died insolvent, by others that run away, and by some that did broke or were broke, before the attorneys of the Vestry got to know their circumstances in this Respect, So, as to Secure the said Subscriptions by the course of the law. The Vestry were therefore necessitated in the year 1772, upon the representation of the present Rector, to draw up a new Subscription for the discharging of this Ballance, and the Rector took peine himself, occasionally when he could spare any time, to get it filled, So as you find it recorded imediatly after the first Subscription on the pages before the general Account of Thomas Denny Esqr. The head manager of this Building a little hereafter, in this book —

And the several charges against the Congregation that make up this Balance are such, as here now followeth from the Several creditors viz—

TO THE PRESENT RECTOR

	£	S.	D.
For his paying Andrew V. Neuman for his mason-work _____	4	17	6
For advancing two years ground Rent from John Cones Lot __	3	0	0
For paying part of the Masons boarding to Andrew V. Neuman	1	13	0
To Andrew Barnet for 3 days worck in tending the masons at 3. 6. p. _____	0	10	6
Advancing cash to Peter Dalbou Jnr. for to buy 400 Ceder boards and a quantity of Small Nails _____	1	19	6
For adding ten shillings to the Sum I bouroughed of Will: Homan	0	10	0
For adding 10 shil: towards the pay of Hez: Goodens for hawling the last logs _____	0	10	0
To Jonas Keen acct. of the 6th years Rent of the Glebe, his last demand _____	15	14	6
Towards laying a new roof of Shingles, on one part & Side of the house in Pilesgrove, & for putting in new logs in the Kitchen wall _____	7	9	6
The whole Res. _____	36	4	6
From this Sum must be Subtracted following payments viz.			
William V. Neuman payed to me his Subscription _____	3	0	0
Dito Andrew Matsson Jnr. _____	4	0	0
Ballance due to the Congregation on account of the purse money	1	5	6
	8	5	6
The ballance due to me from the Congregat: is _____	27	19	0

Swedesborough Sept: the 29th 1773. John Wicksell late Rector.

Received this first day of October 1773 the next heretofore mentioned Seventy Seven Pounds Ninetenth Shilling and Six pence from Racoon Congregation by the Several Small Sums payed into my hands by the some of respective Subscribers in April the first in the year 1772. I say received by me £27 19. 6.   John Wicksell late Rector.

Received this first of October 1773 of Racoon Congregation and Vestry Eight pounds Three and five pence, being in pay for the mason work done some years ago on this Parsonage house by me, and this being in full for all demands works and dues done on the said house. I say received by me £8, 3. 6.   Isaac Vanneman.

Received this first Day of October 1773 by way of several small subscription Sums heretofore payed into my hands at sundry times, the Sum of Ten Pounds Currency being the Principal and interest, of a sum, which I Ten years ago advanced in behalf of Racoon Congregation, upon their earnest request, towards the finishing of their parsonage House at that time build at Racoon Creek I say Received by me £10, 0, 0.   John Derickson.

Received this 15th Day of October, of Racoon Congregation by an order of their Vestry, the sum of Six pounds currency, being advanced 9 years ago towards the building of their parsonage House and this in full of all demands dues or interest. I say received by me 6, 0 0.   WILLIAM HOMAN.

No 1 THE LEASE FOR THOMAS DENNY ESQR.[109]

THIS INDENTURE made the twenty-fifth day of March in the year of our Lord one thousand seven hundred and sixty eight by and between The Reverend John Wicksell, John Lock, John Helm, Charles Lock, Lawrence Lock, Mounce Keen, Junr. F., John Rambo, the present minister and church wardens and vestry men of the Sweedish Lutheran church in the Town of Sweedsborough in the Township of Woolwich in the County of Gloucester and Province of West New Jersey elected and appointed Minister Church Wardens and Vestry men for the time being, agreeable to the directions of a Royal Charter, Granted to the Sweedish Society at Raccoon Creek, bearing date the Twenty fifth day of October (1765) and enrolled in the perogarative office at Burlington in Lib: of Commition A A A folio, of the one Part AND Thomas Denny of the same place surveyor, of the other part WITNESSETH that the said John Wicksell, John Lock, John Helms, Charles Lock, Lawrence Lock, Mounce Keen, Junn and John Rambo aforesaid have by the power & strength of the several good assurances in the law as also in the Charter above mentioned given to them and their successors to sell and convey in fee forever or to lease for year or years under the yearly unit rents all or any of lands belonging to the said Society, in the said Province of West New Jersey for the bebefit & behoof of the present minister and his successors.

NOW THIS INDENTURE witnesseth that the said John Wicksell, John Lock, John Helms, Charles Lock, Lawrence Lock, Mounce Keen, Junn & John Rambo the present minister, Church Wardens & Vestry men aforesaid, have for and in consideration of the sum of twenty shillings of current mony of the place aforesaid of quit-rents to them and their successors to be paid yearly and every year for ever hereafter by the said Thomas Denny his Heirs and assigns unto the said John Lock, John Helme, Charles Lock, Lawrence Lock, Mounce Keen, Junn & John Rambo or to either of them or either of their successors in said office yearly forever they have granted, bargained and leased by these presents do grant bargain sell & convey unto the said Thomas Denny his heirs and assigns forever under the quit rents aforesaid a certain lot of land situated in the town of Sweedsborough,

---

[109] The leases pertain to church-owned lands.

on the West side of the Main Street on road leading through the said town called Salem Road and is part and parcell of the said land belonging to the said Society and counties as followeth.

Beginning at the West side of Salem Road and runs first north forty one degrees, West five chain and thirty Linicks to Thos. James line joining on an alley of one rodwide, then joining on said James's land. North three degrees thirty minutes west two chains and twenty Linicks to John Ladds corner, then joining on his land. North sixty four degrees thirty minutes east sixty five linicks to a stake then south forty one degrees East seven chain to the Main Street or road then down the same south forty nine degrees. West two chain to the beginning. In which town is contained one acre and thirty pearch of land together with the free use of the street & alley's and all and singular the rights, liberties, priviledges, ways, waters, proffits and appertenances whatsoever to the said lot or peice of land belonging or in any ways appertaining to have and to hold the said bargained lot or piece of land with the appertenances unto the said Thomas Denny and his heirs and assigns and to and for the only use and behoof of the said Thomas Denny his heirs and assigns for ever without any apeachment for wast he the said Thomas Denny his heirs and assigns yealding and paying the before mentioned sums of twenty shillings current lawfull money unto the said body Politick and corporate or to the then rector or to his or their successors in the said office in manner aforesaid without any reduction or abatement for any matter or thing whatsoever and that at one entire payment on the twenty fifth day of March yearly in every year forever hereafter at such place in Sweedsborough as by the body corporate or Politick or their successors in said office. Attorneys stewards, Bailiffs or deputes shall be yearly notified by Publick advertisement set up in the town of Sweedsborough aforesaid and if it shall so happen that the yearly quite rents of twenty shillings as aforesaid or any part thereof shall be in arrear and unpaid by the space of five days next after either of the days of herein before limited & appointed for the payments thereof as aforesaid that then it shall and may be lawfull to and for these Body Politick & Corporate their successors their attorneys, Stewards, Baily or deputes into the said granted premises or any part thereof to enter and destrain and the distresses then and there found to carry lead or drive, and take away impound a prize and sell and the monies arising by such and due to apply toward the satisfaction and payment of the said quite rent and disstress detain and cost thereof returning the over plus to the owner, if any there be, and if no such distress can be found on the said premises is sufficient to pay and satisfy the said quit rents so in arrears, and cost as aforesaid that then it shall and may be lawfull to and for the said body Politick and corporate or to their successors attorneys bailiffs, deputes to have & take all lawfull ways and means for the recovery thereof or to reimburse on the said premises and the said Thomas Denny doth hereby for himself His Heirs & assigns covenant grant and agree to and with the said Body Politick and corporates and their successors in manner following that is to say that the said Thos. Denny his heirs and assigns shall and will from time to time and at all times forever hereafter pay or cause to be paid into the said body Politick & corporate or to their successors as aforesaid the said sum of twenty shillings on the days and time aforesaid for the payment thereof without any abatement or deduction whatsoever and lastly that the said Body Politick and corporate for themselves and their successors as aforsaid do hereby covenant grant and agree to and with the said Thomas Denny his heirs and Assigns by these presents that the said Thomas Denny his heirs and assigns paying and performing the covenants and agreements herein contained and which he or they ought to pay and perforce shall and may lawfully peaceably and quietly, have, hold, use, occupy and enjoy all the aforesaid demised lot of land containing one acre and thirty pearch and every part and parcell thereof without any lett, suit, trouble, eviction, mollestation or interuption of the said John Wicksell, John Lock, John Helm, Charles Lock, Lawrence Lock, Mounce Keen, Junn and John Rambo or their successors or either of them or any other person or persons by from or under them or their successors. In Witness whereof the said Parties have here unto interchangeably set their hands & seals of the corporation the day & year first above written.

THOS DENNY   [SEAL]

Sealed & delivered in the presence of us

Andrew Jones
Jacob Jones

John Wicksell	Charles Lock
John Lock	The Mark
John Helm	Of
	Lawrence L. Lock
	Mounce Keen
	John Rambo

No. 2 THE LEASE FOR PETER LOCK

THIS INDENTURE made the twenty fifth day of March in the year of our Lord one thousand seven hundread and sixty eight. by and between the Reverend John Wicksell, John Lock, John Helms, Charles Lock, Lawrence Lock, Mounce Keen, Junn and John Rambo, the present minister Church wardens and vestry men of the Sweedish Lutheran Church in the Town of Sweedsborough in the Township of Woolwich in the County of Gloucester, and Province of West New Jersey Yomen elected and appointed Minister church wardens

and vestry men for the time being agreeable to a Royal Charter
granted to the Sweedish Society at Raccoon Creek in the Township
aforesaid in the year of our Lord (1765) and duly enrolled in the
perogative office at Burlington in lib: of Commitions A A A folio
of the one part AND Peter Lock of the township of greenwich in
the county of Gloucester aforesaid yeaman of the other part, WHERE-
AS THE Sweedish Congregation at Raccoon Creek formerly by some
good assurances in the law became lawfully seized in sundry tracts
of land situated in Woolwich aforesaid formerly called Greenwich
and whereas by the aforesaid Charter and Incorporation they have
full power & authority in the law by their minister church wardens
and Vestry men and their successors forever, to sell and dispose or
so lease for year or years all or any part of said land by the name of
incorporation for use of the appointed minister or rector or his successors in said office NOW THIS INDENTURE WITNESSETH
that the above said John Wicksell, John Lock, John Helms, Charles
Lock, Mounce Keen, Junn. John Rambo, the present minister church
wardens and vestry men aforesaid for and in consideration of the
payment of the yearly quit rents and performances and agreement,
herein after contained, mentioned and reserved which on the part and
behalf of the said Peter Lock his Heirs and assigns are or ought to
be performed abserved and kept they the said John Wicksell, John
Lock, John Helms, Charles Lock, Lawrence Lock, Mounce Keen Junn.
John Rambo have by virtue of the said Charter and other good assurances each, either and every of them have granted bargained and
leased, unto the said Peter Lock his Heirs and assigns forever a certain lot of land situated in the town of Sweedesborough in the township aforesaid on the East side of the main street and joining to the
Parsonage House lot beginning at a stone & Post by the side of the
Church run and runs first by church street, north fifty one degrees
west five chain and 75 lincks to the main street, then along the same
south seventy degrees West one chain and 75 lincks to a corner of
the Parsonage lot then joining thereon south fifty one degrees east
five chain and 25 lincks to church run aforesaid then down the same
by the several courses thereof, to the place of beginning, containing
one acre and ten Pearches of land and meadow ground, be the same
more or less together with all and singular the rights liberties, prive-
ledges and appertenances whatsoever the said lot of land with the free
use of the streets to have and to hold the said bargained and leased
lot or peice of land and meadow ground with all and every the appertenances unto the said Peter Lock his heirs & assigns forever without
any appeachment for waste he the said Peter Lock yealding and paying therfore yearly and every year the just and full sum of Twenty
five shillings of current Lawfull Proclamation, money unto the rector
or minister or church wardens or vestry men or to his or their successors in said office or either of them without any reduction or abate-

ment for any quit rent due or to become due to the Lord of the fee or for any matters or thing, whatso ever, and that in one entire payment on the twenty fifth day of March yearly, and every year in each and every year at such place in Sweedesborough aforesaid as by the Body Politick and corporate their successors in said office their attorneys, stewards bailiffs, or attorneys or deputes shall be yearly notified by Publick advertisement set up in the Town of Sweedsborough aforesaid as by the body politick & corporate and their successors in said office shall appoint, and if it shall so happen that, the yearly quit rents of twenty five shillings or any part thereof shall be in arrear and unpaid by the space of five days, next after either of the days of payment therein before limited and appointed for the payment hereof as aforesaid that then it shall and may be lawfull to and for the said body Politick and corporate or their successors in said office or either of them on either of their Stewards or Bailiffs or deputies, into the said granted premises to enter and distrain and the disstress then and there found to carry lead drive, and take away impound impraise sell and dispose of and the money arising from such state to apply towards the payment and satisfaction of the said quit rents and costs thereof returning the overplus, if no such disstress can be found on the paid premises sufficient to pay the said quit rents so in arrear and lost that then it shall be lawfull to and for the said Body Politick & Corporate their attorneys, stewards, bailiffs or deputies or their successors or either of them to take all lawfull ways and means for the recovery thereof or to recontinue the said premises, and the said Peter Lock do hereby for himself his heirs and assigns do covenant, grant and agree to and with the said body Politick and corporate and their successors in said office in manner following that is to say that the said Peter Lock his heirs & assigns shall and will from time to time and at all times forever hereafter pay or cause to be paid unto the said body politick and corporate as aforesaid the sum of twenty five shillings on the day and time as aforesaid for the payment thereof without any abatement thereof or deduction whatsoever and also make such improvements thereon as shall be sufficient to secure the yearly rents and the same to uphold in good order & repair and lastly that the said Body Politick & corporate for themselves and their successors as aforesaid do hereby covenant, grant and agree to and with the said Peter Lock his heirs and assigns by these present that he the said Peter his heirs & assigns paying and performing the covenants and agreements herein contained and which he or they ought to perform, shall and may lawfully and peaceably and quietly have hold occupy possess and enjoy all the aforesaid demised lot of land and meadow be the same more or less and every part and parsell thereof without any let, suit, trouble, eviction, ejectment, molestation or interuption of the said parties or their successors or either of them or any person or persons by from or under them or any them—In Witness where of the said parties to those present have interchangeably set their hands & seals the day and year first above written.

SEALED & DELIVERED

in the presence of us

Jacob Jones

Andren Jones

Thos. Denny

John Wicksell
John Lock
John Helms
Charles Lock
the mark
of
Lawrence L Lock
Mounce Keen
John Rambo

No. 3 THE LEASE FOR JAMES JAMES

THIS INDENTURE made the twenty fifth day of March in the year of our Lord one thousand seven hundred and sixty eight by and between the Reverend John Wicksell and John Lock, John Helms, Charles Lock, Lawrence Lock, Mounce Keen junn John Rambo the present Minister & Church wardens & vestry men of the Sweedish Lutheran church in the Town of Sweedsborough in the township of Woolwich in the county of Gloucester and Province of West New Jersey elected and appointed minister Rector and Church Wardens, and vestry men for the time being agreeable to the directions of a Royal charter granted to the Sweedish society at Raccoon Creek in the Township aforesaid in the year of our Lord 1765 and duly enrolled in the perogative office in Burlington in Lib: of Commitions folio — of the one part and James James of the county of Salem in the township of Pilesgrove and Province aforesaid Merchant of the other part. WHEREAS the Sweedish congregation at Raccoon Creek formerly by some good assurances in the law became lawfully seized in sundry tracts of land situated in Woolwich aforesaid formerly called Greenwich and WHEREAS by the aforesaid Charter and Incorporation they have full power and authority in the law by their minister church wardens and vestry men and their successors to sell and dispose or lease for year or years all or any part of the said land by the name of incorporation for the use of the appointed minister or Rector or his successors in said office. NOW THIS INDENTURE Witnesseth John Wicksell, John Lock, John Helms, Charles Lock, Lawrence Lock, Mounce Keen Junn John Rambo the present Minister church wardens & vestry men aforesaid for and in consideration of the payment of the yearly quit rent and performance of the covenant and agreements herein after contained and mentioned which on the part and behalf of the said James James his heirs & assigns ought to be performed observed and kept. They the said John Wicksell, John Lock, John Helms, Charles Lock, Lawrence Lock, Mounce Keen, Junn. John Rambo have by virtue of the said charter and other good assurances each and every of them have granted, bargained and leased unto the said James James his Heirs and assigns forever a certain lot of land situated on the West Side of the street in the Township of Sweedsborough in the Township aforesaid and bounded as followeth, beginning at a stake set on the West side of the main street near the corner of Thomas James house and runs first up the said street north forty-nine degrees east three chains and seventy five lincks to the corner of an alley then by the same north forty one degrees West four chain and sixty-seven lincks, to a corner in Thomas & Sarah James line then joining thereon south three degrees thirty minutes east, six chain to the place of beginning, *three quarters of an acre and twenty-four Pearch of land* together with all and singular the rights liberties, priviledges and appertenances whatso ever of the said lot of land with the free use of the streets, to have and to hold the said bargained and leased lot or piece of land with all the appertenances unto the said James James his heirs and assigns forever without any apeachment for waste he the said James James yealding and paying therefor yearly and every year forever hereafter the sum of eighteen shillings of currents money unto the rector, minister or church wardens or vestry men or to their successors in said office or to either of them without any deduction or abatement for any quit rents due or to become due to the lord of the fee or for any matter or thing whatso ever and that in one entire payment on the twenty fifth day of March yearly and every year in each and every year at such place in Sweedesborough aforesaid as by the body Politick and corporate their successors in said office their attorneys stewards, Bailiffs, or Deputies shall be yearly Notified by publick advertisements set up in the town of Sweedsborough aforesaid as by the body politick and corporate or their successors in said office their attorneys stewards bailiffs or deputies shall appoint as aforesaid and if it shall so happen that the yearly quit rent of eighteen shillings or any part thereof shall be in arrear unpaid by the space of five days next after either of the days of payment herein before limited and appointed for the payment thereof as aforesaid that it shall and may be lawfull to and for the said body politick & corporate or their successors in said office or either of them or either of their stewards or bailiffs or deputies into the said granted premisses to enter and distrain and the disstress there found so carry lead or drive take away or impound, impraise and dispose of and the money arising from such sales to apply towards the payment and satisfaction of the said quit rents and costs thereof returning the over plus if any be, to the owner thereof and if no such disstress can be found on the said premisses sufficient to pay the said quit rents so in arrears and cost, that then it shall be lawfull to and for the said body politick and corporate their attorneys stewards bailffs or deputies or their successors or either of them to take all lawfull ways and means for the recovery thereof or to re-enter on the said premisses and the said James James do hereby for himself and his heirs and assigns covenant grant and agree to and with the said body politick & corporate and their successors in said office in manner following, that is today that James James shall and will from time to time and at all times forever hereafter pay or cause to be paid unto the said body Politick and corporate. Their successors as aforesaid the said sum of eighteen shillings on the day and times as aforesaid for the payment thereof without any abatement or deduction whatsoever and also to make such improvements thereon as shall be sufficient to secure the said yearly rent and the same to uphold in good order and repair and lastly that the said body politick and corporate for themselves and their successors as aforesaid do hereby covenant grant and agree to and with the said James James his heirs and assigns paying and performing the covenants and agreements herein contained which he or they ought to pay and perform shall and may lawfully and peaceably and quietyly have, hold, possess and enjoy all the aforesaid demised lot of land and meadow be the same more or less and every part and parcell thereof without any lot, suit, trouble aviction ajection mollestation or interuption of the said parties or their successors or either of them or any person or persons whatsoever by from or under them or any of them.

IN WITNESS WHEREOF the said parties to these presents have interchangeably set their hands & seals the day and year first above written.   JAMES JAMES

    Sealed and delivered
  in the presence of us

Jacob Jones	John Wicksell
Andrew Jones	John Lock
James Steelman	John Helms
	Charles Lock
	the mark of
	Lawrence L. Lock
	Mounce Keen
	John Rambo.

No. 4 THE LEASE FOR THOMAS JAMES

THIS INDENTURE made the twenty fifth day of March in the year of our Lord one thousand seven hundred and sixty eight by an between the Reverend John Wicksell and John Lock, John Helms, Charles Lock, Lawrence Lock, John Rambo, Mounce Keen Junr. the present minister church warden and vestry men of the Sweedish Lutheran Church in the town of Sweedesborough in the Township of

Woolwich in the county of Gloucester and Province of West New Jersey elected and appointed minister church wardens and vestry men for the time being agreeable to the direction of a Royal Charter granted to the Sweedish Society at Raccoon Creek in the Township aforesaid in the year of our Lord (1765) and duly enrolled in the Perogative office at Burlington in Libr: of Committions AAA folio of the one part AND Thomas James of the Township and County and Province aforesaid Inn: holder of the other part. Whereas the Sweedish congregation at Raccoon Creek formerly by some good assurances in the law became lawfully siezed in sundry tracts of land situated in *Woolwich aforesaid formerly called Greenwich* and whereas by the aforesaid Charter and incorporation they have full power & authority in the law by their minister church wardens and vestry men and their successors forever to sell and dispose or to lease for year or years allow any part of said lands by the name of incorporation for the use of the appointed minister or Rector or his successors in said office.

NOW THIS INDENTURE WITNESSETH that the above said John Wicksell, John Lock, John Helms, Charles Lock, Lawrence Lock, Mounce Keen Junn. John Rambo the present Minister Church Wardens & Vestry Men aforesaid for an in consideration of the payment of the yearly quit rents and performance of the covenants and agreements herein after contained mentioned and reserved which on the part and behalf of the said Thomas James his heirs & assigns are or ought to be performed observed and kept they the said John Wicksell, John Lock, John Helms, Charles Lock, Lawrence Lock, Mounce Keen Junn and John Rambo have by virtue of the said Charter and other good assurances each either and every of them have granted bargained and leased unto the said Thomas James his heirs & assigns forever a certain lot of land situated in the Town of Swedesborough in the Township aforesaid and is bounded as followeth beginning at a post for a corner standing in the line of said Thomas James land by the side of the Main Street nearly opposite his door and runs first south three degrees thirty minutes, East in chain and fifty lincks to the water course of as mal Branch of church run then second down the same North, seventy degrees thirty minutes East five chain and Twenty five lincks to a post then third north forty one degrees, west four chain to the Main Street then down the same south forty nine degrees West three chain and seventy five lincks to the place of beginning in which bounded is *contained one acre quarter* of an acre and ten pearch of land and meadow ground togeather with all and singular the rights liberties, priviledges street priviledges and appertenances whatsoever to the said lot of land with the free use of the streets to have and to hold the said bargained and leased lot or piece of land and meadow with every appertenances unto the said Thomas James his heirs & assigns forever without any appeachment for waste he the said Thomas

James yealding and paying therefore yearly and every year the just
and full sum of *one pound twelve* shillings and sixpence of lawfull
proclamation mony unto the Rector or Minister or Church Wardens
or Vestry men or to his or their successors in said office or to either
of them without any reduction on abatement for any quit rent due
or to become due to the Lord of the fee or for any matter or thing
whatsoever and that in one entire payment on the twenty fifth day of
March yearly and every year in each and every year at such place in
Sweedesborough aforesaid as by the Body Politick & corporate their
successors in said offices their attorneys, Stewards, Bailiffs, or attorneys, or deputies shall be yearly notified by Publick advertisement set
up in the town of Sweedesborough aforesaid, and if it shall so happen
that the yearly quite rent of one pound twelve shillings and sixpence
or any part thereof shall be in arrear and unpaid by the space of five
days next after either of the days of payment herein before limited
and appointed for the payment thereof as aforesaid that then it shall
and may be lawfull to and for the said body Politick and corporate
or their successors in said office of either of them or either of their
stewards or Bailiffs or deputies into the said granted premises to enter
and distrain and the disstress then and there found to carry lead,
drive and take away impound impraise sell dispose of and the mony
arising from such sale to apply towards the payment and satisfaction
of the said quit rents and costs thereof returning the over plus if any
be, to the owner thereof and if no such disstress can be found on the
said premises sufficient to pay the said quit rent so in arrear and costs
that then it shall be lawfull to and for the said body Politick & corporate their attorney Stewards, Bailiffs or deputies or their successors
or either of them to take all lawfull ways and means for the Recovery
thereof or to recanter on the said premisses and the said Thomas James
do hereby for himself and his heirs and assigns do covenant grant
and agree to and with the said body politick & corporate and their
successors in said office in manner, following that is to say that the
said Thomas James his heirs and assigns shall and will from time to
times and at all times forever hereafter pay or cause to be paid unto
the said Body Politick and Corporate their successors as aforesaid
the sum of one pound twelve shillings and six pence on the day and
time as aforesaid for the payment thereof without any abatement or
deduction whatsoever and also to make such improvements as shall
be sufficient to secure the said yearly rent within three years and the
same to uphold in good order and repair and lastly that the said body
politick and corporate for themselves and their successors as aforesaid do hereby covenant grant & agree to and with the said Thomas
James his heirs and assigns by these presents that he the said Thomas
James his heirs and assign paying and performing the Covenants and
agreements herein contained and which he or they ought to pay and
perform shall and may lawfully and peaceably and quietly have, hold,

possess, and use, and enjoy all the aforesaid demised lot of land and meadow be the same more or less, and every part and parcell thereof without molestation or interuption of the said parties or their successors or either of them or any person by from or under them or any of them. IN WITNESS WHEREOF the said parties to these presents have interchangeably set their hands and seals the day and year first above written.   THO. JAMES —

    Sealed and Delivered
    in the presence of us
        Jacob Jones
        Andrew Jones

                      John Wicksell
                      John Lock
                      John Helms
                      Charles Lock
                          the mark of
                      Lawrence Lock
                      Mounce Keen
                      John Rambo

No. 5—THE LEASE FOR JAMES STEELMAN

THIS INDENTURE made the twenty fifth day of March in the year of our Lord one thousand seven hundred and sixty eight by and between the Reverend John Wicksell and John Lock, John Helms, Charles Lock, Lawrence Lock, Mounce Keen Junr. and John Rambo the present minister Church Wardens and Vestry Men of the Sweedish Lutheran Church in the town of Sweedsborough in the Township of Woolwich in the County of Gloucester and Province of West New Jersey elected and appointed, minister church wardens and vestry men for the time being agreeable to the directions of a Royal Charter granted to the Sweedish Society at Raccoon Creek bearing date the twenty fifth day of October in the year of our Lord (1765) and duly enrolled in the perogative office at Burlington Lib: of Committions AAA folio of the one part and James Steelman of the Township of Greenwich in the county and Province of aforesaid yeaman of the other part. WHEREAS the Sweedish congregation at Raccoon Creek formerly by sundry good assurances in the law became lawfully seized in sundry tracts or parcells of land situated in *Woolwich aforesaid formerly* called Greenwich and WHERAS by the aforesaid charter and incorporation they have full power and authority in the law by their minister church wardens and vestry men and their successors for ever to sell and dispose or to lease for year or years all or any part of said lands by the name of incorporation for the use of the appointed Rector or his successors in said office.

    NOW THIS INDENTURE WITTNESSETH that the above said John Wicksell, John Lock, John Helms, Charles Lock, Lawrence Lock, Mounce Keen Junr., John Rambo for and in consideration of the payment of the yearly quit rents and performances of the covenants and agreements herin after contained mentioned and reserved which on the part and behalf of the said James Steelman his heirs or assigns are is or ought to be performed observed and kept they the said John Wicksell, John Helms, Charles Lock, Lawrence Lock, Mounce Keen Junn and John Rambo have by virtue of the said charter and other good assurances and each, either and every of them have granted, bargained and leased unto the said James Steelman, his heirs and assigns forever a certain lot of land and ground covered in part with water *situated* in the Town of Sweedesborough in the township aforesaid and is bounded as followeth beginning at or near low water mark about fifty lincks below Raccoon Creek Bridge and runs first south sixty six degrees thirty minutes west one chain and sixty five lincks to a White oak on the top of the Hill then by the same North twenty degrees west two chain and sixty lincks to a stake in John Ladds line then by the same North sixty two degrees thirty minutes east one chain and sixty five lincks to the creek at or near low water mark then up the same binding thereon to the place of beginning *containing one quarter and half a quarter of an acre* of land and mud flats be the same more or less, together with all and singular the rights liberties, priviledges, streets, pavements, proffits and appertenances whatsoever to the said lot of land with the free use of the streets to have and to hold the said bargained and leased lot or peice of land with every the appertenances unto the said James Steelman his heirs and assigns for ever without any appeachment for waste, he the said James Steelman yealding and paying therefore yearly & every year the just and full sum of *thirty shillings* of current and lawfull money of the same place unto the beforesaid Rector Church Wardens and Vestry Men or to his or their successors in said office or either of them without any reduction or abatement for any quit rents due or to become due to the Lord of the fee or for any other matter or thing whatsoever and that in one entire payment on the twenty fifth day of March yearly and every year in each and every year for ever at such place in Sweedsborough aforesaid as by the body politick and corporate their successors in said office their attorneys stewards bailiffs or deputies shall be yearly notified by publick advertisement set up in the town of Sweedsborough aforesaid and if shall so happen that the yearly quit rents of thirty shillings or any part thereof shall be in arrears and unpaid by the space of five days next after either of the days of payment herein before limited and appointed for the payment thereof as aforesaid that then it shall and maybe lawfull to and for the said body politick and corporate or their successors in said office or either of their bailiffs or stewards or deputies into the said granted premises so enter and distrain and the disstress then and therefound to carry lead, drive and take away impound impraise and sell and despose of and the money arising by such sale to apply towards the payment and satisfaction of the quit rents and disstresses and costs thereof returning the overplus if any be to the owner thereof, and if no such disstress can be found on the said quit rents so in arrear and costs that then it shall be lawfull to and for the said body politick and corporate their attorneys, Stewards, Bailiffs or deputies or their successors or either of them to take all lawfull ways and means for the recovery thereof or to recanture on the said premisses, and the said James Steelman do hereby for hiself and his heirs and assigns do covenant grant and agree to and with the said body politick and corporate and their successors in said office in manner following that is to say that the said James Steelman his heirs and assigns shall and will from time to time and at all times forever hereafter pay or cause to be paid unto the body politick and corporate their successors as aforesaid the sum of thirty shillings on the day and time as aforesaid for the payment thereof without any abatement or deduction whatsoever and also to make such improvements as shall be sufficient to secure the said yearly rent and the same to uphold in good order and repair and lastly, that the said Body Politick and Corporate for themselves and their successors as aforesaid do hereby covenant grant and agree to and with the said James Steelman his heirs and assigns by these presents that he the said James Steelman his heirs and assigns paying and performing the covenants and agreements herein contained and which he or they ought to pay and perform shall and may lawfully and peaceably and quitely have hold use occupy posess and enjoy all the aforesaid demised lot or piece of land as aforesaid be the same more or less and every part and parcell thereof without any let, suit, trouble eviction molestation or interuption of the said body politick and corporate or their successors or either of them or any person by from or under them or their successors. IN WITNESS whereof the said parties to these presents have interchangeably set their hands and seals the day and year first above written.

Sealed and delivered   James Steelman
in the presence of us
    Jacob Jones   John Wicksell
    Andrew Jones   John Lock
    Thos. Denny   John Helms
                                         Charles Lock
                                             the mark of
                                         Lawrence L. Lock
                                         Mounce Keen
                                         John Rambo

[ACCOUNTS FOR BANKING THE MARSH—RACCOON 1769]

1769 in the faul [fall] the first proposals were made of some Members, for banking in the church marsh upon Racoon Creek. The Minister, who had thought on it many a time before, was not backward to incurrage the thing, but in the insuing winter Season endeavoured to get Sufficient Subscriptions for the purpose, and being favoured, accordingly they went about it in the Spring 1770, after having advised the Managers Lawrence Lock and John Derixcon to draw an Article of agreement betwixt them and the other owners, concerning the doing and finishing of the work and accordingly the church part was well done and compleated before the month of May last year above mentioned. And the subscribers to this bank are these as follows viz.

	£	sh.	d.		£	sh.	d.
Thomas Denny Esqr. the surveying, dividing, inspecting & settling work is more than any else, Mathew Gill the first starter of it, tho' it was much for his own interest	1	0	0	David Hindrickson one dito	0	6	0
John Lock two Rods	0	12	0	John Rambou towards it	0	7	6
John Helms for two Rods	0	12	0	James Pflannigan dito	0	7	6
William Homan for two Rods	0	12	0	Andrew Jones for one dito	0	6	0
James Steelman for two Rods	0	12	0	Hindrich Hindrichson	0	10	0
Jacob Jones for two dito	0	12	0	Peter Lock Junr. for one	0	6	0
William Matsson for two dito	0	12	0	Isaac Justisson tow: it	0	7	6
Elajah Lock for two dito	0	12	0	Andrew Hindrickson	0	6	0
Charles & Peter Lock in Rap: two	0	12	0	Moses Cock for one	0	6	0
Peter Homan for two dito	0	12	0	Mounce Keen tow: it	0	7	6
Charles Cock for one dito	0	6	0	Jonas Hindrichson	0	6	0
Andrew Matsson Junr. one	0	6	0	Following have dug them: viz.			
Jacob Archard for one dito	0	6	0	John V. Newman one Rod Andrew Culen one dito William Prockt one dito William Noble one dito John Halten one dito Benjamin Angelou one Mosses Hoffman & Jacob Callohan one dito Gabriel Sreeng one			
John Derixson for one dito	0	6	0	The Ditchers Thomas Dodd & Robb: Kraighead to give in each of them a Rod, for two pine logs sold of the Church lots here	0	12	0

1772 the 3d of December, made the Rector the last payment of 2 shil. & —— unto Thomas Dodd present, at the house of Lawrence Lock his father-in-law, & to Robbert Kraighaid a partner in the banking work of the Churchmarsh with the said Dodd, but now absent, the marsh on Racoon Creek, opposite Jacob Jones's is here meant, this being the last & full payment of their whole wages for the said worck; Lawrence Lock present, as one of the managers of the said worck, was therefore ordered by me to take a receit in full as of these worckmen for their Wages now payed in full for their whole worck done at the sd. marsh which he promised to do but he thought there would be no occasion for it and the Rector left it to their own choice.

DEBET	£	s.	d.	year day	CREDIT	£	S.	d.
				1769				
The Collection in the year 1769 amounts in all to ____	3	0	7		Towards three quarts of wine the whole year _____	0	6	0
				Feb. 2	Tow: a half Rime of paper _____	0	11	0
				March 9	Tow: an Incorporation Book _____	0	14	0
				April 30	Tow: repairing of the pales fallen down __	0	4	0
				dito	To the Collectors for entering the Churches and the Leases into the Incorp: book __	0	7	6
				Dec. 15	Tow: a new spade the old did brake in mending _____		6	6
					The whole sum ____	2	9	0
The whole sum	3	0	7		The balance due to the Congr: ____	0	11	7
				1770				
The collection in the year 1770 amounts in all to ____	3	1	1	Jan. 3	To Deutch John for hinches etc. for the Stable _____	0	8	0
				Dito	Tow: nails for the Stable _____	0	10	0
					Tow: four quarts of wine for the whole year _____	0	8	0
				Feb. 6	Tow: a half rime of paper _____	0	11	0
				dito	To Deutch John for a crane in the kitchin _	0	15	10
				April 26	To Erick Cock for mending the pales __	0	2	6
					The whole sum ____	2	15	4
The whole Sum	3	1	1		The ballance due to the Cong[regation] _____	0	5	9
				1771				
The collection in the year 1771 amounts in all to ____	3	3	10	March 11	To Erick Cock for mending the pales __	0	3	0
					Towards wine for the Communion _____	0	6	0
				Dec. 24	Towards a half Rime of paper _____	0	11	6
					To Lawrence Straeng Sr. for the Cow in the year 1765 which there was forgotten	2	10	0
				Dec. 31	To Erick Cock, for mending the Spade _	0	1	0

DEBET	£	s.	d.	year	day	CREDIT	£	S.	d.
						The whole _____	3	11	6
						The ballance due to me _____	0	7	8
						The above ballane to me _____	0	7	8
The whole sum	3	3	10	1772					
The collection in the year 1772 amounts in all to ____	2	10	6½	March	2	Bought a new Spade for the church _____	0	7	6
						Towards wine for the whole year _____		10	6
				April	24	To Erick Cock for repairing the church pale _____		6	0
						The whole _____	1	11	8
The whole Sum is _____	2	10	6½			The Ballance due to the Congregat: _____	0	18	10½
				1773					
The Collection in the year 1773 to the 8th of August amounts to __	1	9	5½	April		Towards comunion wine _____	0	8	0
						To Nails & Sundry repairs of the pales __	0	7	6
The ballance due to the Congreg: __	0	18	10½	June		Towards a new burring line _____	0	2	6
				July	28	To Van Dyke for repairing pews & a broken pair of window shutters _____	0	4	9
The whole is __	2	8	4			The whole is _____	1	2	9
The whole sum is _____	2	8	4			The ballance due to the Congregation _____	1	5	6

No. 6—LEASE FOR JOSEPH DEVENPORT

THIS INDENTURE made the second day of April in the year of our Lord one thousand seven hundred and seventy one by and between the Revd. John Wicksell, and John Lock, John Helms, John Derixon, Lawrence Lock, Mounce Keen, Charles Dalbou, Jacob Jones, Charles Cox, the present minister and church wardens and vestrymen, of the Swedish Lutheran Church in the Town of Swedesborough, in the Township of Woolwich in the county of Gloucester and province of West New Jersey, appointed and elected minister, church wardens and vestry men, for the time being agreeable to the directions of a Royal Charter granted to the Swedish Society at Raccoon Creek, bearing date the twenty fifth day of October (1765) and duly enrolled in the perogative office at Burlington (in Libr. of Comss. A.A.A. folio) of the one part and Joseph Devenport of the township county and Province aforesaid yoman of the other part. WITNESSETH, that the said John Wicksell, John Lock, John Helms, John Derixon, Lawrence Lock, Mounce Keen, Charles Dalbou, Jacob Jones and Charles

Cox have by the power force and effect of the several good assurances in the law, as also in the charter above mentioned given to them and their successors in said office, to sell and lease for year or years and forever under the yearly quit rents all or any of the lands, belonging to the said society, in the said province of West New Jersey, for the benefit and behoof of the present minister and his successors, now—

THIS INDENTURE WITNESSETH, that the said John Wicksell, John Lock, John Helms, John Derixon, Lawrence Lock, Mounce Keen, Charles Dalbou, Jacob Jones and Charles Case, the present minister and church wardens and vestry men aforesaid have for, and in consideration of the sum of twenty shillings of current lawful monney of the place aforesaid of Quit-Rents to them and to their successors to be payed yearly and every year forever, being in said office hereafter, by the said Joseph Devenport or his heirs, executors *Admts.* or assigns, unto the said John Wicksell, John Lock, John Helms, John Derixon, Lawrence Lock, Mounce Keen, Charles Dalbou, Jacob Jones and Charles Case, to either of them or to either of their successors in said office yearly and forever, They have granted, bargained and by these presents do grant, bargain lease and confirm, unto the said Joseph Devenport and to his heirs and assigns forever under the yearly quit rent of twenty shillings aforesaid, to be payed yearly, have leased a certain lot of land containing one real acre in the town of Swedesborough on the west side of the main street or road leading through the said town called Salem Road, and is part and parcell of the land belonging to said corporation and society; and bounded as followeth, BEGINNING AT A part set in the side of the road or street near the corner of the parsonage garden, north thirty nine degrees, west four chain and thirty four links, to a post in the line of land, late John Ladds Esqr. Then joining thereon south sixty five degrees west two chain and twenty-one links to a post then joining other land of the society, south thirty nine degrees east four chain and eighty links, to the main streets or road then up the road north fifty one degrees east two chain and twenty one links to the beginning; containing in those bounds one acre of land, together with all and singular the rights, liberties, ways, waters and appertinences to the said lot of land belong, or in any ways appurtaining, to have and to hold the said bargained lot or piece of land with the appartenances, unto the said Joseph Devenport, and to his heirs and assigns and to and for the only use and behoof of the said Joseph Devenport his heirs and assigns forever without any apeachment, for which he the said Joseph Devenport his heirs or assigns yealding and paying therefor the said sum of *twenty shillings* lawful monney, to the said body politick and corporate or to the then Rector or to either of their succes-

sors in said office, in manner aforesaid, without any deduction or
abatement for any matter or thing whatsoever and that, in one entire
payment on the twenty fifth day March yearly and in every year for-
every hereafter, at such place in Swedesborough, as by the body politick and corporate and their successors in the said office their attornies balifs or deputies, shall be notified, by a publick advertisement,
set up in the said town of Swedesborough and if it shall so happen
that the yearly quit rent of twenty shillings as aforesaid, or any part
thereof shall be in arrears and unpayed for the space of five days, next
after any of the said days herein before limited appointed for the payment of aforesaid quit rent that then it shall and may be lawful to and
for the said body politick and their attornies stewards balifs or deputies, into the said leased premises or any part thereof to enter and
distrain for the rent then due, and the distress there found carry, lead
or drive and take away impound impeach and sell, and the monney
arising from such a sale and due, to apply towards the satisfaction and
payment of the said quit rent and distress, expenditure and cost thereof,
returning the overplus to the owner, if any ther be and if no such
distress can be found on the said premises sufficient to pay or satisfy
the said quit rent so in arrears and the cost thereof that then it is covenanted by and between the said parties that it shall be Lawful to and
for the said body politick and corporate their successors, attornies
balifs or deputies to take all lawful ways and means for the recovery
thereof or to reenter the said premises: And the said Joseph Devenport doeth hereby for himself and his heirs and assigns further covenant grant and agree to and with the said body corporate and politick and their successors in manner following, that is to day, that the
said Joseph Devenport his heirs and assigns shall and will from time
to time and at all times forever hereafter payee cause to be payed to
the aforesaid body politick and corporate, or their successors as aforesaid, the sum of twenty shillings of current lawful monney, on the day
and time aforesaid, for the payment thereof, without any abatement
or reduction thereof whatsoever. And lastly, that the said body politick and corporate for themselves and there successors as aforesaid do
hereby covenant grant and agree to and with the said Joseph Devenport his heirs and assigns by these presents, that the said Joseph
Devenport his heirs and assigns paying and performing the covenants
herein contained, which he or they ought to perform shall and may
lawfully peaceably, quietly have, hold use occupy and enjoy all the
aforesaid premises demised, and lot of land containing one acre of
land and every part and parcell thereof without any lett suit trouble
eviction molestation or interruption of them the said John Wicksell,
John Lock, John Helms, John Derixon, Lawrence Lock, Mounce
Keen, Charles Dalbou, Jacob Jones and Charles Cox, or their succes-

sors, or either of them or any other person or persons whatsoever by, from, or under them or their successors as aforesaid.

Sealed and Delivered   Joseph Davenport.
in the presence of us

B. It is farther agreed on that the
said Joseph Devenport his heirs or
assigns shall build or cause to build
a suitable house for a town or other
emprovements on the said lott with-   [SEAL]
in the space of two years from the
date hereof, as shall sufficiently secure the yearly ground rent of the
said lot and from time to time keep
the same in good repair.

Thomas James
John Vandike.

No. 7—LEASE FOR THE PUBLICK SCHOOL HOUSE OF SWEDESBORROUGH

This Indenture, made the second day of April, in the year of our Lord one thousand seven hundred and seventy one, by and between the Reverend John Wicksell, John Lock, John Helms, Lawrence Lock, John Derixon, Mounce Keen, James Steelman, Charles Lock, and Charles Dalbo, the present minister church wardens and vestry men of the Swedish Lutheran church in the town of Swedes-borrough in the township of Woolwich in the county of Gloucester and wester division of the province of New Jersey elected and appointed minister, church wardens and vestry men for the time being agreeable to the directions of the Royal charter granted to the Swedish Society at Raccoon Creek, and bearing date—the twenty fifth day of October one thousand seven hundred and sixty five of the one part — and Thomas Denny, Esq. of the township county and province aforesaid and to best known of Swedesborough, of the places aforesaid Genl. shop-keeper, clerk and chosen subject in conjunction with the Revd. John Wicksell, the present minister of Swedesborough of the other part WITNESSETH that the aforesaid minister, church-wardens and Vestry-men (and others) being moved by the desolate condition the schools and the schooling of children are in and being desirous to promote and encourage learning unto their children and others for the time to come, Do hereby, by virtue of the above raised charter and in pursuance of good assurances in the law, by their worthy ancestors of the Swedish Society have granted bargained convey and leased, and by those presents do grant bargain, convey and lease for ever one-half acre of ground in the said town of Swedesborough laying on the left side of the Main street now called Salem road joining to the south side of Joseph Devenports lot and bounded as followeth, beginning at the post, by the side of the said street, corner, to said Devenport, then joining thereon first North Thirty nine degrees left four-chain and eighty link to a stake in Ladds line, then joining on said Ladds land, south sixty five degrees, left one chain and fifteen links to a stake for a corner, then south thirty-nine degrees, East five chain and twenty links to the Main street, on road called Salem-road, then up the same north fifty one degrees, East one chain, to the place of beginning, in which bounds is contained one half acre of land for the use of a publik and free school and free from all manner of ground rent, or any other incumbrance (the yearly taxes only excepted) forever therein all Christain denomination children, that help and contribute to build and uphold the said school house shall have a full and absolute free liberty there to send their children to be taught the several branches of learning, as shall be thought necessary by the aforesaid manager, trustees and their successors forever—and that all such persons as aforesaid shall forever hereafter have the liberty of building and rebuilding a publick school and other causes for the use of the school on said lott as the Trustees with the consent of the present rector of the church at Swedesborough for the time being and their successors from time to time shall agree on. And the said incorporation, knowing, that their instituent members besides the free gift of this lott will be the most part towards the building of the said house, is desirous, that two or three orphan-children out of the neighborhood of said place, shall have their free schooling in said house or such number, more or less as the present instances at all times shall require and permit of, at the objection of the present teacher and trustees and their successors in said office, from time to time shall approve of—the incorporation acepted and reserve also the priviledge of the said school house at such time as shall be thought proper yearly and every year to meet in, to be taught music or the singing part of learning, by the officiating master, or any other capable person, without interruption, provided such meetings do not interfere with the common school house and the incorporation farther cause to the use of the said house on every Sabboth when divine service shall be performed in the church at Swedesborough then to have free liberty to make use of said schoolhouse, for the use of the congregation which also shall have a free use of taken down and old dead timber of the churchland to the westward of Thomas James plantation at such meetings for fire wood and at all such meetings as at all other times shall the said schoolhouse be under the immediate command and inspection of the present master who is accountable to the rector and the vestry that a strict Decorum is observed at all such meetings and Christian assemblies And also that the said rector or present minister for the time being and his successors shall have the free inspection and ordering of the children learning in the religious parts that belong to the church aforesaid. And in all matters relating to the said schools, the Rector and the trustees are to act in conjunction with each other. And the schoolmaster is to agree with his employers, after approved of by the minister and trustees and their successors The Trustees hereafter to be such as shall be annualy chosen on the third day in Easter Week, in the town of Swedesborrough yearly and every year for ever hereafter and to remain in said office during good behavior on one year, at one time and no longer except elected again by the majority concerned then present of the towns, founders and builders of the said school house and all such, as hereafter shall likewise agree on that a charity sermon be preached one day in each and every year in said house or in the church for the supporting of the said school, and the rector and trustees for the time being, always to be the judges of that number of children shall be taken in yearly and every year and their successors for ever and for all such purposes as aforesaid and under the mentioned several clauses DO WE JOHN WICKSELL, the present minister, John Lock, John Helms, Lawrence Lock, John Dierecson, Mounce Keen, James Steelman, Charles Case and Charles Dalbo, the Swedish church wardens and vestry-men grant, bargain and lease forever, as aforesaid the above mentioned and described lott of land, containing half an acre, with all and singular the rights, liberties privileges and ——————— for the use of a school, as aforesaid unto the said Thomas Denny, Esq. and Robert Brown the present chosen trustee of the school house and lots of land and to their lawful successors in said trust and ofices forever, for them lawfully, peacibly and quietly to have, hold, use and occupy and enjoy all the afore demised and granted premises, containing half and acre of land and every part and parcel thereof, with the houses and improvements thereon for the sole and several uses above mentioned, without any let. suit, trouble eviction molestation or interruption of them, the said John Wicksell, John Lock, John Helms, Lawrence Lock, John Dericson, Mounce Keen, James Steelman, Charles Case and Charles Dalbo or their successors or either of them or any other person or persons by, from, or under them, or their successors claiming or to in witness thereof the said parties have hereunto set their hands and seal of the corporation the day and year above written

JOHN WICKSELL R.
Sealed and Delivered⎫ Tho. Denny
in the presence of us⎰ Robert Brown
    Thomas James
    Joseph Davenport.

[ACCOUNTS OF THE SWEDESBORO SCHOOL 1771-72]

Here followeth the Article and list of subscriptions for the Public Schoolhouse at Swedesborough, intended to be buildt this summer in the year of our Lord 1771 of Stone, 33. by 23. foot dimention, one story high; under the special care and inspection of John Wicksel the present Rector, Thomas Denny Esqr., and Robert Brown, chosen managers and joint-trustees by the inhabitans and neighbourhood of Swedesborough, and by the unanimous voice of the respective subscribers, on the Town meeting day, in the year above mentioned. The article of subscription is as follows viz.

WHEREAS the neighbourhood of Swedesborough being quite destitute of a public schoolhouse, wherein may be taught reading, writting, arithmatick, and other useful knowledge, promoting humain and Christian Societies; The incorporation of the said borough in order to encurrage a such beneficial purpose for the public well, Hath therefore thought proper, to give a lease forever, for an half acre of ground in the said Borough, whereon a schoolhouse may be buildt, free for all christian denominations children there to be taught. And in case a such house, could not be buildt of stone, the said corporation is also willing to give as manny pine-logs or oak as shall be sufficient for the said purpose; and recommend the further provision and work in the most affectionate manner to the neighbouring inhabitants, and to all other charitable, generous and well disposed people to a speedy execution. And for such grant, the said corporation would be desirous, that two, three, four and more or less orphant children might yearly and forever have free schooling therein.

In consideration of the above motives, and by virtue of our own moving inclination and duty; Do we, the subscribers here beneath inhabitants in Woolwich Township near Swedesborough and elsewhere, subscribe each for himself, the several sums here affixed to our names, and promise to pay the same whenever the monney shall be wanted, to the managers of the same work, who shall, or were as above mentioned chosen, by the subscribers and promoters of this design or praiseworthy undertaking. We likewise who live in this neighbourhood engage ourselves to help to break the stones, or to cut and haul the logs and other materials requisite, according to our several abilities and circumstances. On the other side followeth the subscription itself —

	£	Sh.	D.		£	Sh.	D.
John Wicksell the pres. Rector	4	0	0	George Sommerwill	0	10	0
				Jacob Madeira	0	7	6
The Revd. Andrew Joranson Rect. of Vicacoa	1	0	0	Gabriel Dalbou	1	0	0
				Jacob Mullica	0	10	0
The Revd. Law. Girelius Rect: of Christine	1	0	0	Conrade Shoemaker	0	15	0
				Abram Keen	0	15	0
				Andrew Halten	0	15	0
The Rev. Niclas Collin	1	0	0	William Homan	1	0	0
Abram Jones Esqr. at M. River	1	0	0	John Roberson	0	7	6
				Peter Keyer	1	0	0
				John Adams	0	15	0

	£	Sh.	D.		£	Sh.	D.
Robbert Brocon	2	0	0	John Scott	1	0	0
Jacob Spicer	2	0	0	John Kille	1	0	0
Isaac V. Neuman	3	0	0	William Watson	1	0	0
James Talman	2	0	0	Thomas Batten	1	0	0
Thomas James	2	0	0	Andrew Jones	1	0	0
Prisehilla Harrison	1	10	0	William Key	1	0	0
Constantine Wilikens	1	5	0	Nathan Lane	0	7	6
Doctor Bodo Otto Senr.	2	0	0	William Estleack	0	15	0
Joseph Devenport	0	15	0	Asa Beck	0	5	0
Silas Lord	0	15	0	Edward Andrews	0	5	0
Uriah Paul	1	0	0	John Keen	0	7	6
William Kille	0	15	0	William Morgan	0	10	0
Andrew Matsson	1	0	0	Isaac Zane	0	5	0
Simon Harwood	0	7	6	William Ware	0	7	6
Lawrence Strang Junr.	0	7	6	Adam Shytz	0	7	6
John Gill	0	15	0	Thomas Schute	0	7	6

	£	Sh.	D.		£	Sh.	D.
Lawrence Friend	0	5	0	Aleseander Ware	1	0	0
Zebulon Peirsson	0	15	0	Wm. Zanes	1	0	0
Benjamin Cowgill	0	5	0	Isaace Zane	0	10	0
John Fouraires	1	0	0	James Lord	0	7	6
Isaac Justisson	0	10	0	Nathan Horner	0	7	6
James Mathewes	1	0	0	Henry Guest	0	7	6
Simon Linnard	0	15	0	Samuel Teenken	1	0	0
Ebenasser Cook	0	10	0	Gabriel Steeng	0	5	0
John Molloy	0	10	0	Robbert Russel	1	0	0
John Lock—payed by hauling	0	10	0	John Smith	0	5	0
Garret Cavener	0	7	6	James Franklin	0	5	0
Joseph Rice	0	7	6	Friedrick Bullinger	0	7	6
Hendrick Hindrickson	0	10	0	Jno. Richards	0	7	6
David Hindrickson	0	10	0	George Clarck	1	0	0
Perry Ledden	0	15	0	James Steelman	1	0	0
Abram Lord	0	10	0	Robbert Clarck	1	0	0
John Hatten	0	7	6	Peter Homan	1	0	0
Robbert Tayler	0	15	0	Charles Dalbou	0	10	0
Thomas Budd	0	15	0	John Helms Junr.	0	10	0
James Russet	0	7	6	John More 20 load stones	1	0	0
Samuel Stag	0	15	0	Wm. England Sr. Freight	1	2	6
John Richards	0	7	6				
Joseph Richards	0	7	6				

1772—The 27th day of October did the rector ride about in this neighbourhood and got following subscription monney towards buying of glass oil & putty for the school house windows at Swedesborough and for the putting in the said glasses, for hinches to the big writing table, and for a new writting desk for the master viz.

	£	S.	D.		£	S.	D.
John Wicksell p. rec.	0	12	0	George Avis	0	7	6
Moses Cleva	0	5	0	William England	0	5	0
Neigh Maguire	0	1	0	Peter Freyer	0	3	9
Aron Albersson	0	3	0	Samuel Black	0	5	0

	£	Sh.	D.		£	Sh.	D.
George Sommerwill __	0	2	0	Jonas Dalbou _____	0	2	6
Benjamin Thompson _	0	2	0	Jacob Matsson _____	0	2	6
Harrisson Wells _____	0	7	6	Robbert French _____	0	2	6
John Scott _____	0	5	0	John Rambo _____	0	2	6
Bodo Otto Junr. _____	0	2	0	Samuel Chester _____	0	2	6
Thomas Darcy _____	0	2	0	Joseph Schute _____	0	10	0
William Russell _____	0	2	6				

Now followeth the names of those, who with above or without their foregoing subscription have payed towards the said house by work, which turned into monney, after the present rate, amounts and is as followeth viz.

	£	Sh.	D.
William Homan one days hauling and two days digging --	1	1	0
Peter Lock & John, his brother, Rapapo 1 days hauling and digging, 2 days _____	1	1	0
Charles Cock one days hauling --------------------	0	15	0
Andrew Hindrickson one days hauling and two days dig. --	1	1	0
Peter Keyer two days hauling and one day digging __	1	13	0
William Matson one days hauling -----------------	0	15	0
Esajah Lock one days hauling and one days dig. ____	0	18	0
Isaac Justisson, Nathanael Tauders, Jacob Mattsson, Hugh Forbes, Thomas Adams, Hance Urian, Lawrence Lock, Deutch Engletown, William England and Jacob Linnard each of them one days digging at 3 shill: pr. day -----------------	1	10	0
Charles Steelman two days digging ----------------	0	6	0
Gabriel Dalbou one days digging -----------------	0	3	0
John Fouraire one days digging ------------------	0	3	0
Simon Linnard one days digging -----------------	0	3	0
Thomas England two days digging ----------------	0	6	0
Andrew Cock digging the foundation ------------	0	3	0
Erick Cock			
	96	1	3

No. 8 THE LEASE FOR JOHN RAMBO

THIS INDENTURE made the second day of April in the year of our Lord one thousand Seven hundred and seventy one by and between the Reverend John Wicksel. John Lock, John Helms, Lawrence Lock, John Derickson Mounce Keen, James Steelman Charles Cox, Charles Dolbo the present minister and church wardens, and vestry men of the Swedish Lutheran Church in the town of Swedsborough in the Township of Woolwich in the county of Gloucester and Province of West New Jersey elected and appointed minister church wardens and vestry men for the time being agreable to the directions of a Royal Charter granted to the Swedish Society at Raccoon Creek dated the twenty fifth day of October (1765) and enrolled in the Prerogatives office at Burlington in Lib: of Commitiens AAA Fol:) of the one part and John Rambo of the same place Tavern Keeper of the other part WITNESSETH that the said John Wicksell, John Lock, John Helms, Lawrence Lock, John Dereckson, Mounce Keen, James Stillman Charles Cox Charles Dolbo have by the power and strength of the several good assurances in the law as also in the charter above mentioned given to them and there successors, to sell and convey in fee forever, or to lease for year or years, under the yearly quitrents all or any of lands, belonging to said society in the same Province of West New Jersey for the benefit and behoof of the present minister & his successors NOW THIS INDENTURE WITNESSETH that the said John Wicksel John Lock John Helms, Lawrence Lock, John Derickson, Mounce Keen, James Stillman, Charles Cox, Charles Dolbo and the present minister church Wardens and Vestry men aforesaid have for and in consideration of the sum of three pounds ten shillings — of current money of the place aforesaid of quitrents to them and their successors, to be paid yearly and every year forever hereafter by the said John Rambo his heirs and assigns unto the said John Lock, John Helms, Lawrence Lock, John Derickson, Mounse Keen James Stillman Charles Cox Charles Dolbo or to either of them or either of their successors, in said office yearly forever they have granted bargained and leased by these presents do grant bargain sell and convey unto the said John Rambo his heirs and assigns forever, under the Quitrents aforesaid a certain lott of land situated in the town of Swedsborough on both the west and east sides of the main street or road leading through and the first lott is bounded as follows. BEGINING at a post by the main street or road and runs first north thirty degrees, West five chains and sixty links to a post in Hannah Ladds line then joining thereon — then joining thereon south sixty five degrees west one chain and eighty two links to a post then south thirty nine degrees east six chains to the main street aforesaid then up the same north fifty one degrees east one chain and seventy five links to the place of begining *containing one acre of land.* The second lott is situated on the south east side of the main street or road and is bounded as follows, begining at the side of the fast land of church run at a post in the line of Robert Brown's Lott and runs first by joining on the same north thirty nine degrees west five chains and ninety links to the said Browns Corner Post by the main street or road then up the same North fifty one degrees, east four chain to a post for a corner by the aforesaid street then south thirty nine degrees east four chain, and fifteen links to the edge of the swamp next to the run or flatts then joining up the edge aforesaid to the place of begining *containing two acres of land* and swamp being part and

[166]

parcel of the aforesaid land together with the free use of the street and allies and all and singular the rights liberties ways waters profits and appurtanances whatsoever to the said lotts or pieces of land belonging or in any ways appurtaining to have and to hold the said bargained lotts or pieces of land with the appurtenances unto the said John Rambo and his heirs and assigns and to and for the only use and behoof of the said John Rambo his heirs and assigns forever, without any apeachment for waste to the said John Rambo his heirs and assigns yealding and paying the before mentioned sum of *Three pounds ten shillings* currant lawful money unto the said body politick and corporate or to the then rector or to his or to his successors in said office in the manner aforesaid without reduction or abatement for any matter or thing whatsoever and that at one entirement payment on the twenty fifth day of March yearly in every year forever at such place in Swedesborough as by the body politick and corporate or their successors, in said office attorneys stewards baliffs, or deputies shall be yearly notified by publick advertisement set up in the town of Swedesborough aforesaid and if it shall so happen that the yearly quitrents of three pounds and ten shillings as aforesaid or any part thereof shall be in arrear and unpaid by the space of five days, next after either of the days, herein before limited and appointed for the payment thereof as aforesaid that then and shall be lawfull to and for the said body, politick and corporate their successors their attorneys stewards baliffs or deputies into the said granted premisses or any part thereof to enter and distrain and the distresses then or there found to carry lead or drive and take away impound apraise and sell and the moneys arising by such and due to apply towards the satisfaction and payment of the said quitrents and disstress detinue and cost thereof returning the overplus to the owner if any there be and if no such disstress can be found on the said premisses sufficient to be paid and satisfie the said quit rents so in arrears and cost as aforesaid that then it shall and may be lawful to and for the said body politick and corporate or to their successors as aforesaid the said sum of three pounds ten shillings — on the day and times aforesaid for the payment thereof without any abatement thereof or deduction whatsoever and lastly the said body politick and corporate for themselves and successors as aforesaid do hereby covenant grant and agree to and with the said John Rambo his heirs and assigns by those presents the said John Rambo his heirs and assigns paying and performing the covenant and agreements herein contained and which he or they ought to pay and perform shall and may lawfully peaceably have hold use occupy and enjoy all the aforesaid demissed lotts of land containing three acres and every part and parcel thereof without any lett suit trouble eviction molestation or interuption of the said John Wicksell John Lock, John Helms, Lawrence Lock, John Derickson, Mounse Keen, James Stillman Charles Cock, Charles Dalbo or either of their successors or any other person or persons by from or under them or their successors IN WITNESS whereof the said parties have here unto interchangebly sett their hands and seals of the corporation the day and date above written.

SEALED AND DELIVERED
in the presence of us

Peter Lock
John Vandike

It is farther agreed that the said John Rambo his heirs or assigns shall build or cause to be built a suitable house for a town and other improvements on said lots within the space of two years from the date hereof as shall sufficiently secure the said ground rent of the said lots and from time to time keep the same in good repair.

John Rambo.

No. 9 LEASE FOR ABRAM KEEN

THIS INDENTURE made the second day of April in the year of our Lord one thousand seven hundred and Seventy one by and between the Rev. John Wicksel, John Lock, John Helms, Lawrence Lock, John Derickson Mounce Keen James Stillman Charles Cock Charles Dolboe the present minister church wardens and vestry men of the Swedish Lutheran Church in the town of Swedsborough in the Township of Woolwich in the county of Gloucester and Province of West New Jersey elected and appointed minister church wardens and vestry men for the time being agreable to the directions of a Royal Charter granted to the Swedish Society at Raccoon Creek dated the twenty fifth day of October (1765) and enrolled in the prerogatives office at Burlington in Lib. of commitions AAA folio of the one part and Abraham Keen of the same place Taylor of the other part WITNESSETH that the said John Wicksel. John Lock, John Helms, Lawrence Lock, John Derickson Mounce Keen James Stillman Charles Cock Charles Dolboe have by the power and strength of the several good assurances in the law as also in the charter above mentioned given to them and their successors, to sell and convey in fee forever or to lease for year or years under the yearly quit rents all or any of lands belonging to the said Society in the same province of West New Jersey for the benefitt and behoof of the present minister and his successors, NOW THIS INDENTURE WITNESSETH, that the said John Wicksell, John Lock John Helms, Lawrence Lock, John Derickson Mounce Keen James Steelman Charles Cock. Charles Dolboe and the present minister church wardens and vestry men aforesaid have for and in consideration of the sum of twenty shillings of currant money of the place aforesaid of quitrents to them and their successors, to be paid yearly and forever and hereafter by the said Abraham Keen his heirs and assigns, unto the said John Lock John Helms Lawrence Lock John Derickson Mounce Keen James Stillman Charles Cock Charles Dolboe or to either of them or to either of their successors, in said office yearly for ever they have granted bargained and leased by those presents do grant bargain and sell and convey unto the said Abraham Keen his heirs and assigns forever under the Quit rents aforesaid a certain lott of land situated in the Town of Swedesborough on the west side of the main street or road leading through the same and is bounded as follows BEGINING at John Rambo's corner post by the main street or road and runs first joining on John Rambo's lott north thirty nine degrees west six chains to the said Rambo's other corner post in the line of Hannah Ladds, land then joining thereon south sixty two degrees west one chain and seventy links to a post in said line then south thirty nine degrees east six chain and forty links to a post by the main street or road then up the same north fifty one degrees east one chain and sixty five links to the place of, begining *containing one acre* of land together with free use of the street and allies and all singular the rights liberties, privilidges ways waters, proffits and appurtenances whatsoever to the said lott or piece of land belonging or in any ways appertaining to have and to hold the said bargained lott or piece of land with the appertenances unto the said Abraham Keen his heirs and assigns and to and for the only use and behoof of the said Abraham Keen his heirs and assigns forever without any appeachment for waste of the said Abraham Keen his heirs and assigns yeilding and paying the before mentioned sum of *Twenty Shillings* currant lawful money unto the said Body, Politick and corporate or to the then Rector or to his successors in the said office in manner aforesaid without any reduction or abbatement for any matter or thing whatsoever and that at one entire payment on the twenty fifth day of March yearly in every year forever hereafter at such place in Swedsborough as by the body politick and corporate or their successors in said office attorneys stewards baliffs or deputies shall be notified by Publick advertisement set up in the Town of Swedsborough aforesaid and if it shall so happen that the yearly quitrents of Twenty shillings as aforesaid or any part thereof shall be in arrear and unpaid in the space of five days, next after either of the days herein before limited and appointed for the payment thereof as aforesaid that then it shall and may be lawful to and for the said body politick and corporate their successors their attornies stewards bailiffs or deputies into the said granted premises or any part thereof to enter and distrain and the distresses then or there found to carry lead or drive and take away impound apraise and sell and the moneys arising by such and due to apply towards the satisfaction and payments of the said Quitrents and distress detinue and cost thereof returning the overplus to the owner if any there be and if no such distress can be found on the said premises sufficient to be paid and satisfy the said quit rents so in arrears and cost as foresaid that then it shall and may be lawful to and for the said body politick and corporate or to their successors as aforesaid for the payment thereof without any abatement thereof or deduction whatsoever and lastly that said body politick and corporate for themselves and successors, as aforesaid do hereby covenant grant and agree to and with the said Abraham Keen his heirs and assigns by those presents the said Abraham Keen his heirs and assigns paying and performing the covenants and agreements herein contained and which he or they ought to pay and perform shall and may lawfully peaceably and quietly have hold use occupy and enjoy all the aforesaid demised lott of land containing one acre and every part and parcel thereof without any lett suit trouble eviction molestation or interuption of the said John Wicksel John Lock, John Helms, Lawrence Lock, John Derickson, Mounce Keen James Stillman Charles Cock Charles Dolboe or either of their successors or any other person or persons by from or under them or their successors IN WITNESS THEREOF the said parties have here: unto interchangeably sett their hands and seals of the corporation the day and year first above written.

SEALED AND DELIVERED
    in the presence of us

ABRAHAM KEEN.

    NB. It is further agreed upon that the said abraham Keen his heirs or assigns shall build or cause to be built a suitable house for a town or other improvements on said lott within the space of two years from the date hereof as shall sufficiently secure the ground rent of said lott and from time to time to keep the same in good repair.
        THOMAS JAMES
        JOHN VANDIKE

No. 10 LEASE TO JOHN VANDIKE

THIS INDENTURE made the second day of April in the year of our Lord one thousand seven hundred and seventy one between the Rev: John Wicksel John Lock, John Helms, Lawrence Lock, John Derickson Mounce Keen James Stillman Charles Cock Charles Dolboe the present minister and Church wardens and vestry men of the Sweedish Lutheran Church in the Town of Sweedsborough in the Township of Woolwich in the county of Gloucester and Province of West New Jersey elected and appointed minister church wardens and vestry men for the time being agreable to a Royal Charter granted to the Sweedish Society at Raccoon Creek dated the twenty fifth day

[170]

of October (1765) and enrolled in the Prerogatives office at Burlington in Lib of Commitions AAA follio of the one part and John Vandike of the same place carpenter of the other part WITNESSETH that the said John Wicksel John Lock John Helms Lawrence Lock John Derickson Mounce Keen James Stillman Charles Cock Charles Dolboe, have by the power and strength of the several good assurances in the law as also in the charter above mentioned given to them and their successors, to sell and convey in fee forever or to lease for year or years under the yearly quit rents all or any of lands belonging to said society in same province of West New Jersey for the benefitt and behoof of the present minister and his successors NOW THIS INDENTURE Witnesseth that the said John Wicksel John Lock, ohn Helms, Lawrence Lock, John Derickson Mounce Keen James Stillman Charles Cock, Charles Dolboe and present minister chudch Wardens and Vestry men, aforesaid have for and in consideration of the sum of twenty shillings currant money of the place aforesaid of quitrents to them and their successors, to be paid yearly and every year for ever hereafter by the said John Vandick his heirs and assigns unto the said John Lock John Helms Lawrence Lock John Derexson Mounse Keen James Stillman Charles Cock Charles Dolboe, or to either of them or to either of their successors in said office yearly forever they have granted bargained and leased and by these presents do grant bargain sell and convey unto the said John Vandick his heirs and assigns forever under the quitrents aforesaid a certain lott of land situated in the town of Sweedsborough on the West side of the main street or road leading through the same and bounding as follows—BEGINNING at a corner of the schoolhouse lott and runs first joining on the same north thirty nine degrees west five chain and twenty links to a post corner to said schoolhouse lott then joining on Hannah Ladds land south sixty five degrees west two chain to a post corner to John Rambo's lott then joining thereon south thirty nine degrees, east five chain and sixty links to said Rambo's corner post to the main street or Salem road aforesaid then joining on the same north fifty one degree east one chain eighty five links to the place of begining in which bounds is contained one acre of land being part and parcel of the aforesaid land together with the free use of the street and allies and all and singular the rights liberties priviledges ways waters appurtenances whatsoever to the said piece of land belonging or in any ways appurtaining to have and to hold the said bargained lott or piece of land with the appurtenances unto the said John Vandick and his heirs and assigns and to and for the only use and behoof of the said John Vandike his heirs and assigns forever without any appeachment for waste. He the said John Vandick his heirs and assigns yeilding and paying the before mentioned sum of twenty shillings currant lawful money unto the said body politick and corporate or to the then Rector or to his successors in the said office in manner aforesaid without any reduction or abatement for any matter or thing whatsoever and that at one entire payment on the twenty fifth day of March yearly in every year for ever hereafter at such place in Sweedsborough as by the Body, Politick and corporate or their successors, in said office attorney stewards bailiffs or deputies, shall be yearly notified by Publick advertisement set up in the town of Sweedsborough aforesaid and if it shall so happen that the yearly quitrents of twenty shillings as aforesaid or any part thereof shall be in arrear and unpaid by the space of five days, next after either of the days herein before limitted and appointed for the payment thereof as aforesaid that then it shall and may be lawfull to and for the said body, politick and corporate there successors their attorneys stewards bailiffs or deputies into the said granted premisses or any part thereof to enter and distrain and the distresses then or there found to carry lead or drive and take away impound apraise and sell and the moneys arising from such and due to apply towards the satisfaction and payment of the said quitrents and distress detinue and cost thereof returning the overplus to the owner if any there be and if no such distress can be found on the said premisses sufficient to be paid and satisfied the said quitrents so in arrears, and cost as aforesaid that then it shall and may be lawful to and for the said body politick and corporate or their successors, as aforesaid the said sum of twenty shillings, on the day and times as aforesaid for the payment thereof without any abatement thereof or deduction whatsoever and lastly the said body politick and corporate for themselves and successors as aforesaid do hereby covenant grant and agree to and with the said John Vandike his heirs and assigns paying and performing the covenant and agreements herein contained and which he or they ought to pay and perform shall and may lawfully peaceably and quitely have hold use occupy and enjoy all the aforesaid demised lott of land containing one acre and every part or parcel thereof without any sett suit trouble eviction molestation or interuption of the said John Wicksel John Lock John Helms Lawrence Lock, John Derickson Mounce Keen. James Stillman, Charles Cock, Charles Dolboe or either of their successors or any other person or persons by from or under them or their successors IN WITNESS whereof the said parties have hereunto interchangeabley sett their hands and seals of the corporation the day and year first above written.

SEALED AND DELIVERED
    in the presence of us   JOHN VANDIKE.

It is further agreed upon that the said John Vandike his heirs or assigns shall build or cause to be built a suitable house for a town or other improvements on said lott within the space of two years from the date hereof as shall

sufficiently secure the ground rent of
the said lott and from time to time to
keep the same in good repair.
                THOMAS JAMES
                ABRAHAM KEEN

No. 11   LEASE TO ASA BECK

THIS INDENTURE made the second day of April in the year
of our Lord one thousand seven hundred and seventy by and between
the Reverend John Wicksel. John Lock, John Helms, Lawrence Lock,
John Derexson Mounse Keen James Stillman Charles C o c k
Charles Dolboe the present Minister and church wardens and vestry
men of the Sweedish Lutheran Church in the town of Sweedsborough
in the township of Woolwich in the county of Gloucester and province
of West New Jersey — Elected and appointed minister church wardens and vestry men for the time being agreable to the directions of
a Royal Charter granted to the Sweedish Society at Raccoon Creek
dated the 25th day of October (1765) and inrolled in the Prerogatives
office at Burlington in Lib. of Commitiens AAA folio of the one part
and Asa Beck of the same place, carpenter of the other part, WIT-
NESETH that the said John Wicksel, John Lock, John Helms, Lawrence Lock, John Derexson Mounse Keen James Stillman Charles
Cock, Charles Dolboe have by the power and strength of the several
good assurance in the law as also in the charter above mentioned given
to them and their successors, to sell and convey in free forever or to
lease for year or years, under the yearly quit rents all or any of lands
belonging to said society in the same Province of West New Jersey
for the benifitt and behoof of the present minister and his successors—
NOW THIS INDENTURE witnesseth that the said John Wick-
sel John Lock John Helms Lawrence Lock John Dericson, Mounce
Keen James Stillman Charles Cock Charles Dolboe and the present
minister church wardens and Vestry men aforesaid have for and in
consideration of the sum of Twenty Shillings of currant money of
the place aforesaid of Quitrents to them and their successors to be
paid yearly and every year for ever hereafter by the said Asa Beck
his heirs and assigns unto the said John Lock John Helms Lawrance Lock, John Derexson Mounse Keen James Stelman Charles
Cock. Charles Dolboe or either of them or either of their successors
in said office yearly forever they have granted bargained and leased
and by those presents do grant bargain sell and convey unto the said
Asa Beck his heirs and assigns forever under the Quitrents aforesaid
a certain lott of land situated in the town of Sweedsborough on the
West side of the Main street or Road leading through the same and
bounded as follows begining at a post corner to Abraham Keens lott
and runs north thirty nine degrees, West six chains and forty links

[173]

to said Keens other corner post in the line of Hannah Ladds land then joining thereon south sixty five degrees west one chain and sixty links to a corner of Thomas Denny's lott then joining thereon south thirty nine degrees east six chain and eighty links to the main street or Salem road then up the same north fifty one degrees east one chain and fifty five links to the place of begining containing one acre of land strict measure together with the free use of the street and Allies and all and singular the rights liberties, privilideges ways waters proffits and appurtenances whatsoever to the said lott or piece of land belonging or in anyways appurtaining to have and to hold the said bargained lott or piece of land with the appurtenances unto the said Asa Beck and his heirs and assigns forever without any appeachement for waste to the said Asa Beck his heirs and assigns yeilding and paying the before mentioned Sum of Twenty shillings currant lawful money unto the said Body, Politick, and corporate or to the then Rector or to his successors in the said office in manner aforesaid without any reduction or abatement for any matter or thing whatsoever, and that atone entire payment on the twenty fifth day of March yearly in every year forever hereafter at such place in Sweedsborough as by the Body, Politick and corporate or their successors in said office attorneys Stewards Bailiffs or deputies shall be yearly notified by public advertisement sett up in the town of Sweedsborough aforesaid and if it shall so happen that the yearly quitrents of *Twenty Shillings* as aforesaid or any part thereof shall be in arrear and unpaid by the space of five days next after either of the days herein before limited and appointed for the payment thereof as aforesaid that then it shall and may be lawful to and for the said body politick and corporate their successors their attornies stewards bailiffs or deputies into the said granted premisses or any part thereof to enter and distrain and the distress then or their to be bound to carry lead or drive or take away impound apraise and sell and the moneys arising by such and due to apply towards the satisfaction and payment of the said Quitrent and distress detinue and cost thereof returning the overplus to the owner if any there be and if nosuch distress can be found on the said premises to be paid and satisfy the said Quitrents so in arrears, and cost as aforesaid that then it shall and may be lawful to and for the said body politick and corporate or their successors, as aforesaid the said sum of Twenty shillings on the day and times aforesaid for the payment thereof without any abatement or reduction thereof whatsoever and lastly that said body, Politick and corporate for themselves and successors as aforesaid do hereby covenant grant and agree to and with the said Asa Beck his heirs and assigns by those presents the said Asa Beck his heirs and asigns paying and performing the covenants and agreements herein contained and which he or they ought to pay and perform shall and may lawfully peaceably and quitely have hold use, occupy and enjoy all the aforesaid demissed lott of land containing one acre and every part and parcel thereof without any lett suit trouble eviction molestation or interuption of the said John Wicksel John Lock, John Helms Lawrance Lock, John Derexson Mounce Keen James Stillman Charles Cock, Charles Dolboe or either of their successors or any person or persons by from or under them or their successors, IN WITNESS whereof the said parties have hereunto interchangeably sett their hand, and seals of the corporation the day and year first above written.   ASA BECK.

SEALED AND DELIVERED
    in the presence of us
It is further agreed upon that the said Asa Beck his heirs or assigns shall build or cause to be built a suitable house for a town or other improvements on said lott within the space of two years from the date hereof as shall sufficiently secure the said ground rent of the said and from time to time to keep the same in good repair.
      THOMAS JAMES
      JOHN VANDIKE

LEASE TO ROBERT BROWN

THIS INDENTURE made the second day of April in the year of our Lord one thousand seven hundred and seventy one by and between the Reverend John Wicksel John Lock John Helms, Lawrence Lock, John Derexson Mounse Keen James Stillman Charles Cock Charles Dolboe, the present minister church Wardens and vestry men of the Sweedish Lutheran Church in the Town of Sweedsborough in the township of Woolwich in the county of Gloucester and province of West New Jersey elected and appointed minister church wardens and vestry men for the time being agreable to the directions of a Royal Charter granted to the Sweedish Society at Raccoon Creek dated the Twenty fifth day of October (1765) and enrolled in the Proragatives office at Burlington in Lib. of Commitions AAA follio of the one part and Robert Brown of the same place gentleman shopkeeper of the other part WITNESSETH that the said John Wicksel John Lock, John Helms Lawrence Lock, John Derexson Mounse Keen James Stillman, Charles Cock, Charles Dolboe have by the power and strength of the several good assurance in the law as also in the charter above mentioned given to them and their successors to sell and convey in fee forever or to lease for year or years, under the yearly Quitrents all or any of the land, belonging to the said society in the same province of West New Jersey for the benefitt and behoof of the present minister and his successors. NOW THIS INDEN-

TURE witnesseth that the said John Wicksell John Lock John Helms Lawrence Lock, John Derexson Mounse Keen James Stillman Charles Cock, Charles Dolboe and the present minister church wardens and vestry men aforesaid have for and in consideration of the sume of,   Currant money of the place aforesaid of quit rents to them and their successors to be paid yearly and every for ever hereafter by the said Robert Brown his heirs and assigns unto the said John Lock, John Helms, Lawrence Lock, John Derexson Mounse Keen James Stillman Charles Cock, Charles Dolboe or to either of them or to either of their successors, in said office yearly forever they have granted bargained and leased, by those presents do grant bargain sell and convey unto the said Robert Brown his heirs and assigns forever under the Quit rents aforesaid a certain lott of land situated in the Town of Sweedsborough on the east side of the main street or road leading through the same and is bounded as followeth, begining at a post corner to Thomas Jame's lott and runs first joining thereon south thirty nine degrees, east three chain and ninety links to the water course of a small branch of church run to a post then down the same north seventy two degrees east eighty five links to a post, then South eighty nine degrees east three chain and sixty five links to a sassafras for a corner then north eighteen degrees east eighty links to John Rambo's Corner then joining thereon North thirty nine degrees west six chain and thirty eight links to the main street, then down the same south fifty one degrees west three chain and eighty five links to the begining *containing two acres of land* and meadow ground together with the free use of the street and allies and all and singular the rights liberties, priviledges ways waters proffits and appurtenances whatsoever to the said lott or piece of land belonging or in any ways apertaining to have and to hold the said bargained lott or piece of land with the appertenances unto the said Robert Brown and his heirs and assigns and to and for the only use and behoof of the said, Robert Brown his heirs and assigns forever without any apeachment for waste to the said Robert Brown his heirs and assigns yeilding and paying the before mentioned sum of Fifty Shillings currant lawfull money unto the said Body, Politick, and corporate or to the then Rector or to his successors, in the said office in manner aforesaid without any Reduction or abatement for any matter or thing whatsoever and that at one entire payment on the Twenty fifth day of March yearly in every year forever hereafter at such place in Swedesborough as by the body politick and corporate or their successors in said office attorneys stewards Bailiffs or deputies shall be yearly notified by public advertisement sett up in the Town of Sweedsborough aforesaid and if it shall so happen that the yearly quitrents of fifty shillings as aforesaid or any part thereof shall be in arrears and unpaid by the space of five days, next after either of the days, herein before limited and appointed for the payment thereof as aforesaid that then it shall and may be lawfull to and for the said body, Politick and corporate their successors their attorneys stewards Bailiffs or deputies into the said granted premises or any part thereof to enter and distrain and the distress there found to carry lead or drive and take away impound apraise and sell and the moneys arising by such and due to apply towards the satisfaction and payments of the said Quitrents and distress detinue and cost thereof returning the overplus to the owners if any there be and if no such distress can be found on the said premises sufficient to be paid and satisfy the said quitrents so in arrears and cost as aforesaid that then it shall and may be lawfull to and for the said body politick and corporate or to their successors as aforesaid the sum of fifty shillings on the day and times as aforesaid for the payment thereof without any abatement thereof or deduction whatsoever and lastly the said body politick and corporate for themselves and successors, as aforesaid do hereby covenant grant, and agree to and with the said Robert Brown his heirs and assigns by those presents the said Robert Brown his heirs and assigns paying and performing the covenants and agreements herein contained and which he or they ought to pay and perform shall and may lawfully peaceably and quitely have hold use occupy and enjoy all the aforesaid demised lott of land containing two acres — and every part and parcell thereof without any lett suit trouble eviction molestation or interuption of the said John Wicksell John Lock, John Helms, Lawrence Lock, John Derexson, Mounse Keen James Steelman Charles Cock Charles Dolboe or either of their successors or any other person or persons by from or under them or their successors. IN WITNESS whereof the said parties have hereunto interchangeably sett their hands and seals of the corporation the day and year first above written. ROBERT BROWN.

SEALED AND DELIVERED
    in the presence of us
  NB. It is hereby agreed on that the said Robert Brown his heirs or assigns shall Build or cause to be built one and or either of the lotts which he holds in Sweedsborough such building or Improvements as shall secure the rents of the whole lotts he now possesses and keep the same from time to time in good repair.
      THOS. DENNY
      THOMAS JAMES

    The 19th day of December in the year of our Lord, 1771 came Thomas Petersson from Mauritzes River, to me, & of his own accord offered to subscribe five pound, currency towards building of a new

Church at Racoon Creek in Swedesborough, and payed down into my hands two dahlers on the said Sum, as an earnest. For which sum I am accountable to the Respective Vestry of this congregation. And to this note of obligation he then put his hand and name in the presence of Nicholas Collin.　　　　　　　　　　Thomas his Petersson.
John Wicksell P.R.

　　The said money is deposited in my hands by the Rvd. Mr. John Wixell the 27 Aug. 1773.　　　　　　　　　　Nicholas Collin.

No. 13　JOHN RAMBO

　　THIS INDENTURE made the nineteenth day of August in the year of our Lord one thousand seven hundred and seventy three by and between the Reverend John Wicksell and John Lock John Helms John Derickson Lawrence Lock James Steelman and Mounce Keen Charles Cox and Charles Dalbo present minister and church wardens and Vestry men of the Swedish Lutheran Church in the Town of Sweedsborough in the Township of Woolwich in the county of Gloucester and Western Division of the province of New Jersey of the one part elected and appointed minister and church Wardens and vestry men for the time being agreable to a Royal Charter granted to the Swedish Society at Raccoon Creek in the said Township bearing date the Twenty fifth day of October (1765) and inrolled in the Prerogative Court office at Burlington in Libr. of Commns. AAA folio (　) of the one part and John Rambo of the Township of Woolwich and County and Province aforesaid of the other part. WITNESSETH that the said John Wicksell John Lock John Helms John Derickson Lawrence Lock James Steelman Mounce Keen Charles Cox Charles Dalbo aforesaid hath by the power force and effect of the several good assurances in the law as also in the said charter to them and their successors given to lease and confirm forever or for year or years under yearly Quit Rents all or any of their lands belonging to the said society in the said Province of West New Jersey for the benefit and behoof of the minister and his successors in the said office legally qualified and approved of agreably to said Charter NOW THIS INDENTURE WITNESSETH that the said John Wicksell John Lock John Helms John Derickson Lawrence Lock, James Steelman Mounce Keen Charles Cox and Charles Dalbo the present Minister and church wardens and vestry men aforesaid have for and in consideration of the sum of twenty shillings current Lawful money of the said Province to them in hand paid or to their successors in the said office of Quit Rent to be paid yearly and every year for ever hereafter by the said John Rambo his heirs or assigns unto the said John Wicksell John Lock John Helms John Derickson Lawrence Lock James Steelman Mounce Keen Charles Cox and Charles Dalbo or to either of them or to either of their successors in said office yearly and forever, they have granted bargained leased and by these presents do grant bargain lease and confimr unto the said John Rambo and to his heirs and assigns forever under the yearly quit rents as aforesaid A certain lott or tract of land situated in the town of Sweedsborough in the place aforesaid on the East side of the main road called Salem Road being part and parcel of the lands belonging to the said society butted and bounded as followeth: Beginning at a beach for a corner standing by Racoon Creek and bounded on the said road from thence south east twenty degrees two chain to a large black oak for a third corner from thence north fifty degrees east one chain and twenty five links to a post for a fourth corner standing by the aforesaid creek thence down said creek to the first mentioned beach containing thirty eight perches of ground strict measure be the same more or less taking in the whole front on the creek from the King's road up to the said lott together with all and singular the Mines Minerals fishings fowlings huntings pastures libertys priviledges ways waters profits and appurtenances whatsoever to the said lott or piece of land and leased ground belonging or in any wise appertaining. TO HAVE AND TO HOLD the said leased lott of land and premises with the appurtenances thereto belonging unto the said John Rambo and to his heirs and assigns forever without any impeachment for waste, he the said John Rambo his heirs or assigns yielding and paying the before mentioned sum of twenty shillings Current lawful money — unto the said Body Politic and Corporate or to the Rector or to his or their successors in said office or either of them in manner aforesaid without any Deduction or Abatement for any matter or thing whatsoever and that in one entire payment on the Nineteenth day of August next ensuing the date hereof — yearly and ever year forever hereafter at such place in Sweedsborough as by the Body Politick and Corporate and their successors in said office their Attorneys Bailiffs or Deputies shall be notified by a Publick Advertisement set up in the said town of Sweedsborough and if it should so happen that the yearly quit rents of the sum of twenty shillings as aforesaid or any part thereof shall be in arrear and unpaid for the space of five days next after any of the said days herein before limited and appointed for the payments aforesaid that then it shall and may be lawful to and for the said body politic and corporate and their successors their attorneys, stewards bailiffs or deputies into the said leased premises or any part thereof to enter and distrain for the rent then due and the distrees there found to carry lead drive and take away impound appraise and sell and the money arising from such sale and due to apply towards the satisfaction and payment of the Quit Rents and distress detinue and cost thereof returning the overplus to the owner if any be found and if no such distress can be found on the said premises sufficient to pay and satisfy the said quit rent so in arrear and the cost thereof that then it is covenanted by the between the said

[179]

parties that it shall be lawful to and for the said Body Politic and corporate their successors attorneys Bailiffs or deputies to take all lawful ways and means for the recovery thereof or to reenter the said premises and the said John Rambo doth hereby for himself and his heirs and assigns further covenant grant and agree to and with the said Body, Corporate and Politic and their successors in manner following that is to say John Rambo doth hereby for himself and his heirs and assigns further covenant grant and agree to and with the said Body Corporate and Politic and their successors in manner following that is to say John Rambo his heirs and assigns shall and will from time to time and at all times forever hereafter pay or cause to be paid to the aforesaid body politic and corporate or to their successors aforesaid the said sum of Twenty shillings of current lawful money on the day and time aforesaid for the payment thereof without any abatement or deduction thereof whatsoever. AND also shall build a dwelling house, or other suitable improvements answering or sufficient to secure the ground rent of the said lot and the same to keep in constant repair forever, on said lott or cause it to be builded within the space of two years next ensuing the date hereof lastly that the said body politic and corporate for themselves and their successors as aforesaid do hereby covenant grant and agree to and with the said John Rambo his heirs and assigns by these presents that the said John Rambo his heirs and assigns paying performing the covenants and agreements herein contained which he or they ought to perform shall and may lawfully peaceably quitely have hold use occupy and enjoy all the before said demised premises and lot of land containing thirty eight perches of land and premises and every part and parcel thereof without and lett suit trouble eviction molestation or interruption of the said John Wicksell John Lock John Helms John Derickson Lawrence Lock, James Steelman Mounce Keen Charles Cox Charles Dalbo or their successors or either of them or any other person or persons whatsoever by from or under them or their successors as aforesaid. IN WITNESS whereof the said Parties have hereunto interchangeably set their hands and seals the day and year first above written.   JOHN RAMBO.
SEALED AND DELIVERED
    in the presence of us
    JACOB JONES
    ISAAC JUSLANSON

No. 14 (not signed)   HANS COX—34 Perches [110]

THIS INDENTURE MADE   our Lord one thousand seven hundred seventy   by and between the Reverend Nicholas Collin, John Lock, John Helms, Lawrence Lock, John Derick-

[110] See footnote 75.

son Maurice Keen, James Steelman, Charles Cox, William Homan, the Present minister church wardens and vestry men of the Swedish Lutheran Church in the town of Swedesborough in the Township of Woolwich in the County of Gloucester and Province of West New Jersey: Elected and appointed minister, church wardens and vestrymen for the time present, agreeable to the direction of a Royal Charter granted to the Swedish Society at Racoon Creek dated the 25th day of Octobr: 1765 of the one part; and Hans Cox on the other part WITNESSETH, that the aforesaid minister, church wardens and vestrymen as a Body Politic and Corporate have for and in consideration of the sum of twelve shillings lawful money of New Jersey Quit Rents to be paid yearly and every year hereafter by the said Hanse Cox his heirs and assigns unto them or their successors in the said office, granted, bargained and leased, and do by these presents grant bargain, sell and convey unto the said Hanse Cox his heirs and assigns forever under the Quit rent aforesaid, a certain lot of land situated in the town of Swedesborough between the Churchyard and the wharf, and bounded as follows: Beginning at the Churchyard corner next the street it runs N 34 E 1.92 links on the hill side towards Mr. Browns landing; then N 20 W 1.14 along his wharf lot; then S 84 W 78 links to the corner of the churchyard, then S 43 2.63 links along the churchyard, containing thirty perches. Together with the free use of the street, and all the singular rights libertys profits and appertenances whatever to the said piece of land belonging, to have and to hold the same, to and for the only use and behoof of the said Hanse Cox his heirs and assigns forever, he or they yielding and paying the mentioned sum of Twelve shillings lawful money unto the said Body Politic or to the Rector or his successors without any reduction or abatement whatsoever, and that at one entire payment on the Twenty fifth day of March every year for ever hereafter at such place in Swedesborough as by the said Body Politic and corporate or their successors in said office, attorneys, Stewards, Bailifs, or deputys shall be yearly notifyd by Public advertisement, set up in the town aforesaid, and if it shall so happen that the said yearly quitrents of twelve shillings or any part thereof shall be in arrear and unpaid by the space of five days next after the day mentioned, it shall be lawfull for the said body politic and corporate, their successors, attorneys, stewards or deputies into the said granted premises or any part thereof to enter, and distrain, and the distresses there to be found to carry, lead, drive take away, impound appraise and sell, and the money arising by such to apply towards the satisfaction and payment of the said quitrents, and distress, detinue and cost thereof, and if no such distress can be found on the said premises, to pay the said quitrents so in arrear, and cost aforesaid, that then it shall be lawful for the said body politic, their successors, assigns of the said sum of twelve shillings on the day and time aforesaid without any abatement and deduction whatever by and

[181]

lawful means to recover, or reenter on the premises mentioned, and lastly that said body politic for themselves and successors do hereby covenant and agree with the said Hanse Cox, his heirs and assigns, that he and they shall lawfully peaceably and quietly have hold use and employ the said lot of land without any lett, or suit trouble, molestation of the said Nicholas Collin of or their successors and assigns, on condition of his and theirs paying and performing the covenants heretofore mentioned, and on condition of erecting a suitable dwelling house on the lot aforesaid, without delay, the same being stipulated three years ago when the said Hanse Cox first obtained the said lot from the Rector, Church Wardens and Vestrymen at that time being. In Witness hereof the said parties have interchangeably set their hands and seals the day and year above written.

ALEXANDER WEAR (not signed)

THIS INDENTURE made the twenty fourth day of March in the year of our Lord one thousand seven hundred seventy four between the Rvd. Nicholas Collin, John Lock, John Derickson, Lawrence Lock, John Hellms, Maunce Keen, James Stillman, Charles Cos, William Homan, the present Minister, church wardens and vestrymen of the Swedish Lutheran Church in the Town of Swedsborough, Township of Woolwich, County of Gloucester, Province of West New Jersey, elected and appointed minister church Wardens and Vestry men for the time present, agreeable to the direction of a Royal Charter, granted to the Swedish Society at Racoon Creek, dated the 25th day of October: one thousand seven hundred sixty five: of the one Party, and Alexander Wear of said township, county and Province aforesaid, of the other Party, WITNESSES; that the aforesaid minister, church wardens and vestrymen as a Body Politic and corporate have for and in consideration of the sum of Twelve shillings and six pense of lawful money of New Jersey Quitrents to be paid yearly and every year hereafter by him Alexander Wear, his heirs and assigns, unto them or their successors, in the said office, granted bargained and leased, and do by these presents grant bargain and lease sell and convey unto the said Alexander Wear his heirs and assigns under the quitrent aforesaid, a certain Lott of land situated in the town of Swedsborough on the east side of the Road, and bounded as follows: to wit: on two sides by the lots of John Rambou and Elizabeth Hopman, on the front by the said road, extending from thence down to the march, but not taking in any part of the same, containing half an acre of ground, with the free use of the street, and all and singular the rights, libertys, profits and appartenances whatever to the said piece of land belonging, to have and to hold the same to and for the only use and behoof of the said Alexander Wear, his heirs and assigns, he or they yielding and paying the above mentioned sum of twelve shillings and sixpence lawful money unto the said body politic, or to the Rector and his successors, without any abatement whatsoever and that at one entire payment on the twenty fifth day of March every year forever hereafter at such place in Swedsborough as by the said Body Politic and corporate or their successors in said office, attorneys, stewards, Bailiffs, or deputies shall be yearly notifyd by public advertisement set up in the town aforesaid, and if it shall so happen, that the said yearly quitrents of twelve shillings and sixpence or any part thereof shall be in arrear and unpaid by the space of five days next after the day mentioned it shall be lawful for the said Body Politic and corporate, their successors, attorneys, stewards or deputys, unto the said granted premises or any part thereof to enter and distrain, and the distresses there to be found to carry lead drive take away impound appraise and sell and the money arising by such to apply toward the satisfaction and payment of the said quit rents, and distress detinue and cost thereof: and if no such distress can be found, on the said premises to pay the said quitrents to in arrear and cost aforesaid, that then it shall be lawful for the said Body Politic their successors, assigns etc: the said sum of twelve shillings and sixpence on the time and days aforesaid without any abatement and deduction whatever by any law suit means to recover, or reenter on the premises mentioned. And lastly that said body politic for themselves and successors do hereby covenant and agree with the said Alexandre Wear his heirs and assigns, that he and they shall lawfully peaceably and quietly have hold use and employ the said lot of land without any let, suit, trouble or molestation of the said Nicholas and vestrymen, or their successors and assigns, on condition of erecting a suitable dwelling house on the lott aforesaid without delay: the same being stipulated three years ago when the said Alexander Wear first obtained the said lot from the Rector Church Wardens and Vestry men at that time being in witness thereof the said partys have interchangeably set their hands and seals the year and day above written.

Sealed and delivered
in the presence of us

[RACCOON AND PENNS NECK INVENTORY]

1773 September 30, The Dean, Rev. Johan Wicksell, having received a gracious recall to return home, did in conformity with the kindly Orders of the Very Reverend Cathedral Chaper at Upsala, resign from the pastorate of Racoon and Pensneck, in behalf of his now lawfully ordained successor, and beloved colleague, the Rev. Nils Collin, which duly took place in the Congregations of Racoon and Pensneck on the two preceding Sundays. The articles in the following Inventory were then found belonging to these Churches and Rectory at Racoon Church in Sweabork (Swedesboro), and they are now properly entrusted to him, namely:

Inventory belonging to the church of Racoon, to wit: An old Silver Chalice and Patene, (Plate), An old surplice, A baptismal bowl of pewter,

The great King Charles XIIth Church Bible, The great church Hymnbook in quarto, The large church service-book in the same size, The Charter for Incorporation around [environs of] Sweaborg, 3 Original deeds [or muniment] for the place in Piles Grove; for the place [ground] at Racoon Church, and for the marsh or meadow on Racoon Creek, The Lease for Sweaborg School house, Pastor Lidenius' Inventory and the parish-clerk, And. Hoffman's separate list of births, marriages and deaths.

Inventory belonging to the Rectory of Racoon: 1 old cope, 1 old Pulpit, an old kitchen bowl, an old book-case

[Belonging] to the Church: A good Spade, a mattock, a funeral line, an old Chest in the Church, mostly rotten.

BOOKS

Bishop's Getzelius' work on the *Old and New Testaments*. Dean Halenius' *Concordances*, 2 volumes. Olof Lin's *German and Swedish Lexicon*, gift of deceased Joh. Abr. Lidenius. 35 copies of Doctor Luther's great *Catechism*. Johan Arent's *True Christianity*, loaned during my time to the Lock, Bond, and V. Neuman families. Schriver's *Soul Treasure* [Själa Skatt] 5th volume. The other volumes were loaned out in the congregation before my time. An old *English Bible*, in quarto. The Church Record Book of Racoon and Pensneck from the year 1713, in folio. A New Book of Incorporation, in folio. One dito for the Accounts after this day, in folio.

The Inventory of Pensneck Church consists of the following few articles, namely: King Charles XII's *Large Church Bible*, in the keeping of William Dalbow. One *English Bible*, in Quarto. One Chalice and Patene of Pewter, with a glass, kept in the Church Chest. One English Hymn-book, in large octavo. An Altar cloth, in the keeping of the Church warden, John Beetle. A spade and funeral line.

ACCOUNTS OF THE NEW CHURCH

The old church, a log building erected in the year 1705,* and afterwards repaired from time to time, had for fifteen years been in a condition so ruinous, that public worship could not be celebrated in it without the greatest inconveniences, and no small degree of danger in tempestous weather. My worthy antecessor was prevented by a multiplicity of pressing affairs from commencing a new building; and the distresses of the war delayed it during my time til a late period. In the summer 1783 I turned my sollicitious attention to this important object. Every person acquainted with the present state of ecclesiastical affairs in America, must be sensible of the difficulty of such an enterprise; which morever was the greater in this case, as it was necessary on every principle of prudence and public spirit to form the new church on a plan suitable to the prospect of a future age. Its diminsions ought to correspond with the encrease of population for at least a century and its appearance with the gradual progress of taste in a country advancing fast to the modes of civilized life:— yet, neither the resources nor the general sentiments of the people were equal to my design.

---

*This asterisk refers to a footnote in the original book which appears in this volume on page 209.

The well known difficulty of collecting money even for small public objects, and consequently, the danger of a great undertaking, was so forcibly impressed on the mind of the vestry, that they would not be concerned therein as a body: Which was, however, their official duty. Therefore this trust devolved upon managers chosen by the subscribers; which though a necessary, was not a regular expedient. From the same timed diffidence several good members of the congregation refused their aid though they afterwards made large contributions. A majority of the managers were likewise so much influenced by these fears and other prejudices, that they would not consent to a larger seize than 50 feet by 40, until the trenches of the foundation, being actually dug, showed how small this ground plot really was; nor could without great difficulty be persuaded to allow the number and form of the windows, with other parts of the plan; which are indispensible for convenience, symmetry, and neat elegance after having for several months urged the necessity of the enterprize, both in private conversation and public adresses from the pulpit, I ventured to begin the subscription, and had the satisfaction to find about one thousand pounds subscribed within a few weeks. Upon this the managers ventured to proceed. In the autumn of the year 1783 a contract was made with Mr. Felix Fisler for the necessary quantity of bricks, to be made and delivered at the rate of one pound seventeen shil. 6 d. per thousand. Mr. Isaac van Neaman was also engaged to perform the mason work at the price of two dollars per thousand. He also agreed to furnish stone for the foundation at six shl. a perch. In the spring of the year 1784 Mr. Ezechiel Foster undertook the whole carpentry, and joiners work for the sum of three hundred pounds; stipulating exclusive payment for turning, and other extraordinary services incident to the business.

As the season advanced, the brick-makers begun their work, and continued til late in the autumn. The mason proceeded as the materials were furnished. The carpenter also carried on his business; the managers procuring the timber, planks, boards, etc. from different parts of neighbourhood, and principally from the city of Philadelphia. The season proving very sickly interrupted the several classes of workmen for some weeks. Never the less the work advanced by unwearied exertion so far, that the building was inclosed before Christmas.

Heavy rains in the late months spoiled a considerable quantity of bricks already hauled to the church. The approach of winter and want of money permitted not the purchase of a new supply. It was therefore necessary to contrive small ovens for drying such as were tolerable. I was myself very busy at this work many cold mornings and evenings by which I contracted a severe rheumatic disorder, which continued for a long time.

After all my painful efforts for the public good, I had the vexation to find the roof very leaky from a great number of holes.

This happened not from any defect in the shingles, which were of the best quality, and cost £10 shl. per 1000; but from the neglect of the carpenter, who, notwithstanding my repeated charges, depended too much on the young hands that assisted him.

In the Spring 1785 the carpenter returned, and continued til the month bf March 1786, though with different interruptions. He had then compleated the work according to contract; and previous to his departure made a final settlement with the managers, by which a ballance of sixty pound was found to be in his favour. The reason of this was that his account for extraordinary services, and occasional expenditures amounted to forty pounds, ten shillg. 11d. The principal articles charged were as follows—

	£	Sh.	Pc.
Cash paid out for 450 feet of five quarter board at 9 per thousand	4	1	0
Ditto for Sprigs, nails etc	1	11	0
Expense of journeys for the church	2	7	8½
Total in cash	7	19	8½
For those journeys	3	6	10
For turning the collumns under the galleries	8	0	0
Ditto those at the doors	0	12	0
For turning 522 banisters	10	9	9
Ditto turning caps and bells for the stairs and frontispices	0	18	6
Ditto two posts for the pulpit stairs	0	2	0
Total for turning	20	1	3
For altering the breastwork of the gallery	5	0	0

The remainder is for carting boards, scantling etc. taking out the scaffolding within the church, and for boring the collumns under the galleries. The reason of this operation was, that the posts were not seasoned, and therefore would have split into pieces, if they had not been thus bored, through by a long auger used for hollowing pumps.

(NB. As notwithstand they are all split from top to bottom. Green timber should never be introduced for such purposes.)

Again the altering of the breastwork round the galleries became necessary from the dull and heavy appearance of the boardwork, which was at first resolved upon as the cheapest. As the general account for extraordinaries was accepted by the managers at the time of the above mentioned final settlement and not particularly taken up in the accounts of Mr. Foster with Robert Brown Esq. and myself; I deem it most proper to mention it here with the principal ingredients. The sums paid by us to him, hereafter specified in the general account of receipts and expenditures for the church will amount to the total of £340 10 shil. 11 D. as Mr. Foster after all complained of a hard bargain a generous donation was also collected for him, though it has no concern with the contract, and therefore is not inserted. The carpentry, and joiners work of the church being indeed very extensive and multifarous, the gratuity bestowed on Mr. Foster was not superflous; yet his neglect of the roof can be forgiven only from a sense of his good intention.

From the beginning it was exceeding difficult to collect the subscriptions. In the Spring 1786 a considerable part remained unpaid; wherefore the managers were obliged to issue the following adress— "It is nearly three years "since the new church was first begun. "It has been an irksome task for the "managers to bring it so far. We have done everything in our power, but have reason to complain of the backwardness and ungenerous neglect of many subscribers, who have paid little or nothing. We know well who can plead inability, and who in conscience cannot. To support publick worship is a sacred duty: a voluntary promise to do it is to men of principle equally binding as the most solemn oath: not to perform is impious, it is glaring injustice to those who have done their part, and after bearing the heaviest part of the burden must behold their noble design and spirited efforts defeated by the fault of others! it is cruelty to the managers, who have involved themselves for the public good in reliance on the faith and probity of subscribers; more especially to those among them who have advanced their own cash. We therefore earnestly request every person of ability speedily to pay his ballance, and if he cannot command money, to give his note to such of our creditors as will accept of it: and we must plainly tho' with reluctance, declare, that we shall be under necessity of compelling the negligent by the authority of law. We also beg leave to request all those who have honourably paid their subscriptions, to subscribe again according to their ability, in order to make up unavoidable deficiencies, and to compleat the building at least so far as to render it decently fit for divine service: for which we deem an hundred and fifty pounds sufficient. They may depend on a faithful discharge of the trust reposed in us, and be assured that no part of their contribution shall be expended to pay the debts of careless and selfish subscribers. We deem it needless to persuade persons of sense and goodness; they know how necessary this building is, what ornament to the adjacent country, and what honour to all the generous promoters of it.   NICHOLAS COLLIN May 27, 1786.

> Frederic Ato.
> William Matson
> Andrew Henricson
> Felix Fisler
> Robert Brown.

After my removal to Philadelphia[111] the business was yet very unsettled and notwithstanding the greatest exertions during my frequent visitations of the congregation, it could not be finished until the fifteenth of Aug. 1791.

---

[111] Collin removed to Philadelphia in 1786. See Johnson, *Journal and Biography of Nicholas Collin*, p. 34-35.

It would have been impossible to erect this building by mere dint of money. The managers were therefore obliged to act as brokers, exchanging subscriptions for work, or home produce, orders upon other persons, etc. This roundabout way of dealing was, however, attended with great trouble and lots of time. Another disadvantage from the scarcity of cash was the multiplicity of receipts, and memorandums. To avoid errors I gave and took receipts for the smallest payments, and from time to time exchanged many small ones for one of their total amount: without this expedient my accounts would have made a large volume. The greatest payments made in the country were effected by these slow and perplexing methods. The mason received the chief part of his wages in notes of hand from subscribers. Mr. Fislar obtained very little cash, and kindly took in pay several considerable subscriptions; among these the sixty £ from James Stillman, 15 £ from Andrew Homan, 7 £ 10 shil. from Charles Cox etc. Besides, he dealt with several subscribers for the workmen. Robert Brown Esq. supplied the carpenter and others with articles from his store to a large amount. For my own part I advanced my Swedish Salaries, and kept frequently one hundred pounds in circulation, besides giving my bonds for large sums: which was necessary in the purchase of various costly materials from Philadelphia, principally transacted by me. It is also proper to mention for the information of those who may hereafter wish to know the present state of things, that all the travelling I have performed from first to last in this business would amount to three a four thousand miles.

The articles of the subscription were these.

Whereas a well ordered public worship is an excellent means for the promotion of true piety, and consequently of the salvation of souls, and the temporal happiness of men; we the subscribers do hereby from motives of christian zeal, and public spirit contribute, each of us, the sums annexed to our respective names, for the rebuilding of the Swedish Lutheran Evangelical Church in Swedsborough: for the payment of which well and truly to be made we bind ourselves, and heirs, executors, and administrators, and everyone of them, on the following conditions.

1. The church shall be constituted and administered in the same manner as heretofore; the minister to be commissioned by the crown of Sweden: the church wardens and vestry men to be appointed agreeably to the charter—which minister, church wardens, and vestrymen are to keep and exercise all the rights and privileges vested in them by the said charter.

2. All the subscribers that are or will become, and remain true members of the Lutheran Evangelical Church, shall have a right to seats for themselves, and their families, and to lots in the burying ground, which is to be enlarged to the southwest so far, as only to leave a sufficient road between the pales

and the garden of the parsonage: This right to descend to their heirs while remaining in the said communion and no longer; which is hereby granted by the Swedish corporation, as by their open act and deed.

3. One fourth of the money subscribed shall be paid on the last day of November this year; the second fourth on the first day of May; the third on the first day of August; and the remainder on the last day of November next year.

4. The following persons: to Wit. the Revd. Nicholas Collin, Robert Brown Esq., Doctor Fredric Otto, Robert Clark, William Matson, Felix Fisler, Andrew Henricson, Isaac Vanneaman, Samuel Denny, as managers for the building are to have full powers, jointly and separately, for the recovery of the money subscribed. Three of them as treasurers to wit, Nicholas Collin, Robert Clark, Robert Brown, shall have power to receive any sum, for which they shall give receipt, and be accountable, each for what he receives.   September 1st. 1783.

The first and second articles may to some appear less consistent with that liberal principle of toleration which is now become very general, or with the actual state of the congregation. But these were necessary for the preservation of unity and order, as this country presents many examples of discord and lawsuits about places of worship erected at the joint expense of intermixed denominations. The cessation of the Swedish Mission was indeed a probable event; but it was deemed an easy matter to make suitable alterations in such a case.

The above articles were prefixed to the subscription - list, which circulated for several years while there was any prospect of additional sums. Doctor Otto deserves great credit for his activity in promoting both subscription and collection. The greatest part of the money subscribed was at last obtained, and though with great troubled, yet without legal compulsion, except in a very few cases. The deficiency happened from some of the subscribers dying, and from others proving really unable to pay the whole or any part of their engagement. It would be pleasing to record those who with alacrity paid according to ability, whether more or less, but that such distinction might be prejudicial to Christian harmoney. It is needless to insert a copy of this original subscription list, as the sums paid by the respective subscribers are placed to their credit in the accounts here exhibited by Sq. Brown and myself. All the money collected by the late Robert Clark a very worthy member of the church, was by him transferred to me, and is acknowledged in my debt. I received also a few new subscriptions from well-disposed persons which I have added to their list, and given them credit for the whole in one sum. During the course of the business the treasurers often presented their accounts to the managers, and those of the subscribers who chose to attend:

A measure very expedient for securing the public confidence in transactions so difficult and tedious.

The deficiency of subscribers was made up by moneys arising from the sale of several materials of the old church, and of those purchased for the new building, which were unfit or superflous; but principally from a part of the church revenue during the vacancy, which was in that respect a fortunate circumstance. The several sums thus obtained are specified in the accounts.

I received also from Mr. Charles Lock, to satisfy the urgent demand of Thomas Batton, a loan of twenty four pounds and 10 shil. This I replaced, and therefore do not take up in my accounts. But Robert Brown esq. states the interest paid thereon.

[CREDIT]

NICHOLAS COLLIN in account with subscriptions
from the following persons

	£	Sh.	D.
Doctor Fredric Otto	10	0	0
Mathew Huston	3	0	0
Mrss Cathrine Otto	3	6	8
John Stille in Philadelphia	7	10	0
Samuel Hews	3	0	0
Conrad Shoemaker	12	0	0
Miss Hanna Cox	7	10	0
Peter Lock in Rapapo Vest. Man	15	0	0
Charles Lock	7	10	0
Andrew Henricson	13	18	4
Benjamin Rambo	12	0	0
George Vanlear	30	0	0
Abraham Boice	1	5	0
James Flannigan	10	0	0
William England	5	0	0
SUM	141	0	0

	£	Sh.	D.
BROUGHT OVER	141	0	0
Cornelius Bryan	3	0	0
John Helms Jun.	5	0	0
Mouns Keen	23	6	6
Thomas Dodd	3	0	0
Mrss. Harris	4	0	0
Andrew Stillman	2	5	0
William Homan	18	0	0
Peter Lock, son of Peter	7	10	0
Cudjo, a Black	0	15	0
James Early	0	7	6
Daniel Chew	0	7	6
Hans Hellms	5	0	0
Mrs. Zilla Gwill	7	10	0
John Kelly	10	0	0
Andrew Matson Jun.	10	0	0
Mrss. Phebe Cox	1	5	0

	£	Sh.	D.
Thomas Carney Esq.	6	0	0
Nicholas Collin	15	0	0
SUM	263	6	6

	£	Sh.	D.
BROUGHT OVER	263	6	0
Peter Lock, son of John	6	0	0
Dr. James Stratton	10	0	0
James Stilman	60	0	0
Andrew Homan	15	0	0
Jeffrey Clark	10	10	0
Felix Fisler	30	0	0
Henry Myers	0	18	9
Christian Siren	1	10	0
John Forest	4	0	0
Joseph Blackwood	6	0	0
Isaac VanNeaman	15	0	0
John Runnels	3	0	0
Nathan Fosset	6	0	0
Charles Winemuller	3	0	0
John Huling	3	0	0
Leonard Fisler	6	0	0
Gideon Urian	0	8	4
Michael Stout	3	0	0
Ezechiel Lock	5	0	0
SUM	451	13	7

	£	Sh.	D.
BROUGHT OVER	451	13	7
Daniel Southerland	20	0	0
Jones Lock	10	0	0
David Henricson	15	0	0
Martin Staet	3	0	0
Abraham Jones son of Meredith Jones	1	10	0
Joseph Rice	3	0	0
Daniel Stanton	3	0	0
Peter Kyer	10	0	0
Joseph Harker	3	0	0
John Hellms Sen.	12	0	0
Colonel Joseph Ellis	6	0	0
James Lord	5	0	0
William Dericson	2	5	0
John Cox	3	0	0
George Wiser	2	5	0
Joshua Lord	3	0	0
John Dericson	7	10	0
John Rambo	10	0	0
David Harker	3	0	0
SUM	574	3	7

	£	Sh.	D.
BROUGHT OVER	574	3	7
John Halton	2	10	0
Gabriel Cox	3	0	0
Lewis Fisler	1	2	6
John Sommerlind	3	0	0
John Lock in Rapapo	5	0	0
Ruben Keen	3	0	0
Peter Harden	1	10	0
Francis Stinger	3	0	0
Christian Griner	0	7	6
Valentine Foster	1	10	0
James Tallman	20	0	0
William Watson	4	0	0
John White	3	0	0
James White	1	10	0
Vade Dicson	2	5	0
Andrew Sennecson Esq.	10	0	0
Hans Urian at Racoon	1	10	0
Silliam Underwood	2	5	0
SUM	642	13	7

	£	Sh.	D.
BROUGHT OVER	642	13	7
Jasper Lock	6	0	0
Christian Stinger	1	10	0
Philip Stinger	1	10	0
Jacob Hammit	2	5	0
Ephraim Seley	3	0	0
Owen Conelly	1	10	0
Peter Carney	3	0	0
Thomas Denny Jun.	3	0	0
Moses Hoffman	6	0	0
John Lock Sen.	10	0	0
Richard Batton	15	0	0
John Keen	2	5	0
Archibald Scott	3	10	0
Meredith Jones	3	0	0
Andrew Jones	10	0	0
Jonathan Russel	4	0	0
John Henrickson	3	15	0
William Denny	3	0	0
Nathan Boice Jun.	3	0	0
Gustave Lock	1	0	0
SUM	728	18	7

X—June 10 1785 33 £ 17 shi. 9 d and Nov. 21st
1785 12 £

	£	Sh.	D.
BROUGHT OVER	728	18	7
Jonathan Simkins	2	0	0
John Light	5	0	0

	£	Sh.	D.
Samuel Denny	20	0	0
Jacon Henricson	11	2	6
Jacob Madera	3	0	0
Peter Stinger	1	10	0
John VanNeamen	2	10	0
Daniel England	4	10	0
Job Key	4	0	0
Miss Priscilla Adams	1	2	6
Mary Sommervill	5	0	0
Roberts Kitts	0	15	0
Abel Biddel	3	0	0
Robert Clark	50	0	0
James Clark	20	0	0
Thomas Clark	15	0	0
Elizabeth Sennecson	5	0	0
SUM	882	8	7

Ns: All the money received by me from Robert Clark collected by him as treasurer, was: the subscription of Elizab. Sennecson; ten pound of James Clark's ditto, and three pounds 15 shi. of Thomas Clark's.

	£	Sh.	D.
BROUGHT OVER	882	8	7
Gustave Halton	5	0	0
David Loyd	3	0	0
Charles Halton	10	0	0
John Currey	7	10	0
Robert Harbeson	2	5	0
Catherine Hellms	3	0	0
Lawrence Cox	3	0	0
George VanNeaman	4	10	0
William Riggens	2	0	0
John Daniels	10	0	0
Jacob Stille	5	0	0
Gideon Denny	15	0	0
Leonard Stanton	15	0	0
James Avis	1	10	0
Thomas James	6	0	0
Caleb Henricson	3	0	0
Fredric Pullinger	2	0	0
Samuel Hulings	12	0	0
Daniel Adams Sen.	3	0	0
William Swieten Sen.	2	15	0
SUM	997	18	7

	£	Sh.	D.
BROUGHT OVER	997	18	7
William Svieten Jun.	0	7	6
Magdalena Linch	3	0	0
By the hand of Sq. Brown			
James Tomlin	2	5	0
Samuel Shreve	5	0	0

	£	Sh.	D.
Leonard Velday	1	10	0
John Regu	1	10	0
Joseph Davenport	2	0	0
Francis Turner	5	0	0
William James	2	5	0
Charles Cox	7	10	0
William Scott	5	0	0
Valentine Runnels	2	0	0
Adam Schyz	3	0	0
Michael Wolsh	5	0	0
William Huling	4	0	0
Isaac Lock	3	0	0
Jacob Shoulders	3	0	0
Mrss Hannah Ladd	6	0	0
George Braght	2	0	0
SUM	1061	6	1

	£	Sh.	D.
BROUGHT OVER	1061	6	1
Eeric Petersson	3	0	0
Mary Henricson	3	0	0
John and William Course	5	0	0
Henry Stream	0	8	4
Gabriel Dahlbo	0	8	4
Zebulon Lock	0	12	0
Francis Batton 500 Shingles, and in cash	1	10	0
Tobuis Paulson	0	10	9
Widow Mary Stilman	1	3	4
Peter Morgan	0	8	4
Ebenezer Adams	1	15	0
Robert Craighead	0	7	6
Mathew Lord	0	7	6
Abraham Keen	0	15	0
Lawrence Friend	1	10	0
Executors of Mounse Henricson	2	0	0
Nicholas Fittis	1	2	6
Jacob Jones	3	0	0
Paultes Prisener	2	0	0
SUM	1090	4	8

	£	Sh.	D.
BROUGHT OVER	1090	4	8
Jonathan Matson	1	19	0
Moxes Cox (on Mant. Creek)	5	0	0
James Nail	4	0	0
George Pile	0	10	0
Thomas Jones	1	2	6
James Russel	7	10	0
Thomas England	5	8	0
James Mathews	4	10	0
William Matson v. man	9	3	4
Peter Applin	4	2	11

	£	Sh.	D.
Malachy Horner ----	1	5	0
William Mecum Esq. ----	1	13	4
Abraham Matson ----	5	0	0
William Eckart ----	15	0	0
John Vandike ----	7	10	0
John Cole ----	1	2	6
Nicholas Fustis ----	1	2	6
x - Thomas Batton ----	15	0	0
Lewis Fisler ----	0	11	3
* - Rachel Boon ----	3	0	0
Thomas Peterson ----	1	10	0
SUM ----	1186	4	0

x ns. He has paid and equal sum before, as credited.
* paid before as credited 22 sh. 6 d.

	£	Sh.	D.
Brought over the total sum of subscriptions ----	1186	4	0

	£	Sh.	D.
For materials belonging to the new building, and sold as unfit or useless to wit empty lime hogshead to the amount of five pound 17 shil. 1000 feet of boards for 6 £ 15 sh.: 672 feet of damaged half-priced boards with 211 feet of sap-boards for 2 £ 11 shil. 6 d. posts ribs of plank, small parcels of boards etc.—the whole amounting to ----	18	0	0
For materials, part of the old church, sold by vendue and by the hand of Isaac VanNeaman ----	5	13	9
From the sale of the old wood cut upon the church and in the years 1785 and - 6 for the benefit of the church--	7	9	6
SUM ----	1217	6	3

	£	Sh.	D.
BROUGHT OVER ----	1217	6	3

	£	Sh.	D.
From the vestry, as appears by a settlement between me and them the 26 of April, 1791 ----	88	12	0
From them by the rent of Mr. Mouns Keen 15th of Aug. 1791 ----	3	9	5
SUM ----;----	1309	7	0

	£	Sh.	D.
BROUGHT OVER ----	1309	7	0

	£	Sh.	D.
A subscription from Thomas Peterson at Mourices river of fifteen Shillings, which he left with Mr. Wicsell for the use of a future new church and which Mr. Wicsell deposited with me as is recorded on the old church book ----	0	15	0
Drawback on John Elliots bill, who placed a pair of spectacles for Mr. Foster for which he paid ----	0	6	0
TOTAL SUM One thousand three Hundred and ten pounds eight Shillings ----	1310	8	0

	£	Sh.	D.
BROUGHT OVER 111a _____	1310	8	0

*	*	*	*	*	*	*	*	*	*
*	*	*	*	*	*	*	*	*	*
*	*	*	*	*	*	*	*	*	*

	£	Sh.	D.
BROUGHT OVER _____	1310	8	0

*	*	*	*	*	*	*	*	*	*
*	*	*	*	*	*	*	*	*	*
*	*	*	*	*	*	*	*	*	*

	£	Sh.	D.
BROUGHT OVER _____	1310	8	0

NB Several persons performed various kinds of work without pay or valuing of it in money: to wit.
Samuel Chester,
Abner Batton, by hauling sand
Jacob Urian by freight from Philadelphia
The sons of Joseph Humphreys by ditto.
Samuel Pickin
Jacob Fisler senior, and his son Jacob gave and hauled 1000 feet of pineboard each.

	£	Sh.	D.
BROUGHT OVER	1310	8	0

*	*	*	*	*	*	*	*	*	*
*	*	*	*	*	*	*	*	*	*
*	*	*	*	*	*	*	*	*	*

111a In the original manuscript credits and debits in these accounts were alternately entered. When the number of pages needed for debit entries exceeded those required for credit entries, it was necessary to fill several pages with asterisks (as above) to keep the ledger in the proper alternating order. Each entry on this page thus represents an individual page on the credit side of the ledger in the original.

For convenience in make-up the credit entries have been printed consecutively, followed by the debits in the same order.

	£	Sh.	D.
BROUGHT OVER -------------------------------	1310	8	0

*	*	*	*	*	*	*	*	*	*
*	*	*	*	*	*	*	*	*	*
*	*	*	*	*	*	*	*	*	*

[DEBIT]

The Managers for the New Church

To Issac Venneamen for the stone in the foundation furnished and hauled; and for the whole mason-work in stone and brick the following sums according to corresponding receipts:

	£	Sh.	D.
Jan. 14th 1785 ---	74	1	0
June 24th 1785 ---	13	15	0
December 23d. 1785 --	12	10	0
Febr. 23d 1786 ---	19	15	0
Febr. 25th 1786 ---	4	0	0
May the 6th 1786 --	5	15	9
Sept. 21st. 1786 --	10	13	9
Nov. 20th 1786 ---	6	2	6
27th of Jan; 1787 ---	2	0	0
April 10th 1787 ---	7	3	9
April 20th 1787 ---	5	0	0
Nov. 3d 1787 in full -------------------------------------	23	10	0
SUM --	184	6	9

Nt. Mr. Vanneaman received something above his due in consideration of his taking many bad notes.

	£	Sh.	D.
BROUGHT OVER ------------------------------	184	6	9

	£	Sh.	D.
To Felix Fisler on his bill of 143500 Bricks at £1 17 sh. 6 d. per thsd. with a great number of scaffold, poles furnished and hauled, as per corresponding receits of the 6th day of June 1785, and 23d. day of Febr: 1786, for two hundred and 43 1£, 7 sh. 6 d, and seven £ 14 shi. in full respectively—total ------------------------------	251	1	6
To Samuel Richards in Philadelphia for 48 hsds. of lime as per receits of the 23d of March and 10th day of June 1786, of sixty six pound 7 shil. 3d, and one pound 6 shi. respectively, total in full ---------------------	67	13	3
To William Stiles in Philadelphia for the four hewn stones as doorsills as per rec't Oct. 14th 1784 ---------	14	16	10
SUM ---	517	18	4

	£	Sh.	D.
BROUGHT OVER _____	517	18	4

To Thomas Batton his bills of scantling for the roof, of which the principal articles are: big rafters 2877 ft; inferior ditto 1080; king post 443; Brackets 726; wall plates 736; feet of rafters 276; rig plank 143; gist 242; joists 2547; purline 420; bottom 140; Starts and braces 510 lath 3900, all feet.) as per corresponding receits; Dec; 6, 1784 three pounds; Oct. 1st 1785 six pounds, 2 shil 6 D. Febr. 3d 1786 twelve pds. 15 shi. April 5th 1786 forty one £ 10 shi. Total in full _____ 63 7 6

To Leonard Fisler for 1000 feet of boards delivered at the church, as per rect. 15 day of June 1785 _____ 6 0 0

To Samuel Hewlings for 1000 feet of half-price boards as per receit 20th of June 1785 _____ 2 10 0

SUM _____ 589 15 10

	£	Sh.	D.
BROUGHT OVER _____	589	15	10

To Fithian Stratton for about 3000 ft. of half price and scaffold, boards, as per Mr. Foster receipt of Apr. 15 1785 _____ 9 0 0

To Ezechiel Foster for 600 feet of inch and ¼ seasoned boards, as per rec. of Sept. 22d 1784 _____ 6 12 0

To David Harker for 503 feet of pine, boards as p. rect. 18th of July 1786 _____ 3 5 5

To Hanna Ellis for 1000 ft of boards pine as p. rect. Nov. 5th 1787 in full _____ 5 10 4

To Richard Fittermery C. Executor of Robert Clark for materials of wood, furnished by the said Clark (among those, the posts and beams under the galleries) as per rect. of May 2d 1786 _____ 13 4 0

For 1200 shingles brought from Pilesgrove in sumer 1784 6 1 4

SUM _____ 633 9 5

Nts Huling forgot the recript.

	£	Sh.	D.
BROUGHT OVER _____	633	9	5

To Jacob Madeira for 3126 feet of joists and sleepers under the floor, furnished, served and hauled as per corresponding receipts Febr. 24th 1786 to £ 5 shi; April 10th 1787 12 shi. 6 d; April 27th 1787 15 shi. 5th of Nov. 1787 Thirteen£. Total in full _____ 16 12 6

To Jones, Clark and Cresson in Philadelphia for 1362 feet heart pine scantling, and 568 feet heart pine plank reduced, and for carting the same to the wharf as per rect. the 20th of May 1784 _____ 24 4 0

To the same company for 1867 feet 5 pine boards as per rec'ts Nov. 21st 1785 twenty three £ 7 shi 7d; and Febr. 21st 1787 five £—Total in full _____ 28 7 7

SUM _____ 702 13 6

	£	Sh.	D.
BROUGHT OVER ----------------------------	702	13	6

To M'Colloh and Peterson in Philadelphia for 5000 Indian River Shingles at 7 £ 10 Shi. per thd; 2000 feet of whole price pine, boards a ditto price; and 1000 feet of damaged boards at 4 £ 10 shi. per Tsd, as per corresponding receits thirteen pounds 10 shi. the 2d of Aug. 1784, and forty-three pounds 10 shi. the 4th of Sept. 1784. Total ---------------- **57   0   0**

To the same company for 1200 rough Ind. River shingles at 15 pd. with carting of them to the boat, as per receipts of the 16th of Sept. 1784 ---------------- **9   5   0**

To ditto company for 3000 feet. of pine boards at 7 £ 10 shi. per thd; 1000 ft. Pannel cedar at 11£ 5 shi. p. thd. 500 ft. hard 5/4 pine do at 15 shi. 287 ft. Scantling at 18 sh. 9 d. p hred; 94 feet of plank at 5 d. per foot, as per rec'ts. ---------------------------- **45   17   9**

SUM -- **814   16   3**

	£	Sh.	D.
BROUGHT OVER ----------------------------	814	16	3

To Ditto M'culloh and Petterson for 3000 feet of comon pine board at 7 £ 10 shi. per th.; 300 feet of heart pine plank a 45 shilling per hundred 500 feet of common pine boards at 15 shil. per hrd; 303 ft; of heart 5/4 pine at 1£ 10 Shi per hd with carting, as per corresponding receipts, may the 3d 1786 16 £ 15 shi., Nov. 6th 1786, one pound 10 shilling; March 14, 1787 eleven pounds; April 13th 1787 ten pounds at nine pence the total including interest 1 £ 11 shi 1½ d. in full of all accts for the Sweedsborough Church ---------------------------- **39   5   9**

To Turner and Tomson for an old mast for making the door columns as per Rec't Nov: 18, 1785 ------------ **1   18   8**

To Samuel Fletfher calso in Philadelphia for tunning the 6 columns as per corresp. rec'ts of Dec. 16th 1785 and Jan: 17th 1786 in full total ---------------------------- **7   12   6**

SUM -- **863   13   2**

	£	Sh.	D.
BROUGHT OVER ----------------------------	863	13	2

To Huhn and Risberg in Philadelphia for three boxes best sand on crown-glass 9 by 11 at 6 £ 7 sh. 6 d per box; Three dito common at 5 £ 11 sh. 3 d: ⅛ ditto 10 by 12 a 6 £ 5 shl. as p. rec. 27th of July 1785 ---------------- **28   18   9**

To Poultney and Wisler in Philad. for 64 panes of Square glass specified in the. bill as per rec't in full 26th of Jan. 1786 ---------------- **4   18   6**

To William Skinner for glazing, with the cutting of some glass, and bringing it from Philadelphia as per corresp. rec's. 14 of Febr: 1786 three £ pounds 4 shil. 4 d; and May the 3rd 1786 three £ 17 shl. 8 d in full. total **7   2   0**

	£	Sh.	D.
To Jacob Stall for 15 Pounds of putty, half a gallon of oil, and 6 pints of drying struff as p. re't. 2nd of Febr. 1786	0	19	0
SUM	915	11	5

	£	Sh.	D.
BROUGHT OVER	915	11	5
To Pinkerton and son in Philadelphia for 3 pounds of glue, 1500 sprig and 2½ oz. of screw as p. rec't June 10th 1785	1	0	3
To John Elliot in Philadelphia for a keg of putty w. 81 pound, and 12½ pound of ground white-lead as p. rct. of Aug. 1785	4	1	5
To Ordand Blewr for a keg of whitelead 28 pound, a gall. of oil, a jug, and 10 wt. of putty as p. r. 28th of July 1785	2	4	10
To Bringhurst in Philadelphia, 2 gall of oil a jug and 4 wt, of putty as p. r. Aug 27th 1784	2	2	0
To Abel Biddel for 1500 sprigs bought in Phila; as by his bill			
To Thomas Pascal for 5 lb. of nails and 1300 sprigs bought by Tobias Paulson as per bill	0	10	9
SUM	926	0	8

	£	Sh.	D.
BROUGHT OVER	926	0	8
For 304 inch screws, hinges, ½ a gallon of oil and white-lead bought in Phila. by Nathan Boys as per his bill, 31st of Dec. 1785	0	16	6
To George Roberts in Philad. for 42 pair of pew hinges; 4 groce of screws for the hinges 2 par of spring bolts, a trunk of nails, a large iron rim-lock with traprings etc., four pair of large hinges and screws, as per rcts. Sept. 13th and Nov. 2nd 1786 in full	7	18	6
To Ezech Foster for nails and sprigs as per Rect. July 20, 1789	0	9	8
To Joseph Harker cash for the purchase of iron as p. rct. Oct. 26th 1784	6	0	0
To ditto, cash as per rect. 6th of Nov. 1784	2	1	3
To him ditto for ironwork for the church-roof of 300 weight; for 166 plates; a rod for the pulpit canopy; spikes, rivets, hinges, mending and augur ch. as per receits 16 of July 1785 and 20th Sept 1786 in full	10	17	7
SUM	954	4	2

	£	Sh.	D.
BROUGHT OVER	954	4	2

To William Hulings for making devises, bolts and spikes keys and collers, the whole wieghing 463 at 14 pence per pound as by correspond. receipts 1st of March 1785 2 £ 5 shil; Oct. 25 1784 3 £; June 7th 1785 15 shil. 13th of Febr. 1786 4 £ 10 shil. 10th of April 1787 four

	£	Sh.	D.
pounds; April 26th 1787 twelve pounds 10 shil 2 d in full total _____!	27	0	2
To Robert Harbeson for nails Febr 2d - and May 8th, 1786 as per rec'ts _____	5	0	0
To treat for the brickburners on finishing the first clamp, and for the carpenters on raising the 1st and second stories _____	0	12	6
To Peter Lock for 72 wt. of young pork, ½ a hundred of ryeflour baked into bread, and ½ a basket of turkeys provided for the people at raising the rafter, as per rec't Jan 13 1785 _____	2	8	0
SUM _____	989	4	10

This irregularity arose from others collecting and making a late return.

	£	Sh.	D.
BROUGHT OVER _____	989	4	10
To Mounce Keen for entertaining Mr. Foster while he was formong the draught of the church, as per rec't Apr. 5th 1784 _____	0	10	9
To Mr. Rice for his dinner, lodge etc. when he came to Swedsborough for the money due to him the 20th of May 1787 _____	0	6	0
To Mathew Huston for transcribing 8 copies of the subscription list, as per rec't Nov. 10th 1783 _____	0	8	4
To Lawrence Friend for digging at the foundation heating bricks, and sundry kinds of work as P. rct. May 8, 1785 _____	3	0	0
For unloading boards from a shaloup and other small jobs at sundry times _____	0	5	0
To Samuel Davenport for hauling up shingles and the stones for door sills as witness F. Rice _____	0	7	6
SUM _____	994	2	5

	£	Sh.	D.
BROUGHT OVER _____	994	2	5
To Mounce Keen for hauling scantling water, lime, sand, lath, arch pieces, and other sundries as per rect. the 19th of Aug. 1785, five pounds, 1 shil; and for hauling water sand, scantling with two loads of boards from Dearfield, as per rec. Sept 20th 1785 three pounds 6 shil: and 6 d: Total _____	8	7	6
To John Hulings for hauling 1200 shingles from Pilesgrove, 6 loads from Batton's Mill, lime from the bridge; and for a barrel of cyder used at the raising as per rect. 18 of Jan. 1785 _____	3	10	6
To Joseph Rice for going on several errands and journeys, and sundry kinds of works as per rect. May 31st, 1784	3	0	0
To Nathan Boys for carrying from Philad. 6000 feet of boards and one hd. of lime as per rec't Febr; 18, 1786	3	0	0
SUM _____	1012	0	5

[201]

	£	Sh.	D.
BROUGHT OVER	1012	0	5
To William Denny for going on an errand and for 5 pieces of carpenters stuff, as p. rect. 18th of Febr. 1786	0	14	0
To Jacob Madera for hauling boards from Woodstown as P. r. 24th of Febr. 1786	2	5	0
To Richard Batton for hauling for four days and ½ as p. rct. 13th of Febr. 1786	3	0	0
To Jacob Hendricson for 250 wt. of stuff hauled and sawed as p. rect. 23d of Febr. 1786	2	6	0
To Nichlas Carlson for making a fence round the church and removing the shavings as per rect. Apr. 6 1786	0	16	0
To Lawrence Cox for hauling boards etc. p. rect. Apr. 26, 1786	16	5	0
To Gustave Halton for carrying from Philad. and unloading at the bridge 3000 feet of boards and for two gallons of oil as p. rec't May 6th 1786	2	1	3
SUM	1023	7	8

	£	Sh.	D.
BROUGHT OVER	1023	7	8
To James Clark for hauling a gallery as p. receipt Oct. 24th 1785	1	0	0
To Gideon Urian for the freight of 1200 shingles 16th of Sept. 1789	0	8	9
To Ephraim Seley for cedarboards furnished and brought	1	15	0
For the loan of a diamond to cut glass	0	3	9
A treat to the carpenters and people assisting on raising the pillars	0	7	6
Ditto to the carpenters on finishing the banisters altar, and front-door	0	4	2
To Jacob Fisler for hauling boards as p. receipt Apr. 10th 1787	1	0	0
To William James for hauling scantling 5 days as p. rct. Apr 20th 1787 in full	2	5	0
To Thomas England for the freight of 5 hds of lime p. re'ct May 27th 1786	1	5	0
To Abraham Matson for freight of 300 scantling 30 cases of lime, 8000 boards and shingles 3000 other boards and for a bucket, as p. re'cts Oct. 8, 1786 4 £ 14 sh. 2 d; and 10 £ 10 d the 28th of April 1787 in full		14	15
SUM	1046	11	5

	£	Sh.	D.
BROUGHT OVER	1046	11	5
For grindstone and freight of it	0	13	3
Expense of moving the kitchen garden of the parsonage from the area of the new church	1	0	0
To David Harker for 10 wt. of nails a 10 d.	0	8	4
To Mr. Foster for 60 ft. of cedar board as p. rct. 1st of March 1786	0	6	2

	£	Sh.	D.
For nails to make up the temporary fence around the church	0	1	6
For a blank quarter book and paper used in keeping the accounts	0	7	6
Expense of my journeys to Philadelphia on business of the church, to wit. in Apr. 1784 with Mr. Foster for veiwing public building in order to form the plan 15 shil: in the summer and fall the same year 1 £ 2 sh 6 d.: the 9th of June 1785 12 Sh. 6 d. L in ful. ditto to purchase glass 15 sh. L in Sept ditto to pay for wooden materials 15 sh in Nov. ditto to get the collumns, boards etc. 12.2.6 2d ct 3d of May 1786 to settle with Tittermery* 12 Sh. 6 Total	5	15	0
SUM	1055	3	2

*Son in law and executor of Robert Clark.

	£	Sh.	D.
BROUGHT OVER	1055	3	2
To Ezechiel Foster for extraordinary services to the church, as p. Rec't Decemb. 22d 1764	5	7	6
To him for carpentry and joiners work as per corresponding receipts: Deceb. 22d 1784	14	12	6
22d ditto 1784	3	5	0
Decemb. 20th 1784	57	1	9
Septemb 14th 1785	20	0	0
October 18th 1785	6	10	0
Decemb. 7th 1785	6	5	8
Decemb 24th 1785	3	0	0
1786 Jan. 16th	4	0	0
Ditto Jan. 30	3	15	0
Ditto Febr. 4	20	8	3
Do. Febr. 9th	3	15	0
Do. Febr. 14th	9	18	2
Do. Febr. 18th	2	6	0
Do. Febr. 25	2	1	9
Do. March 1st	1	5	0
Do. 22d by Robert Jordan as per his rec't	3	7	3
1786 ditto April 18 by Isaac Prester as per order and rec't	3	15	0
Do. May 14	1	10	0
SUM	1227	7	0

	£	Sh.	D.
BROUGHT OVER	1227	7	0
1786 May 27th by his son Jeremiah Foster as per order and Rec't	3	5	0
Do. May 27th per order on the final settlement to Reuben Keen as by his receipt	7	9	0
Do. June 24 as per order and receipt by his son Jeremiah	1	2	6
Do. July 18 by David Harker as per order and receipt	4	0	0
Do. Same day by David Harker	3	11	2
Do. Sept. 20 by order and rec. to Joseph Harker	0	19	0
1786 Oct. 18 as by rec. in Philadelphia	3	0	0

	£	Sh.	D.
Do. Nov. 21 by Reuben Keen	0	10	0
1787 May 20th	1	10	0
1788 June 9th by Reuben Keen	7	0	0
To Joseph Harker as p. rec't of November 5, 1785	2	0	7
To William Eckart on his and compan's bill of May 3d— 1785 for 3720 feet of scantling, 223 dd. of promiscous stuff, amount. to 17 £ 9 sh. and 5 d; for carving 2 long poles 15 shil. and for hauling 7 loads from the mill, as per rec't on paid bill April 25, 1791	15	0	0
SUM	1276	14	3

NB—This was omitted in the foregoing statement but is found on his second bill.

	£	Sh.	D.
BROUGHT OVER	1276	14	3
To John Vandike for glasing painting and other work as per recpt 26th of Apr. 1791	13	0	11
To Doctor Otto for travelling expenses, as per rec'pt of April 1791	4	8	10
To Him ditto for travelling expenses in settleing business for the church as per rec'pt 27th of April 1791	0	15	0
To William Eckart and co.p. the ballance of their acct. as by recp't 11 of Aug. 1791	3	9	5
* A drawback on a receipt of Mr. Isaac Van Neaman	0	3	0
To Charles Winemuller for digging etc.	1	0	0
By lots on Thomas England's note	1	2	6
* Expense of eight journeys from Philadelphia for settling the church business	9	14	1
TOTAL	1310	8	0

* by an error p. 1 on a receipt of 5£ 15 sh. 9. in leu of 5£ 18 9 d.
* These journeys were different from those I came to perform divine service on Sundays though I did something towards as settlement even then, and was often detained for a day or two.

TOTAL—ONE THOUSAND THREE HUNDRED AND TEN POUNDS EIGHT SHILLINGS.

SWEDESBOROUGH 15th OF AUG. 1791

We underwritten managers for the new church have examined the foregoing accounts of the Rvd. NICHOLAS COLLIN, and hereby certify that said accounts are true and just: the several receipts and bills being by him exhibited: and the respective sums in his debet being exactly as by him presented.

We members of the vestry have as evidences assisted at the above settlement.

Mounce Keen
Benjamin Rambo
George Vanleer
Gideon Denny

William Matson
Andrew Hendrickson
Felix Fisler
Samuel Denny

We the underwritten do hereby declare that we have no demand against the managers for the Sweedsborough church.

Swedsborough
April 26th 1791
   WITNESS
John Cross

Isaac Vanneman
Felix Fisler
Mounce Keen

Received from Nich. Collin this 15th of Aug. 1791 the ballance of my loan of twenty four pounds ten shil. to the church.   Charles Lock.

SWEDSBOROUGH 15' OF AUG. 1791

DR. ROBERT BROWN ONE OF THE TREASURERS FOR ERECTING THE NEW CHURCH AT SWEDESBOROUGH, IN ACCOUNT WITH THE VESTRY OF SAID CHURCH[112]

1786		£	Sh.	D.
Jany. 25	To John Key's note given to him for his subscription	4	0	0
" "	To Thomas Jones do do	1	17	6
" "	To Jacob Laum's do do	4	-	-
" "	To Henry Shute's do do	3	0	0
Feby. 28	To Cash from Andrew Makon Sr. for his Subscript.	1	13	6
	To do Thomas England do	4	12	0
	To do Thomas Denny Esq. do	30	0	0
	To do James Mathews' do	13	10	0
	To do Joseph Rice's do	1	0	0
	To do Daniel Adams Junior do	3	0	0
	To do Daniel Hooper's do	6	0	0
	To do his own subscription do	30	0	0
	To do Simon Leonard do	3	0	0
	To do from John Sparks Esqr. left as a donation to the church by the late Alexander Randale Esqr.	11	0	0
	To do from Michael Ross' do		16	0
	To do Benjamin Aryelo's __ do	3	0	0
	To do Magdalina Lynch's do	3	0	0
	To do James Tomlin's do	2	5	0
	To do Mayor Elias Boys' do	3	0	0
	To do William Matson's do	5	16	9
	To do George Homer's do	3	15	0
	To do John Ware's do	3	0	0
	To do John Morn's do	6	10	0
	To do Andrew Matson senr. do	3	6	6
	To do Daniel Wells' do	6	0	0
	To Henry Louderbach's note for his do not yet paid	7	10	0
	Carried to next page	£157	12	3

[112] The identity of Robert Brown is uncertain. He may have been a Justice of the Court of Common Pleas.

				£	Sh.	D.
1784						
Sept.	5	By 395 ¼ to furnished at different times		14	0	2
		By sundries		0	11	4
Aug.	21	By 1 gallon rum			4	4
Nov.	11	By 4 quarts do			5	-
	19	By 3 do do			3	9
	20	By sundries		1	9	7
	22	By do		2	19	42
	29	By I Gall. rum			5	0
Dec.	3	By I quart do			1	3
1785						
June	14	By Chalto			1	0
July	9	By 2 Quarts rum			2	2
1786						
Jany.	24	By 2 quarts Brandy			2	10
	25	By cash and goods furnished Ezekiel Foster		59	17	5½
		By Cash for 1 Hd. Lime		1	8	6
		By cash paid Felix Fisler		31	11	9
		By cash paid Ezekiel Foster at 7 different times		47	6	9
		Carried to next page		160	11	1

AMOUNT OF ROBERT BROWN'S ACCOUNT—Brought over

				£157	12	3
1786						
Oct.	31					
		To cash from Samuel White for his subscription		3	0	0
		To Thomas Key's Note for do		2	5	0
		To Joseph Conway's do do		2	10	0
		To sundries purchased at the sale of the old church		4	13	0
1788		To balance of rent due for his ground lots		4	15	2
March 25		To amount of the rent of his lots for 1 year		7	3	0
Oct.	9	To cash for Andrew String's subscription		2	0	0
1789						
March 25		To 1 years rent of his lots		7	3	0
		To 1 year's rent of Meadow		2	10	0
		To cash		1	0	0
				£194	11	5

				£160	11	1
1786						
Sept.	11	By cash paid Ezekiel Foster		2	5	0
		By do. paid N. Collin		5	5	0
1787						
Feb.	20	By do do Ezekiel Foster		12	12	0
May	19	By Ezekiel Foster's accoung in my book		6	7	2
1789						
Apr.	16	To cash paid Charles Lock		1	10	0
		To do in full do		6	1	2
				£194	11	5

The debt and credit of this account have been W. Charles
   Lock appointed for the purpose as signed by the said
   gentlemen—to which this—
Dr. Robert Brown to sundries furnished towards erecting
   the new church _____ £194   11   5
To Dr. The Revd. Docr. Collin as above _____ 1310   8   0
                                                              —   —   —
      SUM TOTAL _____ £1504   19   5
   Examined and compared by the Revd. Docr. Collin & appears by a certi-
ficate in Coll. Brown's Ledger if we add Docr. Collin's account the whole will
stand.
Contra Cr. by sundries expended in erecting the new
   church _____ 194   11   5
Contra Cr. as above _____ 1310   8   0
                                                              —   —   —
      SUM TOTAL _____ £1504   19   5

   I have received from the vestry by Mr. Mouns Keen Three pounds, nine
shil. and 5 being part of his ground rent for the use of the new church.
   I have received from the vestry, by the hand of Mr. Charles Lock a collection from the congregation five pound, one penny: box-money six pounds
1 in shil. five pence; and by Mr. Huston rent for the house five pounds.—total
sixteen pounds, six shil. and 6 pence, as a satisfaction, according to agreement for occasionally preaching and attendance during two years of the
vacancy.   NICHOLAS COLLIN.
   Received from the vestry two pounds for the grain-boxes in the garret.
                                              Nicholas Collin.
   NT. This made about 18 shillings for each sunday.
                        date as foregoing.
   Received from the vestry two pounds eighteen shilling 42, arrears on the
lot of Moses Hoffman til 25 of July 1786.   NICH. COLLIN.
   Received also from them the arrears on Lawry Friends lot one pound
and sixteen shil.   NICH. COLLIN.

   On a settlement between the vestry and Revd. Nicholas Collin,
it appears that he has from time to time received the following sums
of money accuring from rents during the vacancy, to wit.

	£	S	D
Rents on lots in Swedesborough directly received by him from			
Mrss. England _____	2,	1,	8
From Thomas James _____	1,	1,	8
From Lewis Fisler _____	1,	0,	10
From Mrss. Rambo _____	1,	0,	0
Rent from Mr. Rice for the pasture_____	1,	10,	0
Rent of the house from John Mulica by Mr. Charles Lock_____	12,	0,	0
From the Vestry the 10 of Apr. 1787_____	10,	2,	0
From Mr. Charles Lock _____	44,	4,	11
From John Vandike received by him this day_____	5,	10,	11
	Sum	78, 12, 0	
From Felix Fislar one years meadow rent_____	10,	0,	0
	Total _____	88,	12,	0

         Signed by us this 22 of April 1791
Witnesses   NICH. COLLIN
   John Croes   Charles Lock
   John Wade   Peter Lock
            in behalf of the Vestry

A BRIEF ACCOUNT OF THE SWEDISH MISSION FROM ITS COMMENCEMENT TIL ITS CESSATION[113]

The first Swedish colony in North America arrived in the year 1634, and was followed by three or four reinforcements during the succeeding years til 1654.[114] The Swedes acquired by a fair purchase from the natives all the Western coast of Delaware from Cape Hinlopen to Trenton, and extending due west to a distance of 40 miles.[114a] Their first principal settlement was at Christina creek,* where they had a considerable fort, and a church. After some years their establishments extended along the river 40 or 50 miles beyond Philadelphia;** and they had a church at Tinicum; where also the governor did reside. The low Dutch had sometime before the arrival of the Swedes taken possession of North river; and founded New Amsterdam, now New York. They had also got a slender footing on the eastern shore of Delaware; and built a fort, called Nassau, where Gloucester now is. This vicinity naturally created a jealousy, which produced contests, and finally hostilities, that terminated in the conquest of the infant-Swedish colony; as it was not supported by Sweden, which at that time was engaged in war with several of the first powers in Europe.

After the death of those clergymen, who accompanied the first colonists from Sweden the people became very destitute, until on their humble adress to Charles XIth—King of Sweden, the mission was instituted, which has continued without intermission til this time. This mission was composed of three distinct Rectorships, to wit—

All footnotes with asterisks were made previous to the present edition. It is difficult to determine their authorship. Some are obviously by Nicholas Collin, others are possibly by Edgar Campbell. See note page 209.

* Near Wilmington.
** Then yet not existing.

113 The title would indicate that the "Brief Account", written by Nicholas Collin, gives a short story of all the Swedish Churches in the Delaware Valley; but the narrative confines itself to the Raccoon and Penns Neck parishes. In this (first) account, which Collin entered into the Raccoon Church record book, he gives a consecutive story of the mission from the beginning to the end of the Swedish period, when he ceased his labors on the Jersey side of the River.

In the second account, which was entered into the Penns Neck Church record book, he begins with his desire to return to Sweden and then presents a statement about his labors in the New Jersey churches, until he moved to Philadelphia.

Thereupon follows a resume of the church work before he arrived. This account (p. 216 ff. below) is more detailed than that of the first. Both accounts (with the exception of the date of the arrival of the Swedes and some details about New Sweden) are very accurate.

114 The date should be 1638. It is curious that Collin, who knew the work of Acrelius, should have followed Campanius Holm in making 1634 the date of the first arrival of the Swedes. Twelve expeditions in all were sent to New Sweden between 1638 and 1655.

114a The purchase extended westward "several days' journey" and not definitely "forty miles"

Wicacoa with Kingsessing and upper Merion in Pensilvania; Christina in Delaware. And Racoon with Pensneck in West Jersey. The clergy consisted of the 3 respective Rectors, and, in latter times, a minister extraordinary, or common assistant. One of the ordinary Pastors was also provost or Commissary, having a degree of superintending authority over the whole mission. The extraordinary had from Sweden a yearly salary of Thirty three and 1/3 £ Ster. The commissary office has had from time of Mr. Sandin fifty £ ditto. The crown bestowed every coming missionary fifty do, to defray the expense of the voyage. And an equal sum on returning. While waiting for preferment after the return, they had adequate pensions: The commissaries one third more than the others. They also obtained very good employments; several having been rewarded with the best Rectorships in Sweden

At the beginning of this century, Racoon and Pensneck made parts of the congregations over the river: the first of Wicacoa, and the other of Christina. In the year 1704* a church was built where the new church of Swedsborough now stands, and endowed with the lands yet preserved: to wit, the hundred acres of which Swedsborough makes a part; and the march, meadow of six acres, four miles from thence down Racoon-Creek. Their first minister Tolstadius was drowned in Delaware 1706. The second Mr. Aurén died 1713. He was succeeded by Abraham Lidenius who also became pastor of Pensneck: A church was erected there 1717, and by Yaquet[115] endowed with 4 acres of land. From that time both congregations have been united, and both con-joined in the commissions of the Rectors.

By the unwearied sollicitude of said Lidenius the congregations were after eight years consultation prevailed upon to purchase the glebe in Pilesgrove, which contains two hundred thirty five acres, and cost one hundred forty five pounds.

In 1724 M. Lidenius went home to Sweden with his wife Maria Van Neaman, and three children.

Peter Tranberg arrived in 1726, with Andrew Windrufwa, who as assistant had charge of Pensneck til 1728, when he died. In 1741 Tranberg was promoted to the Rectorship of Christina, where he died.[116]

---

*In this place and on P. 105 Dr. Collin becomes confused as to dates, giving both 1705 and 1704 as the year when the first church was "buildt". The actual date was either 1703 or perhaps 1702. The deed of purchase says (1703) whereon the church is now erected, and an old survey of the 100 acres, dated 1702, gives a view of the church a little north of the centre facing Racoon Creek.

August 1912.   Edgar Campbell.

The congregation of Raccoon was formed in 1702, but the church was not built until later. It was dedicated on the Second Sunday after Trinity, 1704. [Editor's Note.]

115 For Lidenius, Aurén, Tollstadius, see notes 3a, 6, 123b.
116 For Windrufwa and Tranberg, see notes 30, 30a.

The vacancy was in some measure supplied by William Malander. This person had come to America with Dylander Pastor of Wicacoa, as Schoolmaster. Being a student of Divinity he obtained permission to preach, and baptise children, and would by a mandate of the Arch-bishop have received holy ordres from the said Dylander and Tranberg, if the first mentioned had not in the meantime departed this life. During the vacancy the Moravians created a Schism, and buildt the meeting house on Oldmans Creek. Pastor Nesman from Wicacoa, and Tranberg from Christina did, however, occasionally supply the congregations.

John Sandin arrived the first of April 1748 with his wife and a young child. After a tedius and perilous voyage, he died after six months. Professor Kalm, who at this time by the King of Sweden's order travelled through North America, resided for the winter at Racoon, and preached in the church. He afterwards married Mrss. Sandin, and went with her to Sweden, encountering on the passage a tremendous tempest.

Eric Unander, who came in as minister extraordinary, became in 1751 pastor of the two churches. In 1756 he was promoted to Christina church; and afterwards went home.[117]

John Abraham Lidenius, son of the above mentioned Lidenius, succeeded as Rector, after having since 1751 served as assistant, in these congregations, and those of Pensilvania. He obtained his recall, but in the meantime died in Pensilvania.

His successor John Wicsell became rector 1762, his active zeal for the spiritual and temporal concerns for the congregations is yet remembered. By his exertions the parsonage house in Swedsborough was erected; the lots leased; the marsh meadow banked, and tossack'd; and the swamp near Swedsborough cleared out for pasture. He has also the principal credit for the charity Schoolhouse in Swedsborough.

In Autumn 1773 he returned, and was promoted to the important Rectorship of Munktorp in the central part of Sweden; where he is yet living.*

Nicholas Collin arrived in 1770 the 12th of May, as minister extraordinary, and officiated through the mission, but especially at Racoon and Pensneck at the departure of John Wicsell. Since that time til July 1786 he was Rector of these congregations, and for seven years provost of the Mission.[118]

By letters to the arch-bishop and consistory of Upsal Dat. 8th of July 1778 I sollicited in pressing terms for my recall. I had then officiated for above eight years within the mission; and was consequently entitled to preferment at home. There was moreover a strong

---

* He was provost (or comissary) for the mission, during two years.

[117] For Dylander, Malander, Näsman, Moravians, Unander, see notes 34, 37, 40, 42, 65a.

[118] For Wicksell and Collin, see notes 69 and 89.

necessity for my departure:— The rents of the churchlands had by the depreciation of the current money, and the dearness of many necessary articles, fell to a tenth part of their usual value. The congregations had suffered great distress from the war; and many of the more able members, were, as is common in America, unwilling to contribute for the support of public worship. There was no prospect of peace or civil order for the several years; and consequently no hopes of relief. A temporary vacancy, though prejudicial to the congregations, was therefore inevitable; at the same time a saving of the title church revenue after my departure would shorten this vacancy by adding to the support of my successor. All this was fully represented in the mentioned letter, with an express declaration that without a speedy alleviation of my sufferings I should not even wait for the recall, but depart next spring. It must be observed that my want of subsistence would not have been grievous, if I could have drawn my commissary salary; but this was impracticable as all communication with Sweden was cut off by the dreadful disorders of those times. When the seat of war was removed from the Delaware, I obtained at least more tranquility; and therefore resolved to wait for my recall; repeating my sollicitation for it by several letters for two years. My request was at last granted by the King's resolve of the 22d. Nov. 1782. The reason of this delay was, that the consistory had not sooner presented my petition, because his majesty had by a previous order signified his pleasure that the American Missionaries should remain in their stations, until the event of the war was known. In May 1783 I received this recall. I should then with pleasure have returned to my dear native country; but personal concerns and anxiety for my ecclasiastical trust determined me still to continue for some time; especially as the urgent plea of necessity had now ceased with the return of peace. I therefore informed the consistory of my resolution to remain for a short while, until the congregations could be supplied with a successor: declaring also, that in case the King was pleased to continue the mission, I was willing to take upon me the charge of Wicacoa, Kingsessing and Upper-Merion, which churches were becoming vacant by the recall of the Rd. Mathias Hultgren; as a newcomer, however deserving, could not be useful in that station because of the extinction of the Swedish language:—I also expressed my readiness to assist my successor in Racoon and Pensneck by all the influence I derived from long service and personal connections.

On this request his majesty was pleased by resolve of the 10th of Aug. 1785, to appoint me Rector of those congregations; and also to leave Racoon and Pensneck vacant, until they should express their option of the Kings future regulation for the Swedish Mission. This was—"that whereas the congregations in their present mature state must be sufficiently able to support their ministers; and whereas they had nearly lost the language of their ancestors, which was a principal tye of their connection with Sweden;—Therefore the congregations could not in future obtain any ministers from Sweden without a formal stipulation to defray the whole expense of the voyage in coming and returning, and to afford them a decent support during their continuance in the ministry." The King was pleased to add, that future ministers who might choose to go upon these terms, should not be entitled to the superior privileges of pensions and preferments heretofore granted to the American Missionaries.

The congregations of Racoon and Pensneck yet feeling the distress of a calamitous war; and the first being moreover involved in a most difficult enterprize of erecting the new church, could not immediately comply with these conditions. I therefore informed the archbishop that for the present a temporary vacancy was eligible; and that I would to the utmost of my power lessen the disadvantages thereof.

It must be remarked, that the Swedish government had already in the year 1773 by the ministry of the Mission proposed to the respective congregations a partial reform of the former plan: to wit, "that they should bear the expense of the voyage from London to America, and from here again to that place for their pastors; the crown, as usual defraying the remaining part. The intervening war prevented any attention to this proposal. It was laid before the respective vestries on the restoration of peace:—Those of Wicacoa with its annexes, and of Christina resolved to comply with the demand, in case they should request the favour of Swedish successors after their present pastors: that of Racoon and Pensneck promised to contribute according to the ability of their less opulent congregations.

In the meantime the Swedish language decreased continually by decrease of the ancient people. The clergy themselves were sensible of the great disadvantages attending the usual change of missionaries every 7 or eight year; and represented the matter in its true light to the archbishop and consistory. The vestry of Wicacoa, K - - ss and U. Mer.[119] received with grateful respect my appointment to their churches; and acknowledged their great obligation to the King and his illustrious predecessors for the long continued care of their spiritual wellfare;—but at the same time declined a continuance of this favour, as the great change of circumstances must hereafter make the mission a burden to the Crown of Sweden, without an adequate benefit to the congregations, which had totally lost the language of their ancestors—; they therefore signified their intention of providing for themselves after my departure.

The vestry of Christina church expressed the same sentiments.

The congregations of Racoon and Pensneck did not come to an immediate resolution on this affair; but by my advice waited until the debt incurred for the new church was somewhat reduced by the rents falling due after my removal; and in the view of knowing how

---

119 K - - ss, and U. Mer., must mean Kingsessing and Upper Merion.

long the mission might be kept up in the other churches under the Rvd. Lawrence Girelius,[119a] and myself. The daily decay of the Swedish tongue by the death of ancient and respectable members; the probability of our speedy return to Sweden; the unpleasant situation of a solitary missionary, and the great expense of a probably frequent change of ministers, insupportable for the small revenue of their churches, finally determined their coincidence in sentiment with their sister-congregations.

The arch-bishop of Sweden having submitted to his majesty these sentiments of the congregations, received the Kings final resolve, which he communicated in a letter addressed to the vestries of the churches that compose the mission, dat. Upsal 25th of June 1789, of which the following is the principal matter accurately translated.

The King approving of the reasons that induce the congregations henceforth to choose their ministers, rather than to be supplied with Swedish Missionaries at the expense of the Swedish Crown—has thereunto given his gracious consent; and in consequence thereof permits the yet remaining Swedish Missionaries, the commissaries, Lawrence Girelius and Nicholas Collin to return to their native country, as soon as their circumstance may render it convenient. At the same time the King, from the love he bears to the Swedish name, appreciates unto all the members of these congregations, as in part descendants from Sweden, all manner of felicity spiritual and temporal; and will have them assured of his royal favor.

It shall also ever be my sincere wish and ardent prayer, that allmighty God may with his grace and mercies embrace the members of these congregations, jointly and separately; and that the Ghospel-light which was first kindled in those parts by the tender sollicitude of Swedish Kings and the zeal of Swedish clergymen, may there, while days are numbered, shine with the perfect brightness, and produce the most salutary fruits.

The grace of our Lord Jesus Christ, the love of the Father, and the fellowship of the Holy Ghost, be with and over you all; Wishes from a most sincere heart.

Your Affectionate Servant

UNO VON TROIL.

119a Lars (Lawrence) Girelius (1739-1805), was appointed assistant pastor in the Swedish American Mission in 1767. He arrived in Philadelphia in October of the same year and was assigned to the Holy Trinity (Old Swedes') Church in Wilmington. On June 10, 1770, he was installed as rector of the parish.

Girelius remained in Wilmington until the spring of 1791, although he had permission to leave the country as early as September 2, 1775. He married Christina Lidenius, the daughter of the late pastor

During the vacancy I gave the congregations every attention consistent with my distant situation, and multiplicity of business. At Swedsborough I performed Divine service every third sunday during the summer and autumn 1786; and by longer intervals the two following years. I likewise visited some worthy members in their sickness; and preached some funeral sermons. Besides, I made frequent journeys for settling the business of the new church. Pensneck could not possibly obtain the same share of service; yet I officiated for a few times at that church, and also preached occasionally at houses on afternoons after finishing the service at Racoon.

Having no doubt but that the Swedish government would take the above final resolution upon the mission, I consulted with the vestry on the means of providing an American Successor. We determined to make proposals to the Rvd. Christian Streit, Pastor of a Lutheran Church in Virginia. He paid a visit to Swedsborough in the fall 1788, and expressed great satisfaction in the honour conferred upon him, desiring time for consideration. By letter of the 1st. Sept. 1789 he notified that he must with regret decline the offer, because of a precarious state of health, and of the impossibility of providing a successor in his congregations.* This gentleman had been educated by Dr. Wrangel when Rector of Wicacoa, and afterwards ordained by the German Lutheran Ministry. With knowledge of the German tongue, he has, being country-born a perfect expression in the English.

After failing in this I intended to try other means for an auspicious settlement of the churches. In the meantime the vestry of Swedesborough engaged Mr. Croes[120] to give what service he could; and after a few months satisfactory trial called him to the pastoral charge; which, I hope and sincerely pray! may promote the glory of God, and the happiness of souls.

In the meantime Mr. Wade had for a twelve month served the congregations by agreement between him and them; without any interposition of mine.

The foregoing narrative sufficiently accounts for the gradual cessation of the Swedish mission; first in Racoon and Pensneck, and afterward in the Christina Church,[121] by the return of Doctor Girelius to Sweden in the month of May last,** with his wife and four children.

Every person of reflection must be sensible, that the Swedish mission has in a considerable degree contributed to the moral civilization of this young country. This great blessing claims the more gratitude from all concerned, as the kindness of their mother country was perfectly gratuitous, and yet very troublesome. The total expense of the mission for near a century amounts to seven or eight thousand

---

* Those congregations are German.
** He lately obtained this distinction from the College of Philadelphia.
120 Rev. John Croes remained in Swedesboro for some years. He and Rev. Collin became fast friends and often corresponded.
121 The Old Swedes' Church in Wilmington.

pounds ster. The missionaries have encountered great hardships, by long and perilous voyages; many years absence from a native land peculiarly dear to Sweeds; by the indigent circumstances of a new country; and by the difficulties of a clerical charge, where the interest of religion is not supported either by laws, or public opinion. The pastors of Racoon and Pensneck have allways borne the heaviest burden, from the insalubrity of a low swampy and less improved country;* the scattered situation of the people for thirty miles in length, and twelve in breadth** and from the scanties of support: the revenue of the churchlands being small; and the ministers never having any regular salaries, but depending on the presents of a few generous members. My sufferings have been very severe:—During the war the rents of the church-lands were insignificant by the incredible depreciation of the congregations money; which finally passed one hundred and fifty to one specie dollar, and sunk in the hands of the unfortunate holders. The congregations did but little for my relief; because several of the best members were distressed by the barbarous devastations of parties. From these causes, and the failure of my supplies from home I was at times in want of necessaries. Yet, this indigence, however disagreeable to persons accustomed to the conveniencies of life, and placed in respectable stations, would have been very supportable in a firm state of health;—but unfortunately my constitution, allready in the second year after my arrival much injured by the Fever and ague, was every year harassed by various painful disorders, and finally so reduced, that a change of place, or the grave seemed to be the only alternatives; especially as I could not as a Swedish missionary have relinquished the fatiguing charge of Pensneck.

May divine grace enable the pastors of souls in every nation, to approve themselves in all things as the ministers of God: in much patience, in afflictions, in necessities, in distresses, in imprisonments, in tumults, in labours, in watching, in fastings, by pureness, by knowledge, by long suffering, by kindness, by love unfeigned, by the word of truth, by the power of God, by the armour of righteousness on the right hand and on the left.* Then shall they turn many to righteousness, and shine as stars forever and ever.† May the incorruptible seed, which Swedish Missionaries have sown in these congregations, sometimes with joy, and sometimes with tears, produce abundant fruit

---

* The Swedes had been settled forty years on the west coast of Delaware before they began to improve the Jersey side.

** Not including Mauritzes River distant fifty miles from Racoon, which is an original Swedish settlement was frequently visited by the Racoon ministers, even in later times. Mr. Wicsel attended it very regularly and I did for several years, both as minister extraordinary, and rector of the congregations.

* 2 Cord.

† Dan. 12.

of the spirit in all goodness, righteousness and truth,‡ and flourish an eternal glorious planting in the land of living.

NICHOLAS COLLIN
late rector of Racoon and Pensneck, and Provost of the Swedish Mission, yet Rector of the Swedish churches in Pensylvania.

PHILADELPHIA
DEC. 10, 1791

A BRIEF ACCOUNT OF THE SWEDISH MISSION, FROM ITS COMMENCEMENT, AND CESSATION IN RACOON AND PENSNECK [122]

Since the building of the church in Swedesborough, on the Racoon Creek, the congregation is generally called by it.[122a]

By letters to the Arch Bishop and Consistory of Upsal dated the 8' of July 1778 I sollicited in pressing terms for my recall. I had then officiated for above 8 years within the Mission: to wit, as Minister extraordinary in all the Congregations from my arrival the 12' of May 1770 til the 19' of Aug. 1773; from that time as Rector of Racoon and Pensneck; and since the year 1775 as Commissary of the Mission. I had conseqvently not only served the usual term required for obtaining preferment at home, but was moreover under absolute necessity of departing;—The rents of the Church lands had by the depreciation of the current money, and the dearness of many necessary articles, fell to a tenth part of the real value. The congregations had suffered great distress from the war, and many of the more able members were, as usual, unwilling to contribute for the support of Public Worship. There was no prospect of peace or civil order for several years, and consequently, no hopes of relief. A temporary vacancy, though prejudicial to the congregations, was therefore inevitable; at the same time a saving of the little Church revenue after my departure would shorten this vacancy by adding to the Support of my Successor. All this was fully represented in the mentioned letter, with an express declaration, that if no speedy alleviation of my present distress could be effected, I should not even wait for the recall, but depart the next Spring. It must be observed that my want of subsistence would not have been grievous, if I could have drawn my Commissary salary; but this was impracticable, as all communication with Sweden was cut off by the dreadful disorders of the times.

After the seat of war had been removed from the Delaware, I obtained at least more tranquillity; and therefore resolved to wait for my recall, repeating my sollicitation for it by several letters for two

‡ Eph. 5.

122 This title is more apt than the one of the "first account". Collin omits the early history of the colony in the first part of this account of Penns Neck and transfers it to the end of the essay.

122a By this name (Swedesborough).

years. My request was at last granted by his Majestys gracious resolve of the 22d Nov. 1782. The reason of this delay was that the Consistory had not sooner presented my petition, because the King had by a previous resolve signified to them his pleasure, that the American Missionaries should remain in their stations until the event of the war was known—Probably this arose from an opinion that the Swedish interest in America was considerable, and might in case of independency be of some advantage in Sweden.

In May 1783 I received this recall. With the greatest pleasure I should then immediately have finished a long and painful exile from my dear native country; but personal concerns and anxiety for the Congregations determined me still to continue for some time; especially as the urgent plea of necessity had now ceased with the return of peace. I therefore informed the consistory of my resolution to remain for a short time, until the congregations could be supplied with a successor; declaring also, that in case his Majesty was pleased to continue the Mission, I was willing to take upon me the charge of the churches of Wicacoa, Kingsessing and Upper Merion, which were becoming vacant by the recall of the Rev. Mathias Hultgren;[123] as a new comer, however meritorius, could not be useful in that station, because of the extinction of the Swedish language;—I also expressed my willingness to assist my successor in Racoon and Pensneck by all the influence I derived from long services and personal connections.

On this request his Majesty was pleased by resolve of the 10' of Aug. 1785 to appoint me Rector of the before mentioned congregations, and also to leave Racoon and Pensneck vacant, until they should express their option of his Majesties future regulation of the Swedish Mission. This was, that whereas the congregations in their present mature state must be sufficiently able to support their ministers, and whereas they had nearly lost the language of their ancestors, which language was a principal tye of their connection with Sweden, therefore the congregations could not in future obtain any ministers from Sweden, without a formal stipulation to defray the whole expense of the voyage in coming and returning, and to afford them a decent support during their continuance in the ministry." The King was pleased to add, "that future Missionaries, who might choose to go upon these terms, should not be entitled to the superior privileges of pensions and preferments granted heretofore to the American Missionaries. The congregation of Racoon, yet feeling the distresses of a calamitous war, and being also involved in a most difficult enterprise of erecting the new Church* could not immediately comply with these conditions. I therefore informed the Arch Bishop, that for the present a tempor-

---

[123] Matthias Hultgren (1744-1809), was appointed assistant pastor of the Swedish Mission in America in 1775, but was delayed by the Revolutionary War in taking up his duties at Gloria Dei until 1779. He served there until 1786.

* The members of Pensneck were not obliged to contribute for this, but some did voluntarily.

ary vacancy was eligible, and that I would to the utmost of my power lessen the disadvantages thereof.

It must be remarked that the Swedish Government had allready in the year 1773 by the Ministry of the Mission proposed to the respective congregations a partial reform of the former Plan; to wit "that they should defray the expense of the voyage from London to America, and from here again to that place for their respective pastors: the Crown, as usual, defraying the expence from Sweden to London, and from thence home." The intervening war prevented any attention to this proposal. It was laid before the respective Vestries on the return of peace: Those of Wicacoa with its annexes, and of Christina, resolved to defray the said part of the voyage, in case they should request the favour of Swedish successors, after their present pastors: That of Racoon and Pensneck promised to contribute according to the ability of their less opulent churches. In the meantime the Swedish language decreased daily by the decease of the ancient people. The clergy themselves were sensible of the great difficulty attending the usual change of Missionaries every 7' or eighth year, and represented the matter in its true light to the Arch Bishop and Consistory. The Vestry of Wicacoa, Kings. and Upper Merion received with grateful respect my appointment to their churches, and acknowledged their great obligation to the King and his glorious Antecessors for the tender care so long displayed for their spiritual wellfare; and at the same time declined a continuance of this favour, as the great change of circumstances must hereafter make the mission a burden to the Crown, and a painful task to the missionaries, without an adequate benefit to these congregations, which had totally lost the language of their ancestors: They therefore signified that on my departure the Mission would cease in their congregations. The vestry of Christina church in like manner expressed their intention to choose for themselves a successor after the Rev. Laurence Girelius. The Congregations of Racoon and Pensneck did not immediately resolve on this affair; but by my advice waited for a year, until the debt incurred for the new Swedsborough church was somewhat reduced by the rents falling due after my removal; and in the view of knowing how long the mission might continue in the other congregations, under Mr. Girelius and myself. The continual decay of the Swedish tongue by the decease of ancient respectable members; the probability of our speedy return to Sweden; the unpleasing situation of a solitary missionary; and the great expense of a probably frequent change of ministers, scarcely supportable for the small revenue of their churches, finally determined their coincidence in sentiment with their sister congregations.

The Rev. Laurence Girelius went home in May 1791 with his wife and four children.

The Arch Bishop of Sweden Doctor Uno Von Troil having submitted to his Mty. these sentiments of the Congregations, received the King's final resolve, which he communicated in a letter adressed to the Vestries of all the churches that compose the Swedish Mission dated Upsala, 25′ of June 1789, of which the following is an extract.

"The King approving of the reasons that induce the Congregations henceforth to choose their ministers rather than to be supplied with Swedish Missionaries at the expense of the Swedish Crown, has thereunto given his gracous consent; and in consequence thereof permits the yet remaining Swedish Missionaries, the commissaries Lawrence Girelius and Nicholas Collin to return to their native country as soon as their circumstances may render it convenient. At the same time the King, from the love he bears to the Swedish name, apprecates[123a] unto all the members of these congregations, as in great part descendants from Sweden, all manner of felicity spiritual and temporal; and will have them assured of his royal favour.

It also shall ever be my sincere wish and ardent prayer, that Allmighty God may with his grace and mercies embrace the members of these congregations jointly and individually; and that the Ghospel light, which was first kindled in those parts by the tender sollicitude of Swedish Kings, and the zeal of Swedish Clergymen, may there, while days are numbered, shine with perfect brightness, and produce the most salutary fruits.

The grace of our Lord Jesus Christ, the love of the Father, and the fellowship of the holy Ghost, be with and over you all.
Wishes from a most sincere heart,
Your Affectionate servant
UNO VON TROIL."

The first Swedish Colony arrived in the year 1634, and was followed by three or 4 reinforcements during the succeeding years til 1654. The Sweedes acquired by a fair purchase from the natives all the Western coast of Delaware from *Cape Hinlopen* to Trenton* and extending due west to a distance of 40 miles. Their first principal settlement was at Christina Creek, where they had a considerable fort and a church. After some years they formed considerable establishments along the river 40 or 50 miles beyond Philadelphia, and had a church at Tinnicum, where also was the Swedish Governor's residence. The Low Dutch had some time before the arrival of the Swedes in America taken possession of North river and founded, *New Amsterdam,* now *New York.* They had also got a slender footing on the eastern shore of Delaware and built a fort, called Nassau, where Gloucester now is. This vicinity naturally created a jealousy, which produced contests, and finally opened hostilities, which terminated in conquest of the infant Swedish Colony; as it was not supported by Sweden

---

123a *apprecates*—an obsolete term meaning "to pray earnestly".
* This according to the best intelligence from old narratives,

which at that time was engaged in a war with several of the first powers of Europe.

After the death of those clergymen, who accompanied the colonists from Sweden the people became very destitute until on their humble adress to *Charles the 11th* King of Sweden the mission was instituted which has continued without interruption til this time. This Mission was composed of three distinct Rectorships to wit, Wicacoa with Kingsessing and upper Merion in Pensilvania; Christina in Delaware; and Racoon with Pensneck in West Jersey—The clergy consisted of the 3 respective Rectors, and in the later times, a minister extraordinary, or common assistant. One of the ordinary pastors was also Provost or Commissary, having a degree of superintending authority over the whole Mission. The Extraordinary had from Sweden a yearly salary of Thirty three and 1/3 pound Ster. The Commissary office has from the time of Mr. Sandin had Fifty pounds ditto. The Crown bestowed every coming Missionary ab. fifty £ ditto money to defray the expense of the voyage, and an equal sum on returning. While waiting for preferment after the return, they had adequate pensions: the commissaries one third more than the others. They also obtained very good employments; several having been rewarded with the best Rectorships in Sweden.

Til the beginning of this century Racoon and Pensneck made parts of the congregations over the River; the first of Wicacoa, and the other of Christina—In the year 1704 a church was built where the New Racoon church now stands, and endowed with the lands yet preserved; to wit the 100 acres, of which Swedsborough makes a part; and the marsh-meadow of 6 acres 4 miles from there down Racoon Creek. Their first minister *Tolstadius*[123b] was drowned in Delaware 1706. The second *Auren* died 1713. He was succeeded by *Abraham Lidenius,* who also became pastor of Pensneck: a church was erected there in 1717, and by *Jaquet* endowed with four acres of land. From that time both congregations have been united, and both conjoined in the commissions of the Rectors.

[123b] Laurentius (Lars) Tollstadius applied for permission to go to America (even at his own expense), but due to a "bad report about him" he was not accepted by the Consistory. However, he left Sweden "without a passport, authority or recommendation" and proceeded to Philadelphia, where he arrived in November, 1701. Here he represented himself as "the legally appointed pastor for Gloria Dei". Accordingly "he was allowed to perform services in the congregation for some time" and, due to the illness of Rev. Rudman, the "Wicaco (church) was at once given into (his) hands". In the midst of his activities the regularly appointed minister, Johan Sandel, arrived in Philadelphia, on March 18, 1702. Tollstadius had to move. Instead of returning to Sweden, as he was advised to do, he began preaching on the Jersey side of the Delaware River and erected a church at present Swedesboro in 1704. His labors, however, were of short duration. On May 29, 1706, he was drowned in the Delaware River,—probably committing suicide to escape appearing in court to answer a charge, as his canoe drifted ashore with a plowshare and his travelling cloak in it, showing that it did not capsize.

By the unwearied sollicitude of said Lidenius the congregations were after eight years consultation persuaded to purchase the Glebe in Pilesgrove, which contains 235 acres, and cost one hundred forty five pounds. In 1724 Mr. Lidenius went home with his wife *Maria Van Neaman* and three children. *Peter Tranberg* arrived in 1726, with *Andrew Windrufva*: who as assistant had charge of Pensneck til 1728, when he died. In 1741 Tranberg was promoted to the Rectorship of Christina.

The vacancy was in some measure supplied by *William Malander*. This person had come to America with *Dylander*, Pastor of Wicacoa, as schoolmaster. Being a student of Divinity he obtained permission to preach and baptize children, and would by mandate of the Archbishop have received orders from said Dylander and Tranberg if the first mentioned had not in the meantime departed this life. During the vacancy the Moravians created a schism, and built the meeting house in Oldman's Creek Pastor *Naesman* at Wicacoa, and Tranberg from Christina did however occasionally supply the congregations. *John Sandin* arrived the 1st. of April 1748 with his wife and a young child after a tedious and perilous voyage. He died after six months. Professor Kalm, who at this time by the King of Sweden's order travelled through North America, lived for the winter at Racoon, and preached in the church. He afterwards married Mrss Sandin, and 1751 went with her to Sweden. *Eric Unander* who came in as minister extraordinary, became 1751 Pastor of the two churches. In 1756 he was promoted to Christina church. *John Abraham Lidenius,* son of the before mentioned Abraham Lidenius, succeeded as Rector, after having since 1751 served in these congregations and those in Pensilvania. He was recalled, but in meantime died in Pensilvania. His successor *John Wicsell* became Rector 1762. *Nicholas Collin* arrived 1770 as Minister Extr. and officiated through the Mission, but especially at Racoon and Pensneck til John Wicsell's departure in autumn 1773. Since that time till July 1786 he was Rector of the congregations.

The Function of Commissary has according to circumstances been connected with all the Rectorships of the Mission: it has been conferred on three Pastors of these churches, namely Sandin, Wicsell, and Collin.

The hardships naturally attending the charge of missionaries, have been felt in a superior degree by the pastors of these churches; from the insalubrity of the climate;* the scattered situation of the people for thirty miles in length and twelve in breadh; and from the insufficiency of support—The ministers never had regular salaries; and the revenues from the church estates were small. My sufferings have been extreme, and in a great measure occasioned by the terrible disorders of the Civil war. When this commenced, the Glebe was rented out for 12 years; and the lotts in Swedsborough were let on permanent ground

_____

* From the unimproved marshes on Delaware and the several creeks.

rent. All was paid in that currency of the Congress, which from a constant depreciation became 150 for one, and finally sunk to nothing in the pockets of the unfortunate owners. Besides, many members of the congregations became extremely distressed by the ravages of parties, while the seat of war was upon Delaware, and by the cruel animosities, which kindled them to reciprocal injuries. May God in his mercy ever for the future forbid such madness. May righteousness and peace forever bless this western world.*

For the information of posterity, when the Swedish origin may be quite forgotten, I have left on record the above narrative. Every person of reflection may judge how much the Svedish mission has contributed to the moral civilization of this young country. This great blessing claims the more gratitude from all concerned, as the kindness of the mother country has been quite gratuitous, and yet very troublesome. The total expense of the mission for near a century amounts to seven or eight thousand pound Sterl. The Missionaries encountered great sufferings—by long and perilous voyages, by many years absence from a native land peculiarly dear to Swedes; by the indigent circumstances of a young country; and by the difficulties of a clerical charge, where the interest of religion is not supported either by law or public opinion. May the incorruptible seed, which Svedish Missionaries have sown in these congregations, some times with joy, and sometimes with tears, produce abundant fruit of the spirit, in all goodness, righteousness and truth,** and flourish an eternal glorious planting in the land of the living!

Nicholas Collin

Late Commissary for the Swedish Mission, and Rector of Racoon and Pensneck, yet Rector of the Svedish churches in Pensilvania.

Philadelphia
12th Dec. 1791

REGISTER OF THE SWEDESBORO AND PENNS NECK PARISHES [123c]

A regular account of the Members being very useful, the following was begun. The majority of the families attended Divine Worship frequently: the others were coming into regular membership.

A

APPLIN Peter, born the 1st. of July 1753 of Dutch Parents. His wife Sarah, born in June 1758, Halton of Swedish Par: Their child: Charles b. 7th of Aug. 1782. Her daughter Rebecca with her former husband Andrew Hellms.

---

* The good members of the Sweedsborough and Pensneck churches did not partake in wicked excesses.
** Eph. 5.
[123c] Compiled by Nicholas Collin, probably in 1786.

B

BERTILSON, John, Rachel his wife. Children Wiljam b. 3 Nov. 1773. Cathrine 12 March 1777, Rachel 14 Febr. 1786.

BERTILSON, Andrew, Mary his W. Child Wiljam b. 12 of Febr. 1775.

BAKER, Wiljam, B. 12 Sept. 1773, the mother is living now know [not known] whether the father is.

BIDDLE WILJAM, (nephew of Aaron next following) his mother was a Sweede, Van Neaman. Born 31st Oct. 1759. Rebecca his wife, b. 14 Febr. 1759 of Swedish-Moravian Par. Their children Wiljam b. Febr. 22 1781. Sara Oct. 2, 1784. Bound to this W. Biddle Rebecca b. 14 June 1773. Her father Laurence Peterson deserted her mother Susanna, who is yet living.

BIDDEL ARON b. 29th of July 1736. Elizabeth his wife, b. 7th of March 1739. Maiden name Stonmez. Their children yet unmarried Jesiah B. 1st of March 1763. Wiljam b. 15th of Jan. 1765. Sara b. 22d of Sept. 1767. John B. 22d of Feb. 1770. Aron b. 11th of Febr. 1772. Elizabeth b. 18th of Jan. 1774. Barbary b. 3d of April 1776. Samuel b. 15th of Novemb. 1780. Jacob b. 31st of Sept. 1783.

BIDDEL, George, (Son of the above Aron) b. 9th of Febr: 1761. Mary, his wife, born Hancock, now about 25 years old. Their children: Wiljam b. 15th of March 1780. Rachel b. 13th of March 1782. George 23 July 1786.

BIDDEL (John, Brother of the above Aron Bittel), born about the year 1733, his father English, mother Low Du[t]ch. Christina his wife, about 6 years older, born Halton, her mother. Their children Abel, married Anne, married to Clark, Elizabeth b. 24 of Decemb, 1762. Barbary b. 15 of Apr. 1764. Mary b. 18th of Jan. 1766. John b. 7th of Apr. 1768. Bound boys, John Stedham, and Samuel Stiner.

BIDDEL, Abel, son of John above, b. 30th of May 1759. His wife Sarah b. Cox, 15 of Jan. 1757, her mother also a Sweed. Her son with Dahlbo deceased, John. Their common child. Abel b. 20 Dec. 1784.

BILDERBACK, Daniel b. in 1768, of John et Elizabeth Billerback, deceased. he lives now with Andrew Stanley.

BIDDEL, Wiljam son of Aaron. Hanna his wife. Child Rebecca b. 29 July 1786.

BARNET, Elihu, Irishman, about 42 years old, not baptised, but inclined for our church. Marget his wife born Corydon of Irish descent, baptized by Mr. Lidenius, b. 22d of Sept. 1751. Their children, Elizabeth b. 17th of March 1772. Wiljam 8th of Nov. 1773.

BARRET, Cathrine, about 36 years old, at present deserted by her husband. Her parents were Mackintosh, and Corneliusson a Swedish woman.

BROWN, John about 30, not baptized. Elizabeth his wife born Jacquet Sept. 8th 1756. Children: Isac b. 5th of Oct. 1772. Jonathan 21st of Febr. 1780.

BOON, Rachel, Widow of Cornelius Boon, b. 29th of Apr: 1743. Children with him: Peter 8th of Nov. 1765. Elizabeth and Andrew twins b. 12th of Decemb. 1768. Magdalena December 19th 1771. Gertrud 26th of March 1781. Her black servants: Anne, educated a Presbyterian and attached thereunto. Robin preferring the church. Both about 36 years.

BARNEY, Elia. Alice h.w. Ch. Jeremia b. 6 of Feb. 1787.

BURTON, Jonas. Elizabeth his wife, born Cole. Child Rebecca 9th Aug. 1784.

C

CABEL, Jacob. Rachel his w. Child John B. 20 July 1786.

CALEB, Daniel. Deborah, his wife, d' Ann b. 26 Sept. 1778.

CARNEY, Thomas, Justice of the peace. His wife Mary b. the 12th of January 1755, not baptized 23d of June 1783. Their Children: Ruth b. 17th of May 1773. Hanna b. 27th of July 1778. Thomas b. 5th of March 1783. These baptised on the same day with their mother, born Harris.

CATTS, Lewis b. about Christmas 1725. Cathrine his wife b. Euler, about 3 years younger, both natives of Germany. Their children: John, George, Elizabeth, Lewis, all married. Samuel b. 1769.

CATTS, John, son of the above Lewis b. 1749. Cathrine his wife. Their Children. Cathrine, b. 13th of Dec. 1773. Elizabeth March 13th 1776, Christina 13th of May 1778. John 26th of Dec. 1781. All at once baptized in year 1782.

CATTS, George, son of Lewis above, born 1751. His Wife Agnes, born Powers of German Par. Their children Hanna.

CATTS, Lewis son of —— His wife Mary b. Hudson the 25th of Sept. 1759, her mother a Sweede. Their child: Michael b. 21st of Nov. 1783.

CATTS, Jacob, b. 11 of Febr. 1760. Emilia his W. daughter of Currey, b. 11 of June 1764. Their ch. Mary b. in Oct. 1782—John b. 18 March 1784.

CRIPPS, (John) b. Nov. 24th 1747. Leureiny his wife, born Billerback, b. 2d. of Jan. 1749. Their children: Witton b. 26th of May 1771. Sara b. 26th of March 1773. Cathrine b. 14th of Nov. 1777. Thomas b. 4th of Sept. 1779. Reiny b. 1st. of Febr. 1782.

COLE, John, 57 or 8 year old now in the year 1784. His par. both Germans. His wife Mary b. Cades of English Parents, about 52 year old. Their children, Cathrine, wife of Hugh Gunning. Adam, married. Marget b. 25th of Aug. 1766, John b. 10th of Jan. 1771. Charity 1st. of Dec. 1773. Hanna b. 6th of May 1778.

COLE, Adam son of the above John, b. 14th of Apr. 1762. His wife Susanna Dahlbo.

COLE, Adam, his parents both Germans, born about the year 1742. His wife Maria, born Hawk in the beginning of Dec. 1746. Their children: Mary b. 3d of Sept. 1767. Cathrine 25th of Nov. 1769. John 14th of May 1772. Jacob 1 of Apr. 1775. Adam in the last of March 1778. Casper 14th of March 1780. Sara last day of Oct. 1783.

COLE, Andrew, Anna Statia, his wife, their common child Samuel, about three April 1781—Priscilla b. 26 of June 1782. His own with a former wife:— Sarah, b. in 1775—Stacy, b. in 1777.

D

DAHLBO, Rachel, widow of Charles, born Lock about 1735 or 6 of Swed. Par. Her children with him. Lydia b. 13th of Dec. 1761. Rachel b. 20th Sept. 1764. Charles 31st Oct. 1770. John 1st. Apr. 1775.

DALBO, Andrew, son of Gabriel deceased, with the first wife Mary b. Embson.

DALBO, Wiljam, son of John, and Alice, b. 2d of June 1756. His wife Ann. Their Ch. Henry B. 5 of June 1781.

DALBO, Rebecca, widow of Gabriel, born Vanneaman of Swedish par. about 1747. Her children with him, Daniel, married. Magdalena b. 5th of March 1763. Wiljam 2d of July 1765. Elizabeth, 11th March 1770. Laurence— Oct. 1775.

Magdalena Dahlbos (the above) illegal child Samuel b. Aug. 31st. 1783.

DAHLBO, Charles, b. 2d of Jan. 1757. Elizabeth, his wife, born Johnson, the 2d of Novembr. 1764, baptized 25th of Apr. 1784. Children, Joseph b. 25th of May, 1783, Charles 22 of Jan. 1787.

DAHLBO, Abel, b. 9th of May 1770. The only living child of Israel and Gertrude Dahlbo, deceased.

DAHLBO, John, b. 3d of Decemb. 1779 son of Samuel Dahlbo deceased, and Sara, now wife of Abel Biddle.

DAHLBO, Cathrine, widow of —— Dahlbo, born 23d of Nov. 1731 of Swedish parents. Her children with him. Andrew b. 25th of Febr. 1758. Magdalena 11th of June 1762. Israel b. 7th of July 1764. Mary 25th of July 1767. Sara wife of John King.

DAHLBO, Daniel b. 22 of Oct. 1761. Son of Rebecca—Widow of Gabr. born Van Neaman. his wife Barbara, daughter of George Peterson b. 17, Febr.

[224]

1764. Their children. George b. 15 Febr. 1783, Gabriel 12 Aug. 1784. Rebecca 18 March 1786.

DAHLBO, William, Mary his wife—son Wm. b. 5 Dec. 1778.

DELANY, (Mathew) b. —— Christina his wife born Hopman. Their children. Mathew b. 15 of March 1776. Christina 22d of June 1778. Jestis 20th of Jan. 1781. Edward 20th of Febr. 1782.

DENNIS, George b. 8th of Nov. 1753, baptised by me. His wife Eleonore, born Peterson 2d of Nov. 1752. Their child, Sara b. 13 of Nov. 1774.

DELAVOU, James, b. 29 Dec. 1758. Mathias DELLAVOU, his brother.

E

ELLVIL, John, b. 28th of Apr. 1747. Sare his wife, born Mecum of Swedish parents about the year 1750.

F

FLOID, David b. about the year 1734, his mother was of English descent. Elizabeth his wife about the same age born Scaggin, her mother was a Swede. Their children, Joseph, b. 8 May, 1760. Isac 25th March, 1764. Solomon 20th of March 1766. Wiljam 4th Febr. 1769. David 5th March 1771. Henry 17 Oct. 1773.

FLOYD, Cathrine, widow of John Floyd, a son of the above David, born ——. Her daughter with him. Elizabeth b. 29th of Apr. 1783.

FARROW, Thomas. Mary h. W.—Ch. Charlotte b. 29 March 1785.

G

GUNNING, Hugh. His wife Cathrine born Cole 14th of Apr. 1761.

GRYFFITH, Laurence, b. about 1757. Susannah, his wife, about 9 years younger—son John. b. 16 Febr. 1786.

GARDINER, James and Sarah—Son Henry, b. 27 March 1779.

H

HALTON, Charles, b. 18 Decemb. 1752, his father was a Sweede, his mother a sister of John and Aaron Biddel. Mary his wife daughter of Jacob Archer, b. 22 Jan. 1760. Childr. Wiljam b. 7 March 1785. Dodo b. 14 Apr. 1787. With his first wife Alice born Dahlbo, Charles b. 19 June 1776. Bound to him Robert Hoffman a foundling b. Oct. 1767. Sarah Savoj, daughter of Jacob and Alice, b. 3d of Febr. 1773.

HALTON, John, brother of Charles, b. 22d 1758. Cathrine h. W. child John b. 14 Febr: 1786.

HALTON, Jesse, a brother of the same b. 7th Jan. 1769.

HARDIN, Peter (his mother was Anne Peterson) b. Sept. 29, 1757. His wife Rebecca b. Peterson the 20th of Nov. 1757. Their child. John, b. 24 Nov. 1776, Henry, Jan. 17th 1779. Sarah 5th of Apr. 1781.

HAWK, but properly Haag, John Casper, born in Germany 27th of Jan. 1723. His wife Susanna Margareta, one year and 6 months older. Their children: Jacob, married. Maria wife of Adam Cole, Susanna b. 15th of May 1764.

HAWK, Jacob, son of the above Casper, b. 20th of Decemb. 1755. His wife Mary, born Dahlbo of Swedish parents, about the same age. Their child. Susanna b. Aug. 1781.

HELMS, Cathrine, widow of Andrew Helms, born Boon about 46 or 6. Her children with him. Helena b. in January 1763. Sara b. 8th of June 1764, married to Ebenezer Pitman. Mary b. 11th of Jan. 1770. John 24th of Febr. 1772

HELLMS, Rebecca born 15 Julii 1778, Par. Andrew Hellms, deceased, and Sara now wife of Peter Applin.

HYLER, Henry. Mary h. W. Child. Wiljam b. 6 May 1782. Henry 9 Dec. 1783. Elizabeth 12 March 1786.

HEWS, Wiljam, b. 20th of March 1770. Par. John Hews deceased, and Marget, now wife of John Holston.

NB. The proper Swedish name is Hollsten, but some call it Holston, others Holson, as the English maim all foreign names, and many here cannot *spell their own.*

HOLSTON, John b. in Febr. 1738. His father Swedish. Martha his wife, born Hardin, 25th of March 1746. Their children Rebecca b. 18th of Apr. 1781. John b. in the last of Apr. 1783.
With his first wife Susannah Scott, Wiljam b. 3d of Jan. 1770. Her son with a former husband. The above Wiljam, both are now living with them.

HOOPER, Alexander and Elizab.—Son Benjamin b. 17 Jan. 1776.

J

JACQVET, (Hans) b. —— Barbara his W. born Austin, the 30th of August 1737. Their children yet unmarried. John b. 11th of Dec. 1754. Joseph 9th of Apr. 1769.

JAQVET (Paul) son of the above Hans et Barbara, b. 11th of Jan. 1757. Anne his W. born Kitts the 28th of Febr. 1760. Children: Jane b. 2d of April 1781. Hans b. 14th of Apr. 1783.

JAGVET, (Peter) son of the same parents b. 13th of July 1763.

JAQUETT, Hanse born Nov. 11, 1728. Died Nov. 11, 1803. Paul, son of Hance, born Jan. 11, 1757. Peter, son of Hanse, born July 13th, 1763. Hanse, son of Paul, born July 13, 1763

JUSTIS, JACOB. Mary his W. Child. Nicholas b. 30 Dec. 1786.

K

KING (John) about 35 years old, baptised at Christine, Sara, his wife, born Dahlbo, the 29th of March 1759. Their children Jacob b. 13th of August 1777. Laurence, b. 25th of March 1779. Rebecca b. 10th of April 1781. Cathrine b. 21st of March 1783. John b. 6 March 1784. Andrew b. 22d March 1787.

KAMP, Hanna, widow of Mathias Kamp, born Johnson the 10th of March 1759, baptised 26th of April 1784. Children with him: John b. 24th of June 1778. Joseph b. 19th of May 1781. Wiljam b. 11th of Aug. 1783.

KEEN, Jonas, of Swedish par. born 7th of Apr. 1742. Christiana his wife, born Van Neaman of Sw. Parents, their children John, b. 28th of Nov. 1763. David 13th Oct. 1766. Jonas 9th of June 1768. Henry b. 1772. Marget 20th Febr. 1782.

KITTS, Robert, b. about — year 1736 with his departed wife. John married; Anne wife of Paul Jacquet. Rusilla b. 1771. Felix 1774. Lives with him Mary Lansbury b. 12, Oct. 1757.

L

LAURENS, Wiljam, b. about the year 1749. Elizabeth his wife born Rauson the 3d of March 1760, baptised by me the 29th of Mai 1778. Her father yet living in Pensilvania, of Swedish descent, her mother Irish. Their child: Wiljam b. 3d of May 1782.

LUMMUS, Jane, daughter of Andrew et Christina Stanley her husband Edward Lummus. Their children not christ[ened].

M

MACKGILL, Cathrine, born Catts in the year 1741, A Lutheran German, married to John MackGill a Roman Catholic. Their son James b. 4th of Febr. 1789 baptised by me: the other children baptised by a Roman Priest, where they formerly lived.

MECUM, Wiljam, born of Swedish parents the 12th of June 1730 with his wife Sara born Sennecson, deceased, Children: Sarah b. 19th of Sept. 1767. Margaret b. 23d of Aug. 1770, Wiljam b. 22d of Nov. 1772. Rebecca 7th of Oct. 1774. George Washington b. 10th of Oct. 1777. Andrew b. 23d of Febr. 1780. Eleonore 6th of February 1782.

MACKELROY, William and his wife Rachel. Son John b. 20 March 1783.

MCGILL, James and Cathrine. Son James, b. 4 Feb. 1784.

MEREDITH, Richard. Ann his w. Child. Jacob Jones b. 16 of May 1773. Daniel b. 9 of Nov. 1778. Diana b. Nov. 21 1780.

MORTON, Erasmus and Kesiah—son John, born 9 Sept. 1776.

P

PENTON, James. Elizabeth h. W. Child. Rebecca b. 4th Nov. 1784.

PARKER, Thomas and Cathrine—Childr. Mary, b. 15 July 1775—George, b. 9 Sept. 1778—John Leif, and Margret Ann b. 11 Jan. 1779. Thomas b. 2d May 1781.

PETERSON, Thomas, ——

PETERSON, Henry b. 17th of Decemb. 1727 of Swedish Parents (his mother was Cobb. Sara his wife b. 17 of Febr. 1728. Her father was Barber an Englishman, her mother Sweede, Peterson. Their Children: Eleonore wife of George Dennis. Thomas Married. Rebecca wife of Peter Hardin, Wiljam, married. Sarah b. 3d of Nov. 1762. Christiana 8th of June 1767.

PETERSON, Thomas, son of the above Henry b. 17th of Oct. 1753. Charity h. W. d. of James and Sara Dennis b. 5 March 1760. Child. Anne Oct. 16 1779. Sara 22d March 1782. Wiljam 25 Sept. 1784.

PETERSON, Wiljam, son of the above Henry, b. 26th of Aug. 1760. Rebecca his wife, born Peterson, 29 Dec. 1761. Their children, Thomas b. 15th of March 1784. Eric 5 March 1786.

PETERSON, Eric, b. about the year 1748 of Swedish Parents. Widower after an English wife.

PETERSON, George, (brother of the above Eric(b. 21st of Aug. 1739. Emily his wife, born Currey of baptist parents 20th of June 1761. Their children, Emily, b. last of Decemb. 1782. Wiljam 22d Jan. 1784.
His children with his first wife Sarah Biddle, sister of John Biddel above: Rebecca wife of the above Wiljam Peterson. Barbara marr. to Daniel Dahlbo. Mary b. 7th June 1767. Sara 1st of Jan. 1776.

POULSON, Paul, about 43. Rhody his wife, born Van Neaman 5th of May 1736. Children: Charles her own with Dahlbo, the above Dahlbo. Common, Darias Nov. 1st. 1763. Debora 19th of Jan. 1768. Anne 18th of Febr. 1770. Joseph 13th of March 1772. Andrew 24th of Nov. 1776. Peter 7th of Apr. 1781. With them lives, being kept by the town, Abigail about 29, her father was a quaker, and her mother Eleonore Van Neaman, sister of this Rhody Poulson.

POULSON, Joseph, born in — year 1743 of Swedish par. Mary his wife, born Allen, of English decent, about — year 1744. Their children, Elizabeth b. Nov. 1763. Marget Nov. 1765 Jeremiah Dec. 14th 1767. Thomas 17th of March 1770. Hanna 16th Febr. 1772. Richard Dec. 1773. Joseph 21 June, 1775. Andrew 28 Jan. 1777. George Nov. 1779. Mary Nov. 1783. Sara 3 Sept. 1786.

POULSON, Jesia. Children with his deceased wife. Charles b. 22 June 1786. With Hanna born Dahlbo. John b. 25 of Febr. 1788.

PITMAN, Ebenezer, of English parents, his mother living and married to John Sparks, not baptised, born 26th of Jan. 1761. His wife Sara born Hellms 8th of June 1764

R

RAWSON, Robert. Sara h. W. Ch. Rebecca b. 20 of Nov. 1785.

RAWSON, Wiljam, Elizab. h. W. Ch. Isaac b. 27 of Feb. 1785.

RISENER, Paultes, born about 1744 of German Parents. Martha his wife, born Jemmerson, her mother was Brita Stilman, a Sweede, born Febr. 1744. Their childr. Hanna 18 Oct. 1767. Elizabeth 2d Oct. 1769. John 10 Dec. 1775. Lydia 21 Jan. 1777. Mary 26 Dec. 1779. Wiljam 19 Oct. 1782.

ROBERTS, Edward, born in Ireland 1st. of Febr. 1725, bred to the church of England, Marget his wife, born Hains 16th of Febr: 1749, bred to the Swedish church. Children, James with his first wife, with this Rebecca b. 2d of Octobr. 1778. Marget 4th of Jan. 1781.
Her children with the first husband Michael Cornelius, who deserted her. Elizabeth b. 21st of Aug. 1767. Peter b. 1st of Sept. 1770.
Bound to them Mary Griffith, b. 18th of Aug. 1768. daughter of John and Mary Griffith both deceased.

ROBERTS, James, son of the above Edward, b. Jan. Priscilla his wife, born Dalbo. Their children: Mary b. 30th of November 1776. Elizabeth b. the last of July 1781. Edward b. 1st of March 1784.

RUSSEL, Rachel, b. 3d of Febr. 1765 of John and Alice Russel, who are baptised, — but baptised 25th of Apr. 1784

S

SAVOY, John b. —— Rebecca his wife born Dahlbo. Their children: Rebecca b. Jan. 26th 1777. Sara last day of Sept. 1780. Anne 30th of Oct. 1782.

SAUNDERS, Duncan and Elizab. d Mary, b. 24 Apr. 1769.

SENNECSON, Andrew b. —— Sara his W. born ——.

SENNECSON, Andrew, son of the above b. 19 of Febr. 1749. Margaret h. W daught. of Sq. Johnson, b. Aug. 2d 1756. Their ch. Robert b. 15 of Apr. 1780. Mary b. 27 of Aug. 1781. His child with first wife, Henry b. Oct 6, 1773, Andrew 14 July 1775.

SENNECSON, John. Susanna h. W. Ch. Francis b. 15 of Dec. 1781. Hester b. last of March 1778.

SEVIL, David. Sara h. W. Ch. Hanna B. 28 Dec. 1785.

SIMMONDS, Wiljam, his wife Elizabeth. Their child. Charity b. 14th Sept 1784. Wiljam 12 Dec. 1786.

SPARKS, Henry, Child Mar.

SPARKS, John born 1759, his father is a Presbyterian his mother was Marget, born Jarret a Swedish churchwoman. Cathrine his wife, daughter of Leonard Stanton. Their child. Marget b. 4th of Aug. 1781. Mary b. 30th of Aug 1782. Sara b. 23 of Febr. 1785. George 10 Nov. 1786.

SPARCS, Henry, brother of the above John. Mary his wife b. Stanton, sister of above Cathrine, 9th Nov. 1760. Child. Hanna b. 14 Jan. 1784. Mary 6 Dec. 1785.

STANLEY, Andrew, b. in Aug. 1723, his mother was a Sweede, Christina his wife, born James in 1729. Their childr. Onesiphrus 24th Dec. 1750. Jane, wife of Lummus, Nathanial   Sennic 4th Febr. 1762. Anne 17th Apr. 1765. Margaret 8th May 1767: Henry 13 Sept. 1772. Bound to them Daniel Billerback.

STANLEY, Nathaniel son of above Andrew. b. 14 Oct. 1757. Child. with his deceased wife Marget born Peterson, Andrew b. 29 June 1781.

STEDHAM, John, an orphan, now bound to John Biddle, his mother was Judith Hellms, b. 25th of March 1767.

STINER, b. 5th of Febr. 1769. Par. —— bound to the same.

STEPHENS, John. Ursula his wife. Their ch. John, b. 21 of Febr. 1783.
STRIMPLE, John. Mary, his wife, born Burton. Their children: Wiljam b. 7 Nov. 1784.

T

TOSSA, Samuel. Sara his W. Child. Marget b. 20 of Dec. 1778. Andrew 15 of March 1780.
TUFT, Brathwaite, 28 of March 1741. Children with his wife Dorothy born Fledger, deceased, Brathwaite, b. 28 July, 1763, baptized by me 12th of March 1775. With his second wife Mary, born Marshall, deceased Mary b. 16 Aug. 1767, baptized by me 12 March 1775 with his third wife deceased, Christina born Richmond, he had Sarah b. 26 Decemb. 1774. Christened by me the above 12 of March with the other two, NB she is dead.

V

VANNEAMEN, Alexander, son of Wiljam and Christina Van Neaman deceased, b. in — year 1751, or 52. Rebecca his W. d. of John and Rebecca Paget deceased. b. —— Children: Mary b. 12 Sept. 1780. Rebecca 16 Nov. 1783.
VANNEAMEN, Garret. Barbara, his W. Child. Elizabeth b. 18 of Apr. 1778. John 26 of March 1774. Isaac 22 of Jan. 1776.
VELIN, Hanna daughter of David Billerback and Sara Poddy, b. 1 July 1763 Her child Sara b. in mid. Apr. 1782.

W

WEBBER, Thomas. Mary h. W. Ch. Thomas b. 9th of Jan. 1782.

My intention was to have completed the foregoing register of the members, on the plan I begun; from which the number and connections may appear under an easy and comprehensive view. But my removal, and the change that gradually took place, prevented it.

The records of baptisms, marriages, and burials for Pensneck are by Mr. Wicsell placed on the Racoon Church book, because, as his mention thereof is in the Swedish records in this book, this Pensneck book of records did not come into his hands before 1767. As the local distinction between the two congregations was never accurately fixed, some baptisms, and most of the marriages are by me recorded on the Racoon books.

[229]

RECORDS OF BAPTISMS, MARRIAGES
AND DEATHS

RECORDS OF BAPTISMS

PENS NECK 1713

Olof and Magdalena von Neeman's daughter, Elizabeth, born ——, christened on September 14. Godparents: Jacobus von devair, Gabrielsson Petersson, Catharina von devair, and Elizabeta von Neeman.

William and —— Philpot's Anna, born ——. Christened on September 20. Godparents: Johannes Senek, Jacob Savoj, Ingrid Hindersson and Margareta Philpot.

Henric Wainam's daughter, Anna, baptised on October 4. Godparents: Anders Hindricsson, Anders Seneck, Ingridh Hindersson and Beata Hindersson.

On October 7 baptised Laurentz Cock's Son, Thomas, in Salem in English.

Cornelius Wallraven's daughter, Elizabeth, baptised on October 25. Godparents: Mathias Starck. Zacharias Berthilgren,[124] Catarina Savoj and Sara Berthilsson.

Anders and Johansson's daughter, Margareta, baptised on November 1. Godparents: Thomas Guilliamsson, Hans Shiere, Beata Hindersson and Catarina Guilliamsson.

Anders and Maria Senecks[son's] Andreas, baptised on November 17. Godparents: Albert Billerback, John Hindricsson, Ingrid Hindricsson and Catarina Wainam.

Albert and Margareta Billerback's son, Daniel, baptised on November 17. Godparents: Anders Senecks, Seneck Senecks, Anna Shiere and Beata Hindersson.

John and Elizabeth Minck's son, Johannes, born on November 25, baptised [the] 26th of the same. Godparents: Lucas Petersson, Johan von Neeman, Anna Jansson, Christina Fransson.

Elizabeth Donet's son, William, baptised on December 13. Godparents: Jacob von Devair, Hinric Johansson and Elizabeth von Neeman.

RACOON 1713

Anders and Maria Hoffman's daughter, Beata, born on December 24; christened on March 4, 1713. Her godparents were: George Kyhn, Måns Kyhn, Gertrude and Christina Petersson.

George and Ella Kyhn's daughter, Helena, born on January 1, christened on March 1. Her godparents were: Laurentz Hollsteen, Gabriel Petersson, Magdalena Kyhn and Brigitta Hoffman.

Hans and —— Halton's son, Lars, was christened on January 11, born on the 1st of the same. His Godparents were: Johannes Hoffman, John Sträng, Ella Sträng and Catharina Hoffman.

On January 12 was christened Fredrick Dinnehs' daughter, named Catarina. Her Godparents: Jonas Aureen, Fredrick Dinnehs, Ingrid Homman, Catharina Dinnehs.

Samuel and Margareta Von Neeman's son, Olof, was christened on January ——. His Godparents: Michael Homman, Maria Rambo and Elizabeth Mulicka.

Thomas and Maria Dinnehs' daughter, Christina, was born on January 26, and christened on May 16. Her Godparents: Nils Qwist, Jöns, Catharina Dinnehs and Christina Didricksson.

Gunnar and Helena Arched's son, Anders, born on February 7, [was] christened on May 16. Godparents: John Arched, Joh: Geörgen, Elizabeth Geörgen, —— Arched.

---

[124] *Berthilgren* is an unusual form. Berthil (Bertil) is a Christian name (as for instance, Prince Bertil, son of the Swedish Crown Prince) and we would expect Bertilsson.

Peter and —— Lock's son, Jonas, born on January 17, [was] christened on
——. Godparents: Anders Lock, John Geörgen, Åsa [Osa] Jones and
Brigitta Hoffman.

Olof and Eva Mulicka's son, Olof, born on July 3, [was] christened on the
2nd. Godparents: Fredrick Dinnehs, Stephen Mulicka, Elizabeth Dinnehs,
Gina Petersson.

Mickail and Judith Homman's son, Gustaf, [was] christened on August 2.
[Godparents:] John Hoffman, Jonas Cock, Elsa and Beata Jones.

Peter and —— Mattsson's son, Pehr, born on June 9, was christened on ——.
His Godparents: Bengt Bengtsson, Erik Mulicka, Maria Sandell, [Bri]
gitta Ramboo.

Lorentz and Hiertrud [Gertrude] Hollsten's daughter, Susanna, born on
Aug[ust] 31, [christened] on September 13. Godpar[ents]: George Lyke
[Lykian?,] Lars Hoffman, Catharina Hofff[man], Christina Fransson.

RACOON 1713

Matts and Julie Mattsson's son, Peter, born on Sept[ember] 6, baptised on the
13th of the same month. [Godparents]: Johan Ramboo, Gabriel Dahlbo,
Brigitta Culn and Brigitta Ramboo.

Anders and Magdelina Dahlbo's daughter, Sarah, born on Septemb[er] 7,
[baptised] on the 13th of the same. Godparents: Gabriel Dahlbo, Carl
Strängs (Streng, Strengs), Anna Cock and Elsa [Cock].

On September 13 christened John Pålson's (Paulsson's) two daughters, one
—— the other 12 years old, called Rebecca and Maria. Witnesses: Jacob
——,[125] George Kyhn, Brigitta Ramboo and Elizabeth Ramboo.

Johannes and Anna Nilsson's son, Johannes, born on S'ept[ember) 19, baptised
on the 9th. Godparents: Joh[an] Nilsson, Stephen Jones, Maria Dinnehs,
Rebecca Cock.

James and Brigitta Guarring's daughter, Elizabeth. Godparents George ——,
Olof Homman, Elizabeth Guarring and Catharina Halton. She [was]
born on Sept[ember] 7, and christened on October 18.

Anders and Maria Mattsson's daughter, Maria, born on Nov[ember] 27, baptised on January 24, 1714. Godparents: George Kyhn, John M——,[126]
Beata Jones, Christina Fish.

Olof and —— Homan's daughter, Anna, baptised on ——. Godparents: Fredrick Hoffman, Manne Didricsson, Catharina P——, Anna Halton.

PENS NECK ANNO 1714

On February 4. Göran Latien's Christina. Godparents: Jacob Hindersson,
Hans Shiere, Christina Göransson, and Ingrid Hindersson.

John Rinkman's Daniel [baptised] on February 1. Godparents: Andreas
Seneck, [Seneck] Seneks[son], Magdalena Hindersson.

Timothy and Margareta Stedham's Henric, born —— February. Godparents: Gabriel Pehrsson, Christina Petersson, Maria Sluby.

John and Gunilla Berthilsson's Andreas, born ——, baptised on April 4. Godparents: Mathias Starck, Hans Shiere, Hiertrud Corneliusson, Elizabeth
Minck.

Peter and Christina Petersson's Sarah, born ——, baptised on April 26. Godparents: Lucas Petersson, Matthias Shogen and Ingridh Petersson.

Marta and Carin Guilliamsson's Johannes, born ——, baptised on June 27.
Godparents: Olof von Neeman, Johan Hindersson, Magdalena Hindersson and Catharina Litien.

---

125 Jacob is perhaps Jacob Savoj.
126 John M. is perhaps John Mink.

Thomas and Margareta Wiggorie's Johannes, born on ——, baptised on August 8. Godparents: Johan Hindersson, Seneck Senecks:[son], Anna Shiere, and Margareta Billerback.

Zacharias and Sara Betrthilsson's William, born ——, baptised on September 12. Godparents: Olof von Neeman, John Berthilsson, Anna Petersson and Magdalena v. Neeman.

John Göransson's Laurentz, baptised on November 21. Godparents: Olof v. Neeman, Marten Johnsson, Anna Petersson and Magdalena von Neeman.

Lucas and Ingridh Petersson's Abraham, born on November 24, baptised on the 29th of the same. Godparents: Abraham Lidenius, John Minck, Elizabeth Minck.

Stephen Mulicka's son, Eric, born on ——, baptised on January 24. His Godparents: —— ——, Catharina Petersson, Ingridh M——.

Fredrich Petersson's daughter, Christina, born on January ——, baptised the 11th. Her Godparents: John J. Hoffman, John F. Hoffman, Magdalena Kyhn, Elsa Runnels.

Peter Cock's son, Gabriel, born on January 31, baptised on Febr[uary] 14. Godparents: Peter Lock, Gabriel Cock.

Michael Laikian's son, born on February 17, baptised on the 27th of the same. Godparents: M. Laikian, Elias Fish, Eva Mulicka, Armgodt Hoffman.

Lars Cock's, Elizabeth, born on ——, baptised on May 9. Godparents: Thomas Johan Ramboo, Jr., Magdalena Kyhn, Maria Ramboo.

Elias and Christina Fish's Rebecca, born on June 24, baptised on the 4th. Godparents: Johan Mulicka, Peter Rambo, Maria Mattsson, Abigail Fish.

Thomas and Maria Dinnehs' Catharina, born on July 21, baptised on the 25th. Godparents: Anders Hoffman, Fredrich Halton, Helena Dinneh and M. Petersson.

Johan and Hiertrud [Gertrude?] Senecksson's Ingridh, born on the 5th [of Sept.], baptised on the 3 October. Godparents: John Cock, Guarret von Neeman, G. Cock and Anna Cock.

Åke and Catharina Helm's Magdalena, born on September 20, baptised ——, Godparents: Elias Fish, John Ramboo, Jr., Sarah Dahlbo and Maria Ra[mboo].

Lars Petersson's Olof, born on ——, baptised on October 17. Godparents: —— Arched, Michail Hoffman, Maria Dinneh, Margareta Petersson.

Jona and Ambora Bjurström's Andreas, born on October 25, baptised on November 2. Godparents: Anders Hoffman, George Kyhn, Maria H.

Gabriel and Christina Petersson's Peter, born on November 4, baptised —— Godparents: John v. Neeman, Olof v. Neeman, Hiertrud Holls, Sarah Petersson.

Gustaf and Magdalena Lock's son, Anders, born on Nov[ember] 20, 1713. Baptised on January 24. Godparents: Anders Lock, John Lock, Christina and Maria Lock.

Stephen and Anna Jonsson's Abraham, born on December 4, baptised the 11th of the same. Godparents: Abraham Lidenius, Laurentz Hollsten, Anna Cock.

Peter and Catharina Matsson's Maria born on ——, baptised on December 12. Godparents: Matts Mattsson, Johan Ramboo, Jr., Catharina and Maria Ramboo.

Johan and Berthil Hoffman's Måns, born on ——, baptised on December 12. Godparents: Måns Kyhn, Joh: F. Hoffman, Catharina Petersson, Brigitta Hoffman.

PENS NECK 1715

Hans and Anna Shiere's Maria, born on ——, baptised on February 28. Godparents: Johan v. Neeman, Carin Stahlkopp and Carin Guilliamsson.

Jean Richman's Maria, baptised on April 10. Godparents: Anders Hindersson, Margareta Billerback.

Robbin Pickman's Anna. Godparents: Anna Petersson, Sarah Berthilsson, Abraham Savoj and Jacob Savoj. Baptised on May 15.

Cornelius Corneliusson's Jacob, born on —— May, baptised on the 15th of the same. Godparents: Jacob von Devair, Hinric Petersson, Anna Fransson, Gunilla Berthilsson.

Jean Classon's Oney, baptised on June 8.

Item Henric Vaiman's Lars.

Olof and Catharina Stahlcopp's Anna, born on ——, baptised on July 4. Godparents: Tim: Stedham, Christiern Petersson, Sara Petersson and Christina Petersson.

Olof von Neeman's Jacob, born on July ——, baptised on the 24th of the same. Godparents: Abraham Lidenius, William Englander, Helekia Masslander and Maria Sluby.

Johan von Neeman's George, born on September ——, baptised on the 25th [of Sept.]. Godparents, Jacob von Devair, Jean Minck, Anna Petersson, Christina Petersson.

Anders Henricsson's Henric, baptised on October 30. Godparents: Cornelius Corneliusson, Johan Savoj, Christina Petersson.

Item, Påwel Jansson's Christina. Godparents: Henric Billerback, Catharina Petersson.

Thom: Gillets Josua, baptised on November 11. Godparents: Lucas Petersson, John Minck, Anna Petersson, Margaretta Minck.

RACOON CREEK 1715

Hans and Brigitta Halton's Sarah, born on December 28, baptised on the 9th [of January]. Godparents: Anders Dahlbo, Magdalena Dahlbo and Fredrick Pettersson.

Jöns and Catarina Halton's Maria, born on January 20, baptised on the 29th of the same. Godparents: Johan Mulicka, Anders Petersson, Maria Dinneh, Margareta Petersson.

Carl Hoffman and Elsa Hoffman's William, born on ——, baptised on February 6. Godparents: Gabriel Petersson, Lars Hoffman, Magdalena Kyhn and Brigitta Hoffman.

James Guarring's James, born on ——, baptised on March 20. Godparents: James Guarring, Senior, Anders Hoffman, Berthil Petersson.

Johan Fred: Hoffman's Fredrich, born on ——, baptised on April 3. [Godparents:] Lourentz Hollsten, Andrew Petersson, Christina Petersson, Christina Didricsson.

Hermanus Helm's Åke, born on ——, baptised on April 4. Godparents: John I. Hoffman, Hindric Hindricsson, Margareta v. Neeman, Regina Hinderson.

Hans and Sara Petersson's Hans, born on ——, baptised on May 8. Godparents: Jan Göring, Abr. Lidenius, Catharina Hoffman, Mary Stedham.

Peter Cock's Anna. Godparents: Anders Lock, Jean Rambo, Gunnar Arched's wife, Eva Mulicka.

Michael Homman's Johannes, born on ——, baptised on June 6. [Godparents:] Anders Lock, Johan Petersson, Regina Henricsson, Debora Hoffman.

Johan and Anna Mulicka's Catharina, born on July ——, baptised on the 25th. Godparents: John Cock, George Kyhn, Christina Fish, Elsa Runnels.

Michael Laikian's Fredrich, born on ——, baptised on August 7. [Godparents:] Fredrich Hoffman, Pehr Cock, Christina Fish, Maria Rambo.

Item Anders and Magdalena Dahlbo's Olof, on July 4.[127] Godparents: Lars Halton, Gabriel, Enoch, Maria Halton, Sarah Dahlbo.

---

[127] *Faddrar d. 4 Julii,* "Godparents, on July 4". The original is confused. *Faddrar,* "godparents", was written first and then it was discovered that the date was omitted, whereupon the date was inserted after *faddrar,* preceding the names of the godparents.

Måns and Magdalena Kyhn's Måns, born on August 18, baptised the 23rd. Godparents: Anders Hoffman, Laurentz Hollsten, Elsa Hoffman, Stina Qwist.

John and Elizabeth Georgen's Maria, born on ——, baptised on the 21st. ([God-parents:] James Guarring, Sr., Manne Dircksson, Berthil Hoffman.

Peter and Maria Lock's Johannes, born on August 29, baptised on September 4. [Godparents:] Anders Matthsson, Joh. Fr. Hoffman, Eric Steehlman's wife.

Item Fredric and Helena Dinneh's Olof, born on August 30. Godparents: Anders ——, Lars Hoffman, Eva Mulicka, Anna Lock.

Laurentz and Hiertrud Holsten's Johannes, born on ——, baptised on September 5. Godparents: Gabriel Peterson, Olof von Neeman, Christina Petersson, and Elizabeth Lidenius.

John and Debora Hoffman's Lars, baptised on September 18, born on the 7th of the same. Godp[arents]:[128]

Anders and Maria Hoffman's Rebecca, born on September 8, baptised on the 17th. Godparents: Jean Göding, Johan Hoffman, Margareta Petersson.

Gunnar and Helena Arched's Elizabeth, baptised on October 2.

George and Ella Kyhn's Rebecca, born on October 2. Baptised on the 15th of the same. Godparents: Johan Mulicka, Lars Hoffman, Christina Petersson, Elsa Runnels.

PENS NECK 1716

Albert Billerback's Sarah, baptised on January 22. Godparents: William Philpot, Jean Hindersson, Magdalena Hindersson, Ingridh Hindersson.

Tim. Stedham's Ingeborg, baptised on January 26.

Geen and Catarina Billerback's Anna Maria, illigitimate, baptised on ——. Godparents: Jacob von Devair, Jacob Savoj.

Johan and Catharina Philpot's Nicolas, born and baptised on April 18. [God-parents:] Abraham Lidenius, George Litien, Elizabeth Lidenia, Anna Shiere.

Olof and Anna Fransson's Maria, baptised on April 22. Godparents: Lidenius, Jacob Hindersson, Magdalena Hindersson and Ingrid Hindersson.

Jean Robbinsson's Elizabeth, was baptised on May 13.

Anders Jansson's Morris, on July 22.

Jona and Christina Shagen's Anna, baptised on August 26. Godparents: Lour. Hollsten, John Minck, Anna Fransson and Elisabeth Minck.

John and Gunnilla Berthilsson's Johannes, born on ——. Godparents: Jonas Shagen, Jacob Wainam, Christina Shogen and the Widow Coltzberg.

Marten and Elizabeth Johnsson's Nicolas, baptised on October 21. [Godparents:] Jean von Neeman, Olof von Neeman, Catharina von [devair],

George and Christina Litien's Eric, baptised on November 1. Godparents: Abraham Lidenius, Elizabeth Lidenia.

Lucas Petersson's and Ingridh Petersson's Maria, born on ——, baptised on November 17. [Godparents:] Jonas Shagen, Anna Fransson.

RACOON CREEK 1716

On January 1 Lars and Gunilla Cock's Olof, born on ——. Godparents:

Gustaf and Magdalena Lock's Rebecca, born on December 10; baptised on January 2. Godparents: John Fr. Hoffman, John F. Hoffman, Debora Hoffman, Helena Lock.

Hindric Hindricsson's and Regina H. Andreas, born on ——, baptised on January 2. Godparents: Peter Lock, Maria Lock and Helena Lock.

---

[128] No names are given in the original.

Manne and Christina Didricsson's Helena, born on ——, christened on January 29. Godparents: Johan Cobb, Johan Kyhn, Helena Arched, Christina Qwist.

Thom. Dinneh's and Maria's Maria, born on February 15, christened on the 22nd of the same month. Godparents: Johan Cobb, Fredrick Dinneh, Olof Persson's Wife, Fredrika Qwist

Frederick and Hanna Halton's Johannes, baptised on February 26. Godparents: George Kyhn, Nicolas Hoffman, Magdalena Kyhn.

Sam. and Marg. von Numan's Margarit, born on February 2, baptised on the 9th of the same. Godparents: The Father and the mother.

Fredrick and Elsa Petersson's Hans, baptised on April 2. Godparents: Jöns Halton, Påwel Kjempe, Catharina Halton.

Olof Homman's Andreas, baptised May 23. Godparents: Lars Petersson, Nils Qwist, Maria Dinneh, Margareta Petersson.

Stephen Mulicka's Thomas. Godparents: Eric Mulika, Nils Qwist's wife.

Olof Mulicka's Maria, baptised on May 27. Godpa[rents]: Matts Mattsson, Peter Cock, Anna Mulicka, Elsa Runnels.

Johan Cock's Johannes, baptised on June 4. Godparents: Peter Rambo, Margareta Mattsson, Elsa Pålsson [Paulsson].

Matts Mattsson's Catharina. Godparents: Stephan Jones, Johan Mattsson, Lisa Lidenia.

Margareta Mattsson, born on June 25, baptised on July 5.

Peter Mattsson's Johannes, baptised on Aug[ust] 12. Godparents: John Cock, John Mattsson, Pehr Cock's wife, Elizabeth Rambo.

Åke Helm's Catharina, born on August 16, baptised on the 21st of the same month. Godparents: Abraham Lidenius, Lars Dahlbo, Brigitta Petersson, Maria Rambo.

Peter Cock's Elias. Godparents: Manne Dircksson, David Cock, Peter Cock's wife, Helena Cobb

Carl Hoffman's and Elsa's Carl, baptised on October 28. Godparents: George Kyhn, Nicholas Hoffman, Ella Kyhn and Helena Cobb.

Johannes and Anna Nilsson's Carl, baptised on November 25. Godparents: Elias Fisk, Anders Dahlbo, Elsa Runnels, Berthil Dahlbo.

Hans and Brigitta Halton's Susanna, born on December 6, baptised on the 9th of the same month. Godparents: Abr. Lidenius, Anders Hoffman, Olof Homman's wife.

Peter Cock's Maria, the same day [December 9]. Godparents: Peter Mattsson, Peter Rambo, Eva Mulicka.

Jöns and Catharina Halton's Måns, baptised the same day [December 9]. Godparents: Thom. Dinneh, Anders Mulicka, His wife, Margareta Petersson.

Fredrick Dinneh's Thomas [baptised on the same day, December 9?]. Godparents: Thom. Dinneh, Brigitta Mulicka, Nicholas Hoffman.

Almgott Hoffman, baptised on December 22.

PENS NECK 1717

Marten and Catharina Guilliamsson's Christina, on January 6. Godparents: Marten Jansson, Peter Hindricsson, Marg. Billerback and Margareta Minck.

Hans Shiere's Catharina, baptised on January 20. Godparents: Jean ——, Elizabeth Lidenius, Maria Litien.

Zacharias and Sarah Berthilsson's Richard, baptised on January 20. [Godparents]: Jacob Hindricsson, Henric Petersson, Hiertrud Corneliusson, H. Petersson.

Jean Suggar's Maria, baptised on January 25. Godparents: Simon and Jean Eaton, Margareta Eaton and Elizabeth Lidenius.

Thom: and Margarita Wiggorie's William, baptised on February 21. [Godparents]: Hans Shiere, Eric Fransson, Catharina Ruckman and Maria.

Christiern and Catharina Petersson's Brigitta, baptised on May 3, [Godparents[: Jacob Hindersson, Sarah Seneck, Anna Fransson.

Olof and Magdal. v. Neiman's Johannes, baptised on May 19. Godparents: —— von Neiman, Guarret v. Neiman, Hiertrud Hollsten, —— Petersson.

Eric and Catharina Jansson's Regina, baptised on May 19. Godparents: Lucas Petersson, Johan Hindricsson, Margareta Billerback.

Johan Robbinsson's Catharina, the same day.

On June 14, baptised Thom. Lambstone's Helena, being as to her (?)[129] She had Thom. Pennington for Godfather.

Abraham and Lisa Lidenius' Johannes, born on October 14, baptised ——. Godparents: Jacob Hindricsson, Olof von Needham, Ingridh Petersson, —— Marslander.

Tim. and Margareta Stedham's Catharina, baptised on October 20. Jean v. Numan, Lucas Petersson, Hiertrud Senecksson, Elizabeth ——.

Jean Caspar's Rebecca, baptised on November 14. Godparents: Caspar, and Elizabeth Jansson.

Josias and Helena Pennington's Thomas, baptised on November 17. [Godparents]: Sennecksson, Sara Petersson and Margareta Wiggorie.

RACOON CREEK 1717

Gabriel Petersson's and Christina's Gabriel, born on December 29, 1716, baptised on January 3. Godparents: Laurentz Hollsteen, Guarret von Numan, Anna Petersson, Magdalena v. Numan.

Elias and Christina Fisk's Elias, baptised on January 23. Godparents: Per Cock, Maria Cock.

Lars Petersson's Thomas, on January 13, baptised. Godparents: Maria Petersson, Catharina Petersson, Thom. Dinneh, Zacharias Petersson.

Jonas and Amborah Biurström's Margareta, born on January 24, baptised on February 5. Godparents: Jacob von devair, Hans Petersson, Ella Kyhn.

Michael and Judith Homman's Olof, born on ——, baptised on February 9. Godparents: Jacob v. devaire, Olof von Numan, Debora Hoffman.

John and Catharina Hoffman's Måns [Mons], born on ——, baptised on March 22. Godparents: Fredrich Hoffman, Påwel Hoffman, Carin Qwist, Margaret Petersson.

Laurentz and Hiertrud Hollsten's Lars, born on March 19, baptised on the 24th. Godparents: Guarret v. Numan, Johan Hoffman, Magdalena v. Numan, Maria Cock.

John and Cath: Lock's Beata, born on March 18, baptised on April 7. Godparents:

Item an illigitimate child, Rebecca Gilbert. The Mother, Maria Magdaniel. Godparents: Berthil Supply, Joh. Georgen's wife. The mother was brought in on the stool of repentance.[130]

Hermanus Helm's and Catharina's Maria, born on ——, baptised on May 26. Godparents: Berthil Dahlbo, Anna Kock.

James and —— Guarring's Helena, born ——, baptised on May 26. Godparents: Helena Arched.

Anders and Magdalena Dahlbo's Lars, born on July 28, baptised on August 11. Godparents: Anders Hoffman, Gabriel Dahlbo, Maria Halton, Elizabeth Dahlbo.

---

[129] *warande till sin,* is an incomplete phrase, which perhaps should be *warande till sin* [*börd oäkta*], "being as to her birth [illegitimate]".

[130] *Plicgtepallen,* "stool of repentance". Stool of repentance, formerly in Scotland, the *cutty stool,* a small raised seat on the gallery in old Scottish churches, where female offenders against chastity were seated during services for three Sundays, and publicly rebuked by their pastors.

Thom. and Maria Dinneh's Elizabeth, born on September 9, baptised on the 15th of the same. Godparents: Frederich Hoffman, Lars Pettersson, Catharina Hoffman, Anna Sträng.

John and Anna Mulicka's Magdalena, born on September ——, baptised the 29th of the same. Godparents: Olof Petersson, John Mattsson, Eva Mulicka, Sarah Dahlbo.

Michael and —— Laikian's Catharina. Godparents: Peter and Gunilla Cock.

George and Ella Kyhn's George, born on October 14, baptised on the 27th of the same. Godpa[rents]: Gustaf Lock, Peter Dahlbo, Catharina Hinricsson.

Pehr Cock's Maria, born on ——, baptised on November 24. Godparents: Måns Kyhn, Johan Jönsson, Catharina Hoffman, Maria Lock.

John and Elizabeth Geörgen's Helena, born ——, baptised on December 8. Godparents: Hans Petersson, Måns Kyhn, Hiertrud Hollsten, Elsa Hoffman.

Hindric and Regina Hindersson's Christina, born ——, baptised on November 10. Godparents: ——

PENS NECK 1718

John Minck's and Elizabeth's Maria, born on January 19, baptised on the 23rd of the same. Godparents: Abraham Lidenius, Jonas Shagen, Lisa Lidenius, Ingrid Petersson.

John von Neeman's Henric, baptised on March 9. Godparents: Abraham Lidenius, Guarret von Neeman, Catharina Guilliamsson, Elizabeth Jansson.

Jonas and Christina Shagen's Wallborg, baptised on March 9. Godparents: Anders Hinricsson, Gabriel Petersson, John Savoj, Catharina Savoj, Gunnilla Berthilsson.

Anders Henricsson's Peter, baptised on April 20. Godparents: Abraham Savoj, Ingrid Hinricsson, and Maria Hinricsson.

Albert and Margareta Billerback's Peter, baptised on June 1. Godparents: Jacob Hinricsson, Lucas Petersson, Dorothea Seneck and Ingrid Hindricsson.

Peter Paulow's and Margareta's Alekie, the same day. Godparents: Lucas Petersson, Guarret v. Neeman, Catharina Savoj, Helena Minck.

Seneck Senecksson's Andreas, baptised on September 21. Godparents: Johan Savoj, Marten Shiere, Ingridh Hindricsson, Margaretta Wiggorie.

Guarret and Maria von Neeman's Christina, baptised on October 11. Godparents: Abraham Lidenius, Olof von Neeman, Magdalena von Numan, Helena Lock.

Lars and Sara Nilsson's Ingridh, baptised on November 30. Godparents: Philip Fransson, Guarret von Neeman, Ingridh Petersson and Helena Fransson.

David Strahen's David. Godparents: Adam Strahen, John Eaton, Catharina Stahlkopp and Anna Shiere [and the] Mother: Susanna.

Christiern Petersson's Peter, baptised on December 18. Godparents: Olof Shahlkopp, Ingrid Hindersson, Margareta Wiggorie.

RACOON CREEK 1718

Magdalena Påwclsson's Catharina, illegitimate [child] was baptised on February 2nd. Godparents: James Guarring, Lars Straeng, Elizabeth Geörgen, Catharina Paulsson.

On the same day was baptised, or confirmed, Charles and Elsa Dahlbo's Maria, baptised in emergency. Godparents: Mr. Jesper Swedberg, Matts Mattson, Sara Dahlbo, Elsa Påwlsson.

Lars Cock's and Gunnilla's daughter, born ——, baptised on February 15. Godparents: Elizabeth Kock, Hiertrud Lock, Michael Laikian, Sam. v. Neeman.

Item: Desiderius Debora v: Numan's Helena. Godparents: The Father and the mother.

Gunnar and Helena Arched's Helena, born ——, baptised on February 16. Godparents: Henric Henricsson, And. Petersson, Christina Didricsson, Beata Jönsson

Anders and Maria Hoffman's Margarita, born on February 21, baptised on March 21. Godparents: Abrah. Lidenius, John Jonsson, Magdalena Kyhn, Maria Petersson.

On March 9, was baptised Anders Jones' Maria, they do not belong to our Church.

Gustaf and Magdalena Lock's Magdalena, born March 6, baptised on the 15th of the same month. Godparents: Mr. Jesper Swedberg, Peter Lock, Eric Steehlman's wife, Elsa Paulsson.

Johan Mattsson's and Annicka's Johannes, born on March 30, baptised on April 6. Godparents: Pehr Cock, Jacob Mattsson, and Maria Rambo.

Fredrick and Hanna Halton's Peter, baptised on April 27. Godparents: Thom. Dinneh, Catharina Hoffman, Judith Mattson.

Hans and Sara Petersson's Sarah, baptised on June 7. Godparents: George Kyhn, Guarret von Numan, Elsa Hoffman, Magdalena von Numan.

Berthil and Maria Supply's daughter was baptised on June 8. Godfather: Johan Anders Hoffman.

Peter and Maria Lock's Jesper, born on May 25, baptised on June 22. Godparents: Jesper Swedberg, Henric Hinricsson, Catharina Lock and Beata Jonsson.

Matts and Judith Mattsson's Lydia, born on July 24, baptised on August 3. Godparents: Anders Hoffman, Jacob Mattsson, Annica Matsson and Maria Petersson

Jöns and Catharina Halton's Jöns, born on August 10, baptised on the 17th of the same month. Godparents: Johannes Hoffman, Zacharias Petersson, Helena Dinneh, Ingrid Runnels.

Lars Sträng and Rebecca's John, baptised on September 22. Godparents: Hans Halton, William Cobb, Brigitta Halton, Maria Sträng.

Item: Måns Kyhn's and Magdalena's Johannes, born on September 25. Godparents: Joh. Hoffman, Alexander King, Ella Kyhn and Maria Hoffman.

Eric and Margareta Mulicka's Johannes, born on October 2, baptised on the 12th of the same month. Godparents: George Kyhn, Catharina Halton and Anna Mulicka.

Åke Helm and Cath[arine's] Israel, born on Octob[er] 8, baptised on the 12th of the same.

Item: Olof Homman's Margareta.

Thomas Chieu and his sister Elizabeth, both brought up as Quakers, baptised on October 29.

William and Almgott Cobb's Christina, born ——, baptised on November 23. Godparents: Johan Hoffman, Påwel Hoffman, Maria Dinneh.

Manne and Christin Didricsson's Eric, born ——, baptised on Decemb[er] 7. Godparents: William Cobb, Joh. Hoffman, Elsa Hoffman, Margareta Guärring.

Stephen Mulicka's Catharina, baptised on Decemb[er] 28. Godparents: Anders Hoffman, John Cock, Hiertrud Cock, Christina Qwist.

PENS NECK 1719

William and Maria Philpot's Nicolas and Thomas, baptised on January 6, at home, in English. Godparents: The Father and Mother.

Johan and Gunnilla Berthilsson's Philip, born on February 12, baptised on the 15th of the same. Godparents: Olof v. Numan, Zacharias Berthilsson, Magd. v. Numan, Lisa Lidenius.

Zacharias and Sarah Berthilsson's Anna, born on February 25, baptised on March 1. Godparents: Abraham Lidenius, Johan Savoj, Lisa Lidenius, Catharina v. Devaire.

Thom. Gillet's, from Duck Creek, Catharina, born on February 19, 1718, baptised on June 3. Godparents: John Minck, John Berthilsson, Helena Minck, Brigitta Minck.

Marten and Catharina Guilliamsson's George, born on ——, baptised June 21. Godparents: Jacob Hindricsson, Jonas Shagen, Catharina Von Numan.

Philip and Helena Fransson's Christina, born ——, baptised on July 5. Godparents: Lars Nillsson, Willm. Pukman, Carin Savoj, Sarah Nillsson.

Abraham and Lisa Lidenius' Christina, born on August 20, baptised on the 24th of the same. Godparents: Rev. Andreas Hesselius, his wife, Mr. Jesper Swedberg,[131] Magdalena v. Numan.

Olof and Magdalena v. Numan's Catharina, born on October 16, baptised on October 20. Godparents: John Seneck[sson], Gabriel Petersson, Hiertrud Seneck[sson], Maria von Numan.

Marten and Elizabeth Jansson's Margareta, born on December ——, baptised on the 26th of the same. Godparents: David v. Numan, Jonas Shogen, Catharina v. Numan, Christina Shiere.

RACOON CREEK 1719

Fredrick and Elsa Peterson's Johannes, born on January 26, baptised on February 8. Godfathers: Jöns Halton, Britta Mulicka and ——.

Hindric and Regina Hindricsson's Susanna, born ——, baptised on February 22. Godparents: Guarret von Numan, Maria von Numan, Fred. George, Beata Jönsson.

Eric and Brita Steelman's Hans, born ——, baptised on March 7. Godparents: Manne Dircksson, Judith Mattsson, and Berthil Dahlbo.

Anders and Maria Mattsson's Rebecca, born on March 27, baptised on April 19. Godparents: Måns Kyhn, John Dahlbo, Brita Steehlman, and Brita Hoffman.

The same day, Manus Helm's and Catharina's Catharina.

Elias and Christina Fisk's Susanna, born on April 3, baptised on the 29th. Godparents: Åke Helm, Gustaf Lock, Susanna Laikian, Marg[areta] Mulicka.

Gabriel and Christina Petersson's Annicka, born on April 17, baptised on the 27th of the same month. Godparents: Mr. Jesper Swedberg, Lisa Lidenia, Anna Fransson.

Hans and Brigitta Halton's Rebecka, born on May 29, baptised on the 31st of the same month. Godparents: William Cobb, Lars Hoffman, Armgott Cobb, Maria Petersson.

Peter and Maria Kock's Margareta, born on June 14, baptised the 28th of the same month. Godparents: Lars Cock, John Rambo, Margareta Mulicka, Beata Jones.

Anders Dahlbo's and Magdalena's Andreas, born on June 27, baptised on the 28th of the same month. Godparents: Lourentz Hollsten, Måns Kyhn, Ella Kyhn, Maria Halton.

Fredrick and Elizabeth Geörgen's twins, Elizabeth and Maria, born on July 10, baptised on the 12th. Godfathers: Gustaf Lock, Edward Hadtfield, Hiertrud Hadtfield, Annicka Jönsson.

John and Catharina Hoffman's Andreas, born on August 17, baptised on the 23rd of the same month. Godparents: Jacob Lundbeck, Nicolas Hoffman, Gunnilla Cock, Ingrid Runnels.

---

[131] Jesper Svedberg, the brother of Emanuel Swedenborg, and son of Bishop Svedberg, spent several years here as a school teacher.

Olof and Eva Mulicka's Jacob, born on August 16, baptised on the 23rd of the same month. Godparents: John Mulicka, Michael Laikian, Brigitta Mulicka, Maria Cock.

John's and Elizabeth Geörgen's Hans, born on August 24, baptised on September 6.

Lars and Cath: Petersson's Lars, born on September 3, baptised on October 17. Godparents: Gustaf Qwist, Påwel Kempe, Judith Mattsson, Christina Dircksson.

George and Ella Kyhn's Elizabeth, born on October 24, baptised on the 26th of the same month. Godparents: Olof von Numan, John Hoffman, Hiertrud Steehlman, Magdalena Dahlbo.

Jacob and Christina Lundbeck's Jacob, born on October 25, baptised on November 8. Godparents: Thom. Dinneh, Lars Hoffman, Gunilla Cock, Brigitta Hoffman.

Hans and Elsa Steehlman's Jöns, born on November 17, baptised on the 21st of the same month. Godparents: Hinric Hindricsson, Zach. Petersson, Elsa Dahlbo, Bea.[ta] Jones.

Michael and Anna Laikian's Maria, born on November 17, baptised on December 5. Godparents: Olof Petersson, Cath. Cock, Brigitta Hoffman.

Thomas and Maria Dinneh's Gunnilla, born on December 18, baptised on the 20th of the same month. Godparents: Jacob Lundbeck, Gustaf Qwist, Cath. Halton, Maria Petersson.

PENS NECK 1720

Peter and Margareta Enlow's Elizabeth, born ——, baptised on February 11. Godparents: Seneck Senecksson, Christina Litien.

Guarret von Numan's and Maria's Johannes, born on February 11, baptised on the 14th. Godparents: Lars Lock, Peter Justice, Lisa Lidenia, Maria Lock.

Jacobus and Catherine Von Devair's William, born on February 11, baptised on the 21st. Godparents: Olof Sluby, Olof von Numan, Christina Litien and Catharina Sluby.

Albert and Margareta Billerback's Ingrid, born on ——, baptised on July 3. Godparents: Joh. Seneck, Magdalena Hindersson, Christina Shiere

The same day was baptised Thomas and Margaret Wiggorie's Ingridh, born ——. Godparents: Lucas Petersson, Ingridh Hindersson, Helena Minck.

On August 14 was baptised a servant,[132] James Price, about 27 years old Witnesses: Captain Strahyn, Jacob Hindersson, Magdalena Hindersson.

Jonas and Catherine Shogen's Jonas, born September ——, baptised on the 18th of the same month. Godparents:[133]

Abraham and Lisa Lidenius, their [daughter] Christina, born on October 28, baptised on the 30th of the same month. Godparents: H[onorable] Mr. Jesper Swedenborg,[134] Guarret von Numan, Maria v. Numan, Christian Pedersson.

Anders and Beata Hindersson's David, born on ——, baptised on November 27. Godparents: David Billerback, Helena Fransson, Regina Guilliamsson. Hiertrud [Gertrude] Corneliusson.

Tim: and Margaret Stedham's Maria, born on March 13. Godparents: Olof Sluby, Olof von Numan, Lisa Lidenia and ?

Olof von Numan's Olof, born ——, baptised on November 20. Godparents:[135]

Marten Guilliamsson's Maria, born ——, baptised on December 11. Godparents: Hindric von Numan, Jonas Shagen, Ingrid Hindersson.

---

[132] *en dräng,* may mean "a lad", "a man", but usually "a servant", "a man-servant".
[133] No names are given in the original.
[134] The Svedberg family had now been enobled and assumed the name of Swedenborg.
[135] No names are given in the original.

RACOON CREEK, 1720

Peter and Gertrude Steehlman's Maria, born on January 5, baptised on the 17th of the same month. Godparents: Hans Petersson, And: Dahlbo, Debora Hoffman, Elsa King.

Elias and Elsa King's Elias, born on February 12, baptised on the 15th of the same month. Godparents: Peter Steehlman, Alexander King, Debora Hoffman, Marg[areta] Guarring.

Eric and Margareta Mulicka's Maria, born on February 15, baptised on the 29th of the same month. Godparents: Charles Dahlbo, Zacharias Petersson, Judth Mattsson, Maria Petersson.

John and Anna Mulicka's Helena, born on February 24, baptised on the 29th of the same month. Godparents: Manne Didricsson, Anna Runnells, Maria Cock.

Fredrich and Helena Dinneh's Eric, born on February 25, baptised on March 13. Godparents: Jons Halton, Gustaf Qwist, Magd[alena] Kyhn, Marg [areta] Guarring

John and Anna Mattsson's Eric, born on March 13, baptised on April 3. Godparents: Matts Mattsson, Mr. Jesper Swedberg, Helena Justice, Lydia Colin.

Carl and Elsa Dahlbo's Anna Catharina, born on May 20, baptised on the 29th of the same month. Godparents: Gabr. Dahlbo, Jacob Mattsson, Magd. Dahlbo, Ingrid Runnels.

Lars Lock's and Gunilla's Lars, born on May 31, baptised June 26. Godparents: Jacob Lundbeck, Peter Cock, Maria Cock and Elizabeth Rambo.

Lars and Maria Lock's Anders, born on September 12, baptised on the 25 of the same month. Godparents: Guarret von Numan, Cath. Sluby.

Peter and Hiertrud Cock's Måns born on September 13, baptised on the 25th of the same month. Godparents: ——, ——

Fredrich and Elizabeth Georgen's Hans, born on the 1st, [baptised] October 18. Godparents: Matts Mattsson, John Rambo, Regina Hindricsson, Anna Laikian.

Olof and Ingrid Homman's Maria, born on October 2, baptised on the 8th of the same month. Godparents: James Guarring, Johannes Georgen, Christina Lundbeck, Christina Dircksson.

Peter och Helena Justice's Marta, born on October 28, baptised on November 6. Godparents: Matts Mattsson, John Cöln, Magd. Kyhn and Lydia Cöln.

Peter Mattsson's and Catharina's Matts, born on October 29, baptised on November 6. Godparents: ——, ——

Anders and Maria Mattsson's Matts, born on December 5, baptised on the 18th of the same month. Godparents: Peter Mattsson, Gabriel Dahlbo, Elsa Steehlman and Catharina Jones.

Fredrick and Hanna Halton's Fredrick was baptised at home in Coahaking, on March 18. Godparents: The Father and Mother.

PENS NECK 1721

Johan and Maria Eaton's George, born on December ——, baptised on January 1. Godparents: Simon Eaton, Lucas Petersson, Ingrid Pettersson.

Item Oney Standlye's Oney

John and Hanna Jaquet's John, born on ——, baptised on April 23. Godparents: Carin Savoj, Sarah Nilsson, and Jean Savoj.

John and Gunnilla Berthilsson's Anna Catharina, born ——, baptised July 2. Godparents: Philip Fransson and Catharina Savoj.

Johannes and Catharina Shagen's Jonas born ——, baptised September 3. Godparents:

David and Susanna Strahen's Johannes, was baptised on the same day.

[244]

Zacharias and Sara Berthilsson's Johannes, born on ——, baptised on September 17. Godparents: Henric von Numan, Peter Berthilsson, Gunilla Berthilsson and Catharina Corneliusson.

Anders and Beata Petersson's Twins, Rebecca and Susanna, born ——, baptised on October 1. Godparents: Zacharias Petersson, Magdalena v. Numan.

Johan and Elizabeth Månsson's Johannes, born ——, baptised on October 1. Godparents: Olof v. Numan, Charles Halton, Gunnilla Berthilsson, Maria Halton.

On the same day was also baptised: William Wiggorie's negro, Tobias.

Guarret and Maria von Numan's Elizabeth, born on December 16, baptised on the 26th of the same month. Godparents: Peter Lock, Hindric Hindricsson, Maria Hoffman, Christina Petersson.

RACOON CREEK 1721

Hermanus and Catharina Helm's Joseph, born on January 10, baptised on February 3. Godparents: Hans Halton, Peter Dahlbo, Catharina Dahlbo, Maria Cock.

Anders and Maria Hoffman's Susanna, born on January 25, baptised on February 2. Godparents: Lourens Hollsten, Guarret von Numan, Elizabeth Lidenia, Maria von Numan

Gunnar and Helena Arched's Israel, born on January 28, baptised on February 5. Godparents: Manne Didricsson, Johan Hoffman, Julia Mattsson, Cath. Pålson.

Jöns and Catharina Halton's Magdalena, born on March 15, baptised on the 16th of the same month. Godparents: Maria Dinneh, Brigitta Mulicka.

Åke and Catharina Helm's Elizabeth, born on April 8, baptised on the 16th of the same month. Godparents: Matts Mattsson, Jacob Lundbeck, Julia Mattsson, Ingrid Homman.

Måns and Magdalena Kyhn's Nicolas, born on May 11, baptised on the 14th of the same month. Godparents: Abraham Lidenius, Olof von Numan, Maria Hoffman, Christin Kyhn.

Gustaf and Magdalena Lock's Elizabeth, born on May 23, baptised on the 24th of the same month. Godparents: Anders Hoffman, Hindric Hindricsson, Eva Mulicka, Brita King.

Matts and Julia Mattsson's Maria, born on May 27, baptised on the 29th of the same month. Godparents: Jonas Jones, Peter Mattsson, Helena Justice and Lydia Cöln.

Herman and Maria Richman's Ulrich, born on September 1, 1719.

Item, Anna, born on March 20, 1721, Both baptised on July 3. Anders Hoffman, Måns Kyhn, and their wives were the Godparents.

Lars and Maria Påwelsson's Lars, born on August 9, baptised on the 13th of the same month. Godparents: Manne Didricsson, Joh; Hoffman, Ingeborg Homman, Catharina Pålson.

Elias and Christina Fisk's Christina, born on September 7, baptised on the 15th of the same month. Godfathers: Peter Lock, Hinric Hinricsson.

William and Almgott Cobb's Johannes, born on September 29, baptised on October 8. Godparents: Guarret v. Numan, John Arched, Maria Lock, Maria Hoffman

Anders and Magdalena Dahlbo's Gabriel, born on September 23, and baptised on October 1. Godparents: Lourentz Hollsten, Zacharias Peterson, Hiertrud Hollsten, Lydia v. Keuhlen.

Thom. and Maria Dinneh's Thomas, born on October 16, baptised on the 22nd of the same month. Godparents: Abrah. Lidenius, Lars Hoffman, Catharina Dahlbo, Julia Mattsson.

Fredrich and Elsa Petersson's Timotheus, born in October baptised on the 22nd of the same month. Godparents: Fredrich Görgen, Tim. Reehn, Catharina Standley, Elizabeth Dahlbo.

Eric and Margareta Mulicka's Brigitta, born on October 20, baptised on November 5. Godparents: And. Petersson, John Arched, Elsa Dahlbo, Catarina Mattsson.

Michael and Anna Laikian's Johannes, born on Nov 4, baptised on the 18th of the same month. Godparents: Johan And. Hoffman, Anders Fredricsson Hoffman, Anna Jones, Maria Jones.

Hans and Brigitta Halton's Johannes, born on November 9, baptised on the 19th of the same month. Godparents: Manne Didricsson, Charles Sträng, Anna Mulicka, Helena Justice.

Hindric and Regina Hindricsson's Jonas, born on Nov. 29, baptised on December 3. Godparents: Gunnar Arched, Anders Mattsson, Elizabeth Georgen, Catharina Jones

An illegitimate child, the Mother Brita Halton, the father said to have been John Kempe, was born on November 24, baptised December 4, named Walborg.

Sam. and Margareta von Numan's Jones, born on December 22, baptised on the 31st of the same month. Godparents: Henric v. Numan, Johan Mattsson, Gunnilla Cock, Deborah v. Numan.

Johan and Maria Arched's Brigitta, born on December 26, baptised on the 31st of the same month. Godparents: Zacharias Petersson, William Cobb, Helena Arched.

PENS NECK 1722

Jacob and Catarina von Devair's John, born on January 11, baptised on the 21st of the same month. Godparents: Jacob von Devair, Junior, Henric von Numan, Sarah Berthilsson, Margareta von Devair.

Mårten and Elizabeth Jonsson's Elizabeth, born on January 24, baptised on February 4. Godparents: Guarret von Numan, Peter v. Numan, Catarina Shogen.

Johan and Maria Casper's Tobias, born on February ——, baptised on March 4. Godparents: Peter v. Numan, Margareta Guarring, Maria von Devair.

Joshua and Helena Hawkes' Joshua, born on ——, baptised on March 18. Godparents: John Minck, and Elizabeth Minck.

Seneck and Maria Senecksson's William, born ——, baptised on May 6. Godparents: Jonas Shogen, John Seneck, Ingrid Hindricsson.

Aldert Aldersson's Nicolaus, baptised on May 6, born on ——. Godparents: John Eaton, Margareta Billerback.

Henric and Christina Gun's Sarah, born on ——, baptised on ——. Godparents: John Minck, Jacob Danielsson, Brigitta Minck and Margareta.

Philip and Brigitta Cannoway's Jacob, baptised on November 16. Godparents: John Eaton and Carin St.

Jonas and Catarina Shogen's Elizabeth, born on November 22, baptised on the 25th of the same month. Godparents: Jean Eaton, William Mecum and Maria Eaton.

Tim. Damsey's and Anna's Johannes, born on December 27, baptised on the 30th of the same month. Godparents: The Father, Ingrid Hindricsson and Brigitta Minck.

RACOON CREEK 1722

Peter and Catarina Dahlbo's Helena, born on January 6, Christened on the 28th of the same month. Godfathers: Lourens Hollsten, Matts Mattsson, Regina Hindricsson, Elizabeth Dahlbo.

Note: This Dahlbou asked me to make a memorandum of this: that he was 32 years old on March 5, when he had his last daughter, Hellena.

Jonas and Sarah Kyhn's Sarah, born on January 26, baptised on the 30th of the same month. Godparents: Carl Halton, Anders Bonde, Elizabeth Lidenia, Magdalena Dahlbo.

Johannes and Catharina Hoffman's Petrus, born on February 3, baptised on the 7th of the same month. Godparents: Anders Hoffman, Almgott Cobb, Maria Hoffman.

Jacob and Christina Lundbeck's Nils, born on January 27, baptised on February 11. Godparents: Åke Helm, John Hoffman, Elsa Dahlbo, Anna Qwist.

Fredric and Helena Dinneh's Jonas, born on February 20; baptised on the 24th of the same month. Godparents: Jöns Halton, Gustaf Qwist, Helena Kyhn, Catharina Halton.

Johan and Maria Kempe's Catharina, born on March 16, baptised on the 24th of the same. Godparent: Gun Kempe.

Berthil and Maria Supply's Margareta, born on March 18, baptised on the 24th of the same month. Godparents: Carl Halton, Lars Påwelson, Margareta Mulicka, Lydia Köln.

Johan and Catharina Runnel's Johan, born on May 8, baptised on the 13th of the same month. Godparents: Jacob Lundbeck, Lars Påwelsson, Maria Påwelson and Rebecca Sträng.

Påwel and Gun Kempe's Påwel, born on September 21: baptised on the 23rd of the same month. Godparents: John Hoffman, Gustaf Qwist, Maria Dinneh and Catharina Halton.

John and Anna Mulicka's Sarah, born on October 22, baptised on November 6. Godfathers: Staphan Mulicka, Thomas Dinneh, Catharina Halton, Margareta Mulicka.

Peter and Maria Cock's Mons, born on November 13, baptised on December 16. Godparents: Peter Rambo, Peter Gustis [Justice], Julia Mattsson, Ingrid Runnilsson.

John and Debora Hoffman's Elizabeth, born on November 15, baptised on the 24th of the same month. Godparents: Alexander King and Brigitta King.

Guarret and Debora von Numan's Margareta, born ——, baptised on December 1. Godparents: Olof v. Numan, and Isabel v. Numan.

Lars and Maria Påwelsson's Christina, born on December 22, baptised on the 28th of the same month. Godparents: Jöns Halton, Påwel Hoffman, Catharina Halton, Christin Lundbeck.

PENS NECK 1723

Jean and Hanna Jaqvet's Peter, born on December 27, baptised on January 1. Godparents: Lars Nilsson, Ingrid Petersson and Christina Petersson.

On February 10 was baptised Anders Hindersson's child, Anders, without godparents, brought in by a little girl.

Thom. Wiggorie's and Margareta's twins, Sarah and Margareta, born on April 20, baptised on May 5. Godparents: Jacob Hindricsson, Marten Shiere, Sara Hind[ricsson].

Jacob and Maria Danielsson's Magdalena, born on May 12, baptised on June 2. Godparents: ——, Brigitta Minck, Christina Guns.

Item, Påwel Jansson's Christina, without godparents. The parents do not go to Church.

Olof and Magdalena von Numan's Elizabeth, born on June 16, baptised on the 23rd of the same. Godparents: Rev. Sam[uel] Hesselius, Gustaf Hesselius, Sara Hesselius, Lisa Lidenia.

Jacob and Regina Savoj's Isaac, born on June 18, baptised on the 30th. Godparents: Gabriel Petersson, John Seneck, Anna Petersson, Christina Petersson.

[247]

Lars and Sarah Nilsson's Påwel, born on July 6, baptised on the 14th. Godparents: Lars Petersson, Margareta Wiccorie, Maria Shiere.
Johannes and Catharina Shagen's Maria, born on August 4, baptised on the
11th of the same month. Godparents: Timotheus Stedham, Henric Guns,
Carin Savoj, Maria von Devair.
Carl and Gunnila Halton's Maria, born on September 17, baptised on the
22nd of the same month. Godparents: Philip Fransson, Zacharias Peters-
son, Helena Fransson and Beata Petersson.
Oney and Dorothea Standley's Anreas, born on August 23, baptised on Sep-
tember 22. Godparents: Seneck Senecksson, Margareta Billerback and
Brigitta Minck.
Jacob and —— Von Devair's Magdalena, born on October ——, baptised on
the 21st of the same month. Godparents: John Savoj and Carin Savoj.
Guarret and Maria von Numen's Andreas, born on November 1, baptised on
the 3rd of the same month. Godparents: Henric von Numan, Peter von
Numan, Helkia Marslander and Margareta Stedham.

RACOON CREEK 1723

Peter and Helena Justice's Lydia, born on February 1, baptised on the 3rd
of the same month. Godparents: Hindrick Hindricksson, Olof Kulen,
Julia Mattsson, Anna Mattsson.
Måns and Elizabeth Kyhn's Peter, born on March 21, baptised on April 7.
Godparents: Johan Hoffman, Elizabeth Lidenia.
David and Maria Von Numan's Johannes, born March 22, baptised on the
25th. Godparents: Peter Rambo, Jacob Mattsson and Catharina Long.
Georgen and Ella Kyhn's Susanna, born March 22, christened on the 30th.
Godparents: Lars Hoffman, John Hoffman, Brita Shogen, Anna Mattsson.
Lars and Gunilla Kock's Sara, born March 24, baptised April 13. Godparents:
Lars Kock, Eric Kock, Maria Jones, Maria Kock.
Manne and Christina Didricksson's Johannes, born May 1, christened June
9th. Godparents: Joh: Hoffman, Påwel Hoffman, Catharina Dahlbo and
Christina Hoffman.
Eric and Margareta Mulicka's Helena, born on June 9, baptised on the 23rd.
Godparents: Samuel von Numan, Jacob Forsman, Elizabeth Dahlbo,
Margareta v: Numam.
Joh: and Helena Jones' Johannes, born on July 2, baptised on the 7th. God-
parents: Nils Laikian, Jacob Mattsson, Catarina Mattsson, Catharina
Jones.
Peter and Maria Kock's Abraham, born July 10, baptised on the 2nd. God-
parents: John Mattson, Jacob Forsman, Maria Påhlsson, Gertrud Seneck
[son].
Gustaf and Maria Lock's Zebulon, born on July 4, baptised on the 21st. God-
parents: John Arched, Anders Hoffman, Elizabeth Steehlman, Maria
Hoffman.
Hindricks and Regina Hindricksson's Magdalena, born on July 23, baptised
August 4. Godparents: Joh: Jones, Johan Hindersson, Magdalena Lock.
Maria Hindersson.
Manus and Catharina Helm's Andreas, born on July 26, baptised August 4.
Godparents: Sam: Von Numan, Johannes Hoffman, Margareta v: Numan,
Anna Mattsson.
Michael and Judith Homan's Abraham, born on August 9, baptised on the
30th. Godparents: Edward Hadtfield, Zacharias Petersson, Christina
Homan.
Peter and Catharina Dahlbo's Catharina, born August 24, christened on the
30th. Godparents: Henric Henricsson, Guarrett von Numan, Helena Jones,
Lydia Kyhlen.

Alexander and Brita King's Andreas, born on August 25, baptised on September 15. Godparents: John Hoffman, Joh. Kulen, Maria Hoffman, Catharina Hoffman.

Gunnar and Helena Arched's Magdalena, born on September 1, baptised the 15th. Godparents: James Guarring, Jacob Arched, Maria Arched, Christina Didricsson.

Edward and Maria Hadtfield's Maria, born September 25, baptised on the 27th. Godparents: Elizabeth Georgen, Christina Kyhn.

Åke and Catharina Helm's Brigitta, born on October 17, baptised on the 27th. Godparents: John Arched, Lars Hoffman, Elizabeth Dahlbo, Maria Arched.

Laurents and Giertrud Hollsten's Elizabeth, born on June 26, baptised on the 20th. Godparents: Olof v: Iman, Lars Lock, Maria von Iman and Maria Lock.

NB Gabriel Friend's Child. see 1740.

Thomas and Maria Dinneh's Helena, born November 2, baptised on the 10th. Godparents: Johan Hoffman, Andreas Hoffman, Anna Gustafsson, Christina Didricsson

Staphan and Catharina Jonsson's Sara, born on November 5, baptised on the 10th. Godparents: Anders Mattsson, Maria von Numan.

William Cobb's and Armgot's Fredrich, born on December 26, baptised on the 1st of January. Godparents: Hindrick Hind: Sam: Cobb, Christina Lundbeck, Christina Didricksson.

PENS NECK 1724

John and Maria Eaton's twins, John and Simon, born on January 18, baptised on the 19th of the same month. Godparents: Olof von Iman, Guarrett von Iman, Gabriel Petersson, Ingrid Petersson, Christina Petersson and Catharina Shagen.

John and Helena Jaqvet's Maria, born on March 14, baptised on the 22nd *dito*. Godparents: Henric Petersson, Maria Guns and Helkia Masslander.

Item was baptised Joseph and Helena Hawkes' Joseph on March 14. Born ——, Godparents:

Henric and Christina Guns' Anna, born on May 11, baptised on the 17th. Godparents: Jean Jaqvet, Henric von Iman, Anna Damsey and Elizabeth Mink.

William Philpot's Maria, born ——, baptised on July 12.

Lars and Anna Nilsson's Maria, born October 24, baptised on [November] 1st. Godparents: ——.

Anders and Beata Petersson's ——, born on November 12. Godparents: Henric Petersson, John Savoj, Anna Petersson, Hiertrud Corneliusson.

James and Catharina Butterwood's Helena, born on December 25 [1724], baptised on January 1, 1725. Godparents: Matthias Petersson, Henric Petersson, Helena Fransson, and Ella Corneliusson.

RACOON CREEK 1724

Jacob and Maria Forsman's Maria, born December 30, 1723, baptised on the 3rd of January. Godparents: Måns Laikian, Eric Kock, Maria Kock, Maria Jones.

Hans and Elizabeth Stulman's Susanna, born December 30, 1723, baptised January 12th. Godparents: Måns Laikian, John Jones, Brita Stuhlman, Maria Jones.

John and Catarina Standle's [Stanley], David, born November 28, 1723, baptised February 2nd. Godparents: Lars Sträng, Lars Påwelson.

John and Anna Mattsson's Peter, born on January 6, baptised on February 2. Godparents: Zacharias Petersson, John Kulen, Catharina Halton, Maria Mattsson.

Elias and Christina Fisk's Israel, born on January 5, baptised February 2nd. Godparents: Matts Mattsson, Olof Kulen, Gunnila Kock and Anna Mattsson.

Samuel and Margaret von Iman's Gabriel, born January 7, baptised February 16. Godparents: Jacob Mattsson, Eric Mulicka, Anna Runnels, Lydia Kuhlen.

Matts Mattsson's and Julia Mattsson's Matts, born February 5, baptised on the 16th. Godparents: Åke Helm, Jacob Lundbeck, Brita King, Lisa Dahlbo.

Michael and Anna Laikian's Ezechiel, born February 11, baptised April 5. Godparents: Lars Kock, Gunnila Kock and Maria Hoffman.

Abraham and Elizabeth Lidenius' Elizabeth, born February 18, baptised on the 23rd. Godparents: Samuel Hesselius, Brigitta Hesselius, Peter Van Iman and Maria Holsten.

Nathaniel Taily's and Anna Taily's Anna, born February 19. Godparents: Gabriel Rambo and Sara Chester.

Olof and Ingrid Homman's Ingrid, born March 6, baptised on the 15th. Godparents: John Hoffman, Gustaf Qwist, Christina Homman and Maria Hoffman.

Jonas and Sara Kyhn's Catarina, born March 9, baptised on the 15th. Godparents: Manna Didricsson, Margareta Sträng, and Elizabeth Dahlbo.

Gabriel and Christina Petersson's Abraham, born April 7, baptised on the 12th. Godparents: Henric von Iman, Peter von Iman, Margaret Stedham.

Anders and Magdalena Dahlbo's Carl born April 8, baptised on the 19th. Godparents: Peter Dahlbo, Anders Hoffman, Catarina Dahlbo, Helena Justice.

Jacob and Christina Lundbeck's Catarina, born April 9, baptised on the 19th. Godparents: John Arched, Gustaf Qwist, Armgot Cobb, Catarina Halton.

Anders and Catharina Hoffman's Catharina, born May 17, baptised on the 24th. Godparents: Jacob Mattsson, Anders Rambo, Catharina Hoffman and Lisa Dahlbo.

Eric and Brita Stuhlman's Carl, born July 5, baptised on the 8th. Godparents: Peter Lock, Anders Mattsson, Maria Lock, Elsa Stuhlman.

RACOON CREEK 1724

Anders and Maria Hoffman's Magdalena, born July 11, baptised on the 19th. Godparents: Lourentz Hollsten, Andreas Hoffman, Elizabeth Kyhn, Catharina Hoffman.

Herman and Maria Ritzman's Catharina, born on July 20, baptised on the 28th. Godparents: John Hoffman, Måns Kyhn, Elizabeth Kyhn, Christina Kyhn.

John and Elizabeth Geörgen's Lars, born July 27, baptised August 17. Godparents: Lars Kock, Powel Hoffman, Elizabeth Hoffman and Sara Flower.

Fredric and Helena Dinneh's Fredric, born August 22, baptised on September 6. Godparents: Elias King, Jacob Lundbeck, Helena Justice and Sara Flower.

David and Maria von Iman's Abraham, born September 5, baptised on the 6th. Godparents: Samuel von Iman, Desiderius von Iman, Märta Rambo.

John and Maria Arched's Catharina, born on September 8, baptised on the 27th. Godparents: Jacob Lundback, Christina Didricsson, Magdalena Petersson.

Påwel and Gun Kempe's Elizabeth, born on September 11, baptised on the 27th. Godparents: Jöns Halton, Georgen Kyhn, Christina Lundbeck and Christina Didricsson.

Lars and Maria Påwelsson's Tobias, born September 26, baptised on the 27th. Godparents: Desiderius von Iman, Anders Hoffman, Debora von Iman, Cath Hoffman.

Joh. and Cath. Hoffman's Maria, born December 3, baptised on the 25th. Godparents: Måns Kyhn, Zacharias Petersson, Hiertru [de] Hollsten, Debora Hoffman.

John and Helena Jones' Brita, born on December 4, baptised on the 25th. Godparents: Lourentz Hollsten, Anders Mattsson, Lydia Mattsson, Margarita Mulicka.

Måns and Maria Laikian's Catharina, born on December 21, baptised on the 27th Godparents: Eric Kock, Zacharias Laikian, Anna Laikian and Rebecca Jones.

Cristoffer and Cath. Gerrisson's Christoffer, born on May 23, 1721, baptised on April 5, 1723. Godparents: Peter Justice, Anna Mattsson.

Item: Darby and Lisa Floyd's Marta, born August 21, 1723, baptised on April 19, 1724. Godparents: Jacob Lundbeck and Maria Dinneh.

PENS NECK 1725

James and Catharina Butterwood's Helena, born on December 25, baptised on January 1. Godparents: Matthias Petersson, Henric Petersson, Helena Fransson and Ella Corneliusson.

John and Elizabeth Månsson's Sara, born on January 4, baptised on the 17th of the same month. Godparents: Olof von Iman, Guarret von Iman, Sara Berthilsson, Judith Corneliusson.

Jacob and Catharina von devair's Henric, born on January 13, baptised on the 17th of the same month. Godparents: Cornelius Corneliusson, Guarret von Iman, Sara Berthilsson, Judith Corneliusson.

Anders and Anna Hendricsson's John, born on ——, baptised on the 31th of the same month. Godparents: Martin Shiere, Seneck Seneckson, Cartharina Standly and Maria Nilsson.

Joseph and Helena Pennington's Joseph, born on March 29, 1724, baptised on January 31. Godparents: Marten Guilliamsson and Christina Petersson.

Marten and Maria Shiere's Maria, born ——, baptised on March 7. Godparents: Jacob Danielsson and Christina Guns.

Guarret and Maria von Iman's Christina, born on March 7, baptised on the 12th of the same month. Godparents: Gabriel Petersson, Jonas Biurström, Anna Fransson, Maria v: Iman.

Jacob and Maria Danielsson's Henric, born on March 9, baptised on the 20th of the same month. Godparents: Henric Guns, Lucas Petersson, Margareta Petersson.

Hen[ric] and Maria Senecsson's Anna, born on February 1, baptised on March 24. Godparents: John Senecssons, Senior, and John Senecsson, Junior; also Anna Senecksson.

Eric Shiere's and Stänkil Guilliamsson's illigitimate child, Eric, was baptised on May 19. Born ——. Godparents: Gillus Guilliamsson and Anna Seneck.

Jonas and Catharina Shogen's Maria, born on April 3, baptised on the 11th of the same month. Godparents: William Mecum, Marta Jansson, Elizabet Jansson and Lisa Jaqvet.

Tobias and Brigitta Casper's Maria, born on July 6, was baptised on the 11th of the same month. Godparents: Olof von Iman, Gabriel Petersson, Carin Savoj and Magdalena Eaton.

Simon and Magdalena Eaton's Elizabeth, born on January 11, was baptised on the 17th of the same month. Godparents: Olof von Iman, Guarret von Iman, Brigitta Casper.

Henry and Ann Petersson's Christina, born on September 1. Godparents: Mattie Petersson, Luke Petersson, Ellena Fransson, Barbro Marsland.

Zach Bartholson's Zacharias, born on September 24. Godparents: Philip Fransson, and his wife, Henry Guans, Helky Petersson.

Olof von Jman's Abraham, born on September 1, christened on the 10th of the same month. Godparents: Jacob von Devair, Cornel. Cornelson, Pet. von Jman, Maria von Jman, Guarrit's Wife, Peter Von Jman's wife.

Henry von Jman's and Maria von Jman's Johannes, born on December 26, christened on January 1.

At the home of Peter von Jman, [baptised?] the farmer of —— Von Jman, Junior

RACOON CREEK 1725

Jacob and Leddi Matson's Brigitta, born on January 10, baptised on the 15th. Godparents: Mattis Mattson, Jean Colen, Annicka Mattson, Cathrina Jonson.

Erik and Annicka Kock's Annicka, born January 5, christened on February 7th. Godparents: Anders Mattson and Maria Forssman.

Barthel and Maria Suffle's Johannes, born January 5, christened on the 7th. Godparents: William Coll [Cobb] and Regina Hindersson, Cathrina Hoffman.

Johan and Maria Gillmor's Maria, born 1724, on the 29th of February, baptised on February 7, 1725. Godparents: Jacob Lundbeck and Maria Archett.

Lars and Maria Lock's Cathrina, born February 21, and baptised March 6.

Peter and Helena Justice's Christina, born March 2, baptised on the 8th. Godparents: James Halton and Mali Dahlbo.

Anders and Elisabeth Jonson's Stephan, born January 7, baptised on May 16. Godparents: Peter Rambo and Cathrina Jons[son].

Peter and Cathrina Dahlbo's Rebecka, born April 30, baptised on May 16. Godparents: Jacob Lundbeck and And. Rambo, Maria Archet and Helena Stillman.

Lars and Rebecka Strang's Lars, born May 7, baptised on the 30th. Godparents: Ante Hoffman, Jacob Forsman, Christina Lundbeck and Nanni Kock.

Peter and Maria Lock's Susanna, born June 20, baptised July 4th. Godparents: Hans Stillman, And. Mattson, Judith Homman and Maria Mattss[on].

Anders and Ceteris Hinderson's Annicka, born August 1, baptised on the 29th. Godparents: Mattias Skagen, Peter Billerback, Geen Donker and Margeth Hindersson.

Carl and Sara Halton's Sara, born September 8, baptised on the 19th. Godparents: William Cobb, Niclas Hoffman, Sara Keen and Annicka Gustafson.

Israel and Regina Hindersson's Israel, born on October 1, christened on the 10th. Godparents: Zacharias Petersson, Israel Lock, Maria Archett and Cathrina Hoffman.

Anders and Maria Hoffman's Johannes, born October 28, baptised on the 31st. Godparents: Garrit von Nehman, Johan von Nehman, Elena Justice and Isabel von Nehman.

Johan and Annicka Mullicka's Ingri, born on October 23, baptised on the 31st.

Pähr and Maria Kock's Adam, born on October 8, christened on the 13th. Godparents: Peter Kock, Lars Kock and Cathrina Koch.

David and Maria von Nehman's Isak, born on November 16, christened on the 26th. Godparents: Åke Helm, Cathrina Helm.

Dissi von Nehman and Debora von Nehman's Andreas, born on November 19, baptised on the 26th. Godparents: Garrith Von Nehman, Tobias, Britta, and Margeth von Nehman

Peter Rambo's and Christina Rambo's Johannes, born on November 21, baptised on the 27th. Godparents: Gabriel Rambo, Elizabet Smith, and Cathrina Rambo.

Lars and Gunnilla Kock's Maria, born on November 24, baptised on the 27th. Godparents: Jonas Lidman, Peter Rambo, Annicka Laikian and Sara Cock.

RACOON CREEK 1726

Peter von Nehman's and Maria von Nehman's Son, Andreas, was born on December 6, baptised on the 1st of January. Godparents: Gabriel Petersson, Matthius Holsten, Maria von Nehman, and the maiden Christina Petersson.

Peter Kock's and Maria Kock's Juli, born November 16, baptised January 2nd. Godparents: Carl Streng, Rebecka Sträng, Maria Gurren, maiden.

Thomas Dennis and Maria Dennis' Johannes, born on January 20, baptised on February 27. Godparents: Niclas Hoffman, Gustaf Gustafsson, Debora Hoffman, Maria Hoffman, maiden.

Heddert Hatfiell's and Gertrud Hatfiell's Adam, born on January 6, baptised on February 27. Godparents: Olof Petersson, Nils Gustafson, Mali Petersson, maiden.

Jacob Lundbeck's and Christina Lundbeck's Johanna, born on February 19, baptised on the 27th. Godparents: James Halton, Zacharias Petersson, Brigitta Halton, Elisabeth Dahlbo, maiden.

Anders Fridrichson Hoffman's and Cathrina Hoffman's Abraham, born on February 27, baptised on March 20. Godparents: Jac. Lundbeck, Niclas Hoffman, Mali Petersson, maiden, Cathrina Hoffman, maiden.

Jacob and Maria Forsman's Margareta was born on March 10th, baptised on the 20th. Godparents: Påvel Hoffman, Annicka Gustafsson.

Gustaf and Mali Lock's Gustaf was born on March 7, baptised on the 20th. Godparents: Jacob Mattsson, Måns Hoffman, Maria Mattsson, Giärtrud Hatfiel [Gertrude Hatfield]

Gabriel and Christina Petersson's Jonas, was born on March 20, baptised on April 5th. Godparents: Jacob Savoj, Jonas Petersson, Margret Wickri [Wiggore].

Erik and Margreta Mullicka's Jngri [Ingrid] was born on April 8, baptised on the 11th. Godparents: Henrik Henrikson, And. Andersson Hoffman, Helena Jonss[on], maiden, Mali Petersson, maiden.

John and Annicka Mattsson's Elisabeth, was born on May 21, baptised on the 30th. Godparents: William Cabb, Enok Enockson, junior, Maria Archiet, Batti [Betty?] Dahlbo, maiden.

William and Armgott Cabb's Pavel was born on June 9th, baptised on the 19th. Godparents: Anders Fredrichson Hoffman, Niclas Hoffman, Maria Hoffman, a wife, and Cathrina Hoffman.

Elias and Elsa King's Twins, Johannes and Susanna, born on May 27, baptised on June 19th. Godparents: Mattias Mattsson, Alexander King, Johannes Swenson, Gustaf Gustafson, Mali Mattson, a wife, Elizabeth Mulicka, maiden. Brigitta King, a wife, Debora Dedricsson, maiden.

Johan and Elena Jonson's Jonas, was born on June 14, baptised on July 10. Godparents: Henrik Henrikson, Carl Lock, Gertrude Holsten, wife, Cath. Hoffman.

Hans and Elsa Stillman's Israel was born on July 7, baptised on the 10th. Godparents: Anders Mattson, Måns Lock, Margret Stedom, Cath. Keen, maiden.

Johan and Maria Gillman's Sara, born April 7, baptised on July 10. Godparents: Gustaf Lock and Sara Halton, wife.

William Lamtsberg's and Maria Morgen's William, born on June 14, baptised on July 10. Godparents: Anderissi von Nehman, Niclas Dahlberg, Maria Morgen, wife, and Debora von Nehman, wife.

Johannes Noal's [and] Rebecka Jonsson's ——, born July 15, 1725, baptised on July 10, 1726. Godparents: Pet. Cock, Jonas Cock, Elena Dahlberg, wife, Cathrina Cock.

Zacharias and Mali Petersson's Magdalena, born on September 9, baptised on the 12th. Godparents: James Halton, Carl Hansson Halton, Cathrina Halton, wife, Cathrina Halton, maiden.

Tobias and Elena Brejet's Erick, born on September 9, baptised on the 10th. Godparents: Anderisse von Nehman, Niclas Dah[l]berg, Debora von Nehman, wife, Brigitta Stillman, maiden.

Stephan and Cathrina Jons[son]'s Marta, born on September 12, baptised on the 23rd. Godparents: Fredrich Hoffman, Gustaf Lock, Margret von Nehman, wife, Els[a] Stillman, wife.

Johannis and Elisabeth Georgen's Fredrich, born on September 15, baptised on the 26th. Godparents: Gunnar Archiet, Peter Guarren, Eva Mullicka, wife, Brigitta Halton, wife.

Påvel and Geen Kemp's Maria, born on September 29, baptised on October 10. Godparents: William Cabb, Lars Hoffman, Elena Gustafs, wife, Mall Petersson, maiden.

Jonas and Sara Keen's Christina, born on October 11, baptised on the 23rd. Godparents: Enok Enockson, Matthias Skaggen, Cathrina Dahlbo, wife.

Anders Rambo's and Cathrina Rambo's Maria, born on October 11, baptised on the 23rd. Godparents: Peter Rambo, Måns Hoffman, Christina Rambo, Maria Hoffman, maiden.

Lars and Maria Påvelson's Andreas, born on October 17, baptised on the 23rd. Godparents: Zacharias Petersson, Armgott Cobb, wife, Christina Dedriksson, maiden.

Andreas Dahlbo and Mali Dahlbo's Johannes, born October 19, baptised the 23rd of the same month. Godparents: Måns Keen, Giöran Keen, Juli Mattss[on], wife, Cathrina Keen.

Stephan and Elisabeth Mullicka's Johannes, born on October 29, baptised November 6. Godparents: Jacob Lundbeck, Nils Gustafson, Margret Steddom, Mali Hoffman, wife.

Carl and Sara Halton's Christina, born on December 19, baptised on the 25th. Godparents: Gustaf Gustafson, Peter Halton, Elizabeth Georgen, wife, Maria Gerren, maiden.

Erick and Hanna Cock's Debora, born on December 11, baptised on the 25th. Godparents: Erick Kock, Ephraim Kock, Margret Sträng [Streng], and Maria Kock.

PENS NECK ANNO 1727

Catharina Petersson, born on February 11. Godparents: Henry von Jman, Lars Nilson, Christina Petersson, Fransina Cornelson.

Jacob Danielson's Gabriel, born on September 26, christened on October 8. Godparents: Peter von Jman, Henry Petersson, Junior, Lena Franson, Sara Fors.

John Philpott's Anna Maria, born on July 27, christened on October 8. Godparents: Senek Senekson, And. Liten, Elizabeth Johnson, Maria Senekson.

And. Henrikson's Andreas, born on July 5, christened on October 8. Godparents: Olof von Jman, Margret Wikry [Wiggorie], Annicka Cornelson.

Olof von Jman's Cathrina, born on October 25, christened on the 29th of the same month. Godparents: Magister [Rev. Mr.] Windrufwa, Cornel. Cornelson, Sara Petersson, Fransina Cornelson.

Luke Petersson's Ingrid, born on October 22, christened on the 31st of the same month. Jacob Danielson, Henry Petersson, Ingry Petersson, Debora Dedrikson.

Own Standly's William, born on November 20, christened on December 3. Godparents: Jonas Skaggen, Oney Henrikson, Albert Billerback's wife, and John Standly's wife.

RACOON CREEK ANNO 1727

Samuel and Margret Von Eman's David, born on December, 1727, baptised on January 8. Godparents: Johannes Hoffman, William Cabb, Maria von Eman, Cathrina Jönsdotter.

David and Susanna Kock's Leddi, born on January 12, baptised on the 15th. Godparents: Carl Strang, Anders Dahlbo, Christina Homman, Anna Kock.

Elias and Christina Fish's Elena, born on January 15, baptised on the 22nd. Godparents: Lars Kock, Johannes Andersson Hoffman, Annicka Mullicka, Cathrina Jonsdotter.

Olof Homman and Ingri Homman's Elena, born on February 26, baptised on March 5. Godparents: Johannes Hoffman, Peter Halton, Elisabeth Georgon, Cathrina Halton.

Anders Andersson's and Maria Hoffman's Beata, born on March 22, baptised on April 2. Godparents: Anders Dahlbo, Thom. Denny, Mali Dahlbo, Maria Denny.

Måns Keen's and Elisabeth Keen's Maria, born on April 6, baptised on the 11th. Godparents: Elias King, Anders Rambo, Anna Cathrina Tranberg, Cathrina Keen.

Mans Petersson's and Maria Peter's Thomas, born on August 19, 1724, baptised on May 28. Godparents: Zacharias Petersson, Mali Petersson.

Fredrich and Elena Denny's Johannes, born on May 24, baptised on the 28th. Godparents: Mattias Skaggen, Johannes Enok, Christina Lundbeck, Geen Kampe

Peter and Cathrina Dahlboo's Gabriel, born on June 29, baptised on July 2. Godparents: Anders Andersson Hofman, Joh. Enokson, Sara Friend, Brigitta Stillman.

Erik and Annicka Kock's Margret, born on June 25, baptised on the 2nd. Godparents: Gabriel Rambo, Gunnilla Kock.

And. Mattisson's and Maria Mattsson's Anders, born on July 15, baptised on the 30th. Godparents: Peter Lock, Enok Enokson, Cathrina Dahlbo, Elena Jonsson.

Peter and Elena Justice's Susanna, born on July 22, baptised on the 30th. Godparents: Gustaf Lock, Carl Lock, Regina Hendricksson, Maria Andersson Hoffman.

Johannis and Maria Archet's Jacob, born on July 26, baptised on the 30th. Godparents: Henrik Henrikson, Lars Lock, Sara Keen, Margret Mullicka.

Anders and Elisabeth Jonse[son]'s Judith, born on June 15, baptised on the 30th. Godfather: Jacob Forsman.

John Sleters and Maria Sleter's Maria, born on July 15, baptised August 10. Godparents: David Kock, Johannes Niclas, Anna Lajemett, Brigitta Strang.

Peter and Anna Cathrina Tranberg's Andreas, born on April 18, baptised on the 20th. Godparents: the Rev. Mr. Lidman, the Rev. Mr. Windrufwa, Mrs. Taylor and Gertrud Holsten.

Gustaf Gustafson's and Annika Gustafsson's Gustaf, born on September 21, baptised on October 8. Godparents: Johan Fredrichson Hofman, Nils Gustafson, Cath. Halton, Annicka Gustafsson.

Olof and Maria Culen's Cathrina, born on October 30, baptised on November 5. Godparents: Jacob Mattson, Zacharias Petersson, Annicka Mattsson, Maria Lock.

Lars and Maria Lock's Måns, born on October 7, baptised on November 5. Godparents: Thom. Denny, Lars Hoffman, Maria Denny, Elsa Stillman.

Henrik and Regina Henrik's Henrik, born on November 1, baptised on the 12th. Godparents: Joh. Archet, Olof Culen, Elena Archiet, Cathrina Homman.

And. Fredrichson and Cathrina Hofman's Elena, born on November 20, baptised on the 26th. Godparents: And. Andersson Hoffman, Paul Hoffman, Maria Paulsson, Maria Hoffman.

David and Maria Von Jman's Aaron, born on October 28, baptised on November 4. Godparents: Gabriel Petersson, Dishe von Jman, Debora von Jman, Margret von Jman.

Alexander and Brigitta King's Frederich, born on January 2, baptised on the 23rd. Godparents: Elias King, Betty Keen, Maria Hoffman.

Timot. and Margret Stedom's Christina, born on January 8, baptised on the 28th. Godparents: Stephan Mullicka, Lars Lock, Maria Mattsson.

PENS NECK ANNO 1728

Senek and Maria Senekson's Johannes, born on January 19, christened on the 25th of the same month. Godparents: Martin Johnson, John Fillpot, Anti Henrikson's and Erik Ellionson's Wives.

John Jaquet's Joseph, born on February 19, christened on the 25th of the same month. Godparents: Luke Petersson, Senior, Henry Petersson, Junior. Annicka Franson, Britta Cannow[ay].

Henry von Jman's child, Elizabeth, born in January, christened on February 25. Godparents: Olof von Jman, Jonas Skaggen, Cathrina Skaggen, Fransenthi Cornels[son].

And[ers] Liten's Christina, born ——, christened on May 5. Godparents: Martin Gill Johnsson, Martin Skeer, Alberth Billerback's and Luke Pettersson's Wives

And. Boon's Peter, born on May 17, christened on the 19th of the same month. Godparents: Luke Petersson, Junior, Peter Boon, Sara Nilson, Fransenthi Cornelson.

Erik Skeer's [Shiere] child, born on July 23, christened on the 28th. Godparents: Senek Senekson, Martin Skeer, Albert Billerbak's wife, Christina Guans.

Martin and Elizabeth Johnson's Twins, Göran and Johannes, born in April, christened ——. Göran's Godparents: Rev. Mr. Windrufwa, Joh. Casparson, Elizabeth Windrufwa and Anna Casparson. John's Godparents: Charles Bukly, Tobias Casparson, Grace Bukly and Judith Casparson.

Carl and Gunnilla Halton's child, born on May 31, christened on June 7. Godparents: Lars Nilson, Peter Von Jman, Sara Nilson, Lena Franson.

RACOON ANNO 1728

Peter and Christina Rambo's Elizabeth, born on January 2, christened on the 7th. Godparents: Thomas Deny, Henrik Henrikson, Juli Mattson, Debora Rambo.

Edward Niclas, 20 years old, christened on January 28. Witnesses: Jacob Lundbeck, Enock Enockson.

Johan: Niclas, 18 years old, christened on January 28. Witnesses: Georg Cotz, Christina Lundbeck.

Ephraim and Maria Kock's Maria, born on January 29, baptised on February 11. Godparents: Jacob Matson, Gabriel Rambo, Maria von Jman [Neeman], Elena Halton.

Jonas and Sara Kock's Måns, born on January 28, baptised February 11. Godparents: Samuel von Jman, —— Bull, Maria von Jman, Maria Bull.

Mich. Lycon and Annicka Lycon's Annicka, born on April 2, baptised on the 21st. Godparents: John Culen, Gabriel Kock, Maria Lock, Cath. Kock.

Dishe and Debora von Iman['s] ——, baptised on the 21st. Godparents: Jacob Forsman, Guarrit von Jman, Margreta Mullicka.

Måns and Maria Petersson's Samuel, born on February 15, 1725, baptised in June. Godparents: Jöns Halton, Thomas Denny, Cathrina Halton, wife, Malin Petersson.

Pähr and Maria Kock's Johannes, born on July 9, baptised on July 21. Godparents: And Dahlbo, John Culen, Margret Von Iman, wife.

John and Annicka Mullicka's Jonas, born on July 18, baptised on the 21st. Godparents: Jöns Halton, Jacob Forsman, Christina Lundbeck, Elena Jönse.

John and Annicka Matson's Israel, born on July 15, baptised on August 11. Godparents: Lars Kock, Gabriel Kock, Maria Von Jman, Brigitta Lock.

And. Enock and Cath. Enock's Rebecka, born on August 13, baptised on the 18th. Godparents: Thom. Bull, Erik Runolls, Regina Henriks, wife, Annicka Niclas, maiden.

Lars and Rebecka Streng's Anders, born on July 11, baptised on August 18. Godparents: Lars Kocks, Jöns Halton, Christina Sträng, Juli Kock, wife.

Jacob and Maria Forsman's Cathrina, born on September 8, baptised on the 15th. Godparents: Jacob Lundbeck, Jonas Kock, Lenora Von Jman, Maria Hoffman.

Jonas and Sara Keen's Maria, born on September 29, baptised on October 26. Godparents: Peter Lock, And. Matson, Cath. Tranberg, Maria Hoffman, Jacob and Leddy Matson.

Jacob and Christina Lundbeck's Henrik, born on November 20, baptised on the 24th. Godparents: Petter Tranberg, William Cabb, Maria Denny, Maria Hoffman.

Gabriel and Betty Rambo's Thomas, born on September 24, baptised on the 26th of December. Godparents: Thom. Bull, Christina Rambo, Martha Rambo.

RACOON ANNO 1729

John and Elizabeth Georgen's Catharina, born on January 6, baptised on the 12th. Godparents: Carl Strang, Petter Homman, Debora Dedricks, maiden, and Betty Guarrem, maiden.

Carl and Sara Halton, born on January 21, baptised on the 26th. Godparents: Christina Lundbeck, Anicka Justice.

Israel and Rebecka Lock's Cathrina, born on January 24, baptised on the 26th. Godparents: Henrik Henrikson, Carl Lock, Cath. Dahlbo, Malin Hoffman.

John and Elizabeth Plomli's Maria, born on January 6, baptised on February 9. Godparents: Margret Mullicka and Annicka Mullicka.

Hans and Elsa Stillman's Johannes, born on January 27, baptised on February 9. Godparents: William Cabb, Måns Hoffman, Maria Mattsson, Maria Lock

Samuel Enkow, born 1699, on March 15, baptised on the 9th. Godparents: Jöns Halton and Thom. Denny.

Lars and Maria Påvelson's Cathrina, born on February 25, baptised on March 9. Godparents: Jacob Lundbeck, Johannes Hoffman, Elizabet Georgen, Maria Guarron.

Anders Andersson and Maria Hoffman's Maria, born on February 24, baptised on March 9th. Godparents: Jons Halton, Måns Hoffman, Cathrina Hoffman, Beata Hoffman.

Thomas and Maria Berry's John, born on March 8, baptised on the 9th. Godparents: John Bars and William Thoms, Maria Guilmor.

John and Margret Smit's Anna, born on September 25, 1716, baptised on May 4 Godparents: John Mullicka, Jacob Lundbeck and Annicka Lundbeck.

Påvel and Jeny Kamp's Sebulon, born on May 11, baptised on the 18th. Godparents: John Georgen, Lars Påvelson, Malin Lock, Christina Halton.

William and Armgott Cobb's Cathrina, born on May 18, baptised on the 26th. Godparents: Henrik Henrikson, Gunnar Orisent, Christina Lundbeck, Maria Hoffman.

Erik and Hanna Kock's Susanna, born on April 27, christened on May 28. Godparents: Lars Cock, Lars Hoffman, Maria Guarron.

John and Margret Enock's David, born on August 4, baptised on the 10th. Godparents: Samuel Von Jman, Enok Enokson, Cathrina Enokson, Ann Niclas.

John and Maria Bright's Elizabeth, born on July 26, baptised on August 10. Godparents: William Bright, Isabel Von Jman, Elizabeth Bright.

George and Lysi [Lucy?] Howels' Maria, born on July 15, baptised on August 24. Godparents: Erik Cock, Elena Bright, Maria Hoffman.

William and Maria Culen's Johannes, born on August 28, baptised on September 8. Godparents: Henrik Henrikson, Carl Lock, Juli Matsson, Christina Henriks.

Jacob and Maria Forsman's Daniel, born on September 9, baptised on the 21st. Godparents: Samuel von Jman, Jacob Forsman, Debora von Jman, Elena Kock.

Peter and Elena Justice's Andreas, born on September 29, baptised on October 5. Godparents: Andreas Stalcop, Nils Justice, Maria von Jman, Cath. Halton.

Peter and Cathrina Dahlbo's Sara, born on October 3, baptised on the 5th. Godparents: Gunnar Arian, Lars Lock, Betty Helm, Beata Lock.

Åke and Elizabeth Helm's Andreas, born on September 25, baptised on October 5. Godparents: Peter Tranberg, Anna Cathrina Tranberg, Sara Keen.

Anders and Malin Dahlbo's Daniel, born on December 5, baptised on the 25th. Godparents: Jöns Halton, Carl Halton, Cath. Halton, Cath. Dahlbo.

John Slaughter and Mali Slaughter's Elizabeth, born on December 5, baptised on the 28th. Godparents: Petter Guarron, Paul Guarren, Christina Sträng, Betty Sträng.

RACOON ANNO 1730

David and Susi Kock's Ezechiel, born on December 24, 1729, baptised on January 4. Godparents: John Niclas, Frenne Kock, Margret Sträng, Maria Lycon.

Benjamin Liddon, born in 1713, on March 16, baptised on January 4. Witnesses: Michel Hoffman, Enok Enokson.

John and Annicka Cherregen's Fredrick, born on March 1, baptised on the 3rd.

Anders and Maria Matson's Peter, born on February 22, baptised on March 3. Godparents: William Cobb, Erik Runolls, Christina Dedriks, Maria Runolls.

Jonas and Sara Kock's Marget, born on February 19, baptised on March 15. Godparents: Israel Lock, Samuel Cobb, Elena Dahlberg, Debora Rambo.

Anders and Cathrina Enok's Prisilla, born on March 17, baptised on the 29th. Godparents: Enok Enokson, Marget Enoks, Elena Jonson.

Peter and Anna Cath. Tranberg's Rebecka born on June 23rd.[136]

Alexander and Britta King's Elizabeth, born on March 14, baptised on the 29th. Godparents: John Hoffman, Carl Lock, Maria Culen, Maria Lock.

Erik and Margret Mullicka's Erik, born on May 1, christened on the 10th. Godparents: Stephan Mullicka, Erik Ronolls, Maria Forsman, Christina Halton.

John and Maria Guillmor's Cathrina, born on April 18, baptised on May 10. Godparents: Lars Hoffman, Mali Hoffman, Britta Stillman.

Zacharias and Malin Petersson's Britta, born on August 26, 1729, baptised on May 18. Godparents: Jacob Danielson, Jacob Matson, Regina Henriks, Malin Petersson.

Lars and Cathrina Petersson's Samuel, born on May 3, 1722, baptised on the 18th. Godparents: Mattias Martenson, Elena Justice.

Lars and Cathrina Petersson's Maria, born on June 1, 1725, baptised on May 18. Godparents: Johannes Hoffman and Cath. Hoffman.

Lars and Cath. Petersson's Marget, born on June 1, 1725, baptised on May 18. Godparents: Påvel Hoffman, Gundela Kock.

Lars Petersson's and Cath. Petersson's Leddi, born on March 3, 1728, baptised on May 18. Godparents: Gustaf Justice, Christina Denny.

Thomas and Anna Bond's Anna, born on January 1, baptised on May 29. Godparents: Jacob Lundbeck, Christina Dedriks, Christina Lundbeck.

Peter and Anna Cathrina Tranberg's Rebecka, born on June 3, baptised on the 7th. Godparents: Colonell Rolf, Captain Vining, Mrs. Hollbrook, Elizabeth Keen.

Gustaf and Annicka Justice's Cathrina, born on August 15, baptised on the 23rd. Godparents: Jons Halton, Erik Keen, Cath. Hoffman, Maria Hoffman.

John and Annicka Mullicka's Christina, born on October 15, baptised on the 18th. Godparents: Pehr Kock, Deshi von Jman, Sara Halton, Maria Ronols.

---

[136] Date of birth of Tranberg's daughter is given below as June 3rd.

Henrik and Regina Henrik's Sara, born on November 14, baptised on December 6. Godparents: Garriet von Jman, Lars Lock, Armgott Cobb, Beata Lock.

John and Maria Orchiet's Jonas, born on November 22, baptised December 6. Godparents: Carl Lock, Påvel Guarron, Cath. Halton, Maria Ronols.

Dishi and Debora Von Jman's Debora, born and baptised on December 20. Godparents: The Parents themselves.

Anders and Christina Stalcop's Johannes, born on December 15, baptised on the 27th. Godparents: Lorens Holsten, Lars Hoffman, Helena Barber, Christ. Petersson.

RACOON ANNO 1731

Joseph and Elizabeth Leddon's Henrik, baptised on January 17, born on April 15, 1715. Godparents were the Parents themselves.

Item on the 17th of the same month baptised Mary Leddon, born on February 5, 1720. Godparents: The Parents themselves.

Anders and Mary Hoffman's Abraham, born on January 30, christened on February 3rd. Godparents: Gustaf Justice. Nils Justice, Annicka Justice.

Carl and Sara Halton's Magdlena, born on February 26, baptised on the 28th. Godparents: James Halton, Lars Pavelson, Christina Hoffman, Elizabeth Guarron.

Thomas and Maria Denny's Twins, Samuel and Debora, born on March 11, christened on the 13th. The former's Godparents: Johannes Hoffman, Samuel Cabb, Armgott Cabb, Malin Peterson. The Latter's [godparents]: Manna Dedrikson, William Cabb, Annicka Justice, Elena Dedriks.

Håkan and Elizabeth Helm's Gabriel, born on March 6, baptised on the 14th. Godparents: Jöns Halton, Carl Lock, Cathrina Halton, Maria Lock.

Johan and Elizabeth Georgon's Johannes, born on March 25, baptised on April 4. Godparents: Stephan Mullicka, Lars Påwelson, Mary Enocks, Mary Guarom.

Matthias and July Mattson's Olof, born on April 8, baptised on the 18th. Godparents: Olof Culen, John Swenson, Catharina Halton, Maria Culen.

Bartholom and Mary Suply's Aron, born on March 23, baptised on April 21. Godparents: Jacob Lundbeck, Christina Lundbeck.

Israel and Rebecka Helm's Sara, born on April 3, baptised on the 21st. Godparents: Anders Mattson, Gabriel Peterson, Diana Holten, Beata Lock.

Pär and Maria Kock's Marta, born on April 7, baptised on the 23rd. Godparents: John Mullicka, Andrew Enoks, Catharina Hoffman, Elizabeth Guarron.

Johan and Catharina Hoffman's Gabriel, born on May 18, baptised on June 6. Godparents: Jacob Forsman, Swen Lock, Annicka Justice, Christina Halton.

Israel and Rebecka Lock's Hermanus, born on July 15, baptised on August 1. Godparents: William Cabb, Lars Lock, Regina Henriks, Catharina Hoffman.

Richerd and Cathrina Lorrence's Israel, born on August 1, baptised on the 25th. Godparents: Anty Hoffman, Maria Halton, Christina Halton.

John and Maria Fisk's Casparus, born on August 15, baptised on the 29th. Godparents: Gustaf Lock, Caspar Fisk, Anna Mullica, Dina Fisk.

William and Armgott Cabb's Sara, born on August 24, baptised on the 29th. Godparents: William Cabb, and Erik Keen, Maria Lock and Malin Keen.

Gabriel Enocks and Mary Enok's Gabriel, born on September 21, baptised on the 25th. Godparents: Jöns Halton, Mary Mattson, Margret Enoks.

Olof and Maria Kulen's Rebecka, born on September 29, baptised on October 10. Godparents: William Cabb, Erik Keen, Catharina Henrikson, Sara Friend.

Erik and Maria Ronold's Johannes, born on October 7, baptised on the 10th. Godparents: Johannes Helm, Gilbert Runolds, Catharina Keen, Maria Runnolds

Michael and Anna Lykon's David, both on August 26, baptised on October 10. Godparents: Jacob Forsman, Michael Hoffman, Maria Denny, Maria Bull.

Andreas and Catharina Hoffman's Thomas, baptised on October 24, born on the 16th. Godparents: Påvel Guarron, Jonas Keen, Elizabeth Guarron, Malin Keen

Pavel and Jeny Kamp's Lars, born on October 20, baptised on the 25th. Godparents: William Cabb, Lars Peterson, Malin Dahlbo, Maria Guarron.

Johan and Mary Keen's William, born on September 25, baptised on October 25. Godparents: Jöns Halton, Samuel Cobb, Catharina Hoffman, Christina Halton

Johan and Maria Hoffman's Rebecka, born on October 27, baptised on November 7. Godparents: Alexander King, Johannes Hoffman, Catharina Hoffman, and Elizabeth Keen.

Samuel and Ann Enlow's Benjamin, born on October 12, baptised on December 5. Godparents: Lars Pavelson, Christina Lundbeck, Malin Peterson.

Anders and Catharina Long's Maria, born on November 15, baptised on December 19. Godparents: Maria von Jman,[137] Elena Dahlberg.

Jona and Sara Keen's Mattis, born on November 15, baptised on December 26. Godparents: Lars Sträng, Alexander King, Sara Friend and Catharina Keen.

Jacob and Maria Forsman's Olof, born on December 23, baptised on the 26th. Godparents: Desiderius V. Jman, Guarit Von Jman, Annicka Mattson, Helena Denny.

RACOON ANNO DOMINI 1732

Pet[er] and Anna Cath. Tranberg's Elizabeth, born on November 7.

ANNO 1733

N.B. After the request made, the Minister was desired to write the Records in the English Tongue & Characters that others may have the benefit of reading them. This was granted and beginns as followeth.[138]

RACOON ANNO 1733

Daniel Lamson aged 13 year was baptised February 2d. Godfathers Thomas Denny, Andrew Stalcop.

John Chester's Daughter Prishilla was born the 4 of Decemb. & baptised 19th. Parents witnesses.

Andrew Dahlbo's son Israel born febr: 28, baptised ——. Witnesses John Helm Jonas Keen Sarah Keen.

Peter Halton's Jonas born March 1st. & baptised—witnesses Gustaf Gustafson, James Garron Catharine Hoffman, Cath: Keen.

Ephraim Friend's John born March 12, baptised, witnesses Andrew Stalcop, Stephen Seneks Catren Rambo Mary Ronolls.

John Geöron's James born Aprill 11. Baptised. witnesses John Mullicka, Pet. Halton, Rebecka Lock, Mary Mullicka.

Dishe Vanimans John born May 16 & baptised. Witnesses the Parents.

David Flid born March 31 & baptised. witnesses Jonas Keen and his wife.

John Davi's Frank born Febr. 6 & baptised. Godfathers Mounce Keen, Jacob Matson, Judy Matson, Magd. Keen.

Mary Parker aged 19 years was baptisd: August 13. Witnesses: Cath: Justis Christian Lundbeck.

---

[137] See note 31, above.
[138] English in the original. Birth records from this entry to 1741 were written in English.

Charity Hult born July 24. & baptisd Sept. 23. Godfathers Willm. Culen, Pet. Justis, Mary Culen Bridgit Henricks.

John Orchad's Mary was born September 23 & baptisd. Godfathers Andrew Hoffman, Cath. Halton.

John Gelmor's daughter Margret Gelmor born Sept: 23 & baptisd witnesses Deshy Voniman, Mary Hoffman.

And: Orcheds Catharina born Octob. 2 & baptisd 8th. Godfathers Zach. Peters, James Keen, Magd. Dahlbo, Mary Halton.

Israel Helm's Hermanus born Octob. 24 & baptisd. witnesses Israel Helm, Sara Peters, Magd: Vaniman.

Oke Helm's Oke born Octob. 23 & baptisd. 28th. Godfathers Gabriel Enokson, Gunnar Kock, Magd. Dahlbo & Magd. Peters.

John Jameson's Mary born Octob. 28th Witnesses the father & Ellen Bright.

Jacob Forsman's Abraham born Octob. 27 & baptised Octob. 30. Godfathers Erick Mullicka Nichlas Dahlberg, Ellen Dahlberg Annicka Kock.

Mathew Farel's Rebecka born August 30 & baptisd. Octob. 28. Witnesses Jzabel Jsly, Rebecka Vaniman.

Henry Henry's Regina born Novemb. 16. & Baptisd. Decem: 2d. Godfathers Charles Lock, Otte Lock, Mary Lock, Christina Henriks.

William Williams John born Octob. 24 & baptised Decemb. 28. Witness the Parents.

RACOON ANNO 1734

Israel Lock's Christina, born January 3d. & baptisd. Jan. 20th. Godfathers: Henry Henrys, Andrew Mattson & Mary Mattson, Regina Henrys.

Willm. Culens Jacob born January 9th baptisd. 20th. Godfathers Nicklas Dahlberg Pet. Matson, Brigitta Culen, Annicka Morten.

John Slater's Margret, born January — 1734 & baptised Jan. 20th Godf.[athers] Andrew Streng, Margret Streng, Deborah Dedricks.

Pet. Lagemeti['s] Susanna was born January 14, baptised 20th Godf. James Hoffman & Betty Seneks.

Pet. Dahlbo's Andrew born febr. 2d. & baptised. godf: Thomas Denny, Charles Lock, Susanna Cock, Sarah Dahlbo.

Stephan Mullicka's Annicka, born febr. 10th baptisd. 24th. Godf. Dishy Voniman Deborah Voniman.

Jonas Keen's Magdlena, born febr. 13 & baptisd. 24. Godf. Erick Keen, Christian Rambo, Christian Orched.

Benjamin Wordenton's Hannah, born March 31. Godf. John Enocks, Abraham Jonss[on], Mary Forsman, Margretta Vaniman.

Richerd Lorens Mary, born March 7 & baptised April 3d. Godf: Lorens Polson, Andrew Hoffman, Mary Garron & Magd.[alena] Peters.

Jonas Keens Rebecka, born March 4 & baptisd. Aprill 14 Godf: Jonas Keen, John Enoks, Brigitta Henrys, Cath.[erine] Helm.

Paul Garron's Catharine, born Aprill 5. baptisd. 14th. Godf: Lorens String, Lucas Peters, Armgot Cabb, Cath:[erine] Lock.

Erik Mullickas Jonas, born 1734. April 2d. baptised 14th Godf. Gilbert Runnolls, Cath: Kock, Cath. Keen

Erick Runolls Rebecka born Aprill 25th, baptisd. May 5 Godf: John Hoffman Lorens Lock, Christian Rambo, & Rebecka Hoffman.

John Plumly's Elizabeth born March 27, baptisd. June 2d. Godf. Dishy Voniman, And: Mullicka, Anna Mullica & Anicka Mullicka.

Hans Hillman's Charles born March 5 & baptised May 5 Godf. Charles Lock Garret Voniman, Brigitta Henriks, Cath: Stillman.

And: Mullicka's Adam born Aprill 4, baptisd. May 5 Godf. Jacob Forsman Erick Kock Ingry Mullicka and Cath. Mullicka.

Andrew Enok's Abraham born June 21. baptisd. June 23 Godf. Lucas Peters Peter Matson, Mary Ronolls, Mary Lock.

Andrew Hoffman's Andrew born June 25. Baptisd. 27. Godf. Johannes Gorgen Peter Justice, Christian Orcherd Mary Hoffman.

Gustaf Justice's Rebecka born July 12, baptisd. 14th Godf. Thomas Denny William Cabb, Margret Justice Christian Denny.

John Nicols's John born August 4, baptisd. Godf. John Enocks, Margret Enoks, Margret String.

Carragens Twins Elizabeth & Catherine were born Sept. 7 & baptisd. Godf: John Hoffman, Pet. Halton, Annicka Mullicka, Elizabeth Jerron.

Pet. Halton's Andrew was born Sept. 7 & baptised Sept. 15. Godf: James Justice, John Hoffman, Ellen Justice, Cath: Mullicka.

Jonas Kock's Mary born Sept. 21. baptisd. Octob. 6. Godf. Jonas Kock Gabriel Kock, Ellen Kock, & Cath. Kock.

Jacob Mattson's Anna Cathrina born Novemb. 11 baptised 17th Godf. Andrew Rambo, Pet. Matson. Cath. Culen, Cath. Mattson.

Erik Kock's Erick born Novemb. 10. baptisd. 17. Godf. John Enock, Erik Kock, Magd. Keen, Cath. Lock.

Pet. Kock's Margret born Decemb. 1st. & baptisd. Godf. Gustav Justice Cath. Denny, Mary Denny.

Willm. Cobbs Ellen born Novemb 30th. baptisd. Decem. 5th Godf. Willm. Cobb Gustav Justice, Christian Orched, Ellen Lock.

RACOON ANNO 1735

Lorence Hoffman Catharine born in the year 1734 Decemb. 24, baptised February 16. Godfathers Andrew Hoffman, Cath. Hoffman, Ellen Lock.

Andrew Long's Ellen born Decemb. 24 1734 & baptised Febr. 16, Godfathers Andrew Rambo, Abraham Jones, Deborah Voniman & Cath. Homman.

Guarret Hommans Ellena born 30 of Decemb. 1734 baptisd. 16 Feb. 1735. Godf. Martens Mortens, Guarret Voniman, Mary Voniman & Cath. Denny.

Zacharias Peter's Sarah born January 10th, baptisd. Jan. 12th. Godf. Zacharias Peters, Willm. Cabb Sarah Kean Christian Orcherd.

George Avis's Jzabell born January 25 & baptised March 2d. Godf. Guarrit Voniman, Christian Voniman & Elizabeth Avis.

John Hoffman's Margret born Aprill 12. baptisd. 20th. Godf. Andrew Hoffman, Charles Lock, Mary Ronnolls, Beata Lock.

Mounce Keen's David born Aprill 28, baptisd. May 4th Godf. Mounce Hoffman, And Rambo, Martha Rambo, Christian Kock.

Andrew Hoffman's Peter born Aprill 21. baptisd. May 4. Godf. Peter Matson, Lorens Lock, Cath. Halton, Mary Denny.

Aron Huets Jzaak born February 26th baptised May 18th. Godf. Jonas Kock, Willm. Guest, Cath. Matson, Christian Kock.

Peter Justice's Peter born May 22d. baptisd. 26th Godf. Jonas Keen, Fredrick Hofman, Mary Hofman, Mary Matson.

Nils. Justices John born July 7th baptisd. July 20th. Godf. Willm. Cobb Gustav Justice Christian Voniman, Cath. Denny.

David Kocks Joseph born July 1st. baptised August 3d. Godf. Manna Dedericks, Enok Enockson, Ellen Orched & Elizabeth Halton.

Ephraim Friends Annicka born June 26th, baptisd. August 17, Godfathers And: Seneks, Eliz: Senek, Cath. Kock.

RACOON ANNO 1736

Benjamin Morgans Susannah born 1735 Novemb. 5th & baptisd. January 18th 1736. Godfathers Gunnar Orched, Christian Dedricks.

Benjamin Morgon's Benjamin was born July 29, 1733; baptised January 18, 1736. Godf. Gunnar Orched, Christian Dedricks.

Jonas Keen's Rachel born Sept: 14 1736. baptisd. Sept. 21, Godf. Andrew Hoffman, John Helm, Elizabeth Helm, Sarah Helm.

John Richardson's Gunnilla born March 7th, baptised 28th January Godf. Erick
Kock, John Hoffman, Gunnella Kock, Ellena Georgon.
John Gergons Andrew born febr. 7 & baptisd. 12th of March Godf. John Hoff-
man, John Weeler, Ellena Lock, Magdlen Peters.
John Woodenton's Stephan born March 1st, baptised 21st. Godf. Peter Garron,
John Lock, Mary Lock, Margret Mullicka.
Peter Haltons Brigit born March 21. baptisd. Aprill 4th. Godf. Peter Masson
Mary Mullicka Mary Denny.
Joseph Woods Prishilla born Aprill 12. baptisd. 16 May Godf. Peter Rambo
Erik Keen, Sarah Keen & Magdal. Keen.
Jacob Mattson Son Jonas born 1736 October [on the] 12th & baptisd. ye
14th. Sureties Peter Rambo, Erik Ronolls, Mary Mattson, Mary Dahlbo.
John Orcheds Sarah born January 7th baptisd. 12. Godfathers: Gunnar
Orched, Christian Orched, Christian Cock.
Jonas Keen's Susanna Born June 13th baptisd. —— Godfathers Jonas Keen John
Hoffman, Mary Dahlbo, Elizabeth Denny.
Peter Dahlbo's Jonas born June 27th, baptised July 4th. Godf. Abraham Jones
Andrew Henricks, Swen Lock, Beata Lock, Ellena Dedrickson, Mary Runolls.
Doct. Humphreys Daughter Mary born June 8, baptisd. 22d of July Godf. the
Parents.
Paul Gorron's James born Septemb. 25 baptisd. 24 of Octob. Godf. John Hoff-
man James Garron Mary Hoffman.
Israel Helms Catharine born August 16th, baptisd. Octob. 3d. Godf. Ake Helm
Gustaf Homan, Cath. Helm, Mary Mattson.
Andrew Morten's Hannah born May 9th baptisd. Octob. 17th Godf. Parents
themselves.
Ephraim Friend's Andrew born August 30, baptisd. Octob: 17. Godf: James
Justice Annicka Cargen, Magd. Kock.
Samuel Cobb's Erick born Octob. 3d. & baptised 17th Godf. Erik Keen, Magd.
Peters Elizabeth Denny
Andrew Hoffman's Jzabell born Octob. 19, baptisd. 31st Godf. Erik Runnolls
John Clark, Cath. Halton, Cath. Cabb.
John Jones's Ellena born Octob. 23d. baptisd. 14th Godf. Gunnar Kock, Abraham
Jones, Regina Henry's Christina Kock.
Daniel Sutton's Mary born Septemb. 11, baptisd. Novemb. 9, Surities,[139] the
childs Mother & Cath. Matson.
Oke Helm's Deborah was born November 30. baptisd. Decemb. 15, Godf. Henry
Henrys, Andrew Hoffman, Christian Rambo Mary Runolls.
Gustaf Justice Ellen born Decemb. 12; baptised 19 of Decemb: Godf. Thomas
Denny, James Justice, Mary Hoffman & Cath. Cabb.
Pet. [and] Anna Cath: Tranberg's Rachel [born on the] 9 Januari.

RACOON A. D. 1737

Willm. Hoffman's William born february 19th baptisd. March 20. Godfathers
Guarret von Iman Mary Denny & the Parents.
Jeffry Clark's Thomas born february 18, baptised March 20th. Godfathers Guar-
ret Von Iman Mary Conner, Annicka Voniman and Martha Voniman.
Abraham Lord's Abraham born March 10th baptisd. March 20. Godfathers Jacob
Mattson, Gabriel Rambo, Judy Mattson & Mary Mattson.
John Hoffman's Daniel born March 5th baptisd. March 20th Godfathers Erik
Ronolls, Swan Lock, Mary Guarron, Ellen Gergon.
John Rein's Elizabeth born March 4th baptised May 2. Godfathers Peter Rambo,
Margret Mullicka Mary Runolls.

---

[139] *Surities*. It was a custom in the Swedish Lutheran Church at the time to require godparents who would take it upon themselves "to stand security for the child", guarantee that it
would be brought up in a Christian manner, that it would never suffer want, etc.

Peter Rambo's Magdlen born Aprill 10th baptisd. April 17th, Godfathers Erik Runnolls, Jonas Keen, Mary Matson, & Margret Jones.

Henry Morgons Joshua born Aprill 23d, baptisd. May 22d. Godfathers Willm. Cobb, Ellena Dedricks and the Parents.

George Howel's Ann born Aprill 1st. baptisd. ——. Godfather and Godmother the Parents.

Item his son Jsaak born 17 Decemb. 1735 baptisd. May 22d. 1737 Surities Parents.

John Richerdson's Elizabeth born May 14th, baptisd. May 20th Godfathers Jacob Forsman, John Richardson, Magdalen Mullicka Magdalen Kock.

George Ave's's Son George born March 26, baptised 19 of June, Godfather Thomas Denny, Mary Hoffman, Rebecka Voniman.

Peter Justice['s] Brigitta born July 18th baptised July 24, Surities Andrew Hoffman, Morten Stille, Ellen Kock, Ellen Gergen.

Hans Stillman's Daniel born August 10th. baptisd. Decemb. 25th. Surities Andrew Hoffman, Mary Helm.

Stephan Mullicka's Jonas born August 14th baptisd. December 25. Godfathers, Gunnar Kock, Peter Kock, Magdlen Mullicka Mary Dahlbo.

Andrew Enok's John born August 18, baptisd. —— Surities Gunnar Orched, Christian Kock, Deborah Dedricks.

Mounce Keen's Mounce born Octob. 8 & baptisd. Octob. 9th.

Erick Keen's Mary born Octob. 17 baptisd. Octob. 29, Surities Jonas Keen, Peter Mattson, Catharine Cabb, Elizabeth Denny.

Robert Husbands John born Novemb. 26th baptised —— Surities Jacob Voniman John Voniman.

Willm. Culen's Willm. born August 12th, baptisd. —— Surities Andrew Henriks Thomas Denny, Judy Mattson, Helena Justice.

RACOON A. D. 1738

Andrew Rambo's Son Andrew born December 23, 1737 baptised January 1st. Surities Andrew Hoffman, Erik Runolls, Mary Runolls.

Israel Lock's Sarah born February 9th, baptisd. febr. 12. Surities Lars Lock, Gustaf Homman, Beata Lock, Elizabeth Orherd.

Nicholas Justice's son Niclas born December 3d. 1737. baptisd. february 25 Surities Gabriel Rambo & the Parents.

Peter Halton's Deborah born February 7th baptisd. 26th Surities John Weeler, Annicka Justice.

Andrew Mortin's Annicka born January 2d. baptisd. March 12th Surities Morten Stille Alexander King, Mary Stille, & Elizabeth Denny.

John Plumly's Sarah born January 27th baptisd. 25 of february.

Samuel Voniman's Deborah born March 8, baptisd. Aprill 3d. Surities John Lock, Erik Kock, Cath. Richerdson & Ellena Lock.

Willm. Guarrets Twins Thomas & Margret born August 4th baptisd. 13. Surities Willm. Cobb, Willm. Denny, Erik Dedrickson, Joseph Ballengen, Helena Dedricks, Elizabeth Denny, Sarah Keen, Cath. Keen.

Daniel Suttons Elizabeth born September 23, baptisd. 21 of Octob. Surities the childs mother & Ellen Voniman.

Guarret Vonimans Mary was born December 6th. baptisd. —— Surities Willm. Jsly, Jeffry Clark, Rebecka Voniman Cath. Halton.

RACOON A. D. 1739

Jonas Keen's William born January 27th, baptisd. Aprill 1st. Surities And. Dahlbo, Ellena Voniman, Susanna Keen.

Peter Kocks Valentine born January 14th, baptisd. Surities Gunnar Kock, And. Lock, Christian Kock, Cath. Lock.

Willm. Culen's Sarah born March 30th, baptisd. Aprill 15. Surities Erik Runolls, Jonas Lock, Regina Henrys, Rebecka Hindrys.

Frans Gervis's John born March 31, baptisd. Aprill 15. Surities Morton Stille Swan Lock, Mary Reim & Christian Cobb.

Lars Hoffman's son Fredrick born February 15, baptisd. 15th. Surities Erik. Kock, Mary Stillman, Magdlen Kock.

Mounce Keen's Jones born Aprill 7th baptisd. —— Surities Willm. Voniman & John Hoffman, Helena Voniman, Sarah Keen.

Peter Rambo's Gabriel born Aprill 19 baptisd. 23d. Surities Gilbert Runolls Lars Lock, Els Hillman Malg. Smith.

Andrew Hoffman's Jonathan born March 21st. baptisd. 23 Aprill Surities Morten Stille, Fredrick Hofman, Gunnilla Jones, Ellena Dedricks.

Andrew Hoffman's Noah born March 5th, baptisd. 18th Surities John Orched, Willm. Denny, Elena Denny & Christian Voniman.

Jacob Forsman's Mary born January 10th. baptisd. January 20th. Surities Willm. Cobb, John Lock, Margret Jones.

John Richedson's Marg. born January 14th, baptisd. 21st. Surities, Willm. Kock, Gustaf Justice, Mary Voniman, Helena Voniman.

John Orched's John born January ye. 4th, baptisd. Jan: 7. Surities Gunnar Kock, Erik Kock, Margret Mullicka Elizabeth Orched.

Israel Helm's Mary born Decemb. 20, baptisd. Febr: 4th.

John Hoffman's John born February 16th, baptisd. 18th Surities Jacob Forsman, James Garron, Cath. Keen, Mary Stille.

Erik Runolls Rachel born february 12th, baptisd. 18th Surities Andrew Henrys, Charles Lock, Margret Mullicka Elizabeth Keen.

Lars Povelson's Brigitta born January 20th, baptisd. 4 of March. Surities James Garron, John Hoffman, Ellena Voniman, Ingrid Camp.

Pet. Dahlbo's Peter born february 28, baptisd. March 4th. Surities Gunnar Kock, Jesper Lock, Cath. Justice Christian Henrys.

RACOON A. D. 1740

Gabriel Friends Rebecka born Aprill 13th. 1723 & baptisd. of Mr. Humphrey in Chester County.

Gabriels Friends Mary born Aprill 13, 1726, & baptised of Mr. Hesselius Surities Charles Grant, John Culen, Cath. Boon, Annicka Boon.

Gabriel Friends Gabriel born Aprill 19 1728, baptisd. of Mr. Lidman in Chester County. Surities Mr. Lidman, George Culen, Margret Culen.

Gabriel Friend's John born Aprill 5th 1703, baptisd of Mr. Backhouse in Chester Surities John Backhouse, Willm. Treehaven Cath. Treehaven.

1740 Andrew Morten's son George Morten born 23 of february, baptisd. March 30. Surities, Jacob Mattson, Willm. Culen, Mary Culen, & Mary Mattson.

Morten Stille's Johannes born March 2d, baptisd. March 9th. Surities James Halton, Elizabeth Denny, Erik Keen, Mary Garret.

Zacharias Peter's son Zacharias born February 28th baptisd. March 9th. Surities James Halton, Erik, Kock, Elizabeth Denny, Mary Mullikca.

Abraham Mullica born December 14, 1739, & baptisd. March 9th, 1740.

John Jemeson born 1740 June 12 & baptisd. Surities the childs father and John Wood.

Niclas Justice's son Andrew was born 1740 & baptisd. July 3d. Surities John Joffman & Mary Mullicka.

Peter Justice's Rebeckah born Decemb. 7th & baptisd. —— Surities Jesper Lock, Erik Dedrickson, Mary Mattson Elizabeth Denny.

Erik Kocks, Lars born December 4 baptisd, ye 14th Surities Richerd Longoker Hans Gergon, Mary Longoker, Magdlen Kock.

RACOON 1741

1741 Joseph Woods Catharine born Decemb. 26 1740 & baptisd ye 26 of March 1741. Surities Erik Dedrickson, Mounce Keen, Christian Cabb, Eliz. Lock.

John Hoffman's Prissitta [Priscilla?] born 27. of March 1741. baptisd. Aprill 26 1741. Surities Thomas Denny, Elizabeth Denny, Sussanna Hoffman.
John Richedson's Joseph born March 16, 1741. baptisd. Aprill 26 1741 Surities Thomas Denny, Elizabeth Kock, Elizabeth Forsman.
Andrew Long's Jonathan born 3d of December 1740. baptisd. Aprill 26, 1741. Sureties Jonas Kock, Cath. Rambo, Mary Lock.
Pet. Rambo's Martha born June 12th 1741; baptisd. June 21. Sureties Alexander King, John Mattson, Elizabeth Helm, Lydia Mattson.
Pet. and Anna Cath. Transbergs son Peter born January ye 15th.
Jacob Richman's son John born January 1st. 1737 & baptisd.
Jacob Richman's son Mattias born 23 December 1739 & baptised.
Jacob Richman's daughter Lydia born March 22d 1741 & baptised.
At the house of Dickeson baptised 1741. May 29 following children

Ann Moddy born 1731. September 2d.
John Fenik Dickeson born 1726. May 2d.
Joseph Fenick Dickeson born 1728 June 22d.
Abraham Fenik Dickeson born 1731. Febr. 11th.
Isaak Fenick Dickeson born 1732/3 March 10th.
Isabel Fenick Dickeson born 1736 March 15th.
Ellenor Fenick Dickeson born 1737 May 17th.
Thomas Murphey born 1740 March 10th
$\overline{41}$

} Surities Parents themselves.

John Killy born 1734. August 25th.
Maleky Killy born 1737. Septemb. 4th.
George Killy born 1740 March 24.
$\overline{41}$
Rachel Dickeson born 1736. feb. 12.
Thomas Dickeson born 1739 January 15th.
George Dickeson born 1740 febr. 15.
$\overline{41}$

} Surities Parents themselves for want of others.

RACOON AND PEN'S NECK, 1741, 1742

1741

Justa Justason's Elizabeth, was born Sept. 30, Baptised Nov. 5.
Simon Kriesman's Maria Cathrin, baptised Novemb. 9., at the Glasshouse.
Item, two children baptised at Geo. Hochscieldt's, viz. Johan Martin, and Johan Jacob, Nov. 10. at Cohansie.

1742

Olof Malander's Deborah, was born at Piles Grove, Febr. 23, baptised March 10, 1741/2.
Heinrich Rotgab's Johan Georg, baptised March 9
Mathias Keiger's Susanna Cathrin, March 9
Johan Georg Couger's Eva Maria, March 9
Philip Sauter's Hans Peter
Hans Georg Hochschieldt's Johan Heinrich, baptised May 17
—— Hochschieldt's, Senior's Johan Adam

} at Cohansie[140]

[140] Cohansy

Laurence Juranson's Lydia, baptised Nov 22, 1741, at Pen's Neck, dead.
Sale [Sally] Keen. Born on the 2nd Day of may, 1737.
Moses Keen. Born on the 21st Day of march, 1739/40.
John Keen. Born on the 4th Day of July, 1742.
Nicolas Keen. Born on the 24th Day of Desember 1744.
Biniaman [Benjamin] Keen. Born on the 7th of febervary[141] 1744. 1747.

PENSNECK 1742, 1743

Children Baptised by Mr. Gabr: Falck & here to be Recorded.

1742. Sept. 15th Sarah, daughter to Tobit & Elizabeth Copner.
    Abraham, son to John & Christine Philpot.
    Benjamin, son to John & Anne Marshall.
17th Elizabeth, D[aughter] to Matthias & Mary Dervas.
    Anne, D. to Peter & Catharine Bilderback.
    Prudence, Bastard-Child, the Mothers name Catharine Buckly.
ye 19th Mary, in the House of Archibald Taylor, Mr. Daniel Bilderback.
    William S. to Walter & Christine Joyce.
Oct ye. 20th Samuel Copner, aged 21 years.
    Rachel D. Patrick & Catharine Has.
Nov: ye. 5th Mary, D. to Cornelius & Margareth Copner.
1743. Jan ye. 7th Thomas, born Dec: ye 28th, 1742. Son to Charles & Jane
    Scott
15th John Cornelius, aged 23 years.
    Eleonora, D. to Andrew & Sarah Sine.
    Isaac, S. to Matthias & Marget Lambson.
    Daniel, S. to John & Rebecka Richmond.
    Mary Anne, D. to Thomas & Mary Elwell.
ye. 23d. Cathrine D. to Charles & Anne Cornelius, born ye. 20th. of the Same
    Month.
ye. 24th. Mary, D. to John & Elizabeth M. Kenally.
Febr: ye. 4th. Tobitha, D. to Andrew & Elizabeth Holstein.
ye. 6th. Anne, D. to Jonas — Jane Stallkop.
    Thomas, about 21 years of Age, Stepson to Walter & Christina Joyce.
    Jane, D. to Lorenz & Mary Göranson.
ye. 9th. Margareth, 3 years old. D. to Robert & Mary Smith.
ye. 13th. Isaac, b. Jan. ye 18th S. to Gvarret & Mary Vanneeman.
ye. 21th. Jane, D. to John & Margareth Vanneeman.
    George S. to James & Hannah Orwen.

RACOON 1749

James and Magd[a]lena Steelman's Jeremiah, born in September, baptised on
    November 10. Godparents: Niclas Keen, Hans Steelman, Sarah Steelman,
    Brita Petersson.
Charles and Sarah Dahlbo's Amariah, born ——, baptised on November 1.
    Godparents: Erick Reinolds, James Steelman, Ellena Lock, Sarah Steel-
    man
Thomas and Elisabeth Denny's Rachel, born on October 30. Godparents: the
    Parents, Fredrick Georgen, Cathrina Georgen.

PENSNECK 1750

Peter and Margreta Dereckson's Rebecka born ——, baptised on March 4.
    Godparents: the Parents.
John and Maria Van Neeman's Rebecka, born on February 26, baptised on
    March 4. Godparents: ——.

---

[141] Thus in the original.

George and Magd[a]lena Van Neeman's Three daughters: Elisabeth, 4½ years, Cathrina 2½ years, Gunila, 1 year old, were baptised on March 8. Godparents: the Parents.

Don Bar's Son, Alexander, born ——, baptised on April 3.

Johan Christian's and Elisabeth Ziren's Daughter Elisabeth was born the 8th of May, 1757, and their other daughter, Cathrina, was born the 27th of June, 1759, and baptised by the Revd. Doct: Wrangel, in the year 1761.[142]

PENSNECK 1750

Time of Birth			Time of Baptism
Month	Day		
		Peter & Margreta Didrickson's Rebecka	March 4
Feb.	26	John & Maria Van Neeman's Rebecka	March 4
		George & Magdalena Van Neeman's three Daughters—Elizabeth 4 & ½ years Catharina 2 & ½, Gunila one year old	March 8
		Jacob & Maria Vandever's Margreta	March 18
		Alexander & Don Bar's Alexander	April 3
		Olof & Elizabeth Dahlbo's Magdlena Sureties: their Parents, Cornelius Cornelius-son & Mary Van Neman	Sept. 17
		John & Anne Philpot's Sarah, Sureties: the Parents	Sept. 17
		Eric & Margreta Johnson's Sarah	Sept. 17
Jan.	8	John & Rebecka Riehman's William	Oct. 14
Sept.	15	William & Margreta Bitle's Barbara	Nov. 11

RACOON 1750

Swen Lock's Son, Andreas, born on February 4, baptised on the 10th. God-parents: Jesper Lock, Gustav Lock, Ellena Georgen, Maria Hendrickson.

John and Gertrud Beesly's Maria, born ——, baptised on February 25. God-parents: the Parents.

Peter and Cathr.[ine] Halton's Maria, born on February 27, 1749, baptised on February 25, 1750. Godparents: the Father, Debora Denny, Maria Justice.

Morten and Ellena Stille's Johanna, born on March 16, baptised on the 25th. Godparents: the Father, Thomas Denny, Elizabeth Denny, Brita Peterson.

John Didreckson's Son, Wil[l]iam, born on May 1, Christened on the 26th. Godparents: Israel Arched, Debora Peterson.

John and Sarah Denny's Priscilla, born in April, baptised on May 24. God-parents: Lars and Brita Lock.

Henry and Elisabeth Liddon's Henry, born on April 27, baptised on May 24. Godparents: Joseph and Rebecka Stenyeard.

Charles and N. Rile's Samuel, born on December 6, 1749, baptised on May 24.

PENSNECK 1751

Time of Birth			Time of Baptism	
Month	Day		Month	Day
Dec. 1750	12	James & N. Morries' Simon	Jan.	2
Dec. 1750	18	Jacob & N. Esler's John	Jan.	2
Jul. 1750		Jacob's & N. Kats' Anna Barbara	Jan.	2
Nov.	9	Jacob & Cathrina Corneliusson's Cathrina Surities: John & Helena Mounceson	Nov.	11
Nov.		William & Christian Van Neeman's Alexander		

---

[142] These birth records were obviously inserted at a later date; very likely the writer made the entry on a page which had been partially filled in 1750.

RACOON 1751

Date of birth				Date of Baptism		
year	month	day		month	day	year
1750	Dec.	7	Peter and Magdelena Matsson's Helena	Febr.	23	
1750	Oct.	5	Jonas and Helena Denny's Margreta	Febr.	23	
			Anna Barbara, a German girl, Godparents: the Parents	Febr.	23	
	March	16	Thomas and Elisabeth Denny's Maria	March	25	
	May	11	David and Eleonora Loyd's son, Dahlbow			
	Febr.	13	Gilbert and Maria Reinold's Walentine	August		
			Mounce and Elisabeth Hoffman's Jeremiah			
	August	16	John and Brigita Halton's Joshua			
	Sept.	30	Lars and Brigita Lock's Ruth			
	Sept.	30	Erick and Maria Unander's Gustav Godparents: Dean Israel Acrelius, Dean Olof Parlin, Mr. Adolph Benzel, Mr. Mons Keen, Mrs. Elisabeth Parlin, Madam Sarah Porter, the Mother, Helena Von Neeman.	Octob	4	

PENSNECK 1752

Time of Birth				Time of Baptism	
Month		Day		Month	Day
Nov.	1751	26	Mary Anne, daughter of Philip & Christina Soutor	Jan	20
Jan.		10	Christian & Margreta Nahels John. Surrities John Suimlay (?) & Hannah Abel	Jan	20
Jan.		20th	Henry & Sarah Petersons' Helena	Febr	3
Nov.	1751	29	Michael & Margreta Harps, John Michael at Cohansie. Surities. John Michael & Cathrina Miller	Feb.	8
Feb.		19	Anne Mary, daughter of Michal & Anne Mary Kats	March	8
			John & Mary Sandelins Children John, Jeremias, Schedick & Priscilla.	March	30
March		18	Daniel & Catharina Bilderbacks' Hans	April	26
Nov.	1751	8	Peter & Cathrina Bilderbacks' Henry	April	26
Dec.	1751	28	Peter & Margreta Dedricksons' Jack	May	10
May		6	Cornelius & Anne Corneliussons' Peter Surrit: Peter & Anne Petersson, Henry & Sarah Petersson.	May	10
			Paul & Mary Kamps Mathias	May	18
Feb:			Thomas & Elvils	Jun	14
Feb		12	Edward & Elisabeth Laurence's Elisabeth Surrit: Wiljam Von Neeman & Rachel Keen	Feb.	18
Nov.		3	George & Anne Ejler Surrities	Dec. 31	
Nov.		15	John [and] Maria Barbara Smith's Maria	May 1753	21

Date of Birth				Date of Baptism	
	month	Day		month	Day
	Febr.	21	James and Maria Tomlin's Elisabeth	March	12
1751	Sept.	25	Daniel and Maria Forsman's Margreta	March	12
	Febr.	18	Jonas and Maria Hendrickson's John	March	15
	Jan.	20	Walter and Cathrina Harris' Philip Gottfried	March	29
	Jan.	21	John and Gertrud Beesley's John	April	5
	Febr.	25	Israel and Magdlena Halm's Andrew	April	5
1751	Dec.	3	Hans and Sara Steilman's John	Jan.	5
1751	Nov.	14	Carl and Helena Lock's Debora	Jan.	1
	March	1	John and Elisabeth Delawuh's John	May	24
1752.	Nov.	13	Daniel and Rebecka Adams' Rebecka, Godparents: The Parents	Dec.	24
	Nov.	11	Petter and Magdlena Mau's Jacob, Godparents: the Parents	Dec.	24
1751	Dec.	3	Vallentin and Magdlena Praght's Margaretha, Godparents: the Parents.	Nov.	7
1752	Sept.	2	Adam and Anna Margreth Mour's Elisabeth, Godparents: the Parents	Nov.	7

PENSNECK 1753

Time of Birth				Time of Baptism	
Month		Day		Month	Day
Jan.		1	George and Mary Kats' Michael. Godparents: Michael and Rosina Hirreheis, Michael Kats and Magdalena Christein	Jan.	2
			John Bilderbach's Wife Elizabeth	Feb.	14
Sept.	1752	14	John and Elizabeth Bilderbach's Elizabeth	Feb.	14
Oct.	1752	24	Andrew and Christina Standley's Jane	Feb.	14
Sept.	1752	21	Oliver and Cathrina Webb's Mary	Feb.	14
Sept.	1752	21	Peter and Anna Petersson's Sarah	Feb.	14
Feb.		1	Lars and —— Halton's ——	March	11
Jan.		25	Daniel and Rebecka Dahlbo's Cathrina	March	11
March		9	Olof and Elizabeth Dahlbo's Cathrina	March	11
April		11	Gottfried and Maria Lisa Lauren's Anna Maria Cathrina. Godparents: William Contryman, Abr. Zimmerman, Anna Zimmerman, Anna Cath. Contryman, Anna Margreta Reis	May	21
April		21	Peter and Mary Marget's Adam. Godparents: Adam and Barbara Lieberger	June	10
May		8	Friedrick and Hannah Brita Baker's Mary Magdlena. Godparents: George Stanten, Henry Ejler, Mary Ejler, Magdlena Ponharten	June	11
Sept.		20	Philip and Cath. Mintz' Adam. Godparents: Adam Leiberger and the Parents.	Oct.	29

Date of Birth Year Month Day				Date of Baptism Month	Day
			John Richardson, nearly 40 years old	Jan.	12
			Joseph Richardson, 35 or 36 years old	Jan.	12
			Benjamin Richardson, 32 or 33 years old	Jan.	12
			John Sweeten, 22 or 23 years old.	Jan.	12
1746	March	8	Charles & Mary Slaid's Philip	Jan.	12
1749	Sept.	30	Charles & Mary Slaid's Ruth	Jan.	12
1748	Febr.	12	Robert and Anna Monjon's Sarah	Jan.	12
1751	Sept.	3	Robert and Anna Monjon's Mary Anna	Jan.	12
1752	Dec.	21	Joseph and Maria Richardson's Johanna	Jan.	12
1752	Dec.	3	Thomas and Cathrina Chester's Samuel	Jan.	12
1753	Jan.	22	Eric and Elisabet Coke's Hance	Jan.	12
1752	Dec.	8	Jeremia and Maria Burch's Hannah, Godparents: the Parents	May	11
	March	22	Robert and Abigail Turner's Maryall, Godparents: the Parents	May	11
	March	10	Daniel and Rebecka Förssman's Daniel. Godparents: the Mother, And. Hoffman	May	21
	May	18	John Tomlin	May	24
1730	April	11	Elizabeth Tomlin, his wife	May	24
1725	Febr.	2	Maria Thomas, her Husband, a Quaker.	May	24
1730	Febr.	28	John Wilkinson	May	24
1733	Febr.	8	Marta Chester, a maiden	May	24
1740	Nov.	1	Marta Thomas, Daughter of Absalom and Maria Thomas	May	24
1742	Sept.	14	Joseph Jackson, Godparents: Martin and Maria Tomlin	May	24
1752	Dec.	10	Henry and Elisabeth Liddon's Johanna. Godparents: the Parents	May	24
1750	Dec.	27	Elisabeth Clark's daughter, Maria Flan. Godparents: the Mother, Wil. Wiks	May	24
	March	19	Marrieddi and Elisabeth Jones' Debora. Godparents: the Mother.	May	24
1752	Dec.	31	Peter and Margrita Cox' Jacob. Godparents: the mother	May	24
	Jan.	10	Martin and Maria Tomlin's Elishu. Godparents: the Parents		
1749	July	19	John and Elisabeth Tomlin's Elisabeth. Godparents: the Parents	May	24
1750	Nov.	11	John and Elisabeth Tomlin's Mathew. Godparents: the Parents	May	24
1752	Sept.	28	John and Elisabeth Tomlin's Drusilla. Godparents, the Parents	May	24
1752	April	10	Absalom and Maria Thomas's Ephraim. Godparents: the Mother	May	24
	May	19	Erick and N. Moulika's John. Godparents: And. Hoffman	May	24
	March	11	Charles and Anna Reily's Elisabeth. Godparents: the Parents	Aug.	11
	Dec.	11	John and Hannah Herwind's Maria. Godparents: the Parents	May	11
1749	Octob.	16	Jacob and Cathrina Ruchman's William, Godparents: Judith Matson and Parents.	Aug.	12

[271]

Time of Birth Year	Month	Day		Time of Baptism Month	Day
1751	Oct.	20	Jacob and Cath. Richman's Maria. God-parents: Mr. Olof Parlyn and Elisa-beth Parlin.	Aug.	12
1753	Sept.	10	Johan and Susannah Helm's Hans, God-parents: Johan Steelman and the Parents.	Oct.	8
	May	11	Johan and Maria Von Neeman's Elisa-beth, Godparents: the Parents	Oct.	8
	June	14	Patrick and Cathrina M'lain's Daniel, Godparents: the Parents	Oct.	8
	Aug.	15	Erik and Maria Unander's Christina Lydia. Godparents: Mr. Gustav Hes-selius, Dean in Weto, in Sweden, the Rev. Joh. Novelius, Mr. Johan Hes-selius		

PENSNECK 1754

Time of Birth Year	Month	Day		Time of Baptism Month	Day
	April	21	Cornelius and Anne Corneliusson's John Godparents: John Mounceson, Thom-as Carney	April	21
1753	Nov.	2	Cornelius and Caspar's Sarah. Godpar-ents: William Bitly, Sr. and the Mother	April	21
	March	8	William and Prilchet's Mary Godparents: the Parents	April	21
1730	March	25	A Quaker, John Ambler	Sept.	8
1754	May	11	John and Elsa Gill Johnson's Elsa God-parents: the Parents and Erick Gill Johnson	Sept.	22
1754	July	10	George and Anna Ejler's Stephen Suri-ties: Henry Ejler, Christina Sack	Oct.	29
1752	June	18	Henry and Elizabeth Faver's child, George Godparents: Cathrina Baker and Jo-seph Fadder, Margreta Gam	Oct.	29

RECORD OF BIRTHS AND BAPTISMS IN RACOON, 1754

Date of Birth Year	Month	Day		Date of Baptism Month	Day
1754	Jan.	4	Hinrich and Maria Crip's Catharina, God-parents: Jonas Lock, Jesper Lock, Helena Lock, Magl.[Magdalena] Keen	Jan.	14
1753	Nov.	22	Olof and Elisabeth Kock's Jechonia, God-parents: the Parents	Jan.	20
1753	Dec.	5	Petter and Elisabeth Halton's Helena, Godparents: Joachim Reincke, the Mother, Märta [Martha] Jones	Jan.	20
1753	June	22	Tobias and Brita Van Neeman's Marga-retha, Godparents: the Mother, Erick Moulica and Sarah Mulica.	Jan.	30
1754	Feb.	8	Lars and Cathrina Cock's Christina, God-parents: Lars Lock, Gabrl. [Gabriel] Dahlbo, Christina Cox, Brita Dahlbo	Feb.	11

Date of Birth				Date of Baptism	
Year	Month	Day		Month	Day
1754	March	3	John and Elisabeth Tomlin's William, Godparents: the Parents	March	30
1754	March	14	Daniel and Rebecca Adams' Daniel. Godparents: the Parents, Zebulun Lock, Magdlena Keen.	April	14
1754	March	23	Jonas and Maria Hendrickson's Elisabeth. Godparents: Johan and Sarah Denny, Gabriel Dahlbo, Susanah Keen	April	14
1753	Dec.	24	Ebenezer and Brigitta Adam's Ebenezer. Godparents: the Mother, Zebulon Lock, Beata Kock, and Rebecca Dahlbo.	April	14
1753	Dec.	22	Mounce and Elisabeth Hoffman's Thomas. Godparents: the Parents	April	14
1754	March	31	George and Maria Griis's Isack. Godparents: Andr. [Anders] Hoffman, Edward Laurence, Isabella Hoffman	April	14
1754	Feb.		James and Maria White's Samuel. Godparents: the Parents.	April	15
1755	March	13	Garret & Mary Cavender's Susanna		
1759	March	5	Garret & Mary Cavener's George	Aug. 20	1762
1762	Aug.	13	Garret & Mary Cavener's Wiljame [William]	Aug. 20	1762

[RACCOON]

Monce & Sarah Keen's { Sely, born 1738 May the 2nd.
Moses, born 1740 March 21st.
John, born 1742 July 4th.

John & Rachel Keen's Christian, born 174- December the 6th.
Nicolas, B. Dec. ye 24th, 1744. S. [on] to Mounce & Sarah Keen.
Benjamin, B. febr. ye 7th, 1747. P.[arents] Mounce & Sarah Keen.
N.B. Peter Keens three Sons with his first wife, a friend, [Quaker?] not yet baptized, but their age, upon his desire, still here recorded. viz.
Elijah, B. Oct: the 22nd 1748.
Peter, B. Aug: the 27th 1752.
Daniel, B. April the 15th 1755.
His present wife, Cathrine Keen, is born May the 23d, 1742.

RACOON, 1756

1730	Nov.	8	John Keeper's Wife, Elisabeth, 26 years old.
1753	June	5	John and Elisabeth Keeper's Thomas.
1755	Jan.	29	John and Elis. Keeper's Elisabeth.

RACOON 1761

BAPTISMS OF THOSE CHILDREN WHO WERE [BAPTISED BY] The Revd. Mr. John abr. Lidenius in the year before—Racoon.

Dec: Andrew & Mary Matssons Mary B. Dec: the 2d 1761. S. Deb: Angelou.
Willm. & Mary Englands Elias B. March the 11th 1760 S. Sarah Steelman.

Andrew } Andrew & Mary Jones, Mary. B. May the 18th 1760.
Jones } Andrew and Mary Jones William B. Jan: the 14th 1762.
Children } Andrew & Mary Jones, Rebecka B. May the 1 1766.

BAPTISED of the Revd. Doct: Wrangel and Pastor Loci [before] my arrival and accession to the Ministry in these Congregations.[143]

RACOON 1762

Church-record over persons and children being baptized in Racoon Pensneck, Mauritzes River and Salem Congregations from the first day & introduction to my Ministerial functions in the aforesaid Congregations which happined to be the 11th day of July 1762. Wherein the big letter B. signifieth Born, the small letter b. baptized, P. Parents S. Surities as followeth.

Baptisms in Ra[c]oon from the 11th July 1762, to the end of the same year, wherein the children or persons baptized at Mauritzes River will be set down with a marck of MR. in Margine.[144]

1762
This Column sheweth
the time when
baptized. ——

1762 July	Jonas & Eleanora Denneys G. Wiljame, B. the 9th June 1762. b. 11th July 1762. S. P. themselfs.
11th.	Joseph & Mary Richards Isac, B. ye 17th maji 1762. S. Isac Justice.
	Jacob & Mary Archets Jacob B. ye 14 June 1762. S. the P. thems: [selves].
	Abram & Rachel Matssons Hannah B. ye 13th June 1762. S. they [the] P.
11th.	John & Sary Locks Cathrine B. ye 13th June 1762 S. John Wicksell vice Pastor, loci & Regina van Neuman.
August	
the 1st	Jacob & Anne Johnsons Jacob. B. July ye 10th 1762 S. they P.
	Andrew & Mary Johnses Wiljame B. January ye 14th 1762. S. they P.
	John & Sary Denneys Isac B. July the 22nd S. Lars Lock & Deborah Denny.
Sept: ye 12th.	Thomas & Marta Fischers Thomas B. July ye 30th 1762. S. George & Mary Catt.
20th.	Peter & Cathrine Keens Elisabet B. April ye 3 1762. S. they P.
	Moses & Sary Locks Emy B. Oct: ye 27th 1760 & Israel B. Sept. ye 3rd 1762. S. they P.
	Niclas & Elisabet Keens Rebecka B. May ye 4th 1762. S. P.
Oct. the 28th.	Job Ramford B. Oct: ye 27th 1737 and the same day his wife Mary Ramford. B. Oct: ye 23d 1735.
	Job & Mary Ramfords Anne B. Sept ye 7th 1761 S. P.
24th	Wiljame & Britta Homans Vandewar B. Oct: ye 19th 1762. S. Fran[c]is Auers, Magdlene Linch & Britta Lock.
Nov. the 15th.	John & Susanah Cables Jacob B. ye 8th Nov: 1762. S—P.
21	Robert & Marta Padricks Robert B. April ye 15th 1762. S. the mother.
Decemb. the 5th	Benjamin & Deborah Engelous Aukenius B. Oct: ye 27th 1762. S. P.
	Barthol & Elisabeth Supplys Garret B. Nov: ye 25th 1762. S. P.

---

[143] The list of baptisms is missing.
[144] Wicksell's baptismal records (1762-1773) are in English in the original.

9th.	Maride & Elisabet Jones. Abram B. Nov: ye 11th 1762. S. Sally Lock.
	Andrew & Debora Locks Isaac B. June ye 2d. 1761. S. Hance Urian (Rapapo) & Drusilla Lock.
Decemb, the 26th.	John & Mary Amblys Edeth B. Feb: ye 20th 1762.
	Philip & Susannah Eulers Margreta B. Aug: ye 18th 1762. S. Leonhard & Marget Kam.
	Charles & Betty Kocks John B. Dec: ye 20th 1762. S. John Wicksell V. P. loci & Regina van Neuman.

PENSNECK 1762

1762	Niclas & Marget Nilssons —— B. ye 2d April 1762. S. they P. themselves.
July the 25th.	Laurens & Elisab: Haltens Drusilla B. ye 19th of June 1762. S. P.
	Wiljame & Elis: Dalbous Regina B. May ye 14th 1762.
August 8th.	Patrick & Cathrine Doffye Abram, B. June ye 15th 1762. S. they P.
25th.	Andrew & Patience Hoppmans Maria, B. Aug: ye 22. 1762. S. Cath: Taylor.
Sept. ye 5th	John & Anne Penningtons Rebecka B. Feb. ye 18th 1762. S. they P.
	Jacob & Susanah Howells Elisabet. B. March ye 28th 1762. S. they P.
	John & Rebecka Hickmons John. B. March ye 15th 1762. S. they P.
	Hance & Anne Sears Else B. January ye 22. 1762. S. they P.
19th.	Andrew & Cathrine Standlys Senex B. Feb. ye 4th 1762. S. they P.
Oct. the 4th.	Jacob & Ester Catts Michel. B. July ye 7th 1762. S. they P.
M.R. 30th.	Gabriel & Marget Trollingers Sary. B. Jan. ye 19th 1760. & her brother Philip B. May ye 4th 1762. S. they P.
31st.	Abram & Gunills Jones Abram B. Jan: ye 8th 1759 S. they P.
	Jonas & Helena Hoffmans Eli. B. Dec: ye 30th 1761. S. they P.
	Laurence & Susannah Peterssons Hinrich. B. May ye 13th 1761.
	Philip & Cath: Grace Wiljame B. April ye 12th 1761 S.—P.
	John & Sary Cobbs Jonathan B. June ye 4th 1759. S. — P.
	Friedrich & Helena Cobbs Christopher B. Sept: ye 1st. 1760. S.—P.
	Dito Prudence B. Jan. ye 26th 1758. S—P.
	Daniel & Priscilla Petterssons Marta B. May ye 25. 1761 S—P.
	Paul & Priscilla Cobbs Caleb B. Dec: ye 7th 1761. S—P.
	John & Jane Peterssons John B. May ye 8th 1761. S—P.
Nov. the 1st.	John & Elisabeth Hoffmans Mary B. April ye 5. 1760 S—P.
	Gabriel & Rachel Van Neumans Gabriel B. May ye 12th 1760. S—P.
	George & Mary Meyers Charles B. Aug. ye 31. 1756 Mary B. may 1st. 1762.
	John & Susy Erichssons John B. Aug. ye 13 1762. S.—P.
Dec: 12th.	John & Marget Dickssons Marget B. Nov: ye 30th 1760. S.P.
	Eduard & Jane Tests Priscilla B. Oct: ye 28th 1762. S.—P.
	John & Elisabet Thomssons Elisabeth B. Nov. ye 29th 1761. S—P.
25th.	Baptized Sary Bremen, full grown, did not know her age.

RACOON 1763

1763 January the 7th.	Andrew & Cathrine Balls Prudens. B. ye 5th 1762. S. Wiljame and Elisabet Tuff. & Elisabet Senex.

Samuel & Jane Greffins Sary B. Sept: ye 8th 1762. S. Elis. Prise.

Feb. the
9th
Hendrick & Sary Hindrichssons Hindritte. B. Feb: ye 6th 1763 S. Lars & Britta Lock & Elisab: Hindrichson. his youngest son Hindrich B. Feb: ye 13th 1761. Bapt: of Mr. Wrangel D.D. the last year.

23d.
Antony & Regina Taylors Regina B. Dec: ye 12th 1762. S.P.

March the
5th.
James & Cathrine Clarcks Wiljame. B. Dec: ye 14th 1762. S.P.

20th.
Linnert & Mary Stantens Linnert B. Feb: ye 21 1763. S.P.

27th.
Zacharia & Rachel Schaus Sary B. March ye 12th 1763. S. Gilb: & Elisabet Runalls.

April
the 1st.
Joseph Caremon 30 years old. died the 8th after.

the 10th.
Erich & Anne Cath: Mullikas Sary. B. March ye 29th 1763. S. Abr: Matsson.

May the
4th.
Robbert & Mary Kragheads Elisabet B. May ye 9th 1761.
dito their Rebecka B. March ye 14th 1763. S. the mother only.
Hugh & Mary Forbes Anne. B. April ye 23d. 1761.
dito their son James B. April ye 26th 1763.

8th.
John & Rebecka Strengs Sary. B. March ye 29th 1763. S. Isac Justiss & Rebecka Strang.
Thomas & Christine Clercks Nanzy B. March ye 4th 1763.

June the
21st.
Francis & Anne Battins Thomas. B. Jan: ye 29th 1737. His brother Richard B. June the 19th 1740

MR. 26th.
Lawrence & Susannah Peterssons Wiljame B. Feb. ye 18th 1763.
Daniel & Priscilla Peterssons Absalon B. May ye 15th 1763.
David & Mehatable Van Neumans Richard B. Jan: ye 24th 1761.

27th.
Samuel & Sary van Neumans Lucas B. March ye 8th 1759. his syster their Cathrine B. March ye 15th 1762. S.P.
Abram & Grace Masslanders Wiljame B. Aug: ye 18th 1756. their Abram B. May ye 30th 1757. their Cherin B. June ye 20th 1759.
Gipson & Hannah Worells Lowis B. Aug: ye 23d. 1757. their Hannah B. July ye 25th 1762.

PENSNECK 1763

1763.

January
the 23d.
Senex & Mary Senexes John B. Dec: ye 25th 1762. S. Anne van Neuman.

Feb. the
19th.
Andrew & Mary van Neumans Mary B. Feb: ye 10th 1763. S.P.

20th.
James & Mary Thomases John B. Jan: ye 23d. 1761. S.P.
Joseph & Marta Allmans Anne Sept: ye 25th 1762. S.P.

23d.
Francis & Abellona Readkaps George Leonhard. B. Feb. ye 9th 1763. S. George Linnert.

March the
16th.
Jeremia & Britta Allens Mary B. Sept. ye 11th 1762. S.P.

20th.
Ehrent & Elisab: Biedles Esaia. B. March ye first 1763 & his brother George B. Feb: ye 9th 1761. of the Revd. Mr. Wrangel D.D.

the 22d.
Mathias & Anne Suluvans John B. July ye 18th 1762. S. the father only.

25th.
Peter & Cathrine Haetens Elisabet. B. April ye 8th 1762. S.P.

May the
15th.
George & Anne Stantens John B. May ye 3d 1763. S.P.

June the 19th.	John & Elisabet Bilderbacks Mary B. Aug: ye 3d 1762.
	Thomas & Cathrine Pattissons Elisabet B. Oct: the 19th 1761.
	Mathias & Sary Lambssons Kezaia B. March ye 23d. 1762.
	Joseph & Santy Pattissons Thomas B. July ye 4th 1761.
Salem 20th.	
	Wiljame & Susanah Philips Mathias B. Oct. 23d. 1762.
	James & Brigitte Mullings Hannah B. January ye 4th 1762.
	Thomas & Mary Margeens Thomas B. Sept: ye 20th 1760. His brother Joseph B. Sept. the 6th 1758.
	Salomon & Hannah Drapers Mary. B. Dec: the 28th 1762.
M.R. the 28.	
	Lazarus & Alander Riggins Lazarus. B. Jan: the 2d. 1762.
	Peter & Mary Massys Samuel B. March ye 18th 1759.
	John & Christine Peterssons Priscilla. B. Sept: ye 18th 1757.
	Jacob & Zephaya Jamis Thomas B. Sept: ye 25 1761.
	Mary Brannens Joseph Brannen B. Sept: ye 1760. the father unknown.
	Philip & Elisabet Hoopers Hindrick B. Oct: ye 30th 1758.
	Their Nanzy B. Feb: ye 28th 1754.
	Ebenezer & Sary Riggins Benjamin B. Nov: ye 18th 1762.
29th.	James & Elisabeth Garryns James B. Jan: ye 27th 1754.
	dito their Ebaya B. April ye 8th 1756. dito their Levaysy B. Aug. ye 17th 1759.
July the 3d.	Dito their Urias B. Feb: ye 13th 1763.
	Hance & Marget Lambssons Anne B. June ye 3d. 1763.
July ye 17th.	Conrad & Mary Caintylys Andrew B. ye 15 March 1763. S. Jacob & Cathrine Sly.
Aug: the 31.	George & Mary Starcks Cathrine B. ye 5th of Aug: 1763.
	John & Mary Caremons Joseph B. the 5 Oct: 1762.
Sept: 25. M.R.	Ebenaser & Debora Emssons Marget. B. ye 21 Aug: 1763.
Oct. 11.	Ebenaser & Sara Riggins Judith B. Aug. ye 4th 1763.
	Wiljame & Mary Jones Mary. B. ye 10th June 1757.
	Thomas & Christine Fowlers Thomas. B. ye 18th Nov: 1761.
Oct. 25.	Hance & Barbary Duquettes Peter. B. July ye 15. 1763.
Nov. the 6. M.R.	Thomas & Marget Webbers Marget B. Sept: ye 18th 1763.
Dec: 4th.	Jonas & Lyddy Van Neumans John B. July ye 31. 1760.
5.	Baptized Elisabeth Powel. 19. years of age & married to Wiljame Powel.
18th.	Jacob & Cathrine Slys Jacob. B. Nov: ye 26. 1763. S. Michel & Ursilla Catt Jacob Rather & Mary Catt.
19th.	John Ab: & Britta Lideniuses Abram Garret B. Dec: ye 15, 1763. S. the Revd. Mr. And: Borell. John Wiksell. Andrew & Betty van Neuman with their wifes & John Lock with his wife.
27th.	John & Mary Mountains Mary. B. March ye 19th 1761. S. Becky Tailor. Their James B. Nov: ye 13th 1757.
	Rocher & Junass Sherins Rebecka. B. Jan. ye 14. 1760.

RACOON 1763

July the 10th.	Isaacs & Sara Van Neumans John B. July ye 4th 1763. S. John Rambou, John Runnals, Mary Archet & Mary van Neuman.
	Fredrick & Sara Urians Andrew B. ye May 1763. S. Sara Kocks.
	Abram & Jane Laeddens Jane b. ye 11th of June 1762.

the 24.	Philip & Anne Laurences John B. ye 15th of Jan: 1763. S. Mathew & Cathrine Phall. their Mary B. ye 31. of March 1741.
Aug. the 7th.	Gabril & Mary Dalbous Lyddy. B. ye 1 of April 1763.
	Wiljam & Elisabeth Sweetens Wiljame B. ye 25 of Jan: 1763.
17.	Martin & Eva Bals John B. the 7th April 1763. S. John Dendelspeck.
	Jacob & Anna Leissingers Andrew. B. ye 24th April 1763. S. Erich Bloomer
	Hindrich & Cathrine Streems Sara B. ye 22. July 1763 S. George & Cath. Weiser.
	Melchior & Elis: Horners George B. ye 17th July 1763 S. George Horner & Hannah Weaver.
	Michel & Salome Bauers Anna Maria B. ye 1 May 1763. S. Peter & Anna Margett.
Sept. 18th.	John & Becky Homans Jacob B. ye 1. Aug: 1763 S. Noach Hopman.
19th.	Jacob & Zephaya Fishlers Hannah B. the 30th of Sept: 1749. dito their Zephaya B. the 24. Feb. 1752. Dito their Jacob B. the 8th of March 1754. Dito their Linnert B. ye 30th of May 1756. dito their Elisabeth B. ye 2d. of April 1758. dito their Rachel B. 30th of March 1760. dito their Samuel B. ye 18th July 1763. S. Lars & Britt: Lock.
Oct: 16.	Eric & Hannah Coxes Mary B. ye 28th of Aug: 1763.
30th.	Andrew & Anne Van Neumans John B. Oct. ye 20th 1763.
	Jacob & Anne Pipeperts Anne Mary B. ye Sept: the 5 1763. S. Francis & Lizy Ouers.
Nov: 27th.	John & Elis: Delavoos Rachel B. Sept: ye 30th 1763. Their Anne B. Oct: ye 16th 1761.
	Thomas & Elisabeth Dennys Rebecka: B. Nov: ye 17th 1763. S. John Rambou & Christina Van Neuman.
the 30th.	Wiljame & Christine Van Neumans Wiljame. B. Oct: ye 12th 1763.
Dec: 25.	Gilbert & Mary Runalses Sara. B. Sept: ye 28th 1763.
	Daniel & Judy Strengs Rebecka. B. Sept: ye 30th 1763.
	Friedrich & Hannah Winholtz Samuel. B. Nov: ye 26th 1763.
	Jacob Homan. Sara his Sister widow Tossa 41 last 10 of Apr. Elizabeth Conor 28 17 next Oct.

PENSNECK 1764

Jan. ye 9th.	Daniel & Anne Nilssons Hannah B. June the 3d. 1763. S. Cornel: & Anne Cornelsson.
	Richard Allen a married man B. Nov. ye 5 1737 P. Thom & Hannah Allen.
	Thom and Hannah Allens Sidony B. in March 1749.
	Richard and Hannah Allens Joseph B. Oct. the 18th 1762.
	John and Mary Gressys Israel B. June the 9th 1763.
the 22d.	Isaac & Mary Nilssons Levy. B. Decemb: ye 26th 1763.
the 23d.	James & Mary Thomasses Erich B. Decemb: ye 8th 1763.
Feb: 4th.	Thom & Hannah Alleens Thomas B. Dec: 9th 1747. and their John B 9th of March 1748.
	Thom & Marta Fishers John B. Jan: the 20th 1764.
the 6th.	John & Jane Flyeds Jane B. Nov: ye 18th 1763.
the 20th.	Daniel & Mary Morssys James B. Dec. ye 11th 1763.
the 28th.	Peter & Elisabeth Heins Hance Georg. B. Oct. ye 23d. 1763. S.
March	
	Hance & Anne Cautch.
	Adam & Elisabeth Fyx Charlotta B. Dec: ye 23. 1763. S. the same Cautch.

ye 4th.	Joseph & Mary Duquettes Nathanael B. Nov: ye 27th 1763.
	John & Anne Penantons Richmomd B. April ye 20th 1763.
April ye 7.	Hawes & Susannah Davids. David B. January ye 21. 1764.
	John & Jane Joressons John B. Feb: ye 18th 1764.
the 2d.	George & Sary Peterssons Barbora B. Feb: ye 17th 1764.
	John & Else Dahlbous Magdlene B. March ye 16th 1764. S. Mary Beedle.
	Jacob & Susy Howels Moses. B. March ye 7th 1764.
	Laurence & Anne Morris Rachel & Sary Tweens B. March ye 14th 1764.
Mr.R. 15.	Jonas & Hellena Hopmans Hellena B. Jan: the 6th 1764.
	Philip & Cath: Grace Silvy B. Decemb: ye 11th 1763.
	Friedrich & Hellena Cobbs Elisabeth B. Sept: ye 12th 1763.
the 16th.	Wiljame & Elis: Mauglouclen Elisabeh B. Feb. 1 1762.
	John & Jane Peterssons Anne B. March ye 16th 1764.
the 23d.	John & Christine Beetles Barbary B. April the 15th 1764.
	Paul & Rodee Paulssons Darias B. Nov. ye 1. 1763.
the 24th.	John & Sary Goldsmith Esaia B. Feb. ye 20th 1764.
May the 6th.	Alpheus & Brigitte Borteens Mary B. April ye 2d. 1763.
June	Hindrich & Charity Savels Elisabeth B. May ye 19th 1763.
the 11th.	Wiljame and Sary Prichets Elisabeth B. Feb: ye 23d. 1761.
	Andrew & Cathrine Helms Sary B. June the 8th 1764. S. Mary Helm.
the 24th.	Senex & Mary Senexons Andrew B. March ye 21. 1764.
June the 24th.	George & Rosee Alkorns James B. July 17th 1759.
	Francis & Mary Nails Sary B. May the 30th 1764. S. Elis: Borten & Mary Potter.
the 25.	Mathew and Anne Sullivans Mary B. Oct: ye 29, 1763.
July ye 8th.	Wiljame & Elisab: Dalhbous Rebecka Elisabeth. B. June ye 7th 1764.
	Lawrence & Cathrine Dalhbous Israel B. July ye 7th 1764. S. Gab: & Reb: Dalbou & Sara Helm.
Aug. ye 6th.	John & Jemamy Tooders Peter B. Oct. ye 2d. 1753, and John B. March the 6th 1757 his Brother—Wiljame & Isabella Huttsons Assaria B. July ye 31, 1764.
the 26.	John & Sara Makoms Lyddy B. Dec: 29 1763.
	Tobias & Cathrine Caspers John B. March the 17th 1764.
Salem.	Cornelius & Patty Aunails Peggy & Richard tweens B. Aug. 23d. 1764. S. John Borden, Mary Canaday & Francis & Mary Aunail.
Sept: 7th.	John & Rebecka Hichmons George B. Aug: the 7th 1764.
Oct. 8th.	Clemy & Mary Sinnerts Clemy. B. Jan: the 15th 1764.
	Nicolas & Rosannah Foys Peggy B. July the 7th 1764.
	Williame & Elis: Hockets Sarah B. Oct: the 3d 1761 & Elisabeth born April the 12th 1764.
Nov. 11th.	Robert & Plony Thomssons Wiljame B. Oct: the 7th 1764.
the 18th.	John & Mary Makoms John B. Oct: the 29 1758 & Mary B. Dec: the 2d. 1759 S. Sara Makum.
	Mickel & Barbora Butlers Mary B. Dec: the 9th 1760. Their Anne B. Oct: the 6th 1764.
Dec. 9th.	Giles Lamssons Wife Elisabeth 23 years of age. last Nov. S. her Husband & Francis Miles.
	Philip & Mary Pentons Philip B. Feb: the first 1763.
NB.	Cesar & Phillis Sandys Cesar Nigroes B. March the 20th 1761. belonging to Fran: Miles.
	Hance & Margery Lamssons Lyddy B. Dec: the 27th 1761.
10th.	Elisabeth Asly a young woman B. Nov: the 30th 1744. S. Francis

	& Mary Auknail.
the 31.	Laurence & Elisabeth Haltens John B. Dec: the 22d. 1764.
	Laurence & Susanna Peterssons Peter B. Oct: the 13th 1757. Their Anne B. Dec. the 20th 1764.
Ap: 5.	Ebenezar & Anne Peakmans Elisabeth B. Jan. the 11th 1762.
the 6th.	Andrew & Mary Paussons Barcas. B. March the 30th 1764. Their Tobias B. Oct. 8th 1761.
13.	John & Else M. Keans Rosey B. Ap. the 9th 1764.
19th.	John Vallentine & Anne Margret Baumans John Vallentine, B. March the 23d. 1764.
30th.	Daniel & Rebecka Dalhbous Levina B. Dec: the 9th 1761, their Ester B. Feb: the 10th 1764.
	Yet more Baptisms this year performed by the Revd. Mr. Lidenius in the Neck.[144a]
April the 5.	Ebenezar and Anne Peackmons Elisabeth B. Jan: the 11th 1762.
the 6th.	Andrew and Mary Paulssons Barcas B. March the 30th 1763. NB. Tobias their son, B. Sept: the 8th 1764. Baptized by Dr. Wrangel.
April ye 13.	John & Else Keans Rosy B. April the 9th 1764.
the 19th.	John Vallentine & Anne Marget Baumans John Vallentine B. March ye 23d. 1764.
the 30th.	Daniel & Rebecka Dalbous Livinah B. Dec: the 9th 1761. And their Ester B. Feb: the 10th 1764.
May the 13th.	Gideon & Judith Clarcks Bathsebah B. March the 28th 1763.
the 15.	Ebenezar & Anne Peackmons Silvanus B. May the 6th 1764.
the 20th.	David & Elisabeth Floyds Isaac B. April the 25. 1764.
the 27th.	Caspar & Susannah Hankes Susannah B. May the 15th 1764.
July the 8th.	William & Elisabeth Dalbous Rebecka Elisabeth B. June the 7th 1764.
the 9th.	Laurence & Cathrine Dalbous Israel B. July the 7th 1764. S. Sarah Helm.
the 28th.	John & Susannah Goldsmith Lydiah B. February the 16th 1759.
August the first.	Robert & Sary Whites Sarah B. July the 19th 1764.
the 5.	Andrew and Cathrine Hoffmans Anne B. June the 4th 1764.
Sept. the 11.	John and Margareth Mullickas Esther B. August the 25th 1757 & their Son Edward B. Oct: the 15th 1761.

RACOON 1764

Jan. the 1.	Joseph & Mary Paulssons Elisabeth B. Nov. ye 14th 1763.
13th.	Andrew & Elisabeth van Neumans Alexander & Wiljame tweens B. the 12. of Jan: 1764. S. Fredrich King & Wiljame & Christine van Neuman.
15th.	Jonas & Christine Keens John B. Nov. ye 28th 1763.
Feb. ye 13th.	Abram & Rachel Matssons Mary B. Dec: ye 3d. 1763.
26th.	Peter & Mary Strickers Anne Judith. B. Feb: ye 5, 1764.
	Jacob & Marget Johnssons Mary B. Feb: ye 9th 1764.
	Jonas & Anne Joneses Jonas. B. Sept: ye 11th 1763.
the 27th.	Charles & Britta Steellmans Prishilla. B. Sept: ye 1, 1763.
	George Brouns wife Elisabeth. B. Dec: ye 28th 1741. & their chil-

[144a] It will be noted that five April entries are repeated. The original was badly confused, but it appears that a later entry was made to specify the baptisms of Lidenius.

dren Mary B. Nov: ye 28th 1760. And Sary B. Jan. ye 16th. 1762.

March 4th. Robbert and Brigitta Clarcks Isaac. B. Feb. ye 9th 1764.

the 8th. Gabriel and Rebecka Strengs Hellena Rein B. Feb: ye 10th 1764. S. Gotf: Köhler & Wiljame Noble.

the 11th. Wiljame & Mary Englands Sary B. Feb. ye 3d. 1764. S. Sary Homan. Charles & Rebecca Coxes Peter B. Feb: ye 27th 1764. S. John & Peter Lock and Rachel Dalhbou.

the 14th. Dennys & Sary Bargains John B. Feb: ye 16th 1760.

ye 22d. Isaac Schoote B. ye 26th 1741 a married man.

April 4th. John & Cath: Sweetens Benjamin B. Jan: ye 20th 1763.

the 7th. Nathan & Mary Boys Cathrine B. Feb. ye 22d. 1764. S. John Runals & Elis: Hindrickson. Wiljame & Sary Lowis John B. 1761. & Wiljame B. April ye 15th. 1763.

the 26. Hance Michel & Anne Mary Eulers Hance Mickel B. Feb: ye 20th. 1764. S. John and Sary Powers.

the 7th. Alexander & Elisabeth Coopers Wiljame B. March ye 10th 1764.

the 22d. Andrew & Mary Matssons Jonathan B. May ye 7th 1764. S. Benjamin Angelou & Marta Jamesson.

the 10th. Andrew & Cathrine Justissons Rebecka B. May ye first 1764. John & Rachel Middletowns Nathan B. Feb: the 15th 1764.

the 17th. Wiljame & Betzy Tuff Senex B. May the 4th 1764. S. Britta Clarck. Mary Dellyns Levaisy B. Dec: ye 22d 1763. the Hues [husband] ran away.

the 28th. Mathew & Susannah Lords Joseph B. Sept: ye 28th 1761. John and Cathrine Eulers Cathrine B. April ye 18th 1764.

M.R.

July the 1. Paul & Prishilla Cobbs Paul B. June ye 2d. 1764.

the 2d. Joseph & Mary Lords Mary B. June ye 19th 1760.

the 9th. James & Magdlena Steelmans Isaac B. June ye 15th 1764.

the 22d. Andrew & Debora Locks Andrew B. July ye 13th 1764. S. Zebulon & Sary Lock.

29th. John & Elisabeth Tills Wiljame B. April ye 29th 1764. S. Jac: & Elis: Paulin.

Coh:

ye 30th. John & Mary Hamlers Patience B. Jan: ye 12th 1764.

Aug. 12th. John & Rebecka Strengs Abram B. June ye 30th 1764.

the 14th. Peter & Sara Longåkers Hellena B. Aug: ye 30th 1763. S. James

M.R.

Wale.

the 30th. Jacob & Zephaya Kimmys Wiljame B. June the 26th 1764. David & Christina Goldens Sary B. Jan: the 11th 1764. Samuel and Cath: Erickssons Andrew B. June the 26th 1764.

Sept: 9th. Nicolas & Elis: Hollands Thomas B. May the 14th 1764. S. Thom. Jones.

the 10th. John & Mary Stillmans Sarah B. Sept: the 1st. 1764.

the 23d. Thomas & Cathrine Adams Susannah B. Aug: the 27th 1764. S. Erich Cox.

Oct: 12th. Charles & Anne Raylys Jonathan B. March the 31st 1764. Their Susannah B. March the 12. 1756 their Charles B. Apr: the 13th 1753. their Mary B. May the 10th 1760. their Sary B. July the 17th 1762. the follow: were Bapt: before namely

M.R. Thomas B. Dec: the 17th 1748. Samuel B. Dec. the 9th 1750 & Elisab: B. March the 12th 1752.

the 16th. Jonas & Lyddy van Neumans Samuel B. April the 11th 1764.

the 21. Charles & Rachel Dalhbous Rachel B. Sept: the 20th 1764. S. Cath: Hindrickson.

Nov. 4th.	Peter & Regina Locks Rebecka B. Oct. the 28th 1764. S. John Lock & Elis: Keen.
	Jacob & Regina Elkhorns Sagina B. Aug: the 2d. 1764. S. Mick: & Susan: Powers.
the 25.	Mathew & Susannah Lords Rebecka b. Oct. the 15th 1764.
	Robbert & Mary Kragheads Job. B. Oct: the 12th 1764. S. Esaia Lock.
Dec. ye 2d.	Jeremia & Britta Allens Wiljame B. Oct: the 7th 1764.
	Isaac & Susannah Shootes Mary. B. Sept: the 23d. 1764.
	John & Hannah Arveens Prudence B. March the 14th 1764.
the 23d.	Peter & Anne Justice Bakum B. the 22d. Dec: 1764. S. Rebecka Justice.

PENSNECK 1765

Jan: the 1.	Thomas & Jane Howards Lemuel B. June the 23d 1764.
the 15.	John & Elisabet Barons Marget B. Dec: ye 4th 1764. S. Cornel: Snell & Mary Lowise.
the 20.	Patrick & Cathrine Doffys Cathrine B. Dec. ye 13th 1764. S. Peter & Patient Hopman
Feb:	
the 10.	Aron & Elisabet Beetles Wiljam B. Jan: ye 15th 1765.
April the 5.	Augustine & Mary Petersons Hindrick B. March the 4th, 1765.
the 14.	John & Mary Dickssons Anne B. June the 13th 1764 S. Marget Philpot.
the 14.	Mathias & Anne Sullivans Mathias B. March the 10th 1765.
May the 26.	John & Sary Standlys Susanna & Elisabet tweens B. May the 13th 1765 S. Joseph Dunham & Anne Green.
the 28.	Jacob & Anne Leissingers Jacob B. Dec: the 14th 1764. S. George & Elis. Blumer & Anne Beiry
the 28.	George & Anne Mary Catts Annamaria B. April ye 4th 1765. S. Carles & Dor: Winemyller & Hans & Elisabet Blumber.

M.R.	
June the 7	John & Sary Cobbs Sary B. April the 18th 1765.
the 7	David & Mehittable Van Neumans Judith. B. Jan: the 11th 1765.
the 7	Samuel & Sarah v: Neumans Elias. B. feb: the 12th 1765.
the 23	John & Charity Greens George. B. April the 14th 1765.
the 23	Hindrich & Charity Savels Abel. B. May the 4th 1765.

M. R. the 7.	
	S. Susy Caple
	Gabril & Marget Trollingers Michel B. Dec: the 3d. 1764.
July 28.	Gipsson & Hannah Worells Jonathan B. Dec: the 7th 1764.
Aug. 18.	Moses & Sary Locks John B. April the 8th 1764.
	Gabril & Rebecca Dalbous Wiljam B. Julii: the 2d 1765.
	Joseph & Cathrine Allmons Salomon B. April the 13th 1763 their
Salem the	Daniel B. July the 18th 1765.
same day.	Wiljam & Susanah Philips, Mikel Phillips B. May the 6th 1765.
	Stephen & Mary Rays, Abram B. April the 16th 1765.
Sept. the 9.	John & Susy Elisab: Bodenhagens Anna-Margreta B. Aug: the 25. 1765. S. Annemary: Tailor

M.R.	
Sept: 17	Wiljam & Elisab: Makgloucklens Wiljam, b. Feb: the 2d. 1765.
P.N	Peter & Cathrine Haltens Rebecca B. Aug: the 18th 1765 S. Isaac
Sept: 22.	& Elizabeth Justice and Rebecca Streeng.
M.R.	Georg Philips & Eva Maria Carmans Philip Carl. B. Oct. the ——
Oct. the 22.	1764. S. Carl Ludv: & Maria Walter.
the 25.	Eduard & Marget Crows James B. Jan: the 12th 1764.

P.N.
Oct. the 7.   John & Mary Greffys Samuel B. March the 14th 1765.
7th.   Isaac Sommers & Marget Grefys Milly B. March the 31. 1765.
               oäckta [illegitimate].
Dec. the 22.   Isaac & Mary Anne Nilssons Elisabeth B. Nov: the 7th 1765.
dito   Charles and Sary Greens Marget B April the 9th 1765.
Nb. the 1.   Cornelius & Rachel Boons Peter B. Nov: the 8th 1765 S'. Peter
               Boon & Wiliam Dalbou
the 29.   Andrew & Christiane Standlys Anne B. April the 17th 1765.

RACOON 1765

Jan: the 27.   Laurence & Sary Friends Wiljam B. Dec: the 6th 1764.
Feb. the 5.   Joseph & Sary Schootes Sary B. Jan: the first 1765.
the 17.   Gabrial & Mary Dalbous Mary B. Dec: the 8th 1764.
the 24.   Moses & Elisabet Hopmans Moses B. Jan: ye 1765. S. Wiljam
               Matsson.
the 25.   Job & Mary Rampfords Thomas B. Dec: the 31. 1763.
March
the 2.   James & Cathrine Clark's Hindrich B. Dec: the 22d 1764. And
               their James B. Nov: the 30th 1760 S. Thomas Carney & Robert
               Clarck.
the 5.   Hindrich & Sara Hindrichsons Caleb B. March ye 5th S. Magdlena
               Lock.
the 10.   Wiljam & Christ: Stremples Moses & Aron tweens B. Jan. 11th
               1765 S. Reb: Angelou.
the 31.   Jonas & Christine Keens Rebecka B. Feb: the 24th 1765.
April the 7.   Isaac & Sarah Van Neumans Susannah B. Feb: the 14th 1765.
the 7.   Samuel & Elisabet Linches Wiljam B. Feb: the 21. 1765 S. Wiljam
               & Christ: van Neuman and Magdl: Linch.
the 21.   John & Cathrine Winssons Anne B. Feb: the 10th 1765.
May the 3.   Thimothy & Margery Clarcks Garret B. Feb: the 23d. 1765. S.
               Christ: V: Neuman.
the 9.   Cleften Rouls & Cathrine Hindrichsons Joseph bast:[ard] B.
               March the 31, 1765. S. Elisabeth Hindrichson & Jonas Hind-
               richson her brother.
the 19.   Moses & Elisabet Coxes Rebecka B. March the 24th 1765.
the 19.   Theresia Nicolasson B. Aug: the 31. 1745 S. Elis: Senex & Emy
               Chester.
the 19.   James & Mary Whites John B. Aug: the 10th 1760 S. Laur: &
               Britta Lock.
19.   their James B. Jan: the 1st. 1765. S. Mary Kraghead.
the 27.   Zacharias & Rachel Schaws John B. Ap: the 20th 1765 S. Gilb:
               Runals.
June the 2.   Benjamin & Debora Angelous David B. May the 22 1765. S. Mary
               Matsson & Gab: Streng.
the 23.   Charles & Anne Raylys Wiljam B. March the 25. 1765.
the 23.   Eric & Hannah Coxes Anne B. June the 3d 1765.
the 23.   Leonhard & Mary Stantens John B. May the 5th 1765.
the 30.   Thomas & Christine Clarcks Elisabeth B. Dec: the 29th 1764. S.
               Mary Clarck.
the 30.   John & Elisabet Keepers Rebecca B. June the 27th 1762 and their
               Judith B. Aug: the 11th 1764. Their Cathrine B. March the 23d.
               1759. their Bathniphleoth B. June the 10th 1760 their Thomas
               B. June the 5th 1753. their Elisabeth B. January the 29th 1755.
               their Sarah B. Aug: the 19th 1757.
Aug. the 1.   John & Sary Locks Prischilla B. this morning S. Cath: Hindrichson,
the 8.   Charles & Rebecka Coxes Anne B. Aug: the 6th 1765.

the 25.	Daniel & Prischilla Peterssons Matsson B. May the 21. 1765.
	Abram & Jane Laiddens Mary, B. Aug. the 15th 1764.
the 30.	Wiljam & Cathrine Sauderses Marget B. May the 17th 1765. S. Marget Kalm & Mary Stricker.
Sept.	
the 15.	John & Elisab: Fourakers Deborah, B. July the 8th 1765.
the 27.	Peter & Elisab: Keyers David B. Nov: the 30th 1763.
	Ephraim Waas & Elisab: Matlocks Maryanne B. Aug. the 17th 1760. were promised, but died both before they were married.
the 22.	Zebulon & Prischilla Locks Lydia B. Aug: the 26 1765. S. Susannah Lock.
Oct. the 15.	John & Mary Reaves Rachel B. Jan: the 12th 1757 S. Charles Hopman.
the 27.	John & Nanzy Higners Nanzy B. Feb. the 11th 1765.
Novemb	
the 1.	Gilbert & Mary Runnalls Rebecka B. Oct. the 11th 1765.
the 17.	Mary Wilkesson B. July the 27th 1738 wife of the English Clerck. Her Sons John B. Oct. the 5th 1757 & Samuel Feb: the 27th 1759 P: John and Mary Wilkesson.
the 17.	John and Mary Derexons Mary B. Oct: the 1. 1765.
the 20.	George & Barbora Krumreins Susannah B. Aug: the 2d. 1765.
the 28.	Jonas & Mary Hindrichsons Israel B. Sept: the 6. 1765 S. Israel Helm.
Dec.	
the 25.	William & Christine van Neumans Sarah B. Nov: the 9th 1765.
the 26.	Hughes & Mary Forbes Mary B. Sept: the 13th 1765.
the 30.	Jonas and Anne Jones Mary B. Sept: the 1. 1765.
May 21.	Jacob & Marget Johnssons Elisabeth B. April the 4th 1765. baptized by the Revd. Andrew Borell. and their Son Mathias was born the 3d of Feb: 1755 & bapt: at Nordeast — River by the Revd. Mr. Hamilton

PENSNECK 1766.

April the 6.	David & Elisab: Floyds Solomon, B. March the 20th 1766.
	Joseph & Mary Nails [Nagel] Christine, B. July the 17th 1765.
	John & Susannah Cabels John, B. July the 19th 1765.
	Paulus & Rody Pouhlsons Sary, B. Nov: the 2d 1765.
	Daniel & Rebeckah Dalbous Magdlenah, B. March the 27th 1766.
the 20.	Jacob & Susannah Howels George, B. March the 5th 1766.
	Robert & Susannah Woodsides Robert, B. June the 20th 1762.
the 23.	Gabriel Peterssons & Eleonor Butterworth Priscilla B. Feb: the 7th 1750
May the 11.	Benjamin Trustin & Barborah Coles Elisabeth, B. Nov. the 20th 1765 S. Elisab: Cooper & the mother
the 25.	Christopher & Lydia Graigs Robert, B. May the 28th 1765.
the 8.	Gideon & Judith Clarcks Mary, B. January the 11th 1765.
June the 10.	Adam & Mary Coles Susannah B. May the 9th 1766.
the 14.	Ebenezer & Anne Peakmans Sarah B. May the 13th 1766.
July	
the 11th.	Thomas & Mary Webbers John B. June the 4th 1766.
the 15.	Andrew & Elisab: V. Neumans Friedrick B. July the 17th 1766.
May the 4.	Hance & Barbora Jaquettes Hance B. Feb: the 18th 1766.
	Joseph & Mary Jaquettes Joseph B. March the 14th 1766.
the 7.	Joseph & Mary Lords Absalon B. Sept: the first 1765.
M.R.	Abram & Grace Marlanders John B. Aug: the 13th 1765.
	Lazare & Hellena Riggins Gracy B. Aug: the 28th 1764.

June 29.	Schedrick & Mary Sunderlins Joseph B. Sept: the 15th 1765.
the 30.	Cornelius & Marget Dailys Robert B. the 16th of April 1765.
Aug. the 23.	Jacob & Cathrine Slys Sarah B. May the 13th 1766.
Sept: 3.	William Smith & Sara Bremens Elisabet B. 17th of Dec: 1764.
the 14.	John & Maria Mackrays Amos B. July the 24th 1766.
	Hugh & Susannah Davis Hugh B. Dec: the 19th 1765.
Oct. 25.	Jacob & Anna Leissingers John-George B. Sept: the 16th 1766.
	S. Hance & Elisabet Blumer.
Nov: 17.	Albert & Sary Bilderbacks Rebecca B. Sept: the 8th 1766.
Dec. 8th.	John & Jane Jouranssons William B. Aug: the 14th 1765.
	Joseph & Marget Pennintons Joseph B. June the 13th 1766.
	These following children were bapt: of the Revd. Mr. Lidenius.
April	
the 2.	David & Elisabeth Floyds Solomon B. March the 20th 1766.
	Joseph & Mary Nails Christina B. July the 17th 1765.
	John & Susannah Gabels John B. July the 19th 1765.
	Paulus & Rhody Pohlssons, William B. Oct: the 4th 1765.
	Andrew & Mary Pohlssons, Sarah, B. Nov: the 2d 1765.
the 3.	Daniel & Rebeca Dalbous, Magdalena B. March the 27th 1766.
the 20.	Jacob & Susannah Howells George B. March the 5th 1766.
	Robert & Susannah Woodsides, Robert B. June the 20th 1762.
the 23.	Gabriel Peterssons Eleonor Butterworth Priscilla B. Feb: the 7th 1750.
May the 11.	Benjn. Trustin & Barbora Coles, Elisabeth B. Novbr: the 20th 1765.
the 25.	Christopher & Lydia Craigs Robert B. May the 28th 1765.
the 28.	Gideon & Judy Clarcks, Mary B. January the 11th 1765.
June the 10.	Adam & Mary Coles, Susannah, B. May the 9th 1766.
the 14.	Ebenazar & Anne Peakmans, Sarah B. May the 13th 1766.
July the 11.	Thomas & Mary Webbers, John B. June the 4th 1766.
the 15.	Andrew & Elisabeth Van Neumans, Friedrick, B. July the 7th, 1766.
Aug: the 3.	Michel & Sarah Noers Sarah, B. Nov: the 25th 1748.
the 17.	Robert & Martha Pedricks Silas, B. June the 14th 1765.
Sept: the 7.	John & Mary Coales Cathrine B. Feb: the 15th 1762. Adam B. April the 15th 1763. Margareth B. Aug: the 14th 1766.
	Israel & Gertrud Dalbous Sarah B. Sept: the 3d. 1766.
the 23.	Hance Cownrad & Mary Fautzers John B. Sept. ye 19th 1766.
	Peter Stonemetz & Deborah Hoffmans, Mary, B. July the 18th 1766.
the 28.	Duncan & Elisabeth Saunders, John, B. March the 11th 1766.
Oct. the 4.	Alexander & Elisabeth Coopers John B. Sept. the 27th 1766.
Nov. the 16.	John & Sarah Goldsmith, Samuel, B. Novemb: the 3d. 1766.
the 20th.	Anne Readh, widow to Niclas Read, baptised in heavy sickness.
Dec: the 21.	Robert & Jane Kitts Martha B. May the 23d. 1766.
the 31.	William & Christine Strimples William, B. Dec: the 30th 1766.

RACOON 1766

January	
the 26.	Marget B. Nov: the 9th P: Joseph & Mary Paulsson.
Feb.	
the 2.	Carles & Helena Locks Hellenah B. Dec: the 31. 1765.
the 16.	George & Anne Stantens Anne B. Jan: the 2d 1766.
March	
the 9.	Bartholom: & Isabella Supplys Aron B. January the 1. [date torn] S. John and Mary Steelman.
the 18.	John & Marget Mullickas John B. April the 17th 1765.

the 22.	Michel & Salome Powers Samuel B. December the 16 1765 S. Jacob and Regina Eickorn.
the 22.	Hindrich & Anne Cathrine Streems Anne-Cathrine B. Jan: the 11th 1766. S. George & Anne Cath: Weiser & Louis Catt.
the 23.	John & Else Dalbous Andrew B. Feb: the 10th 1766.
the 24.	Isaac & Marget Howells Marget B. Jan: the 26. 1766.
the 28.	John & Christine Beetles Mary B. Jan: the 28 1766.
the 28.	William and Mary Loves Marget B. Feb: the 28th 1766. S. Rob: & Britta Clarck.

M. Riv:
April the

7th.	James & Elis: Garrins Israel B. Feb: the 6, 1766.
the 7.	Philip & Eva Maria Corvins Christiana Cathrina b. March the 2d. 1766 S. Maria & Cathrina Walter.
the 20.	Joseph & Mary Richards Mary, B. Feb: the 27th 1766.
May the 11.	Gabriel & Rebecka Strengs Ephraim B. Feb: the 17th 1766.
the 11.	Jacob & Anne Jones, Anne, B. Sept: the 9th 1765.
the 25.	Jacob & Mary Orchards William B. Ap: the 19th 1766 S. Sary V. Neuman.
the 25.	Andrew & Mary Jones Rebecka N. May the 1. 1766.
June 29.	Peter & Regina Locks Ananias B. May the 28th 1766. S. John Lock.
July 24.	Jonas & Hellena Dennys Elisabeth B. June the 19th 1766.
Aug. 3.	Jacob & Anne Papperts Fransiscues B. May the 16th 1766. S. & Else Ours.
Aug. 10.	John & Cathrine Sweetens Michel B. Sept: the 26th 1765.
	Malachia & Elisabet Horners, Cathrine B. Feb: the 27. 1766. S. John & Cathrine Euler.
Oct. the 6.	Robert & Britta Clercks Priscilla B. Sept: the 3d. 1766.
the 19.	John & Charity Greens, Hezekia B. Aug: the 15th 1766.
Nov. the 4.	John & Sary Dennys Debora B. Nov: the 12th 1766.
Nov. 15.	Jacob & Sophia Fislers Joseph B. Oct: the 3d 1766.
	John & Cathrine Eulers Hannah B. Sept: the 12th 1766. S. George Horner, & Hannah Weawer.
Nov. 27.	Daniel & Judith Streengs Daniel B. Oct: the 29th 1766. S. John & Rebecka Streeng.
	Andrew & Mary Matssons William B. Nov. the 26th 1766.
Dec: 9.	John & Beatha Hommans Debora & Rachel Tweens B. Dec. 7th 1766.
Dec. 24.	Jonas & Christine Keens David B. Oct: the 13th 1766.
the 28.	William & Elisabeth Tuffs John B. Oct. the 23d 1766.
Sept: 3.	John & Cathrine Runnels Nathan B. Nov: the 2d. 1765.

PENSNECK 1767

January

the 11.	William & Margaret Smiths, Mary, B. April the 9th 1766.
the 15.	Mallacky & Cathrine Kellys Anne B June the 7th 1762 Joseph B. Jan. the 19th 1764.
the 19.	Gideon & Judith Clarcks, Jacob, B. Jan: the 9th 1767.
	James B. Dec: the 24th 1765.

March

the 25.	James & Sary Dilcks James B.

At Dilcks.

	John and Emy Duffils Charity B. Feb. ye 14th 1762 & Elisabeth B. Oct. the ―― 1765.
May 3.	William & Sary Lues Anne, B. April the 5th 1765. Joseph B. March the 9th 1767.
March 29.	Jacob & Ester Catts Jacob B. Oct: the 13th 1764. Rebecca & Isaac, tweens B. March the 14th 1767.

April 25.   Augustine & Mary Peterssons Else, B. April the first 1767.
            William & Isabella Hauttssons Esajah, B. March the 13th 1767.
            William and Lucretia Smiths Johnsson, B. January the 12th 1767.
M.R.
May 10.   Paul & Priscilla Cobbs Aron. B. Feb: the 16th S. John & Sary
            Cobb.
June 7.   Patrick & Marget Doffys Mary, B. Dec: the 9th 1766.
the 8.   George & Mary Catts Dorothea, B. May the 6th 1767. S. Charles
            & Doroth: Winemiller.
the 21.   Senex & Mary Senexons Anne, B. January the 28th 1767.
            Gabriel & Rebecca Dalbous Sarai B. May the 4th 1767.
            George & Sary Peterssons Mary B. June the 8th 1767.
            John & Prudens Stedhams John B. March the 26th 1767.
            Ehren & Elisabeth Beetles George B. Feb: the 9th 1761. & bapt:
            of Mr. Wrangel.
            John & Christiane Beetles Anny, B. Feb: the 12th 1761 & bapt:
            of the same.
the 22.   William & Rebecca Slydes, Mary, B. Dec: the 26th 1764 & their
            Marta, B. Feb: the 27th 1767.
M.R.
June 16.   Lawrence & Susy Peterssons Aron B. Dec: the 29th 1766.
Aug: 2.   Benjamin & Marget Howels Philotaty B. March the 16th 1767.
Salem
the 3.   Joseph & Anne Dennums Joseph B. Feb: the 23d. 1767.
            Andrew & Mary Wides Jane B. April the —— 1767.
Sept: 3.   Darias & Ruth van Neumans William B. Feb: the 20th 1764 &
            Thomas B. March the 22d. 1766.
Salem 3.   John & Cathrine Allbrights William B. March the first 1767.
the 14.   Mathias & Anne Sullivans Marta B. Nov: the 15th 1766.
Oct: 4.   Aron & Elisabeth Bietles Sary. B. Sept: the 22d 1767.
the 7.   Lawrence & Cathrine Dalbous Mary B. July the 25th 1767.
Nov: 4.   William Longlys Sary old last May 16 years. S. her present
            mother in law Mary.
the 15.   Michel & Marget Cornellissons Elisabeth B. Aug: the 21 1767.
Dec. 6.   Andrew & Christiane Standlys Marget B. May the 8th 1767.
Salem   Henry & Mary Crebbs James B. Nov: the 15th 1767. S. Arthur
the 7.   Holland & Hannah Mannen.
            John & Annie Mae Kassons Mary Marget B. Sept: the 22d 1767
            S. William M. Kasson.
            Baltsar & Mary Heils Anne B. March the 15th 1767.
the 25.   Cornel: & Rachel Boons Elisabeth tweens B. Dec: the 17th 1767.
the 26.   Louis & Cathrine Catts Samuel B. Oct: the 31. 1767 S. James
            Fricke.
            Throsy B. March the 20th 1767 P. Cesar & Phillis Negroes the
            mother a xstian [=Christian].

RACOON 1767
Jan:
the 18.   Hindrich & Sary Hindrichssons Andreas B. Dec: the 9th 1766. S.
            Andrew Hindrichssons and Sary Lock.
            Magnus & Elisabeth Dragströms William B. Dec: the 2d. 1766.
the 28.   John & Mary Wilkessons Silas B. Dec: the 22d 1766.
March 15.   Charles & Rebecca Cocks Andreas B. March the 4th 1767 S. Cath:
            Keen.
the 17.   Alexander & Cathrine Forsters William B. Dec: ye 10th 1764 &
            Rachel B. March 7th 1767.
the 23.   Marta Boys wife to John Boys B. March the 6th 1736 and their

children Mary B. Dec. the 23d 1753. Susannah. B. March the 24th. 1760. Robert B. Sept: the 8th. 1762. Nathan B. Oct: the 10th 1764. John B. Jan: the 15th 1767 P. John and Marta Boys.

April 5. Isaac & Sary van Neumans Mary, B. Dec: the 14th 1766.

the 19. James Pflannigan B. May the 1st. 1741 and his son John B. April the 9th 1767. His mothers name Sary.

May the 3. Lawrence & Sary Friends Elisabeth B. March the 28th. 1767.
Thomas & Marta Fischers Sary B. Sept: the 12th 1766.

the 12. Isaac & Susannah Schootes Isaac B. May the 7th 1767.

the 24. Thomas & Christiane Clercks Thomas B. Jan: 18th 1767 S. John Stillman.
Robert & Mary Kragheads Hannah B. April the 12th 1767.

June the 8. John & Mary Stillmans Deborah, B. April the 3d. 1767.

the 14. Nathan & Mary Boyss John B. Feb: the 7th 1766.
Remhard & Marget Taylors Rebecca B. Oct: the 27th 1765.

Aug: 9 Charles & Rachel Dalbous Elisabeth B. July the 5th 1767.

the 16. Mathew & Susannah Lords Peter B. May the 6th 1767.

Salem
the 25. Rodger & Junes Sherrins Hannah B. July 21, 1764.

Sept. 27. John & Sary Locks David B. Sept: the 15th 1767 S. Peter Lock & Sary Lock.

Oct. 1. James & Cathrine Clarcks John B. Sept. the 14th 1767.

the 11. William & Hellena Brights Elisabeth B. Aug: the 20th 1762. S. Math: & Tobita Margen.

the 12. James & Sary Dilckses Elisabeth B. June the 30th 1762.

M.R.
the 21. Philip & Cathrine Graces Andrew B. April the 10th 1766.
Jonas & Elleonora Hopmans Pamela B. Aug: the 28, 1766.
John & Janes Peterssons Benony B. Sept. the 27th 1767.

Nov. 1. Andrew & Cathrine Justices Cathrine B. Sept: the 15th 1767.

the 22. Thomas & Cathrine Adams Isaac B. Oct: the 17th 1767.
John & Rebecca Streengs John B. Oct: the 25th 1767.

the 29. Andrew & Deborah Locks Zebulon B. Oct. the 19th 1767 S. Zeb: Lock & Mary Neuman.

Dec. 13. Moses & Elisabeth Coxes David B. Aug: the 9th 1767.
Baltzar & Marta Risseners Hannah B. Oct. the 18th 1767.

PENSNECK 1768

Feb: 6 Thomas & Elisabeth Jones Mary B. December the 4th 1767 S. Ab: & Jane Jones.
Thomas & Rebecca Shopschires Anne B. Nov: the 8th 1767 S. dito grand Par:

the 14. Andrew & Rebecca Minks John B. Jan: the 8th 1768.

the 21. Malachi & Mary Kellys Cathrine B. Jan: the 3d 1768.

March 7 James Embssons 41 year of age.

the 27 Ebenaser & Deborah Embssons Ebenasser B. February the 7th 1768.
Paul & Rody Pohlssons Deborah b. January the 19th 1768.

Salem Robbert & Cathrine Cannadays Robbert b. 1768 and their Orphan child Cathrine.

the 28

April 4 John & Mary M'Krays Lydiah B. Feb: the 27th 1768.

the 5 Darias & Ruth van Neumans John B. Feb: the 9th 1768.

May 29 George & Mary Starks George B. April the 16th 1768.
John & Christiane Beetles John B. April the 7th 1768.

June 6	John King in Helsingborough 29 year old next Sept: John his son 6 years old next fault [fall], William 3 year old Aug: the 7th next, Elisabeth 4th year old orphan child.
	Joseph & Märta Dods Joseph B. July 2d. 1765 & Richard B. March 5th 1768.
the 19.	John & [J]öransons Mary B. February the 2d 1768.
Salem.	Eduard & Prudence Tunkeens John B. May the 14th 1768.
July 10	John & Elisabeth Hollidays Sarah B. April the 27th 1768.
M.R. 23.	By the Revd. Andrew Jöransson Deborah B. Jan: the 14th 1753 and Rebecca B. Jan: the 7th 1768. P. Samuel and Sarah van Neuman.
the 31.	Jonas & Christine Keens Jonas B. June the 9th 1768.
Salem	Richard & Rebecca Garrets John Garret B. March the 6th 1768.
	Friedrick & Eva Hoffmans Anne-Christine B. May the 12th 1768. S. Cathrine Klein.
Aug: 1	John & Susannah Bottenhagens Conrad-Judah B. March 22d 1768 S. Conrad & Mary Bradly.
	James & Elisabeth Fords Anne Mary B. June the 24th 1768.
the 21.	Isaac & Mary Anne Nilsons William B. July the 23rd 1768.
	John & Marget Woostards William B. July the 15th 1768.
Sept. 11	Allexander & Marget Browns Else, B. Dec. the 29th 1767.
Oct: 2.	Zacharias & Marget Jordains Michal B. Sept: the 11th 1768 S. Michel & Marget Jordain.
	George and Elisabeth Myers Marget B. August the 26 1768 S. the same.
the 25.	John and Mary Greffsys Mary B. Aug: the 18th 1768.
	Daniel & Rebeccah Dalbous Rebeccah B. Sept: the 14th 1768.
Salem the 24.	Mathew and Elisabeth Morrissons Anne B. July the 3d 1768.
Nov: 16.	James and Elisabeth Sanderssons Isabella B. Oct: the 6th 1768.
	Isaac and Marget Howells Mary. B. Nov. the 8th 1768.
Dec. 27.	Elwell and Marget Moors Elisabeth B. Jan: the 11th 1767 S. his Parents.
	Robbert & Edy Fitlens Mary B. Feb: the 5th 1764. S. Pat: & Elis: Moore.
	Joseph Bilderbacks and Sary Minks, *oackta son* [= illigitimate Son] Joseph B. July 1768.
NB the 23.	Cornelius and Rachel Boons tweens, Andrew & Elisabeth B. Dec: the 12th 1768.

RACOON 1768

Jan: 14	Leonhard & Mary Stantens Sary B. Decemb: the 13th 1767.
	Alexander & Elisabeth Coopers Anne B. Novemb: the 3d 1767.
the 23.	William & Cathrine Loves James B. Decemb: the 31 1767.
Feb: 17	George & Anne Stantons George B. Decemb: the 26 1767.
the 28	John & Cathrine Runnals Abram B. Feb: the 22d 1768.
March 5.	John & Mary Gittis Anna Maria, b. July the 3d 1761. and their Dorothea B. Decemb: the 20th 1768 S. Charles & Doroth: Winemyller, John Friedrick Kuckerow, & John Adam Schütz.
the 13.	Peter & Elisabeth Keyers Sary B. July the first 1767.
	Jacob & Mary Gosslins Hannah B. Jan: the 31. 1768.
April 3	Benjamin & Elisabeth Duffils Mary B. Jan: the 22d 1768.
	Joseph & Mary Pohlsons Jeremiah B. Decemb: the 14th 1767.
the 16.	Malachi & Elisabeth Horners Malachi B. Feb: the 17th 1768.

the 24.	Elisabeth Hewett wife to Isaac Hewett 33 year old and their follow: children Hezekiah B. Sept. the 16th 1761. Elisabeth B. Dec. the 25th 1763. Isaac B. Dec: the 22d 1765. Ester B. Oct: the 31 1757 Delilah B. Oct: the 27th 1757. Robbert B. Novemb: the 26 1767.
May 6.	Daniel & Susy Strengs Charles B. April the 14th 1768.
the 15.	Zachariah & Rachel Schaws Zachariah B. March the 20th 1768.
the 28.	Friedrick Foulks old 36 year last Octob: Patience his wife 24 year next July. Hannah their daughter B. June the 15th 1767.
	Sary James wife to Thomas James 30 year old the 10th last Decemb:
June 10	Peter & Cathrine Keens Sarah B. Feb: the 8th 1768.
	Mounce & Sarah Locks Isaac B. May the 2d 1766 & Sarah B. March 7th 1768.
the 26.	Jacob & Rebecca Kalloways Gideon B. May the 22d 1768.
	Hindrick & Magdl: Fabers Elisabeth B. April the 23d. 1768 S. Hance & Elis: Blumer.
July 3.	John & Sarah Hullings Marcus B. April the 26. 1768.
the 17.	John & Jöransons Mary B. February the 2d 1768. Powers.
the 26	John & Sarah Dennys John B. July the 7th 1768.
the 30	Hindrick & Joannah Paxtons Elisabeth B. Aug: the 3d 1765 and their Sary B. June the 4th 1768.
Aug: 15	John and Elisabeth Jones Deborah B. Feb: the 12th 1760 their Priscilla B. May the 12th 1763 their Lydiah B. Nov: the 31 1764, their Sarah B. Nov: the 27th 1766.
	Andrew and Sarah Jones Andrew B. Oct: the 15th 1763.
	William & Cathrine Linnards Hindry B. Feb: the 15th 1761. Their William B. July the 21 1764. Their Samuel B. April the 2d 1767.
the 12	Gabriel & Rebeccah Strengs Elisabeth B. July the 28th 1768.
the 28	Peter & Anne Margret Morgens Wilhelm B. June 28th 1768 S. William Saunders.
Sept: 25	Thomas & Deborah Clarcks Elisabeth B. Aug: the 13th 1768 S. the grand-Parents, both sides.
the 23.	James & Sary Pflannigans James B. Oct: the 16th 1768 S. John & Sary Helms.
Nov. 6	Joseph & Mary Richards Joseph B. Sept the 13th 1768.
Dec. 10.	Jacob and Cathrine Slys Elisabeth B. Sept: the 28th 1768. S. Jacob and Anne Leissinger.
the 25.	Magnus and Elisabeth Dragströms Gustavus B. Oct: the 19th 1768.
the 27.	Jacob and Marget Madairys, John, B. Oct: the 15th 1768. S. John Kyckerou, and Dorothea Winemyller.

Whereas, the paper appears to be, too much blouting in the place, hence I advice my worthy and kind successors to loock for the continuation of my Records, more forward, in this boock. I have proposed it several times to the Vestry to purchase or get a new one; But they have not, as yet complyed to my desire; But for [to] do them justice I declare that the mean-reason hath been, the want of cash or monney, in this country, in our days. But we live in a good hope of better times and then, hopefully, will this dessign be excuted; Meanwhile I must behelp myself with this boock, so, as I have found it, and so as it is. And leave the satisfaction, to get a better one, to my successor in the ministry, of these my dear Congregations.

Feb.
the 5.   Lawrence and Elisabeth Haltens Jesse b. Jan: the 7th 1769.
          Michel & Sary Powers Hannah b. Sept: 14th 1768. S. Mathew &
          Hannah Rose.

March   Jacob & Hannah Leissingers Elisabeth b. Feb. 1. 1769 S. Hance
the 9.   & Elisab: Blumer.
the 11.   Hinry and Mary Janes Thomas B. March the 4th 1769. S. Hannah
          Carney.
          John & Sary Browns Thomas b. Feb. the 7th 17699.
the 19.   Augustine and Mary Pettersons Beetle b. Feb: 26th 1769.
April
the 16.   Thomas and Marget Webbers Sarah B. Oct: the 6th 1768.
          Patrick and Marget Duffys Hannah b. March the 20th 1769.
          William & Christiane Stremples Christina b. Feb: 5th 1769 S.
          Susy Cable.
the 17.   David and Elisabeth Floyds William b. Feb: the 4th 1769.
          Alpheus & Brittie Burtens James b. July the 7th 1765.
May the 7. Gabriel and Rebecca Dalbous Elisabeth b. March the 12th 1769.
          Conrad & Rachel Faussers Elisabeth b. Oct. 18th 1768.

Egharbour
June the 4. Peter and Mary Frambes' Susannah b. Feb: the 9th 1769.
the 7.   John and Susannah Bailys Charles b. Oct: the 10th 1767.
          Samuel and Pheby Snells Samuel B. April the 6th 1768.
          David and Hellenah Richmons Sary b. Jan: the 5th 1769.
M.R. the 9. Thomas and Elis: Jones Stephen b. May the 12th 1769. S. Esqr.
          Jones & his wife.
          Nathan and Mary Schaws James b. Jan: the 12th 1769. S. dito
          Grand P.
          Philip and Cathrine Graus Priscilla b. Dec: the 23d 1768.
the 11.   Lawrence and Susannah Petterssons Hannah b. Dec: the 20th
          1768.

N.B. May
the 21 in
the Neck. Hance and Barborah Jaquets Joseph b. April the 9th 1769.
July the 2. John & Anne M'Carsons Hezekiel B. May the 12th 1769.
          Michal & Cathrine Powers Christine b. Oct: the 28th 1768.
          Jacob & Susannah Haltons Andrew b. Nov: the 3d 1766.
          Alexander & Margreth Browns Alexander b. May the 5th 1769.
          Charles & Margreth Greens George b. Feb: the 5th 1768.
the 3.   Hance & Margeth Lambssons Hance b. March the 26th 1769.
          William & Jane Aschlys Mary b. August the 22d. 1768.
the 13.   Andrew & Elisabeth Van Neumans Susannah b. March 28th. 1769.
the 16.   Thomas & Elisabeth Barens Mary b. Decemb: the 10th 1768.
the 23.   Thomas & Mary Richardsons Sarah b. April the 23d 1769.
Aug. the 13. Senex & Mary Senicksons William b. May the 30th 1769.
Sept. the 3. John & Cathrine Parkers John b. August the 26th 1769.
Sept. the 3. Joseph & Mary Jaquets John B. June the 13th 1769.
          John & Ruth Starcks Mary B. July the 22d 1769.
the 24.   Schedrich & Mary Sunderlens Rebecca B. Sept. the 15th 1768.
          John & Cath: Allbrechts Friedrich B. July 8th 1769 S. Will: &
          Marg N. Casson.

Salem
Oct: the 4. Joseph & Anne Dennums William Confirmed, B. April the 3d. 1769.
          Gau Kollins Antony. B. Sept. the 13th 1769. His fath: name con-
          cealed.

the 16.   Samuel & Sarah Pedrichs Mary. B. May the 1. 1765 & Elisabeth
                 B. July 14th 1769.
Nov. 5.   William and Elisabeth Tuffs Mary B. Sept: the 24th 1769.
                 William & Anne Bilderbacks Daniel B. June the 7th 1769.
                 William and Isabella Houtsons Elisabeth B. Novemb: the 1 1769.
the 26.   Jacob & Anne Pipparts Jacob B. Novemb: the 15th 1768.

RACOON 1769

January
the 1.   Erick and Hannah Cocks William B. nov. the ——— 1768.
the 11.   Carl and Rebecca Cock's Abram b. January the 2d. 1769.
                 Peter and Reginah Locks John b. December the 29th 1768.
the 14.   William and Sary Nobles Archabel B. Dec: the 19th 1768 s. Dennis
                 W. Whire.
the 19.   Jacob & Marget Johnsons Jacob b. Sept: the first 1768.
March
the 12.   Jacob and Mary Archers Sary B. March the 2d 1769.
                 Cathrine a Negroe-child the mother bapt: S. John & Cathrine Strat-
                 ton collector.
the 24.   Mathew & Susannah Lords Samuel b. Jan: the 23d 1769.
the 26.   Daniel & Sary Suderlands Magdlene b. Feb: the 26th 1769. S. the
                 Grand Par.
April
the 11.   Robbert & Mary Kraigheads William b. March the 17th 1769.
the 30.   Isaac and Sary V. Neumans Johannah. B. April the first 1769. S.
                 Johns Adams and Hannah Steelman.
May
the 15.   Timothee and Margery Clarks Nanzy b. March the 9th 1769.
                 Thomas and Christian Clarks Lyddy b. March the 26th 1769.
                 William and Mary Englands James b. April the 5th 1769.
the 28.   Cornelius and Marta Bryants William b. May the 5th 1769.
June
the 13.   Eseyah and Susy Fowlers Aron b. Nov: last 1768 died the same day.
the 25.   William & Cathrine Sauders Charles B. April the 28th 1769.
July
the 9.   John & Anne Mary Millers Cathrine Dorothea b. Oct. 12th 1768
                 S. Carl & Dor. Wineryller.
the 30.   Jacob & Sophia Fishlers Benjamin b. Jan: the 11th 1769.
August
the 13   Moses & Mary Jones Sarah b. May the 30th 1769.
                 James & Cathrine Clarks Carney b. May the 2d. 1769.
the 20.   Zebulon & Drusilla Locks Prisehillah b. July 2d. 1769 S. Mary v.
                 Neuman.
                 Hindrick & Sary Hindricksons Isaac b. July the 19th 1769 S. Prise-
                 hila Denny.
                 John & Margreth Löckners John b. May 18th 1769 S. Francis &
                 Barb: Holtz.
Oct:
the 5.   Lawrence & Sary Friends John b. Aug: the 29th 1769.
the 6.   Gabriel & Rebecca Streengs Elisa. b. Sept. the 5th 1769.
the 3.   John & Mary Derichsons Nathan b. Sept: the 17th 1769.
                 Andrew & Rebeccak Mincks Hannah b. July the 27th 1769.
the 22.   Jonas & Mary Hindrichsons Jonas b. Aug: the 22d. 1769.
the 29.   Baltzar & Marta Riseners Elisabeth b. Oct: the 2d. 1769.
                 Jeremia & Bitta Allens Zedony b. Aug. the 3d 1769.
                 Friedrick & Elis: Bullingers Peter b. Dec: the 26th 1769.
Nov.
the 8.   Friedrick & Patience Foulks Christiana b. Feb: the 5th 1769.

[292]

the 22. Dec.	Carl & Britta Steelmans Jonas b. Sept. the 23d 1769.
the 18.	Thomas and Deborah Clarcks John b. Nov: the 6th 1769.
the 17.	John M. Kallums & Mary Boys Mary B. Oct: the 7th 1769 Bapt.
the 18.	Thomas and Deborah Clarcks John B. Novemb. the 6th 1769.
the 31.	George & Sarah Peterssons Aron B. Dec: the 27th 1769.

PENSNECK 1770

Feb: 4	Andrew and Cathrine Helms Mary B. Jan. the 11th 1770.
	John and Mary Savoys Elisabeth B. Jan. the 26th 1770.
the 5	Henry and Charity Savills Samuel B. July the 24th 1769.
	Jacob and Anne Steinheusers Jacob B. Sept. 27th 1767. & Samuel B. Feb. 1, 1769.
	Alpheus & Britta Burtens Rebecca B. Nov: 2d. 1769.
the 25	Darias and Ruth V. Neumans Dishee B. Dec: 28th 1769.
	John and Sarah Browns Hannah B. Feb: 28th 1761. Susannah B. Dec: 29th 1763. And William B. Nov. 16th 1766.
the 26	Jonas and Anne Jones' Sarah B. January the 1. 1768.
the 28	James and Rachel Cahallens Mary B. Sept: the 17th 1769.
March 18	Jonathan & Ebaya Beeslys Morris B. Dec: the 6th 1769.
April 8	Aron and Elisabeth Beetles John B. February the 22d. 1770.
	Paul and Rody Paulssons Anne B. Feb: the 18th 1770.
May 13	George and Mary Starks Mary B. Dec: the 10th 1769.
	Joseph and Mary Paulssons Thomas B. March the 17th 1770.
June 4	Eudard and Prudence Tunkens Elisabeth B. April the 5th 1770.
	William and Jane Ashlys Sarah B. March the 2d. 1770.
the 24	Ebenesser and Margeth Embsons Charles B. May the 9th 1770.
the 26	Israel and Gertru Dalbous Abel B. May the 9th 1770.
	Patrich and Margeth Duffys Neomy B. July the 28th 1770.
	Andrew and Patience Hoffmans Patience B. June the 14th 1769.
the 31.	Michel and Mary Crouhans Benjamin B. April the 15th 1769.
Oct. 28	John and Jane Youranssons Andrew B. Aug: the 17th 1770.
	Mallacky and Mary Christ: Kellys John B. Sept: the 19th 1770.
Oct: 28	Adam and Mary Coles Cathrine B. Nov: the 15th 1769. S. Casp: ——N.B. Here is filled up from the Racoon list.
Sept. 30	Friedrich & Elis: Bollingers Susannah B. July 28th 1770. S. Jacob & Elis: Bollinger.
Oct: 7	Andrew and Mary Jones' Andrew B. Sept: the 4th 1770.
	Peter and Elisabeth Keyers Joseph B. Aug: the 23d. 1770.
	George and Anne Stantens Hannah. B. Aug: the 2d 1770.
the 9th.	John & Elis: Fouraires Sarah B. Sept: the 10th 1767 & Elisabeth B. Aug. the 19th 1770.

RACOON 1770

Jan. 7.	Andrew and Deborah Locks Deborah B. Nov. 29th 1769. S. Andrew Keealen and Lyddy Lock.
the 27.	John & Cathrine Sweetens Rebecca B. Oct: the 31 1767 and her brother John B. Maye the 9th 1769.
Feb. 2.	William and Cathrine Nilssons Priscilla B. Jan: the 31 1770.
the 11.	George & Jane Oaklys George B. July the 26th 1767.
the 18.	Noah & Agnes Hoffmans John B. Dec. 3d. 1769 & their Robber: an adopted child and its parents concealed but B. Oct. 1767.
the 22.	Joseph Chesters & Hannah Lords Maria B. Dec. 3d 1766 A. B.
March 30.	John and Sarah Goldsmidts William B. Dec. the 14th 1769.
April 8.	Leonhard & Mary Stantens Elisabeth B. Feb: the 11th 1770.
	John and Charity Greens John B. Dec: the 6th 1769.

the 15.   Richard & Sarah Wests Edmond B. Sept: the 9th 1766.
           James Bryant a young man old 21 year next 15th may.
May 6.   Jacob & Regina Jones Caleb B. March the 28th 1770.
the 9.   Robbert & Sarah Clarcks Jane B. April the 15th 1770.
the 20.   Jonas and Susannah Madeiras Johannes B. Sept: the 19th 1769 S.
           Jacob and Margeth Madeira.
June 26.   Benjamin and Deborah Angelous Jehu B. May the 18th 1770.
July 1.   Christopher and Barborah Arnolds Johan Michael B. May 19th
           1770. S. Johan Michael Engeltown & Elisabeth Scheuer.
the 22.   Johan Joseph & Anne Mary Millers Elisabeth B. Feb: the 25th
           1770. S. John Mickel Engeltown & Dorothea Winemyller.
Aug. 9.   Gabriel & Mary Dalbous Hannah B. Dec. 31. 1767. and their Wil-
           liam N. Nov: 28th 1769. S. Silas Fowler & Cathrine Adams.
the 19.   Jacob & Rebecca Callohans Susannah B. June the 1st. 1770.
           Isaac & Elisabeth Hewets Edmond. B. June the 8th 1770.
M.R.
Sept: 4   John & Jane Peterssons Jane B. April the 3d 1770.
the 6.   Job & Prischilla Glassbys Aron B. Nov: the 10th 1768.
the 23.   John and Mary Pintens Andrew B. Sept: the 17th 1770.
the 26.   John & Mary Cunninghams John B. March the 22d 1769.
Oct. 13   Peter and Mary Strickers John B. June the 30th 1766 and their
           Mary B. Feb: 25th 1768. S. John & Cath. Euler and Margeth
           Kalm.
Nov: 10   Conrad and Susannah Schoemakers George B. Sept: the 18th 1770.
the 11   Magnus and Elisabeth Dragströms Hellenah B. Oct. the 12th 1770.
the 23   Benjamin & Elisabeth Duffils Joseph B. May the 3d. 1770.
the 26   Isaac & Elisabeth V. Neumans Rebecca B. Oct: the 24th 1770.
Dec: 9   William and Elisabeth Sweeteens Elisabeth B. June the 24th 1770.
the 11.   Francis and Elisabeth Chattens Mary B. Sept: the 18th 1761. Their
           Rebecca B. Sept: the 26th 1763. George B. July the 26th 1765.
           Jane B. Nov. the 23d. 1768 and Clarck B. July 10th 1770. S.
           George & M: Clarck.
the 16   Isaac and Silly Justissons Mary B. Nov: the 22d 1770.
the 26.   John and Sarah Locks Garret B. Dec: the 1 1770.
the 30.   Charles and Rachel Dalbous Charles B. Oct: the 31 1770.
the 31.   Thomas and Hellena Taylors Andrew B. Nov: the 21. 1770.

PENSNECK 1771 [145]

Sept: 29   Isaac & Anne Nilssons Isaac B. Aug. the 11th 1771.

M.R.   Jonas & Hellenah Hoffmans Aram & Talitha tweens B. May the
Oct. 16.   first 1771.
           Abram & Grace Marslanders Joab. B. Oct. the 29th 1767 and their
           Marta B. December the 11th 1769.
the 21   Thomas Bright 40 year of age his Son Jesse B. June the 13th 1765.
           his Charles B. April the 26th 1768. His Ruth B. Feb. the 19th
           1771 with his pres: wife Isabella.

NB. the 14 Joseph Connover about 30 year of age at great Eggharbour.
Nov. 3.   John & Elizabeth Corrys Margeth B. Sept. the 17th 1771.
Dec. 1.   Hance & Margeth Lambssons Mecum B. January the first 1771.
the 2   Andrew & Margeth Senicksons Rebeccah B. Oct. the 27th 1770.
           John & Hannah Dillmores Thomas B. March the 26th 1769.
           John & Anne M'Carssons Marta B. April the 24th 1771.

---
[145] Incomplete in the original.

the 15	John & Lorena Crebs Whitton B. May the 26th 1771.
	Albert & Sarah Bilderback's Francis B. April the 7th 1771.
the 24	Cornelius & Rachel Boons Magdlene B. Dec. the 19th 1771.

RACOON 1771

January the 20th	Josias N. June the 1st. 1767. The mother Hanna Plomblin the father concealed.
Feb: 13	Andrew & Judith Hindrickssons Isaac B. Jan: the 16th 1771.
the 20	Jacob & Margreth Madeiras Adam B. January the 10th 1771. S. Adam & Elis: Schytz.
March the 28	George & Hannah Horners Friedrich and Abigail tweens B. Jan. the 23d 1771. P. Surities Friedrich and Abigail Weaver.
April the 14:	Samuel & Lovisa Laidens Abigail B. Jan: the 10th 1771. S. Fredrich & Abigail Wiver.
the 31	Thomas & Cathrine Parkers Jacob B. Feb the 4th 1771. S. Jacob & Cath: Sly & Ursilla Catt.
M. River. the 7th	Samuel and Ambrosia Cobbs Erick B. March the 3d 1770.
the 10	Thomas and Elisabeth Jones' Lydia B. March the 11th 1771.
	Thomas and Rebeca Shopshires Lovisa B. December the 14th 1770.
	Nathan and Mary Schaws Henry B. March the 8th 1771.
the 28.	Mathew and Susannah Lords Annanias B. April the 15th 1771.
May the 14	Cleft and Susannah Ronils John B. May the 7th 1771.
	Eduard and Dina Hamptons William B. October the 20th 1770.
the 4.	John and Sara Goldsmiths Charles B. May the 1st. 1771.
the 14	Jonas & Christina Keens Isaac B. Dec. the 28th 1770.
	Jonas and Anna Jones William B. March the 11th 1771.
	Thomas and Mary Webbers Mary B. October the 30th 1770.
the 12.	James and Sara Pflannigans Elisabeth B. April the 31 1771.
	John and Maria Savoys Rachel B. April the 6th 1771.
the 27	John and Susannah Richards Jacob B. May the 10th 1770.
the 29	John & Mary Stillmans Edmond B. Oct. 31 1770.
	Charles and Rebecca Cocks Isaac B. May the 18th 1771.
the 31.	Marten and Hannah Dylanys Isaac B. Sept: the 5th 1767 their Daniel B.: June the 3rd 1769. Their Elizabeth B. Oct: the 3d 1770 S. [Surities] Dr. Bodo & Marg: Otto.
June 8	John and Elisabeth Keepers John B. Sept: the 18th 1766. Their Rachel B. March the 29th 1769. Their Rody B. Sept: 27th 1770 S. [Surities] Dr. Bodo & Marg: Otto.
NB.	Conrade and Cathrine Nails Joseph B. August the 26th 1770.
March 14	Was Mary Welch baptized by me on her sickbed near 50 year old.
the 16	Jacob and Mary Gosslins Mary B. Jan: the 8th 1770.
the 30	Cornelius and Marta Briants Sarah B. Dec: the 7th 1770.
	Thomas and Elisabeth Barns Blair B. Feb: the 25th 1771.
July 7	James & Sara Dilcks Sara & Anne tweens B. Sept. the 17th 1770.
	John & Emy Duffields James B. May the 14th 1767 their Sara B. Sept. the 18th 1769. Their John B. May the 24th 1771.
Nb.	The continuation of this & the following year see a litle before the accounts here next forgoing.
July 7	Jeremia & Jane Carters Emy B. march the 16th 1757. their son Samuel Aug: the 12th 1760. Their John B. Sept: the 27th 1769. Their Sarah. B. February the 4th 1771.
	John & Elisabeth Jones John B. Oct. the 8th 1770.
the 21	William and Mary Englands Mary B. June the 13th 1771.
the 25	Mary Roulens Edward b. April the 22d. 1771. attrib. fath: Dr. Lithgow.

the 28	John and Cathrine Culens, Jacob. B. April 28th 1771. s. Jacob Calan & Eliz. Pile.
the 29	David & Elisabeth Pfloids David B. March the 15th 1771.
Aug: 10 M.R.	James & Cathrine Scotts Sarah B. Oct. the 25th 1770.
the 18	Laurence & Susannah Peterssons Elizabeth B. April the 4th 1771.
Sept. 1	Jacob & Anne Leissingers Peter B. Feb: the 4th 1771. S. Pet: Green & Mary Catt.
the 10.	Isaac & Sarah V. Neumans Hellena B. August the 23d. 1771.
Dec. 13.	George & Magdlene Sommerwills James B. Nov: the 13th 1771.
Dec. 13.	George & Magdlene Sommerwills James B. Nov: the 13th 1771.
the 24	Abram & Christine Keens Cathrine B. Dec: the 3d. 1771.
the 29.	Adam & Elizabeth Schytzes Cathrine B. Decemb: the 7th 1771.

William and Mary Englands Children you find here recorded, all in one place for better conveniency sake.—Viz:
Thomas, born April the 17th, 1753.
William, born December the 8th, 1757.
Daniel, born January the 27th, 1760.
Elias, born March the 11th, 1762.
Sarah, born February the 3d, 1764.
James, born April the 5th, 1769.
Mary, born June the 13th, 1771.

PENSNECK 1772

Feb.9	Alexander & Margeth Browns Rebecca B. May the 18th 1771.
the 23	Aron & Elisabeth Beetles Aron B. Feb. the 11th 1772.
March 8	Andrew and Cathrine Helms' John B. feb. the 24th 1772.
April 17	Alexander & Elisabeth Coopers George b. July the 19th 1770.
dito	Joseph and Mary Pohlssons Hannah B. Feb. the 16th 1772.
	Conrade & Rachel Fautzers William B. August the 24th 1771.
the 16	John Crebs a married man brought up a friend B. Nov. 24th 1747.
May 17	William and Hannah Rights Rebeccah B. April the 3d 1772.
June 7	Darias & Ruth V: Neumans Priscilla B. March the 28th 1772.
the 10	John & Susannah Lee's Mary B. December the 10th 1771.
the 28	Swen & Mary Senicksons Elisabeth B. February the 12th 1772.
	John & Jane Bootens George B. September the 11th 1771.
	William & Jane Gill Johnssons Andrew B. October the 28th 1771.
July 12	Jacob & Susannah Halliards Mary B. March the 10th 1771.
Aug. 2	Richard Merrides and Rachel Burcks illeg: Child Richard B. June the 7th 1772.
Oct. 12	Curtis & Elisabeth Tranchards Elisabeth b. May the 6th 1772.
	William & Jane Ashly's William B. July the 2d. 1772.
Dec. 25	Niclas & Cathrine Keens James b. Nov: the 12th 1771.
the 28	Andrew & Margreth Standly's Henry B. September the 27th 1772.
	Thomas & Cathrine Pattersons Mary B. Aug. the 17th 1764.
the 18	Augustine & Mary Peterssons Abram b. November the 18th 1772.

RACOON 1772

Jan: 1	Nathanael & Margeth Sanders John B. Nov. the 3d 1771.
the 12	Thomas & Deborah Clark's Mary, B. Nov. the 28th 1771.
Feb. the 2	Adam & Eliz: Schylz Anne Mary B. Oct. 21. 1771. S. Conrade & Susy Schoemaker.
the 2	Henry & Sary Hindricksons Peter B. Dec. the 5th 1771 S. And: Mattson.
March 3	John Fredrich & Elis: Bollingers Friedrick b. Feb. the 26th 1772.
the 4	Peter & Mary Keyers Benjamin B. Feb. the 29th 1772.

| the 5 | Peter & Regina Locks Lydia B. Feb. the 12th 1772. |
| the 29 | John & Mary McDarmuts Isac. B. feb. the 17th 1772. |

April

the 12   Elisabeth Johnsson about 24th years old, and her Son James B. Feb. the 20th 1772. Her husband and the fathers name George Johnsson.

the 28   Lawrence & Sarah Friends Sarah B. March the 15th 1772.

May 10   Jonas & Mary Hindrichsons Gabriel B. Feb. the 10th 1772.

Dito his daughters Elisabeth ill: child Cathrine B. in March dito year.

the 17   Daniel & Sary Sutherlands Sary B. April the 17th 1772.

the 10   Baltzar and Marta Riseners Lydia B. March the 27th 1772.

June 1   Thomas & Christiane Clercks Jeffry B. Nov. the 27th 1771. NB this is Clemell Clerk.

the 6   Samuel & Lovisa Laiddens Mary B. February the 3d. 1772.

the 19   John & Elisabeth Rambos Jacob B. December the 31st. 1771.

the 21   Andrew & Mary Mattssons Aron B. May the 13th 1772.

Alexander & Cathrine Forsters Deborah B. February the 27th 1769.

July 8   Abram & Cathrine Lords Zephayah B. June the 30th 1771.

July 12   James & Cathrine Clarck's Peter B. February the 23d 1772.

Aug. 9   John & Susy Madeirah's Margreth B. April 4th 1772 s. Jac: & Marg: Madeira.

the 11   Joseph & Merry Westerns Elisabeth B. July the 26th 1772.

the 16   Elisabeth Pintons, Jacob, illeg: B. May the 28th 1772.

Jeremiah & Britta Allens John B. June the 23d 1771.

James & Cathrine Scott's Rebecca B. July the 9th 1772.

Sept. 11   John & Cathrine Reynolds Elias B. January the 4th 1771.

Octob. 13   Isaac & Sarah V. Neumans Sarah. B. August the 26 1772.

the 18   Joseph & Elisabeth Rise's Jacob B. September the 25th 1772.

the 26   Conrade & Mary Kertzly's Barborah B. May the 24th 1767 their Son John b. March 8th 1772. S. John & Mary Kyckerau.

Nov. 23   Benjamin Jnr. & Margreth Richards Cathrine B. September the 24th 1771.

Dec. 6   Andrew & Lyddy Hindricksson's Peter B. November the 27th 1772.

the 26   John & Mary Codd's Mary B. Sept: the 10th 1759. Their Hellenah B. February the 7th 1762. Their John B. Aug: the 4th 1767. James B. Sept. the 20th 1769.

PENSNECK 1773.

Jan. 31	Erick & Anne Peterssons Henry, N. Jan: the 22d. 1773.
Feb. 10	William & Mary Johnston's Mary b. Oct. the 22d. 1772.
the 21.	Jacob & Else Savoy's Sam. B. Feb. the 4th 1773.
March 14	Hance & Margreth Lambsson's Lawrence B. Jan. the 14th 1773.

Salem 15   Edward & Prudence Tunkens Samuel B. October the 24th 1772.

the 28   Conrade & Cathrine Neal's Philippina B. Aug. the 25th 1772 S. Philippina Wagener.

Benjamin & Susy Pedricks Thalitha B. Feb. the 18th 1773. S. Bricks Barton.

April 25   John and Sarah Catt's Sarah B. June the 25th 1772.

Thomas and Cathrine Parkers William B. Feb. the 7th. 1773 S. Jacob and Cathrine Sly, & Ursilla and Mary Catt.

May 4   Casper & Regina Sacks, Jacob B. March the 31 1773.

the 23   Mallacky and Mary Kelly's Sarah B. January the 23d. 1773.

June 20   Richard and Christine Merides Alles, B. January the 23d. 1773.

July 11   Andrew and Margreth Senicksons Henry B. April the 14th 1773.

Aug. 1	Alexander & Elisabeth Coopers Alexander B. April the first 1773.
	Thomas & Mary Richardssons Elisabeth B. July the 5th 1772.
the 22	Jacob & Susannah Howells John B. April the 15th 1773.
Oct. 10	Albertus & Sarah Bilderback, Isaac B. March the 14th 1773.
	John and Renah Crabs's Sarah B. March the 26th 1773.
the 11	William & Jane Gill-Janssons Sarah B. June the 19th 1773 S.
	Christiane and Anl Zepherus Handly.
	John and Susannah Howels John B. April the 15th 1773.
the 18	William and Isabella Hutssons William B. Septbr. the 24th 1773.

Here lay thee down thy pen: here thy course takes an end
You've written long enough, let another turn the pages.[146]

RACOON 1773.

Jan. 10	Abram and Cathrine Lords Abram B. Dec. the 4th 1772.
	John & Rebecca Streengs Mary B. Dec. the 17th 1772.
	Isaac & Silly Jiestissons Sary B: November the 28th 1772.
Feb. 14	James & Cathrine Steelmans Elisabeth B. February the 5th 1773
	S. William & Britta Homan & Hellena Lock.
the 17	Charles & Rebecca Cock's Rebeccah B. January the 29th 1773.
the 20	Bodo & Cathrine Otto's Jnrs. D. M. Cathrina Margeta B. Jan.
	the 20th 1773. S. Bodo Otto Jnr. Margretha Schweighauser,
	& Christ: Lockner.
the 26	William & Rebecca Forekers Joseph B. March the 26th 1769, and
	their William B. January the 9th 1773.
the 27	Jacob & Cathrine Hewes Cathrine B. Feb: the 25th 1771 and their
	Hannah B. October the first 1772.
	Gabriel & Mary Dalbous Gabriel B. May the first 1772. S. Jonas
	Dalbous.
April 11	John & Mary Pintons Cathrine B. March the 12th 1773.
the 13	Elizabeth Vanleer wife of George Vanleer Esqr. old 35 years the
	15th day of Jan: Last, and all these following their children
	were baptised the same time viz—Mary Vanleer B. July the
	20th 1757. Hannah B. January the 27th 1759. Beauty B. July
	the 16th 1760. William B. June the 25th 1762. Elizabeth B.
	February the 21st. 1765. Rebecah B. January the 16th 1768.
	Zebeah B. January the 21st. 1770 and their George B. June
	the 17th 1772.
the 27	George & Anne Stantens Friedrick B. January the 10th 1773.
May 2	James and Sarah Gardiners Peter B. April the 4th 1772.
	Jacob and Anne Mary Madeira's Anna Margretha B. March the
	26th 1773. S. Anna Margretha Calm.
May 5	Charles & Rachel Dalbous John B. April the first 1773 S. Eliz V.
	N.Man.
the 20	Phoeby Beetle about 15 years of age ——
June 6	Friedrick & Elisabeth Bullingers Eva Christine B. March the
	28th 1773. S. Living and Christina Gull.
	Christopher & Barbara Arnholds Elisabeth B. Oct. the 10th 1772.
Aug. 9	Thomas & Isabelle Rights, Wade B. June the 13th 1773.
October 12	Thomas and Deborah Clarcks Denny B. Septbr. the 30th 1773.
the 10	Robbert and Rachel Browns Märta B. Septbr. 29th 1773.
the 13	Peter and Elisabeth Keyers Jacob B. Septbr. the 11th 1773.
the 17	William & Elizabeth Sweetens Gideon B. May the 21st. 1773.
the 21	John and Elizabeth Foräkers Edy B. Feb. the 15th 1773.

---

[146] Written in Swedish by Wicksell at the end of his time as pastor. His successor, Nicholas Collin, used English almost exclusively.

PENS NECK 1774

Patric and Margarethe Dauffis their daughter born the 22d Decem: 1773, baptized the 18 Jan:

Febr: 20th Peter born 18 Jan. 1774. Parents Peter and Sarah Angelo.

Mary 9th June 1762. The same Father and his first wife.

13 Elizabeth born 18th Jan. this year. Parents Aaron and Elizabeth Biddel.

April 4 Henry born 17 Oct: 1773 Parents, Henry and Elizabeth Floyd.

John born 1 Apr: Parents Garret and Barbara Van Neaman.

John born 7th February 1774 parents

Dito 11th Deborah born 7th March. Parents Eben Israel and Debora Emson.

Willjam born 15th Apr: 1774. Parents Nicholas and —— Keen.

Sarah born the 4th of Oct: Parents Obadiah and Susanna Allen.

Nancy born 17 Jan. 1765 Parents Nicholas Daniel and Nancy Nelson.

Helena born 15 Dec: Parents Cornelius and Rachel Boon.

Andrew 9th November Parents Andrew and Cathrine Hellms.

Jacob 14th Dec: Parents Jacob Susanna Taylor.

Edward, son of Curtis and Elizab-Trenchard in Salem B. 11 March 1774.

RACOON 1774

Maj [May] 6th Susanna born 19 March 1774. Parents Joshua and Elizabeth Lord.

7th June Willjam born 16th Jan: Hanna and Willjam Forsman.

Cathrine born 8th of May Parents Sarah Tomas Clark.

John 29 December 1773 James and Sara Gardiner.

John Swecks old Jacob and Rebecca Matson.

Linnard Stantons daughter Hanna born 4 Apr: 1774 baptised in Maj.

The 19th June the following baptised.

Richard born 3d December last year. Parents Mary and Joseph Paultson.

Elizabeth born 17 March 1772 Parents Eliah and Marget Barney.

dito Willjam 8th Dec: 1772. Same Parents.

Cathrine born 28 Febr: 1774 Parents Conrad and Cathrine Cole.

John 14 May 1772 Parents Adam and Mary Cole.

Elisha born 11 May 1774 Parents Thomas and Mary Righley.

Elizabeth born 23 Nov: 1774 Parents John and Helena Halton.

John born 15 June Parents Andrew and Mary Jones.

Thomas born the 20th of August Parents Noah and Agnes Hopman.

Parc Garsham and Margrete, Alexander 30 Aug: 1774.

Sarah Laurence and Sarah Friend; Rachel born the 10th of Oct:

Elizabeth born 27 Nov. 1774. Parents Andrew and Judy Henricson.

Rudy the 16th Octobr: Parents Josha and Lissy Rambo.

Isac 22d Dec: Joseph and Elizabeth Rice.

PENS NECK 1775 [147]

Brathwait born the 28th of Julii 1763. Parents Brathwait and Dorothy Tuft.

Mary born the 16th of August 1765. Parents Brathwait and Mary Tuft.

Sarah born the 26th December 1774. Parents Brathwait and Christian Tuft.

Deriah 5th Febr: of the present year. Parents Doris and Ruthy Van Neaman.

Mary 10th Jan: of this year Parents Thomas and Cathrine Parker.

Joseph 15 Dec: 1774 Parents John and Mary McCreed.

RACOON 1775

John the 10th of Jan: Palser and Margreta Reisner.

Sarah born the 7th of January Anno 1775 Parents Charles and Rebecca Cox.

Jacob 26 Sept: 1773 Parents Edward Hamton and Diana H.

---

[147] Incomplete in the original.

Mathew 14th of Sept: 1774 Mathew and Susanna Lord.
Sarah Parents Gabriel and Mary Dahlbo born Dec: 1774.
February
Jane born the 23d of December, baptised the second. Daniel and Sarah Southerland.
April 12th
Johannes 27th September. Michel Power and Sarah.
Jacob and Margret Madeira—Samuel 24th of February.
Richard son of Joseph and Mary Richards born the 21st Dec: 1774.
Sarah born 5th of Apr this year, baptised 11th of June. Parents Jacob and Regina Jones.
Cathrine born April 20th 1775. baptised 18th June.
Sarah born the 15 Apr: this year. Parents John and Sarah Goldsmith.
Cathrine born 25th of Febr: Christened 29th of Julii this year. Parents Conrad and Susanna Shoemaker.
Isac born the 15th of August baptised the 22d of Sept:. Parents Isac and Sarah Van Neaman.
Joseph born 27th of Julii baptised 8th Octobr: Willjam Sweeten and Elisabeth.
Baptised the 27th of October Benjamin born 25th Sept: present year. Parents Jacob and Mary Archer.
Edward born 22d April this year. Parents Edward and Rachel Green.
John born last December 1771. Mary 8th of September this year. Parents of these Robert and Mary Craighead.
William born 30th of August, Parents John and Sarah Booth.
Anne born 3d of August. Parents Isac and Gertrude Dericson.
These baptised the 12th of November.
Elisabeth born 13th of Octr: baptised 26th of Nov: Parents Cliffon and Susanna Roel.
Jane Daughter of James and Mary Brown born the eigth, baptised the 18th of December.
Gideon son of Isac and Cecilia Jestis born 25th November Christened 25th December.

RACOON 1776

Jan: 7th.	Sarah daughter of George and Sarah Petersson born 1st of Jan:
27th.	Elisabeth daughter of Malachiah and Elisabeth Horner. Born 25th of June last year.
Feb: 18th.	Isac born 22d Jan: last Parents Garrit and Barbara van Neaman.
19th.	Samuel born 4th of Sept: 1775 Parents Thomas and Debora Clark.
March	John born 9th of Febr: Parents Charles and Britta Stillman.
last.	John born 28th of November 1775 Parents Andrew and Elisabeth Matson.
Apr: 3d.	John born 2d of November Parents David and Margrete Fox.
Ditto 6th.	John born Febr: 9th Benjamin and Deborah Angelo.
	Jacob 3d of March Jacob and Rebecca Calloway.
May.	William 10th of Apr: John and Brigitta Hennigen.
10th	Mary 5th of Oct: 1775 Peter & Sara Coughlin.
17th	John born 16th of Apr: instant, Parents David and Mary Derricson.
June 2d.	Noah born 9th of March instant Parents William and Sarah Clark.
8th.	Elisabeth born 11th of Febr: instant William and Hanna Fursman.
16th.	Anne 18th of Jan: inst: Par: Thomas and Elisabeth Barns.
	John 9th of Jan: inst: Charles and Mary Bensley.
June 23d.	Mary born 11th of May Inst: P: Thomas and Mary Riley.
10th Julii	Jemymy born 31st of May Inst: Parents James and Cathrine Steelman.

18th	Sarah daughter of Israel Lock and Betsy Cook born in Febr: 1775. Suretys John and Elisabeth Cloyn.
22d.	Cathrine born 30th December last year. Parents James and Cathrine Clark.
4th	Mary born August the 5th of Julii inst: Parents Jacob and Stina Jestison. [Justis].
11th	Sven born 25th of June inst: Parents Zebulon and Drusilla Lock.
13th	Elizabeth born 27th of Julii 1774 John and Cathrine Alexander Parents.
ditto	Ga[r]sham son of Garsham and Margret Alexander.
August.	William born 1st Januari 1772 Parents Patric and Cathrine Boon, Mary daughter of the same born 12th ditto.
	Barbary born 23d Apr: inst: Parents Aaron and Elisabeth Beetle.
Sept:	Martha born 24th of April 1774 Walentine and Sarah Runnels. Hannah ditto 11th of June inst:
	Rebecca born 25th of August inst: Par: Andrew and Judith Henricson.
Octobr 6	William Parents Cornelius and Rachel Boon born this day.
19	Sarah born 21st of Sept: inst: Parents Moses and Rebecca Hopman.
1st.	Mary born 6th of Nov: 1775 Parents Amariah and Lydia Dahlbo.
November	Mary born 15th of Nov: inst: Parents James and Priscilla Roberts.
	Martha 1st of January inst: P: Hewett and Mary Forbes.
Decembr:	John br: 17th of April inst: Mother Elisabeth Sirren.

1777

Elisabeth born 5th of November 1776 Parents Peter and Elisabeth Kayer.
Charles Parents Charles and Alice Halton born 19th of June last. 1776.
Edward b: 20th of March last year. Pars: Elihu and Margrete Barnet.
Eleanore b: 6th of Jan: inst: Parents Morris and Magdalene Welch.
Mary b: 5th of August last, Parents Jacob and Anne Stiner.
Josep b: 21st of June last, Parents Joseph and Mary Poulsson.
Susannah b: 11th of August last P: Mathew and Susanna Lord. Bapt: 8th of March.
Deborah b: 25th of Febr: inst: Pars: Daniel and Sarah Southerland.
Samuel b: 16 Apr: inst: Parents Laurence and Sarah Friend.
Silas b: in May 1776 Parents Joseph and Mary Richards.
Wiljam B: 22d of May inst: P: Jacob and Margaretha Madeira.
John b: 10th of Apr: inst: P: Joshua and Jail Halton.
Lewis b: latter part of June inst: Lewis and Margrete Fisler Parents.
Cathrina Elisabeth b: 28th of May Parents Joshua and Cathrine Lord.
Alexander b: 3d of June inst: Pars: Abraham and Christine Keen.
Samuel b: 14th of August inst: parents Conrad and Susanna Shoemaker.
Elisabeth b: 29 Aug: inst: Parents Augustine and Mary Peterson.
Robert b: last of May Inst: P: Richard and Sara Tittimerry.
Elisabeth b: 28th of Aug: inst: P: Joseph and Elisabeth Rice.
William b: 12 of Dec: 1776 P: John and —— Howel.
John b: 18th of March 1776 Malachia and Elizabeth Horner.
Elizabeth b: 21st of Sept: inst: Parents George and Cathrine Piles.
Rebecca 17th of Sept: inst: Parents Isac and Sarah Van Neaman.

1777-78

Peter b: 14 Aug: 1777 Parents Jonas and Christina Keen.
Cathrine b: 11 Febr: 1777 Parents Thomas and Cathrine Parker.

Charlette b: 26 May 1777 Pars: Conrad and Judy Nail.
Rachel b: 17th of March inst: Pars: Gabriel and Rebecca Dahlbo.
Joseph b: 6th of Apr: inst: Parents Wiljam and Anna Bright.
Jacob b: 28th of Julii 1778 Parents George and Mary Stanton.
Mathias b: 23d of Jan: 1777 Steven and Elizabeth M'Gill.
Hannah b: 5th of Sept: inst: Parents Jacob and Christina Justis.
Rebecca b: 15th of July inst: Par: Andrew and Rebecca Hellms.
John b: 3d of May inst: Mathew and Susanna Lord Parents.
Mary daughter of William and Hanna Fursman b: 27 of Julii 1778.
John Laurence son of John and Cathrine Carey b: 20 Julii, 1777.

1779

3d. William b: 1st of August 1778 Parents Walentine and Sarah Runnels.
Feby: Hanna b: 17th of March 1778 Jacob and Rebecca Matson Parents.
Elizabeth b: 15th of Apr: 1776 Parents Samuel and Louisa Lidden.
Rebecca b: 1st of July 1778 Parents—same.
Deborah b: 15th of Nov: 1778 Parents Benjamin and Deborah Angelou.
David b: 29th of Oct. 1778 Parents William and Elizabeth Roy.
John 5th of Nov: 1778, Parents James and Cathrine Stillman.
Sarah b: 23d of Nov: 1778 Parents John and Sarah Clark.
John Nicholas Parents Sarah Goldsmith and Somebody.
Andrew b: 12th of March inst: parents Andrew and Elizabeth Horner.
Wiljam b: 3th of May inst: Parents John and Sarah Richards.
Michael b: 29th of Octobre 1778 and Magdalena b: 10th of March 1775.
both children of Christopher and Barbary Arnot.
Sarah b: 24th September 1778 Parents Gustaf and Hanna Halton.
John ditto b: 15th June 1775.
William b: 16th of Junt Inst: parents Luke and Margret Fisler.
William b: 30th of April 1779 Parents Fredric and Elizabeth Pullinger.
James 21st of Aug: inst. Parents Daniel and Sarah Southerland.
Charles Simon b: 31st of July Jacob and Elizabeth Linnardt Parents.
Sarah b: 5th of Oct: 1778 Jacob and Deborah Urian.
John b: 3d of Sept inst. Parents Samuel and Sarah Dahlbo Pensneck.
John b: 16th of Oct: inst. Parents James and Elizabeth Bryant.
Susannah b: 13th of Sept: inst: parents Jacob and Margrete Madeira.
Kesia daughter of Edward and Diana Hampton b: 3d of April 1779.
Mary b: 20th of Oct: George and Cathrine Pile.
Peter and Susannah Hunters children: Samuel b: 10th of March 1764. Aaron
  b: 14th of Sept. 1766. Enoch b: 1st of July 1770. Hannah b: 14th of Oct.
  1771. Mary b: 29th of June 1773. Isac and Jacob twins b: 1st of June
  1776. Peter b: 4th of June 1778.

1780

Elizabeth b: 12th of Apr: 1777 Parents Edward and Diana Hampton.
Esrah b: 29th of Jan: inst. Parents Andrew and Judith Henrickson.
Jesse b: 28th of Jan: inst: Malackia and Mary Christina Kelly.
Mary b: 1st of March 1777 ditto parents.
David b: 12th of December 1779 Par. David & Eddy Henricson.
David b. 16th of Febr. Inst: Jacob and Rebecca Calloway.
Mehetebel daughter of John and Margareth Lock, b: 6th of Febr: 1780.
Anne b: 16th of March last Parents Wiljam and Elizabeth Runnels.
Sarah 26th of Sept. 1779 Jacob and Anne Middleton.
Willjama Hellms b: 15th of June inst. Parents Isac and Sarah Van Neaman.
Charles b: 31st of May inst: Parents Samuel and Judy Pickin.
John b: 1st of Jan. 1780 Parents John and Susannah Mc Leman.
Benjamin b: August 22d.

Priscilla b: Oct. 2d.
Richard b: 3d of Novembr: 1778 Parents John and Susanna Richard.
George b: 20th of April 1780 Parents Adam and Elizabeth Schütz.
Rebecca b: 22d of Sept 1780 Par. Laurence and Sara Friend.
John b: 31st of Jan. 1779, Par. N. and Magdalena Marshal, then living in Rapapo.
1781
Isac b. the 8th of Nov. 1780 Par. Jacob and Christina Jestis.
Isac b. 18th of Decemb. 1780, Parents Daniel and Sally Southerland.
Jan.
Mathew b. 21st. of Feb. inst. John and Mary Cook.
Charles Friedric b. 6th of Febr. inst. Jacob and Rebecca Myer Par.
Louisa Leddon b. 14th of Decemb. 1780 Samuel and Louisa Leddon Pars.
James b. 19th of Febr: 1777 Par. Jacob and Mary Van Neaman.
George Armond Garret b. the 11th of April 1780 Pars. John and Anne Garret.
Wiljam (a black) b. last of Aug. 1776 his mother Cathrine a Negro.
Miles b. 2d. of Oct. 1780 P. David and Hanna Garrison.
Sarah b. 4th of Apr. Pars. Daniel and Rebecca England.
Anne b. 12th of Nov. 1779. P. Joseph and Mary Rice.
Martha b. 16th of May inst. Jacob and Lidia Shoulders.
Martha b. 27th of Novembr. 1780. Pars. —— Gill.
Wiljam b. 7th of Jan. 1781 Pars. Jacob and Rebecca Matson.
Samuel b. 6th of July inst. Par. Peter and Elizabeth Stinger.
Andrew b. 15th of June par. James and Cathrine Stillman.
Catun born Sept. 12th Par. John and Lydia Strang.
Debora b. 18th Nov. 1776 Par. Hue and Hanna Montgommery.
Mary b. 4th of Oct. Jacob and Emilia Catts.
Fredric b. the 4th of May inst. Par. Malachy and Elizabeth Howel.

1782.

Hanna b. 16th day of Novembr. 1781 Par. James & Elizabeth Bryan.
Elizabeth b. 15th of January this year, Par. Isac & Baja Van Neaman.
Susanna b. 20th of December inst. par. Ephraim & Debora Saly.
Cathrine b. Decemb. 13th 1773.
Elizabeth March 13th 1776
Christina May 13th 1778
John Decemb. 26th 1781
          Parents John & Cathrine Catts.
John b. 11th of Jan. inst. Parents Charles and Mary Halton.
Rachel b. 10th of Febr: Mathias & Mary Johnson Par.
Sara b. 25th of December last. Par. Jacob & Margret Madira Ev: John
     Rickers.
Anna b. 2d of Decemb. last Parents Friedric & Elizabeth Pullinger.
Sarah b. 17th of December 1781 Par. Thomas & Debora Clark.
Margareta b. 13th of Aug: 1781 Par. Thomas & Mary Ryley.
Rebecca b. 23d. Nov. 1781 Par. Lucas & Marget Fisler.
Jacob b. 25th of Apr. Inst. Par. Adam & Cathrine Stinger.
Anne Mary b. 11th of Jan. inst. Par. Philip & Dorothy Stinger.
Jacob b. 18th of Decemb. 1781 Par. Valentine & Sophy Forser.
Wilhelm b. March 9th inst. Par. Daniel & Eva Stinger.
Rebecca b. 15th of June inst. P. Malachy & Mary Christine Kelly.
Sara b. 23d of Sept. instant Par. Peter & Elizabeth Stinger.
Samuel b. 20th of June inst. P. George & Cathrine Pile.
Pertina b. 26th of Aug. inst. Parents John and Louisa Regu.
Cathrine b. 4th of July inst. Par. James & Cathrine Flannigan.
Jessey b. 25th of Sept. last. P. Joseph and Mary Rice.
William b. 19th of Oct. inst. Par. Paltes & Martha Reisner.

George b. 13th of June 1782 Par. Conrad & Susanna Shoemaker.

Sarah b. 19th of Aug. 1782 Par. Adam & Elizabeth Schyz.

Hinchman b. 11th of Oct. 1782 Par. James and Paty Tallman.

Priscilla Hewling with her children to Wit. Marget b. 13th of March 1774 Priscilla Jan: 14th 1776. Samuel 8th of Febr. 1778, Wiljam Nov. 20th 1780.

Hanna b. Sept. 13th 1782 Par. William & Sara Noble.

Wiljam b. 18th of Nov. 1782 Parents Jacob & Lydia Sholders.

Danson b. Oct. 14th 1781, Branson b. March 22d 1777 Kesiah B. Apr. 18th 1774. Parents of the three, George and Elizabeth Van Lear.

John b. 29th of July last. Par. William & Elizabeth Runnels.

Elizabeth b. 29th of Jan. 1783 inst. Par. Thomas & Cathrine Parker.

Wiljam Watson England b. 6th of Apr. inst. Par. Daniel & Rebecca England.

Mary b. 27th of March inst. Parents Thomas & Hester England.

Hester, mother of this child 23 years old last Oct. the 18th.

James b. 2d of April 1782 Par. John & Sara Clark.

Benjamin b. the 14th of December 1782, Par. Malachy et Elizabeth Horner.

Zephanias son of Tomlin and his wife deceased, b. 5th of Apr. 1775.

Mary daughter of Eglinton et his wife b. Nov. 1776.

These two orphans brought to baptism by Mathew Morgan et his wife to whom they are bound.

John b. 21st. of May inst. Par. John & Cathrine Hoffman.

Mary b. 30th of March inst. Par. Charles & Mary Halton.

Lydia b. 19th of Sept. P. John & Lidia String.

Wiljam b. 22d of Nov. inst. Par. James & Cathrine Flannigan.

Jonathan b. —+— Par. James et —— Shoulders.

Daniel 12 Dec. inst. Par. Daniel & Sara Sutlerland.

Fredric b. 6th of Febr. 1781, Par. Jacob and Marget Myers.

RECORDS OF MARRIAGES

RACOON 1713

On October 15 were married Carl Hoffman and Elsa Cobb.
On December 29 were married Lars Petersson and Catharina.

RACOON 1714

On May 10 were married Johan Mulicka and Anna Halton.
On November 17, Anders Thaten and Ella Sträng.

PENS NECK 1714

On November 4: Marten Johnsson was married to Elizabeth v. Neeman.
On November 25 were married Johan Philpot and Catharina Litien.

PENS NECK 1715

On May 25 were married, Abraham Lidenius and Elizabeth von Numan.
On October 26 were married, Jonas Shogen and Christina Fransson.

RACOON CREEK 1715

On January 25 were married Johannes Geögen and Lisa Guarring.
On April 20, Fredric Halton and Hanna Ryd.

PENS NECK 1716

On May 10 were married Christiern Petersson and Catharina.
On November 22, Simon Eaton and Margareta Nilsson.

PENS NECK 1717

On January 22, Joh. Shagen and Catharina v. Devair.
On February 27, William Philpot and Maria Mattsson.
On October 10, Peter Enlow and Margareta Minck.
On October 31 were married, Seneck Senecksson and Maria Philpot.
On November 14, David Strahen and Susanna Caspar.
On November 29, Philip Fransson and Helena Kobb.
On December 12 Jacob von Devair and Catharina Forssen.

RACOON CREEK 1717

On March 27: Desiderius von Numan and Debora Long.
On May 1: Johan Mattsson and Annicka Cock.
On June 11: Charles Dahlbo and Elsa Runnels.
On October 22: Samuel Daton and Dorothea Long.
On November 6: Guarret von Numan and Maria Lock.
On November 27: William Cobb and Almgott Hoffman.
On December 4: Eric Mulicka and Margareta Petersson.
The same day: Charles Sträng and Margareta Cock.

PENS NECK 1718

On June 18 were married Lars Nilsson and Sara Jaqvet.
On November 27: Ony Standly and Dorothea Seneck.

---

[148] Referred to in the original as "Bröllop", "Weddings".

RACOON CREEK 1718

On March 4, Berthil Supply and Maria Magdaniel.
On August 11, William Cobb and Anna Hwinscher.
On October 30, Jonas Kyhn and Sarah Dahlbo.
On December 28, Sam. Smith and Elizabeth Jansson.

PENS NECK 1719

On January 6th, Timothy Damsey and Anna Shiere.
On April 23rd, Johan Hansson and Maria Jansson.
On the October 1st, Johan Casper and Maria Baner.
On December 2nd, Marten Shiere and Maria Litien.

RACOON CREEK 1719

On May 5 were married, Elias King and Elsa Hoffman.
On August 7, Jacob Lundbeck and Christina Qwist.
On December 4, Peter Justice and Helena Lock.
On December 11, Lars Lock and Maria Sluby.

PENS NECK 1720

On April 21, Johan Standley and Catharina Billerbach.
On May 5, Jonas Shagen and Catharina von Numan.
On August 18, Samuel Walcketh and Catharina Jansson.
On October 20, James Strahyn and Geen Rickman.
Item Daniel Cole and Maria Hawke.

RACOON CREEK 1720

On July 22 were married Alexander Randel and Sarah Long.
On November 16, Andreas Petersson and Beata Jones.
On November 16, John Arched and Maria Petersson.
On November 23, Lourentz Påwelson and Maria Homman.
On December 5, Thom Tailor and Edeth Boles.

PENS NECK 1721

On February 1, were married Jacob Savoj and Regina Guilliamsson.
On June 21, Henric Guns and Christina Shiare.
On September 3, Joseph Hawkes and Helena Minck.
On December 25, Charles Price and Anna Philips.

RACOON CREEK 1721

On January 4 were married Alexander King and Brigitta Hoffman.
On July 24, Josias Mink and Hanna Algier.
On August 3, Charles Angelow and Gun Miller.
On December 28, Påwel Kempe and Gun Dounkins.
Item, Jean Runnels and Catharina Påwelson.

PENS NECK 1722

On February 4, were married Johan Billain and Margareta Classon.
On the same day, Johan Brooks and Maria Mecum.
On November 16, Philip Cannoway and Brigitta Hindricsson.

RACOON 1722

On February 28 were married, Jacob Forsman and Maria Cock.
On April 17, David von Numan and Maria Rambo.
On June 20, Jacob Danielsson and Maria Petersson.
On July 17, Peter Cock and Maria Sträng.
On June 15, Sam. Taylor and Martha Wilson.
On July 24, Staphan Jones and Catharina Lock.
On August 8, James MacMaine and Catharina Sluby.
On December 7, William Ellwill and Anna La Shamet.
On August 15, Måns Kyhn and Elizabeth Georgen.

PENS NECK 1723

On December 2: William Hill and Anna Cobb.

RACOON CREEK 1723

Matthias Shogen and Brigitta Mulicka were married on January 31.
Sam. Gillard and Joan Parrot, on February 26.
Anders Hoffman and Catarina Long, on June 5.

PENS NECK 1724

On January 26, William Johnsson and Lydia Loveday.
Item, James Parnell and —— ——.
On February 13: Anders Hindersson and Anna Nils.
On the 14th of the same: Edward Cannoway and Maria.
On March 17: John Whenu and Elizabeth Ward.
On June 11: James Hill and Rachel Chandlor.
On July 26: Cornelius Calfey and Maria Palmer.
On August 20: Simon Eaton and Magdalena Minck.
Item: Tobias Casper and Brita Minck.
On October 14: James Butterwood and Catharina Corneliusson.
On the 21st of the same: Henric von Iman and Maria von Devair.
On November 12: Lars Petersson and Helkia Marshlander.
On December 10: Hinric Petersson and Anna Cobb.
On the 22d of the same: Charles Buckley and Grace Willcock.
On December 14: Samuel Angelow and Anna Cock.
Item: Robert Ayres Sharlotti and Marg[areta] Hind[ersson].

RACOON CREEK 1724

On February 2nd were married, James Stule and Cath. Barret.
On —— the 5th, Lars Hoffman and Maria Mattsson.
On April 29th, Jacob Mattsson and Lydia Kulen.
On August 12th, Eric Kock and Anna Jones.
On November 24th, Anders Hoffman and Maria Von Iman.
On December 2nd, Peter Rambo and Christina Kyhn.

PENS NECK 1725

John Seneckson and Anna Guilliamsson were married on January 28.
Thomas Nixon and Catharina Casper on March 29.
Thomas Hicks and Elenor Downs on May 6.

RACOON CREEK 1725

On April 7 were married, Georg Horsel and Lucia Wardety.
On May 7 were married, Anders Stalcop and Christina Petersson.
On November 15, Zacharias Petersson and Magdalena Halton.
On November 24, Anders Rambo and Cathrina Hoffman.
On November 25, Israel Lock and Rebecka Helm.

RACOON CREEK 1726

On April 1 married Erik Kock and Hanna Warrelton.
On May 26 married John Culen and Cathrina Mattss[on].
On November 17 married Lucas Petersson and Christina Dedrichsson.
On November 3 married Georg Pomrai and Susanna Conrari.
On December 27 married Gustaf Gustafson and Annicka Keen.
On December 27 married Michel Hoffman and Juli Jung.
On the 27th married Joshua Hutchinsson and Margreth Smith.

RACOON CREEK 1727

On May 18 were married, Jonas Kock and Sara Bull.
On October 25 were married, Andreas Enock and Cathrina Jonss[on].

RACOON 1728

Åke Helm and Elizabeth Dahlbo were married on December 27.

RACOON 1729

John Enockson and Margret von Jman were married on June 27.
John Thoms and Hanna Parker, on December 11.
John Fish and Maria Bull.

RACOON 1730

John Hoffman and Mary Lock, on December 3.
John Bekom and Elizabeth Morgon, on the 27th.
Daniel Guen and Anna Wood on Decembr 30.
Benjaman Liddon and Susanna Doffell were wedded on January 4.
Israel Henrikson and Emi Jonsson, on February 19.
John Jonson and Christina Hickman, on May 30.
Gabriel Enokson and Maria Guarron, on December 30.
Erik Runolls and Maria Hoffman, on the 31st.
Anders Senecks and Betty Greenoway, on November 12.

RACOON 1731

Anders Mullicka and Maria Georgen, on February 17.
Stephan Mullicka and Christina Homman, on December 16.

RACOON 1734

John Hoffman & Mary Garron were joyned May 24th.
John Helm & Sarah Dahlbo June 6th.
Willm. Thorn & Mary Wood Octob. 29th.
Garret Voniman & Christian Denny Octob. 30.
Lorens Lock & Brigitta Henrys Novemb. 19th.

[308]

Ötte Kock & Mary Lock, Novemb. 22d.
Samuel Cabb & Catharine Keen Decemb. 11.

RACOON 1735

Andrew Tossa & Susanna Hollsten, married febr. 5

RACOON 1736

Joshua Huet & Ann Smith were married on Aprill 26th.
Mortin Stille & Mary Halton on August 29th.
Erik Kock & Magdlen Peters Sept. 18th.
Erik Keen & Cath: Denny Novemb. 17th.
Robert Husband & Elizabeth Oltry Decemb. 23d.
Willm. Roman & Mary Ablert Novemb. 23.

RACOON AND PEN'S NECK 1741, 1742

1741

Hans Georg Hochschieldt and Anna Maria Heim, Nov. 10. } at Cohansie.
1742

Heinrich Rotgab and Barbara Miller, January 18

Henry Liddon and Elizabeth Perrymon, January 28
John Miller and Elizabeth M'Lallin, February 9
Edward Lawrence and Elizabeth van Nieman, Febr. 9
William Ellwill and Sarah Safely, Febr. 10 } at Pilesgrove.
John Keen and Rachel Chandler, February 18
William Hutson and Judida Harker, March 25
Thomas Davis and Elizabeth Basset, April 12
William Dallbo and Elizabeth van Nieman, May 9, of Pen's Neck.
Johan Conrad Cougar and Barbarah Probstin, March 9, at Cohansie, paid
    nothing.
John Martin Halter and Catherin Sautrie, May 13, from the Glasshouse.
Christoph Pfeiffer and Maria Schulem, of Cohansie, May 17.
Thomas Proctor and Sarah Reed, of Pensneck, May 19.
Jesse Wallar and Anne Wallin, of Pilesgrove, July 2.

PENS NECK 1749

Michael Lampson and Christina Philpot, from Pensneck.

PENSNECK 1750

Month	Day	with Licence or Banns	
Jan.	1		Marcus More and Sarah Peterson.
Octob.	25	Banns	David Preis and Maria Judith Sheer.
Nov:	28	Banns	John Scott, and Elizabeth Gullion.
Aug.	24	Banns	Mathias Lampson and Anna Corneliusson.
Aug.	12	Banns	John M'Kansie and —— Sanderlin.

PENSNECK 1751

Jan.	25	Banns	George Leonhard Krumrieen and Barbra Ridman.
Feb.	3	Banns	John Gevall and Susana Sack.
Feb.	10	Banns	Michael Miller and Sarah Holstein.

[309]

Apr.	13	Banns	Obadiah Laid and Rebecka Linch.
May	1	Banns	William Chattell and Anne Kits from Piles Grove.
June	10	Banns	Hendrick Peterson and Sarah Wandaever [Vandevair?]
June	29	Banns	John Davids, and Hanah M'Caeen from Alloway's Creek.
Jul.	17	Banns	Daniel Aloay and Margreta M'Farell.

PENSNECK 1752

June	15	Banns	William Baven and Susanah Peckman from Pensneck.
June	15	Banns	Joh. Gottfrid Laourer and Maria Elis. Welten from Cohansie.
Sept.	27	Banns	Patrick Duff and Cathrina Groom from Pensneck.
Oct.	1	Licence	David Seeley and Johanna Bassat from Manaton.
Oct.	16	Licence	Benjamin Lippencut and Rebecca Hayns from Manaton.
Oct.	23	Banns	Martin Brown and Margreta Duringerin ? from Cohakin.

PENS NECK 1753

| Dec. | 22 | Banns | Hance Jaquette   Barbara Astron. |

PENSNECK 1754

Jan.	3	Licence	Thomas Penington & Mary Jones.
March	4	Publishing	Petter Enloes and Jane Jaquette.
March	28	Publishing	William Barry and Sarah Stiles.

RACOON 1754

January	2	James Jones White and Maria Cock, from Glouster County.
	3	Thomas Pannington and Maria Jones, from Pensneck.
	10	Gustav Lock and Catharina Loikan, from Glouster County.
		John Michael Rieselbrecht and Catharina Palsin, from Cohansie.
	15	John Shemler and Elisabeth Dielshastern, from Cohansie.
February	1	John Phil. Smick and Magdalena Comerin, from Cohansie.
	2	Edv. Tailor and Marta Nicols from Mantelcreek.
	21	John Streng and Rebecca Justice from Glouster County.
March	2	Mathew Morgan and Tobithee Eglington, from Glouster County.
		Connelly and Elisabeth Plomley, from Glouster County.
	6	Peter Enloes and Jane Jaquette, from Pensneck.
April	4	Will. Barry and Sarah Stils, from Pensneck.
	15	Nicolas Mygler and Magdalena Olijn, from Cohansie.
		Daniel Simpkins and Martha Chandler, from Cohansie.
		Paul Johnson and Elisabeth Davis, from Cohansie.
May		Andrew Justice and Cathrina Stanton, from Pensneck.
		Alexander Smith and Ruth Foster, from Cohansie.
		Dost Consler and Catharina Lavie, from Pensneck.
June		Georg Starck and Cath. Petterson, from Pensneck.
		Hans Georg Hierneissen and Magdalena Katzen, from Pensneck.
July		Jacob Kats and Esther Marg. King, from Pensneck.
Aug.	5	Michell Lee and Sarah Dickeson, from Alleways Creek.
Sept.	3	John Rawlins and Elisabeth Stevens, from Piles Grove.
	8	Robert Wilson and Elis. Shearwood, from Pensneck.
	30	Melchior Run and Barbara Relsin, from Cohansie.

Oct.	10	John Ambler from Elsingborough, and Hedda Aplin, from Glouster County.
	14	Henry Furster and Miriam Schneeden, from the Glass House.
	28	Frantz Huver and Margaretha Harrican, from the Glass House.
Nov.		Joseph Philpot and Margaretha Connoway, from Pensneck.
		Salomon Loyd and Prisilla Wood, from Piles Grove.
	10	And. Lock and Esther Cooper, from Glouster County.
	11	Henry Lundbeck and Mary Hyde, from Glouster County.
	12	Lars Vaneman and Hannah Howard, from Pensneck.
	13	John Lock and Sarah Vaneman, from Glouster County.
	19	John Smith and Mary Hill, from Pensneck.
		John Marshal and Marg. Elvil, from Pensneck.
Dec.	31	Peter Johnson and Barbara Miller, from Cohansie.
		Peter Hitzler and Mary Marg. Reize, from Alleways Creek, married on September 22.
		John Pooge and Abigail Tackry, from Pensneck, married on December 14.
	25	Willm. Colline and Phoeby Smith, from Clouster County.
	19	Michael Richman and Rebecka Keen from Piles Grove.

[PENNS NECK ? 1755]

Jan.	26	James Farrell and Mary Pattersson, from Pensneck.
Feb.	12	Zebulon Lock and Magdalena Keen, from Glouster County.
		Hugh Davis and Susanna Keen, from Piles Grove.
		Nathanael Dickinson and N. Thomson, from Mannington.
	18	John Reinolds and Regina Hindrichsson, from Glouster County.
	22	James Pattersson and Francense Butterworth, from Pensneck.
	26	Petter Spengler and Mary Akertin, from Piles Grove.
	30	Georg Mann and Barbara Katzin, from Piles Grove.
April	10	Matthias Johnson and Eleon. Haogks, from Pensneck.
	6	John Bidle and Christ. Halton, from Pensneck.
		William Grasberg and Jane Hill, from Pensneck.
May		Robert Rea and Mary Hill, from Pensneck.
July		James Green and Hedd[a] Grafs, from Mannington.
Aug.		John Hertzhorn and Martha Loo, from Glouster County.
Dec.	2	Georg Reaman and Mary Conningham, from Cohansie.

RACOON 1756

Jan.		Simon Martin and Cath. Starn, from Piles Grove.
Feb.		John Dahlbo and Elsa Bitle, from Pensneck.
		Jsack Howell and Cath. Sanderlin, from Pensneck.
March	7	John Tharrenton and Abig[ail] Allen, from Glouster County.
April		John Jones and Mary Williams, from Piles Grove.
		Aron Bettle and Rebecka Petterson, from Pensneck.
		John Ford and Ruth Jefreys, from Pensneck.
June		John Souder and Margaretha Tilshaven, from Cumberland County.
		Joseph Grist, Jr. and Dorothea Gill, from Pensneck.
Aug.	10	Michael Miller and Marg. Shumaker, from Allaways Creek.
	12	Charles Dahlbo, from Pensneck, and Rachel Keen, from Glouster County.
Sept.	28	Cornelius Trimnal and Anne Mary Read, from Piles Grove.

PENSNECK 1762

No marriages this year.

[311]

RACOON 1762

No marriages this year.

PENSNECK 1763.

Nov:
ye 7th.   Married William Herway & Anne van Heist of Salem & Man.
The rest of the Pensneck were married by the justice Trencher.

RACOON 1763

Jan. 2d.   Married Wiljame Tuss & Betzy Beesly of Salem & Pilegrove.
Feb. 18   Jonas Keen & Christine van Neuman of dito.
22   John Middletown & Rachel van Neuman of Gloucester.
24   Robert Thomas & Mary Briant of dito.
March 16.   Mar: Joseph Paulsson & Mary Allen, the first couple in ye church.
July 26.   Timothee Clarck & Margery van Neuman of Gloucester & Greenwh[ich].
Aug. 25.   Peter Stricker & Mary Euler of this place.
Oct. 19th.   Nathan Boy & Mary Runals of this place.
Dec. 14th.   Lawrence Friend & Sally Kocks of this place.
28th.   Peter Lock & Regina Van Neuman of this place.

PENSNECK 1764

May ye 24th.   Augustine Petersson & Mary Beetle of Salem & Up[per] P.N.
Oct. ye 13th.   Wiljam Slide & Rebecka Pedrick of dito place.
Nov: ye 13th.   Zacharias Stedham and Margary Joice of dito.
Dec: ye 15th.   Wiljame Beetle & Cathrine Archet of dito.
the 20th.   Ananias Ellvel & Prudens Petersson of dito.
The 27th.   Cornelius Boon and Rachel Dalbou of dito place.

RACOON 1764

May ye 28.   Thomas Dodd & Christine Lock of Gloucester & Greenwhich.
Nov. ye 11th.   Anthony Hooper and Sary Eslick of dito.
Dec. ye 24.   James Golden and Margery Laidden of dito.
July the 31st.   Robbert Bonor and Nanzy Smith from Salem.

PENSNECK 1765

Jan. the 1.   Married, Andrew Linmeyer with Elisabet Holstein of Salem & Pilesgrove.
the 11.   Conrad Andrews to Margery Schrotner living in Cohakin.
the 15.   Thomas Ellis to Anne Humphries of Gloucester & Hattenfield.
the 22.   Peter Sauders to Anne Elisabeth Hindrickson from Cohanzy.
the 22.   Johan Coltzly to Maria Margreta Hartman living at the Glasshouse.
Feb. the 7th.   Shadrick Sunderlin to Mary Anne Jaquet of Salem & P.N.
the 10.   Joseph Eduards to Susannah Hilderbrand of dito.
the 14.   Rease Kindle to Anne Borden of Salem & on the 15th Mathew More to Peggy Kindle.
March the 3.   Caleb Darling to Abigail Holliday of Salem & P.N.
April the 15.   Thomas Drake to Thankful Laster living in Salem.

M.R.
Oct. the 22.   Johan Georg Boody to Anne Elisabeth Hartman Maur: River.
Decemb: the 2. Andrew Wike to Mary Marriere Salem.
the 22.   Antony Born to Hannah Jounger. Salem.

[312]

RACOON 1765

Jan: the 10.	Married John Runnals to Cathrine Boys of this place.
the 27.	Adam Kohl to Margery Haak of Salem & Pilesgrove.
the 29.	Jacob Frease Junr. to Elisabet Lauderback from Cohakin.
March the 4.	Eduard Test to Susannah Hencock. in Salem.
March the 7.	John Green to Charity Stanten of Salem & P.N.
May the 28.	Charles Winemyller to Dorothea Abelle of this place.
June the 5.	John Callahan to Elisabet Kidd. living in Cohakin.
August the 6.	Nathan Linham to Mary Stonebanks Pilesgrove.
Sept: the 25.	John Forster to Jane Alexander, Racoon.
Nov: the 15.	Joseph Jackson to Anne Schoote, Racoon.

PENSNECK 1766

Feb. 10.	Eduard Tunkens to Prudy MakWheire [Mac Guire?] of Salem town.
13.	Patrick Duffy to Marget Greffy of Salem & Upper P.N.
Feb. 27.	Jacob Tossy to Sary Homan of Salem & Upper P.N.
March 2.	Elias Nilsson to Sary Eduards of dito.
the 31.	James Dickisson to Anne Kelly of dito.
April 13.	Samuel Smith to Lucrace Johnsson of dito.
May 19.	Francis Treassy to Cathrine Welch of dito.
	Bartimeus Tuff to Mary Marchal of Salem & Mananthan.[149]
Dec. 12.	James Alexander to Cathrine Mackray of Salem Town.
11.	William Pedrick to Anne Daasen of Salem & Upper P.N.
7.	John Holliday to Elisabeth Jouransson of dito & Lower P.N.
May 22.	William Smith to Sarah Dykes both belonging to lower Pensneck.
Oct. 2.	Michael Corneliesson to Margreth Haynes. Salem County & Upper Pensneck.

RACOON 1766.

Jan. 21.	Alexander Hamilton to Jane More of Gloucester.
Feb: 26.	David Davis to Rebecca Derixon of dito.
May 22.	Magnus Dragström to Elisabeth Justisson of this place.
the 25.	Benjamin Howel to Marget Jones of Salem & P.N.
Sept: 15.	Adam Mauer to Anne Cathrine Fultin of dito.
Oct: 16.	Poltens Reissiner to Marta Jamesson of Gloucester.
Nov: 15.	Ehrend Frinkhead to Mary Barber of Salem & Pilesgrove.

PENSNECK 1767

Jan. 15.	Mallacky Kelly to Mary Hopman living in Mananthan.
Feb: 15.	Aron Dunlap to Rebecca Cornellisson out of Upper Pensneck.
July 1.	John M'kasson to Anne Straune from Salem.
Aug: 23.	John Lumly to Grace Junger dito.
Sept: 14.	William Ashly to Jane M'Crau, dito.
the 15.	Danniel Dorrell to Joanna Moore dito.
Oct: 8	William Johnsson to Mary Taylor, from Helsingborough.
the 28	William Longly to Mary Mollen from Mananthan.
Nov: 3	Robert Johnsson Esqr to Miss Jane Gebbens of Salem Town.
the 10	James Moore to Anne Munrow from Allow-Creek.
the 15	John Starck to Ruth Jones from lower Pensneck.
Dec: 7.	James Ford to Elisabeth Stump from Salem.
	Briant Conor to Mary Parker Salem.
the 24.	Francis Marshal to Rebecca Cobener from Lower Pensneck.

[149] Manhattan.

RACOON 1767

Jan. 1.	James Flannigan to Sary Helms living in Salem County.
the 15.	Alexander Brown to Marget GilJohnsson of dito.
the 16.	William Sharpe to Mary Riggens living in Gloucester County.
Feb: 12.	Jacob Miller to Mary Wilkins Pilesgrove.
March 3.	John Lockner to Marget Coale dito.
the 19.	Jacob Gaarslin to Mary Whittin dito.
May 26.	Salomon Smith to Sary Dennys, dito.
June 8th.	Jacob Calloway to Rebecca Angellou out of Gloucest: County.
Aug: 29.	William Briant to Elisabeth Easly Dito.
Sept: 17.	Thomas Clarck to Deborah Denny she dito & he of Salem & Pilesgrove.
Oct: 9.	Joseph West to Mary Jisard dito.
Nov: 24.	Nathan Mills to Marta Waard dito.
Dec. 21.	George Williams to Mary Smith dito

RACOON AND PENS NECK 1768

Jan. 7.	Joseph Munjan, to Ruth Slyde in Gloucester County.
Feb. 7.	Joseph Staton to Hannah Warbitton from Mauritz: River.
Feb. 10.	Andrew Minck to Rebecca Van Neuman. Salem County.
the 11.	Robert Whin, to Mary-Anne Hewitt. Gloucest: County.
the 12.	Thomas Angelou to Elizabeth Cane, from Pilesgrove.
the 15.	James Holliday to Sary Sleepe, Salem County.
the 29.	Isaac Heather to Emy Scott, Salem County.
March 6.	James Sanders to Elisabeth Forster. dito.
April 18.	Walter Wood to Sary Bowen, from Cumberland County.
the 29.	Andrew Kind to Elisabeth Hughs. Gloucest: County.
the 21.	Esajah Parwen to Mary Kirl from Cumberland County.
May 26.	Daniel Lopor to Elis: Sutten, dito.
June 9.	Jacob Bakes to Emy Basset, from Pilesgrove.
the 17.	Erasmus Morten to Susannah Tate dito from New-Castle.
May 7.	William Semeter to Elis: Bast. dito.
July 16.	Jacob Jones to Regina Lock, Racoon-Creek.
Sept. 5.	John Hoffsee to Hannah Middeltown, Gloucester County.
the 6.	John Briarly to Mary Laid. from Pilesgrove.
the 11.	Benjamin Straten to Marget Thomas from Mananthan.
the 28.	Abram Mullicka to Mary Jarel gloucest: county.
Nov. 10.	Eduard Batten to Idy Right, dito.
the 14.	Jacob Woolf to Sary Hawertin dito.
Dec. 26.	Zacharias Jordain to Elis: Myer from Mananthan.

RACOON & PENSNECK 1769

Jan: 15.	John Boothen to Jane Jöransson from Pensneck.
the 19.	Joseph Cobener to Jane Allmond dito.
the 26.	John Savoy to Mary Dalbou, dito.
Feb. the 3.	John Cunningham to Mary Burrens Pilesgrove.
the 12.	James Dilcks to Sary Jones Mantes Creek.
the 23.	John Crebbs to Lorenah Bilderback Pensneck.
March the 10.	Jonathan Beesly to Elaya Peterson of Salem & Pilesgrove.
the 20.	Thomas Cupperwtheith to Mary Wiggins Salem.
the 27.	Thomas Parker to Cathrine Sly. Pensneck.
May the 3.	Benjamin Pedrich to Susannah Andersson of dito.
the 5.	John Adams to Cathrine Collwell. Woodbery.

	William Nilson to Cathrine Mullicka, hereabout.
the 25.	Erick Keen to Mary Lippencot, hereabout.
July 28.	Dean Simkins to Susannah Right Pilesgrove.
Aug. 8.	Edward Leonhard to Sary. Davis Mantes Creek.
the 11.	Thomas Taylor to Helenah Gardiner. Pensneck.
the 14.	Gabriel Trollinger to Philisare Reach Pilesgrove.
Sept.	
the 12.	Isaac Halfpenny to Jane Fearly Mananthan.
the 24.	William M'Dade to Mary Buckly, Salem.
NB. the 27.	Cleft Roael to Susannah Where Rapapo.
NB. Oct:	
the 3d.	Edmond Wetherby to Miss Anne Gebbons of Salem Town.
Nov. the 29.	John Moren to Elisabeth Hewet Gloucester County.
the 26.	John Dillmore to Hannah Emly Salem.
Dec.	
the 4.	Thomas Butterworth to Deborah Carter. Mantes Creek.
the 6.	Esaiah Lock to Judy Matsson Racoons Creek.
Dec.	
the 12.	Ephraim Bee to Anne Jaggard. Mantes Creek.
the 14.	Samuel Wintern to Anne Dawson. Pilesgrove.
	Thomas Schoote to Sarah Munjan—Woolwhich.
the 19.	Patrick Murphy to Barborah Longacre of dito.
the 21.	Andrew Senickson Junr. to Margeth Bilderback. Pensneck.
the 22.	Mathias Lambson to Anne V. Neuman. ditto.

NB. If ever, there be observed faults in any of these my Records it is not my neglect or my own; But entirely, the neglect ignorance & bungling information of some of my hearers, who are not mindful of themselves or of good order or of any other good thing, belonging to their salvation.   Sat. Sap.[150]

THE YEAR 1770

Jan. 11.	John Pinton to Mary Dillin He of Glouster Sche of Salem.
the 22.	James Houlten to Christiane Linmyer of Salem & Pilesgrove.
	Jonathan Bail to Sarah Fiseh of Gloucester & Greenwhich.
the 30.	Isaac Brehmen to Sarah Flitcher of dito.
Feb: 2.	George Verry to Barborah Cole of Salem & Pilesgrove.
the 5.	William Stremple to Hellena Shattly of dito.
the 6.	Isaac V. Neuman to Elisabeth Pedrich of dito.
the 15.	Peter Jaquet to Hanna Elvell of dito and Pensneck.
the 27.	Hindrich Sparcks to Elisabeth Hildebrand of dito.
	William Lawrence to Margeth Sparcks of dito.
the 28.	Conrad Neal to Cathrine Witesell of dito.
	Richard Grimes to Mary Hutehesson of Gloucester & Greenwhich.
March 1.	James Franklin to Sarah Lord, dito.
the 6.	Samuel Laidden Junr. to Lueretia Weaver of dito.
	Andrew Hindrichson to Judy Jones of dito.
the 10.	John Coby to Jamimy Smallwood. He of Philadelphia she Here.
the 11.	John Richards to Susy Hewet of Gloucester and Greenwhich.
the 26.	James Scott to Cathrine Richards of dito.
May 8.	John Eaten to Anne Cattell of Salem & Lower Pensneck.
the 9.	Samuel Cahoon to Hannah Davis of Glocester & Greenwhich.
the 17.	Joseph Dell to Mary Burden of dito.
the 29.	Jacob Cobelt to Mary Barbora Strawben of Salem.
June 23.	Conrad Schoemaker to Susanna Shoulder of Gloucester & Woolwhich.

---

[150] An abbreviation of the Latin *satis sapiensac,* meaning "enough wisdom".

July 4.	Greffey Greffieth to Sarah Hilderbrand of Salem & Pensneck.
Aug. 8.	Abram Simkens to Elisabeth Loper of Salem & Up: Pensneck.
the 9.	Robbert Sparcks to Rachel Sommers of dito.
the 21.	Isaac Justisson to Silly Slyde of Gloucester & Woolwhich.
Sept. 14.	William Smallwood to Mary More, of Philadelphia sche here.
the 20.	John Corry to Elisabeth Heines of Salem & Lower Pensneck.
Oct: 10.	Philip Sauders to Christine Couger of Salem & Cohaken.
the 17.	John Hall to Hannah Walker of Salem & Pilesgrove.
Oct. 23.	William Butler to Zaphira Bishop of Salem & Pilesgrove.
the 30.	Thomas Maffart to Anne Scott of Gloucester & Greenwhich.
Dec: 1.	Jonathan Simkins to Rachel Ratherford of Salem & Up:PN.
the 3.	John Friedrich Kyckerou to Elisabeth Lauderin of this place
the 19.	Samuel Platt to Unice Pinyard of Gloucester & Greenwhich.
	William Pinyard to Elisabeth Roberts of dito She of Woodwhich.
the 20.	Philip Slyde to Mary Lord of dito.
the 31.	Abram Keen to Christine Chester of this place.
NB. May	Mathew Gills Negroeman Cudjo to Ms. Harrissons Negroe Wooman. Venus in the presence of their Masters.

THE YEAR 1771

the 1.	Zebulon Pearsson to Mary Stedham of Gloucester & Woolwhich.
	Joseph Smith to Foeby Chester by the Revd. Niclas Collin.
the 10.	James Holliday to Elisabeth Jouransson of Salem & Lower Pensneck.
the 20.	John M'Williams to Brichet Moony of Salem County & Town.
the 23.	John Turner to Rebecca Linnard of Gloucester & Greenwhich.
the 31.	Samuel Tomlin to Rachel Garslin of dito.
Feb. 5.	Philip Miller to Mary Weeks of dito.
April 3.	Jacob Tomlin to Elisabeth Franklin of dito.
the 12.	Job. Coles to Elisabeth Tomlins of dito and Waterford.
March 21.	Jacob Savoy to Else Balbou of Salem & Upper Pensneck.
April 3.	Samuel Hewet to Lyddy Jones of Gloucester & Greenwhich.
the 8.	Samuel Grigg to Mary Anne Avunjan of dito.
the 17.	Robert Turner to Johanna Richards of dito.
	Joseph Devenport to Cathrine Halton of dito & Woolwhich.
the 21.	Joseph Marchant to Sara Richardsson of Salem & Pensneck.
the 23.	John Catt to Cathrine Powers of Salem & Pilesgrove.
May the 15.	Nathanael Sauders to Margeth Johnsson of Gloucest: & Woolwhich.
the 16	Jacob Hewet to Elisabeth Tomblins Gloucester & Greenwhich.
the 16	Alexander Ware to Sara Batten Gloucester & Woolwhich.
the 12	George Sommerwill to Maria Helms. Salem Co. & Upper P. N.
June 13	John Adams to Lyddy Lock of Gloucester & Woolwhich.
June 16	Solomon Stinger of Alloways Creek Township to Gwyn Blumer of Pilesg: & Salem County.
July 11	Daniel Ligthgold to Gertrue Beesly of Salem County & Town.
the 18	John M'Darmuth to Mary Halten of Gloucester & Woolwhich.
July 24.	John Forest to Cathrine Miller of Salem & Pilesgrove.
the 25	Job Stow to Margeth Roulen of the same place.
Aug. 13	Abram Lord to Cathrine Coock, of Gloucester & Woolwhich.
the 16	Carles Walters to Cathrine Hersin of Mauritzes River.
the 22	Samuel Endicott to Cathrine Walters of dito place.
the 30	Curtes Trenchard to Elisabeth Tuff of Salem Town.
Sept. 26	Isaac Howell to Prudens Stedham of Salem & Upper Pensneck.
Oct. 7	Joseph Rise to Elisabeth Dragström of Gloucester & Woolwhich.
the 14	Joseph Connover to Sarah Steelman of Great Eggharbour.
the 30	Abram Richmon to Sarah Keen of Salem & Pilesgrove.

Nov. 3	Christopher Bench to Mary Bee, of Salem county and town.
the 15.	James Wood to Jane Alexander of Gloucester & Woolwhich.
Dec. 4	David More to Lyddy Richmon of Salem & Pilesgrove.
the 7	William Guin to Elisabeth Huggin of dito place.
the 17	James Briant to Rebecca Dalbou of Gloucester & Woolwhich.
the 24	Simon Hardin to Sarah Denny of dito place.
the 31	Michal Turner to Anne Easly of Gloucester and Greenwhich.

THE YEAR 1772

Jan. 14	Jacob Allcut to Mary Budden of Gloucester and Greenwhich.
Feb. 6	William Dennies to Rebecca Dylap of Salem & Up: Pensneck.
the 9	Samuel Brown to Anne Lambsson dito of dito.
the 10	Jacob V. Neuman to Mary-Anne Krest of Gloucester & Greenwhich.
the 11.	William Forssman to Hannah Plumbly dito of dito.
the 12	James Steelman to Cathrine Keen dito of dito.
March 2.	Henry Weaver to Elisabeth Lidden dito & Woolwhich.
the 20	Mathew Tomblen to Elisabeth Ervin dito & Greenwhich.
the 24.	Vallentine Rynolds to Sarah Simpson dito & Woolwhich.
the 25.	Robbert Brown to Rachel Denny dito of dito.
April 2	Cornelius Embsson to Anne Brown of Salem — Up: Pensneck.
the 6	Thomas Manne to Hannah Mannen of Gloucester & Greenwhich.
the 13	Elia Barber to Elisabeth Hoppman of Salem & Pilesgrove.
the 14	Erich Petersson to Anne Dennies of Salem & Up: Pensneck.
the 16	Philip Jacob Dishlow to Anne Jennet of Gloucest: of Woolw.
the 24	Daniel Smith to Dorcas Smith of Cumberland and Allowes Creek.
the 25.	Phelix Fisler to Ruth Lock of Gloucester & Woolwhich.
May 20	Samuel Hewit to Mary Torch of dito & Greenwhich.
July 2	Michal Triest to Margreth Heils of Salem and Mananthan.
Aug. 4	Isaac Ireland to Mazy Hogben of Salem.
the 5	Joshua Lord to Elisabeth Piles of Gloucester and Woolwhich.
the 6	Francis Green to Cathrine V. Neuman of dito dito.
Sept. 11	Jacob Chester to Deborah Rambo, of Gloucester & Woolwhich.
the 15.	Henry Guest to June Simkens of dito, dito.
Octob. 18	Patrick Barrit to Cathrine Machentosh, of Salem & Pensneck.
Nov: 4	Jesse Winsor to Prudence Wood, of Gloucester & Woolwhich.
the 24:	John Booth to Sarah Powers, of Salem & Pilesgrove.
the 26.	Daniel Penton to Anne Hamton, of Salem & Allowes Creek.
the 29.	John Cambell to Mary Tressy, of Salem.
the 30.	William Leeds to Rachel Hamilton, of Gloucester & Greenwhich.
Dec: 9	Azariah Dickesson to Elisabeth Linsey, of Salem & Pilesgrove.
the 11.	Richard Worth to Lyddy Nilsson, of dito, dito.
the 31.	Andrew Matsson Jnr [Jr.] to Elisabeth Derichsson, Gloucester & Woolwhich.

THE YEAR 1773.

January 2	John Borrodail to Mary Russel both of Gloucester and Woolwhich.
the 4	Isaac Delawoo to Elisabeth Finnemore of dito & Greenwhich.
the 13	John Van Dyke to Prishilla Denny both of Swedesborough.
the 15	Samuel Robesson to Elisabeth Barnet both of Salem & Pilesgrove.
the 18	Israel English to Sarah Davis both of Gloucester and Greenwhich.
the 20	Samuel Farland to Margreth Denny of dito dito.

the 28	Thomas Clarck to S'arah Noah of Salem & Upper Pensneck.
Feb. 3.	John Cunningham a Mallattoe to Elisabeth Horssing of Gloucester & Greenwich.
the 9	Samuel Jackson to Margreth Kelch of Salem and Mananthan.
the 24	Andrew King to Anne Nielsson dito of dito.
March 23	Christopher Graft to Fredrica Taylor of Salem & Upper Pensneck. Aron Ward to Rebecca Fowler of Gloucester & Greenwhich.
the 25	David Weeks to Elisabeth Reed of Salem & Pitchgrove.
April 15	Samuel Hullings to Prishilla Welch both of Gloucester & Woolwich.
the 20	Jacob Matsson to Rebecca Adams of dito & dito.
May 1	Moris Welch to Magdalene Dalbou of Salem & Upper Pensneck.
the 4	John Allen to Sarah Pohlsson dito dito.
the 15	Richard Webster to Hannah Bacon of Cumberland & Stovecreek.
the 16	Ebenassar Bruster to Mary Rowly of Salem & Allowes creek.
the 24	John Nixon to Elisabeth Butler of Gloucester and Woolwhich.
the 27	William Armstrong to Sarah Linmeyer of Salem & Pilesgrove.
June 9	Thomas Hutchisson to Rachel Ellwell of dito & Pitchgrove.
the 10	Moses Hoffman to Rebecca Cock of Gloucester & Woolwhich.
Aug. 4	Aquilla Barber to Meribah Curry of Salem County & Pilesgrove.
the 16	Mosses Dawsen of Pilesgrove to Elisabeth Eastly of Gloucester & Woolwhich.
	William Cowgil and Lydia Lowsen Gloucester and Woolwhich.

PENSNECK FROM 1 OCT: 1773

13th	Samuel Dick and Sarah Sennecson, he from Selim, she from lower Pensneck.
	Garret Van Neaman and —— Halton.
	Isac Howel and Mary Wilder 7th Jan. 1774.
	Doc: Willjam Hanbey Mary Wittemberg.
	Henry Course and Cathrine Nelson.

RACOON FROM 1 OCT: 1773

November the 1st.	Willjam Hall from Philadelphia Printer, and Jane Trenchard Spinster from Selim.
4th.	Mathew Dulany from Manington Township Selim County to Christine Justis in Woolwhich and Gloucester county.
Dec: 14	Benjamin French and Elisabeth Mills.
19	John Halton and Helena Matson.
21	Garsham Alexander and Marget Mappin.

RACOON 1774

[Jan.] 5	Isac Howel and Mary Wilder.
19	Hjob Thomas and Hanna Bennet.
Febr: 2	Samuel Holly and Sarah Randel.
10th	John Hellms and Cathrine Beetle.
22d	Willis Nichols and Rebecca Shaw.
23	Amariah Dahlbo and Lydia Taylor.
March 20	John Firestone and Susanna Sivil.
dito 16th	Moses Cox and Widow.
24th	Charles Halton and Elisa Dahlbo.
April 8	Zachariah Merrow and S'arah Sinkins.
first April	Alexander V: Neaman and Rebecca Page.
May the 4th	John Rouse and Margrete Morrison from Pilesgrove, published.

[318]

8th	John Keen and Mary Matson licensed.
17 Julii	George Johnson and Cathrine Richman licensed.
	Solomon Abrahams and Christine Wall married 22 Julii published.
24 Julii	John Leonard and Sara Woodrough.
	Emanuel Stratton and Sarah Shute the 6th of June.
	John Hutcheson and Rachel Richman the 9th of June.
	Peter Coughlin Sarah Neilson 20 November.
	Alexander Van Neaman and Rebecca Page in June.

ANNO 1775

January 1st. of	John Hampton and Mary Harrys.
Febr: 14	Richard Titymerry and Sarah Clark.
15	Peter Brown and Bridget McBride.
	Barny Bready and Jane Woodside.
April	Joseph Wood and Margrete Raygor [or Rajer].
May	Rowland Bunton and Anne Franklin
	Philip Maj and Mary Shephard.
	James Finlaw and Rachel Simkin.
8th	Abner Batten and Sarah Russel.
11th	David Dericson and Mary Wood.
June 26th	Charles Mohollan and Jane Van Neaman.
2th	William Congleton and Barbary Holloday.
July 20th	John Brown and ——
Aug: 20th	John Marshal and Elisabeth Lipseginer.
the same day.	John Meclaskey and Sary Clansy both from Elsinborough.
September the 5th	Jeremiah Mahony and Mary Willjams from Greenwich Township.
October last.	John Shuhan and Mary Irvin.
Nov: 2d.	Joseph Pinyard and Sarah Humphreys.
Nov: 23th	David Loyd and Sarah Archer.
December 14th	Peter Carney and Margret Duffy from Pensneck.
December 20th	Chatfield Howel and Elisabeth Jones from Manington.
December 25th	William Key and Elisabeth Henricson.
	John Turner and Jane Finnemore Greenwich Township. Marryd 28th December.
	Paul Braght and Rebecca White the same day.

THE YEAR 1776

Jan.	Joseph Key and Rachel String.
16th	Abraham Leonard and Mary Rider.
29th	Samuel Cartwright and Sarah Butley.
Feb: 6th	Gabriel De Vebber and Rosella Eglinton.
5th	Robert Welsh and Eleonora Jones.
19th	Henry Lemon and Sarah Hensey.
22th	Isac Butterworth and Lucrece Smith.
March 20th	William Love and Mary Merrow.
April 2d	Charles Seward and Rebecca Heines.
7th	Peter Pillmore and Jane Finn.
10th	James Roberts and Priscilla Dahlbo.
23d	James Penton and Rebecca Howel.

April 18th.	John Lock and Margreta Van Neaman.
May 21st.	Willjam Quinlin and Sarah Tussy.
19th	John Savoy and Rebecca Dennis.
June 23	Mathias Louderback and Anne Curry.
25	Charles Shulch and Susanna Riley.
Julii 9th	Fredrick M'Kasson and Anne Dritchet from Pensneck.
	Joseph Thom and Sarah Barber.
August	
	William Beetle and Ruth Randel.
	Obadiah Uptin and Sarah Dahlbou.
	Isac Butterworth and Sarah Brown.
	Christopher Moyers and Sarah Andersson.
December	
	Willjam Lamb and ——
	John King and Sarah Dahlbou.
	Wiljam Garret and Susanna Gentry.

THE YEAR 1777

1st.	George Pile and Cathrine Lord Widow.
19th.	John French and Nancy Irvin.
[Oct.?] 1st.	Mathias Valentine Keen and Elizabeth Hood.
3d.	John Bowers and Isabella Isley.
17th.	William Moie and Elisabeth Vily.
ditto.	Samuel McKey and Sarah Penton.
	Thomas Petersson and Charity Dennis.
18th.	Charles Benzley and Mary Barbary Kaiser.
19th.	William Buckit and Susannah Hellms
25th.	John English and Rebecca Cameron.
March 27.	Andrew Hellms & Sarah Halton.
April.	
	Mathias Camp and Hanna Johnson.
	Jonas Johnson and Hannah Jacquet.
Nov:	Stephen Hawkins and Anne Duhany
	Samuel Dahlbo and Sarah Cox.
Dec:	Ephraim Laly and Deborah Lock.
	Isac Lundback and Lydia Pedrick.

YEAR OF OUR LORD 1779

Jan: 7th.	Thomas Curry and Rachel Simkins.
18th.	Richard Gruff and Edy Reeves.
31st.	Gabriel Cox and Sarah Elvill.
Feb: 5th.	Robert Cooper and Elisabeth Homan.
March 5th.	Amariah Warden and Susannah Evans.
24th.	James Stephens and Sarah Reeves.
25th.	Wiljam Runnels and Elizabeth Pullinger.
ditto.	Jacob Stille and Elizabeth Linch.
April.	Ludvig Rudolph and Cathrine Horner.
	Henry Tridway and Patience Dilks.
	Andrew Cole & Anne Statia Ward.
	James Webb and Peggy Thompson.
May	Joseph Turner and Charity Duffil.
June	Joseph Watson & Lydia Dilks.
	Jack & Judy, Blacks.
	Wiljam Cooper and Mary Thomas.
	Wiljam Ford and Lydia Thompson.
	Samuel Davenport and Hanna Simpson.

{ Adam Louderback 29'
& Sara Clark

	Peter Picky & Sara Reed.
Sept.	John Burroughs and Elizabeth Course.
	Hjob Weeks and Elizabeth Barber.
Octobr.	John Richards and Sarah Beale.
	Nathaniel Stanly and Margret Petersson.
	Jacob Hawk and Mary Dahlbou.
	Henry Henricson and Mary White.
July	Samuel Basset and Grace Sharp.
	John Arnold and Martha Slip.
	John Bauks and Deborah Castle.
August	Christopher Four and Margaret Calmon.
	Ishman and Canne, Blacks.
Sept.	Abden Abbet and Margret Bran.
	John Tudor and Margret Davenport.
Oct.	Uriah Nail and Emily Fowler.
Dec.	Peter Inlow and Anne Scott.
	Samuel Wood and Emily Tredway.

THE YEAR OF OUR LORD 1780

Jan: 6th	Jonathan Lord and Sarah Long.
Ditto	John Lord and Mary Svieten.
18th	Andrew Svieten and Mary Van Neaman.
Ditto	George Wall and Elizabeth Bright.
Febr: 24th	Jacob Walker and Sarah Howel.
	Wiljam Pence and Sarah Runnels.
March 16th	Wiljam Dyer and Jane Scott.
April 11th	Jonathan Carter and Rachel Ridcart.
Mary the Seventh	Christopher Lindmyer and Rebecca Mink.
7th	Joseph Paul and Mary Clark.
June	
ditto	Richard Orme and ——
14th	Peter Carny and Mary Roberts.
21st.	Charles Halton and Mary Archer.
23d.	John Lock and Mary Tomlin.
26th	John Dellavou and Sarah Dalbo.
July 3d	Zephaniah Brown and Rachel Reeves
2d	Mathias Johnson and —— Stanton.
12th	John Carter and Marget Kew.
August the 21st.	Joseph Worry and Mary Boyce.
September	
16th	Caleb Stackhouse and Rachel Mulford.
17th	John Walter and Rebecca Caspeson.
18th	Gideon Urian and Mary Jones.
27th	Isac Van Neaman and Hanna Lounsberg.
ditto	Jesper Lock and Christina Starr.
Oct. 12th	Peter Adams and Agnes Garwood.
18th	John Sparks and Cathrine Stanton.
19th	Richard Meredith and Anne Jones.
Nov: 1st	Joseph Myers and Elizabeth Rumley.
8th	George Peter Van Neaman and Susanna Lord (NB he is also called Eric).
ditto	Leaven Velin and Hanna Billerback.
9th	Abraham Jones and Mary Lock.
9th	John Regu and Louisa Ward.
21st	John Titimerry and Regina Clark.

24th	Jonathan Chew and Emilia Smith.
29th	Jacob Justis and Mary Curdin.
Dec: 2d	Jacob Henricson and Hanna Gibs.
27th	David Viley [Vealdey] & Anne Allen.
Ditto	Daniel England & Rebecca Creighead.

THE YEAR 1781

January 1st	Wiljam Atkinson and Rebecca Garrwood.
9th	John String and Lydia Goldsmith.
16th	Francis Elliot and Anne Quin.
18th	Jacob Catt and Emily Currey.
Feb. 22d	James Gardiner and Rachel Howel.
March 15th	Isac Van Neaman and Bajah Denny.
April 1st	John Burroughs and Lea Duboice.
3d	Martin Howk and Margret Fox.
5th	Charles Dalbou and Elizabeth Johnson.
11th	Wiljam Beetle and Rebecca Hoffman.
May 16th	Ebenezer Adams & Rebecca Roberts.
23d	Wiljam Hulings and Abigail Albertson.
31st	George Bright and Elizabeth Halton.
June 25th	Chester Biddle and Joanna De Wall.
27th	James Welch & Nancy James.
20th	Peter Appling & Sarah Hellms.
July 15th	William Taylor and Jane Angelo.
Aug. 5th	William Gregory & Mary Welsh.
Sept. 3d.	John Morris & Mary Breman.
Octobr:	Jonathan Simkins Hanna Harris
	Peter Carney & Marget Clark.
	John Dickinson and Mary Bowers.
	Hezekiah Hewet and Anne Tredaway.
	Charles Stillman and Mary Forbes.
November	
12th.	Wiljam Dalbou and Elizabeth Peterson.
12th.	Charles Lock & Henrietta Henricson.
Decembr:	Asa Lord and Mary Down.
27th	Adrew Cox and Mary Harris.
28th	

THE YEAR 1782.

	John Sparks and Elizabeth Pittman.
Jan. 1st.	Francys Halton and ―― Johnson.
	Thomas England and Ester Adams.
	Joseph Adams and Susanna Rue.
2d.	Moses Shoots and Phebe Butler.
23d.	Charles Melay and Elizabeth Dawdey.
	William Peterson & Sarah Flemens.
25th	Osvald Bush & Christine Stretcher.
28th	James Emmery & Emilia Scott.
February	
3d.	Lewis Catts and Mary Hudson.
13th.	James Stillman & Helena Codds.
19th.	Isac Richards & Mary Fish
20th.	Joseph Rice & Mary Dormit.
28th	John Hoffman & Cathrine Firestone.
March 5th	George Katts and Agnes Bowers
20th	Jeremia String & Jemimy Hewet.
	John Stephens & ―― Sly.

Apr. 2d.	Francis Turner & Cathrine Stillman.
11th	Hans Hellms & Mary Codds.
May 7th	Peter Morgan & Elizabeth Hewet.
9th	Daniel Van Neaman & Mary Dempsy.
June 19th	George Peterson & Marget Currey.
July 18th	Abraham Jones & Elizabeth Hewet.
29th	Thomas Conor & Elizabeth Vallis.
21st.	Peter Jaqvet & Edy Philpot.
August 1st.	John Floyd and Cathrine Cahaly.
8th.	Joseph Parr & Sara Lathburg.
September	James Dodson and Christina M'Cartey.
19th	Thomas Key et Mary Matson.
27th	Thomas Denny et Faithy Ware.
Octobr.	
11th	Benjamin Ford et Sara Key.
29th	Samuel Pickin et Anne Bud.
Novemb.	
3d	John Guest and Priscilla Angelou.
29th	Daniel Dalbou et Barbara Petersson.
Decemb.	Daniel Clark et Anne Beetle.
26th	George Catts & Mary Harris.

THE YEAR 1783

Jan. 9th	Joseph Hickman et Marget Miller.
14th	Christian Rever & Mary Schuck.
Feb. 6th	Leonard Velday & Rebecca String.
March 4th	Jonas Lock & Sara Sparks.
11th	John Mour and Cathrine Clansy.
27th	John Sommers & Debora Batton.
April 1st.	Joseph Van Neaman & Mary Porch.
2d.	Wiljam Petersson & Rebecca Petersson.
2d.	ditto Samuel Stiles & Elizabeth Chew.
3d.	John Key & Sara Bennet.
24th	Thomas Denneway & Anne Jones.
13th	Ebenezer Pitman & Sara Hellms.
May 31st	William Shute & Sara String.
June 4th	Henry Shybly et Maryle Hoffman.
July 12th	John Ozborn et Mary Miller.
ditto	John Crawford et Anne Kelly.
August	None.
Sept. 24th	William Petersson et Mary Parker.
Octobr 29th	Thomas Tire et Mary Hannecy.
December	
5th	Jesia Paulson et Elizabeth Cortis.
9th	Joseph Scott et Elizabeth Davis.
20th	George Myers et Patience Scott.
ditto	Wade Dickson et Elizabeth Fizler.
ditto	ditto Gideon Denny et Mary Claiton.
26th	Levy Gryffy & Elizabeth Morphey.
December	
1st.	Valentine Smith et Dorcas Hope.
2d.	Stephen Kennard et Elizabeth Peckin.
4th	Joseph Turner and Sarah West.
ditto	Restore Carter et Anne Kidcart.
9th	Daniel Pecker & Barshaba Pennue.
10th	Jonas Burton et Elizabeth Cole.
30th	David Henry et Elizabeth Mires.

RECORDS OF DEATHS

PENS' NECK 1713 AND 1714.

On November 4, died Hiertrud Minck, and was buried on the 6th.
On November 11, Baron Isac Baneer,[151] buried the 14th.
On January 4, died Henric Johnsson, buried the 7th.
On March 11, died Anders Senecksson, [and]
On the 13th, his wife Maria, both were buried in one grave on the 14th.
On May 4, died Henric Petersson's daughter, Margareta, buried on the 6th.

RACOON 1713

On January 1, in the night, died the two children of Manne Didricsson; buried on the 3rd of the same month.

RACOON CREEK 1714

On October 6 was buried Fredric Dinnehs' daughter, Catharina.
On November 25, Christina Cobb, William Cobb's former wife
On December 3, Manne Didricsson's daughter, Maria.

PENS NECK 1715

On August 15 was buried, Lucas Petersson's Abraham, ½ a year old, the first in the New Churchyard.
On November 2 was buried, Elisabeth von Numan.
On November 12, Olof Nilsson.
On November 20, Anna Classon.

RACCOON 1715

On February was buried Jean Hoffman's son, Anders.
On the 9th, Johan Hoffman himself.
On April 24, Jean Cock's little daughter, "baptised in emergency".[152]
On October 3, Laurentz Hollsten's son, Johannes.
On October 5, Catarina Kyhn.
On December 27, Gunnar Arched's daughter.

PENS NECK 1716

On March 4 was buried Pawel Minck, shot to death unawares by Matthias Shagen.[153]
On May 3 was buried Elias Fransson, Olof Fransson's Son.
On June 26 was buried Lucas Petersson's son, Johannes.
On December 1 was buried Catharina von Devair, Jacob von Devair's wife.

RACOON 1716

Jöns and Catharina Halton's daughter, on January 24.
Their Son, on February 16.

---

[151] Baron Isaak Banier (Banér) member of the famous Banér family in Sweden, born 1662. After spending some time in Philadelphia, and Wilmington, "he went to Pens Neck, where he married Maria Jaquet, the daughter of a farmer".
[152] *Nöddöpt,* "emergency baptism" was administered in the case of serious illness, when it was feared that the person in question might die.
[153] *Ihjälskuten oförwarandes,* "shot to death unawares". However, *oforwandes* (oforvarandes) probably here means "by accident".

On August 5, was buried Anders Lock, bitten to death by a Rattlesnake.
On September 30: Tim. Stedham's and Margarita's daughter, Ingeborg.
On December 22: Jöns [Jons] Halton's Son, Måns, baptised in the same month.[154]

PENS NECK 1717

On October 8 was buried, Johan Hindersson, Sr.
On October 24, George Kyhn's little son, Eric.
On December 26, Hans Shiere.

RACOON CREEK 1717

On July 9, buried Matts Homman's son, Peter.
On the 20th, Anders Lock, a young lad.
On August 14: Åke Helm's son, Johannes.

PENS NECK 1718

On January 14 was buried Hans Shiere's daughter, Catharina.
On June 16: Elizabeth Guilliamsson.
On the 14th of November, there did drown in the River, between New Castle and Pens Neck: Anna Fransson Christina Shagen with a little suckling babe, Walborg. Margareta Eaton. Giertrud Pettersson. Anna Fransson was found at once and buried on the 9th of November.[155]
On December 18, George Litien was buried

RACOON 1718

On January 10, Carl Hoffman was buried.
On the 22nd of the same month, Ella Steehlman, 80 years old, [who] had come from Sweden.
On February 2nd, Lars Kock's daughter, scalded to death by hot water.[156]
Item: Eric Steehlman's Erik.
On October 12, Berthil Supplye's Step-daughter, Rebecca.

PENS NECK 1719

On January 8th, Johan Hindricsson, Junior.
On February 27th, Sarah Seneck
On April 10th, Johan von Numan.
On April 25th were buried two of those wives who drowned the 4th of last November, and had been recovered, the one, namely Margareta Eaton by Daniell England, on April 22nd, and the other, namely Christina Shagen, by her own Husband on the 23rd of the same month.
On April 27th was buried Eric Jansson.
On October 10th, Olof v. Numan's daughter Elizabeth.
On the 18th, Christina Göransson.
On the 17th, Christina Lidenia, Abr. Lidenius' daughter.
On the 18th, Guarret von Numan's daughter Christina.

---

[154] This phrase is in English in the original as is printed here.
[155] There must be a mistake in the original. If she were drowned on November 14, she could not have been buried on November 9. Under "deaths and burials", below, it is stated that Margareta Eaton and Christina Shagen were drowned on November 4. November 14, is therefore, a mistake for November 4, or the writer might have in mind New Style for November 14, and Old Style for November 9.
[156] *ihjälbränd af hett vatn*, "burned to death by hot water".

[325]

RACOON CREEK 1719

On August 8, Fredrick Geörgen's daughter Elizabeth, one month.[157]
On August 10, Ingrid Mulicka.
On September 3, Fred. Geörgen's daughter Maria, near 2 months.[158]
On October 29, Olof Homman's daughter Britta.
On November 12, Jonas Biurström's wife, Amborah.
On November 23, David v. Numan's Son, John.
On December 13, Elizabeth Cock.
On November 30, Sam.v.Numan's little Son.

PENS NECK 1720

On the 9th of February was buried Jacob v: Devair's Mother, Catharina.
On the 11th of the same month, Abraham Enlow.

RACOON CREEK 1720

On January 3, was buried Ella Laikian, probably widow of Michael; 70 years
    old.[159]
On *dito* 31, John Seneck's daughter, Gertrude.
On February 17, Elias Fisk's son, Elias, 17 years and 3 months.[160]
On March 22, Carin Jones, or Lock.
On March 25, Anders Mulicka.
On *dito* 30, Fredrick Dinneh's son, Eric, five weeks old.[161].
On August 10, Johan Seneck[sson]'s daughter, Margareta.
On November 6, Johan Lock.
On December 15, Peter Steehlman's son, Peter.

PENS NECK 1721

On April 17 was buried Catharina Petersson.
On the 25th, Johan Berthilsson.
On ——, Margareta Enlow.

RACOON CREEK 1721

On February 28, was buried Matts Homan, died on the 26th.
On April 18, was buried Johan Dahlboo, died on the 16th.
On April 22, was buried Carin Dahlbo, died on the 19th. must be widow of
    Olof Dalbo, probably about 60. The three men were [probably] her Sons,
    brothers of Andrew.[162]
Item, Anna Catharina Dahlbo, died on the 21st.
On April 24 was buried Charles Dahlbo, died on the 22nd.
On May 31 was buried Lars Dahlbo, he died on the 28th.
On the 13th dito was buried William Cobb, died on the 11th. prob. old William
    past 60.
On June 6 was buried Helena Seneck, died at the home of her Father, Joh.
    Nilsson on the 4th of the same month.
On the 12th was buried Staphan Jones' wife, Anna, and her Son, Jonas, died on
    the 10th.
On July 11 was buried Catharina, Lourents Hollsten's daughter, died on the 9th.

---

[157] English in original.
[158] The original is as follows: Fred. Georgens dotter Maria, near two months. English words
and short phrases are often interspersed with the Swedish text.
[159] English in original.
[160] English in original.
[161] English in original.
[162] The note is in English in the original; possibly written by Nicholas Collin.

On August 25 died Lars, the child of Lars Påwelson, buried on the 27th.
On October 8 was buried Matthias, the son of Peter Mattsson, died on the 6th.
On October 22 was buried Måns Kyhn's Wife, Magdalena, died on the 19th.

RACOON CREEK 1722

On —— was buried Williamkie Kyhn, died on the ——. Wilamkie, mother of
    Jonas and Eva, was 65 at least.[163]
On March 28, died Peter Mattsson, buried on April 1. 36 and 10 months.[164]
On September 15, died Catharina Runnels with her little son, John, buried on
    the 18th of the same month.
On November 4, died Gabriel Dahlbo, buried on the 7th of the same month.
    Brother of the aforementioned.[165]
On October 24, died Helena Mulicka, John Mulicka's daughter, buried on
    November 6.
On December 26 died Michael Laikian's Maria, buried on January 13, 1723.

PENS NECK 1723

Påwel Nilsson, died on September 7, buried on the 8th of the same month.

RACOON CREEK 1723

Helena Kyhn, died March 4, buried on the 13th. 10 years 2 months.
Susanna Kyhn, died March 13, buried on the 15th. 7½ years.
Rebecca Kyhn, died March 25, buried on the 27th. 1 day old.
Child of George and Ella Kyhn.
Debora Lock, died June 9, buried on the 11th.
Israel Helm, died August 26, buried on the 30th.
The ancestor of the Helm in Rapapo and Jameii, probably.[166]
Thomas Huge, died September 1, and was buried on the 3rd.
Andreas Hoffman, died September 17 and was buried on the 18th.
Catharina Richman, died on September 29, buried on October 1.
George Barber died on October 14, and was buried on the 17th dito.

RACOON CREEK 1724

Lydia Justice, died on August 10th, buried on the 12th.
Abraham von Iman died on September 11th, was buried on the 13th.

PENS NECK 1725

Anna Petersson died on March 20, buried on the 23rd of the same month.
Ingrid Hindricsson died on March 26, buried on the 28th of the same month.

RACOON CREEK 1725

On September 19 died Cathrina Riethman, and was buried on the 22nd.

RACOON CREEK 1726

Måns Halton died on March 24, and was buried on the 27th.
Cathrina Helm, wife, died on June 30, and was buried on July 1.
Johannes Sträng died on July 7, was buried on the 9th.
Elena Archiet died, of a stroke of lightning, on August 8, was buried on the
    10th

[163] English in the original.
[164] English in the original.
[165] English in the original; possibly written by Nicholas Collin.
[166] See footnote 165.

James Guarren, junior, died on August 21, was buried on the 22nd.
Brigitta Rambo died on August 21, was buried on the 23rd.
Peter Petersson died on August 25, was buried on the 27th.
Moses Halton died on September 16, was buried on the 18th.
Israel Henrickson died on November 3, and on the 6th was buried.
Brigitta Stillman died on November 6, and on the 7th was buried.

RACOON CREEK 1727

Peter Janson Kock buried on January 18.
Elizabeth Larsdotter Kock, on March 29.
Elisabeth Kamp, on April 18.
Susanna Henriksdotter, on the 25th.
Anders Hoffman, on May 13.
Maria Hoffman, on September 6.
Cathrina Petersson, on December 28.

RACOON 1728

Thom Happer, buried on January 14.
Maria Helm, buried on the 14th, (daughter of Herman, 10 years, 9 months).
Måns Lycon, buried on the 17th (son of old Michael, deceased, he was near 49).[167]
Ingrid Homman, buried on the 21st.
Fredrich Denny, buried on February 2.
Margret Stedom, buried on the 22nd.
Brigitta Sträng on the 30th.
Erik Steddom, on the 26th.
Catharina Forsman, on the 26th.
John Runolls, on the 20th.
Hans Peterson, on November 18.
Elsa Guarron, on December 17.
Gabriel Petersson on the 2th.

RACOON 1729

William Runols died on January 5.
Elizabeth Mullicka, on the 16th.
Johannes Culen, on the 17th.
Jonas Mullicka, on the 18th.
Lars Stillman, on the 25th.
Petter Homman, on the 28th.
Jacob Culen, on the 30th.
Susanna Halton, on February 1.
Swen Culen, on the 5th.
Hermanus Helm, on the 7th. Son of old Captain Israel Helm deceased, about 54 years.[168]
Lars Lock, on the 18th.
Heddy Mathson, on the 19th.
Eva Mulicka, on the 24th.
Maria Kampe, on the 8th.
Maria Påvels, on the 9th.
Debora Hoffman, on the 18th.
Britta Hoffman, on the 28th.
Elizabeth Hoffman, on the 26th

---

[167] See footnote 165.
[168] See footnote 165.

Anna May died on April 1.
Samuel Peterson, on the 2nd.
Anders Halton, on the 8th.
Nils Lundbeck, on the 27th.
Jacob Lundbeck, on July 20.

ANNO 1730 RACCOON

Paul Kamp died on January 1.
Isak S'eneckson, on the 30th.
Brigitta Skaggen, on August 9.
John Lycon, on October 28.

ANNO 1731 RACOON

Gustaf Justice buried on the 6 January.
Thomas Bull, on the 12 April.
Samuel Denny, on the 18 April.
Catharina Halton, on the 9 May.
Erik Stillman, on the 10 May.
Margareta Kock, on the 23 May.
Samuel Von Iman, on the 23 May.
Vestryman Peter Lock, on the 13 June.
David Lykon, on the 1 July.
Mary Enoks, on the 26 September.
Sara Halton, on the 19 October.
Jeny. Kämpe, on the 26 October.
Maria Halton, on the 7 November.
NB. The greater part died of small-pox, which raged that year.

RACOON 1734

Susannah Lashmet buried January 22d.
Erick Kock August 13th.
Danniel Hatfield Sept. 10th.
Cath. Helm burried September 13th.
John Voniman November 8th.
Deborah Jones December 7th.

RACOON 1735

Rebecka Wood was biurried January 17th.
Johannes Seneck May 5th
Cath. Culen Septemb. 27th.

ANNO DNI. 1736

Hans Peters Buerried January 17th.
Susanna Morgon february 1st
N. Halton February 22d
Catharine Justice March 1st
Hans Halton Aprill 4th
George Keen Aprill 10
He was married the first time with Anna Jestenberg 30 Oct. 1705: and next
    year in Nov. with Ella Mollica that is Mulica).[169]

---

[169] See footnote 165.

Lorens Geron buerried July 28th.
Susannah Peters August 4th
Elizabeth Rudman Sept. 5th.
John Swenson Novemb. 14th
George Friend Octob. 17th
Andrew String Octob. 17

RACOON 1737

Helenah Conolly Decemb. 15th.
Elizab. Conolly   Decemb. 8th.
Jane Conolly   Decemb. 10th.
John Conolly   Decemb. 15th.
Mary Conolly   Decemb. 17th.
    Died by Infectuous dis-temper.

[RACCOON 1739-1741 ?]

Cath. Hoffman died May 31st. 1739.
Andrew Rambo July 27th.
Annica Friend August 11th.
Jonas Jones Septemb. 14.
John Mattson killed by the oversetting of a cart Sept. 11th.
Ellen Jones died Novemb. 23.

RACOON 1741 and 1742

Mr. John Rambo, buried Oct. 17.
Zechar. Petersson's Son, Nov. 20, 1741.

1742

Erik Mullicka's wife, Marget, febr. 5.
Jöns Halton, buried Sept. 14, 1742.
Mr. William Peterson, aged 97 years, buried June 27. 1742, (all at Racoon).

PENS NECK 1762

NO BURIALS IN THE NECK THIS YEAR which I was called to.[170]

RACOON 1762

July the 17th.	Gustav Justisson dead the 15th in an aploplex: fit 65 year & ¾ old.
Nov. ye 8th.	Sary Boys dead ye 6th in her childbirth.
20th	Beata Lock died ye 15th in consumtion old.

RACOON 1763

Jan. 29.	Burried Tamsy Carmon.
Feb. 5.	Alexander Whares wife.
28th.	The widdow Elisabeth Stalton & her daughter Debora Forster.
March 12th.	Thomas Chester.
19th.	Friedrich Hopman.
21.	Åke Helm.

---

[170] The Penns Neck congregation did not consider that Wicksell had been directed to serve their parish as well as Raccoon. It took several years before he was completely accepted, and their reluctance to have him officiate is reflected by several references such as this.

April 10th.	Joseph Carman.
16th.	Jöns Hopman 53 years of age.
May 5.	James Steelhmans son Daniel.
Aug:	
ye 18th.	John Locks daughter Rebecka dead in the flux.
22.	Samuel Linch Esqr.
24.	Alexanders wife. the 25. Nicolas Keen.
Oct. 2d.	John Fisk. the 16th Erich Coxes daughter Mary.
Nov. 30th.	Wiljame van Neumans son Jacob.

PENSNECK 1763

Feb. 6th.	Burried Jacob van Neuman.
Sept: 15.	George Stantens wife.
Oct: 23.	The old school master Christ: Whitehorn.

There were surely great many more dead in both Congregations, but not to my knowledge buried; but after evil custom without a Minister.

PENSNECK 1764

Jan.	
ye 13th.	Andrew and Elisabeth van Neumans Lusinda. dead in small pox.
Feb.	
ye 5th.	John Casys wife dead in pleurisie.

| M.R. Oct. | |
| the 16th. | Friedrick Hoppmans Son Friedrick, killed of the old Laurin by an accident. |

RACOON 1764

Jan: 12th.	Andrew Senexon in his 64th year of age.
the 15th.	Bitta Lidenius wife to the Revd. Mr. Ab: Lidenius dead in child-birth.
May ye 5th.	Mary Runals wife to Erich Runals.
June 23d.	Christine Caremon wife to the deceased Jos: Caremon.

PENSNECK 1765

In Pensneck none but several were buried there without my knowledge.

RACOON 1765

January	
the 20.	Burried James Wallis dead the 18th in consumtion in the 22d year of etc.
May the 12.	Eric Mullika dead the 10th in a decay in his 36 year of age.
the 16.	James White.
the 28.	Jonas Lock died the 26th suddenly in his 52 year of age.
Aug. the 5.	John and Sary Locks Prischilla died in fits 4 days old.
the 11.	Andrew and —— Van Neumans Rebecka 3 years 7 month old.
Nov.	
the 8th.	Gilbert & Mary Runnels Rebecka 27th days old.
Dec. the 7.	Jonas Hindrichsson Junior died in the small pox 20 year & some month old.

PENSNECK 1766

Many were buried here, but I was not called to attend them.

RACOON 1766

Januar : 2	Died his Syster Rachel Hindrichson in the same disorder.
the 3	Died their Syster Cathrine Hindrichson in the same.
Jan : 10	Cathrine Halten died the 8th. 84 years of age.
the 12	William van Neuman died the 10th in small pox 20 years old.
Feb : the 4	John Rambous child died in Small pox before it was baptised.
March 29	Charles Lock child Hellena died in the Hooping cough 3 month old.
July 19	Hance Erichs Shoulder died in the dropsie 50 years of age.
20	Zacharias Schaws child Sary in the Hooping-cough.
Sept. 10	John Mullicka died the 15th. 97 years of age.
26	John Foutch wife a Deutch woman.
Dec. 5	John Jamisson died in pleurisie 57 year 4 month & 24 days.
11	John Homans tween Rachel & the 19th the other Deborah.

PENSNECK 1767

March 25	Peter Halten drowned in the river about 60 years of age.
May 15.	Hellena Måsson died in the dropsy about 60 year of age.
Sept : 14	Deborah Boon wife of Peter Boon died in Consumption old 48 year

RACOON 1767

Feb : 4	Anne Homan died in the dropsy old 48 years & 28 days.
March 4	Mary Ramford died from a gathering inside old 33 years & two month.
the 6.	Peter Dalbou drowned in Racoon Creek old 30. years & 4 days. Elisabeth Caar drowned the same time old about 70 year.
June 3.	Widdow Supplys son Aron died in a soar throath 17th month old.
the 4.	Francis Battin died of decay old 65 years.
Nov. 16.	Else Steelman died in the dropsy. old 73 years.

PENSNECK 1768

Jan. 13.	Cornelius and Rachel Boons child Elisabeth a tween, by decay.
Feb. 26 :	Francis Miles, died by a decay or consumption, 41 year old. Many more died, and were burried, but they did not apply to me, for to attend; as is the bad custom of this Congregation.

RACOON 1768

Jan. 19.	John Dalbou, died the 17th in the pleurisie old 41 year & three month.
the 21.	Thomas Allen, died the 19th in dito, in his 60th year of age.
the 30.	Widdow Chesters young son 6 year old, died in a kind of flux.
Feb. 2.	James Turners daughter was burried, but the parents gave in no account of her death, as is often the case here.
May 3.	Zacharias Schaw, died suddenly in town, 36 year old.
June 23.	James Helms, died of inward decay in his 22d year of age.
Aug. 7.	John Jerves died the 5th, in consumption, 29 year, 4 m. 7 days old.
Sept. 19.	John Denny died in dito, 42 year, 7 m. & 22 days old.
the 16.	Jonas & Christina Keens daughter Rebecah died in fever Negues. old 3 years & 6 m.
Oct : 13.	Nathan Boys Senior died in the Dropsy 63 year old.
Nb. Feb. 19.	Gilbert Runnalls died the 17th in a kind of pleurisie about 60 years old.

PENSNECK 1769

Oct. 20. Benjamin Beetle, son of William Beetle, died in the flux, 17 years two month, and eighteen days old, a pattern for other youth here in my days or stay.

Many more were burried here in Pensneck without my knowledge as lieft among them from many years back. Lord! Inlighten & strengthen better the growing generation.

RACOON 1769

Jan. the 4. Mauritz Connor died the 2d in consumption about 60.
the 12. Thomas Angellow in consumption about 44 years 9. m. old.
Feb. 2d. Britta King, died the first from age 82 years old.

Mr. Haltons Negroes girl bapt: by me, died of fits & buried.

April 3. John Pinter died in consumption old 52 years 2 month.
July 28. Gabriel Straengs son Gabriel died the 26 by womiting & purging.
Oct. 6. John Wilkensons oldest son, died, after having had the flux.
Dec. 8. Talitha Hoffman died the 6th in a nerveous fever old ab: 18th [about 18 years old].
the 19. Abram Hamock died the 16th in consumpt: aged ab: 48th years.

NB. Many more were burried here, but without my knowledge.

PENSNECK 1770

March 12 Old Margeth Senickson died in Pawlsey. Ab: 75 y. of age.
Sept: 25 William Tuff died the 23d. from inward decay about 30 year old.

Several more were buried without any application made to me about any assistance or officiating.

RACOON 1770

Jan. 9 Hoffman—Möses died the 7th by a nerveous fever aged ab: 56. y.
June 5. Moses Keen Senr. died the 3d in a kind of pleurisie ab: 105 year old.
the 22. Jeremia Steelman died in the small pox old 20 Y: & 7 m.
Nov. 26 Peter Longaker died very suddenly in a fit Ab. 50 y. of age.
Dec. 8 Charles Streeng died the 6th of mortification 77 y. old.
Nov. 18 Conrad & Susy Shoemakers son George died in fits ab. am. [about a month] old.

PENSNECK 1771

This year, I was called to no burials in Pensneck.

RACOON 1771

Jan. 12 Magdlene Steelman wife of James Steelman, died in her 49th year. Suddenly, from a shaking aigue & purging.
the 23 John Dilcks up in the woods about 54 years old, died from complic: peines.
the 29 Charles Lock about 62 year died of a paulsy, joined of a plurisy.
March 16 Elizabeth Matsson wife of Peter Matsson, in Pleuristie about 55 y. old.
the 31 Peter Mattsson her Husband at 58 year old found dead in a cannoe.
April 3 Elisabeth Bloomer wife of Hance Bloomer died in head plurisie.

May 16.   Cleft & Susy Rowells child John 9 days old.
June 1   James Halten about 58 years old found dead in the creek.
Aug. 11   William Scharpe about 50 year, died in consumption.
the 25   Samuel Anyelou died suddenly from unknown disorder.
Nov. 7   Erick Cock about 28 year old, died in consumption.
the 11   Elisabeth Cock wife of Moses Cock ab. 49 y. old. died in dito.
    Lyddy Hewet wife of James Hewet died in her first child bearing
    of tweens.
Dec. 16   Maria Matsson 66 year old died of decay.
ns. Jan. 11   Margeth Cock wife to Peter Cock deceased died very suddenly of
    some unknown disorder.

BURIALS IN PENSNECK, To which I was called in the year 1772.

Jan. 19.   William Dalbous wife Elizabeth died of a long purging a cold
    added to it at last. old 51 one month.
Sept. 26   Mathias Lambssons fourth or fith wife, Anne died of old age 66
    y. old.

RACOON 1772.

March 20   John and Magdlene Sommerwills James died in fits about 4 m. old.
the 22   Lawrence Streeng Junr. died the 19th suddenly from unknown
    sickness about 40 y.
April 11.   Peter Mouth died suddenly after a fever and aigue about 50 years
    old.
the 22   Lawrence Strang Senr. died the 20th of old age about 74 year old.
the 26   Jacob Mullica died the 24th from fainting after his first bleeding
    in his 28th year of age. He fainted away and awakened no
    more.
Feb. 6.   Hindrick Hindrickson died in the plurisie the 3d. old, 45 years 3
    m. & 3 days.
the 13   Britta Lock wife of Lawrence Lock died of a lingering fever &
    augue About 50 odd year.
June 5   Rebecca Gooldsmith, died in her 17th year from consumption.
the 15   William V. Newman died suddenly in pleurisie about 60 years old.
the 19   Andrew Hoppman died of consumption 36 years of age.
July 9   Abram Lord died in pleurisie about 35 years of age.
Sept. 5   Joseph Wood Snr. died with the dropsy & consumption both
    about 60 year old.
Sept. 13.   Andrew Hoffman Snrs. Widdow, Mary died of old age about 66,
    years old.
Oct. 6.   Britta Jamesson Widdow of John Jamesson died of a plurisie ab:
    dito age.
the 16   Mary V. Neuman died of vomiting & purging in her 24th year of
    age.
Nov. 15   John Calm died of old age about 74 years old.
Dec. 3   John Melloy Schoolmaster, died in Dropsy in his 56 year.

RACOON 1773

Feb. 11   Sary Hindricksons Son Isaac 3½ years old died by falling in a
    hot pot of Water.
the 13   Sary Helms wife of John Helms died in pleurisie about 60 years
    old.
the 27   Erick Cock, the Clerch, died in pleurisie. about 64 year old.

March 24	The widdow Mary Hoffman died of old age about 80 or more years old.
April 29	John and Sarah Locks daughter Maria died in the Dropsie in her 15th year.
July 11	Simon Hardens Wife died suddenly of an inward disorder not rightly known, in her 45 year of age.
the 19	Hanse Hillmans Widdow's Daughter Sarah, died in a fever after the meesles in her 17 year of age
the 23	Asha Clayton Colonel of a Provincial Regiment in Pensylvany. Died here at his brothers David Claytons house of vomiting & purging, which begun with a fever, about 40 years of age.
Aug. 26	Maria Forssman widdow of Jacob Forssman, died after 13 years dry Peines all over her body, about 70 or more years old.
Octob. 12	Charles Dalbou, a very worthy Vestry man of this congregation died in the small-pox; old 49 years, 6 month & 4 days.
NB.	Andrew Låck from Rapapo born the 20th Nov: 1773.
Nov: 3	See Mr. Wicsels account for the foregoing month.
N N .	Boys son of John et —— Boys the 28th.
Jan:	John Stilman sometime in December. Wiljam Dahlbo 23 December.
1774. 11	Elizabeth Denny aged 46.
Feb: 13	John Håman
14	Amariah Dahlbo Hopman
25	Esaiah Låck

INDEX

Abbet, Aben, 321
Abel, Hannah, 269
Abelle, Dorothea, 313
Ablert, Mary, 309
Abraham, Johan, 3
    Solomon, 319
Acrelius, Israel, 43, 61, 63, 65, 67, 71,
    269
Adam (see Adams)
Adams (Adam)
    Brigitta 273
    Cathrine, 281, 288, 294
    Daniel, 193, 270, 273
    Ebenezer, 194, 273, 322
    Ester, 322
    Isaac, 288
    John, 163, 292, 314, 316
    Joseph, 322
    Peter, 321
    Priscilla, 193
    Rebecka, 270, 273, 318
    Susannah, 281
    Thomas, 165, 281, 288
Akertin, Mary, 311
Albersson, Aron, 164
Albertson, Abigail, 322
Aldersson, Aldert, 246
    Nicolous, 246
Alexander, Cathrine, 301
    Elisabeth, 301
    Garsham, 301, 318
    James, 313
    Jane, 313, 317
    John, 301
    Margret, 301
Alfwin, Dr. (Bishop of Waxio), 56
Algier, Hanna, 306
Alkorn, George, 279
    James, 279
    Rosee, 279
Allbrecht, Cathrine, 291
    Friedrich, 291
    John, 291
Allbright, Catharine, 287
    John, 287
    William, 287
Allcut, Jacob, 317
Allen, Abigail, 311
    Anne, 322
    Britta, 276, 282, 292, 297
    Hannah, 278
    Jeremiah, 276, 282, 292, 297
    John, 278, 297, 318
    Joseph, 278
    Mary, 276, 312

    Obadiah, 299
    Richard, 278
    Sarah, 299
    Sidony (Zedony), 278, 292
    Susannah, 299
    Thomas, 136, 278, 332
    Wiljame, 292
Allman, Anne, 276
    Joseph, 276
    Marta, 276
Allmon, Cathrine, 282
    Daniel, 282
    Joseph, 276
    Salomon, 282
Alm, Petrus, 57
Aloay, Daniel, 310
Ambler, John, 272, 311
Amblys, Edith, 274
    John, 275
    Mary, 275
Anderson, Anders, 255
    Mans, 61
    Sarah, 320
    Susannah, 314
Anderss, John Hoffman, 118
Andrews, Conrad, 312
    Edward, 164
Angellow (see Angelou)
Angelo (see Angelou)
Angelou (Angellow, Angelo, Angelow)
    Anna, 132
    Benjamin, 135, 155, 281, 283, 294,
        300, 302
    Charles, 306
    David, 135, 283
    Deborah, 273, 283, 294, 300, 302
    Jane, 322
    Jehu, 294
    John, 300
    Mary, 299
    Peter, 299
    Priscilla, 323
    Rebecca, 283, 314
    Samuel, 307, 334
    Sarah, 299
    Thomas, 314, 333
Angelow (see Angelou)
Aplin (see Applin)
Appelin (see Applin)
Applin (Aplin, Appelin, Appling)
    Charles, 222
    Hedda, 311
    Joseph, 124, 136, 138
    Peter, 194, 222, 225, 322
    Sarah, 222

Barkley, James, 61
Barn, Anne, 300
  Blair, 295
  Elisabeth, 295, 300
  Thomas, 295, 300
Barnet, Andrew, 141
  Edward, 301
  Elihu, 223, 301
  Elizabeth, 223, 317
  Margete, 223, 301
  William, 223
Barney, Eliah, 223, 299
  Elisabeth, 299
  Jeremia, 223
  Marget, 299
  William, 299
Baron, Elisabet, 282
  John, 282
Barret, Marget, 282
  Catherine, 307
Barrit, Patrick, 317
Barry, William, 310
Bars, John, 257
Bartelson, Andrew, 61
Bartholson (see Berthilsson)
Barton, Bricks, 297
Basset, Elizabeth, 309
  Emy, 314
  Johanna, 310
  Samuel, 321
Batten (Battin, Batton)
  Abner, 196, 319
  Anne, 276
  Debora, 323
  Edward, 314
  Francis, 135, 137, 194, 276, 332
  Richard, 192, 276
  Sara, 316
  Thomas, 164, 190, 195, 276
Bauer, Anna Maria, 278
  Michel, 278
  Salome, 278
Bauks, John, 321
Bauman, Anne Margret, 280
  John Valentine, 280
Baumgartner, Sigmund, 54
Baven, William, 310
Beale, Sarah, 321
Beck, Asa, 100, 101, 164, 173, 174, 175
Bee, Ephraim, 315
  Mary, 317
Beedle, Mary, 279
Beetle (Bietle)
  Aaron (Aron), 282, 287, 293, 296, 301
  Anny, 287, 323
  Barbary, 279, 301
  Benjamin, 333
  Cathrina, 133, 318
  Christine, 279, 286, 287, 288

Ehrent, 276, 287
  Elizabeth, 276, 282, 287, 293, 296, 301
  George, 276, 287
  John, 78, 79, 97, 98, 99, 140, 184, 279, 286, 287, 288, 293
  Mary, 286, 312
  Pheeby, 298
  Sary, 287
  William, 140, 282, 312, 320, 322, 333
Beesly, Betzy, 312
  Ebaya, 293
  Getrud, 268, 270, 316
  John, 268, 270
  Jonathan, 293, 314
  Maria, 268
  Morris, 293
Beete, William, 61
Beette, Marta, 132
  William, 132
Beiry, Anne, 282
Bekom, John, 308
Belcher, Jonathan, 58
Bench, Christopher, 317
Bengtsson, Bengt, 234
Bennet, Hance, 318
  Sara, 323
Bensley, Charles, 300, 320
  John, 300
  Mary, 300
Benzel, Adolf, 269
Benzelius, Henric, 63, 67, 70, 73, 76
  Jacob, 42, 52, 56
Benzelstierna, L., 64, 67, 70
Beronius, Magnus, 37, 52
Berry, John, 257
  Maria, 257
  Thomas, 257
Berthilgren, Zacharias, 233
Berthilsson (Bartholson, Bertilsson)
  Andrew (Andreas), 223, 234
  Anna, 242
  Anna Catharina, 244
  Gunilla (Guinilla), 234, 236, 237, 240, 241, 244, 245
  Jean, 7, 8, 11
  John (Johan, Johannes), 2, 9, 10, 14, 17, 20, 112, 116, 223, 234, 235, 237, 241, 242, 244, 245, 326
  Peter, 17, 116, 245
  Philip, 241
  Rachel, 223
  Richard, 238
  Sara, 233, 235, 236, 238, 242, 245, 246, 251
  William, 223, 235
  Zacharias, 2, 7, 8, 10, 11, 14, 17, 20, 23, 112, 116, 117, 235, 238, 241, 242, 245, 251
Bettle, Aron, 311

Case, Charles, 158, 162
Caspar, Jean, 239
   Rebecca, 239
   Susanna, 305
Casparson, Anna, 256
   John, 256
   Judith, 256
   Tobias, 256
Casper, Brigitta, 251
   Cathrine, 279, 307
   Cornelius, 272
   Johannes, 1, 306
   John, 279
   Maria, 251
   Sarah, 272
   Tobias, 251, 279, 307
Caspersson, Johannes, 23
   Tobias, 23, 99
Caspeson, Rebecca, 321
Casson, Margret N., 291
Castle, Deborah, 321
   William, 291
Casy, John, 331
Catt, Annamaria, 282
   Anne Mary, 282
   Dorothea, 287
   George, 274, 282, 287, 323
   Louis, 286, 287
   Mary, 274, 277, 287, 296, 297
   Ursilla, 277, 295, 297
Catts, Agnes, 224
   Catharine, 224, 227, 287, 303
   Christina, 224, 303
   Elisabeth, 224, 303
   Emilia, 224, 303
   Ester, 275, 286
   Euler, 224
   George, 224
   Hanna, 224
   Isaac, 286
   Jacob, 224, 275, 286, 303, 322
   John, 224, 297, 303, 316
   Lewis, 224, 322
   Mary, 224, 303
   Michael, 224, 275
   Rebecca, 286
   Samuel, 224, 287
   Sarah, 297
Cattell, Anne, 315
Catzen-Ellenbogen, Count of, 45, 64
Cautch, Anne, 278
   Hance, 278
Cavender (Cavener)
   Garrett, 164, 273
   George, 273
   Mary, 273
   Susanna, 273
   William, 273
Celsing, Gustaf, 36
Celsius, Olof, 52, 57, 64, 67, 70, 73

Chandler, Maria, 310
   Rachel, 307, 309
Charles XII, 19
Chattell, William, 310
Chatten, Clarck, 294
   Elisabeth, 294
   Francis, 294
   George, 294
   Jane, 294
   Mary, 294
   Rebecca, 294
Cherregen, Annicka, 258
   Fredrick, 258
   John, 258
Chester, Cathrina, 271
   Christine, 316
   Emy, 283
   Foeby, 316
   Jacob, 317
   John, 260
   Joseph, 293
   Maria, 293
   Marta, 271
   Prishilla, 260
   Samuel, 165, 196, 271
   Sara, 250
   Thomas, 271, 330
Chew (Chiew), Daniel, 190
   Elizabeth, 241, 323
   Jonathan, 322
   Thomas, 241
Chiew (see Chew)
Christein, Magdalena, 270
Christian, Cathrina, 268
   Elizabeth, 268
   Johan, 268
Claiton, Mary, 323
Clansy, Cathrine, 323
   Sary, 319
Clarck (Clark)
   Bathsebah, 280
   Brigitta, 281
   Britta, 281, 286
   Carney, 292
   Cathrine, 276, 283, 288, 292, 297,
     299, 301
   Christian, 292
   Christina, 283
   Daniel, 323
   Deborah, 290, 293, 296, 298, 300,
     303
   Denny, 298
   Elisabeth, 271, 283, 290
   Garret, 283
   George, 132, 135, 164, 294
   Gideon, 280, 284, 285, 286
   Hindrich, 283
   James, 135, 139, 193, 276, 283, 286,
     288, 292, 297, 301, 304
   Jane, 294
   Jeffry, 136, 191, 263, 264

Dicson, Vade, 192
Didrecksson (see Didricsson)
Didricsson (Dedrickson, Didrecksson,
  Dirckson, Dircksson, Dirksson, etc.)
    Christina, 233, 236, 238, 240, 241,
      243, 244, 248, 249, 250, 254, 308
    Debora, 253, 254
    Ellena, 263, 264
    Eric, 241, 264, 265
    Helen, 238
    Jack, 269
    Johannes, 248
    John, 268
    Margaret, 268, 269
    Manne (Manna), 6, 11, 15, 18, 26,
      27, 35, 117, 118, 234, 237, 238, 241,
      242, 244, 245, 246, 248, 250, 324
    Maria, 324
    Peter, 268, 269
    Rebecka, 268
Dielshastern, Elisabeth, 310
Dilck, Anne, 295
    James, 286, 288, 295, 314
    Sara, 286, 288, 295
Dilcks, John, 333
Dilckse, Elisabeth, 288
Dilks, Lydia, 320
    Patience, 320
Dillin, Mary, 315
Dillmore, Hannah, 294
    Thomas, 294
Dinneh, Catarina, 233, 235, 324
    Elizabeth, 234, 240
    Eric, 244, 326
    Fredric, 27, 117, 233, 234, 237, 238,
      244, 247, 250, 324, 326
    Gunilla, 243
    Helen, 235, 237, 241, 244, 247, 249,
      250
    Jonas, 247
    Maria, 233, 234, 235, 236, 238, 240,
      241, 243, 245, 247, 249, 251
    Thomas, 12, 18, 26, 27, 115, 118,
      233, 235, 238, 239, 240, 241, 243,
      247, 249
Dinnehs, Olof, 237
Dinnerhs, Catharina, 233
Dione, Eben Ezer, 61
Dirchsson, Dircksson, Dirksson (see
  Didricsson)
Dishlow, Philip Jacob, 317
Dober, Martin, 51
Dod, Joseph, 289
    Marta, 289
    Richard, 289
Dodd, Thomas, 139, 155, 190, 312
Dodson, James, 323
Doffell, Susanna, 308

Doffy, Abram, 275
    Catherine, 275, 282
    Marget, 287
    Mary, 287
    Patrick, 275, 282, 287
Donaldson, Gabriel, 61
Don Bar, Alexander, 268
Donet, Elizabeth, 233
    William, 233
Donker, Geen, 252
Dormit, Mary, 322
Dorrel, Danniel, 313
Dounkins, Gun, 306
Down, Eleanor, 307
    Mary, 322
Dragstrom, Elisabeth, 287, 290, 294, 316
    Gustavus, 132, 290
    Hellenah, 294
    Magnus, 287, 290, 294, 313
    William, 287
Drake, Thomas, 312
Draper, Hannah, 277
    Mary, 277
    Salomon, 277
Dritchet, Anne, 320
Duboice, Lea, 322
Duff, Patrick, 310
Duffield, Emy, 295
    James, 295
    John, 295
    Sara, 295
Duffil, Benjamin, 289, 294
    Charity, 286, 320
    Elisabeth, 286, 289, 294
    Emy, 286
    John, 286
    Joseph, 294
Duffy, Hannah, 291
    Marget, 291, 293, 319
    Neomy, 293
    Patrick, 291, 293, 313
Duhany, Anne, 320
Dulany, Mathew, 318
Dunham, Joseph, 282
Dunlap, Aron, 313
Duquette, Barbary, 277
    Hance, 277
    Joseph, 279
    Mary, 279
    Nathaniel, 279
Duringerin, Margreta, 310
Dykes, Sarah, 313
Dylander, Jons, 36, 38
Dylany, Daniel, 295
    Elisabeth, 295
    Hannah, 295
    Isaac, 295
    Martin, 295
Dylap, Rebecca, 317

Early, James, 190
Easly, Anne, 318
    Elizabeth, 314
Eastly, Elisabeth, 318
Eaton (Eaten)
    Elizabeth, 238, 251
    Jean, 238, 246
    Johan, 244
    John, 30, 240, 246, 249, 315
    Magdalena, 251
    Margareta, 325
    Maria, 244, 249
    Simon, 10, 11, 22, 33, 112, 113, 116,
      244, 249, 251, 305, 307
Eckart, William, 195
Eduards, Joseph, 312
    Sary, 313
Eglinton (Eglimgton), Mary, 304
    Rosella, 319
    Tobithee, 310
Eickorn, Jacob, 286
    Regina, 286
Ejler (Euler, Eulers)
    Anna, 269, 272
    Anne Mary, 281
    Catherine, 281, 286, 296
    George, 269, 272
    Hance Mickel, 281
    Hannah, 286
    Henry, 270, 272
    John, 281, 286, 294
    Margreta, 275
    Mary, 270, 312
    Philip, 275
    Stephan, 272
    Susannah, 275
Elkhorn, Jacob, 282
    Regina, 282
    Sagina, 282
Ellionson, Erik, 255
Elliot, Francis, 322
    John, 195
Ellis, Joseph, 191
    Thomas, 312
Elwell (Elvill, Ellwell)
    Annanias, 99, 312
    Hannah, 315
    John, 225
    Marg., 311
    Mary, 267
    Mary Anne, 267
    Rachel, 318
    Sara, 225, 320
    Thomas, 61, 267, 269
    William, 307, 309
Embson, Charles, 293
    Mary, 224
Embsson, Cornelius, 317
    Deborah, 288
    Ebenaser, 288, 293
    James, 288

Margreth, 293
Emly, Hannah, 315
Emson, Debora, 277, 299
    Ebenaser, 277
    Israel, 299
    Marget, 277
Endicott, Samuel, 316
Eneberg, Johan, 36, 37
Engelous, Aukenius, 274
    Benjamin, 274
    Deborah, 274
England, Daniel, 193, 296, 303, 304, 322,
    325
    Elias, 273, 296
    Hester, 304
    James, 292, 296
    Mary, 273, 281, 292, 296, 304
    Rebecca, 303, 304
    Sara, 281, 296, 303
    Thomas, 165, 194, 206, 304, 322
    William, 136, 144, 165, 190, 273,
      281, 292, 295, 296
    William Watson, 304
Englander, William, 236
Engleton, Deutch, 165
    Johan Michael, 294
English, Israel, 317
    John, 320
Enkow, Samuel, 257
Enloes (see Enlow)
Enlow (Enloes)
    Abraham, 326
    Ann, 260
    Benjamin, 260
    Elizabeth, 243
    Margareta, 243, 326
    Peter, 243, 305, 310
    Samuel, 260
Enokson (Emokson, Enock, Enockson,
    etc.)
    Abraham, 281
    And., 255, 258, 259, 261, 264
    Andreas, 308
    Catherine, 255, 257, 258
    David, 257
    Enok, 32, 35, 253, 254, 255, 256,
      257, 258, 262
    Erik, 262
    Gabriel, 32, 34, 236, 259, 308
    Johannes, 305
    John, 255, 257, 261, 262, 269, 308
    Margret, 257, 258, 262
    Mary, 259, 329
    Prisilla, 258
    Rebecca, 255
Erickson (Erich, Erichsson)
    Andrew, 281
    Catherine, 281
    Cha., 61
    Eben Ezer, 61
    John, 275

Hugh, 138, 165, 276, 284
James, 276
Martha, 301
Mary, 276, 284, 301, 322
Ford, Anne Mary, 289
Benjamin, 323
Elisabeth, 289
James, 289, 313
John, 311
Wiljam, 320
Foreker, Rebecca, 298
Joseph, 298
William, 298
Forest, John, 191, 316
Fors, Sara, 254
Forser, Jacob, 303
Sophy, 303
Valentine, 303
Forsman (see Forssman)
Forssman (Forsman)
Abraham, 261
Catherine, 256, 328
Daniel, 257, 270, 271
Elizabeth, 266
Hanna, 299
Jacob, 18, 27, 32, 35, 36, 42, 113,
248, 249, 252, 253, 255, 256, 257,
259, 260, 261, 264, 265, 307, 335
Margareta, 253, 270
Maria, 249, 252, 253, 256, 257, 258,
260, 261, 265, 270, 335
Olaf, 260
Rebecka, 271
William, 135, 138, 299, 317
Forster, Alexander, 287, 297
Cathrine, 287, 297
Deborah, 297, 330
Elisabeth, 314
John, 313
Rachel, 287
William, 287
Fosman, Jacob, 26
Foster, Ezechiel, 185
Ruth, 310
Valentine, 192
Fosset, Nathan, 191
Foulk, Christiana, 292
Friedrick, 290, 292
Hannah, 290
Patience, 290, 292
Four, Christopher, 321
Fouraire, Elis, 293
John, 165, 293
Sarah, 293
Fouraires, John, 164
Fouraker, Deborah, 284
Elisah, 284
Foutch, John, 332
Fowler, Aron, 292
Christine, 277

Emily, 321
Eseyah, 292
Rebecca, 318
Silas, 294
Susy, 292
Thomas, 277
Foy, Nicolas, 279
Peggy, 279
Rosannah, 279
Frambe, Mary, 291
Peter, 291
Susannah, 291
Franklin, Anne, 319
Elisabeth, 316
James, 164, 315
William, 126, 140
Franssen (see Fransson)
Franson, Lena, 254, 256
Fransson (Franssen)
Anna (Annika), 113, 236, 237, 239,
242, 251, 256, 325
Christina, 233, 234, 242, 305
Elias, 324
Ellena, 251
Eric, 239
Helena, 240, 242, 243, 248, 249, 251
Lena, 254, 256
Maria, 237
Olof, 237, 324
Philip, 2, 7, 8, 9, 10, 11, 14, 17, 20,
22, 23, 28, 112, 116, 117, 240, 242,
244, 248, 251, 305
Frease, Jacob, Junr., 313
Fred, Johannes, 27, 114, 119, 236
Fredrick, John, 30, 32
Fredrickson, Andrew, 255
Manne, 35
Peter, 35
Freidrich, Adolph (King), 36, 44, 45,
53, 64, 71, 75, 76, 77
French, Benjamin, 318
John, 320
Robbert, 165
Frenne, Gabriel, 41, 42
Freicke, James, 287
Freyer, Peter, 164
Friend, Ambrose, 263
Annica, 262, 330
Elisabeth, 288
Ephraim, 260, 262, 263
Gabriel, 249, 265
George, 330
John, 260, 265, 292
Lawry (Lawrence), 102, 107, 164,
194, 283, 288, 292, 294, 299, 301,
303, 312
Mary, 265
Rachel, 299
Rebecca, 303

Moses, 328
N., 329
Peter Fredrickson, 34
Petter, 32, 34, 254, 260, 262, 263,
    264, 268, 272, 282, 332
Rebecca, 242, 282
Regina, 242
Sarah, 225, 236, 252, 253, 254, 257,
    302, 308, 320
Susanna, 238, 242, 291, 328
Wiljam, 225
Halter, John Martin, 309
Hamen, John, 335
Hamilton, Alexander, 313
Rachel, 317
Rev. —, 284
Hamler, John, 281
Patience, 281
Hammit, Jacob, 192
Hamock, Abram, 333
Hampton, Diana, 302
Edward, 302
Elisabeth, 302
John, 319
Kesia, 302
Hamton, Anne, 317
Diana, 299
Edward, 299
Jacob, 299
Hanbey, Doc. Willjam, 318
Hanke, Casper, 280
Susannah, 280
Hannecy, Mary, 323
Hanson, James, 34
Hansson, Johan, 306
Hantsson, Isabella, 133
Haogks, Eleonor, 311
Harden, Benjamin, 135
Henry, 225
John, 225
Martha, 226
Rebecca, 225
Sarah, 225
Hardin, Simon, 317, 335
Harker, David, 191
Joseph, 191
Judida, 309
Harman, Nicholas, 61
Harps, Margreta, 269
Michael, 269
Harrican, Margaretha, 311
Harris (Harrys)
Catherina, 270
Hannah, 322
Mary, 319, 322, 323
Philip Gottfried, 270
Walter, 270
Harrison, Prischilla, 164
William, 136, 138

Hartman, Anne Elisabeth, 312
Maria Margreta, 312
Harwood, Simon, 164
Has, Catherine, 267
Hatfield (Hatfiell, Hatfill, Hatfiel)
Adam, 253
Danniel, 329
Edward, 249
Gertrud, 253
Heddert, 252
Maria, 249
Hatten, John, 252
Hauttson, Esajah, 287
Isabella, 287
William, 287
Hawertin, Sary, 314
Hawk (Haag)
Jacob, 225, 321
John Casper, 225
Mary (Maria), 225, 306
Susanna, 225
Susanna Margareta, 225
Hawkes, Helena, 246, 249
Joseph, 23, 61, 249, 306
Joshua, 246
Hawkins, Stephen, 320
Haynes, Margreth, 313
Hayns, Rebecca, 310
Heather, Isaac, 314
Hegblad, Johan, 87
Heil, Anne, 287
Baltsar, 287
Margreth, 317
Mary, 287
Heim, Anna Maria, 309
Heins, Elisabeth, 278, 316
Hance Georg, 278
Peter, 278
Rebecca, 319
Hellm (see Helm)
Hellman, James, 94
Jonas, 43
Helm (Halm, Hellm, Hellms)
Ake (Oke), 5, 6, 10, 11, 12, 13, 18,
    21, 30, 35, 40, 41, 42, 113, 115,
    117, 118, 119, 120, 135, 235, 236,
    238, 241, 242, 245, 247, 249, 250,
    252, 258, 261, 263, 308, 325, 330
Andreas (Anders, Andrew), 35,
    99, 140, 222, 225, 248, 258, 270,
    279, 293, 296, 299, 302, 320
Betty, 258
Brigitta, 249
Catherine, 193, 235, 238, 239, 241,
    242, 245, 248, 249, 252, 261, 263,
    279, 293, 296, 299, 327, 329
Debora, 263
Elizabeth, 245, 258, 259, 262, 266
Gabriel, 259

Hakan, 259
Hans, 190, 272
Helena, 225
Hermanus (Herman), 6, 15, 26, 27,
    30, 32, 35, 236, 239, 245, 261, 328
Israel, 35, 241, 259, 261, 263, 265,
    270, 284, 327
James, 332
Johannes, 260, 270, 290, 325
John, 35, 69, 84, 89, 90, 91, 92, 94,
    96, 97, 99, 100, 101, 102, 105, 107,
    108, 125, 126, 127, 130, 135, 138,
    139, 140, 142, 144, 145, 147, 149,
    152, 153, 155, 157, 158, 159, 160,
    164, 165, 166, 169, 171, 172, 173,
    176, 178, 180, 182, 190, 191, 225,
    260, 262, 272, 296, 308, 318, 334
Joseph, 245
Judith, 227
Magdalena, 235, 270
Manus, 18, 115, 118, 242, 248
Mary, 225, 239, 293, 316, 328
Rebecca, 222, 225, 259, 302, 308
Sara, 225, 228, 259, 262, 279, 290,
    314, 322, 323, 334
Susanna, 272, 320
Hencock, Susannah, 313
Hendricson (Hendricson)
    Andrew, 69, 107, 108, 251
    Anna, 251
    Elisabeth, 273
    John, 251, 270
    Jonas, 69, 270, 273
    Maria, 268, 270, 273
    Regina, 255
Hennigen, Brigitta, 300
    John, 300
    William, 300
Henricsson (Hendrickson, Henricson)
    Anders, 236, 240
    Andrew, 187, 190, 240, 254, 299,
        301, 302
    Anti, 255
    Caleb, 193
    Catharina, 259
    David, 191, 302
    Eddy, 302
    Elisabeth, 299
    Esrah, 302
    Henrietta, 322
    Henrik (Henric), 18, 30, 32, 36,
        115, 123, 236, 241, 248, 253, 255,
        256
    Israel, 308, 328
    Jacob, 322
    Jacon, 193
    Jon, 35, 192
    Judith, 299, 301, 302
    Mary, 194

Mounse, 194
Oney, 254
Peter, 240
Rebecca, 301
Regina, 236
Henricksdotter, Susanna, 328
Henrik, Andrew, 263, 264
    Bridgit, 260, 261
    Christina, 257, 261
    Henrik, 255, 259
    Regina, 255, 256, 258, 259
    Sara, 259
Henrys, Andrew, 265
    Brigitta, 261, 308
    Christian, 265
    David, 323
    Henry, 261, 263
    Regina, 261, 264
Hermanson, M. V., 77
Hersin, Catherine, 316
Hertzhorn, John, 311
Herwind, Hannah, 271
    John, 271
    Maria, 271
Hesselius, Andreas, 3, 19, 242
    Brigitta, 250
    Gustav, 62, 247, 272
    Johan, 272
    Maria, 62
    Samuel, 3, 15, 19, 247, 250, 265
    Sara, 247
Hew (Hewe), Catharine, 298
    Hannah, 298
    Jacob, 298
Hewett (Hewet)
    Delilah, 290
    Edmond, 294
    Elisabeth, 290, 294, 315, 323
    Ester, 290
    Hezekiah, 290, 322
    Isaac, 290, 294
    Jacob, 316
    James, 334
    Jemimy, 322
    Lyddy, 334
    Robbert, 290
    Samuel, 316, 317
    Susy, 315
Hewitt, Mary Anne, 314
Hewling, Marget, 304
    Priscilla, 304
    Samuel, 304
    Wiljam, 304
Hews, John, 226
    Margaret, 226
    Samuel, 190
    Wiljam, 226
Hichman, George, 279
    John, 99

Hickman (Hickmon)
  Christina, 308
  John, 275, 279
  Joseph, 303
  Rebecca, 275, 179
Hicks, Thomas, 307
Hierneisson, Hans George, 310
Higner, John, 136
  Nancy, 307
Hilderbrand, Elisabeth, 315
  Sarah, 316
  Susannah, 312
Hill, James, 307
  Jane, 311
  Mary, 311
  William, 307
Hillman, Charles, 261
  Els, 265
  Hans, 35, 261, 335
  Sarah, 335
Hindersson (Hinderson)
  Anders, 20, 23, 116, 235, 243, 247, 307
  Beata, 233, 243
  Christina, 240
  David, 243
  Hinric, 240
  Ingrid, 233, 234, 237, 243
  Israel, 252
  Jacob, 2, 7, 8, 9, 10, 14, 17, 21, 112, 113, 234, 237, 239, 243
  Jean, 113, 237
  Johan, 8, 9, 234, 235, 248, 325
  Magdalena, 234, 237, 243
  Margeth, 252, 307
  Maria, 248
  Regina, 236, 240, 252
Hindrickson, (Hindrichason, Hindrikson, Hindrichsson)
  Andrew, 17, 23, 117, 125, 139, 165, 189, 233, 287, 295, 297, 315
  Anne Elisabeth 312
  Brigitta, 306
  Caleb, 283
  Catherine, 132, 135, 281, 283, 297, 332
  Clefton Rouls, 283
  David, 139, 155, 164
  Elisabeth, 132, 135, 281, 283, 297
  Gabriel, 297
  Henry, 296
  Hindriita, 276
  Hindrick (Hinric), 26, 27, 41, 59, 114, 117, 125, 155, 164, 236, 237, 243, 245, 246, 248, 276, 283, 287, 292, 334
  Ingrid, 233, 240, 246, 327
  Isaac, 292, 295, 334
  Israel, 34, 284

Jacob, 11, 17, 23, 238, 239, 242, 247
Johan, 239, 325
John, 233
Jonas, 331
Joseph, 283
Judith, 295
Lyddy, 297
Magdalena, 248
Mary, 284, 292, 297
Peter, 296
Povel Peter, 35, 238
Rachel, 332
Regina, 244, 246, 248, 311
Sary (Sarah), 139, 247, 276, 283, 287, 292, 296, 334
Hindrys, Rebecka, 264
Hinricson, Catharina, 240
  Henric, 118, 245
  Ingrid, 240
  Jacob, 240
  Johan, 112
  Maria, 240
Hirrehis, Rosina, 270
Hirshfield, Prince of, 45, 64, 71
Hitzler, Peter, 311
Hochschliedt, Hans Georg, 266, 309
  Johan Adam, 266
  Johan Heinrich, 266
Hocket, Elisabeth, 279
  Sarah, 279
  Williame, 279
Hoffman (Hofman)
  Abraham, 253, 259
  Agnes, 293
  Almgott, 238
  Anders Anderson, 255, 257
  Anders Fredricsson, 27, 246, 253
  Anderson, 253
  Andreas, 249, 327
  Andrew (Anders), 3, 6, 11, 14, 15, 16, 17, 20, 26, 27, 32, 34, 41, 42, 99, 113, 114, 115, 117, 118, 119, 184, 233, 235, 236, 237, 238, 239, 241, 242, 245, 247, 248, 250, 252, 259, 260, 261, 262, 263, 264, 265, 270, 271, 273, 280, 293, 307, 324, 328, 334
  Anna Christina, 289
  Annicka, 252, 280
  Ante, 30, 32, 252, 259
  Aram, 294
  Armgodt, 235
  Beata, 233, 255, 257
  Berthil, 235, 237
  Brigitta, 233, 234, 235, 236, 243, 306
  Britta, 242, 328
  Carl, 236, 238, 305, 325
  Catherine, 233, 234, 236, 239, 240, 241, 242, 247, 249, 250, 251, 252,

Cathrina, 249, 252, 253, 308
Elena, 235, 255, 258
Elizabeth, 246, 252, 255
Emi, 308
Ezechiel, 116
Helena, 253
Johan, 240, 253
John, 241, 308
Jonas, 253
Judith, 255
Marten, 246
Rebecca, 253
Sara, 249
Stephen, 3, 6, 235, 249, 252, 253
Joranson (see Joransson)
Joransson (Joranson, Jouranson)
    Andrew, 163, 289
    Deborah, 289
    Elisabeth, 313, 316
    Jane, 285, 314
    John, 285, 290
    Laurence, 61
    Mary, 289, 290
    Rebecca, 289
    William, 285
Jordain, Elisabeth, 314
    Marget, 289
    Michael, 289
    Zacharias, 289
Joresson, Jane, 279
    John, 270, 289
Jounger, Hannah, 312
Joyce, Christine, 267
    Margary, 312
    Thomas, 267
    Walter, 267
Junger, Grace, 313
Jurisson, Laurence, 267
    Lydia, 267
Juslanson, Isaac, 180
Justason, Elizabeth, 266
    Justa, 266
Justice (Justis)
    Andreas, 258, 265, 288, 310
    Annika, 257, 258, 259, 264, 282
    Bakum, 282
    Brigitta, 264
    Cathrina, 258, 265, 288, 329
    Christina, 252, 302, 318
    Elena, 252, 255, 258
    Ellen, 262, 263
    Elizabeth, 282
    Gustav, 258, 262
    Gustav, 61, 258, 259, 262, 263, 265, 329
    Hannah, 302
    Helen, 244, 245, 246, 248, 250, 252, 264
    Isac, 274, 282

James, 262, 263
John, 262
Lydia, 248, 327
Margret, 262
Maria, 268
Marta, 244
Nicolas, 26, 264, 265
Nils, 32, 34, 35, 258, 259, 262
Peter, 11, 18, 27, 30, 32, 34, 114, 117, 118, 243, 244, 247, 248, 251, 252, 254, 258, 261, 262, 264, 265, 282, 306
Rebecka, 262, 265, 282, 310
Susanna, 255
Justisson, Andrew, 135, 281
    Anna, 132
    Catherine, 281
    Elisabeth, 313
    Gustaf, 132, 135, 330
    Isaac, 137, 139, 164, 165, 294, 316
    Mary, 294
    Rebecka, 281
    Silly, 294

Kaiser, Mary Barbary, 320
Kalloway, Gideon, 290
    Jacob, 290
    Rebecca, 290
Kalm, Euler, 294
    Marget, 284, 294
    Peter, 62, 210, 221
Kallum, John, 293
    Mary, 293
Kam, Leonhard, 275
    Marget, 275
Kamp (Kampe)
    Elisabeth, 328
    Geen, 255
    Hanna, 226
    Jenny, 257, 260, 329
    John, 226
    Joseph, 226
    Lars, 260
    Mathias, 226, 269
    Mary, 269, 328
    Paul, 30, 257, 260, 269, 329
    Sebulon, 257
    Wiljaim, 226
Kats (Katts)
    Anna Barbara, 268
    George, 270, 322
    Jacob, 269, 310
    Mary, 269, 270
    Michael, 270
    N., 268
Katzen, Barbara, 311
    Magdlena, 310
Kayer, Elisabeth, 301
    Peter, 301

Richard (Richerd), 35, 259, 261
Lorense (see Lorence)
Love, Catherine, 289
    James, 289
    Marget, 286
    Mary, 286
    William, 286, 289, 319
Loveday, Lydia, 307
Lowis (Lowise), John, 281
    Mary, 282
    Sary, 281
    Wiljame, 281
Lowsen, Lydia, 318
Loyd, David, 193, 319
    Saloman, 311
Lumly, John, 313
Lundbeck, Catharina, 250
    Christina, 132, 243, 244, 247, 249,
      250, 252, 253
    Henry, 311
    Isac, 320
    Jacob, 13, 18, 26, 27, 243, 244, 245,
      247, 250
    Nils, 247, 329
Lue, Martha, 311
Lycon (Lykon, Lycor)
    Annicka, 256, 260
    David, 260, 329
    John, 329
    Mans, 328
    Maria, 258
    Mich, 256
    Michael, 260
Lydman (see Lidman)
Lykon (see Lycon)

M'Caeen, Hannah, 310
M'Carson (M'Carsson)
    Anne, 291, 294
    Hezekiel, 291
    John, 291, 294
    Marta, 294
M'Carty, Brita, 132
    Christina, 323
M'Crau, Jane, 313
M'Dade, William, 315
M'Darmuth, John, 316
M'Farell, Margreta, 310
M'Gill, Elizabeth, 311
M'Kansie, John, 309
M'Kasson, Fredrick, 320
    John, 313
M'Kray, John, 288
    Lydiah, 288
    Mary, 288
M'Lain, Cathrine, 272
    Daniel, 272
    Patrick, 272
M'Lallin, Elizabeth, 309
M'Williams, John, 316

Mac Genis, James, 61
Mac Maine, James, 307
Mak Wheire (Mac Guire), Prudy,
    313
Mc Bride, Bridget, 319
Mc Creed, John, 297
    Joseph, 297
    Mary, 297
Mc Darmut, Isac, 297
    John, 297
    Mary, 297
Mc Gill, Cathrine, 227
    Elizabeth, 302
    James, 227
    Mathias, 302
    Steven, 302
Mc Key, Samuel, 320
Machentosh, Cath., 317
Mackelroy, Rachel, 227
    William, 227
Mackgill, Cathrine, 227
    James, 227
    John, 227
Madeira (Madairy)
    Adam, 295
    Anna, 298
    Anne, Mary, 298
    Jacob, 163, 193, 290, 294, 295, 297,
      298, 300, 301, 302, 303
    Johannus, 294, 297
    Jonas, 294
    Marget, 290, 294, 295, 297, 300, 301,
      302, 303
    Samuel, 300
    Sarah, 303
    Susannah, 294, 297, 302
    William, 301
Maffart, Thomas, 316
Magdaniel, Maria, 306
Maguire, Neigh, 164
Mahony, Jeremiah, 319
Makgloucklin, Elisab, 282
    Wiljam, 282
Makom (see Mecum)
Malander, Olof (William), 37, 38,
    210, 221, 266
    Deborah, 266
Mann (Manne)
    George, 311
    Hannah, 317
    Thomas, 317
Mansson, Charles, 118
    Elizabeth, 245, 251
    Hellena, 133
    John, 245, 251
    Sara, 256
Mappin, Marget, 318
Marchant, Joseph, 316
Margee, Joseph, 277

Joseph, 321
Marget, 289, 304
Michael, John, 269
Michel, Hance, 281
Henry, 135
Middleton, Anne, 302
Jacob, 302
Sarah, 302
Middletown, Hannah, 314
John, 281, 312
Nathan, 281
Rachel, 281
Miles, Francis, 61, 78, 279, 332
Thomas, 99
Miller, Anne Mary, 292, 294
Barbara, 309, 311
Cathrina, 269, 292, 316
Elisabeth, 294
Gunn, 306
Jacob, 313
John, 292, 309
Joseph, 294
Marget, 323
Mary, 323
Michael, 61, 309, 311
Philip, 316
Minck (Mink)
Andrew, 288, 292
Brigitta, 242, 247, 248, 307
Elizabeth, 233, 234, 235, 237, 240,
246, 249
Gertrude, 324
Hannah, 292
Helena, 240, 242, 243, 306
Jean, 8, 10, 11, 22, 23, 112, 116, 117,
236
Johan (Johannes), 2, 20, 233
John, 17, 233, 235, 236, 237, 240,
242, 246, 288
Josia, 306
Magdalena, 307
Margareta, 236, 238, 305
Martin, 61
Pavel, 324
Rebecca, 288, 292, 321
Sary, 289
William, 112
Mintz, Adam, 270
Catherine, 270
Philip, 270
Mires, Elizabeth, 323
Moddy, Ann, 266
Moholan, Charles, 319
Mole, William, 320
Mollen, Mary, 313
Molloy, John, 164
Monjon, Anna, 271
Mary Anna, 271
Robert, 271
Sarah, 271

Monsen, John, 61
Montgomery, Debora, 303
Hanna, 303
Hue, 303
Moony, Brichet, 316
More (Moore, Mour)
Adam, 270
Anna, 270
David, 317
Elisabeth, 270, 289
Elwell, 289
James, 313
Jane, 313
Joanna, 313
John, 323
Marcus, 309
Marget, 289
Mathew, 312
Nicolas, 111
Moren, John, 315
Morgan (Morgon, Morgons, Morgen)
Anne, 240
Benjamin, 262
Elizabeth, 308
Henry, 264
Joshua, 264
Maria, 253
Mathew, 304, 310
Peter, 194, 290, 323
Susanna, 262, 329
William, 290
Morisson, Anne, 289
Eliz, 289
Fred, 304
Mathew, 289
Morphey, Elisabeth, 323
Morray, Timothy, 126
Morrie, James, 268
Simon, 268
Morris, Anne, 279
John, 322
Lawrence, 279
Rachel, 279
Sary, 279
Morssy, Daniel, 278
James, 278
Mary, 278
Morten (Morton)
Andrew, 263, 264, 265
Annicka, 261, 264
Erasmus, 227, 314
George, 265
Hannah, 263
Kesiah, 227
Mounceson (Mounsson)
Helena, 268
John, 126, 268, 272
Mountain, John, 277
Mary, 277
Mour (see More)

Olof, 6, 18, 27, 115, 117, 240, 243, 252
Peter, 26, 34, 61, 113, 115, 119, 234, 240, 269, 280, 328
Priscilla, 275, 276, 277, 284
Prudens, 312
Rebecca, 311, 323
Samuel, 256, 258, 329
Sarah, 234, 236, 239, 254, 261, 262, 269, 287, 293, 300, 309
Sary, 279
Susannah, 245, 275, 276, 280, 287, 291, 296, 330
Thomas, 177, 178, 195, 227, 320
Timotheus, 246
William, 26, 227, 276, 322, 330
Zacharias, 34, 35, 67, 68, 118, 125, 239, 241, 243, 244, 245, 246, 247, 248, 250, 251, 252, 253, 254, 255, 258, 261, 262, 265, 308, 330
Pfeiffer, Christopher, 309
Pflannigan, Elisabeth, 295
James, 155, 288, 290, 295
John, 285
Sary, 290, 295
Pfloid, David, 296
Elisabeth, 296
Phall, George, 282
Mikel, 282
Susannah, 282
Philip, Anna, 306
Wiljame, 277, 282
Philpot, Anna, 233, 254, 268
Catharina, 237
Christine, 266, 309
Edy, 323
Jean, 9
John, 23, 237, 254, 266, 268, 305
Margareta, 233
Marget, 282
Maria, 241, 249, 305
Mathias, 277
Nicholas, 61, 237, 241
Susannah, 277
Thomas, 241
William, 23, 233, 237, 241, 249, 305
Philpott, Erich, 99
Joseph, 311
Pickin, Charles, 302
Judy, 302
Samuel, 195, 302, 323
Pickman, Anna, 236
Robbin, 236
Picky, Peter, 321
Pile, Catherine, 301, 302, 303
Elisabeth, 301, 317
George, 194, 300, 301, 302, 303, 320
Mary, 301
Piles, Samuel, 303
Pillmore, Peter, 319

Pinter, Andrew, 294
John, 132, 294, 332
Mary, 294
Pinton, Catherine, 298
Daniel, 317
Elisabeth, 297
Jacob, 297
James, 319
John, 298, 315
Mary, 298
Sarah, 320
Pinyard, Joseph, 319
Unice, 316
William, 316
Pippart, Anne, 278, 291
Jacob, 278, 291
Pitman, Ebenezer, 228, 323
Elizabeth, 322
Sara, 228
Platt, Samuel, 316
Plomblin, Hanna, 295, 317
Plomli (Plumly)
Elizabeth, 257, 261, 310
John, 257, 261, 264
Maria, 257
Sarah, 264
Plumly (see Plomli)
Pomrai, George, 308
Ponharten, Magdlena, 270
Pooge, John, 311
Porter, Sarah, 269
Potter, Borten, 279
Mary, 279
Powel, Elisabeth, 277
Wiljame, 277
Powers, Catherine, 291, 316
Christine, 291
Johannes, 300
John, 281
Michel, 286
Salome, 286
Samuel, 286
Sary, 281, 300, 317
Praght, Margaretha, 270
Vallentine, 270
Pressin, Samuel, 137
Price (Preis)
Charles, 306
David, 309
James, 243
Prichet, Eliz, 279
Sary, 279
William, 279
Prilchet, Mary, 272
William, 272
Prisener, Paultes, 194
Probstein, Barbarah, 309
Procket, William, 135
Procter, John, 99
Proctor, Thomas, 309

Shoemaker (Schoemaker)
    Catharine, 300
    Conrad (Conrode), 139, 163, 190,
      296, 300, 301, 304, 333
    George, 294, 304, 333
    Susannah, 294, 296, 300, 301, 304,
      333
Shogen (see Shagen)
Sholder (see Shoulders)
Shoot, Isaac, 282
    Mary, 282
    Moses, 322
    Sarah, 317
    William, 136, 323
Shopschire, Anne, 288
    Louisa, 295
    Rebecca, 288, 295
    Thomas, 288, 295
Shoulders (Sholder)
    Jacob, 194, 303, 304
    Lidia (Lydia), 303, 304
    Martha, 303
    Susannah, 315
    William, 304
Shreve, Samuel, 193
Shuhan, John, 319
Shulch, Charles, 320
Shybly, Henry, 323
Shytz (see Schyz)
Sinic (see Seneckson)
Silvy, Dean, 315
    Grace, 279
    Rachel, 319, 320
Simkens, Abram, 316
    June, 317
Simkins, Jonathan, 192, 316, 322
Simmonds, William, 228
Simpkins, Daniel, 310
Simpson, Hannah, 320
Sinnert, Clemy, 279
    Mary, 279
Sinnicson (see Seneckson)
Siren, Christian, 191
Sirren, Elisabeth, 301
Sivil, Susanna, 318
Skagen (see Shagen)
Skeer, Eric, 256
    Martin, 256
Skinner, Cort., 132
Slaid, Charles, 271
    Mary, 271
    Philip, 271
    Ruth, 271
Slater (see Sleter)
Slaughter, Elizabeth, 258
    John, 258
    Mali, 258
Sleeper, Sary, 313
Sleter (Slater), John, 255, 261
    Margeret, 261
    Maria, 255

Slide, William, 312
Slip, Martha, 321
Sluby, Cathrine, 243, 244, 307
    Maria, 234, 236, 306
    Olof, 243
Sly, Cathrine, 277, 285, 290, 295, 297,
    314
    Elisabeth, 290
    Jacob, 277, 285, 290, 295, 297
    Sarah, 285
Slyde, Marta, 287
    Mary, 287
    Philip, 316
    Ruth, 314
    William, 287
Smallwood, William, 316
Smick, John, 310
Smit, Alexander, 310
    John, 164, 257, 269, 311
    Johnsson, 287
    Margaret, 257
    Mary, 314
    Nanzy, 312
    Phoeby, 311
    William, 286, 287, 313
Smith, Daniel, 317
    Dorcas, 317
    Elizabeth, 252
    Emilia, 322
    Joseph, 316
    Lucrece, 319
    Lucretia, 287
    Margareth, 267, 286, 308
    Maria, 269
    Mary, 267, 286
    Robert, 267
    Salome, 314
    Samuel, 306, 313
    Valentine, 323
    William, 285
Snell, Cornelius, 282
    Pheby, 291
    Samuel, 291
Sommerlind, John, 192
Sommers, Isac, 282
    John, 323
    Rachel, 316
Sommervill, Mary, 193
Sommerwill, George, 139, 163, 165,
    296, 316
    James, 296
    John, 334
    Magadalene, 296, 334
Souder, John, 311
Southerland (Sutherland)
    Daniel, 139, 191, 297, 300, 301, 302,
    303
    Deborah, 301
    Isac, 303

59, 60, 68, 115, 117, 125, 243, 249, 250, 257, 264, 267, 270
Hans, Jr., 242
Isac, 281
Israel, 253
James, 34, 35, 86, 87, 90, 91, 99, 101, 102, 105, 106, 107, 126, 127, 130, 135, 139, 140, 155, 160, 162, 164, 165, 166, 167, 168, 169, 170, 171, 172, 173, 175, 176, 177, 178, 180, 181, 182, 183, 191, 267, 298, 300, 317, 322, 331, 333
Jemymy, 300
Jeremiah, 267, 333
Johan, 272
Johannes, 257
John, 270, 285, 288, 295, 300, 302, 335
Jonas, 115, 293
Jons, 243
Lars, 328
Magdalena, 267, 281, 333
Maria, 244
Mary, 194, 265, 281, 285, 295
Olof, 18
Peter, 18, 115, 244, 326
Prishilla, 280
Sarah, 267, 270, 273, 281, 316
Susanna, 249
Steenhagen, Fred, 45
Steinheuser, Anne, 293
  Jacob, 293
  Samuel, 293
Stenyeard, Joseph, 268
  Rebecka, 268
Stephens, John, 229, 322
  Ursula, 229
Steuchius, Joannes, 37
Stevens, Elisabeth, 310
Stille, Ellena, 268
  Jacob, 193, 320
  Johanna, 268
  Johannes, 265
  John, 190
  Morton (Morten), 35, 69, 264, 265, 268, 309
  Mary, 264, 265
  Peter, 125
  Samuel, 323
  Sarah, 310
Stiner, Anne, 301
  Jacob, 301
  Mary, 301
  Samuel, 223
Stinger, Adam, 303
  Anne, 303
  Cath., 303
  Christian, 192
  Daniel, 303
  Dorothy, 303

Eva, 303
Francis, 191
Jacob, 303
Peter, 193
Philip, 303
Solomon, 316
Wilhelm, 303
Stonebanks, Mary, 313
Stonemitz, Peter, 285
Stout, Michael, 191
Strang (Straeng, Strahen, Straune, Streeng, Streng, Strieng, String, etc.)
  Abraham, 281
  Anders, 256
  Andrew, 27, 32, 261, 330
  Anna, 240, 313
  Betty, 258
  Brigitta, 255, 328
  Carl, 27, 32, 132, 234, 252, 254, 257
  Catun, 303
  Charles, 118, 246, 290, 305, 333
  Christina, 256, 258
  Daniel, 132, 135, 278, 286, 290
  David, 249, 305
  Elisa, 292
  Elizabeth, 290
  Ella, 233, 305
  Ephraim, 286
  Gabriel, 126, 135, 138, 155, 164, 281, 283, 286, 290, 292, 333
  Hellena, 281
  James, 306
  Jeremiah, 322
  Johannes, 249, 327
  Judith, 278, 286
  Lars, 19, 27, 32, 132, 240, 241, 249, 252, 256, 260
  Lawrence (Lorens), 35, 84, 126, 135, 138, 261, 334
  Lawrence, Jr., 135, 164
  Lidia, 303, 304
  Margareta, 250, 254, 258, 261, 262
  Maria, 120, 132, 241, 307
  Mary, 298
  Rachel, 319
  Rebecka, 132, 241, 247, 252, 256, 276, 278, 281, 282, 286, 288, 290, 292, 298, 323
  Sary, 276, 323
  Susannah, 244, 290
Stratton, Emanuel, 319
  James, 191
Stream, Henry, 194
Streem, Benjamin, 313
  Cathrine, 278, 283
  Henry, 278, 283
  Sara, 278, 283
Streeng (see Strang)
Streit, Christian, 214

Margaret, 250, 252, 255, 261, 308, 311
Margarete, 233, 236, 238, 247, 253, 254, 256, 272, 320
Maria, 84, 209, 221, 240, 242, 243, 245, 248, 249, 250, 251, 252, 254, 255, 256, 257, 260, 272, 307
Martha, 263
Mary, 262, 264, 268, 286, 288, 292, 293, 321, 334
Mehatable, 276, 282
Olle, 30
Olof, 7, 8, 9, 11, 13, 14, 20, 21, 22, 28, 73, 112, 116, 117, 132, 233, 234, 235, 236, 237, 239, 240, 241, 242, 243, 245, 247, 249, 251, 254, 256, 325
Peter, 117, 246, 248, 250, 251, 252, 256
Priscilla, 295
Rachel, 275, 312
Rebecca, 224, 261, 264, 267, 294, 314, 331
Regina, 274, 275, 311
Richard, 276
Ruth, 287, 288, 293, 296, 299
Samuel, 18, 26, 30, 32, 35, 36, 115, 117, 233, 238, 240, 246, 248, 250, 254, 264, 276, 282, 289, 326, 329
Sarah, 282, 283, 284
Sary, 276, 277, 288, 289, 292, 296, 297, 300, 302, 311
Susannah, 283, 291
Tobias, 272
William, 23, 39, 99, 120, 126, 135, 141, 265, 269, 278, 280, 283, 284, 287, 302, 331, 332, 334
Von Reulen, Jacobus, 114
Von Troil, Uno, 213, 218, 219
Von Zinzendorff, Count Nicholas, 40, 42, 46, 47, 53, 54, 56, 69

Waard, Marta, 314
Waas, Ephraim, 284
Wade, John, 120, 214
Wagener, Philippina, 297
Wainam, Anna, 233
Catarina, 233
Henric, 233
Stephen, 116
Walcketh, Samuel, 306
Waldius, Eric, 37, 52
Wale, James, 281
Walker, Hannah, 316
Jacob, 321
Wall, Christine, 319
George, 321
Waller, Jesse, 309
Wallin, Anne, 309

Wallis, James, 331
Wallraven, Cornelius, 233
Elizabeth, 233
Walter, John, 321
Maria, 282, 286
Walters, Catherine, 316
Charles, 316
Warbutton, Hannah, 314
Ward, Aron, 318
Elizabeth, 307
Louisa, 321
Statia, 320
Warden, Amariah, 320
Wardety, Lucia, 308
Ware, Alexander, 135, 164, 316
Faithy, 323
William, 164
Warrelton, Hanna, 308
Watson, William, 164, 192, 304
Wear, Alexander, 182, 183
Friedrich, 295
Henric, 317
Weaver, Abigail, 295
Hannah, 278
Lucretia, 315
Webb, Catherine, 270
James, 320
Mary, 270
Oliver, 61, 270
Webber, John, 284, 285
Marget, 277, 291
Mary, 284, 285, 295
Sarah, 291
Thomas, 228, 277, 284, 285, 291, 295
Webster, Richard, 318
Weeks, David, 318
Hjob, 321
Mary, 316
Weeler, John, 264
Weiser, Catherine, 278, 286, 313
George, 278, 286
Weithorn, Elizabeth, 132
Welch (Welsh)
Eleonore, 301
James, 322
Magdalene, 301
Mary, 295, 322
Morris, 301, 317
Priscilla, 318
Robert, 319
Wells, Harrisson, 165
West, Edward, 294
Joseph, 297, 314
Richard, 294
Sarah, 294, 297
Western, Eliz., 297
Merry, 297
Whenu, John, 307

Where, Susannah, 315
White, James, 192, 273, 283, 310, 331
  John, 192, 283
  Maria, 273, 283, 321
  Rebecca, 319
  Robert, 280
  Samuel, 273
  Sary, 280
Whitehorne, Christ., 331
  Samuel, 61
Whittin, Mary, 314
Wiccarie (see Wiggorie)
Wiccorie (see Wiggorie)
Wickery (see Wiggorie)
Wickory (see Wiggorie)
Wicksell, John (Johan), 77, 78, 84,
  88, 89, 90, 91, 92, 93, 96, 97, 101,
  102, 103, 126, 127, 129, 132, 134,
  139, 141, 142, 144, 145, 147, 148,
  149, 150, 152, 153, 154, 157, 158,
  159, 160, 162, 163, 164, 165, 168,
  170, 171, 172, 173, 175, 176, 177,
  178, 180, 183, 210, 215, 221, 274,
  275, 277, 335
Wide, Andrew, 287
  Jane, 287
  Mary, 287
Wiggins, Mary, 314
Wiggorie, Ingridh, 243
  Johannes, 235
  Margareta, 235, 239, 240, 248, 253,
  254
  Margret, 243, 247
  Sarah, 247
  Thomas, 9, 20, 23, 61, 112, 126, 235,
  237, 243, 147
  William, 239, 245
Wikry (see Wiggorie)
Wilder, Mary, 318
Wilikens, Constantine, 164
Wilkinson, John, 271
Willcock, Grace, 307
Wilkesson, John, 287
  Mary, 284, 287
  Silas, 287
Williams, John, 261
  William, 261
Wilson, Martha, 307
  Robert, 310
Windrufwa, Andrew, 29, 30, 31, 33,
  209, 221, 254, 255, 256
  Elisabeth, 256
Winemuller, Charles, 191
Winemyller, Carl, 292
  Charles, 282, 289, 313

Dorothea, 282, 287, 289, 290, 292,
  294
Winholtz, Frederick, 278
  Hannah, 278
  Samuel, 278
Winny, Henric, 23
Winsor, Jesse, 317
Winsson, Anne, 283
  Cathrine, 283
  John, 283
Wintern, Samuel, 315
Wiser, George, 191
Wister, Richard, 125
Witesell, Catharine, 315
Wittemberg, Mary, 318
Wolsh, Michael, 194
Wood, Anna, 308
  James, 317
  Jeremiah, 125
  John, 265
  Joseph, 319, 334
  Mary, 308, 319
  Prishilla, 310
  Prudence, 317
  Samuel, 321
  Walter, 314
Woodenton, John, 263
  Stephan, 263
Woodrough, Sara, 319
Woods, Catharine, 263
  Joseph, 263
  Prishilla, 263
Woodside, Jane, 319
  Robert, 284, 285
  Susannah, 284, 285
Woolf, Jacob, 314
Woodstard, John, 289
  Marget, 289
  William, 289
Wordenton, Benjamin, 261
  Hannah, 261
Worells, Gipson, 276, 282
  Hannah, 276, 282
  Jonathan, 262
Worry, Joseph, 326
Worth, Richard, 317
Wrangel, Carl, 36, 78, 81, 85, 86, 87,
  135, 214, 268, 274, 276, 280, 287

Zane, Isaac, 164
  William, 164
Zimmerman, Abraham, 270
  Anna, 270
Ziren, Elisabeth, 268

www.ingramcontent.com/pod-product-compliance
Lightning Source LLC
Chambersburg PA
CBHW030234030426
42336CB00009B/90